A Cuckoo in the Curriculum

or

A Life of Lessons

Bob Watson

With a Foreword by John Edmonds

ISBN 0-9519236-6-8

British Library in Cataloguing Publication Data.
A catalogue record of this book is available from the British Library.

Published by: Milepost Research,
8 Green Bank, Barnoldswick, BB18 6XHX
01282 850430

Printed by Printdomain

Contents

Illustrations

Front cover: Sailing ship montage — Izzy Kitt
Back cover photo: Oil on Water — Tim Watson.
Maps by Mike Clarke

Notes

References and notes can be found at the end of each chapter. Comparatively few references are to primary sources. This may count as laziness but my brief has not been to present an academic treatise, rather to stimulate thinking and discussion about aspects of current education practice. I hope my sources where quoted, will appear respectable.

Names of beneficiaries have been changed or omitted where appropriate.

Sobriety is used in the text to describe the charity as well as the barge.

The use of the word 'cuckoo' in the title of the book and elsewhere to describe the relationship of informal learning to the curriculum, requires brief explanation. The cuckoo is popularly regarded as a ruthless squatter which occupies the nests of other birds, expels their chicks and destroys their eggs. But another description presents the bird as a homeless wanderer; indeed the RSPB exhorts us to 'take urgent action to secure its future'. It is generally the second interpretation which is adopted in the book, but I do apologise for any inconsistencies, and of course to the cuckoo's victims, whether feathered or human.

The book is not primarily intended to be a vade mecum to youth work or aspects of learning beyond the formal curriculum, but to help those who wish to use it in this way, I have included questions at the end each chapter. The intention is to give the reader the opportunity to draw out the lessons of the events and questions raised in the preceding pages. If this appears to be 'teaching Grandma to suck eggs' or too much like an A-Level exam paper, then please ignore them.

Not all the appendices have references in the text but I hope they will all engage readers who have an interest in waterways politics. The last three appendices should be read by all readers.

Author's Preface

Like the common cuckoo which relies on other birds to hatch its young, education relies on the good sense of government to create a habitat where food is available to feed the soul as well as to meet the requirements of the market.

Whether for children at risk or adults in prisons, the informal, sometimes unorthodox curriculum, like the cuckoo, is always searching for a home to nurture its offspring. I hope that readers who are entertained by the book's drip-feed of ideas through anecdote and allusion, will do everything they can to reverse the decline of the species and secure its future. Some may even be inspired to have a go themselves.

Bob Watson MBE
Withernsea, South Holderness, 2015

Dedications

To the memory of my cousin, the late Joseph Rowell, whose estate made possible the publication of this book.

Then for *Sobriety*'s Treasurers — Sydney Wilks, David Fishburn, George Robinson, Andrew Brett and Bernard Fletcher without whose timely intervention in financial crises, real or imagined, the *Sobriety* Project would have sunk without trace.

Also for teachers, youth workers, voluntary sector practitioners, prison officers and social workers who are enthusiastic for a curriculum that will bring greater benefit to the people in their care.

And finally for successive secretaries of state for education without whose persistent interference in the school curriculum or neglect of it, this book would not have been written.

Acknowledgements

Over the years I have been disarmed by the extent to which *Sobriety* has been supported by colleagues and trustees, many of whom have become friends in spite of the personal price of *Sobriety* they have sometimes had to pay. I am indebted to them. I also owe a practical debt to those who have helped me write the book and made suggestions for its improvement: Simon Ryder: Shirley Collier: Bill and Joyce Petch: Judith Nicholson: Jon and Dot Fogell: Tim Watson: Jenni Watson: Paul Cooper: Peter and Shirley Teed: Ken Lawson: Kathryn Smith: Margaret Rogers: Izzy Kitt: Andy Brownlie: Karen Beaumont: Ilona Csatlos Graudins: David Uffindall: Russell Butterfield: Tim and Amanda Harding: Mike Clarke: Jean Williams: Viv and Eric Morgan: the late Goff Sherburn: Eileen Sherburn: Ernie Sherburn: Chris Sherburn: Bill Sowerby: Steve Gardham: Julie Frost: Rachel Walker: Simon Jarrold: Enid Thompson: Ryan Linley: Curtis Richards: Emma Williams: Steve Robinson: Trevor Cox: James Bryan: Diane Taylor: Trevor Roberts: Clare Hunt: James Bryan: John Hughes: Brian Calvert: George Robinson: Bill and Shan Rigby

FOREWORD

Bob Watson has written a book that crackles with humanity and wisdom. It reflects the nature of the man.

I remember sitting alongside him in the back of a minicab on the way to a waterways meeting. The driver decided to bombard us with his highly prejudiced views on black and ethnic communities. I got angry, but Bob started, quite gently, to ask the driver about his views and whether they were based on real-life experiences. Before we reached our destination, the driver had mellowed and admitted that there are, "*good and bad in everyone.*" It was a remarkable transformation.

'Cuckoo' can be read as a personal memoir, but Bob is careful to say little about his own role as leader and motivator of the small and remarkable group which does such good work in Goole and the wider Yorkshire region. Centre stage is always occupied by *Sobriety*, first by the barge, and then by *Sobriety*, the project, which expanded to include more vessels, the waterways museum, the arts centre and much more besides.

I am not sure if Bob Watson has a hero, but the West Riding's chief education officer, Sir Alec Clegg, must come close. The influence of this celebrated Yorkshire educationalist flows through the book, and he is quoted often as a source of common sense and of inspiration.

Clegg used to recall that his aunt had a text on her sitting room wall which contained the couplet:

Two loaves, sell one, and with the dole
Buy hyacinths to feed the soul.

The loaves are the facts but the hyacinths represent the spirit: they are what make humans into the people they are. 'Cuckoo' is the story of what happened to the hyacinths that Bob planted in Goole.

The philosophy that defines *Sobriety* is described with admirable moderation, but between the lines is a thick seam of frustration and anger. Education is fundamental to the development of the human spirit, but in recent years the powers-that-be have defined the nature of learning ever more narrowly. Why is learning now assumed to be exclusively classroom-based and test-driven? What becomes of the children who do not adapt well to this sort of narrow-minded schooling? And what happens to the poor and disadvantaged who lack the confidence to navigate systems that are hard-headed and bruising? And more widely, what happens to people whose lives go wrong when they reach adulthood? Britain's prisons are full to over-flowing but nowhere in the system is there much concern for rehabilitation or resettlement.

The *Sobriety* barge started as an outdoor classroom, but the project developed a range of programmes where skills are taught in an atmosphere that is sympathetic and supportive. The skills are valuable but even more important is the way that the successful learning of skills raises confidence and self-esteem. The numbers are impressive. 30 pupils a week given a new view of the world; 7000 children, mainly from low income families, travelling to destinations on the Continent and around the British coast aboard *Audrey*, a sailing barge; well over £10million raised to support *Sobriety*'s work.

But the real measure of *Sobriety*'s success is in the transformation of lives. 'Cuckoo' is full of examples of excluded pupils who discovered a better way to learn, people with mental difficulties who gained a fresh exuberance for life, young offenders who discovered new opportunities and prisoners who began to see a path to a happier future.

Sobriety is an extraordinary community, drawing its staff and volunteers from a wide variety of backgrounds — skilled skippers, of course, but also a biology specialist from St Alban's, the spouse of a prison officer, someone with a fine arts degree and Bob himself — a seconded RE teacher. No snobbery of course, cultural or otherwise; the young people aboard the converted lightship *Audrey* would give performances of Mozart's comb concerto and Beethoven's saucepan symphony.

Equality of respect is a key principle. It is difficult for an outsider to tell who are the paid staff, who are the volunteers and where the volunteers have come from. On one of our visits to Goole I still remember the expression on a colleague's face when she found out that the good-looking and well-mannered young man who was driving our mini-bus was an inmate at the local prison.

So many successes but also so many obstacles. For a long time Goole Grammar School was helpful, as were borough and county councils. But managements changed and local authorities were reorganised. Over and over again *Sobriety* has had to prove its worth to people who have a different view of the world, apply rigid targets and are subject to crushing political pressures. And this explains both the triumph of *Sobriety* and the difficulties that *Sobriety* always faces.

Almost without exception, when someone has taken the time to visit and understand what is being done at *Sobriety*, they go away impressed. Visitors have included royalty and celebrities from every part of society. But usually the important decisions have been made by people who judge *Sobriety* on the basis of written reports that include a detailed description of Alec Clegg's 'loaves' but often omit to say much about the 'hyacinths'. *Sobriety* has remained outside the mainstream, which is an uncomfortable place to sit at times when budgets are cut and educational objectives are defined so narrowly.

It is impossible to describe *Sobriety* without being enthused by the optimism and by the sense of fun. 'Cuckoo' is full of humour and the narrative is carried along by stories of victories won, disasters avoided and bureaucracy out-manoeuvred. They are a jolly lot, this community in Goole, ready to see the funny side of life and to make the best of challenges that would defeat so many of us.

'Cuckoo' is an account of what would be possible if we focused more directly on the needs of individuals and helped them to feel better about themselves. Education should be freed from the cramped thinking that puts a higher worth on test results than on self-esteem. We should provide every citizen with the help and support that affluent people take for granted. Side-lining the poor and 'difficult' is inhumane and unworthy. Exclusion and imprisonment are not solutions but declarations of failure.

More opinion-formers should visit *Sobriety* and, to learn a little more of its wisdom and humanity, they should read this book.

John Edmonds
London April 2015

INTRODUCTION

On high days and holidays, at weddings, funerals, christenings and family get-togethers, there are moments between the embraces and quarrels when the world stands still and individuals take stock.

On such an occasion in 2006, while waiting in the galleries of Buckingham Palace for instructions on the etiquette of the MBE ceremony, I stood gazing at life size portraits of imperial statesmen and generals, and asked myself, *"How on earth did I get here?"* I had a third class degree, no famous grandfather, no celebrity presence on TV, nor was I was a football manager or spymaster. I had no record of pioneering new designs of vacuum cleaner or for solving the mysteries of 'dark matter' in the universe. And I had never run a mile in less than ten minutes nor worn lycra in the saddle. My 'gong' was for 'services to young people' but even in this noble field of endeavour I had not been any more than average, either as a classroom teacher or outside the classroom. Many of my projects involving young people had lasted a few years and had then been superseded or had run out of steam. In awe of the men in the paintings and nervous at the prospect of being 'on stage' I decided the answer to my question could only come by story telling and argument; the stories would do the work and be evidence for the argument.

The moment passed and I became pre-occupied with the business in hand — how to address royalty and walk backwards without falling over. In the end I did forget the second bow on exit, but things went well. After the ceremony we enjoyed the attentions of deferential policemen, beefeaters and hard sell photographers. Later at a posh London restaurant we were mesmerised by the obsequious pirouettes of waiters in a ballet of their own. Friends and relations came to a 'midsummer evening' at the Yorkshire Waterways Museum and I was summoned by Radio York to give an account of myself. Time allowed the ideas to mature and become the seeds of the present text which began to take shape five and a half years later in January 2012. The book has turned out to be both an autobiography and an exploration of the initiatives, successes and challenges of the *Sobriety* Project, a small charity which took its name from a Humber barge and began its life in the curriculum of a Yorkshire comprehensive school.

Influences and Transplants in Part 1, describes my time in Kano northern Nigeria in 1972. I then deal with the Outward Bound Trust's personal development courses known as *City Challenge* with which I was involved from 1974, and finally, there are my recollections of an earlier period, beginning with a prep school in Sheffield in the nineteen fifties and ending with teaching responsibilities in Goole Grammar School from 1966. My innate enjoyment of adventure and the pleasure of seeing others blossom from it, led me to believe that just as classroom learning enabled children to make sense of themselves and their surroundings, education *outside* the classroom was indispensable to their personal development and happiness. The one complemented the other. Sadly however the balance has been lost and in many teaching establishments in the second decade of the twenty first century, out of school activity has become a 'cuckoo' with no nest in the curriculum. Monopolised by tests and examinations, the learning process has been governed by the use of narrow performance indicators and is resulting in a culture which seems to be asserting that 'If it cannot be measured, it's not worth doing'. Referring to the value of art in the curriculum in one of his *Guardian* columns, 'Loose Canon' Giles Fraser said, 'There is more to reality than the flat footed empiricism of those who believe that if you can't count it, touch it or weigh it, it doesn't exist.'[1] In the same vein, Yorkshire poet Ian Macmillan has called for more creativity in schools and says that children can be helped by the 'power of words'. Talking about working with teenagers at a pupil referral unit in Doncaster,[2] he said, *"We developed performance poetry and I could see them becoming more confident and articulate in front of me, becoming creators as well as observers. That's the thing about creativity, it's at the heart of us all, it helps us to learn and crucially become better human beings."* The same process was at work on *Sobriety*'s sailing barge during its millennium cruise round Britain in 2000. The presence of professional artists on every leg of the voyage created opportunities for personal achievement as well as contributing to the team effort.(Chapters 7 and 8)

In its examination of all aspects of the creative arts sector in 2015, the Warwick Commission deplored the decline in arts activity in schools. Insisting that 'arts education should be an entitlement for all children', the report complained that 'policymakers are obsessed with a siloed subject-based curriculum and early specialisation in arts or science disciplines that ignore and obscure discussion about the future need for all children to enjoy an education that encourages creativity.'[3] And, it might be added, education for independence and self confidence is under the same threat, not just in schools, but in prisons, day centres and in the field of informal youth work.

It is not difficult to apply these comments to some of the methods used by government in the crusade to 'raise standards'. For the future of many children if not of government ministers, out-of-classroom learning is just as important as the knowledge tested in examinations. It may be eulogised by politicians but is often sidelined in favour of more fashionable initiatives which invoke 'standards' as a vote winning excuse for oppressing children and their teachers with endless inspection and assessment.[4] However, despite appearances, the book is not an attack on the classroom curriculum or an unjustifiable elevation of the alternatives to it. It is more a plea, expressed through story and anecdote, for a balance of opportunities to be restored.

In Parts 2 and 3, *A Curriculum for All* and *Changing Agendas* my experiences have hardened into convictions, and autobiography evolves into narrative centred on the *Sobriety* Project. The chapters cover a period of 42 years from 1973 to 2015 and explain how the *Sobriety* Project has applied the principles of an out-of-school curriculum more widely in the battle against misfortunes which condemn people to the scrap heap. The charity has used the surprising and underused resource of the UK inland waterways to show how private and public interests can come together to combat the futility and destructiveness of exclusion from society. In Chapter 11, Women and Children in Trouble, there is an exploration of the varying quality of women's prisons and a view of the plight of young people who have been expelled from school. In both instances, *Sobriety* had a part to play in the rescue of individuals. But the chapters are not primarily about boats and waterways; they are about a broad view of education which shows how people pushed to the edge have regained their confidence and begun the struggle back to normal life. They may be young people leaving prison and looking for work, men and women overwhelmed by mental illness or personality disorders, or children languishing in the academic 'sumps' of big schools. The chapters also describe the forces that have hindered *Sobriety*'s curriculum, or on the other hand, have created the opportunities to expand and spread the word about it.

The obstacles in the battle for the mind of government and the world at large find a place in Part 4 — *The Future*. Chapter 14 examines the work of the National Community Boats Association, the Inland Waterways Advisory Council and British Waterways, (now the Canal & River Trust). The concluding Chapter 15 returns to earlier themes and reflects on the future of informal learning in schools and other institutions.

Finally, the word 'curriculum' is not limited to describing what goes on in schools. It is also used, often by implication, to describe the approach to education by other institutions such as prisons, day centres, and by the *Sobriety* Project against a background of ever narrowing public education policy.

Notes

1   Canon Dr Giles Fraser writing in his regular column 'Loose Canon': *Guardian* 18.5.2013
2   Ian MacMillan giving the David Fickiling lecture at Newcastle University. The lecture was set up 10 years ago to examine the contribution children's literature makes to British culture.
3   Warwick Commission: Guardian 18.2.2015 under heading 'Creativity draining away from schools…'
4   This is the theme of journalist Warwick Mansell's *Education by Numbers: The Tyranny of Testing*: POLITICO'S: 2007.

A Cuckoo in the Curriculum

Part 1

Setting the Scene

Influences and Transplants

Christopher Mbonu and family, the author, and Simeon Ayeni (in the dark glasses).

Pounding millet in the Fulani village, a few yards from Sulieman Crescent.

Tuareg.

Chapter 1

NIGERIA: SOME LESSONS

'We overvalue what can be measured and undervalue what cannot'
Sir Alec Clegg, Chief Education Officer, West Riding Education Authority (1945-1974)[1]

Kano: A Personal Adventure

December 1972 saw my return from Kano in northern Nigeria to the chilly gloom of pre-Christmas Yorkshire and my teaching job in Goole, a small inland port on the Yorkshire Ouse.

Walking through the terraced streets of the little town at dusk with their half hearted illuminations of reindeer, I knew I was being reclaimed. The adventure had finished. I was coming back to mass unemployment, a miners' strike, blackouts, violence on picket lines and a state of emergency.

I had to forget a thousand year old mud-walled city: sword-carrying Tuareg 'blue men' from the desert crossing the airport's runway on camels: hobbled donkeys loaded with panniers of sand waiting to be ridden side saddle to Sabon Gari market:[2] a landscape of guinea savannah and granite inselbergs: Fulani cattle nomads making music with three-stringed pigs bladders and baked bean tins: city people walking through winding streets of adobe houses lit by hurricane lamps in the sand: Haille Selassie, Emperor of Ethiopia and Lion of Judah, guest of honour at a durbar in Katsina: calabashes, small hand-carved 'native tea sets' (nativity sets), camel blankets, baby shawls and other village objects waiting for a Trade Winds aircraft to take them to England and the West Riding schools museum service. My secondment had come to an end with a plane into Gatwick and a shivering train north; an eight hour journey had frozen my year in Nigeria into a diary of distant but hardening memories.

For a year since January, I had been living in a balconied flat on Sulieman Crescent on the outskirts of Kano and teaching English in one of the city's schools as part of an exchange programme between Kano and the West Riding Local Education Authority. My spacious five room accommodation designed for families who would be government guests at the opening of the new Bagauda Dam, was in an apartment block of plate glass and concrete. At the front there was an open garden with a resident chameleon and at the side a village of mud and straw huts, home to cattle-minding Fulani.

Along from Nasarawa (Victory) Gate and the ten metre high groundnut pyramids was Government Boys College. It gave a boarding education to boys who had come top of their village primary schools. They had arrived in secondary education in spite of a questionable selection process which could see a boy do well in the examinations but then be impersonated by another who adopted his name, and with money and influence, elbowed his way through the system. There was no free universal secondary education and it was the fierce competition for places that led to this corruption. Some would say that in England such bribery took a middle class, more outwardly respectable form. Parents and teachers did not steal children's identities but they did find ways of getting round the 11+ exam to secure a place in 'the grammar school' and to lift a family a few rungs up the class ladder.[3]

Today the purpose of Government College, Kano and schools like it, is stated in very British language:[4]

Federal Government Colleges in Nigeria were conceived to be unifying institutions, bringing together young Nigerian students from diverse ethnic and religious divides, with the purpose of providing them with high quality education in an environment of academic and developmental excellence devoid of ethnic, religious or social stratification that ruled Nigeria then, and unfortunately continues to plague Nigeria today.

The schools were set up to provide high quality education to children from different social strata, ethnicity, religion and geographic locations within Nigeria, while the teachers were drawn from around the world.

Kano students had great enthusiasm for education. It would bring advancement, mobility and wealth. I remember Shehu Abdullahi standing up in my class and announcing while rubbing his tummy, *"My mother and father, they bring me food, but you sir, give us Education!"* Shehu was not wrong. That was why I was in his classroom teaching English to him and other young men who in their villages spoke only Hausa or Fulani. If they could not speak English they knew they would not get the job and salary to match their parents' ambitions.[5]

Less demonstrative but no less enthusiastic for learning, was Saleh Suleh, a young man from Birnin Kudu a town 75 miles south of Kano, famous for its neolithic cave paintings. When I took two visiting West Riding education advisers to see the town's rocks and drawings during the school holidays, he was on hand to welcome and show us round. As part of an English language project in school, he sang and recorded the legends of Kano's long history, telling of the achievements of the early kings and explaining how the city acquired its walls in the eleventh century.

The Kano-West Riding exchange, like many good developments, had not come about through civil servants' calculations but as a result of a chance meeting in London between the West Riding's Chief Education Officer, Sir Alec Clegg, and Alhaji Dambatta who, in today's local authority language, held the Education portfolio for Kano. Reg Eyles, Sir Alec's deputy with responsibility for further education, had then been invited to Kano where he spent a fortnight cycling round schools and government ministries to make the practical arrangements for a link. The outcome was a brief circular to West Riding heads asking for volunteers to teach at the two federal secondary schools in Kano – Government Boys College and Government Girls College. I was the only volunteer for the boys' school and in mid 1971 began making arrangements for what promised to be an adventurous year.

A preliminary obligation was to obtain medical clearance from Britain's Overseas Development Administration, a part of the Foreign & Commonwealth Office whose job was to foster good relations with developing nations. I was instructed to attend upon Surgeon Colonel Hayward. As I walked into the room he greeted me with, *"You're Watson aren't you? Had the pox recently?"* and with some irritation, obviously wanting to make the interview more exciting, asked, *"D'you smoke? — I mean d'you use hash, man?"* Then having remarked that people with my physique were perfect victims for 'the white man's grave',[6] he allowed me a clean bill of health.

At Heathrow I met Kay Hudson, lately vice-principal of Lady Mabel Women's PE College near Rotherham, which in 1949 had been housed in Wentworth Woodhouse, home of the Fitwilliams before their estate was taken over for coal mining after the second world war. Kay had just retired, and Sir Alec, always with an eye for a good appointment, had persuaded her to take on the headship of Government Girls College which needed some reform if its students were to have any chance of personal independence let alone academic success.

A five hour Nigeria Airways flight via Rome, Tunis and the Sahara Desert took us to an early morning meeting with Sheila Everard, deputy head of Government Girls College and her bush dog *Banza* ('bastard' in the Hausa language), and the school which was to be Kay's home for the next four years.

Kano was amazing: Black Africa buzzing: humped zebu cattle wandering in narrow streets of adobe houses with horn shaped roof ends: cars and motor bikes going anywhere to avoid overloaded donkeys: the smell of desert heat and crowds of jet black faces: women carrying water in calabashes on their heads and babies strapped by shawls to their backs: travelling beggars with stumps for limbs — the final triumph of leprosy. It was another world.

Like me, Nigeria also was finding its feet at the beginning of the seventies. The country had become independent of British administration in 1960 and by 1972 was training its own teachers to replace expatriate staff. However the indigenisation timetable at Government Boys College was slow to get off the ground and the majority of staff were from overseas and on short term contracts. The staffroom was an interesting mix. Bashir Mohidien from Kerala in south India, was an imam who taught Islamic studies. Francis Katookaren, his friend, was a devout Christian also from Kerala, who taught chemistry. Other staff, mainly men, came from Egypt, Australia, Canada and the UK, including the head of English who had taught in Fiji before coming to West Africa. Two successive heads were from England but by the end of my year the post of principal had been filled by a northern Nigerian, Malam Ibrahim (malam is a respectful form of address in Hausa, somewhere between mister and sir).

For the students, the day began early with breakfast, which, like lunch and tea, consisted of an unidentifiable meat stew laced with peppers and boiled in cauldrons. It was advertised as beef but often suspected to be donkey, camel, or any other roaming game, much as in England 40 years ago when, before the EU made it illegal, fallen stock (animals which had died of natural causes) was sent for manufacture into 'pork' pies. Pepper stew was not good as a permanent diet and in the dining hall there were disagreements, sometimes violent, between cooks and boys.

Classes began at 8.00am and finished at 1.00pm with a quarter hour break from 10.45 to 11.00. English had to be taught from dry text books; classroom facilities were non existent and to breathe life into lessons teachers had to rely on their inventiveness. Students were generally well motivated, invariably courteous and had a great sense of humour but it was important to remember that they came from an independent and proud Hausa-Fulani culture with more than a thousand years of documented history. Their religion was Islam and ties were with the Magreb rather than Black Africa. No matter how benevolently the British administered the northern states, by the middle of the twentieth century they and other westerners were still regarded as colonialist incomers and a threat to the Hausa-Moslem way of life.[7] On the other hand they appeared to be bringing a design of education that promised prosperity.

Ramadan was a particularly difficult time for the school especially if it fell in May, June or July, the hottest months. Believing that the Koran forbids swallowing anything during the day, students would hasten to spit out of the classroom windows. This was not an easy situation for a young non-Moslem teacher to manage in the middle of a lesson. Nor was the comment of an Egyptian maths colleague when, in conversation about the Middle East (1972 was the year of the notorious Munich Olympics), I happened to tell him that three years previously I had spent a month on the Israel-Lebanon border picking peaches on a kibbutz. *"Fatah will be coming to get you"*, he said — jokingly of course!

In her position, Kay Hudson was much more at the sharp end and fiercely protective of her girls who were often regarded as fair game by passing Kano aristocrats. She had incessant arguments with the Ministry of Education in pursuit of more resources. Officials respected her ambitions for the students; it was impossible not to. But in spite of lip service to equality of educational opportunity, many had secret suspicions about girls being educated to the point where they might question the world around them and especially the social order. By contrast, women in the south of Nigeria were well represented in local government and frequently owners of small businesses.[8]

Twenty years later my own views on women's education would gain substance when I promoted a home grown training course for women to become barge skippers on the Yorkshire waterways, much to the disgust, only temporarily I am pleased to say, of the local boating fraternity. In 2012, the world took notice when the Pakistani Taliban shot and seriously injured schoolgirl Malala Yousafzai for daring to criticise their ban on women's education. She recovered, and in 2014, went on to win the Nobel Peace Prize. Today the UK Department for International Development is assisting the Nigerian Government to remove the barriers to girls' primary education and to extend and improve teacher training in rural areas, where only about 60% of children go to school. The problems are big. There are two different cultures at work, one Moslem, the other western. There may be as many as seventy pupils in a primary school class and they may be any age from six to thirty. Teacher training courses generally take place in the summer holidays and are more about learning English and basic skills than how to perform effectively in the classroom. Primary teachers' pay and conditions are inconsistent and there is violent hostility to girls being educated on Western principles from the Islamic fundamentalist group, Boko Haram. Its name which means 'Western education is sin' effectively condemns women to lifelong servitude; it also creates a fierce new military and political challenge to the Nigerian Government. Little else has changed except that by all accounts Kano now is a dangerous place where politically inspired murder and the massacre or kidnap of school students are commonplace.

A long suffering Suzuki 100 took me from Sulieman Crescent to school each morning and in the summer break carried me and maths colleague Simeon Ayeni on a six week journey round Nigeria. After first travelling north east through Potiskum to Maiduguri on the border with the Republic of Chad we turned south towards Cameroon and then west to Lagos where we were to photograph the grave of Vernon Hunt, a former pupil of Goole Grammar School and co-pilot of a Nigeria Airways aircraft which crashed on landing at Lagos aiport in 1969. The plan at the end of the expedition was to return to Kano on the main road through Ibadan and Zaria.

During 1972 Nigeria was moving to driving on the right and generally re-organising its traffic arrangements. It was an ideal time to be using a machine incapable of more than 40 mph. One would expect that the change in direction would take place at the same time all over the country. At midnight on the appointed day, traffic would stop and move over to the right. But this was not the way it was. The change was spread over three months and it was not unusual to be faced by three cyclists in line abreast on the 'wrong' side of the road. Self restraint was necessary. Unrestrained comments implying white superiority would be answered with an indulgent grin, a fist in the air, and then loudly in Hausa, 'Baban bature' – 'O great son of the Englishman!' regardless of whether one was English, French, Swedish or from Kazakhstan. Humour and polite questions were the best response to the impasse. *"What are you doing Malam? Why are you driving on the wrong side of the road?"* Invariably the incontrovertible answer was, *"We're practising."* It was an attitude not too concerned with death or even life but with an inclination to stick firmly to tradition without reference to a changing world. However, this detachment could occasionally be reconciled with twentieth century expectations as when I came across one of Kay Hudson's staff breezing along in a new Toyota in Kano city centre, *"Aminu, I didn't know you could drive."* *"I couldn't; Patrick Itomo taught me yesterday."*

Of course the great thing was that Aminu recognised the need to learn to drive! Less of a laugh was an accident on our summer expedition. The cheapest form of transport in West Africa at this time was the lorry, the sides of which would be decorated with injunctions and prayers in Hausa or English from the Koran or Bible, depending on the owner's religious inclinations. A vehicle was delivered as a simple chassis just as it would have been in Britain in the nineteen forties and fifties. A wooden superstructure was then erected on the chassis using a hammer and nails. As a consequence the front seat was best avoided. The rows of six inch nails a few inches from the passenger's chest were a vivid reminder of the fate of Saint Catherine of The Wheel.

After crossing the river Niger at Jebba, my friend Simeon and I were following a wagon loaded with cola nuts which are turned into sugary drinks by western manufacturers but habitually chewed for their bitter taste by Africans. Riding on the sacks of nuts were about twenty people bound for the city of Sokoto in the north-west of Nigeria. The wagon suddenly left the road, overturned and disintegrated into a cloud of sand and debris as if in an earthbound air crash. With the help of an official from Jebba railway station, we rescued the injured passengers and laid them in the shade on the platform, but few of them would survive: the nearest doctor was eighty miles away in Ilorin.

There was a sadness and conflict in rural Nigeria's encounter with the West, a topic that has been well aired over the years by African writers like Chinua Achebe [9] and Cyprian Ekwensi and which more than anything occupied my thoughts when I returned to England. The contrast between the traditional culture of the villages and the lifestyle of the cities highlighted the responsibility of governments not just to be mindful of rural minorities but, as in some parts of China, to adopt policies which protected village interests and provided amenities hitherto available only to big centres of population. That the mismatch of town and country could also lead to catastrophe was evident when the unreported tragedy at Jebba was more than equalled by a plane crash at Kano in 1973 which killed 200 pilgrims returning from Mecca. They had tried to cook food on camping gas stoves in the pressurised cabin of the aircraft.

Kano itself was a city of contrasts. The Emir lived in a palace, kept retainers and advisers, and was generally the guardian of Hausa culture. Even though like the British monarchy he had no substantial powers, he did retain influence over local officials. A few yards from the palace were the regional headquarters of the federal military government. Yacubu 'Jack' Gowon was head of state and committed to re-uniting the nation in the aftermath of the Biafran War, and, as is generally understood, to undoing the effects of the colonial power's attempts to introduce democracy to ethnic groups with irreconcilable political interests. It was a situation made worse by boundaries drawn without regard to tribal allegiance. Twenty million Hausa people occupy an area of sub-saharan West Africa stretching from Chad to Sierra Leone but there was no recognition of this by map makers or politicians.

Simeon Ayeni was from Lagos and being Yoruba, represented 'the enemy' to politically minded Hausas and Igbos who were jumpy about Yoruba influence. He and I had a taste of these simmering hostilities when we arrived in the newly designated South East State, the former 'breakaway Biafra' as it had been known to the BBC. The purpose of our detour into South East State was to visit Christopher Mbonu, an Igbo friend of mine who had been an Anglican curate in Goole and now, as Archdeacon of Onitsa, was living with his family near the regional capital, Enugu. His son had spent three years of the war from 1968 to 1970 hiding in the forest to avoid conscription into the army of Odumegwu Ojukwu, the Biafran leader. In spite of a federal victory and forty years of attempts at reconciliation, the war continues with grim ferocity into the twenty first century. Violence between Hausa Fulani Moslems and Igbo Christians is endemic and incessant.

After our visit to Enugu we travelled to the Cameroon border at Mfum which lay in a ravine of the Cross river. Our intention was to climb Mount Cameroon, a dormant volcano and the highest peak in West Africa. We had been assured by colleagues in Kano that it would be wet and foggy but as long as it did not erupt, would be well within our capability to climb. However the border was more of a problem than the mountain. I had a Cameroon visa but Simeon did not, having assumed that Nigerian nationality would be enough to get him across the border, and we were refused entry. At Ikom a few miles back we asked a gentleman in army uniform if he knew of anywhere to stay for the night. He was Sergeant Gabriel and he did know where 'spies' could stay — in the lock-up of his barracks. He could not understand why anyone would want to climb Mount Cameroon, and two hours of interrogation got the three of us nowhere. Appeal was useless. The commanding officer was at a meeting in Lagos and the second in command was, figuratively speaking or perhaps actually, tied up in the local brothel. However we came to no harm and the next day, reluctantly, he let us go.

Riding for hours on a small motor bike on bush roads was stressful for both of us. The heat, the bike's vibration and the possibility of an accident miles from anywhere were a worry. The aftermath of Nigerian road accidents was not reassuring. While crossing a narrow bridge near Makurdi in the east of the country we came across an articulated lorry in the middle of a field. It had left the road and jack-knifed, crushing a VW Beetle and presumably its occupants, between the cabin and trailer.

One way of relieving the tension, as friends do, was to have the occasional punch up — a war of civilisations, black against white, but disappointingly not the eschatological battle between Christian and Moslem which would have completed the picture (Simeon was an atheist). Although this cleared the air and produced the adrenalin needed for overtaking wagons with swinging trailers on the laterite gravel roads of eastern Nigeria, it was not our only remedy. One idyllic day we climbed through mountain mist up a dirt road to the Obudu Cattle Ranch, a resort in the highlands of Cross River State where waiters in bow ties served cold beer and ham sandwiches with the crusts removed. The motorbike had a fit of mountain sickness but its riders were well refreshed.

Going south we arrived in Jos, capital of Benue Plateau State which was 5,000 feet above sea level and had an agreeable climate. However, long distances on the bike led to dehydration and this, with the doubtful hygiene of Nigerian roadside eating places and a diet of beans blended with several species of coleoptera, made me a casualty of what in Nigerian English was called 'dysentry'. Having passed out in Jos museum, I woke in the Sudan Inland Mission's Evangel Hospital with a saline drip in my arm. It was a comfortable way to spend two days but I felt slightly guilty about not being down the road with the locals in the more austere government hospital. In spite of this excitement I had to remember that my real business was teaching, not getting into scrapes around Nigeria on what was little more than a motorised bicycle with a maths teacher who was only just a little less irresponsible than me.

Early in 1973, after I had been back at Goole Grammar School for a few weeks, Reg Eyles asked to see me. He and Sir Alec wanted to know what I had learned from my secondment. At the time it was a difficult question to answer and I mumbled some clichés about good practice in the classroom and expounded on the help Kay Hudson had given me. I was relieved that I was not being interviewed for a job but they must have been reasonably satisfied that my secondment had been a good investment because three Goole Grammar School colleagues were already planning for a year in Kano. I was pleased that Simeon Ayeni, my Yoruba friend, was coming to teach maths for a year at Goole, and two young people from Kano were on their way to Ripon Grammar

School, the West Riding's only boarding school, with the intention of going on to read medicine at Leeds University. Coincidental with Simeon's and my summer exploration of Nigeria, Francis Katookaren and Bashir Mohidien had turned up at Goole Grammar School as part of a family visit to England.

If I had been asked now what I had learned, I would still have touched on the importance of imaginative teaching but would have added that being pummelled with the 'African' experience had given me insights and warnings that would not have been available at home. Nigeria was my own personal development course, my out-of-school activity, hard work physically, intellectually and emotionally. It was an experience in technicolour, frustrating but unmissable, a year of exploration during which many aspects of my life before Kano were questioned. The challenges were, firstly, the contrast in outlook between colleagues at Government College who were 'old colonials' and, albeit secretly, were convinced of their own 'European' superiority, (even though they might be Indian, Egyptian or even African), and those of us who came from a younger generation with no experience of imperial protocols. Secondly, in contrast, the Hausa people were full of pride in their culture but unconcerned about any obligation to get a job done *tomorrow*. The day after tomorrow — (in the vernacular, 'jibi' rather than 'gobé') would do. Thirdly there was the climate which was very hot in a city on the southern edge of the Sahara. Lastly there was Simeon. He and I spent six weeks on a small machine with all our belongings packed into two panniers, not knowing where we would sleep at night and for much of the time driving on dirt roads with corrugations deep enough to wreck the bike. It was an expedition with all the features of a 'spaghetti' Western.

Having been educated at Government College, Lagos and the University of Ibadan, Simeon was very westernised, perhaps even to the point in his younger days of being a 'typical' public school boy, always courteous and wishing to please, but perhaps thinking secretly that I needed taking down a peg or two. We rubbed along, but never really became bosom buddies. His politics were those of a radical free thinking African and I represented a throwback to the days of British colonialism, perhaps not to slavery, but certainly to the era of the white overlord.

So self restraint became a necessity in daily life, not just in encounters on a motor bike, but also in the classroom. Pupils spoke a foreign language and came from a cultural mixture of Islam and animism in which the prayer mat and the ju-ju tree provided equal re-assurance. They were powerful influences tempered by humour deriving from fables of animal or human misfortune, the best of which were collected into an anthology of Hausa stories [10] given to me by West Riding education advisers, Jean Imrie and Joan Bloomfield who were visiting Kano to help with primary school science courses.

Where are the Hyacinths?

Kano had been a healthy test of patience and resilience. It had also been an adventure I wanted to share. I realised that this short year, as well as my teaching prior to Kano, had done much to reinforce my ideas about education. They are best summed up in Sir Alec Clegg's reference to his aunt who had taught many girls including Margaret Thatcher. On her sitting room wall hung the text:

If thou of fortune be bereft
And of thine earthly store hath left
Two loaves, sell one, and with the dole
Buy hyacinths to feed the soul.

Sir Alec interpreted the lines in this way, *"The loaves are mainly concerned with facts, and their manipulation, and with the intellect; the hyacinths are concerned with a man's loves, hates, fears, enthusiasms, and antipathies: with his courage, his confidence and his compassion and in short, with a whole range of qualities which will determine not what he knows but the sort of person he is."* The 'loaves' were of the mind; the 'hyacinths' were of the spirit.[11] Experiences in Nigeria as well as a natural inclination were leading me to think that these 'hyacinths' were probably best found in an informal curriculum beyond the classroom.

Mr A. B. Clegg, as he was before being knighted in 1965, was a member of the committee which in 1963 presented *Half Our Future*, sometimes known as the Newsom Report.[12] In the part of the report dealing with out-of-school activities his influence is clear:

There are many positive reasons why 'extra-curricular' provision is important. For the individual boy and girl, it can mean the discovery of new interests. Some they may carry with them into adult life; others will vanish as quickly as many adolescent enthusiasms naturally do, but there may have been profit as well as pleasure in the experience. It is often a chance for the odd-man-out to come into his own, among the staff as well as the pupils, revealing an unsuspected talent; and for some of our pupils, especially, there may be a gain in confidence from being a member of a much smaller social and working group than is normally possible in class.

In later years he told a sad little story showing what he meant by 'hyacinths' (and the lack of them). It was of a young boy who had been asked to write a composition about his father. He wrote several lines: *"My dad is very tall. He has a soft voice and was full of fun. He played with me and my brothers and we all love him. He died last week."* All the boy's teacher was able to write at the end of the composition was one word — Tenses!

For me the Kano 'hyacinths' had been teaching and living with young people brought up to be very proud of their Hausa culture. If my first 'hyacinth' was to experience their anxiety at being educated for a way of life which had its currency in faraway cities and unpredictable futures, my second was to hold tightly to a view of education often outside the classroom that would give young people the confidence to become independent and compassionate adults. I like to remember a saying of Abbott Lawrence Lowell who was President of Harvard and a reformer of university education in the United States:[13]

Columbus, when he set out did not know where he was going. When he arrived he did not know where he was. When he returned he did not know where he had been. But all the same he discovered America.'

I, too, was not entirely sure where I had been, but I did feel older and perhaps a little wiser. Kano had re-inforced my conviction that the classroom should not have an exclusive claim on children's minds. It had been an adventure I wanted to share but in the short term it was not going to be easy to work out how my Nigerian experience could find its way into the broader curriculum of a new comprehensive school.

Back in England in 1973 I did not realise it at the time but I was in the right place with the right people: people whose convictions about the real nature of education had not only been tried and tested but had taken them into positions where they could have a direct and lasting effect on the curriculum. One whom I had the privilege to know for several years, during his time as Sir Alec's deputy, was Jim Hogan who had been the first warden of the Outward Bound Trust's sailing school at Aberdovey, set up after the Second World War by Kurt Hahn, a German educationist, and his friend Laurence Holt, owner of the Blue Funnel Line in Liverpool. Looking back over his time at Aberdovey, Jim said many of his students were far from bright. They came from homes and schools that had never encouraged them to be anything but doubtful about their abilities and this had led them to be defensive and hostile. What was important for his sea-school staff was not so much the teaching of skills as helping the young people to be more mature and tolerant. He was often surprised by what they would achieve in unexpected circumstances. In his book *Impelled into Experiences* Jim told the story of an intending seaman: [14]

> *…who came from serving as a pot boy in an East End pub to face the ordeal of our demanding regime. Small, self effacing and pathetically humble, he was patronised by all and showed no signs of resenting it. He was one of a watch of twelve who formed the schooner's crew on a particularly unpleasant passage. By a pure quirk of providence he was entirely unaffected by the sickness which obliterated his companions. Throughout the trip he manned the galley, producing hot meals and drinks for the officers and himself, and regularly patrolled the lee side of the ship so as to redistribute those of his comrades who were disposed to lie drowning in the scuppers, which were well awash.*
>
> *As things got worse his cheerfulness, not to say cockiness, visibly increased. When the watch shamefacedly struggled back to consciousness the old relationships were patently inappropriate. Not only was he treated with respect; he was in fact a changed person and he did not look back. Previously the pet of the watch, henceforth he accepted the role of potential bulwark'.*

In his preface to Jim Hogan's book, Sir Alec Clegg expressed the hope that:

> *…we may at long last have escaped from the practices of talent spotting, training the strong and ignoring the weak, and cultivating failure by praising the adept and ignoring the inept.*

He was over optimistic. Twenty-one years later, the National Curriculum arrived with such an obsession for testing that by 2003 some primary schools were spending over ten hours a week cramming children to pass tests in English, Maths and Science. Like the pot boy from the East End pub, children who could not keep up were constantly reminded of their failings.

In mainstream secondary schools slow learners with special educational needs could find themselves being physically included but emotionally excluded and sometimes bullied because they could not keep up and were regarded as different. [15]

Inspection of schools and testing of pupils became the responsibility of an arm of government, the Office for Standards in Education, Children's Services & Skills. It was founded by Ken Clarke MP in 1992, and from 1994 until 2000 was led by Chris Woodhead: [16]

...who is one of the most controversial figures in the debates about the direction of English education policy. He is particularly associated with support for 'traditional teaching methods' and for taking a scornful view of 'progressive educational theories' introduced into English schools from the 1960s onwards...(Wikipedia entry unattributed)

Critics argued that he was generating poor morale, that he rarely identified successes in schools, and that the progressive teaching he attacked was a 'straw man', with little resemblance to actual classroom practice.

Woodhead most prominently identified weaknesses in schools with poor teaching and repeatedly asserted this view. Amongst his controversial remarks he claimed there were '15,000 incompetent teachers' and said, *"I am paid to challenge mediocrity, failure and complacency."* His blunt approach gained him many enemies, especially in teaching. [17] To many teachers it seemed like a witch hunt, and the consequences for many hardworking and dedicated headteachers were dire. His policies led to widespread distress and the ruin of some people's careers. For some staff his inspection regime had the hallmarks of the McCarthy era [18] in America and it was not without justification that at the time of his resignation a dark tale was told about his departure from office:

On the day Chris Woodhead resigned from Ofsted a man came to his office and said, "Is it possible to have a word with Mr Woodhead?" The receptionist said, "I'm very sorry but Mr Woodhead doesn't work for Ofsted any more. He left yesterday." "OK", replied the man and he left the building. The following day the same man came and in a dapper tone asked to see the former Chief Inspector. The incredulous receptionist gave him the same answer. When the episode was repeated for the third time the receptionist said indignantly, "He's resigned I tell you. Mr Woodhead has gone! Why do you keep coming here only to get the same answer?" The man replied cheerfully, "I just love to hear you keep saying that he's gone." [19]

There is an opinion among teachers that Woodhead confused 'informal' with 'progressive'. Be that as it may, he was seen by many to have introduced a brutal and undiscriminating regime of school inspection.

More recently in 2011 the senior political editor of the *New Statesman* writing in the *Guardian* maintained that:

...endless preparation for tests is killing the enthusiasm of teachers for teaching, exam costs have doubled to £300 million in the last ten years and the tests don't even bring good results. When compared to results of nations which scorn the need for incessant measurement, our results in science, literacy and maths, so dear to the hearts of the testers, are increasingly unsatisfactory. The danger of imposing too much bureaucracy on teachers is that through no fault of their own they cease to excite their children and curiosity dies. [20]

13

In a depressing study of what he calls 'hyperaccountability' in pupil testing, *Times Educational Supplement* journalist, Warwick Mansell, says:

Take the case of an eleven year old. Let us call her Michelle. Imagine she is sitting down to take tests in English, maths and science. On her performance rest the future of her teacher, her headteacher, the local authority's director of children's services, the director of the National Strategies, the Education Secretary, and, ultimately, the Chancellor and the Prime Minister. But to Michelle, the result is actually, on the face of it and in its own right, of very little significance. [21]

Oscar Wilde said that education begins only when a child leaves school, but the young people leading the 2011 riots in London *had* left school and, in the eyes of the Coalition Government at the time, there was an urgent need to find ways of identifying and measuring the personal and social outcomes that contributed to 'character building' in young people of all ages. This led to the publication of *A Framework of Outcomes for Young People* which attempted to measure the elusive 'soft' outcomes governing their lives. [22] The report was the latest in libraries of academic research (beginning with Plato) in the quest for this 'golden fleece' of education. It was praiseworthy but pointless in the light of cuts that were going to destroy the Youth Service, and a regime of testing in schools that could not afford the time for such luxuries.

Sir Alec Clegg did not need expensive research to tell him education should only incidentally be concerned with the gross national product and material advance. But in 2011 the headteacher of Crown Woods College in London was imposing different coloured uniforms for pupils with differing levels of tested ability:

They are taught in separate colour co-ordinated buildings, play in fenced-off areas and eat lunch at separate times. At 11 years old, all pupils at the college are streamed according to ability in what the headteacher argues is the only way to survive in the brave new world of market-driven education. [23]

The article records some of the side effects of the policy of splitting the college into three schools:

One girl aged 15 who attends Sherwood school says that students in the top school 'look down' on students in the other ability schools like hers. She says arguments and fighting have broken out between different schools… "If you were friends with someone in Delamere, you are kind of enemies now, because you don't want to talk to them. If you talk to them you kind of feel you're betraying your school… There was an argument in the school the other day and the girls were arguing between the fences… it just feels like we've been cut off from them."

How sad. How dangerously close to the mindset of the adversaries in the Balkan wars of the nineteen nineties or of Christian and Moslem neighbours in the Middle East. What a far cry from John Buchan, Lord Tweedsmuir's understanding of education: [24]

The object of humane studies is the understanding of human nature, the broadening of human interests and the better appreciation of the purpose of human life. Technique raises none of these questions. It is the mastery of brute fact for a definitely utilitarian end. Its concern is with material things and not with those of the spirit.

At a less exalted level, the children's author, Michael Morpurgo,[25] has written that he:

…abandoned classrooms altogether because I felt that for so many children not nearly enough education could be achieved within their confines. I exchanged mine for a farm and…began to bring city children to the countryside…They help to lamb the sheep, milk the cows, feed the pigs, collect the eggs, watch the sun rise and set, and go for long muddy walks along the Torridge…That's the kind of classroom that can really change things.

But interference is multi-faceted and recent proposals by government to abolish farm related examinations in secondary schools bode ill for the future. Put simply, if school farms do not contribute points in league tables, schools will cease to teach the disciplines associated with them, and the farms will be abandoned.

In *Memoirs: Of a Deskert Loon in the Hungry Thirties*, George Anderson Clarke was less concerned with testing than with education. He recalls his school in Deskford, Banff, which had a headteacher who 'could change things':

John Beveridge was an unusual headmaster by introducing many novel ideas. For example all boys from 11+ had to join the girls in their weekly cooking class. Another innovation was to hand out two or three of his daily newspapers, asking us to see if we could spot the political slants of each paper. This helped us understand their politics and so understand better the power of the press. We also did the crosswords which helped expand our vocabulary. When teaching us geometry he gave us a surveyor's tape and told us to measure the school's exterior and draw up a plan of it: an enjoyable way of learning.

Scorning an approach to education which disregarded such teaching by experience, Sir Alec told a famous fable:[26]

There was a small boy called Fred and he lived on an island with his father and mother and nearby lived his uncle and aunt. His father kept pigeons and bees and a garden of flowers and vegetables. His uncle was a forester and planted acre after acre of trees in rows. The boy did not go to school; there wasn't a school on the island, but his mother taught him to read and write and encouraged him to draw and paint pictures. She also recited poetry to him and sang to him when he was little…telling of family visits to York and Malham Cove and of how the child grew up in understanding of many things. Then came the Fall: One day a learned educationist visited the island and met the boy and was astonished at his understanding of many things and at the knowledge which he had developed round these things. And the educationist said to himself how wonderful it would be if every child in the land had the learning which this boy had built around the simple experiences which he has had with bees, pigeons, flowers, vegetables, forestry and visits to York and Malham. And the learned educationist reasoned thus: 'It is impossible for every child to lead the life that this boy had led and to develop the knowledge which this boy's way of life has given him. But what we can do is give the children all the knowledge that this boy has, without the experiences.

First of all we will look at his numerical and mathematical ability which he has gained from reckoning areas from odd shaped bits of land and working out the number of trees they will take, and from his mother's shopping expeditions, and we will reduce these to simple symbolic formulas and tables and make children learn a lot of them very quickly. Then we will take the boy's speech and writing which is so good, and subject it to careful analysis and if we teach the other boys whose speech and writing is not so good how to subject what they say to this kind of analysis, they will realise how badly they speak and write and will promptly set about trying to improve the way they speak and write…

The fable sends the learned educationist home to divide Fred's knowledge into parcels which he hands out to various textbook writers. Inexorably the fable continues:

And so it came about that all over the land the children were assembled in groups of 40 and made to learn the facts set out in the books written by Messrs Hall & Stevens, Warner & Martin, Durrell & Palmer, and Potter and Ridout. And the learned educationist began to entertain a horrible suspicion that the reverse process didn't work. In other words, whereas Fred grew in understanding because he started with experience and read to feed the interest which derived from it, those who started with the reading failed to develop understanding because the interest was not there.

No doubt their interest would have been revived by the measured transfer of soft outcomes!

Like Fred, Jim Hogan's pot boy had learned by experience and become a leader not through information and instruction but by his response to the circumstances of the people around him. Jim was Deputy Chief Education Officer of the Wet Riding until he and Sir Alec retired in 1974 when, following the Redcliffe-Maud report on local government, the Authority was abolished. However my acquaintance with him was not through the LEA, but through a new development of Outward Bound, pioneered in Leeds during the late sixties and known as City Challenge.

Clegg and Hogan were among the last educationists of the twentieth century to have a vision of education undistorted by politics and sectional interests. It is apparent that the true locus of education has moved out of schools; the curriculum is now in the hands of government rather than teachers, governors and local authorities and the 'tyranny of testing' is making the classroom less attractive. The question is where and how can education be conducted so that it does make a difference to people's lives. I hope that the chapters which follow will be pointers to an answer but we should be aware in the meantime that a curriculum which is the target of so much political interference, itself perhaps the result of an unstable politics, cannot be good for either children or adults. Heads are hobbled by intrusive paperwork and many classroom teachers have simply had enough. This book is partly about the value of informal learning in the broader setting of prisons and other institutions, but it also broods over and deplores the grotesque state of affairs found in many schools and within the teaching profession. The account of the progress of an eleven year old pupil, Mandy, told to me by her classroom teacher, says it all:

Mandy is more hungry to learn than the rest of the class put together. She comes from a traveller family. Her mother cannot read or write. She is absent from school nearly as much as she is present, but when she is in class she soaks up knowledge and skills like no other. She approaches teachers to ask for assistance out of lessons (where other children don't) and takes responsibility for her own learning, not out of some instilled duty but out of a real wish to expand and find out about her world.

She came to the school five months ago, and at age 11 could not form words or read even the simplest of books. She was in Year 6 but was working at or below the level of a child in a Reception class. Her progress since then has been exponential. Orally she is brilliant and her grasp of concepts way above her prescribed 'level' is often suprising. She is obviously very intelligent and as sharp as a razor: on one recent occasion I collected the class from the door into the playground after lunch and said in teachery voice "Right, lunchtime's over, it's time to quieten down and get on with the afternoon". I happened to look at Mandy. Without a word, and with a glint in her eye she pointed to a school poster on human rights with an excerpt which read 'We have a right to play'. I laughed out loud and was made speechless by her wit! Her ever-opening world is alive because she is learning to read.

A fortnight ago, the head teacher came into a meeting I was having with another Year 6 teacher, with an air of excitement. "Great news!", she said, "Mandy is leaving! This means she won't ruin our end-of-year data!". The information was met with a congratulatory reception from the other member of staff and they both seemed much the happier for knowing that the girl was going to depart from the school.

In that moment they had both forgotten they were teachers. They had been hypnotised by a system whose raison d'être has freakishly morphed so that children have become products; their SAT results and the effect they have on schools' perceived 'success' now outweighs any idea of the rounded education that can assist a pupil's wellbeing. Yes, there is sound methodology in current pedagogy and Michael Gove's 2014/2015 curriculum has much to benefit children, but head teachers are so in fear of the consequences of failing an Ofsted inspection that, as this story of Mandy shows, children now almost stand in the way of the machine's momentum and many teachers are left wondering what it all is for. Any week now, Mandy will not arrive in class on a Monday morning. Her family will have moved on and she will have gone for good. She may continue in full time education; she may not. What is sure is that her moving from the school is a loss. It is a loss for her and certainly one for the school.

The final comment of my young teacher friend was *"She will 'ruin' any school's data but surely there are more important things than that!"*

Questions

What were the lessons of Kano?

Was it a hyacinth?

Where are the hyacinths to be found in the current school curriculum (2015)?

Chapter 1 Notes

1. This was a recurring theme in Sir Alec Clegg's speeches and conversations. The context is best explained in his after dinner speech given on 3rd August 1972 at the end of a vacation course for teachers at Bingley College of Education. It also features in his book *About Our Schools* — see note 11 below.

2. Sabon Gari means Stranger's Quarter in the Hausa language. Stalls were owned by people from other parts of Nigeria, very often Igbos. In times of ethnic violence, the market was an easy target. On a lighter note it was here that you could buy a mug of tea for a penny, a mug of coffee for a penny or *teacoffee* mixed, for three pennies.

3. 11+: A headteacher now working in the south of England said that many schools including his own, operated a two entry point system. Pupils made a straight entry if they passed the 11+ and middle class children were usually prepared more thoroughly. But for those middle class children who slipped through the net, there was a second chance through the scholarship system which meant that their parents could pay a contribution and get the place at the grammar school.

4. Excerpt from Nigerian Ministry of Education brochure.

5. Shehu: His parents knew the truth of the saying that if you give a hungry man food, you feed him for a day. Teach him how to fish and farm and you feed him for life. A more modern take might be that if you train him to become a banker or lawyer or even better, a professional footballer, he will have access to a very good salary.

6. White man's grave: A term coined in the 19th century to describe Sierra Leone, Britain's first colony in West Africa. Before the widespread use of the prophylactic, quinine, malaria was thought to bring certain death to explorers and merchants who lingered on the West African coast.

7. Even after 12 years of independence this remained the central theme of many Nigerian newspapers.

8. A highly readable and often hilarious up-to date account of life in modern Nigeria is *Looking for Transwonderland: Travels in Nigeria* by Noo Saro-Wiwa. Her description of the University of Ibadan's dog show of is worthy of a literary prize on its own merits alone. The author's father Ken Saro-Wiwa was hanged in 1995 for publicly opposing the regime of General Sani Abacha and fighting for the rights of the Ogoni people whose livelihood was being destroyed by the Royal Dutch Shell company's oil exploration. His execution led to Nigeria being suspended from the Commonwealth for three years.

9. In his book, *There was a Country*, Chinua Achebe (1930-2013) says that Hausa Fulanis and Yorubas do not like Igbos because they (Igbos) have a cultural ideology which emphasises individualism and competitiveness.

10. Oxford Library of African Literature: *A Selection of Hausa Stories* compiled by H. A. S. Johnston: OUP 1966. See also *Islam in West Africa* by J. S. Trimingham: OUP 1959.

11. See page 17 of *About Our Schools*: Alec Clegg: published by Basil Blackwell: 1980

12. HMSO: A report of the Central Advisory Council for Education: DES: 1963. J H Newsom CBE was chair of the Council.

13. Lowell was President of Harvard University from 1909–1933.

14. *Impelled into Experiences* — The Story of the Outward Bound Schools: JM Hogan: EP Publishing: 1968

15. Baroness Mary Warnock was chair of the committee which in 1978 had called for a re-think of the education of children with special educational needs.

16. For a summary of Chris Woodhead's views on education see the (unedited) online encyclopaedia Wikipedia.

17. The political events leading up to the creation of Ofsted and the appointment of Mr Woodhead are comprehensively covered in chapter 7 of Derek Gillard's *Education in England: A Brief History* (2011)

18. McCarthyism: 'Joe' McCarthy (1908-1957) was an American politician who served as a Republican US senator for the state of Wisconsin from 1947 until his death in 1957. Beginning in 1950, McCarthy became the most visible public face of a period in which Cold War tensions fuelled fears of widespread communist subversion. He was noted for making claims that there were large numbers of communists and Soviet spies in the United States federal government and elsewhere.

19 For opinions of the Chief Inspector of Schools see: BBC *Talking Point* 9th November 2000 – *Resignation of Chris Woodhead*. The story told here came from the former headteacher of a school for children with special educational needs.

20 *Guardian* 17.12.2011. This trenchant and disturbing article by Mehdi Hasan is well worth reading.

21 *Education by Numbers: The Tyranny of Testing* — Warwick Mansell: published by Politico's in 2007. In his Guardian article Mehdi Hasan (note 20 above) says 'Mansell's book should be required reading for the test obsessed education secretary Michael Gove, and his Labour shadow, Stephen Twigg. Politically motivated meddling in the examination system by both Conservatives and Labour has done little to boost schools standards or pupil performance. Over the past decade, according to the OECD Programme for International Student Assessment (PISA) global survey of 15 year olds, Britain has slipped from fourth to 16th in Science, seventh to 25th in literacy and eighth to 28th in Maths'. Mansell was writing at the end of the Blair era and before Michael Gove and his successors respectively, became secretary of state. However the findings of his research should be taken very seriously in the current climate of frustration and misery affecting many teachers.

22 *A Framework of Outcomes for Young People*: Researched by Catalyst and published by the Young Foundation for the DfE in July 2012. The report looks at different ways of measuring so called 'soft' outcomes for young people: 'soft' as opposed to 'hard' examination results.

23 *Education Guardian* 25.7.2011: article by Rowenna Davis.

24 John Buchan, author of the Hannay novels and many other works of fiction, history and political comment. He was also Governor General of Canada 1935-1940. The excerpt is from *The Interpreter's House: 'The Chancellor's Installation Address Delivered Before the University of Edinburgh July 20th 1938'*.

25 In 1976 author Michael Morpurgo and his wife, Clare Morpurgo (the oldest daughter of Sir Allen Lane, the founder of Penguin Books), established the charity Farms for City Children, with the primary aim of providing children from inner city areas with experience of the countryside. The programme involves children spending a week at a countryside farm, during which they take part in purposeful farmyard work.

26 This is one of Sir Alec Clegg's most famous parables and has been re-told many times in many publications.

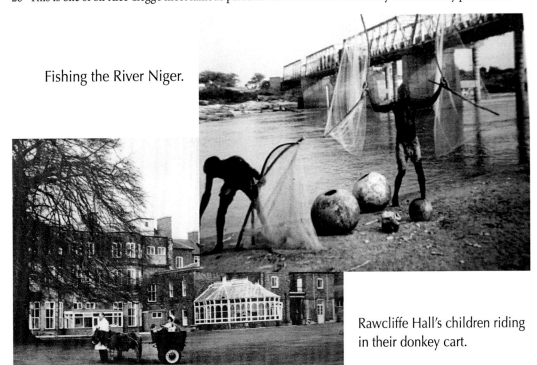

Fishing the River Niger.

Rawcliffe Hall's children riding in their donkey cart.

Chapter 2
CITY CHALLENGE

To Serve, To Strive And Not To Yield

An inscription on a cross in McMurdo Sound, Antarctica, commemorating those who died in Captain Robert Falcon Scott's 1911 expedition to the South Pole. This line from Alfred Lord Tennyson's *Ulyssses* was later adopted by the Outward Bound Trust as the organisation's motto.

City Challenge adopted a different kind of testing — one to give young people a personal foundation of achievement not limited to market driven knowledge. It was conceived in 1967 after 10 years of thinking and planning by Captain Freddie Fuller who followed Jim Hogan as warden of Outward Bound's Aberdovey Sea School.

In 1942 Fuller's ship, *MV Medon*, was torpedoed in the south Atlantic and for the next five weeks he was responsible for a lifeboat of 16 survivors, all Chinese. After days at sea with few rations and little hope of rescue, his companions had begun to throw themselves overboard, not wishing to be a burden to their friends. Fuller's conviction that there must be a better way of responding to misfortune became the inspiration behind the Outward Bound Trust's use of the hardships of the sea and mountains as paths to personal development.

By the early sixties Outward Bound had expanded into the Lake District and Scotland with schools at Ullswater, Eskdale, Moray Firth and Loch Eil, and was successfully helping young people to learn skills and principles of lifetime value. Students came from many different backgrounds and beliefs but worked together in facing common tasks and common hazards. At the same time Freddie Fuller was asked by President John Kennedy to set up the American Peace Corps in Puerto Rico. From seeing young people at work in the Puerto Rican slums, he (Fuller) realised that it was not only the mountains and ocean that could provide opportunities for young people to learn about themselves; so too could the cities. Fuller's obituary in 1993 [1] recorded that

> *...whilst tailoring the first courses for the corps in Puerto Rico, he saw the success and enthusiasm with which volunteers tackled the challenges of an urban environment. The idea was brought back across the Atlantic to become City Challenge. Today another quarter of a century later, City Challenge still thrives in the UK and has spread to northern Europe and back to the US with Outward Bound education centres established in New York and Boston.*

The same impulse was later to be engrained in the fabric of the *Sobriety* Project. It took people who had life-challenging experiences and allowed them to build on the personal strengths which would help them overcome their difficulties. In future years *Sobriety* would owe a great deal to this urban version of Outward Bound.[2]

The headquarters of City Challenge were in Canal House, a former lock keeper's residence near the canal basin in Coventry. It shared the premises with a scheme to bring the waterways into the mainstream of the city's education provision, a brainchild of Sir Robert Aitken, Director of Education, who was also Chair of City Challenge and a member of the Schools Curriculum Development Committee. Like Alec Clegg and Jim Hogan he believed that education should build on the strengths and enthusiasms of young people, not confront them with demoralising targets invented and supervised by politicians.

In a belief that school was only one part of an individual's education, the Department for Education was using its resources at that time to promote best practice rather than testing. The eleven plus exam which had been the cornerstone of selection in the tripartite system was becoming obsolete. Meanwhile a growing number of comprehensive schools was adopting a curriculum for life (not just work) which had originated in the public school concept of an all-round education. At the same time a report, *The Youth Service in England and Wales,* published in 1960 and commonly known as the *Albermarle Report*, was highlighting the need for local authorities to share in providing leisure activities for young people. 1965 saw the *National Association of Youth Clubs* publish *The Unattached*, a non-statutory sector report about experimental street projects which catered for young people excluded from youth centres and regarded as 'unclubbable'. The emphasis was changing from *provision* of activities to *involving* young people in the planning of services. This period of the mid sixties to the mid eighties was one of optimism inspired by some distinguished practitioners and it remains a mystery why the world of education stopped listening to them.

In summer 1975, two and a half years after returning from Kano, I was in Edinburgh to help with a City Challenge course being led by full-time Director David Gibson who had previously been a youth worker in Castleford, a mining town in the West Riding. Just before the demise of the West Riding Authority, Sir Alec Clegg and Jim Hogan had appointed him to develop City Challenge in line with Fuller's suggestions. Edinburgh City Challenge was not the first on the scene; in 1967 Leeds Education Authority had hosted an experimental course and the resulting format had been repeated in Pontefract, Batley, Belfast and elsewhere. By 1975 many of the teething problems had been solved and a standard pattern of placements, seminars and recreation had emerged.

For the month of August, nine tutors and forty young people aged between 17 and 25 and mostly sponsored by their employers, schools, colleges or young offender institutions, became temporary residents in Edinburgh's Royal High School which in 1968 had abandoned its palladian home on Calton Hill and moved to the northern suburbs. In preparation for the course, staff borrowed beds from the army, turned classrooms into dormitories and requisitioned city council minibuses laid up for the summer to take students to the placements.

The placements which had been arranged with agencies in the city were not to be sniffed at. Staff as well as students found them hard and exhausting. A four day stint at Goggaburn was the biggest shock. This was a hospital of a type common until the early nineteen eighties, full of 'patients' with what in those days was described as 'mental handicap', a term later replaced by 'learning disability'. Some had been there for years and were compliant with the institution's regime; others were rebellious and angry at their confinement in a place they did not like or understand and in spite of being given generous doses of largactil and other drugs, shouted, screamed and had to be restrained. Inmates were commonly labelled high grade and low grade, eugenic terms invented by institutions that, like a prison, had the power to rob a person of dignity or individuality and make it impossible for them to achieve independence. It was a misguided policy based on the view that it made for a better society.[3] The 1975 film *One Flew Over The Cuckoo's Nest* made the point well. Set in a fictional psychiatric ward it followed patients' tragic decline into a subservience not too far removed from that inflicted on Nazi concentration camp victims. Methods of persuasion were similar: forced electro-convulsive therapy administered without anaesthetic: head shaving: teeth removal, and sterilisation. If all these measures failed there was a resort to frontal lobotomy. The notorious 1971 Zimbardo Stanford Prison Experiment[4] in the USA illustrated the plight of prisoners (which is what these patients were) and their appointed guards who on a whim could abuse them with impunity.

Students were surprised and upset and came back to evening seminars determined never to return to the hospital. But four days on the wards getting to know the patients often led them to take a different view. Some transformed their terror into compassion, some remarked on the resilience and humanity of the hospital staff while others were sceptical about staff competence and wanted to see the end of such institutions. Whatever their view they depended on one another for sorting out their feelings. An academically minded trainee police constable might well understand the sociology of mental illness or learning disability but be less inclined to muck in. On the other hand a young woman from prison might have the emotional edge when it came to working closely with noisy patients but be less able or willing to communicate her feelings in seminars. The challenge in the placements and back at base was for students to support one another in spite of their different backgrounds. This central aspect of the course was brought home to Edinburgh course tutor David Uffindall[5] who thirty years later recalled a 19 year old man 'who had had a couple of difficult days at the Sally Army in Edinburgh where he found talking to the inhabitants a bit daunting'. *"I tried to reassure him"*, said David, *"by pointing out that it wasn't a great problem because it had taken him over a week to start talking with other course members of (his) similar age." "No, Dave,"* he said, *"it's taken me 19 years." "It was a response I have never forgotten."*

Students were stretched to the limit. Any idea of 'going it alone' was impossible. In the hospitals, playschemes, hostels, night shelters, soup runs and on busy geriatric wards where they might find themselves having to feed and toilet elderly incontinent residents, they were continuously dependent on each other for re-assurance and sympathy. It was a small step to take these feelings back to seminars where with their tutor's help they could unravel opinions and entrust their worries and fears to a group that had shared their experience. Other placements were a playscheme on the Craigmillar council estate known for its bleak architecture as Little Moscow, at a Salvation Army hostel for homeless men in the Pleasance, and at a night shelter in the Grassmarket.

Rivalling Goggaburn Hospital was a fifth location arranged with Edinburgh Social Services, which required students to go into private homes. If the placement was with a family, the students would play with the children, do the decorating or tidy the garden. If it was with someone old or disabled, they would spend the time listening to their stories and talking about their own hopes and plans. From evening seminars and social workers' briefings, the students were guided to the view that they had to make a more than routine effort.

For staff and students alike, living together in the course base was as much of a challenge as the placements. There was little privacy and no entertainment except what staff and students organised themselves. However, there was plenty of drama when the course was struck down with a three-day bug. Bugs can be a great leveller; they bring down the mighty and the stroppy. One hapless young man, who had taken longer than most to get used to the course and indeed was stroppier than most, announced he was feeling sick. He then vomited a liquid projectile twenty feet down the middle of the men's dormitory. It was a spectacular but not particularly life enhancing experience for the spectators and an achievement only equalled at my school in Ely when one winter evening, the school's dramatic society was performing Dorothy Sayer's *The Zeal of Thy House* among the huge Norman columns of the cathedral nave. A sudden pause in Gabriel's lines was filled by the echoing sound of liquid splashing across the flagstones. This told the audience that the unfortunate archangel, who in the daytime was a large prop forward in the first rugby fifteen, was indisposed.

The courses lasted a month but by the end of ten days, students and indeed staff had invariably moved into a realm of understanding and friendship they would never forget. The pressure was relentless but they knew they had discovered something indefinable that could perhaps only be expressed through the language of poetry or religious symbolism. Freddie Fuller had been right; this was the spiritual equivalent of Aberdovey's rough seas or Loch Eil's mountains. But the staff team was more ordinary than the sailing instructor or mountain leader. The course director, David Gibson had been a youth worker and would later become chief executive of the Association of Further Education Colleges. Helping him were David Uffindall, a youth tutor from Ripon, Liz Thompson, a domestic science teacher from Leeds, Benny and Clive, youth workers from Edinburgh, and me, an RE teacher from Goole. David Gibson's remarkable personality and the ever present duty to support students in seminars and placements made us feel we had a special mission. By the end of the course the prospect of returning to class room teaching was a challenge in itself.

Peter Teed, head of Goole Grammar School, and officers of the new Humberside Education Authority generously allowed me to take occasional days off during term time to make behind-the-scenes arrangements for courses to be held in Humberside in three successive years from 1975: two in Hull, at the Albermarle Centre and Chapman Street Infants School respectively, and one in Grimsby at Havelock School. Each course took the best part of a year to arrange, mainly because head teachers were reluctant to hand over their schools for use by strangers during the summer holidays and large institutions like Brandesburton Hospital (The 'Goggaburn' of the East Riding) were not keen to have students with prying eyes on their wards, asking questions best left unanswered.

I myself directed three summer courses: one in Rotherham based at Old Hall School: another in Bradford at Ilkley Grammar School and the other in Westminster, based rather curiously in a college in Tooting. Not having quite the same 'Pied Piper' qualities as David Gibson, I found it tough at the helm. It was difficult for me to reconcile differing opinions of staff and I was unsure how far to tolerate unconventional behaviour by students. I quickly learned that solutions to problems came more easily when staff and young people arrived at them together. As a result I had no qualms about holding long staff meetings or insisting that students spent at least two hours in evening seminars. The course had to listen as well as persuade. Even so there were moments. The Rotherham course for example had few rules but one of them was that it was 'dry'. Students were briefed by their sponsors before joining, and at the beginning of the course, staff argued that alcohol was a distraction that could impair relationships and create difficulties with placements. It was a pity we did not stick to this to the very end. Having navigated our way through four intensive weeks and feeling proud of our students, we decided that prior to the farewell dinner, the bottles should be opened to encourage guests to socialise and the students to let their hair down more willingly than they had tied it up! The result was disaster. The dinner was semi-formal with top table dignitaries who included the Directors of Rotherham's Education and Social Services Departments, the headteacher of Old Hall School and senior personnel from the Outward Bound Trust. In the middle of the Director of Education's speech, there was a disturbance at the table to my left. A student was abusing David Gibson with powerful obscenities; he then collapsed face down on the table and was carried out on the shoulders of four less inebriated students. There were similar episodes at ten minute intervals through the evening. Needless to say, later courses celebrated their success with orange juice, sandwiches, no top table and no distinguished guests. Instead, local authority officers were invited to visit students in their placements and to come and talk to staff at the course base.

A well tried timetable required staff to arrive five days before the students so that they could get to know one another, organise the placements and iron out any problems. One such problem arose when the transport manager of the London Borough of Wandsworth which was lending us the vehicles for the Westminster course, insisted that City Challenge staff should take a minibus driving test. Six of us failed and it was only at the end of the first week of the course that our two more capable colleagues were able to get from behind a steering wheel.

The course venues in Hull were memorable. One was in the middle of the city; it was a large youth centre which was surprisingly closed for normal business during the summer holidays. Accommodation was in the sports hall with an imported division down the middle. Twenty men slept in one half and twenty women in the other. The other Hull base was Chapman Street Infants School in Cleveland Street, situated between a motor cycle stadium and a tar factory. The school was grudgingly allocated to us by a city education officer who had fallen out with Humberside County Council. I am still amazed that 50 young people and staff were able to live for four weeks in premises with no bathroom and where the washbasins and toilets were designed for five year olds. It said a lot for David Uffindall's good humoured leadership and the resilience of his staff and students that they survived this peacetime equivalent of Freddie Fuller's lifeboat!

As at Goggaburn hospital in Edinburgh, it was predictable that the old fashioned 'mental handicap' hospitals at Grenoside in Rotherham, Menston near Bradford and Brandesburton near Beverley would absorb most thought and discussion in evening seminars. Morag Smith was a youth tutor at Minsthorpe Community School at South Elmsley near Pontefract and later became director of City Challenge. On her first day as a tutor on the Rotherham course, she and I had agreed to work together at Grenoside Hospital. We were welcomed by staff and then led on a tour of the hospital during which we were confronted by three naked men smearing excrement on a basement wall. Students could not be expected to face this kind of behaviour on the first day of a placement so we prepared them by inviting representatives of the different agencies to come every few days to brief the students and answer questions.

At Menston, students coped bravely and quietly with patients suffering dementia who had to be washed, taken to the toilet, fed, but above all, befriended and listened to. At Brandesburton the course had to deal with a different kind of problem — a chief nursing officer who refused to take seriously the students' complaints about staff abuse of patients. He was later dismissed, for bullying and offering favours to hospital staff in return for sex.

Buttershaw estate in Bradford was a social priority area. Its social workers felt that City Challenge could give them useful help with families who were disorganised and generally finding life difficult. It was with these vulnerable and dependent families, sometimes comprising three generations, that students were most impressed. They played with the children and did everything they could to help with household chores.

But it wasn't always easy. I visited a group working with a family that was friendly and outgoing — a man and two young children. But they couldn't cope. During breakfast the dog jumped on the table and cocked its leg up against the cornflakes packet. The bathroom was indescribable and the students had to wear masks as they scraped the dirt off the walls and prepared to redecorate. In that evening's seminar two of them said they weren't going back. After the group had spent some time exploring the possible reasons for the family's difficulties they decided they would go back. By the end of four days they had made good friends of this little family. It was City Challenge at its best; students being put under carefully managed pressure in the work placements, having plenty of opportunity to explore successes and failures through discussion, and as members of a group, listening to one another's answers; and after that, to go home and befriend people facing similarly hard times.

Under the heading *Outward Bound in the Urban Situation* the City Challenge brochure described the purpose of the courses:

City Challenge is designed to stimulate self knowledge and understanding of others…

It offers a valuable programme to Industry, Commerce and Public Services for the non-vocational training of their employees. The nature of the projects gives the students an insight into the social problems of our time and some of the ways in which they may help to ensure that these are alleviated. The course provides an opportunity for the students to:

- *reach a greater understanding of themselves*
- *make a personal re-assessment*
- *re-examine their own attitudes and prejudices*
- *develop the capacity for understanding and compassion*
- *discover they have a responsibility to society*
- *understand the need for self discipline*
- *discuss freely their own ideas and problems*

For City Challenge students the experience was much less crystalised. When reading their diaries, it is easy to become dewy-eyed. The students overcome their early fears, act heroically, and tell a story that with its soft texture, makes comfortable reading and confirms the belief that City Challenge was without equal. I believe it was, but I also know that not all students found themselves in a fairy story with a happy ending. For some, the loose ends would remain untied and the courses would raise more questions than they could answer. The ground was moving from an idea of unquestioning personal service to the exploration of the politics of reform and social action, and in some quarters this was not seen as a welcome development.

A Student's Diary

The observations of Judith Holmes, a VI form student from Goole Grammar School attending the 1978 Bradford course, are not sentimental or romantic. The conclusion of her 17 page report is limited to a mere five lines in which she says she enjoyed the course and 'was pleased that I had the opportunity to take part in such a scheme. I learnt a lot'. And indeed she had. There are parts of her narrative that read more like the messages of a war correspondent than the comments of a young student on a personal development course in an English city. Here is a small selection of her thoughts and reactions:

Monday 31st July: Green Lane Playscheme, Manningham

For six weeks during the summer holidays the playscheme catered for about 200 children per session. They were Asian, West Indian and white, the whites being in the minority. The age groups were from four to fifteen.

I was sitting sewing a doll's dress for an Asian girl when Jennifer a little plump white girl came to sit on my knee. We were talking about animals. Apparently her father had starved their dog which had to be put down. He had then left the family to go and live with another woman. I clung to the child wondering why someone so young should be caught up in such matters. Then I realised where I was different from these children; they all seemed so much more responsible than I was at their age. This was because of the large families. Everyone was expected to do their bit. The older kids (those about seven years old) were expected to take care of the younger ones and do errands such as shopping and taking the washing to the lauderette. They all took on responsibilities within the family and it was this that made them appear so grown up.

Wednesday 2ⁿᵈ August: Shelter for Homeless People

Local people were signing a petition to get rid of the tramps. It was the job of City Challenge to make a paved path down to the shelter with a border of plants and vegetables to make the premises more attractive. All of this would cost about £200. I thought the money would have been better spent on the men themselves.

As it was raining it was impossible to work on the path so we spent the morning inside the shelter. I helped make the soup. The kitchen was filthy and I'm sure the soup wasn't edible. We had to cut up endless sacks of carrots, some of which were going bad. Old bones were stewed up to make the stock. The smell of the soup, mixed with the smell of the shelter gave off a revoltingly sickly smell. It was vile.

Friday 4ᵗʰ August: Cheshire Home

We went up a beautiful tree lined drive which swung round to the house. The house was old and large. Together with the trees and flowers it looked lovely.

There were 29 residents, the majority of whom had multiple sclerosis or had suffered a stroke. All of them had led normal lives, were married and had children. They then found it impossible to move their arms and legs without thinking about it. If only they could live at home surrounded by their families I'm sure they would be much better off. Instead they all had to adjust from an active to a passive life in a Cheshire Home. As most of the visitors came on Saturday afternoon, I spent most of the time bathing and dressing a few of the women so they would be clean. At one point Dawn, a course member, told me that Jennifer, a resident, wanted to go to the toilet. Could I fetch someone? I went to the staffroom as most of the staff were having a tea break. I rushed in and asked the Sister if she would come and help lift Jennifer. She said, *"This is my tea break; ask one of the other staff."* I told her they were all busy. To that she just replied, *"Well, leave her then."* I was appalled. How could she treat people like that? I rushed back to Jennifer and between us, Dawn and I struggled to lift her from the wheelchair to the toilet. In the end we managed. How would that Sister like to be treated like that? I was talking to one lady who told me that that morning she had been sitting on the commode from seven o'clock until nine.

Wednesday 9ᵗʰ August: Westwood Hospital, Meanwood

We arrived at the unlocked but fenced grounds. The volunteer organiser gave us a grand tour. I don't know if I agreed with this. I felt as if I was looking at caged animals.

As I ventured onto Alexandra Ward, the smell was far worse than at the shelter. As the patients were incontinent and being sick the smell was overpowering. There were about 25 people on the ward, two of them males. Only three of them could communicate verbally. The rest dribbled, laughed or shrieked but most of the time the ward was silent until one of them became frantic for some reason.

Carol was a bonny girl with fair hair but only one eye. The other had been poked out by a woman on another ward. She dragged me past a tiny building which was the mortuary. We sat down on a seat when suddenly she grabbed my hand and bit my knuckle. The staff said that if I hit her she would not attempt to harm me.

It was as if the staff rushed everything so that once jobs were done they could laze about for a few hours. This I thought was totally the wrong attitude. Food was shovelled down patients' throats. After breakfast nappies were soiled and dripping. The floor was wet with urine. I paddled about trying to avoid it. I would not want a child of mine to be treated like this; nappies would be changed as soon as they were soiled. But not here; there was a timetable to be followed. Nappies were changed in the morning, at half past one and at six o'clock. Never mind the smell and constant dripping.

It seemed awful that the patients were left all day and every day to stare into space or gaze unknowingly at the television. What sort of existence did they have? Life on this ward was certainly not doing them any good. If they were given more love, care and attention, things would have been so much better for them.

I passed a long row of tooth brushes hung up in the bathroom but their teeth were not cared for. They went from day to day without being cleaned. Teeth were bad and breath smelt. I asked a nurse why teeth were not cleaned. *"We haven't the time,"* came the reply. What an excuse. They didn't care.

Next I went over to Linda and while playing with her I noticed her long filthy finger nails. After rooting round I found a pair of scissors. I then cut her tiny nails which smelt of sick and faeces. Once finished I moved on to the person next to her. I unclasped the saliva wet hand and cut the nails while trying to hold my breath.

Monday 14ᵗʰ August: Community Service, Berkeley House

Ann Ryan was the occupant of 6, Berkeley House where we were to decorate. Ann was 20 with a son Timothy, aged two. She was unmarried. Her second child was due at Christmas. Tim went to playschool each day where he was provided with meals. Ann was rather distressed because he would not eat at all at home. Looking round at the filth of the place I was not surprised. Tim was only sent to playschool because Ann had been violent with him. After introductions I looked out of the open bathroom window onto the rest of the council estate. It all looked grey and dismal. There were no trees and the only patches of grass were covered in rubbish. The flats and houses were scruffy and dirty. It all looked so artificial and manmade. Dirty faced kids were fighting and screaming on the path.

The End of City Challenge

I had the good fortune to do this work in the seventies and eighties, decades of blossoming excitement for City Challenge. In the early nineties however, the Outward Bound Trust, not for the first time, ran out of funds and was temporarily taken over by the Duke of Edinburgh's Award (DoE). There were similarities between City Challenge and the ethos of its new owner, not least the expectation of service to the community, but there were also differences. City Challenge courses were one month residentials creating a community of spirit rather than a pathway to achievement and awards. Living and working together were young people aged 17 to 25 from many different backgrounds; the prisoner and the policeman, the university student and the unemployed labourer. For young people who had no means of financial support there were bursaries provided by sponsors like IBM, Volvo, and local authorities. They invited young people to attend the courses not to meet any prescribed targets, but because they knew that they would return with new horizons and aspirations. And judging from the reports that the tutors agreed with the students, they were right. An example from the August 1977 Hull course will suffice. The young man in question was Asian and had been sponsored by S. R. Gent & Co, the clothing manufacturer. At the end of a detailed two page report describing his work in the placements and his relationship with other students, his tutor wrote:

> Having seen what Umar had to give in response to the intense demands of people with a learning disability, I had hoped that his apparent philosophy of passive acceptance would resolve itself into a more definite meeting of challenges. By the end of the course he was coming to terms far more with certain facets of his own personality and is learning to consider criticism from a more constructive and rationalised angle. He has made great steps forward in his understanding of people and begun to develop a more compassionate disposition. I wish him well for the future.

Reading between the lines tells us Umar had learned quite a lot from his City Challenge course.

The courses were in the end a casualty of the merger between Outward Bound and the Duke of Edinburgh's Award (DoE). The name itself was hi-jacked by a Conservative government to advertise its competitive bidding proposals for urban renewal funds. Now the term is being used by a commercial company which arranges day courses for the corporate sector. It was sad that the DoE chose to ditch these urban courses which with volunteer staff and the co-operation of local authorities cost a tiny fraction of Outward Bound's outdoor programmes. What a pity the DoE did not preserve and develop City Challenge rather than concluding that it was at best superfluous and at worst a threat to its own schemes. Regrettably in the end the people making the decisions were not in the mood to listen. However it must be said that even in the heyday of Outward Bound, the courses never found favour with the principals of the outdoor centres who venerated sailing and mountaineering as the Holy Grail of personal development. Russell Butterfield, a former headteacher and outdoor education specialist puts a gloss on this:

> It wasn't just funding. Outward Bound lost its way by moving upmarket; it became increasingly market orientated when the real need was to provide for some of our most disadvantaged youth. Also the 1990s saw a growing disenchantment with outdoor education following a succession of appalling accidents (unrelated to Outward Bound) to young people. The mountains and the sea were swapped for the zip wires of a more domestic environment.

As a founding father of Outward Bound, Jim Hogan did his best to persuade the traditionalists that the courses did not represent a communist conspiracy and at a residential conference at Rhowniar in mid Wales in 1981, he endeavoured to persuade them that City Challenge was a powerful complement to Outward Bound's original purpose. It could come up with as many surprises as the hills and seas and for many it was more accessible. The bursary scheme enabled young people to enrol for an experience so memorable that it would be a guide for the rest of their lives.

But we must ask what, in Clegg's terms, were the 'hyacinths' of City Challenge? I think students went away with more confidence and knowledge gained by having their eyes opened in placements. In seminars they had the opportunity to re-appraise their prejudices and opinions. In the social life of the course they were learning from people from different backgrounds and lifelong friendships were often formed. No student ever found the course easy but the staff had to make sure that students went home with enough understanding to explain what had happened to them. Sometimes this would lead to a major review of career plans, a new light on a close relationship or a determination to remedy the kind of injustice manifested in some of the placements. For staff, the reward was seeing students better able to cope with themselves and the world when they left than when they arrived. The message for education practice was to treasure the City Challenge legacy by making adventurous use of resources, by having unlimited patience with young people and above all by not allowing institutional interests to smother personal development.

In 1977 I was offered the post of national director of City Challenge but by then Goole Grammar School and the *Sobriety* Project were becoming far too exciting to leave for what would have turned out to be only temporary excitement in London.

Questions

Was City Challenge simply a product of its time?

Would it have any relevance today?

Would you encourage young people to get involved in this kind of intensive service to the community?

Would they gain anything?

Was Judith Holmes right to be angry about the attitude of staff in some of the placements?

Chapter 2 Notes

1 Captain Freddie Fuller. Obituary, *The Independent*, 22nd April 1993.

2 For a comprehensive history and appraisal of the Outward Bound Trust see Basil Fletcher's, *The Challenge of Outward Bound,* published by Heinemann in 1971.

3 For a story about Darren O, a West Indian boy, showing the futility of this kind of approach to learning disability, see Sally Tomlinson's, *A Sociology of Special Education*, Routledge 1982 and new edition in 2012.

4 The Stanford prison experiment was a study of the psychological effects of becoming a prisoner or prison guard. The experiment was conducted at Stanford University USA from August 14 to August 20, 1971, by a team of researchers led by psychology professor Philip Zimbardo. Twenty-four male students were selected to take on randomly assigned roles of prisoners and guards in a mock prison situated in the basement of the Stanford psychology building. The participants adapted to their roles well beyond Zimbardo's expectations, as the guards enforced authoritarian measures and ultimately subjected some of the prisoners to psychological torture. Many of the prisoners passively accepted abuse and at the request of the guards, readily harassed other prisoners who attempted to prevent it. The experiment even affected Zimbardo himself who in his role as superintendent, permitted the abuse to continue. Two of the prisoners quit the experiment early and the entire experiment was abruptly stopped after only six days. Parts of the experiment were filmed and excerpts of footage are publicly available. (Information from Wikipedia)

5 I am indebted to David Uffindall for the loan of his reports on the City Challenge courses which he directed, and in particular his copy of Judith Holmes's account of her experiences of the placements on the 1978 Bradford course.

Chapter 3
EARLY WANDERINGS

School and University

Steered by parental wishes, I travelled through a fairly traditional education in the fifties and sixties beginning with weekly boarding at a prep school in Sheffield, continuing with five years at the King's School Ely and ending with a theology degree at Jesus College Oxford. My parents had little money but they did have a knack of persuading me to work hard enough to win any available awards.

I was nine when I left home with a small suitcase to travel each week by train and tram from Ordsall, a suburb of Retford in north Nottinghamshire where my father was rector, to Westbourne School on the far side of Sheffield. On Monday mornings my father and I would climb into a 1934 Austin Seven [1] and rattle our way to Retford station in time for the 7.00am train to Sheffield Victoria. My companions were a group of businessmen who always seemed to occupy a compartment full of steam and tobacco smoke. In charge was Dennis Bramhill, a potato wholesaler who worked at Castlefolds Market and was a churchwarden and friend of the family. At Victoria station we all went our separate ways and for me that meant getting a tram to the cathedral. The fare for adults was a penny and because I counted as half an adult I paid for a halfpenny-half ticket which was square and red. It was a novelty to sit on the top deck but the cost of getting there was knees bashed painfully against the stairs while the tram lurched and swayed at a speed that made me wonder how it could possibly stay on the lines. At the cathedral I boarded another tram, this time marked Crookes, for the same fare, to Broomhill which was my destination. A five minute walk took me to school on Westbourne Road. On Friday afternoons I made the same journey in reverse except that there was a through tram from Broomhill to Handsworth via the station. There were no businessmen in a steam and tobacco filled compartment but worse, there were giggling girls from Notre Dame High School on West Street who could have been as old as fourteen or fifteen and more wordlywise than me. I could never understand their conversation and found that the safest tactic was to hide behind *Radio Fun* and *The Beano* until they got out. Meanwhile we crawled along, stopping at every station: Darnall for Handsworth: Waleswood, Kiveton Bridge: Kiveton Park: Shireoaks: Worksop. After Retford the train was bound for Immingham, Cleethorpes, Grimsby Town and Grimsby Docks, places so distant they were in a foreign country. After an agreeable half hour's walk from the station to Ordsall, I would get home in time for a welcome tea of stew and vegetables. In spite of being desperately homesick for the first few weeks, Westbourne taught me a good deal of independence and was perfect training for going away to school in Cambridgeshire when I reached 13.

A scholarship of £120 took me to the King's School Ely. In the late nineteen fifties, life there was exciting and despite being an all boys school in buildings that were part of a 14th century monastery, it was not monkish. We had the freedom to wander the town, make friends where we liked and at week-ends within reason, go where we pleased. On several occasions just after I had passed my driving test, one of the staff lent me his Bedford van for visits to Cambridge. It was much less restrictive than being at home where as an only child I was kept on a short lead. I was never homesick or lonely; there was too much to do, too much call of adventure in and out of school, not to be completely absorbed. The head, Ben Fawcett, made no bones about where the emphasis would lie in his school — 'to help boys become individuals with points of view based on their own reasoning and thinking'. In the VI form I did Latin, Greek and Ancient History and became a King's Scholar, an appointment bringing a £10 a year scholarship and the lifetime right to play marbles and bowl hoops in the cathedral nave. It was all pretty easy going. Even the traditional public school expectation of a 'stiff upper lip' was only occasionally in evidence, one concession to it being the rule that dormitory windows must be kept open even in winter. As Ely was the east wind's first stopping place on its way from the Ural mountains, those of us on the 'wrong' side of the dormitory sometimes woke in the middle of the night with our faces buried in snow. What a difference from boarding schools today which advertise individual study bedrooms en suite with shower and toilet and supplied with TV and DVD.

I went to Oxford in 1961 and it took some getting used to. I wanted it to be like Ely but it could not be. It was intellectually very tough and as someone who had not done Scripture at A-level and had a simple Sunday School understanding of the Bible, it took me some time to realise that the Old and New Testaments were not history books in the usual sense. My comfortable journey through rectory and cathedral was over. For the first time I had no protection against a position in the wider university where 'God' was at best irrelevant and at worst the enemy. Influences were many. In 1960 Luis Buñuel had made *Viridiana*,[2] described as 'one of the great feelbad movies of all time'. It was an attack on the Catholic Church for its support of Franco but also on Christianity generally for its unrealistic expectations of holiness. Another ambush came from biology. In 1963 after winning the Nobel Prize for his discovery of the structure of the DNA molecule, Francis Crick gave a lecture in Oxford's Taylorian Institute which made it difficult to believe there was much connection between God and the double helix.[3] I myself was coming to the brutal conclusion, no doubt obvious to many, that theology and religious belief did not go hand in hand. My discomfort had begun with scepticism about the 'after life' supposedly evidenced by the gospel writers' story of the empty tomb. I was dismayed to find in FW Beare's *The Earliest Records of Jesus* which was a standard reference book for analysing the differences between the texts of the first three gospels, that 'the story of the empty tomb did not form part of the earliest tradition of the Resurrection'. The author says 'what we have here is a legend of relatively late growth…the Resurrection is not conceived in terms of the re-animation of the corpse…there is not a word to suggest that he (St Paul) has ever heard of the story of the empty tomb or that such a story would be relevant to his doctrine…'.

The plan was that after Oxford I would go to Wells Theological College in Somerset and become a Church of England parson like my father. He had spent his ministry in the Diocese of Southwell primarily as a parish priest but also as the founding chair of a diocesan committee for improving the living conditions of Nottingham's single parents. He was something of a romantic who had spent his school and university holidays working for the Caledonian Steam Packet Company on the river Clyde. In a rakish letter to my mother when he was sixteen, he had revealed his yearning for a ship's storm-lashed quarter deck; there was, he wrote, 'no better place to be.' My experience of Oxford was similarly tempestuous.

In 1964 I did go to Wells. After the social freedom of Ely and the intellectual freedom of Oxford, theological college routine was oppressive. I felt marked as a rebel especially by older men who had come to the end of a professional career in another field and wanted to make the Church their last resting place. There were too many assumptions that seemed absurd. The college did not help to boost my creative energies and I made good use of Somerset's notorious scrumpy which if one could ignore the fermenting pips and stalks, was available at 5d a pint in *The Fountain*. Quite amazing theological constructs came to mind even after half a pint but they were not going to find a home within the definitions of the Thirty Nine Articles of Religion.[4] In the circumstances I was grateful that I was five hundred years late for the Inquisition.[5] The worst punishment I could expect would be a blessing with holy water from the chaplain and a hot water telling off by older students who were more certain in their beliefs. It would be unfair however to be critical of a college that was doing its best not only to educate its ordinands in the 'God' problem but also to give them first hand experience of west London's 'Poor' problem. At that time in the mid sixties, Notting Hill was a long way from emerging into the floodlit comedy of its eponymous movie. Landlord and tenant legislation was still in the dark ages and Rachmanism[6] was rife.

A leader in the fight against housing exploitation was Tony Bridge, artist turned priest, vicar of Christchurch, Lancaster Gate and a friend of Congregationalist minister Bruce Kenrick who founded Britain's first housing association, the Notting Hill Housing Trust. For two weeks the entire population of Wells Theological College moved from the untroubled comfort of Vicars' Close and as guests of Tony Bridge, experienced the world of evictions, poverty and racism that characterised Notting Hill at that time. Even so, a break with Wells was inevitable and it arrived with the chance to spend a week helping out in a local secondary school. I loved the challenge of the classroom and immediately applied and was accepted to do a postgraduate Certificate in Education at Birmingham University during the academic year 1965-1966. The college principal, Tom Baker, who later became Dean of Worcester, was understanding if not relieved and took me and two friends on a ten day holiday to the Costa Brava. My mother and father loyally acquiesced in my decision to go to Birmingham and perhaps thought the church would be a less dangerous place if I was on the outside.

In my own case I inherited particularly from my mother a great sense of urgency. She had trained as a primary school teacher at Beckett Park,[7] Leeds, specialising in needlework. But those were the days when married women were barred from the profession and she had given up teaching in 1939 to marry my father. In her opinion there was no time for idling, whatever the circumstances; the job had to be done as if the Apocalypse[8] were upon us. This kind of clerical household is precisely described in *A History of Christianity* by Professor Sir Diarmaid MacCulloch who himself came from an Anglican parsonage in Suffolk:

> *(The parsonage)…was perhaps not the most comfortable place to live, on a modest income and under constant public gaze, but children there grew up surrounded by books and earnest conversation, inheriting the assumption that life was to be lived strenuously for the benefit of the entire community — not least in telling that community what to do, whether the advice was welcome or not. It was not surprising that… thoughtful and often troubled, rather self conscious parsonage children took their place in a wider service.[9]*

The sixties were gathering pace and although not quite understanding what was happening around me, I relished opportunities for the adventures they seemed to promise. My tutor was Edwin Cox who, through his later work at the London Institute of Education, was to help transform the understanding and practice of religious education (RE) in schools. He would persuade teachers and local authorities to get away from the confessional approach which assumed Britain was comprehensively and exclusively Christian and accept that the function of RE in school was not to implant children with a package of eternal truths guaranteeing them a place in heaven, so much as to give them the insights and encouragement to cope with their present existence. In more secular ways this was what the *Sobriety* Project would be setting out to achieve ten years in the future.

It was at Birmingham that I abandoned any ambitions towards academia. I had enjoyed A-level Classics but had struggled with Greek Prose Composition which required candidates to translate, for example, an excerpt from Milton's *Paradise Lost* into verse in the style of Euripides.[10] At Oxford I had managed a third class degree, perhaps the rough equivalent of today's 2.2 but nevertheless modest when compared with the performance of many of my contemporaries. My tutor in Jesus College, Denys Whiteley, who was an authority on St Paul, had said at an end of term appraisal (known as a 'don rag') in front the college's principal and fellows, *"Mr Watson must learn not to cut through the jungle of theological problems with the intellectual panga[11] of generalisation."* Signs of failure were everywhere. However the discovery that Edwin Cox was thinking like me was a pleasant surprise and after reading Harold Loukes's *Teenage Religion,*[12] a survey of the religious attitudes of young people in secondary modern schools, I knew I was on the right track; it would be the practical rather than proseletysing end of Christianity that would claim my interest and commitment as a teacher.

My first teaching practice was in autumn 1965 at Bordesley Green Secondary Modern School for boys, twenty one years after the Butler Education Act which introduced the tripartite system of grammar, modern and technical school and determined through a written examination at 11, which of these schools a child would attend. Segregation was theoretically based on the results of the 11+ but could also be influenced by parental pressure.[13] Located in a downtown area near Birmingham City football ground and with few resources, Bordesley Green was typical of its kind. Many of the all male staff were Welsh rugby players who had a 'scrum down' relationship with the pupils. Sometimes it was the turn of the boys to prevail as when they filled the petrol tank of the head's car with sand; at other times it was the turn of the staff to use the cane with a good deal of energy. Lessons would be interrupted by the shrieks of victims of an iron Christianity inherited from the coal mines of the Welsh Valleys. The school's understanding of RE was best observed in morning assembly. On the head's call for silence, a pair of doors would open at the side of the hall and four pupil slaves groaning under the lash of the deputy head's tongue would wheel a dais into the congregation. At the front, on balustrading, was a shield with TRUTH chiselled in bas relief. In the middle, raised up, the deputy head stood in suit, gown and mortar board. After a timid congregational rendering of 'O God our help in ages past,' he would step forward, lean over the shield and shout, *"Right you lot, let's see if you can pray a bit better than you can sing. Close your eyes."* After making a few pestering requests to the Almighty and barking, *"Open your eyes"*, he ended assembly and was wheeled back to where he had come from. He seemed to be using morning assembly to impose control on a group of boys who were already timid and self conscious. It was a reincarnation of *Dotheboys Hall* in Charles' Dickens' *Nicholas Nickleby*, a sad urban mockery representing everything wrong with religious education at the time. It was so shocking as to be almost blasphemous and I was glad that in my years at school living in the shadow of Ely Cathedral I had been part of a different experience. However I had a good understanding with the children and got a distinction for this part of my teaching practice. My second school, the following term, was Sheldon Heath, an 11-18 twelve form entry comprehensive school opened in the 1950s in east Birmingham as part of the post-war education reforms.[14] It was a very big school and there were nearly as many staff at Sheldon Heath as there were pupils at Bordesley Green. The student teachers from the university were welcomed by Rosabelle Tulloch, a Scottish deputy head who took a personal and somewhat severe interest in our progress. However it was good that expectations were high and in addition to the RE teaching I was given a class to look after. This included taking the register and collecting dinner money, procedures often helped by one or two children who sat at the front of the class, knew everyone's business and acted as spies. I was calling out the names one morning, but got no answer from a boy called Peter Robinson. The two at the front seemed to be saying, *"He's away because of the gas strike."* By coincidence that week, the nearby Tipton gasworks, one of the biggest producers of town gas in Europe, had exploded, but I was not aware of any strike. After further interrogation it dawned on me that the two at the front were saying in a flawless Birmingham accent that Peter was away because of the 'gastric'!

Goole Grammar School

After Birmingham I had to find a job, so in spring 1966 I began reading the back pages of the Times Educational Supplement, home at that time to most of the advertisements for education posts in England and Wales. Wanstead High School turned me down at interview but I was much cheered by an advertisement for an RE teacher at Goole Grammar School in the West Riding of Yorkshire. It said exam work was well established but that other aspects of the subject such as community service, needed attention. Until then my only experience of Yorkshire was of Eddie Waring, known as 'Mr Rugby League', whose speech in contrast with the received pronunciation of most 1960s

Goole Grammar School.

television presenters, seemed a hilarious distortion of the mother tongue. Neither did I know anything about Goole. I learned only later that its rivers, canal and docks made it 'The Venice of the North', a description which led a wit in *The Yorkshire Post* to ask if the citizens of Venice thought of their own city as 'The Goole of the Adriatic'. However a more true to life portrayal of ships moving through the countryside towards their inland destination was *The Port in Green Fields*, a book by a local historian.[15]

From my first impressions on interview day, I knew Goole Grammar School was going to be home. There was a warmth about the place that I had not felt on teaching practice. It was the same feeling of excitement I had had in the school in Wells and I was given every chance to talk about it to the school's senior mistress, Jean Williams, as we walked round the school rugby field before the formalities. My only blunder was to mistake the interview with the West Riding's Religious Education Adviser, Alan Loosemore, as a conversation with someone I thought was another candidate. He must have put me at ease because I was offered the job. The appointment was conditional on a successful outcome to my Education year at Birmingham. Assuming that my coursework was complete, I got a temporary job in a paint factory in Erdington, across the city from the digs in Harborne. Unfortunately my coursework was not complete and I received a sharp note from Edwin Cox reminding me that I still owed him an essay on the effects of the 1870 Forster Education Act.

During the long holidays before going to Goole in the September I went to America and stayed with some of the people I had met the previous summer while working for Undergraduate Tours. This was a company based in Paddington that used the snob value of Oxford and Cambridge to advertise tours round London for foreign visitors, mostly American but also French and South American. The work involved meeting clients at a London hotel or at Southampton docks if they had come by ship, and showing them the sights. The pay was £4-10s-0d for a day in London and £5-0s-0d for a tour further afield. It was a great way to get to know London and the people I met were delightful. Among them were the literary critic Lionel Trilling and Diana his wife, who I collected from Oxford and took on a tour of Devon and Dorset.

With a map and bus ticket America was easy. The map joined up the places where I was going to stay and a '99 days for $99' Greyhound Bus deal took me to them. American hospitality knew no limits and I spent only three nights in hotels during the six weeks I was there. The first occasion was in the YMCA in Dallas which was dirty, the second was in Reno, Nevada, the poor man's Las Vegas, and the third, on the way to the Grand Canyon, was in Flagstaff, Arizona where I shared a bed with a Pakistani and a Frenchman. I had met these two travellers in Flagstaff bus station at 2.0am. The arrangement was a solution to the problem of finding somewhere to stay at that time in the morning and was a fine example of international co-operation. At the time I fancied the episode might be a sign of the 'Last Days', the end of the world foretold in St Luke's gospel which says 'I tell you in that night there will be two men in one bed; one will be taken and the other left'. It was a relief that there were three of us rather than two in one bed, that is until I surmised that an increase in bedfellows might bring on the last days more quickly than St Luke had imagined and went on to ask whether it would still be one that would be taken or would it be two? As the one in the middle of the bed what would be my chances of survival? Would it be settled by a throw of dice or would our lives be measured and scored for virtue? But sunrise brought reassurance and after hiring a car to take us to the rim of the canyon, we spent the day in awe of this natural wonder.

All my American hosts were warm hearted, generous, open-handed and proud of showing me what they could only tell me about when they had been in England. A judge's daughter taught me to water-ski in the Ozarks of south eastern Kansas and an eye surgeon in Philadelphia took me to watch a cataract operation at his hospital. After passing out in the operating theatre and becoming a casualty myself, I was taken swimming by his wife who was a Daughter of the American Revolution, an organisation with the motto 'God, Home and Country'. Members have to be able to prove bloodline descent from participants in the Boston Tea Party or other events which directly helped the United States achieve independence. The competition size pool where we swam was located in the basement of one of the city's banks and ornamented with statues of gods and heroes. I was not sure at the time whether swimming pools below British banks were similarly garlanded.

I had taken the Greyhound bus to Flagstaff from Austin, the capital of Texas where I had been staying with a professor of junior college administration, Colvert C. Colvert and his wife, Lottie May Colvert. I had watched England win the World Cup in Texas University's student common room and spent a good deal of time in the university, but had not reckoned with a gunman, Charles Whitman, climbing the university tower and shooting sixteen people dead just after my departure the next day. It was an unpredictable tragedy, apparently the consequence of a brain tumour found at Whitman's post mortem, which I had escaped by a hair's breadth. The Colverts had nearly persuaded me to go with them two days later to visit the Houston Astrodome, a covered-in baseball park described by some as the Eighth Wonder of the World but more recently condemned by a Houston resident as a *sweaty, unventilated temple to Texan athleticism*. Had I decided to stay two extra nights with the Colverts I would have been on the university campus on the day of the shootings. In Los Angeles I landed on the Mormon relation of one of my friends at Jesus College. Rather riskily I thought, he took me for a ride in his red Ford Mustang through Watts, the city's black ghetto. The previous year 1965, had seen a Long Hot Summer when five days of civil disturbances had resulted in 34 deaths, 3,438 arrests and over $40 million in property damage.

By contrast there was the buzz of being at the crossroads of Haight-Ashbury and Berkeley Avenues on the University of California Berkeley campus where the Free Speech Movement, antecedent of the Vietnam War protest demonstrations, had taken root, and Joan Baez had sung *We shall overcome* for the first time. In spite of the Cold War and nuclear arms race between the West and the Soviet Union and their allies which had continued since the end of the Second World War, the 1960s were for young people a few years of optimism. They embraced a counter culture which looked doomsday and injustice in the face and gave rise to the peace movement, women's rights, the Beatles, and in August 1962 Martin Luther King's *I have a dream* in which, from the steps of the Lincoln Memorial in Washington, he called on America to abandon racial segregation. These and other memories captured in photo transparencies were invaluable teaching aids for my first term at Goole.

With America in support, I was able to dive straight into classroom discussions about race, war, slavery, cities, riots, free speech, government and so on. Conveniently they were all topics prescribed by the West Riding Agreed Syllabus for Religious Education published under the liberating title of *Suggestions for Religious Education*. It seemed a far cry from the drills of Bordesley Green Secondary Modern. The syllabus also accorded with Edwin Cox's antipathy to classroom preaching. It took a lead from Harold Loukes' *Teenage Religion* which earlier in the decade had used the results of an enquiry into young people's attitudes, to highlight the futility of using RE to indoctrinate children with incomprehensible formulae. The West Riding's *Suggestions*, augmented by selective use of Roger Young's *Everybody's Business*,[16] raised questions that invited young people to express an opinion: What is snobbery? Why should I work to make my employer richer? Have people the absolute right to strike? Who is my neighbour? Is there a superior race? Why should I forgive someone who seems completely unforgivable? Does forgiveness rule out the need for punishment? Is declaring war ever justifiable?

The two people at Goole who gave me the encouragement and guidance to align these ideas with activities beyond the classroom were Peter Teed, Head from 1964 until his retirement in 1985, and Jean Williams who until 1970 was my head of department as well as being Senior Mistress. Jean was a Quaker with a scholarly no-nonsense approach to the curriculum, who had known Edwin Cox at Birmingham. She taught Scripture to Ordinary and Advanced levels of GCE but allowed me to make the running with non-examination RE. As Senior Mistress, she was also responsible for girls' welfare. I never knew her predecessor 'Dinger' Bell, but it was clear that Jean's regime was a breath of fresh air. She abolished segregated stairs for boys and girls and had an eagle eye for any hint of sex discrimination whether in the staffroom or the classroom. Her wit was sharp and she was unbeatable in debate. Even though it allowed my promotion to head of RE, I was sorry when she left the school in 1971 to become a senior adviser in the York area of the West Riding. Peter Teed's headship on the other hand, is described by a 2012 blogger in *Goole on the Web — School Memories*:

I think Peter Teed was a visionary. As I recall he came in for some stick from hang 'em and flog 'em locals, but I think his interest in the wider world, notably Europe and America, was timely and brought a refreshing new dimension to school life. His passion for the arts filtered into school life and made my Goole Grammar School days richer than they would otherwise have been.

I suspect however that Peter wondered whether this 'new' RE was not simply a rest stop on the way to outright atheism. As a lay reader at Goole Parish Church he had a broader, less technical interest in RE but he never interfered either with my approach to teaching or with some unorthodox ideas for morning assembly. In extending the influence of RE beyond the classroom I think we were unconsciously marketing a brand. Unlike a commercial brand it was not always visible and it persisted in raising questions that could not easily be answered. With a 'take it or leave it' approach it was generally rough at the edges and had no audience except the school and local community. Some said it was so far from traditional Christianity that it was not religious. But its questions were certainly educational and their answers which I do believe had a religious inspiration, came to pupils not just through classwork but through morning assembly and service in the community. The curriculum beyond the classroom would complement what was learned in the classroom.

It was my job to keep up with the debates and organise the activities. Against the Cold War's ever present background of political and military tension, imagine an assembly beginning with an alarm recorded from a Second World War air raid siren; then comes the opening lines of Peter Porter's poem *Your Attention Please* [17] read through a loudspeaker by a drama teacher playing the part of the radio announcer:

> *Your Attention Please*
> *The Polar DEW has just warned that*
> *A nuclear rocket strike of*
> *At least one thousand megatons*
> *Has been launched by the enemy*
> *Directly at our major cities.*
> *This announcement will take*
> *Two and a quarter minutes to make,*
> *You therefore have a further*
> *Eight and a quarter minutes*
> *To comply with the shelter*
> *Requirements published in the Civil*
> *Defence Code — section Atomic Attack…*

With memories of Hiroshima and Nagasaki much less distant than they are now, my response to the Cold War and Vietnam War was to join the Campaign for Nuclear Disarmament and take interested pupils down to Trafalgar Square to hear EP Thompson and Bruce Kent asking whether a philosophy of Mutually Assured Destruction (MAD) was not suicidally risky. Stanley Kubrick's film, *Dr. Strangelove* and Peter Watkin's *The War Game* in their own ways give us the answer to their question! [18]

The West Riding syllabus may have justified a less conventional approach to statutory RE but the Ordinary and Advanced Level GCE requirements of the Northern Universities Joint Board prescribed the synoptic gospels for study at O Level and a number of biblical and non-biblical texts at A level. It was always a pleasure to teach this scriptural 'hard core' of the gospels with their message that the Kingdom of God was about to replace Roman imperial oppression, and their assertion that Jesus Christ was the Messiah of a humane and just society longed for by the Old Testament prophets.[19] It was also necessary to keep some sort of theological integrity in lessons and the wider curriculum by making a connection between the New Testament gospels and the ideas evolving in Europe and America during the mid twentieth century.

Among them was the 'religionless Christianity' of Dietrich Bonhoeffer's *Letters and Papers from Prison*, written in 1945 while he was awaiting execution for plotting against Hitler. Bonhoeffer was a Lutheran pastor who had not only criticised the Nazi euthanasia programme and persecution of Jews, but had also raised questions about the role of Christianity and the Church in a world where human beings no longer needed a God as a means of explaining human limitations.[20] Also, in 1942, Albert Camus had written *The Outsider*, a novel which perhaps in the finality of its despair comes near to the stories of Christ's Passion. He was a proponent of *L'Absurd*, an idea that it is fruitless for human beings to search for metaphysical meaning in existence. Jean Paul Sartre's play *In Camera*, written in 1944, was saying that it is experiences of life that make us human, not the plans of a Creator. Neither Camus nor Sartre were theologians but they helped set the scene for the western Protestant churches' realisation that they had to square the 'God' problem with the purpose of the Church and its view of Christ. It boiled down to two crunch questions: Can you be a Christian without believing in a transcendent God, and if you can, where does Christianity make its mark? In 1963 in England, the SCM Press published *Honest to God*. It was written by John Robinson, Bishop of Woolwich and remarkably became a best seller, nearly as widely read as DH Lawrence's *Lady Chatterley's Lover* which had arrived on the book stalls in 1960 following the outcome of the trial of Penguin Books on a charge of obscenity. John Robinson had been witness for the defence. *Honest to God* proposed abandoning the notion of a Creator existing somewhere out in the universe. Complementing Robinson, 'Death of God' theologians like Thomas JJ Altizer in America,[21] were saying that the concept of divine transcendence had lost any meaningful place in modern thought. In the minds of many people God *was* dead. The function of the Church therefore, was not to evangelise on behalf of a distant God but to present Jesus as the model human who acted in love and faith in a universe without 'transcendent' meaning and to offer hope through engagement with the 'here and now' where meaning might be found.

Another influence was 'the social gospel' or 'liberation theology' which, beginning as a radical movement in South America in the 1960s, had persuaded many Roman Catholic priests that by sharing in the poverty of the city slums, they would bring attention to the appalling living conditions suffered by the urban poor. With political emphasis on the humanity of Christ they had abandoned the Church's traditional view that poverty was good for the soul, a way to eternal life with Jesus in Paradise, and asserted that Resurrection could be real and in the present. In April 1968 Martin Luther King was assassinated. In South Africa, Trevor Huddleston, Canon John Collins of CND fame, and later, Desmond Tutu, were fighting for the black franchise against Apartheid. Later, in February 1977, Oscar Romero, Roman Catholic Archbishop of El Salvador who spoke out against poverty and social injustice in his country, was shot by government agents while celebrating the Mass in a hospital. The following month in March 1977, Janani Luwum,

Archbishop of the Church of Uganda was kidnapped and shot by the Ugandan dictator, Idi Amin, also for speaking out against the oppression of the poor. It was the tragedy and bravery of these individuals that was inspiring. God might be dead but he was on their side, and their fortitude and sacrifice seemed to allow an understanding of Resurrection as the transformation of human beings in this life, which did transcend their fate. For my own part, like many heretical, some would say spineless, Anglicans, I compromised and decided it was legitimate to pick and choose what to believe. I was glad the rectory and the cathedral had not allowed me completely to throw out the baby after I had emptied the bathtub.

Salvation Army

At Goole Grammar School the 'social gospel' had begun in 1967 with an eight mile sponsored walk in aid of the homelessness charity *Shelter*,[22] to the village of Adlingfleet near where the Ouse and Trent become the Humber. Along the road, like Joan Baez, we sang the anthem of the American Civil Rights Movement, *We shall overcome*. A few years later two of my former A-level students, Joan Burton and Margaret England, became officers in the Salvation Army and went to Brazil to work in the slums of São Paulo. After thirty years they are still there, caring for the poor and building schools and community centres. Another pupil, Judith Lawson, soon took word back to her father Ken, another Salvation Army officer in charge of the Goole Corps, that there was a new kid on the block teaching O and A-level. At the time, Ken was reading for a Theology degree at Hull University and needing some help with New Testament Greek. I was happy to oblige and soon had a regular date which included a meal with him and his family on Thursdays after school. In the course of conversation, Ken mentioned that Major Fred Brown, officer in charge of Regent Hall, the only church on Oxford Street in London, was looking for volunteers to help with the adjacent Rink Club. It was an all night rendezvous for tired and sometimes drug addicted young people with no home. It was also a haven for suburban Flower Children who were in London at weekends to express their 'free love' amidst a climate of sex, drugs and rock and roll.

This kind of voluntary work seemed a suitable enterprise for the 1967 summer holidays and after meeting Fred Brown, I joined his staff in a house on Christchurch Hill in Hampstead. My instructions were to spend weekends at the Rink Club and to help out from Mondays to Fridays at an addiction centre in a Salvation Army hall next to the World's End pub in Chelsea. Regent Hall dated back to the eighteen eighties. The Salvation Army had been without a dedicated place of worship in London's West End so that when the Princess Skating Rink on Oxford Street became vacant, General William Booth, the founder of the Army, had bought the lease. Following renovation, Regent Hall, thereafter known as The Rink, opened its doors on 18th March 1882. Eighty years later, a club of the same name opened on the same premises. '2012 Urban Army' blogger, Gordon, looked back:

> *Nestling among the classy frontage of designer shops on Oxford Street is a wooden door next to Regent Hall's main entrance and behind it are wooden steps leading up to the Rink Club's former premises where from the mid 1960s until the early 1970s the Salvation Army engaged in a level of mission that was not only intense but pioneering. The unimpressive wooden door became a 'portal' that blurred the distinction between church and community.*

It was my job in the 'mornings after' to mop out the entrances to the shops on each side of this wooden door.

Fred Brown himself was a controversial figure. After writing *Secular Evangelism*[23] which reflected on the Salvation Army's work and values against a background of mid 20th century liberation theology, he was forced to resign his commission. The Army hierarchy was particularly appalled by his assertion that:

> *We should stop thinking of evangelism as a means of inflating our congregations. Since the days of which I am writing, a lot of troubled water has flowed under the bridge of evangelical debate and now most of us are agreed that to treat people as pew fodder, and little else, is, considerations of effectiveness apart, a denial of everything central to Christianity…it represents nothing less than devout blasphemy, a spirit that has done more harm to the cause of Christ's kingdom than multitudes of non-churchgoers. It is devout because its sincere aim is to serve God and further his cause. But it is blasphemy because it uses God's name to manipulate and condition other people.*

There was no possibility of manipulating or conditioning the people spending Friday and Saturday nights at the Rink Club. They were there because they wanted somewhere safe in central London, a place where they could sit out the night drinking coffee, chatting and listening to a continuous performance on the juke box, of Procul Harum's *A Whiter Shade of Pale*. It was a time when many young people romantically equated drug use with protest. In the Soho clubs, Bert Jansch, the Scottish songwriter and guitarist who died in spring 2012, was singing *Needle of Death*, while the Brain Committee, having reported in 1961 that there was no significant addiction to dangerous drugs in Britain, fed a popular view that cannabis might soon be legalised. (The Committee naïvely attributed the rise in heroin addiction to a small number of over-prescribing doctors). In its second report in 1965, Brain recommended the establishment of special centres in London where addicts could be isolated from the community and treated. The hall at World's End was a social club set up to meet this requirement. Treatment in the form of methadone substitution was provided by two doctors in an adjacent surgery. For me, this was an utterly different way of life. At The Rink I was excited by personalities like Anton Warlich-Clifford (and his dog), who was setting up the Simon Community at 129, Malden Road in Kentish Town, an organisation which still provides refuge and welfare for London's rough sleepers. I was also intrigued by policemen disguised as hippies who, moustached and sitting alone, found it difficult to maintain their flowery camouflage. At the World's End centre, addicts, volunteers and staff sat round a table and drank tea and chatted. The outcome of discussions was unpredictable. Sometimes they ended in sulks, bad temper and tears: sometimes in cheerful intentions to make plans. Altogether I took the work very seriously, probably too seriously, and against the rules, befriended John Cochrane, a 17 year old from Glasgow who was homeless, out of work, drug dependent and in his overall state at that time, unemployable. I suggested to my landlady back in Goole that she might make space for him in her house. Much to my surprise she demurred!

Two weeks after I had been back at school, Fred Brown wrote to ask if I wanted the job of running St Martin's Crypt[24] in Trafalgar Square which, like the Simon Community, was providing support for homeless people in central London. The salary would be £1,500 a year. I was flattered to be asked but felt more at home in school and was grateful for an experience that had given me insights and questions I could share and raise in lessons, assemblies and the school's community service programme; they were the seeds of the ideas that would lead to the *Sobriety* Project.

Rawcliffe Hall

In the 16th century, the Boynton family, whose principal seat was Burton Agnes Hall near Bridlington, had built a second home in the village of Rawcliffe, about three miles from Goole. In 1794 this rather modest pile had passed into the hands of the Creyke family who as farming pioneers and railway enthusiasts were eager for the economic development of this part of Yorkshire. In 1919 they had sold their home to the West Riding County Council which gave it the name Rawcliffe Hall Hospital for Mental Defectives and used it as an overspill for Barnsley workhouse. In the late nineteen sixties, well before the arrival of 'Care in the Community' and the closure of Victorian psychiatric hospitals, there were about 100 women in residence, some with a learning disability and some who, years before, had borne children out of wedlock and become homeless. After 50 years of being sectioned and detained there was not much to choose between the two groups; the Hall was their home and its staff worked to make it welcoming and comfortable.

School organised expeditions to Ban-the-Bomb and other events in London were not for younger children but another venture certainly was. With elderly ladies to befriend and a matron with a boxer dog called 'Bonkers', how could it be otherwise? Here were opportunities for school pupils of all ages. Hospitals, like Goggaburn in Edinburgh and Grenoside in Rotherham, were crying out for volunteers to help their patients with feeding, bathing and toileting. But Rawcliffe Hall was not a hospital; it was a community, and its residents were not patients in the usual sense; they were middle aged and elderly ladies who, although having nowhere else to go, had ambitions to look after themselves and one another.

Groups of younger children would visit every few weeks on Friday evenings and play games and dance with residents who soon became friends. Then the word got to a men's hostel near Selby and to Whixley Hospital near York which was also for men, that their residents would be welcome to join the fun at Rawcliffe. Back in the classroom children learned about Joey Deacon, a resident of St Lawrence's Hospital, Caterham, who with the help of his friends had written *Tongue Tied*.[25] Joey begins the book by telling how, as a result of his mother falling down stairs before he was born, he was unable to walk or talk. He then goes on to describe his early family life with great warmth and affection:

> *Annie cooked the dinner, we had rabbit pie, and dear old Grandma washed up while Annie tidied me up ready for the pictures. Our next door neighbour carried me down the stairs and put me in my wheelchair. On the way to the pictures my chair started squeaking so Annie pushed me into a butcher's shop and she asked her friend Jack if he could oil it for me.*

It was remarkable how the book was written. Until Joey met his friend Ernie Roberts, no one but his close relatives could understand what he was saying. Ernie, who also lived in the hospital, translated the story for another friend, Tom Blackburn, who used one finger to type the manuscript. In 1974, the book *Tongue Tied* was published by the National Society for Mentally Handicapped Children with the sub title *Fifty years of friendship in a subnormality hospital.* Joey's book and a later television documentary helped to alter public understanding of learning disability in much the same way as the film *Cathy Come Home*[26] had sparked a national debate about homelessness in the mid 1960s. No longer were patients' abilities to be left dormant; they were to be discovered and developed in new ways, and young people could help with the process.

Meanwhile the response of older students was to make a film to promote Rawcliffe Hall to the outside world. They used a simple 8mm Bolex camera and added a synchronised sound track using the school's language laboratory on two consecutive Sundays. The recording was then transferred to a tape which was glued to the edge of the film so that it could be played on an 8mm sound projector. The students wrote the storyboard themselves and kept things simple by filming activities around the institution: residents cleaning, cooking, learning to read and write, doing arts and crafts and looking after the donkeys and goats in the walled garden. Staff explained the backgrounds and problems of the residents and how under the 1958 Mental Health Act, they were voluntary patients and needed to prepare to live independently. Matron Phyllis Lacey rounded off the 20 minute production by explaining how all the different routines helped achieve the magic formula of *stimulation, occupation and rehabilitation.* In 1969 the school raised £800 to buy a new Ford Transit minibus for excursions and holidays and in 1970 sixth formers took residents on holiday to a Quaker centre at Hutton-le-Hole on the North York Moors.

Rawcliffe Hall's end was predictable. The Care in the Community agenda of the nineteen eighties led to its closure and the site of the hospital is now occupied by a middle class housing development. All that remains is the wall that protected residents from traffic on the A614 and a hopper ornamented with the Creyke family crest which is in the collection of the Yorkshire Waterways Museum. As for the residents, they went to live on council estates if they could look after themselves or in hostels if they needed continuous support. 'Care in the community' was right for the long term future of people with a learning disability; they were to become part of a local community rather than shut away in institutions. The policy was laudable but never properly implemented. The spiralling cost of public services and the drives to ensure health and safety meant that making good provision was always a process of swimming against the current. Where it worked well it was inspirational but where it worked badly it turned out to be high-cost and low quality care. In 2014, thirty years after Rawcliffe Hall closed, there is still concern about the care and treatment of people with a learning disability and disturbing stories are circulating about mental and physical abuse. Inspectors are condemning some privately run hostels and saying publicly that standards are low. On the other hand some social workers are hailing 'community care' as a new discovery.[27]

One of the most important effects of the school's involvement with Rawcliffe Hall was to break barriers between the institution and local people. The first message was that the women were not 'mad' or a useful subject for humour, but had simply been shut away for many years; the second was that they loved people coming to their home and as always, the children's enthusiasm disarmed their parents. In subsequent years the link would become an accepted element in the coursework for a CSE (Certificate of Secondary Education) in Home Management, an umbrella term for cookery, needlework, childcare and home economics which were so important for generations of boys as well as girls leaving school. The demise of these subjects in the school curriculum was arguably one of the biggest educational setbacks of the 20th century. While Kenneth, now Lord Baker of Dorking, Secretary of State for Education, was planning the National Curriculum in 1989, he is said to have come to the conclusion that children did not need to be taught the skills associated with these subjects. *"Their grandmas will show them how to do things like that"*, he is alleged to have said.[28] In one sentence a school's opportunity to shape and improve the lives of its most vulnerable children was taken away. Would it be unreasonable to ask whether the increase in obesity and a decline in parenting and other home skills are not partly the result of Lord Baker's decision? Celebrity chef appearances on television are no substitute for what was, for tens of thousands of children, a popular two year course in skills to last a lifetime. Twenty years later the Coalition Government under David Cameron was hailing the possibility of cookery in schools as new and 'innovative' and promising to review the National Curriculum accordingly. Here is Russell Butterfield again, commenting on the broader picture:

> *The assault on child-centred, needs-referenced learning continues. Some 4,500 vocational training courses for 14-17 year olds have been abolished by the present government. GCSE is now everything, even though every child and every employer knows that a GCSE below grade C is worthless. This follows from a drive in government to identify failure — as if the red underlining of failure was itself a strategy to reduce it. ('It is not enough if some are to succeed — others must fail': Vidal)*

Presumably some of the local 'failures' can be counted among the 3,230 children who were excluded from Hull and East Riding schools in 2012-2013. Without further research it is impossible to say how many exclusions were a direct result of children's frustration with the 'tyranny of testing' but it would be interesting to discover from the children, the extent to which an exam filled curriculum had an effect on their behaviour. Looking forward to Chapter 11, we may get a clue from the backward slide of Liam Ventris.

The late Ted Wragg, Professor of Education at Exeter University, saw the benefits of a broader approach:

> *…the haunting memories of the excitement of the 60s, for me the best decade for curriculum development, only underline the odiousness of central demand for drab uniformity and lack of adventure in the 1980s. It was good to be a teacher in the 1960s, nothing to be ashamed of or defensive about, and my nostalgia for that time could easily become overwhelming.*[29]

Community Relations: Batley And Dewsbury

Another example of RE in action was the school's link with the Asian community in Batley and Dewsbury in West Yorkshire. It was a project less to do with community service and more about discovering cultures and beliefs different from those of Britain's traditionally white population.

In the late nineteen sixties Asian economic migrants living in the Yorkshire wool towns hailed from Gujarat and Punjab provinces of India, and from Pakistan. There were also those expelled from Uganda where they were being punished by President Idi Amin for their success in business. In Yorkshire they found work in textile mills, biscuit factories, local government offices, small businesses and the professions. Their communities were well established and had their own gudwaras, mosques, temples and churches. Enoch Powell's *Rivers of Blood* speech in April 1968 [30] had caused disquiet, but with plenty of jobs available and the outlawing of racial discrimination, new arrivals were reassured by government policies of respect for their traditions. Unlike in France where immigrants were expected to conform to the cultural patterns of the majority, a policy of multi-culturalism in England encouraged the different communities to hold on to their own customs. It was a standpoint that, with 30 years of hindsight and the subsequent rise of Islamic fundamentalism, some may say was misguided. While agreeing that the policy was more difficult to implement within single ethnic communities, I would not agree that it was wrong. In any event helping young people discover the beliefs and problems of cultures new to Britain had to be part of the RE teacher's practical curriculum. Discovery could chase away prejudice; memories of friendships could replace xenophobia.

At a West Riding conference for headteachers, Peter Teed met Harry Lodge from a Batley primary school with a 70% Asian intake. The two heads aired the idea that their respective schools would have a lot to gain if they found out more about each other's way of life. Eyes would be opened and new friendships would reject the racism satirised in Wole Soyinka's *Telephone Conversation* between an African man who wants to rent a flat and the landlady who owns it:

The price seemed reasonable, location
Indifferent. The landlady swore she lived
Off premises. Nothing remained
But self-confession. "Madam", I warned,
"I hate a wasted journey - I am African."
Silence. Silenced transmission of pressurized good-breeding. Voice, when it came,
Lipstick coated, long gold-rolled
Cigarette-holder pipped. Caught I was, foully.
"HOW DARK?"...I had not misheard..."ARE YOU LIGHT OR VERY DARK?"......

It was in a spirit of curiosity and duty that in January 1971 I found myself in an adult education class in Batley, puzzling over William St Clair Tisdall's *Simplified Grammar of the Gujarati Language,* written in 1892 and dedicated to the members of the Irish Presbyterian Mission to Gujarat. However, learning a smattering of Gujarati was more mood enhancement than serious endeavour. I had no ambition to become expert in the language but did think it important to learn the alphabet and to be able to recognise and speak a few common phrases.

Both schools agreed there would be three early objectives; the most important would be a series of week long joint holidays in Goole Grammar School's outdoor centre in Nidderdale, North Yorkshire. To help with their preparation we would make a film about the Asian community in Batley, and thirdly, organise a Sixth Form conference to unravel the political complexities of multiculturalism. In support was John Concannon, Batley's Community Relations Officer. Popularly known as 'Con', he was fluent in Urdu, a language he had learned when serving in the Parachute Regiment in East Africa. As a trusted go-between, he introduced us to families and community leaders, and even persuaded the local imam to let us film in Dewsbury Road mosque.

I quickly recruited three sixth form boys, one of whom had helped with the Rawcliffe Hall film and we landed in Batley on the day when decimal currency made its first appearance in the UK — 15th February 1971, which fortunately coincided with the half term week's holiday.

The work proceeded apace. For four days we toured the community and with Con in tow, interviewed white and Asian children, teachers, youth club workers and employers and came up with a half decent 8mm film. It wasn't going to win any awards but it did present an intimate local picture of Pakistani and Indian people living in the area and was a useful way of persuading Goole staff and pupils to be interested in the idea of camping with Batley children in the great outdoor wilderness of Nidderdale. As a result of our efforts there was a month of 'Batley Camps' in the summer term of each year from 1971 until 1978. Children and pupils from six primary schools and three secondary schools in Batley and Dewsbury came together with young people from all years in Goole Grammar School to take part in a weekly programme of adventure. For many Batley children this was the first time they had explored the countryside and for the Goole young people it was their first contact with Moslem and Hindu children. Sometimes it rained and sometimes there were midges, but our memories were of the sun shining forever over the hills, becks and gorges of Upper Nidderdale.

The weeks were not always without incident. Con thought that since few of the primary school children had ever been to the seaside, it would be good for each camp to have a day out at Morecambe. After a coach journey that turned the Asian children white and the white children green, we recuperated with games on the beach. After a couple of hours it began to rain and the children, who were equipped with the cheapest and thinnest rain gear, got very wet. We found a launderette but forgot to empty the children's pockets before putting their anoraks into the tumble driers. Peering into the revolving cylinders one could make out a whirling liquid mass of chocolate, chewing gum and half eaten cheese sandwiches. While we waited for the anoraks to re-appear, two large Lancashire women glared at me and muttered to one another, *"D'you think these kids are all his?"*

The Nidderdale centre's accommodation made mixed camps possible and when there were too many children and young people for the dormitories, we used tents. In the light of world events since 2001 it was easy by comparison to persuade parents and community leaders to allow Asian girls of primary school age to attend the camps. It was also remarkable even at that time, before the spread of political Islam into Europe, that we were able to run camps for teenage Asian girls. They came from Howden Clough Girls High School in Batley and spent five days at the Centre. I am sure that the venture was only possible because the head of Howden Clough school, David Bennett, who had previously been head of VI form at Goole Grammar School, was able to re-assure parents that their daughters would come to no harm.

With changes of personnel the camps came to an end in the late seventies but by then more than a thousand children from both communities had lived together and learned about one another's way of life. Perhaps memories of the camps in Upper Nidderdale would sow the seeds of tolerance and be a guide for those young people's understanding of race relations. They had found that there was no reason to treat anyone as 'the enemy'. One has to ask whether the young Moslems who seek adventure on the battlefields of the Middle East, would have found something of what they were looking for in this less classroom centred school curriculum. It is absurd to claim any direct connection between the curriculum and Islamic jihad but a man or woman's desire for adventure can be satisfied in many different ways. Is it naïve to suggest that a preoccupation with testing can deny access to courses and activities that might divert young people from getting involved in life and death struggles far from home? The 2012 Ofsted report on one of the schools represented on the Batley camps in the 1970s makes no mention of out-of-school activities and confines its assessment entirely to classroom learning. It says:

> Around 90% of students are from either Pakistani or Indian heritage with the remaining few of White British heritage; a higher number than in most schools speak English as an additional language or are in the early stages of learning English...Some find learning tasks too difficult...Some students find it hard to learn because the literacy levels of some learning materials are too difficult.

Is it not time to put the clock back and allow pupils more adventure, more discovery and more out-of-school opportunities for the kind of learning that harnesses compassion and understanding unburdened by tests? The Yorkshire Dales are easily accessible from any direction and constitute a wonderful resource for city children. For many years Nidderdale provided Goole Grammar School with a playground that was remote, beautiful, and brimming over with social and economic history and geology. The following pages describe what it offered and give a taste of its interest.

How Stean Centre Nidderdale

Despite the Ramblers' mass trespass of Kinder Scout in 1932, access to wild country was more restricted in the nineteen sixties than it is now. In Nidderdale, the landowners often treated ramblers as trespassers if they had the cheek to wander across the grouse moors between Pateley Bridge and Grassington. For permission to visit Bradford Corporation's reservoirs and to walk in the surrounding hills at the head of Nidderdale, one had to apply for a written permit which was not always granted, and there were gamekeepers and council officials eager to enforce the restrictions. In spite of such discouragement, the British public was determined to enjoy the countryside when and where it liked and many schools followed in its footsteps. They acquired redundant village schools, churches or farm buildings and turned them into moorland classrooms and outdoor centres which fostered a love and respect for the countryside. Children and young people studied landforms, geology and botany and trained in hillcraft. Perhaps above all, the centres gave children from urban areas the chance to leave their noisy streets and find pleasure in the natural world. Goole Grammar School made an early start in the movement and by the late fifties was renting the disused Cosh House near Foxup, a village high up in Littondale in the Yorkshire Dales. Approached by a rough track and lacking all basic amenities, the house was remembered with affection by staff and pupils used to the privations of wartime, but regrettably shunned by pampered generations thereafter. Its isolated location as well as its distance from Goole meant it was used only by the most determined enthusiasts — that is until it was renovated fifty years later and put on the market at £495,000.

When I arrived in September 1966 the school had given up Cosh House and was using an old cricket pavilion owned by Batley High School, at Stainforth near Settle, not far from Pen-y-Gent, the hill of Three Peaks fame. The hut was an improvement on Cosh House but the limitations were that it was often fully booked and like Cosh, too far from Goole. The time had come for the school to acquire its own outdoor centre.

On the Nidderdale moors beyond Pateley Bridge, above where a tributary of the river Nidd flows through How Stean Gorge, was High Blayshaw, an inaccessible farm with few prospects except the occasional pheasant shoot and a farmer who told hikers to, *"bugger off back to your towns!"* He looked down with envy at his brother in the farm below who made a good profit from city dwellers wanting to park their holiday caravans in his field. It was a contrast between lives in which one seemed to be a prisoner of nature, doing battle with the land to make it profitable, and the other who was making an enterprising living from tourism in one of Yorkshire's most attractive dales.

The field with the caravans was at Studfold Farm, between Lofthouse and Middlesmoor, the last village at the top of the dale, and it was here in 1967 that Ken Ibbotson, a woodwork teacher at Goole Grammar School, met the farmer and owner, Herbert Walker, and persuaded him that allowing the school to erect a modest outdoor centre on his land would augment his income and be a lively complement to the caravans. Meanwhile fifty miles south, at Ferrybridge, Christiani Construction was finishing work on a new bridge to carry the A1 across the River Aire and advertised for sale its wooden site office. With a floor area of 1,200 square feet, it was tailor made for Herbert Walker's farm. Staff and parents dismantled it and got permission from the landlord of the adjacent Red Lion to store it in the pub yard until it could be transported to Nidderdale. Its re-erection took a few months. The plumbing was to an original design by the department heads of history and geography, apparently direct descendents of Archimedes, who were assisted by admiring parents and pupils. A pump in How Stean Beck, which had to be primed each morning, sent water to a header tank in the roof of the hut: electricity came from an authorised hook-up to the farm and sewage went into a septic tank. The building had two dormitories, staff bedrooms, kitchen, common room, toilets and shower rooms. 'Snagging' was complete after a year and the centre became fully operational for teachers and groups of pupils to use for field studies and more generally for exploration and adventure; the dale was the centre's home and offered something for everyone.

The names on the Nidderdale map [31] have the ring of *Treasure Island*: Foggyshaw Lodge: Foul Hole: Thrope Lodge: Dead Man's Hill (where hangings took place): Goyden Pot: Trapping Hill: Blue Burnings: Jenny Twigg and her Daughter Tib (two rocks): Acoras Scar: Meugher (a hill pronounced Mewfa) and Tom Tiddler's Cave. They could all find their place in children's books.

Add to this the exploration of footpaths, moors, woodlands, ponds, dams, caves, gorges, becks, the remains of a light railway, a ghost-town in the hills, a waterwheel and a gunpowder factory and you have a prescription of sublime happiness for a child of any age and background. The highlight of the week for some children was a ride on Basil, a sheep as big as a donkey. He hung around the centre in the mornings, waiting for aspiring riders to emerge and, as payment for service to be rendered, feed him the breakfast leftovers. For the more serious social geographers and historians, the dale was a curriculum goldmine; the centre was the way to it and there was no shortage of books and photographs to help.

An important source of information about the dale's development was Harry Speight's *The Garden of the Nidd – A Yorkshire Rhineland*, written in 1894. From this and Bernard Jennings *History of Nidderdale*, researched by the Pateley Bridge Local History Class, it is easy to understand why Nidderdale was never included in the Yorkshire Dales National Park and why it took forty years from 1954 when the Park was established, for Nidderdale to be given the status of an Area of Outstanding Natural Beauty. The reason was that for a large part of its history, the dale was industrialised and generously populated. In the Iron Age, farmers felled the trees to make way for cattle; in later Roman times there were millers. From the sixteenth to the twentieth centuries its industries were cotton and flax spinning at the hamlet of Glasshouses (which survived until 1986), rope manufacture, corn milling, linseed crushing and lead mining using a fire engine that could pump water from a depth of 200 feet. There were factory schools in the 1860s for children to be educated in the morning and to work in the mills in the afternoon. In the 20th century these were followed by primary schools sending children to what eventually became Upper Nidderdale High School. For religious devotion every small community had its church or chapel and by the end of the Victorian era there were at least 15 places of worship in the dale.

In a second volume, *Nidderdale from Nun Monkton to Whernside* written in 1906, Speight refers to the Nidderdale Light Railway to be opened the following year, which would carry the public from from Pateley Bridge to Lofthouse. Above Lofthouse the line would be reserved for taking construction workers and materials up to Scar Village, a temporary shanty town in the hills beyond Middlesmoor where Bradford Corporation was to build Scar House and Angram reservoirs. As well as 62 bungalows and a canteen providing 1,000 meals a day, there was a mission hall, a hospital, a school and a concert hall which doubled as a cinema and made a charge of 3d (1.5p) for customers to watch silent films. The author continues:

With the opening this year of the railway up dale to the romantic region of Middlesmoor,
it seems likely that Pateley Bridge will become a great centre of attraction to visitors in the
summer season. The population of the township has been declining over several decades
but despite this tendency in agricultural districts, there is hope that the new railway, with a
station at Ramsgill, will revive its fortunes.

Harry Speight was promoting the economic value of tourism and good communications just as much as he was writing history. Later, he says

An entirely new road has been made for the permanent way, and this road has been
continued to Angram, a distance of about seven miles…Should this road eventually be

open to the public it will form a grand driving route through the romantic portion of the
upper dale as well as a means of access into Coverdale in place of the old mountain road
over Rainstang.

Such was the power of Bradford Corporation's bureaucracy, it would take eighty years for Speight's dream of open access to become a reality. When the road eventually opened to the public, the precision of its construction by the railway engineers became clear. The gradient of the road linking the reservoirs to Lofthouse is constant and a vehicle will free wheel for all of the three miles downhill at exactly 25 mph. The trains on the 'gravity railway' did the same. Sadly the line closed in 1937 after 30 years service and its metalwork was auctioned to pay for armaments. Otherwise it might have survived to be restored in the light railway preservation movements of the 1950s. In an informative little book published by The Oakwood Press, DJ Croft quotes from *The Railway Magazine* of September 1937:

When all this (Scar village) is cleared away and the last train has gone clanking down
the lonely valley, there will be little to show besides the two towering dams and the great
tranquil lakes, what a hive of industry this bleak and desolate spot once was.

For the geologists and students of landforms the features of Upper Nidderdale met syllabus requirements perfectly. Here is Speight's extravagant description of How Stean Gorge, advertised locally as 'Little Switzerland':

Among the most interesting 'sights' conveniently accessible from Lofthouse is the romantic
gorge of How Stean which has been produced in a similar manner to the mighty ravines of
Colorado. The resulting scenery of the Nidderdale canyon is infinitely more pleasing and
picturesque…In some places the ravine is nearly 80 feet deep richly draped with mosses,
ivy, wild flowers and spreading trees.

Walks for all shapes, sizes, ages and capacities begin at How Stean. The 'old mountain road over Rainstang' (above), made to sound like a 6,000 metre pass through the Himalayas, is in fact an easy ramble through Middlesmoor and Inmoor Lane to the reservoirs. From the moors on the other side of the Scar House dam is a path to Little Whernside with a branch up Great Whernside and the village of Kettlewell. To the south of How Stean one can negotiate the bogs and tussocks of Raygill House Moor to get to Greenhow on the Pateley to Grassington road. To the east are Goyden Pot, New Goyden Pot and Manchester Hole, caves through which the subterranean Nidd goes on its way to empty into Gouthwaite reservoir. There was an opportunity for children to explore some of the caves when Tom Price, outdoor education adviser in the West Riding, visited one of the Batley camps. Having previously been warden of the Eskdale Outward Bound School in the Lake District in succession to Eric Shipton, the famous mountaineer, Tom was generally regarded as the expert in outdoor education. His philosophy was down to earth. *"Anyone"*, he said, *"can make adventure training safe by taking all the adventure out of it. The best safety lies not so much in the avoidance of danger but in learning how to deal with it."* Like Jim Hogan he inspired young people to lose their fear and achieve more than they ever thought possible. Such people are not 'crag rats' but neither do they look down or turn back. Tom was still climbing at the age of 93.

Although staff and students loved the centre and its setting, relations with the farmer were not always easy and there was the occasional clash of interest, understandable when one remembers that the Walker family were pioneers in making a business of tourism in the upper dale. On one celebrated occasion, the head of geography, irritated by the farmer's refusal to agree a short landlease, admonished him with 'Now let's be reasonable Mr Walker!' It was another clash of civilisations. Exhortations like this were not going to change the mind of a Dales farmer who was manifestly in favour of tourism development but definitely on his own terms. On the other hand his stubborness was puzzling to a teacher used to a logical and scientific approach to the landscape of geographical problems.

Farmer Herbert Walker was cautiously go-ahead and by no means as cynical as the Wensleydale farmer who, when it was suggested at a meeting organised by the regional development agency that farmers should work collaboratively, came out with a conference stopping, *"In the War we used to shoot collaborators."* Other problems were caused by restrictions on the use of the caravan site toilets, considered by school parties to have a more reliable flush than the centre's own loos which were dependent on a good flow of water in the beck. In times of drought the submersible pump failed to raise enough water to the tanks and life became difficult. Another expectation was that the farm shop would be the main provider of groceries and that there would be a stream of children queueing to buy sweets.

Goole Grammar School's Nidderdale hut lasted longer than the railway — just over 30 years. Parents and friends of the school raised £40,000 for its renovation in 2001 but a new head with harder business sense, decided in 2003 that enough was enough and that it should be sold.

The reason for its closure was the burden of maintenance and a decline in use, attributable partly to teachers not wanting to take the risks associated with outdoor education. After payment of a nominal sum, its ownership reverted to the Walker family and they have re-opened it as an outdoor activity centre, all in contradiction to the prophets of doom at Goole who reckoned its final purpose would be to serve as a tearoom. With competition from another centre only yards away at How Stean Gorge it would be curmudgeonly not to applaud the family's services to the dale over the years and to wish them well with the venture. We may hope that trends in education will observe a 25 year cycle and that in the unlikely event of a future government moderating its obsession with testing, we may see a return to the popularity of outdoor residentials at places like Studfold Farm. As settings for personal and social education they are second to none.

Nowadays the dale is different from what it was forty five years ago. In the pubs at Lofthouse and Middlesmoor, local customers do not go silent and stare threateningly at visitors when they walk into the bar; they make them feel at home and happily share their knowledge of the dale. Predictably the entrance fee for How Stean gorge has increased from one shilling to £4.75. The farmers do not shout 'bugger off' to visitors but welcome them with a smile and offer accommodation in their holiday cottages. Some, though not many, have even stopped using barbed wire in their fences, and several are refugees from the cities whose schools years ago brought them to Nidderdale and enthralled their imaginations. Universal tourism has changed everything and the dale is better for it.

There is however a more worrying postscript. It is that Goole Grammar School (now Goole High School Academy of Excellence) should perhaps have noticed that in an era governed at home and at school by digital communications and entertainment, its Nidderdale centre could have been used to counter the declining role of nature in its pupils' lives. In his research for a TV documentary, *Project Wild Thing*, film maker David Bond discovered that his daughter's days were restricted to play indoors, at school, on car journeys and at home. Four percent of her time was spent outside. In contrast, his 81 year old mother, growing up in Hornsea in the Holderness area of east Yorkshire, roamed across 50 square miles at the age of 11. When he was a boy in the mid seventies, Bond says he roamed within one square mile but that his children wander freely only in their own garden. If it thinks about it at all, the school may have cause to regret parting with its own 'gateway to the Dales', the like of which may yet need to be rediscovered as a very relevant component of the curriculum.

Looking back over those first years at Goole, I am not ashamed to say that they were so exciting as to appear fanciful. Classroom teaching was enjoyable, often entertaining, and the only condition of admission to the staffroom was second sight in card games, usually Bridge. Always a stranger to divination, I trumped the soothsayers by helping to organise a chess tournament.

There were also many personal pleasures, the most thrilling being a discovery of Yorkshire's heather moors and limestone dales which the school rambling club visited most weekends. Until I went to Goole, all my time had been spent in the midlands and south of England. I had enjoyed the beaches and woodlands of Hampshire where there were family connections and the Mendip hills in Somerset when I was in Wells, but now I was routinely walking fifteen miles over the Yorkshire hills and being invited to go on expeditions to the Scottish Highlands. The first of these in spring 1967, was in the company of Bill Petch, head of history. We walked and scrambled for a week in the Cuillin Hills on the Isle of Skye and camped among ptarmigan on the slopes of Blaven. Out of these early introductions came a compulsion to discover more of the the 'great outdoors'. It led to an irresistible appetite for adventure and many years walking in mountains not just in the UK and Europe but on the Tibetan Plateau in western China where twenty five years in the future, during the summer of 1993, I would be leading a young people's expedition sponsored by the Yorkshire Schools Exploring Society.

China '93

China '93 was an expedition involving 40 young people and 20 staff, including five doctors. The expedition was to learn about the geography of the Plateau and the history and way of life of its Golok inhabitants who, like the Mongol peoples, operated an economy based largely on the yak which in Tibet grazed the summer pastures of the high plains. Young people and staff had to raise the money to pay for their 'ticket' and to take part in a year long training programme. There were five groups of eight expeditioners, each with a distinct objective: trekking the route of an ancient Bhuddist pilgrimage, climbing in the Anyemachin mountains, making a film about life on the Plateau, mountain biking, and lastly a group which undertook a detailed study of two villages, one Bhuddist and the other Moslem.

The expedition began and ended in Beijing and in that great city we were able to explore the Great Wall, the Forbidden City and the Ming Tombs. On the train journey from Beijing to Xining we stayed a night in Xian and visited the Terracotta Army. Several expeditioners were from Humberside schools, including two from Derringham School for children with additional learning needs and two from Goole Grammar School. Humberside County Council made available bursaries which augmented what they had already raised themselves.

For the young people, the expedition bore a resemblance to City Challenge. Albeit in a different, more attractive setting, they had to learn to live together under pressure and to lend a helping hand when circumstances demanded. For all of them and for the staff, it was 'the journey of a lifetime' not only because they were living for five weeks 10,000 feet up on the Plateau but because of what they learned about their strengths and weaknesses. It was the same for me but I had to have that extra 'management resilience'. This came in useful when a well known British bank managed to lose (temporarily) £40,000 in the process of transferring the expedition money to China.[32]

Questions

'From my first impressions on interview day, I knew Goole Grammar School was going to be home'. What did I mean?

How would you interpret 'Religious Education' in today's curriculum? Does it represent an outdated view of the world or is its politics too important to ignore?

Why do you think, perhaps surprisingly, that young children (11-13 years) took so enthusiastically to visiting Rawcliffe Hall?

Chapter 3 Notes

1   A 'Ruby'(1933) two door saloon with a registration number that these days would belong to a water company boss – EAU 100. I seem to remember the car belonged to the diocese of Southwell and was on loan to my father. Our own vehicle was a more upmarket 1935 Austin Ten.

2   *Viridiana* was voted the 37th greatest film of all time in *Sight & Sound* magazine's 2012 poll. The film's plot concerns the trials and tribulations of a novice nun and was regarded by many as blasphemous. There is a scene where a group of drunken beggars appear to represent Leonardo's *Last Supper* to the accompaniment of the Hallelujah Chorus.

3   The lecture in January 1963 was arranged by the Oxford University Humanist Group and was entitled *The Molecular Basis of Life*. Crick had won the Nobel Prize in 1962.

4   *The Thirty Nine Articles of Religion* dating from 1563 and the reign of Elizabeth I, are a statement of the principal doctrines of the Church of England which it was expected would govern the lives of the population of England and protect them against popery on the one hand and Puritanism on the other. Articles XXXII – XXXIX deal among other things with celibacy and excommunication.

5   The Inquisition was a procedure for rooting out heresy from the medieval church. Suspected heretics were interrogated and given an opportunity to recant. If they were unwilling to do so they were punished. Galileo and Joan of Arc are probably its most famous victims. Galileo acknowledged his heresy and survived; Joan was obdurate and did not.

6   Peter Rachman (1919–1962) was a landlord in the Notting Hill area of London in the early 1960s, who became notorious for tenant exploitation. He built up a property empire in west London of more than a hundred mansion blocks and several nightclubs. The first house he purchased and used for multi-occupation was in now fashionable St Stephen's Gardens, W2. In adjacent areas including Powis Square, Powis Gardens, Powis Terrace, Colville Road and Colville Terrace, he also subdivided large properties into flats and let rooms, often for prostitution. Nowadays the housing situation in the capital is much the same, in spite of the rent acts. Thousands of people living in sheds and warehouses are being forced to pay high rents for dangerous and unhealthy accommodation. (John Waite: *Face the Facts* BBC Radio 4 April 23rd 2014)

7   Beckett Park: a teacher training college for women which later became Carnegie College for Physical Education. Leeds Metropolitan University has recently been renamed Leeds Beckett University.

8   The Apocalypse: the end of the world described in the Book of Revelation, the last book of the New Testament. There is a flippant reference to St Luke's account of the 'Last Days' in my story later in this chapter, about a visit to the Grand Canyon

9   *A History of Christianity*, Penguin Books, 2010: page 686.

10 Euripides: a Greek tragedian (480-406 BC)

11 Panga: A broad heavy knife or machete found in east Africa.

12 *Teenage Religion*, H.Loukes, SCM Press 1961. The author was Reader in Education at the University of Reading. His book resulted from an enquiry into religious belief in secondary modern schools on behalf of the Institute of Christian Education. It contained transcripts of tape-recordings showing the religious attitudes of young people. Pupils commented on the problems discussed and there was an analysis of the teacher's task in making Christian education relevant to boys and girls in their last year at school.

13 Parental pressure – See Chapter 1 Note 3.

14 Raising of the school leaving age and the movement towards the establishment of comprehensive schools to replace the tripartite system of grammar, modern and technical schools implemented by the Butler Act of 1944.

15 *Goole: A Port in Green Fields*, Joyce Mankowska, 1973.

16 *Everybody's Business*, Roger W Young, OUP, 1968

17 Peter Porter was an Australian poet who died in April 2010 aged 81. The notice of his obituary in the Daily Telegraph commented that after his broadcast of 'Your Attention Please', a spoof warning of imminent nuclear attack, the BBC felt bound to issue an apology to listeners who had taken the instructions seriously.

18 *The War Game* was a one hour documentary made for TV in 1965 by Peter Watkins and is about the effects of a nuclear attack on Britain. The BBC refused to show it. *Dr Strangelove* or *How I Stopped Worrying and Love the Bomb*, released in 1964, starred Peter Sellers and George C. Scott in a black comedy about how a nuclear war could begin by accident. One realises that the possibility is still real when a Russian official could declare in connection with the problems in Ukraine in 2014, that 'Russia is the only country which could reduce the United States to nuclear ash'.

19 For the concept of a future king coming to rescue the Jews from themselves or from persecuting nations see *He That Cometh: The Messiah Concept in the Old Testament and Later Judaism*, Sigmund Mowinckel, Eerdmans, 1956 (revised 2005).

20 *Letters and Papers from Prison*, SCM Classics, 1953. The book is still in print.

21 The *Death of God* found expression in the thought of a number of mainstream Protestant theologians such as Thomas JJ Altizer, William Hamilton, John Robinson, Paul Tillich, Gabriel Vahanian, Paul van Buren. Their ideas are difficult to handle but may form the instinctive beliefs of many Christians, especially in the middle-of-the-road, muddling-along Church of England. 'God is dead' was a saying originally used by Friedrich Nietzche. God's response was supposedly 'I *may* be dead, but Nietzche is certainly dead'.

22 Shelter was launched on 1 December 1966 and evolved out of the work with homeless people at St Martin-in-the-Fields. A major spur to the setting up of the charity was the public outcry which followed the transmission in November 1966 of the BBC television play *Cathy Come Home*.

23 Published by SCM Press, January 1st 1970.

24 St Martin's Crypt is now a café and popular tourist rendezvous with art gallery and brass rubbing centre.

25 A 44 page book published in June 1974 by the National Society for Mentally Handicapped Children.

26 See note 22.

27 See for example 2013 research report by University of Glamorgan *Looking into abuse: Research by People with Learning Disabilities*.

28 I have not been able to find evidence for this utterance. Perhaps it is part of the subversive oral tradition. The point is that Domestic Science aka Home Management aka Home Economics *was* abolished by Ken Baker and absorbed into 'Technology'. See also an article in the *Times Educational Supplement* by Peter Wilby – *Storming of the Classroom Castle*, May 19th 2006, updated in 2012.

29 Ted Wragg's article *Flowers from a Secret Garden* appeared in a special supplement to mark the 75th year of publication (1910–1985) of the *Times Educational Supplement*.

30 The full text of Enoch Powell's speech delivered to a Conservative Association audience in Birmingham on 20th April 1968 can be found on the *Daily Telegraph* website http://www.telegraph.co.uk/comment/3643823/Enoch-Powells-Rivers-of-Blood-speech.html.

31 OS Explorer Map 298.

32 For a superbly illustrated account of life on the Tibetan Plateau see *Mountains of the Middle Kingdom: Exploring the High Peaks of China and Tibet*, by photographer Galen Rowell. The book is published by Sierra Club Books, San Francisco. ISBN: 0-87156-829-2.

A Cuckoo in the Curriculum

Part 2

A Curriculum for All

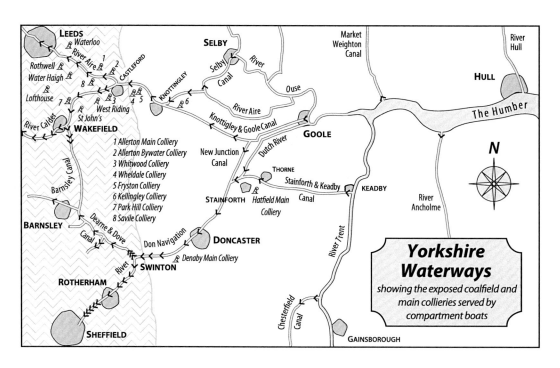

Yorkshire Waterways
showing the exposed coalfield and main collieries served by compartment boats

1 Allerton Main Colliery
2 Allerton Bywater Colliery
3 Whitwood Colliery
4 Wheldale Colliery
5 Fryston Colliery
6 Kellingley Colliery
7 Park Hill Colliery
8 Savile Colliery

A barge similar to *Sobriety* passing Eastwood Lock in the 1970s.

Chapter 4
SOBRIETY: A BARGE APPEARS

"Let you steer?" replied the barge-woman, laughing.
"It takes some practice to steer a barge properly."
"You common, low, fat barge-woman," he shouted.
(*The Wind in the Willows* – Kenneth Grahame)

The *Sobriety* story is of a charity founded in 1973, four months after I returned from Kano. From the beginning the charity was intent on using the history, arts and environment of the UK waterways and near European coast in a curriculum to balance more formal aspects of education. In this respect the Project's development was inevitably influenced by national politics and policies, and events in Yorkshire and the East Riding town of Goole. This book is now concerned with the circumstances of a development which has sometimes been frightening, at other times amusing, but never less than exciting; it is the story of an attempt to use the inland waterways and coast of Britain as a resource, not only for a broader school curriculum, but also to combat the social and economic exclusion of a significant proportion of the UK population. St Matthew's gospel sums it up: his Chapter 25 makes the point:

'I was hungry and you gave me food, I was thirsty and you gave me drink, I was a stranger and you welcomed me, I was naked and you clothed me, I was sick and you visited me, I was in prison and you came to me.'

'Lord, when did we see thee hungry and feed thee, or thirsty and give thee drink? And when did we see thee a stranger and welcome thee, or naked and clothe thee? And when did we see thee sick or in prison and visit thee?'

(Edited from Revised Standard Version)

A New Authority And A New School

The school I had come back to in December 1972 was different from the one I had left. I felt like Washington Irving's Rip van Winkle. He was beguiled into sleeping for twenty years and missed the American War of Independence which replaced the British monarchy with a republican presidency. When Rip awoke and went home, his wife was dead and no one recognised him. In Goole Grammar School there were new staff who spoke and acted like old hands. *"Who's this new guy?"* I heard them ask. And one of them was running the RE department. I had to be ready for a new start. Nigeria had taught me a degree of resilience which was coming in useful. I could think back to the episode at Ikom and observe that I probably had more of a future in Goole Grammar School than in Sergeant Gabriel's lock-up. As well as changes in me and the school, changes were imminent in local government and in the organisation of education in the Goole area. The first to affect us, only marginally at first, was the 1974 local government boundary changes proposed by the Redcliffe-Maud Report [1] which saw the end of the West Riding. There was a new Humberside authority covering the north and south banks of the Humber estuary with the market town of Beverley as its administrative centre. During Humberside's first few years, the new Humber Bridge appeared on its notepaper as an optimistic symbol of the advantages of joining the two banks of the river in economic and administrative union. Boundary change is not always popular but protest by 'Yorkies' and Lincolnshire 'Yellow Bellies' against the new authority was formidable. The most picturesque objection came from the Earl of Yarborough whose estate on the south side of the Humber straddled the proposed border with Lincolnshire. After making it clear that being embraced by the hated new county would be worse than being snatched into East Berlin, he persuaded the Commission to put a kink in his northern border. The Yarborough enclave between Scunthorpe and Grimsby survived further boundary changes in 1996 but to be on the safe side the Earl would probably have preferred a wall and razor wire.

The second change occurred during my year away. In 1972 Margaret Thatcher was Education Secretary in the Heath government and was hovering over the parliamentary order to turn Goole Grammar School with its 1,000 square mile pupil catchment area into a local comprehensive. The change came two years later but for sentimental reasons the school kept its old name until 1987, when, following Peter Teed's retirement, a new head renamed it Vermuyden School after the Dutch drainage engineer Cornelius Vermuyden. No one knew how to spell, let alone pronounce the name, (at various times Verm*oo*den, Verm*ow*den, Verm*oi*den or Verm*er*den or even *Ferm*er*den), and two headteachers later in 2009, it became Goole High School, the name of the town's former secondary modern which with the grammar school had been abolished in 1974. In 2011 the new High School became an Academy of Excellence and cut its ties with East Riding of Yorkshire Council. Two years later an Ofsted report [2] concluded that the school was less than 'excellent'. However its headteacher was in no mood to take this lying down and stated publicly that her school was the 'latest victim of a brutal inspection regime'. She insisted that it was 'now better than when Ofsted had rated it as 'good''.

In 1973 the school had no such problems but it did have only a year to transform itself from a traditional 11-18 grammar school, taking the fifteen per cent of children who had the highest scores in the 11+, from the area formed by the Pontefract, Hull and Scunthorpe triangle, into a 13-18 comprehensive catering for all of Goole's children in that age range. It would be the top of a pyramid of six 5-9 primary schools and three 9-13 middle schools, one of which would be housed in the former secondary modern buildings across the road from the grammar school. The first group to arrive in the new school would be 120 children aged 13; thereafter pupil numbers would steadily rise each September until they reached 1,500; the curriculum would change from being O and A Level GCE orientated to providing for a population with a much bigger range of interests and ambitions. The absurd practice of streaming fourth and fifth year pupils, which had seen 'D' stream children in the grammar school become university lecturers, would be abolished and children would work largely in class size social groups. My worries about how I would fit into the new school disappeared when soon after I had unpacked the camel blankets and bottles of native medicine, I found myself being interviewed for the post of head of a faculty of social and community studies by Peter Teed and Bill Morrell, the West Riding's Chief Adviser. Their questions made it clear that the priority was to give the new curriculum an underlying consistency of purpose, sympathetic to the needs of all pupils. Arrangement of naturally linked groups of departments by faculty would break down subject barriers, encourage teachers to be enthusiastic about children with varying interests and send to the dustbin the seemingly indelible labels of 'less able' and 'more academic.' The content of the curriculum had to be relevant not in the first instance to the vocational requirements of the market place but, as a reflection of Alec Clegg's 'hyacinths', to the hopes and expectations of children. And where there appeared to be no hope and expectation, the curriculum should come to the rescue. As Tony Little, headmaster of Eton said in 2012, '*A good school will want young people to develop the self confidence to stand up for themselves and the desire to stand for a purpose higher than themselves.*'

A New Faculty

It would be fair to say however, that it was in spite of some reservations that Peter Teed recommended my appointment to head of faculty. He may have been impressed, if occasionally puzzled, by my approach to religious education but I knew that he was not entirely sure of my ability to lead a group of nine teachers who had little in common except membership of the faculty. During my five years (discounting Nigeria) at the school, I had shared with Jean Williams the teaching of statutory RE to all pupils as well as Ordinary and Advanced level GCE Religious Studies to specialist groups. I had also taught VI form General Studies and developed community service projects. These were responsibilities that had been fortified by my own 'extra curricular' interests: City Challenge, work in London with the Salvation Army, and in local youth clubs, teaching evening classes at Hatfield Borstal, six weeks on an Israeli *kibbutz* and my year at Government College, Kano. Add to this a growing love of hillwalking and camping and a newly discovered enthusiasm for directing school plays, and you have an individual who was mesmerised by adventure. On the down side I had a tendency to carry on regardless and was certainly a 'late developer' but I also had ideas which seemed to fit with the planned scheme of things in the new comprehensive school. What I had not learned in Goole or Kano was administrative responsibility for matters such as timetabling, nor did I have experience of staff management. I had no idea of how I was going find common ground between subjects as far apart as Stage 1 RSA Typewriting and A level Economics, or Careers Guidance and O-level Accounts.

Meanwhile the faculties of Maths-Science, Humanities, PE, Languages and Creative Arts were hard at work. Their staff, who now included colleagues from the secondary modern school, would use new techniques for teaching across traditional subject boundaries. At the point where they became reasonably convinced of their interests and had an inkling of their intentions after leaving school, children would choose specialised courses leading to appropriate qualifications. For the Humanities faculty it was comparatively easy to organise its member subject areas to contribute to a course of study, for example, on Victorian England; staff would meet to plan lessons using resources from one another's subject areas and remove any obstructions to cross departmental teaching. Up to a certain level the Maths-Science faculty was able to do the same. For the performing and visual arts it was a gift: for language teaching more difficult: for PE it was stating the obvious; they had always done things in this way. Some courses and activities would be shared between faculties, and staff would be expected, when and where necessary, to teach in areas outside their own faculty. For the Faculty of Social and Community Studies however, the future looked mysterious.

In spring 1974 a few months before the Great Change, Peter Teed led a staff conference at Bretton Hall which in 2001 would become part of the Yorkshire Sculpture Park but was at that time a teacher training college founded by Alec Clegg. It specialised in design, music and the visual and performing arts. At the conference I was much encouraged by the presence of Jim Bolton, recently appointed assistant director of education for Humberside, who said that the new LEA would attach the same importance as the West Riding to education outside the classroom. After seven years as a pupil at Batley Grammar School and three years as a student at the London School of Economics, Jim had become deputy director of education for the Borough of Grimsby. It was during this time that he had come under the influence of Jim Hogan and Alec Clegg. He was a lifeline to the future and during the nineteen seventies and eighties would make himself responsible for keeping an eye on *Sobriety*'s relations with the authority.

When I was asked to lead a conference session on out-of-school activities I suggested there was more to them than met the eye. There appeared to be in-school activities out of school, such as geology field studies. Then there were out-of–school activities in school, such as a chess clubs or foreign language societies. Or in-school activities in school — not classwork but involvement in school councils, and with others, the opportunity to make decisions about aspects of school organisation. Finally there were out-of-school activities out of school, such as camping and hillwalking, which would surely play a part in pupils' development. These were merely labels of convenience and in practice there was overlap and sometimes little distinction. Sports activities for example, would certainly be found under all four headings. The terms now sound like a parody on US Defence Secretary Donald Rumsfeldt's 2004 speech about known unknowns and unknown unknowns in America's relations with countries in the Middle East, but at the time it was an attempt to identify the boundaries and reach some conclusions about the faculty's purpose.

With a careers tutor on its staff and responsibility among others for teaching office skills, the faculty was always going to be concerned with Sir Alec Clegg's 'loaves' — with facts, the intellect and training for employment. But for many young people, preparation for work went hand in hand with a need to know how to manage a home and family. In response to this, a team of cross faculty staff led by Eileen Dunford, an outstanding teacher and administrator, designed a set of courses shared with the Creative Arts faculty, which covered nutrition, food preparation, meal planning and cookery (pupils brought their ingredients into school and took home the finished product). There were also courses in pre and post natal advice, the care of babies and toddlers, needlework, the care of fabrics, and safety of household machinery. With a specially designed flat in the teaching area, pupils were able to work together to practise their skills. Another component of these courses in home management related directly to the local community. Every girl and boy on the course was expected to spend a timetabled half day a week in an old people's home, a school for children with a learning disability, a hospital, or a private household where an elderly person was living alone. Pupils kept diaries and submitted them with coursework for assessment in the Certificate of Secondary Education. Standards were high and pupils were proud to be involved. Many 'loaves' were turned into 'hyacinths' by their enthusiasm and commitment. Some would say that the current pressure for the achievement of targets makes it impossible except in the public schools, academies and free schools, to timetable such an experience. Is it not depressing that the freedom to grow Sir Alec's 'hyacinths' is generally restricted to the independent sector while state schools are threatened with return to the old worn out separation of 'the academic' from 'the less able' by single examination? How long will it be before a secretary of state brings back Bordesley Green secondary modern in the name of 'raising standards'? No wonder that many teachers are disillusioned with the endless quest for measurable performance that undermines ambition for their children.

Years later in 1989 when Chris Woodhead, Her Majesty's Chief Inspector, scorning 'progressive theories,' set to work hunting down his '15,000 incompetent teachers', the National Curriculum brought an end to courses in home management. Successive governments then pondered over the cause of unhealthy lifestyles and attempted to combat them with multi-million pound special programmes like the Healthy Living initiative of the late nineteen nineties.

For the first two years of the new comprehensive school from 1974 to 1976, the long established subjects of woodwork and metalwork also found a home in the faculty. The scene in the workshops often resembled a Victorian factory with workers bent like statues over lathes and a 'supervisor' patrolling the aisles to keep an eye on the goods being produced. One of the most dedicated of the happy band of budding engineers in this sweat shop was Jock Mitchell, a Scots boy with very definite opinions about how his education should be conducted. On a casual visit to the workshops I found him at a lathe, standing knee deep in filings and pouring gallons of cooling liquid over a metal bar thick enough to support a building. Not wishing to interrupt the process, I asked him with polite indulgence what he was making. The answer was shouted proudly over the din of the lathe, *"Och sir, I'm making a wee screwdriver."* I was pleased it wasn't a gun barrel.

The faculty was evolving into a bridge between school and work but not just at a practical level. Its Ordinary and Advanced level courses in economics, accountancy, sociology and business studies would give pupils a better understanding of global politics and some help with choosing a future occupation, whether they intended to leave school at 16 or to go via the VI Form into further or higher education. The demands of the new school meant that the social and community curriculum had to be 'preparation for life'. Careers evenings and conferences for pupils, teachers and employers had to be organised and were complemented by 'Design for Living' which brought into the classroom working people from the public services and private industry. An Ordinary Level GCE in Rights & Responsibilities was advertised among older pupils. Supported by BBC radio programmes it required them to have an understanding of the law relating to landlords and tenants, the sale of goods, the provision of services, marriage and divorce, arrest and trial and so on.

At the informal and social level every child coming into the school would spend a week of the autumn term at the How Stean Centre in Nidderdale where there would be opportunities away from the classroom to get to know staff and other children. It would be a springboard for staff and pupils to show themselves during a week of informal activities. There would be no situation as dramatic as that faced by Jim Hogan's pot boy but there would certainly be events and challenges to affect the thinking of staff back in school. Out-of-school activities previously at home in the RE department, now moved into the faculty. But one of these, landing unplanned and unwelcome in the faculty nest, would attempt to link the school to the history and traditions of the port of Goole. This 45 ton cuckoo in the curriculum was a cargo carrying barge called *Sobriety*. As we shall see, it was loaded with 'hyacinths'.

A New Curriculum

During my first few years at Goole, I had come to the conclusion that one of the most important duties of a teacher was to awaken in children, a passion for discovery which played to their sense of wonder and generated a desire to understand the world. There were many ways to enrich the process so that it led to an unmistakable light in pupils' eyes. Knowledge could be turned into learning by a good teacher, but the student was entitled to expect more than a briefing of facts. Tests and examinations had their place but if practised in isolation were more likely to kill than cultivate. Desmond Lee's commentary on the Greek philosopher Plato's view of education states the matter clearly:

> But in all he does the educator should remember that his aim is not to 'put into the mind knowledge that was not there before'…but to turn the mind's eye to the light so that it can see for itself; his business in other words is not to stick thoughts into his pupils' heads but to make them think for themselves.[3]

My own modest contribution to 'turning the mind's eye' was in the organisation of projects to benefit children or students by giving them an insight into other people's predicament. At a grammar school where activities and classwork could be smoothly linked, this was easy. In a comprehensive school where with the increasing influence of right wing educationalists like the MP, Rhodes Boyson, there was less room for classroom spontaneity, I felt myself to be on a stage with a cast and scenery better fitted to the character of a developing *Sobriety* Project than to the prescriptive curriculum foreshadowed by Parliament's Black Papers.[4] I was also fortunate that by 1987, two years before the arrival of the National Curriculum, I was seconded by Humberside LEA to become the *Sobriety* Project's full time organiser. In doing so I left behind the faculty I had been leading for twelve years and abandoned any idea of promotion in mainstream education. I had no regrets. *Sobriety* would give me full time freedom to promote and practise an alternative curriculum represented by City Challenge and some of Goole Grammar School's out-of-school activities. But we need to go back fourteen years to see how this came about.

In 1973 Goole Grammar School had three staff rooms. These were for women, men and one that, for the purposes of Bridge and Chess, ignored gender. It was a perfectly civilised arrangement, preventing men boring women and women boring men, both with their gossip. There was no bar to women coming into the men's staff room and the only condition imposed on men visiting the women was that they did not sit in the chair reserved for Katie Holland, Head of Domestic Science. I was in awe of Miss Holland and usually took a chair in with me or stood near the door. But on this occasion I was sitting in an arm chair and having a relaxed discussion about the timetable recently published by the deputy head after six weeks of work during the summer break. The conversation soon drifted from serious matters into fantasies about the comprehensive school curriculum. Someone said, *"We'll need a Viking ship like the one in Goole Corporation's badge". "Or we could have a barge"*, I said, and we all howled with laughter.

A few weeks later I had the job of producing AA Milne's *Toad of Toad Hall* based on Kenneth Grahame's *Wind in the Willows*. It is not a difficult undertaking; there are only four main characters and a crowd of weasels and stoats. I had a Badger, Mole, Ratty and Toad who were tailor-made for the parts and we all enjoyed the rehearsals. After the performance in Goole Youth Centre, Peter Teed came to me and said, *"Can I have a word? Mr McGrory wants to give us a barge and I think it might be of interest to your faculty as well as to PE and the Geography people. It's called* Sobriety." *"I'm glad it's not called* Chastity *or* Obedience," I said, momentarily recalling Saint Augustine's of Hippo's famous prayer, 'Give me chastity and continence O Lord, but not yet.'[5] A frayed rope hanging from a tie beam and a ladder with missing rungs took us down into the hold of this *Sobriety*, previously home to 120 tons of anything from wet slag to cocoa beans. There were perfunctory grunts of appreciation but for most staff it was an encounter with fantasy; the thing was a wreck, of no educational value, a ridiculous proposition for a school grappling with a new population and a new curriculum. The truth was that John McGrory, a Goole business man with interests in shipping and inland waterways, had heard on the grapevine that a cargo-carrying barge was for sale in Thorne, a small town between Goole and Doncaster. With a view to converting it for the enjoyment of disabled children he had acquired the barge for £600 but had then offered it to the school in the hope that it would deflect young people from trouble and keep alive the history and traditions of Yorkshire s waterways. Although destined for scrap if no one adopted it, the vessel was by no means a wreck and from my point of view was an ideal project for a faculty charged with linking school and community. On the strength of this, John agreed an arrangement whereby if the school ceased to have use for it, the vessel would be returned to him.

Sobriety had been built at Beverley in 1910 and some said that on her maiden voyage she had been overloaded with newsprint and had sunk in the river Hull. She was a Humber sailing barge technically known as a *keel*. This was a term deriving from 'ceolas', an early Scandinavian word for boat. She was 'Sheffield' size, 61ft 6in long and 15ft 3in wide, designed to fit the locks on the canals up to Sheffield which she would have navigated by sail when possible, but, like Toad's barge in *The Wind in the Willows*, would have been pulled by a horse or the captain's wife when there was no wind. The man who hired out himself and the horse in a package-deal with a captain, was known as a horse-marine. By the early nineteen seventies there were not many survivors of this pre-war trade but I did get to know one who could tell a tale. Ben Tether from Old Goole, with horse and barge and crew, would work his way up to Sheffield, perhaps with a cargo of molasses, taking three or four days to get through the locks and bridges between Goole and his destination. When he and the horse and the captain and his wife and the barge arrived in Sheffield, horse-marine Ben would leave the unloading to the captain, go to the pub and at closing time, get on his horse and go to sleep. When he awoke, if he was still on the horse, he would find himself in Doncaster, half way to Goole; the horse was teetotal and so knew its way home. Another character was Jim Rownsley who after getting divorced at the age of 75 was living on a caravan site in Mexborough. As *Sobriety*'s captain in the 1930s he recalled cooking breakfast on the canal bank *en route* to Sheffield.

In 1939 under a wartime scheme for improving waterway transport, *Sobriety* lost her sails and was given an engine. As a motor barge she was less pleasing to look at but more capable of earning a good living for her captain. With a built-in means of propulsion she was also a more plausible addition to the curriculum when she became the responsibility of the Social & Community Studies Faculty in April 1973. One of her first engagements was to spend an afternoon working for the school's Modern Languages faculty by ferrying two groups of 30 French children and their hosts between Goole and a small village up the canal. But as Toad's barge-woman said, *"It takes some practice to steer a barge properly."* And this was no pedalo; it was the size of a small ship and in the wrong hands would sink anything getting in its way. Bill Drakeley, a probation officer friend, solved the steering problem by recruiting Tom Barrass, an ex barge-man with hands as big as shovels. I myself scrounged 30 lifejackets from the local sea cadet unit, otherwise known as the Training Ship *Boadicea*, which was located far from the ocean on the first floor of a building in one of Goole's back streets. But here was our first brush with Authority.

To give approval for the barge to carry more than 12 passengers, an official from the Department of Trade and Industry in Hull had to make an inspection.[6] With amazing urgency the inspector arrived aboard *Sobriety* in an overcoat open to the wind. As he stumbled down the ladder into the engine room, there was no small talk and not much inspection, just a slurred announcement that when he left he would be going to church. I was impressed that the Department for Trade & Industry appeared now to be including prayers for the canal faithful in its regulations and as a teacher of religious education was keen to know if the practice was widespread. However from a hesitant enquiry along these lines came finger to my chest — *"I'm going to church to pray for you! By four o'clock you'll be on a manslaughter charge."* He then climbed the ladder and disappeared. I was grateful that four o'clock came without the appearance of any policemen. Even better was instant fame. The *Goole Times* of the 5th of April 1974 captured the idyll under the heading 'Old barge provides Goole school with floating classroom'. The article continued:

Isabelle Fouchet was on her first visit to England and was enjoying her stay. She has been on barges on the Seine but this was a different experience altogether... The sun shone, farm workers stopped to wave and the skipper mastered the unnerving rules of the road for dealing with oncoming vessels. This involves steering straight down the middle of the channel and veering to starboard at the last moment.

The hard work of development will continue for a long time yet, accompanied by the strict wearing of lifejackets. Not for Mr Barrass though. Resplendent in trilby hat he declared "I've spent all my life on canals but I've never learned to swim".

Mr Barrass would return to haunt us later.

A few weeks after this, in the caption for its back page picture of a group of children on *Sobriety*, the *Guardian* referred to 'a floating classroom'. The *Yorkshire Post* was more ambitious with the headline 'Geography classroom takes to the water'. It was not an entirely accurate description of what we were about but it was good currency for a year or two. Meanwhile Bill Drakeley persuaded the West Riding Probation Service to spend £75 on black varnish for the barge's hull. 'Varnish' was a misnomer; it was liquidised tar containing so much vaporising spirit that even at twenty five yards its effect was to turn the workforce into zombies.

Before becoming a probation officer, Bill had been an education welfare officer, popularly known as a Kid Catcher. Before this he had worked in Goole shipyard. I never found out quite what his job was but he did recall concealing in a large overcoat some weights he had clandestinely fabricated for weight training. As he cycled through the shipyard gates on his way home, his contraband burst his pockets and rolled slowly along the gutter in front of him. He may have been a 'bent' plater but as a probation officer he was indispensable to the development of the barge. As a native of Goole and a former tradesman at the shipyard, he understood the town. As education welfare officer he knew all children who 'twagged' off school, as well as their parents, grandparents, cousins and uncles; he also knew the law and was able to interpret it in everyone's best interest. As a result he was popular and respected. He had taken to probation like a duck to water and hailed *Sobriety* as a resource to be taken seriously. In an article written in June 1974 for the probation team in Wakefield, he described his impressions:

John McGrory - founding benefactor.

She had been lying sadly in her berth for many months, unattended. She was owned by John McGrory, a local lad made good. He has always had a soft spot for lads who get into trouble and rather than sell her for scrap, he decided to give her to the Youth Service on the understanding that they would do something useful with her. They had a look and decided it was not on. Bob Watson of Goole Grammar School who used to be an RE teacher, had a long hard look last summer. "Well", he said, "With all the weight of the school and Probation Service behind us, what might two years of hard graft bring?"

I looked at the rust on the waterline and intimated that she might well end up where Mr McGrory didn't want her to go. Anyway I wrote to Peter Raine who directed the Yorkshire Area Intermediate Treatment Scheme[7] and he came down to Goole to stand on the deck with a faraway look in his eyes and eventually sent us a life saving £75. We got her out of the water (I could write a book) and painted her bottom. I conned three of my lads (probation clients) to help whilst friend Robert (your author) was inundated with willing volunteers from the school (his story) and to cut a long story short we cleaned her out, stripped and re-assembled the engine and rectified the steering gear. Derek Davies is a simple woodwork master but he knows more about wood and metal than the rest of us put together and he produced an intricate costing and work programme for the conversion of the barge into an aquatic minibus to take at least thirty folk where her width and draught will allow. With camping gear stacked under the floor of the converted hold and crew members' accommodation in the fo'c'sle (front) we have fantasised at least one trip to Stratford-on-Avon. So far we have been to Leeds on the Aire & Calder but as the song says, you've got to have a dream.

Sobriety is having a strange Hamelin effect. It's collected Alf Taylor, a local magistrate and youth leader with a talent for summoning up anything from heavy duty plastic bags to lawyers, three barge skippers, and Simeon Ayeni, a Nigerian teacher here on exchange who was found asleep in one of the locker berths by an inquisitive youth who blurted out his story to Mr Davies, saying he had found a bloke who had been in a dark cupboard for so long he had gone f…ing black. It's a rare alchemy: a black teacher, a seventy year old and teenagers all sharing an experience. Doesn't happen all that often these days. I should

Sobriety on the River Ouse near the village of Saltmarshe.

mention the foreman working on the M62 extension who has shown an interest to the tune of 30 tons of sand for ballast (all legit) and the lawyer on board the other evening depressing us with the nuances of Board of Trade regulations for passenger carrying vessels. Our lads listened with silent interest to his explanation of the thinking behind the regulations. And so it goes on, we hope.

The barge presents initial problems of finance. We ought to be able to pay the rent and insurance without having to worry too much. This is the part I see the statutory services playing, provided they are satisfied with the number of clients involved and the measured value of the project. I think it should be given a whirl for a couple of years as I think there is something to be gained in a work-play situation. The groups can be mixed in an infinite variety of ways and at the moment there is a good strong team of adults. We have yet to satisfy the Board of Trade she won't blow up or catch fire and this will involve a lot more hard work and some money, although the latter is not the greatest need. What we do need are more committed adults.

To conclude: Peter (stubborn, immature, poor father relationship) will not wear his hearing aid. He is given the job of blowing the klaxon to warn other shipping of our approach to a bend. We nearly sank a 700 tonne tanker because he did not hear Mr Davies instruct him to blow the horn. He certainly heard what the rest of the lads thought about his competence as a klaxon man and this was taken up later by his supervising officer in an interview when he expressed a desire to become a barge mate. Strong formative forces I would think.

Bill himself was also constrained by formative forces but had the gift of being able to turn the most solemn occasion into a subject for humour. One such episode saw him in the Crown Court being asked to explain his social enquiry report on a defendant accused of stealing 200 feet of electricity board cable. Lying on the table in front of the court was an exhibit produced by the prosecution — a blue axe. The judge was irritated and snappily asked why the case had taken so long to come to trial. Bill answered that his client had been in hospital recovering from injuries received at the time of the alleged offence. These injuries had been caused by the defendant having attempted to steal the cable while it was still attached to the pylon. Later he used to say to me, *"Now Robert, always remember to be thankful to the criminal because without him we'll be out of a job."*

Bill was trying to endear the villains and hooligans of the district to the pleasures of boating. The hope was that first hand experience of the sleet blowing horizontally over the Goole canal in February would lead them to penitence and recantation. The barge would be a kind of waterways boot camp,[8] leading to a different way of life. But of course, the reality was otherwise. If conditions outside were thought to be character building then conditions inside *Sobriety* would have made a medieval prison seem luxurious. The loo was a draw bucket,[9] the bunks were two feet wide and the 'catering' was done a week in advance. The reason for this was that the Rayburn cooker, which admittedly had cost only 50 pence after being craned out of another more derelict vessel, required a week to get enough heat to cook a chicken. Put the bird in on a Monday and hey presto it would be done to a turn by Friday, just in time for the going-home sandwiches.

Bill was a good probation officer until Humberside Probation moved him to Scunthorpe and put him under a manager with a hidden alcohol problem, in a community he did not know, and with an emphasis on enforcement rather than befriending. The situation improved in the end but the damage had been done. Bill's marriage broke down and several years later he was found dead by the roadside near Beverley; he had had a heart attack while climbing a hill on his bike. I lost my Best Man and a good colleague.

An account similar to Bill's, describing one of *Sobriety*'s early expeditions comes from John Hughes, a pupil at Goole Grammar School in the same year, 1974. He wrote the article for the *Sobriety* Project's Review of 2010:

John McGrory had bought an old barge — the Motor Vessel Sobriety *— for scrap, but gave it to Goole Grammar School to use for as long as it was wanted. Bob Watson who was teaching at the school, had a vision of converting this worn out coal barge into a sort of floating hostel.*

There is a key point here. The barge was scrap-heap bound. It wasn't even titivated up to sell. It was filthy and unless you've worked in a coal-mine I doubt you can picture what the insides of a working coal-barge are like; it was rusty! Scraping and re-painting the bottom of a Humber barge with domestic rollers on the end of garden canes is curiously not one of the jobs that I look back on as the most immediately gratifying of my career. And it was mechanically unsound.

A few of us were roped in to service the engine as part of our Engineering Science O-Level classes. At Bob's urging, we also scraped, painted, sledge-hammered and generally tidied up MV Sobriety *until she looked really not much different, but was nevertheless back in the water and the engine did start easily and ran smoothly. The sound of that three cylinder Lister has a special place in my memories. And she was seaworthy — well, perhaps more accurately, canalworthy.*

She was berthed in what had recently become Goole Marina. It was not very swanky but there were a few pleasure boats, mainly dingy old cabin cruisers completely dwarfed by the huge bulk of Sobriety. The Marina wasn't very well maintained and there was one section where boats of almost any draught were likely to go aground. This area was loosely cordoned off with a few small buoys on a rope. But I get ahead of myself…

Bob organised a maiden voyage to Leeds. I think this was partly to advertise the project and also to thank the band of loyal volunteers, as he charitably referred to us bunch of ne'er-do-wells. We were to travel up to Leeds, stay overnight in a Sea Cadet base in the middle of the city's industrial canalscape and travel back to Goole the following day.

We were all very new to this canal lark, but were looking forward to getting involved in working the locks. First up — Pollington. Except that Pollington lock was stuck. They were waiting for engineers to fix it. We didn't have much choice but to wait around until they turned up. The rest of the journey to Leeds doesn't figure very clearly in my ageing memory. I know we hit every lock and I know I became adept at leaping off the barge to tie it up in the lock, keeping the rope taught through the lift and then leaping back aboard. I do remember Knottingley Junction though. It's the bit of the Aire & Calder Navigation system where you are briefly on the River Aire. There was a different feel to the way the boat was moving — being steered more by the breeze than by old Mr Barrass who had been recruited as skipper. For some reason I remember very little about our night in Leeds. All I have is a vague memory of a strange scout hut based on an island in the canal, and little else.

The trip back was uneventful. Well, fairly uneventful. Mr Barrass was preserving his perfect score at hitting the locks. The need for engineering repairs at Pollington didn't seem so strange if Mr Barrass was typical of canal helmsmen. But we were still all in one piece and I was lazing around on the foredeck when we came to Ferrybridge. Mr Barrass had resisted any attempt to allow anyone else to steer so he was in full command as we swept past the right hand fork and continued down the River Aire.

"Shouldn't we have turned right, back there?" I shouted aft, helpfully.

"You mean starboard, lad!" he shouted back, "I know where I'm going!"

Well he may have known where he was going but he didn't know how to get there. When the sign saying DANGER - WEIR AHEAD came into view, even Mr Barrass couldn't keep up the pretence that we were still on course. Trying to stop a heavily-laden barge quickly must create some interesting problems but so does trying to stop an incredibly underweight one with the wind behind her! In an act of inspired seamanship which almost but not quite redeemed him, Mr Barrass rammed the bank head on. After my now customary manoeuvre of leaping off, using the rope to swivel around and leaping back on, we were now heading back the way we came to re-enter the Aire & Calder canal.

Finally, we reached the home marina. We had to turn in quite sharply, so I jumped off at the cut and used the rope to let Mr Barrass get her round the turn.

"Right you are lad!" he shouted and gave it the everything forward and trust in the Lord treatment.

Two things happened here: I decided not to leap back on; it was damned awkward. Mr Barrass had full steam ahead and I could walk around the Marina to where Sobriety would berth anyway. The second was Mr Barrass shouting, "Watch this line of buoys, they may get stuck under the stern" as he headed straight for the line of buoys at full clip.

Again, I don't know what Mr Barrass thought those buoys were there for, but it hadn't changed from the day before. What had changed was the speed that the poor boat was going when she ran aground. This time there was no chance of reversing off. She wasn't exactly high and dry; in fact far from it, but she was surrounded by water and there was no way she was moving! Sobriety was well and truly stuck in the middle of the marina and there was no way ashore for any of her weary crew. This is where having a shore-party (me!) helped. Although the owners of the various pleasure craft weren't so daft as to leave any oars lying around in the various tenders and rowing boats, I did manage to find a plank of wood and a rowing boat that was tied up rather than padlocked, and used these to paddle out to the barge. It was hard work paddling with a bit of planking so we rigged a rope and pulled hand-over-hand to ferry everyone ashore in about ten trips. The end was a bit of an anti-climax, although Bob may be able to tell this bit of the story better than me.

When I came back to the Marina the following morning to assist in the salvage operation, Bob and others had already cadged a tow off a passing barge and Sobriety *was safely berthed after her maiden (of her new life) voyage!*

The aforementioned 'Bob' takes no responsibility for the veracity or otherwise of the above. What your author does remember is how cold was the journey to and from Leeds and how we had no coal for the small fire in the crew cabin. Derek Davies, *Sobriety's* temporary skipper, promoted to assistant skipper on this expedition, said we should fill a couple of draw buckets with coal as we passed Ferrybridge power station. This is one of the biggest electricity generators in Europe with an hourly requirement of 800 tonnes of coal — not best coal that one used to see dumped outside people's houses on coal board estates, but dirty gritty slag that needed a flame-thrower to ignite it. Braving the sleet and rain, one of the crew jumped ashore to collect two small bucketfuls. Suddenly all hell was let loose; klaxons sounded loud enough to be heard in Doncaster and a dozen security men came sprinting to the quayside shouting, *"That's CEGB (Central Electricity Generating Board) coal. Put it back!"* I guess we should have written a letter to Lord Robens, then Chairman of the National Coal Board, to ask his permission.

Reality

For the next few years *Sobriety* was going to lead us temporarily into a world so peripheral to the curriculum that bridges had to be built between it and the school, never mind between school and community. The cuckoo was still searching for a nest and even at this early stage it was unlikely that the school was going to be willing to host the intruder. The first problem was money. Bill Drakeley had been too optimistic. The only way we could buy the materials for getting the barge into shape was through faculty capitation — the money the local authority allocated to the school to cover its expenditure. *Sobriety's* continuing excess of expenditure over income, apparently at the cost of text books and typewriters, did not go down well with the teachers of A and O-level sociology, economics, business studies, accountancy and law. Nor did it please the head of office studies who was being denied the business machinery necessary to teach her syllabus. It was suggested furthermore, that the head of faculty was more concerned with his barge than with the progress of the faculty. I had a hard time at staff meetings and could only console myself with the fact that when George Shields, head of Mexborough Grammar School, had finished building his single seater aircraft in the school's woodwork shop, described by a former pupil as 'all glue and slide rule', he had had to demolish half the school to get it out.[10] The second problem was the distance between school and barge. It was only two miles but it might as well have been twenty two; the school minibus was not always available to ferry staff, pupils and materials to the Dog and Duck Basin where *Sobriety* was berthed. Thirdly, the barge was expensive of staffing. Workshop classes were generally no more than 15 but this was too many if pupils were doing anything more than the scraping and painting described by John Hughes. If the group going to the barge was less than the whole class then two staff would be needed — one on the barge and the other to teach children remaining behind in the workshops. Fourthly there was the timetable which, before the use of computers in administration, saw senior staff complaining about teachers who insisted on exclusive privileges for their own discipline. However if the barge was ever to be developed into a floating 'hostel' or 'classroom' or both, the timetable would have to help. Assuming that the school day consisted of four lessons in the morning and four in the afternoon, we would need full half day sessions. For most subject areas, this represented four lessons on the trot with no break or change, a quite unacceptable arrangement for geographers and language teachers. *"But what,"* I whimpered, *"of the comprehensive ideal and the* raison d'être *of Social and Community Studies?"* The final problem was one of confidence. While most staff were in favour of expeditions to Nidderdale and aware of its benefits, they were less convinced that a Humber barge could provide the same kind of experience. It would only accommodate half a class at a time and after an hour or so, when the excitement had died down, became slow, boring, and an invitation to foolery. And in the middle of the Humber there was no escape — for pupils or staff!

The problems were solved steadily over two or three years: surprisingly we won the battle of the timetable, and were given half day sessions to enable Derek Davies, a teacher who had exchanged the peaceful life of a craftsman for the perils of the deep, to work on the barge with his pupils during lesson time. In *Sobriety*'s hold they fitted out two dormitories of bunks, as well as a saloon and kitchen. The project now had its own bank account in the name of Goole Grammar School Barge Club and repaid the money borrowed from the faculty with a loan of £800 from the Midland Bank, a tidy sum in 1975: we recruited a management committee consisting of Leslie Duckels, company secretary of Croda International, Ann Fox a Humberside education adviser, Derek Davies, Bill Drakeley, Lal Woolass, a boatman from Old Goole, and Peter Teed. I was secretary, scribe and convenor.

Friends Enemies and New Adventures

Sobriety was becoming a separate entity available to the school but not dependent on it. We now had to discover how the vessel could be used for educational and other benefits and to spread the word as widely as possible. It took six years until 1986 to do this and was possible only through the determination of a small number of school staff, the goodwill of maritime businesses in Goole and Hull and the backing of the local education authority (LEA). Notable among sympathetic Humberside officers was Jim Bolton, Deputy Director of Education, who I had first encountered at Bretton Hall. Early in his career and conveniently for *Sobriety*, he had worked for Jim Hogan, as an office boy, he always said. Jim (Bolton) took a personal interest in *Sobriety*'s development and one day in 1976 arrived with his colleague Rex Stott at the barge, carrying two de-luxe porta-potties, priced at £30 the pair. He presented these to the Project with what was then a less worn comment, *"It may be sewage to us but it's obviously bread and butter to you."* (In 2015, these appliances can now be bought online; the Kampa Khazi is the cheapest and sells at a very reasonable £13.48 : the luxurious Thetford Porta Potty Qube 335 will set you back £86.23). Jim's presents were not incorporated into the barge's plumbing system but were freestanding facilities charged with Elsan fluid, a corrosive bright blue liquid which dissolved all solid matter and anything in contact with it, ready for disposal at British Waterways bankside sanitary stations. It is still available, advertised politely at £14.99 for an Elsan Double Blue & Rinse Toilet Chemical Twin Pack. But in those days 'when men were men' we purchased it in 40 gallon drums containing enough fluid concentrate to service the needs of a transatlantic liner. The chemicals did not always end up in the right place, as happened during a day on the Humber when I negligently emptied the contents of an overflowing porta-potty into the wind. A blue mist engulfed the boat and a shower of decomposing toilet paper descended to the deck, settling on the head and spectacles of a hapless young member of the crew. *"Mr Watson, Sir!"* was his heartbroken response. My carelessness was mortifying and I got a justifiable telling off from Derek Davies.

Goole is 52 miles from Spurn Point and about 15 miles upstream from where the Ouse and Trent join to become the Humber, making it the furthest inland port in the UK. Built by the Aire & Calder Navigation in 1826 it allows ships of up to 5000 tonnes to navigate the Ouse seaway and discharge their cargoes for transportation into the Yorkshire hinterland. Until the nineteen fifties this was almost entirely by canal; now it is by road. The Humber and Ouse have some interesting features; they are full of danger but conversely a gift to maritime commerce. The Humber, meaning 'dark waterway', is one of the world's most treacherous estuaries. Ships and small boats running aground can come to a sticky end when the incoming tide tips them over

Sobriety interior.

the edge of a sandbank. At the time of the fortnightly spring tides which never last more than three hours at Goole, an estimated 434 million gallons of water rushes up the narrowing channel at an average speed of six knots — about seven miles an hour. But as Baron Duckham says in his *Yorkshire Ouse – The History of a River Navigation*:

> *The tidal stream in the Ouse has from the earliest times been seen as an incalculable aid to navigation…No waterman of earlier centuries would have thought of isolating the tide's gift of depth from its provision of motive power. He would no more have attempted to stem the tide than he would have spat in the wind.*

Nor would he have emptied the contents of a porta-potty into the wind! The need to work by wind and tide was making a professional skipper, volunteer or paid, indispensable to *Sobriety*'s future. The enterprise was not going to flourish until we had a dependable, skilled person in charge who understood the difference between bales of cotton and living children. But money aside, finding the right person was going to be difficult. The cussing, grumbling and ignorant pronouncements of boatmen who had learned their opinions at the back doors of Goole's public houses, had no place in an organisation trying desperately to commend itself to sceptical head teachers.

For a while we made do. Derek learned the rudiments of river navigation and passed on his knowledge so that between us we ceased to be frightened by coasters and sandbanks. Nevertheless we were objects of curiosity among barge skippers still carrying cargoes. I think they thought *Sobriety* had joined the despised fraternity of pleasure boats and was a traitor to their traditions. On the other hand there were many former bargemen and dock employees who, saddened by the decline of canal transport, took the view that *Sobriety* was finding a new way to value Goole's canal-port heritage. This did not stop the lock-keepers on the docks demanding a bottle of beer every time a barge went through Ocean Lock and making it clear that both bargemen and pleasure boat owners were the scum of the earth wherever they came from. Their rule, 'ships first, barges last', meant that *Sobriety* would have to wait sometimes for as long as three hours to get into the docks from the river. A ship would 'pen' down on its way to the Humber, leaving the lower gates open to an empty lock but no barges were allowed in and the lock gates were closed against them. They did not have to wait their turn; they had to wait until the ships were half way to Rotterdam! But for young people and adults who had never encountered the culture of the north east waterways, the adventure of going down by barge to Hull and Grimsby was a rich experience. Even more so was the discovery of its characters and customs. An intriguing individual was Black Fred of whom it was said he never washed. One morning he turned on the gas in his barge cabin to boil a kettle but then found he had no matches. After scrounging a box from another barge he went back to light the stove. It is said that the ensuing explosion dislodged the grime of years and turned his face snow white.

Once they had got used to us, the staff in all the ports on the Humber invariably gave *Sobriety* a generous welcome. Practical help came from Docks Board electricians and plumbers who finished the conversion of the accommodation and got rid of the porta-potties. The river pilots took children for high speed rides down the river from *Sobriety*'s berth on Hull's Riverside Quay and the dockmasters in Grimsby and Hull allowed us onto quaysides that cars and minibuses could drive to. Twenty miles upstream in York, however, the berthing arrangements were more haphazard.

From Goole to Naburn, a small village south of York, the river is still tidal even though it is 75 miles from the North Sea. Indeed the tide may be gaining at Naburn while ebbing at Goole and flooding at Spurn Point. The channel above Goole gets narrower, which means the tide flows faster and on the sharp bends between Selby and Naburn it is easy to get tangled in overhanging trees. Another hazard is the two bridges at Selby, one for the railway, the other the former toll bridge on the main road into the town. With the tide running at 8 knots it is almost impossible to get safely through the bridges and round a following sharp bend without turning to face the current and going astern, a procedure known as 'rounding up'.[11] Naburn weir and lock are at the end of this tideway. To the right of the lock there is a small palladian building dating from 1823 which was the banqueting house of the Ouse and Foss Navigation trustees. There is evidence that during the 1820s the Trustees spent nothing on the river and everything on their banquets. Duckham observes:

> *The comparatively high cost of the banqueting house represented a real lack of responsibility among the trustees when resources were low…Many citizens were highly indignant at the improvidence and for a time the matter was a local cause célèbre. The building still stands, a little incongruous in its rural setting, as a monument to the civic pomp of a more leisurely age which felt little shame at mingling business with pleasure.[12]*

By the late 1970s the board of trustees had been dissolved and their responsibilities taken over by the city council. York was not as amenable to river tourists as it is today but we rubbed along with the council's requirements and were tolerated, albeit as aliens. Within the city, the riverborne threat comes not from tides but from heavy rain on the North York Moors. The upland torrents and tributary rivers all flow into the Ouse and can cause it to rise two metres, and in as many hours, flood city centre pubs and riverside cellars. In spite of the river's occasional bad temper, York was a place of pilgrimage for any group using *Sobriety*. Children who had hardly been out of Goole had their breath taken away by its walls and minster and the locomotives in its railway museum. And to go there by barge! The only trouble was that the tide below Naburn made it impossible to get from Goole to York and back in a day if one was ashore in the city for more than an hour or so. Under a cloudless sky one Saturday afternoon in July 1981, *Sobriety* was berthed at Skeldergate bridge, the third of the modern road bridges to cross the river at York. The Project had been entertaining aboard its 'flag-barge' the chairman of Humberside Education Committee, Councillor Maxwell Bird. The visit had gone well. Councillor and Mrs Bird were intrigued, even if not overcome with admiration, and at the end of a brief cruise through the city, we made *Sobriety* fast on Hargreaves wharf, had a cup of tea and said our cheerful goodbyes. There would be no one on board until a group arrived the next day but the barge appeared well roped and the weather settled. The gods of the river knew differently. At seven o'clock on the Sunday morning the 'phone rang at home. It was North Yorkshire police.

"Are you the owner of a barge called Sobriety?" said the voice.

"No, but I know who is," I said.

"Well," said the voice, *"there's been a lot of rain and the river's come up in the night. Your barge has slipped her moorings. We've got it tied to a tree in a field at Bishopthorpe. You'd better come and fetch it."*

During the half hour drive to York I reckoned this was not a job for an amateur. How had the wretched vessel got to Bishopthorpe? How would I get aboard if it was in a flooded field? Where would I take it? What if it was aground? Should I petition the Archbishop of York to hold a vigil and say prayers in the Minster? Bishopthorpe was after all where he had his riverside palace and I was sure he would recall sympathetically a visit by a church group from Thorne, part of a pilgrimage organised by John Twistleton, vicar of Moorends. (Mr Twistleton, it was rumoured, had been the brains behind the invention of Teflon non stick frying pans). There had been a shortage of bollards on the palace wall and the skipper had taken a turn with his rope round the sundial which was the centrepiece of the palace rose garden. His plan had been not merely to keep *Sobriety* close to the wall but at the end of the visit to use the sundial as a lever for springing the barge round into the main flow of the river. But a medieval sundial is no match for forty five tons of floating iron and the archbishop turned to see an irreplaceable garden ornament, symbol of mortality, the Fall of Man and witness to six hundred years of learned doctrinal argument, moving inexorably towards the river, while the skipper, with back turned, kept a lookout for oncoming boats. But now, I was on my own. There was no one to answer my questions or stifle my fantasies. I knew that Bishopthorpe even on a sunny September morning would not be a place of relaxation.

In the basin which marks the end of the Foss, a river that rises in the hills to the north of York and joins the Ouse in the city, I found Len Howard, proprietor of White Rose Cruises which ran river trips to Naburn. Without fuss he called his son and asked him to go with me to Bishopthorpe, about an hour's walk by riverside path. At a stile about half way, we met two out of breath policemen in uniform returning to York. They were obviously looking forward to breakfast following their involuntary promotion to barge captain and mate during the night. We found *Sobriety* tied to a tree but she was not in the middle of a field and it was easy to get on board. There were slight problems with her wheel and steering chains but we solved these and cranked her engine, a Lister JP3, which even in those days was a museum piece. The river was very high and we could not find a secure berth until we came into the middle of the city. Eventually we tied up on a wall a short distance above Skeldergate bridge. I was just getting ready to leave when three visitors arrived. Their leader had a shirt open to show a necklace of what looked like crocodile teeth. It was my 'High Noon' moment. The newcomers were not friendly and it was fortunate that *Sobriety* remained close enough to the quay for us to have a conversation, yet far enough away to prevent them getting aboard. *"You've sunk my boat,"* said the one with the necklace. Another looked down at me and said, *"You've smashed my sewage tank." "There's a lot of people after you. My boat"s worth £30,000"*, said the first. After being hectored by the river manager, an officious former sea captain based at Naburn locks and employed by the Ouse and Foss Navigation trustees to keep order on the river, I escaped from York in the late afternoon.

On Monday morning I went in as usual to Goole Grammar School where I was still teaching, and during morning break, with some apprehension, rang Fred Wright, head of the insurance section at County Hall, Beverley. I fully expected this well regarded officer with responsibility for all the local authority's insurances, to tell me to my face that I was an idiot. Far from it. When I had finished the story he said, *"Don't you worry Bob. I'll sort it out."* He had from the beginning taken a kindly and personal interest in the Project. At least that was how it appeared. If he had a more personal opinion, he disguised it well. At tea time the same day I had a call from David Webb, our link with senior management in Humberside Social Services. He asked me if I had seen the *York Evening Press.* I said no I had not and did not want to. He then read out *Sobriety's* full tally of destruction. The front page headline was, 'Two vessels sink in runaway keel havoc'. The editorial described a riverborne invasion. *Sobriety* had sunk *Bywell Princess*, damaged the sewage tank of a pub barge, collided with a wooden fishing boat and finally had run into *Ashanti Gold*, a 50 passenger trip boat. I quickly calculated that the claims against us were in the region of £200,000, perhaps getting on for £1 million in today's reckoning. The word was out. Humberside was paying and suddenly *Sobriety* had damaged every boat on the Ouse within twenty miles of York. *"Anyway,"* David said, *"I'll leave it to you. I don't think we need to be involved."* When, according to the paper, Humberside County Council was asked for an explanation, he had said with commendable *sang froid*: *"Sobriety, her skipper and the children are on their way home today. I can only think that as a result of the accident they may have gone by bus."* The only clue to the fact that the article was perhaps not revealing the whole truth was the 'eyewitness' comment from a resident of a boat, *Little Joe,* who allegedly, *"woke up to some bangs and saw the keel hitting Ashanti Gold. She was just about to smash into us when I pushed her off with my feet."* It is perhaps not unfair to suggest that an iron barge of 45 tons deadweight travelling down a river at four knots would have taken more than a pair of feet to divert it from its target.

Two months later we had a visit from John Fielder, a surveyor with marine solicitors Elborne Mitchell, who at that time had their HQ on Tower Hill in London and whom Fred Wright had asked to investigate the claims. The firm's website highlights some cases in their history:

Since the 1960s, Elborne Mitchell has played a key role in many cases which have made headlines within the insurance industry and beyond. These include the mysterious loss of the MV Derbyshire in the South China seas: sanctions-busting operations in South Africa and the uncovering of the largest ever maritime fraud with the sinking of the MV Salem: the tide of litigation which engulfed Lloyd's in the late 1980s and led to Lloyd's Reconstruction & Renewal Plan in 1996: the invasion of Kuwait in August 1990 and the theft by Saddam Hussein of most of the Kuwait Airways fleet: and the LMX spiral of personal accident and workers' compensation claims.

Unhappily for the enthusiastic claimants neither Humberside nor the Project would be an easy touch. John Fielder spent two days on the river studying paint scratches and dents and all the alleged evidence for the damage. He found that *Bywell Princess* had been moored on short ropes causing her to capsize when the water level rose: the sewage tank of the pub barge was illegally installed and the Council would probably prosecute: *Ashanti Gold*, the trip boat, was not even on the river; it was being repaired on a slipway: and although the fishing boat had been damaged, some of its timbers were rotten. That was the end of the matter until ten years later, when we heard that the man with the crocodile necklace was still arguing and that the insurers had decided to pay him £11,000 to go away.

A Full Time Skipper

I first met Brian on a wet and cold January evening in 1978 when he came to the door of a small house in one of Goole's Victorian terraces. Against the sound of a budgerigar chattering in a room at the back I told him I had been sent by Bill Drakeley, his probation officer, to ask if he wanted to help with *Sobriety*. Standing there he looked pale and nervous but said he would give it a go.

Bill had told me Brian's story. After a difficult childhood when he didn't really get on with his more cerebral brothers and sisters, Brian had gone to work on the waterways, taking cargo barges on the Humber, Ouse and Trent to Grimsby, York, Nottingham and anywhere else he was sent by the carrying company. During this period, for reasons I never knew, he had been sent to prison and had spent much of his sentence in Dartmoor, a grim and isolated granite institution built to house French prisoners during the wars with Napoleon. Before release he had been in touch with Bill and was bravely determined to return to his home town and make good.

The deal was that he would work at first as a volunteer. If all went well he would join the Job Creation Programme being promoted by Prime Minister Jim Callaghan and then graduate to the more exclusive Special Temporary Employment Programme recently launched by the Department of Employment. The government schemes were limited but would give us time to find him a permanent salary from elsewhere. That was the plan, we stuck to it and the effect was remarkable. Brian came from several generations of barge owners and shipbuilders. The family had owned a shipyard on the river Ouse in the village of Hook near Goole. One of his grandfathers had been owner-skipper of two keels, *Guidance* and *Hermes*, which after the widespread abandonment of sail in 1939, had been powered by petrol but later converted to paraffin. His other grandfather was George Tomlinson who had led the rescue of the passengers of an airship which crashed in the Humber. George had been a regimental sergeant major in the Royal Engineers before becoming skipper of the United Towing tug *Welshman* and it was on this vessel that from the age of 10, Brian had learned his trade. *Sobriety* now had an employee who would be in attendance every day to maintain the barge and run residential expeditions to the cities and towns of Yorkshire and the East Midlands. People of all generations and backgrounds would be able to visit new places, meet new people, live together and help one another. The barge would be in use seven days a week and, when it was not on trips, would serve as a base for unemployed young people to learn some work disciplines. Just as an experienced skipper was indispensable for activity on the waterways, so also there was a need for people ashore to look after the Project's administration, bookings and funds. This led us to make full use of current job creation schemes and we were able to recruit a small team, one member of which, Linda Thornton, stayed with the organisation for more than twenty years. Without her work on the typewriter and telephone and later, the computer, the Project would never have emerged from infancy. We were now well set for independent development; no longer Goole Grammar School Barge Club but the *Sobriety* Project.

Questions

Does the chapter's analysis of the school curriculum still hold good? Where are today's 'hyacinths' so beloved of Alec Clegg?

What do you think was Peter Teed's view of education that led him to encourage *Sobriety*'s development? What were the problems that he and I faced as the project advanced?

Is it possible nowadays to arrange secondary school timetables so that they allow for the sort of out of class activities provided by *Sobriety*?

Chapter 4 Notes

1   Lord Redcliffe Maud was chair of the Royal Commission on Local Government in England which began work in 1966. Its recommended root and branch changes finally took effect in April 1974.

2   See www.ofsted.gov.uk for report on Goole High School Academy of Excellence. Also Yorkshire Post 25.2.2014 (Failing Goole Academy 'should be returned to Council') and 6.9.2014 (Teachers suspended as results investigated).

3   Penguin Books, 2003: Translation by Sir Desmond Lee (1908-1993), Classical scholar and Fellow of Corpus Christi College, Cambridge.

4   Five 'black papers' appeared during the period 1969 to 1977 and generally speaking were of right wing origin, advocating a more centralised government controlled curriculum. This led eventually to the National Curriculum, the Ofsted inspection regime and league tables. See *TES* website for *Flutterings from the Tyndale Affair,* an article by Gerald Haigh July 2006, and Gillard D (2011) *Education in England: a brief history*: www. educationengland.org.uk/history

   Haigh says, *'The rather too laissez-faire approach at Tyndale School in Islington was the spark that lit the firework of Jim Callaghan's Ruskin College speech in October 1976 in which he raised doubts about what he described as, "the new informal methods of teaching which seem to produce excellent results when they are in well-qualified hands but are much more dubious when they are not".'*

   He concludes: *'You can read the message of the Tyndale butterfly in various ways. Perhaps it was a much needed catalyst for the restoration of order from imminent chaos, and the development of a strong framework within which leadership could operate. Or, on the other hand, perhaps those teachers, by taking too radical an approach to freedom and choice, opened the door to the new authoritarians and, in doing so set back, perhaps permanently, any prospect of a truly progressive approach to teaching in our primary schools.'*

5   The Confessions, Book 8, Chapter 7.

6   The inspection would be carried out by a surveyor from the Department of Trade and Industry (DTI) to make sure that appropriate safety equipment was in place and that the skipper navigating the barge had relevant experience. The DTI's regulatory powers were later taken over by the Department of Transport. More recently the Maritime and Coastguard Agency has become the statutory authority and has codified the regulations for small passenger boats. The twelve passenger rule has always been strictly enforced and only in exceptional circumstances will permission be given for it to be waived.

7   The Intermediate Treatment of Young Offenders was a government sponsored programme designed to keep children out of the criminal justice system for as long as possible. The scheme as embraced by *Sobriety* is the main subject of Chapter 5.

8   Boot camps have been described as 'correctional facilities for wayward adolescents, found especially in the American penal system'. In spite of government efforts to introduce them in the UK, they never found favour with judges or magistrates. The term now describes activity centres that promote extreme fitness and has nothing to do with criminal justice.

9   A draw bucket hung on the end of a rope and was used to pick up water from canal or river to swill down the deck. The bucket had to be thrown forward and pulled out of the water before the movement of the barge against the flow dragged it from the hands of the skipper or mate.

10 *Sobriety* could not have happened now. In today's test orientated schools we would have lost the argument and the barge would have been returned to its owner.

11 The manoeuvre allows a vessel enough steerage to go slowly astern and avoid hitting the bridges. Just beyond the bridges upstream at Selby there is a sharp right hand bend. In the 1980s ships berthed on Spillers' wharf which was on the outside of the bend. If a vessel failed to come about and then 'shot' the bridges it would in all likelihood crash into the side of a coaster. The town's bye-laws require strict observation of the rules of navigation on this part of the Ouse.

12 Duckham, *The Yorkshire Ouse*: Chapter 6.

The lyrics under the music:
COME LIST-EN TO ME LADS AND A TALE I'LL TELL TO YOU YOU MIGHT
THINK IT RA-THER STRANGE ME LADS BUT EV-ERY WORD IS TRUE IT
HAPP-END ON THE KEL-LY LEE IN NINE-TEEN SIX-TY TWO WHEN THE
DE-VIL PAID A CALL UP-ON THE BRAVE AND GALL-ANT CREW
STOKE-LE UP YOUR BOIL-ER LADS DON'T LET THE PRESS-URE FALL WE
NE-VER WILL FOR-GET THE DAY THE DE-VIL PAID A CALL

The Devil and the Tugman, *by Gezz Overington (see page 102).*

Come listen to me lads and a tale I'll tell to you.
You might think it rather strange my lads but every word is true,
For it happened on the Kellingley in 1962
When the Devil paid a call on that brave and gallant crew

Chorus to each verse:

Stoke up the boilers lads don't let the pressure fall
For we never will forget the day the Devil paid a call.

The night was coming on and the stars began to glow,
The crew was supping tea in the cabin down below
When on the cabin door there came a rat-a-tat-a-tat
And there stood the Devil in a three cornered hat.

Now our skipper Goff he was a friendly sort of chap.
He said "Come right on in my lad and hang up thee cap.
Well now then Mr Devil what can we do for you?
Would you like a mug of tea or a nice plate of stew?"

The Devil said these very words the truth to you I'll tell:
"There's no bloody coal left to stoke the Fire of Hell."
We could see by his face it really weren't a joke,
We offered to let him have a couple of bags of coke.

"Well thanks all the same my lads, it's not enough you know.
It won't keep them buggers shovelling for long down below"
The last thing we saw was our old pal Nick; he was rapping on
Lord Roben's door with a bloody big stick.

He travelled England far and he travelled England wide.
He couldn't get no coal me lads, no matter how he tried
And the last thing we heard he'd gone and spent a lot of brass.
He's had Hell converted on to North Sea gas.

Chapter 5

DEVELOPMENT

A New World

Half term expeditions by barge into Yorkshire's cities were not going to show headteachers how *Sobriety* could transform their curriculum. The antics described by John Hughes were not the best way of persuading schools that a week of privation in the makeshift accommodation of a 1910 barge on the Aire & Calder Navigation could be just as rewarding as a camp in the Lake District. A visit to the nature reserve in the shadow of the Barnby Dun cooling towers near Doncaster could hardly compete with a day on Langdale Pikes or Great Gable. Moreover a campsite or outdoor centre would cater for at least 30 children whereas *Sobriety* had a legal complement of 14 passengers and crew, usually ten children two teachers and two crew. In the face of sceptical staff, how could a head justify a barge 'holiday' to his or her governors, let alone acquiesce in serious disruption to the timetable? Even so there were some heads, generally of schools for pupils with learning difficulties [1] who did take the plunge, mainly because their staff-to-pupil ratios were more generous. Tall Trees, a school for young children with severe disabilities, not far from Goole, used *Sobriety* for a day. The head's account of the outing on 23rd June 1976, shows what an adventure it was:

A barge trip on the canal seemed just right — both banks within easy reach! But would the four hour journey prove too restrictive for some of the children? Would Cathy, rather excitable and 'bad on her pins' ever get on board? And none of them would ever get down that vertical ladder to see the little cabin. Still, they would be on a real boat on real water. So here we were with nine children donning and furiously blowing up lifejackets. On board and quickly away, the children sat rather spellbound at first but soon began to move around the deck. As we neared the first bridge, all heads went down. Workmen repairing the banks waved to us, Cowick Water looked enormous, a mother duck chivvied her family to safety as we passed, and the steady four miles an hour gave plenty of time to look. The vertical ladder proved no obstacle to anyone — incredibly! Happy faces peered up at us through the hatch — "It's a little house!" At Pollington lock, James was rather anxious when the water went down — "Is it Davy Jones's lock?"

Although Peter Teed and the committee were making every effort to involve schools, the marketing process was inevitably slow. To employ a full time skipper, we needed a predictable income. It was Humberside Social Services Department which took up the challenge and decided that *Sobriety* was ideal for a 'curriculum' to keep young people out of trouble or the

Sobriety passing Wilmington swing bridge on the River Hull.

consequences of trouble — usually youth custody or local authority care. As a half way house between community supervision and custody, the intermediate treatment (IT) of young offenders,[2] as it was known, relied for its success on locally based group activities rather than on the rules of an institution. With the opportunities *Sobriety* could create for young people to learn team work and other skills, came the adventure of being away from home and having a hand in organising a week long expedition. These days, the way that social workers were introduced to the magic of the waterways would raise some eyebrows; chief officers would not have the time to spend on such frivolities. But perhaps a reliable hunch is worth a dozen meetings.

On Thursday May 4th 1978, *Sobriety* was berthed at the town end of Beverley Beck and being made ready for a visit by councillors and chief officers who would come the few yards from County Hall to eat lunch prepared by young people from Goole Grammar School. Guests of honour were Muriel Bean JP, Chairman of Humberside County Council and Councillor Dick Emsley, Chairman of Humberside Education Committee. Living on board were the children from Brook Cottage community home in Driffield, with Michael Hunter its officer-in-charge, and his family. They had joined the barge at Goole and after coming down the Humber and up the river Hull had arrived in Beverley the previous day. Brian Calvert was skipper and thoroughly familiar with the tides and currents of the two rivers. Not only was everyone safe and happy but they had been able to help with steering and barge related chores. As well as being Chairman of Humberside County Council,[3] Muriel Bean was a governor of Goole Grammar School. She had been invited by Peter Teed to preside over *Sobriety*'s visit to Beverley in the hope of persuading the Authority to pay the skipper's salary when the government job creation scheme came to an end. The stage was set.

As he came aboard, Humberside's Director of Social Services, Jim Gardham, recognised a demure and confident young woman in a long dress. She was one of the County's most difficult children. Excluded from schools and special units and defying all attempts at reform, she had come to Brook Cottage as a last destination before being expected to go into secure accommodation. He was amazed and went away convinced that if this barge could work wonders for one, it could work wonders for many. My own view was that her conduct was more the result of Michael Hunter's quiet influence than of the barge. But it was a team effort!

Special needs teacher, Russell Butterfield raises a question here. 'What is it about these experiences that time after time, allows 'failed' children to shine? His answer is unequivocal:

It is the patient, kindly development of their self esteem by gifted and inspirational adults. With a blend of a new environment and high adventure mixed with a liberal dash of team responsibility and expectation, they suddenly perform. Or could they always do it but are stifled by classrooms and an alienating curriculum that sucks the life out of them?

A few weeks later I had a telephone call from Humberside Social Services Deputy Director, Geoff Hughes, asking me to attend a meeting at the Department's HQ in Hull. This was a man who in his capacity as regional adviser for BBC's *Children in Need*, would later confront me with a showstopping question, *"What is it then? If we give you the tools, will you finish the job, or is it that we will give you the job and you will finish the tools?"* At the HQ meeting he was more friendly and said the deal was that in return for the skipper's annual salary, *Sobriety* would have to become available for use by Social Services for 30 weeks each year. He conceded that for 10 weeks it could be used by youth clubs and schools and for the rest of the time by old people's homes and groups outside Humberside. In return for the grant of £8,000 a year, the Project would need to register as a charity and undertake to raise funds needed for maintenance. It was expected that all groups including those from Social Services would pay to hire the barge and that I would have regular meetings with David Webb, the department's principal officer in charge of fieldwork. The arrangement ruffled the feathers of some less imaginative social workers, otherwise it was a straightforward contract, honoured by both sides, that worked flexibly and without problems until the break-up of Humberside in 1996. The project would serve the needs of both departments — Social Services and Education — and the overlap in educational terms was plain to see. In 2015 the financial and other arrangements are different, but the groups using the Project remain broadly the same as in the 1970s.

Equally welcome was an article in the *Yorkshire Post* in May 1979 under the heading 'Deal puts barge on an even keel' which quoted Councillor Spencer Rudkin, Chairman of Social Services, as saying, *"My committee has great faith in this project. I think there is tremendous potential for using Sobriety with young people who have been in trouble. I feel that a few days of shared work and experience of sailing and running a barge can help to build up a sense of interdependence and of social responsibility"*. In the *Lincolnshire Times* under the admittedly rather naff title of *Children Learn to Cope on the Crest of the Waves*, an imaginative reporter, David Black, revealed the practicalities:

A barge putters listlessly along the river on a thundery morning looking strange and out of place among motor boats and cabin cruisers. This is the river Ouse — 'gin palace' country- and the barge cuts too functional a dash amid the gaudy look-alike pleasure craft.

The barge's 'cargo' seems a little out of place too. Eight children and three social workers. But the barge and the children together mark the first steps in what could become a revolution in the care of Humberside's deprived children...

Separating the formal from the practical, Black said the barge might be called 'a floating intermediate treatment centre' but was in fact an aid for social workers to show inner city children an aspect of life beyond the corner of their street. Some children on board were on supervision orders imposed by the courts: others were from homes where the parents were alcoholics and the children were routinely beaten and injured: many were excluded from school or pupil referral unit: all were from any of a thousand circumstances that distorted their childhood. The eight children on this expedition were from Hull's Preston Road estate and in an interview for the *Lincolnshire Times*, Andy Busby, the senior social worker on board, explained the work that went into making the trip possible. The first hurdle he said, was the selection of children — who goes and who doesn't. Getting a fair blend was the problem:

"If you get it right, then you get the group working for you. Take the two Andys over there," he said, pointing to his two namesakes, both aged 14 and looking very capable of adolescent devilment given the chance. "I've got a kid that could have come on the trip but he's a real headcase. Now those two lads over there are a pretty bubbly pair but the rest of the group which isn't so bubbly, restrains them".

The article went on to say that the party had arrived on Friday morning and once all the gear was aboard, the working of the barge was put immediately on a ship-shape footing. Each of the social workers appointed themselves head of a watch and a duty roster was posted. From the word go, each boy and girl knew his or her precise job for the whole weekend — 'A' Watch cooks tea Friday: 'B' Watch washes up: 'C' Watch does breakfast on Saturday and so on. But although life on board was to be regulated, Busby was concerned that the atmosphere should be easy going. After every meal the question was the same: 'What are we going to do? Answer — 'We can do this, this, or this'. The alternatives were presented and the babble of preferences began. Without interference from the three leaders, a decision was made. On the Friday afternoon it was the railway museum in York followed by a trip to the swimming pool.

The reporter, David Black, observed a professional commitment that gave the social workers an almost magical way with the children, leading to a constant round of banter, jokes and teasing.

Such loose relations between the social workers and children he said, are all part of the job. For youngsters from homes where parents can't cope or simply cannot be bothered to show affection, it is important that such a gap be filled. These children have to be taught how to relate to adults and to their own feelings years after ordinary children have developed similar abilities. And the delay means other, bad characteristics, have to be unlearned.

Black concluded that the barge itself was just a lump of steel, merely a tool. Only in the hands of people like Andy Busby and his colleagues could the tool be used to do the job. Without them the barge was just another drain on ratepayers' money; with them it was working for a better future for the children and a better future for Humberside.

Sobriety did have its critics among social workers who preferred a more methodical approach to dealing with young people's problems. There were too many unpredictable possibilities on a week long expedition to Nottingham or Lincoln. Plans could easily be scuppered by the tide or weather or a disconsolate skipper. For them the scheme was an intrusion on a purer kind of social work. In contrast, another report, this time in the *Hull Daily Mail*, took a more positive view when a reporter from the paper interviewed senior social worker Chris Graham and children who were on a three day voyage to Hull and York:

*Providing 24 hour contact between the youngsters and the social workers, Sobriety gives
a perfect opportunity to help them build up relationships with adults — something
which many of them find very difficult. It also takes them away from their troublesome
environment and shows them more creative and profitable ways of using their time.*

Chris went on to say, *"There are plenty of things for good kids to do but these children have
excluded themselves through their behaviour and the barge trip is just part of the slow painstaking
work carried out at weekly group meetings with the children"*. She said two of their successes were
a 14 year old boy who was now getting up first in the mornings to put the kettle on for tea and
a 13 year old girl who was volunteering to wash up. The time spent ashore, she said, was just as
important as the time on board. *"It takes the children into the community, helping them deal with
the day to day problems of visiting public places. Being able to cope with a disturbing situation
without blowing a fuse and causing havoc is a big step forward for them."*

The St Thomas's Way: A Curriculum for Young Offenders

Their 'steps forward' were interesting not merely to regional reporters; they were national news.
The 1980 Young Offenders White Paper promoted by Home Secretary, William Whitelaw, was
proposing a menu of remedies for youth crime. At one end were 'short sharp shocks' in detention
centres and a re-packaging of borstal training into 'youth custody'; at the other were proposals to
make more use of supervision orders, community service schemes and intermediate treatment.
While most welcomed an end to remanding 14 year olds in prison, there were many, especially
magistrates, who were less than confident about community sentences. However, a comment in
The Times newspaper tried to look forward:

*The failure of the soft line approach is blamed on woolly-minded do-gooders like social
workers and probation officers, but the soft approach has never really been tried since the
institutions and resources to back up care or supervision orders have not been provided.
The hard line has also clearly failed in the past since 84 per cent of boys sentenced to
borstal training were reconvicted within two years. Intermediate Treatment still looks like
one of the most constructive measures as the White Paper says. Unfortunately, as everybody
also agrees, there are not nearly enough centres, and it is devoutly hoped that pioneering
voluntary organisations and local authorities will provide more of them.*

The article might have added that in the 'hard line' detention centres, life was conducted 'at a
brisk pace'. The centres were intended to give inmates a taste of the fear that the hapless KoKo
experienced in Gilbert and Sullivan's *Mikado*, the comic opera from where Mr Whitelaw had got
the idea for his 'short sharp shock'. But the way it turned out was different. By all accounts the
young people sent to these institutions spent most of the day lying on their beds doing nothing.

The Department of Health & Social Security's (DHSS) Local Authority Circular 83/3 on the
other hand, promised grants of £15 million over three years to voluntary sector organisations to
set up and staff 4,500 alternatives to custody for serious and persistent young offenders. Satisfied
with the way things were going on the barge and having no other organisation in Goole that could
meet the requirements of the circular, Humberside Social Services lost no time in approaching

the *Sobriety* committee with a plan to convert the redundant St Thomas's Roman Catholic Primary School in Old Goole into a place where young offenders would come to do activities and have meetings to consider how they could become better citizens. It was a building with which I was familiar, having worked as a volunteer at an evening youth club run by a teaching order of sisters who lived in the next door convent. Since Victorian times, the nuns had been working in this small but needy area which by the 1980s had become notorious for its levels of unemployment, crime and worsening health.

Sobriety's trustees readily agreed to collaborate with Social Services in setting up St Thomas's Centre, regarding it as a desirable extension of the Project's responsibilities. The main condition of DHSS funding was that centres should be managed by inter-agency committees representative of the police, the local magistracy, social services, education and probation. For *Sobriety* to be linked to the work of these bodies could only help it achieve its longer term purposes. Accordingly between January and August 1984 a full working management committee was recruited and led by Superintendent Malcolm Cairns (later to become Deputy Chief Constable of Greater Manchester). The building was re-furbished by unemployed local people organised by the National Association for the Care and Re-settlement of Offenders. Staff were appointed to work under the leadership of Catherine Smith, the centre's supervisor, and policies and working practices were agreed. But it was not all plain sailing.

The first unpleasant surprise was a letter from Maynard Cox, the Clerk to the Justices, saying that *Sobriety* had no right to invite magistrates to sit on an intermediate treatment committee; it would compromise their duty of impartiality. The second was a letter from the DHSS awaiting my return from holiday, saying that the committee should not have used its grant to purchase materials for the repair of the building and that I should forthwith put in the post a cheque for £49,000 to re-imburse government for mis-spent funds.

It was a big relief that both problems were solved within a few days. A meeting with the Bench resulted in two magistrates, Harold Mason and Mary Hilborne, joining the committee and we were able successfully to assure the DHSS that its money had been used properly.

The centre opened on September 1st 1984 as a 'satellite' of the *Sobriety* Project. Its job was to provide a programme of group work, meetings and activities which could be accepted by the magistrates as a legitimate alternative to detention centre, youth custody or local authority care. Children could come to the centre only as a result of referral by the local courts. Those who might get into trouble were not eligible to attend.

The treatment programme was 90 days long and when they were not at the centre or at school, the children were expected to keep in touch with their 'tracker', an adult who would keep a parental eye on their progress. During the first month, five young people under 17 were referred, one of them by Beverley Crown Court and the others by the Goole Bench. During the second month two further groups were set up for children who would not have been sent away but who had begun to commit serious offences which if repeated, might result in a custodial sentence. The *Goole Chronicle* of December 13th 1984 introduced St Thomas's Centre to its readers:

Against a background of rising crime and the continuing national debate about old fashioned or new fangled forms of treatment for young offenders, our reporter Kassie Robinson visited the Old Goole Intermediate Treatment Centre to see how the staff and boys react to current methods and new suggestions:

It is tea time, Monday evening, at the St Thomas's Intermediate Treatment Centre for Young Offenders in Old Goole. The boys have chosen egg, beans and chips, followed by rice pudding. Finally they finish their meal amid high jinks and sit down briefly to talk about their time at the Centre. The group who are between the ages of 15 and 17 all take part in a combination of activities whilst there.

The *Chronicle* report explained that the boys would attend two four hour sessions a week during the day or in the evenings, and spend all day Saturday at the centre. At weekends they would tidy up old people's gardens and remove graffiti from public places. The work was based on their own ideas and suggestions. One boy said, *"I don't find it hard work. It's all right sometimes."* Bill Gilpin, one of the supervisors, said that during the evening sessions the group took part in woodwork classes and had recently made some toys for a local playgroup. As well as the craft sessions, he said, they played darts and made a video of the activities each evening. They also held group discussions about themselves and their offences. He said they all agreed that, *"It's better than sitting at home and being bored."*

Reporter Kassie Robinson observed that the supervisors had devised a points system for the boys, both individually and collectively. They could gain a maximum of 20 points per session — 10 of these being for the tasks they have to do, such as cooking and washing up, and 10 for good behaviour. She went on to say that the group as a whole had a target of 250 points each session. If they achieved an adequate number of points they were treated to a day out. If any of them failed to get sufficient points they did not go. All the boys were juvenile offenders on 90 day orders. If they were not attending St Thomas's they would be in a penal institution. Unsurprisingly the boys in Old Goole were all unanimous in their preference for the 'St Thomas's Way'.

We also learned from the Chronicle's report that during their 90 days, they were on report at school. One of them remarked, *"I can't stand school."* Asked whether they had any ambitions, one said he'd like to be an engineer and another, that he would like to go into catering. Some had hobbies of their own; one liked fishing and another weight lifting at the Leisure Centre. They all agreed they got on well together and would remain mates after they had left St Thomas's but that a serious problem was that the police knew them and went to them first when there was any trouble. They said the police were always after them. Kassie concluded her article by saying that Cath Smith and the other supervisors would like to involve the boys in projects in the town, since one of their main aims was to get them to be socially responsible individuals within the community rather than against it.

In due time St Thomas's acquired an identity which was administratively and operationally independent of Sobriety but in spite of good results, the number of so called 'heavy end' offenders referred by the courts was too small to justify the level of expenditure on full and part time staff.

Humberside Social Services' laudable response was to ask the DHSS for permission to broaden the centre's remit. The upshot was a new agreement which opened the door to boys and girls who had committed less serious offences. They might be young people of school age with severe behavioural or family problems for whom a temporary connection with the centre would be beneficial, or young people repeatedly cautioned by the police or even young people in the 17 to 21 age range who were the concern of the Probation Service.

The changes revived staff morale and enabled the centre to become more involved with young people living in Old Goole, many of whom were already in some kind of trouble with the police. As a result Catherine Smith's reports became noticeably more relaxed:

Staff were to receive their just desserts for the hard time they had given their clients when they were well beaten at darts and dominoes and completely put in the shade at windsurfing and ice skating. During the last activity one member of staff spent more time sitting on the ice than skating.

Another member of staff was John Drakeley, son of Bill Drakeley, who became a part time skipper with *Sobriety* and used the barge to help his work with St Thomas's clients in much the same way as the social workers described earlier. But John believed that the severity of the treatment should increase with age and in the view of a young man of 17, whom John had conscripted to help with bringing a barge called *Eden* back to Goole from Wigan, the 89 locks and 178 bridges encountered on their journey over the Pennines, made prison look like a soft option.

It was probably to be expected that the final consequence of broadening the centre's remit was a dilution of staff expertise. Combined with the ending of DHSS support, this made St Thomas's an easy target for local authority budget cuts and the centre ended its days as a family centre for local people, staffed by local social workers. The question has to be asked whether or not St Thomas's Intermediate Treatment Centre was a success. If we accept the definition of intermediate treatment as a 'form of care that provides opportunities for children in trouble to learn patterns of behaviour that replace potentially criminal ones', then yes. However if we ask about its effectiveness strictly as a statutory alternative to custody then the answer is yes in respect of individual children but no in terms of overall value for money. There were too few referrals from the courts to justify the location of an IT centre in Goole. By contrast in Hull, Scunthorpe and Grimsby, demand for places outstripped supply and there was a procession of referrals. Certainly St Thomas's was less expensive and less damaging than custody and kept the flag of compassion and reform flying high during the 1980s — a flag which, with a new government's policy of 'getting tough' in the 1990s and turning probation and youth services into agencies for law and order during the decade from 2000, dropped steadily to half mast.[4] Contributing to this decline in sympathy for young people was the complete closure of all youth provision in Goole by the end of the nineteen eighties. Staffed mainly by volunteers, it had been for some club members an early deterrent to crime.

David Our Bishop

Although St Thomas's Centre was the responsibility of *Sobriety* it was a sideline, an independent offspring set up to enable Social Services to experiment with government policies. The Project had an office in the building which was preferable to its cubby hole in the Grammar School but St Thomas's staff were employed to do the bidding of the Social Services area manager, not to implement the policies of the *Sobriety* trustees. It was however, an equitable *quid pro quo* for the skipper's salary and *Sobriety* certainly did not lose by it. More on my mind and occupying the thoughts of the *Sobriety* committee was coping with engine breakdowns, sub-standard accommodation, an overworked skipper and the old problem of how to get schools more involved.

Sobriety's Lister JP3 engine had three cylinders and a starting handle. Getting it going would have tested the agility of an Olympic gymnast. In preparation for the main performance, a line of wheels on the side of the cylinder block known as compression valves had to be rotated in a clockwise direction to allow the engine to be turned by hand. The next stage was to put the handle in place on the shaft and beginning slowly, to turn it faster and faster until gyrating like a whirling dervish, the skipper reached the climax of the entertainment. As soon as the exhaust began to ejaculate black smoke the operation was completed with a vault over the engine to close the compression valves, a routine which if executed successfully, would have brought glory to a Cretan bull dancer.[5] If the serious student of the Lister JP3 wishes to explore YouTube, they will find short videos of the monster in action, accompanied by the wailing and tears of enthusiasts mourning its passing.

Having been an irritation to users and the despair of skipper Brian Calvert, the barge's engine finally gave up and was sold for £120 to local engineer, Tommy Simms, who in his devotion to curing its sickness had been like a vet caring for an ailing donkey. It was eventually installed in another barge at Beverley, an intimation of its stubborn immortality.

We were able to sell the engine as a result of intercession by David Lunn, Bishop of Sheffield who had recently become the Project's patron. The manufacturers R. A. Lister & Co had agreed to repair the engine free of charge but when it arrived at their factory in Dursley near Gloucester, David Esse, the firm's manager, said it was beyond repair and generously offered to present the Project with a new unit. The first duty of the reinvigorated barge was to visit Leeds, Cleethorpes and other similarly exotic resorts in the course of a holiday for the men from Coltman Street Day Centre in Hull. The men, organised by their indefatigable leaders, Larry Saunders and Phil Teale, were worthy souls, the poor of the world, most of whom were homeless and suffered chronic mental illness. As examples of the Project's clientele they were excellent hosts to the small team from the Lister factory keen to see their engine at work on the Humber.

A local newspaper's farcical report of the visit was a wonderful example of lazy punctuation. Read aloud slowly it could have been straight from the TV comedy news programme *Have I got News for You!*

The men from the centre had been on the barge taking care of themselves, all thanks to
Rallister and Co. which donated a much needed engine. And to show their thanks the

*holiday-makers **cooked** the company's engineering manager, the senior designer and the **parts** executive, lunch when they visited the barge.*(My emphases)

David Lunn, Bishop of Sheffield from 1980 to 1997 had come in for a lot of stick for his opposition to the ordination of women. His view was that this was a question to be settled by the whole Christian Church not just the Church of England. But in spite of his apparently reactionary views, he was regarded with affection and respect by *Sobriety*, and rightly so. Prior to becoming a bishop, he had been vicar of Cullercoats, a fishing village between Tynemouth and Whitley Bay with a long sea related history. When he arrived in Sheffield the only place he could find with any maritime links was Goole at the far end of his diocese, *'beyond the Coalfield, dark, dominant and entrenched in its own horrific experiences.'*[6] And there was a barge, *Sobriety*, which could take him on a ten day visitation of his parishes, northwards from Sheffield through Rotherham and Doncaster, back to faraway Goole.

On July 16th 1982, *The Times* had a back page picture of the Bishop complete with crozier and mitre emerging from Sobriety's hold. The caption was 'From pulpit to bilges: the Bishop of Sheffield aboard *Sobriety* yesterday, his floating home as he and his crew tour towns alongside the Yorkshire Canal'. But it was the *Guardian* reporter Michael Parkin who on the same day joined 'a sweat shirt cleric on a canal crusade'. Under the heading '*Sobriety* and a bishop who went to see', he told the story:

The Bishop of Sheffield, the Rt. Reverend David Lunn, is visiting 40 of his parishes by sailing along the quieter waters of his see in a borrowed canal barge with the improving name of Sobriety.

"I don't suppose", the bishop said at a reception attended by four mayors at one stop along the canal, "that any of you here know much about sobriety".

From later evidence this seems to have been no artless remark. "I am not prepared to say whether it was deliberate or accidental," the bishop said cheerfully yesterday.

From the story so far it will be clear that the bishop is a singularly unstuffy prelate. He walked through Doncaster yesterday with a rustic shepherd's crook and wearing over his purple bishop's smock a navy blue sweat shirt adorned with a picture of the barge and the words, 'I'm one of the crew in the Diocese of Sheffield'.

Earlier he had been greeted by Canon Geoffrey Lawn, vicar of Doncaster, who said he had already approached one of his parishioners, Mrs Winnie Cutts, to ask: "Can you give the bishop a bath?" The Sobriety *is lacking in some of the amenities of Bishopscroft, the episcopal residence in Sheffield.*

Sailing with the bishop are his chaplain, the Rev. Tom Harris (rather unkindly described as 'travelling vicar' in the programme, as if he were some kind of luggage), four sixth form girls from Goole Grammar School who are cooks and hostesses on the trip, the skipper and a barge apprentice.

So far, the bishop has held services along the route, has prayed, visited the old, the educationally subnormal and industry, has gone on picnics and has chatted on board.

One of the highlights for him was at the Dell at Hexthorpe where hundreds of children combined in the presentation of pageant, play, and music.

At an open air service at Mexborough the bishop licensed an unemployment officer for the diocese, Mr Michael Keen, from Telford, Shropshire, who enlivened the scene by bringing along a party of punks.

As the sweat-shirted bishop walked through Doncaster he was greeted by people who had heard of this unconventional visitation. He was on his way to visit First Aid, a support centre for young people in a former church.

Today the journey continues along the South Yorkshire Navigation with the bishop stopping off to go down Bentley Colliery. Tomorrow, after watching a medieval pageant at Barnby Dun, he will tour working men's clubs and pubs in the area.

It will be the day on which he celebrates his 52nd birthday. We can be sure that, as a bishop, he will be ever mindful of the wise advice contained in the name of his barge.

What the *Guardian* article did not mention was my sudden recollection during tea with the bishop at home in Goole, that I had encountered him in a 'previous life'.

While at Oxford I had a good friend, Andrew White, also a theologian, whose father was vicar of Shepton Mallet in Somerset, home to Showerings, makers of *Babycham*. In the class of his degree he had matched my own dismal performance, but this did not prevent him from becoming marketing manager at *The Economist*, and after that, from setting up a successful horticulture business near Oxford. At the time in question, after university, he was, like me, on the way to becoming an Anglican priest. While I was at Wells, near Shepton Mallet, he was at Lincoln Theological College, a short train journey from my home in Nottingham. When terms allowed, we held symposia in Lincoln's Lion & Snake, or in a similar public house in Bath, to reflect on the future — whether it would be the sheer tedium of everlasting life in the celestial choir, or the more exciting possibility of meeting a few Hellfire chums in 'the other place'. As the family drank tea with the bishop, it struck me that this was the same David Lunn who had been chaplain of Lincoln Theological College and had not been amused when after one of our more jubilant evenings, he had discovered the men's toilets six inches deep in water — the result of our modifications to the college plumbing. I never had the courage to remind him of the episode and I hope he will forgive Andrew and me in our absence for having caused him such bother all those years ago. Memory of the incident certainly prevented me from getting too excited about children's behaviour on *Sobriety*. The bishop's next formal engagement with the Project would be two years later in 1984 when he presided at the commissioning of *Sobriety*'s second boat, *Eden*, which John Drakeley had brought by canal from Lancashire with his hapless volunteer from St Thomas's.

David Lunn was very good value. Not content with doing a canal tour of the diocese and securing a new engine for *Sobriety*, he decided he wanted to do something more, by telling the people of Sheffield about the Project's work. Accordingly, on July 14th 1987 Hull and Humberside were linked with Sheffield by the arrival of the newly acquired *Eden* on the Sheffield Canal. At the top of the Tinsley flight of locks, the bishop welcomed a group of elderly and disabled people from Jack Harrison Court, a sheltered housing complex off Beverley Road in Hull. Helping to look after their guests were Joe Kelso and Dean Ross from Compass Youth Training Scheme. Les Middleton was skipper and Terry Clarke who had accompanied the bishop on his *Sobriety* trip, was assisting him.

The following evening the bishop entertained representatives from public life at Bishopscroft, his residence in Sheffield. It was a working evening with slides, discussion and a series of vignettes presented by people who subsequently worked regularly with *Sobriety* including Moira Bartlett, assistant governor of Hatfield Youth Custody Centre and two Sheffield probation officers. One of these, Mike Glover, had responsibility for the pre-release training of men coming to the end of a life sentence at Lindholme Prison near Finningley, a former RAF station and now the site of Doncaster's Robin Hood airport. As a result of the evening, it was not long before three 'lifers' from Lindholme and three young men from Hatfield were coming each day to the Project to lend a hand in the workshops as part of their pre-release training. But this was not the last time we should be grateful to our bishop. A few years later he persuaded John Laing & Co to build a *Sobriety* HQ on derelict land between the two waterways south of Goole.[7]

We Built A Ship

The search for a second vessel began in 1983 with a visit by Charles Quant, Director of the Rainbow Boats Trust,[8] and a drunk on Thorne Lock who had some random knowledge of working boats being sold off by British Waterways (BW). The trail eventually led to the office of Mr L. W. Croft, manager of BW's repair yard in Wigan and a stunted Leeds & Liverpool Canal boat going into retirement after 30 years of patching up the canal's banks. We bought it for £300 and rebuilt it for the waterways that were too small for *Sobriety*. The man who organised the reconstruction was Geoff Walton.

Five feet seven tall with a jet black beard and a tone of voice that let you know he was not to be contradicted, Geoff could easily have been mistaken for a reincarnation of Leon Trotsky. At various times branch secretary and shop steward of the GMB (General Municipal, Boilermakers & Allied Trade Union), he was a relentless agitator and the scourge of small town 'moneybags', as when working for a local firm on grass verge improvements, he requested a portable toilet. The boss called him a 'communist bastard', threw him in the ditch and sacked him. Geoff was definitely a picturesque victim but he was also an eloquent and persuasive organiser who could if necessary, shame his union members into toeing the line. So when a scruffy little vessel with the appearance of a homemade landing craft arrived in Goole to be converted into *Sobriety's* second 'ship', he seemed to be the one individual capable of recruiting and managing a workforce to do the work for nothing. And he did.

Two years previously the merger of his union with the Amalgamated Society of Boilermakers, Shipwrights, Blacksmiths & Structural Workers had brought into Geoff's sphere of influence a number of tradesmen from Drax power station with the skills between them to rebuild not just *Eden,* but a replica *Titanic*. There were five scaffolders, a shipwright, three burners, five erectors, ten platers, six welders, a shot blaster and, in addition to Geoff, two people expert in scrounging materials and equipment from big companies.(quarter inch plate from British Steel and welding equipment from Babcock & Wilcox were only the start). They were all on short time and available to help during the winter. I myself was still on a full teaching timetable of 28 lessons a week and it was fascinating for my classes when Geoff came into the room with ultimatums like, *"We've got to have a crane by three this afternoon or the job stops. The crane driver is OK but the Docks Board people say they'll need all the cranes to unload two ships. Can you discuss it with them — pronto!"* He would wait until the break between lessons and then accompany me to the faculty office where he would hover until I made the necessary 'phone call. By comparison when Brian Calvert arrived in school, often with his dog, he would put the problem into a respectful, more philosophical context but with a no less final conclusion:

"We've got a problem mister".

"What, Brian?"

"We can't take Sobriety *to York any more".*

"Why?"

"Because the hose pipe at Foss Basin won't reach the barge".

My faculty of business, social and community studies was building bridges between school and work in real time.

The 'job' in Geoff Walton's mind was a complete re-construction of *Eden*, meaning that below deck level there would be a fourteen foot extension to her hull, new bows and a remoulding of her stern end. When this was finished she would be given a 40 foot steel deckhouse to enclose her living area. Her overall length of 57 feet would get her into most of the locks in the Yorkshire, Lancashire and Midlands navigations. The job went well. British Shipbuilders on the Tyne and Cochrane's at Selby helped with the technical drawings: Nick Allon, a young naval architect recently made redundant from Dunstan's shipyard in Hull, designed the living area and galley: the new privately owned Associated British Ports (ABP), successor to the British Transport Docks Board, gave us space on the docks and handed over its former mortuary on Copenhagen Road near number two dry dock, to serve as a 'snap' room and equipment store. Always restless for progress, Geoff decided that his union band could do more than build; they could also train four young people to be welders and platers. The Project for its own part, went to Hatfield Youth Custody Centre near Doncaster and recruited two young men to be trained as skippers for the new barge. One of them, from the Bransholme estate in Hull, stayed with *Sobriety* for seven years and then got a job on the North Sea oil rigs.

On Thursday 27th June 1985 the new *Eden* was lifted into Goole's Railway Dock by a Hewden Stewart 300 ton crane (loaned free of charge for the occasion) and commissioned by Bishop David Lunn in front of a congregation of 200. Goole Jubilee Jazz Band provided the music and ABP was happy for its Thursday lunchtime to be disrupted. In my short speech I paid tribute not just to the people who had been involved in the operation but to Geoff Walton's long-suffering wife Chris and the wives and partners of the workforce.

She is married not to an ordinary husband who helps about the house and garden and

washes the car, but to one in whose faraway look are wheels and anchors and steel plates and engines. She is the Barge Widow.

The telephone rings at all hours and uncouth voices ask for him, but he is not at home. He sits bolt upright in the night and barks instructions to the phantom welders in his dreams. He is always late for meals. He sometimes speaks as if possessed and mutters incoherent words —Docks Board compressor: Woodward's propellor: Paint! He disappears on the pretext of doing family errands. A recent investigation into his condition brought to light a large quantity of family shopping under the decking and in a kitchen cupboard at his home between the cornflakes and the porridge oats, were found a quadrant and a bilge pump…

But Geoff himself had the last wistful word:

All my references and there are many, all my 30 years experience since I started work at 15 for the British Transport Commission and my qualifications as a skilled craftsman, cannot secure me a regular job with a wage and a future. The very personality and character that 'begged, borrowed and stole' materials, 'conned, kidded and cajoled' volunteers to undertake an operation of such proportions, cannot be trusted with a brush to sweep the streets!

So in fact the right man was asked to build Eden. *Not only was it built for the handicapped and under privileged but was also for my part, built by the handicapped and under privileged. If the people who sail in her get half as much pleasure out of her as the pain I had getting her built, then she will be as happy a ship as she is beautiful.*

The landscape of the port where Geoff and his colleagues rebuilt *Eden* thirty years ago, has changed out of all recognition. Instead of today's barren concrete platforms for containers, were sheds filled with cargoes which were loaded 'over the side' from barge to ship and ship to barge. The docks were choked with canal craft carrying wire, steel, nuts, coal, gravel, sand, petrol and fertlisers. And there were the *Tom Puddings* — trains of compartment boats pulled by tugs, bringing coal from the West Riding mines for onward movement by sea to London's power stations. On the skyline across the *Port in Green Fields* were tall cranes on tram lines, their drivers like owls in a tree, calling to men below. There were Cold War timber ships from Russia with numbers instead of names, showing the hammer and sickle on their funnels, and with aerials wreathed in espionage. And towering over the docks just as their inventors had towered over Victorian ingenuity, were the Number 3 and Number 5 Boat Hoists, part of the compartment boat transportation system still unchanged after one hundred and twenty years of operation. On the docks were electricians, plumbers, storekeepers, joiners, roofers, engineers, all employed by the British Transport Docks Board to maintain the sheds, capstans, cranes, bridges, locks and hoists to keep ships, wagons and barges on the move twenty four hours a day. On the waterways of the Aire & Calder Company, so powerful in Yorkshire that it was dubbed the Fourth Estate after Queen, Parliament and Church, were barges carrying everything from molasses to dog food. Their names like *Sobriety* and *Service* paraded their owner's virtues, but some like *Prodesse* (To make a profit), left no doubt of their owners' intentions. The most celebrated of the company's engineers was William Hamond Bartholomew. Born at Stanley near Wakefield in 1831, five years after the company had opened the Goole canal and its entrepôt (entry port), he eventually succeeded his father as engineer to the navigation and experimented with steam powered tugs using the screw propellor rather than paddles. By 1864 his tugs were pulling trains of compartment boats or 'pans' (colloquially known as *Tom Puddings*), each with a coal carrying capacity of 30 tonnes. When the train arrived in Goole docks, its twenty pans were lifted one by one in the hoist's cage until they reached the point at which they could be tilted and the coal emptied into the hold of a waiting ship.[9]

Associated British Ports, now owned by Singaporean and Canadian pension funds, employs half a dozen people to run the docks and ships are loaded and unloaded by private contractors. Only a few sheds remain, while the South Dock Hoist, orphaned survivor of a family of five, stands neglected near the entrance to the canal. Transportation of bulk cargoes has almost finished. John Branford still runs barges taking sand and gravel from Hoveringham to Leeds but Whitaker tankers no longer bring fuel from Immingham via the Humber, Ouse and Aire & Calder to Castleford and Leeds.

A Loyal Skipper

An internet review of Goole's *Jailhouse* pub says, '*Take a crash helmet and don't make eye contact if you from outta town*'. Then it adds dismissively, '*Beer crap too*'. It does not mention the habit of spitting in beer, 'crap' or not, to secure recognition of ownership, but the advice to strangers to stare straight ahead would certainly have made sense to some of this little building's reluctant customers when it was opened in 1857. It was built by the Aire & Calder Company to be the town's police station and court, with detention cells for suspects and felons. In 1891 it ceased to be a 'nick' and was turned into a cottage hospital which it remained until 1912. Sixty years later it became a Job Centre with administrative ties to Moorfoot, a building in Sheffield with the appearance of a Babylonian ziggurat and the only public or private place of work I have known, where the visitor had to sign a receipt for a cup of tea. Moorfoot was the headquarters of the Manpower Services Commission (MSC), a gigantic quango (quasi autonomous non governmental organisation) set up in the early 1970s by Edward Heath's government to reduce unemployment. Its schemes took advantage of the needs of towns and villages to improve their amenities and put money into the hands of parish councils and charities to organise projects that would give work to people who were unemployed. It was indispensable for *Sobriety*'s development. Without the fifteen years of MSC programmes from 1974 until 1989 the Project could not have expanded its workforce and capital assets to cope with the business coming its way. An article in the Project's Review of 1985 under the heading *Unemployment, Young Offenders and MSC Schemes* showed the importance of this source of income. It noted that the first full time skipper was recruited in 1978 through the Labour government's Job Creation Programme. The WEP (Work Experience Programme) paid for the Project to train young people to be assistant skippers from 1978 onwards. By 1985 *Sobriety* was employing 12 people on the MSC's Community Programme (CP). In 1984 the scheme paid for the materials for *Eden* and five years later, just before the quango's functions were taken over by the Training & Enterprise Councils (TECs), the Project converted a disused lightship into a sailing barge utilising funding exclusively from MSC to pay the wages of a ten strong workforce. As a bonus, the management arrangements for the different phases of the MSC's work, brought useful contacts through its staff in Leeds, Hull and latterly Grimsby.

Brian Calvert *Sobriety*'s first skipper.

Brian Calvert was an example of volunteer turned employee, his salary being paid by the MSC's Special Temporary Employment Programme before becoming available from Humberside Social Services. After six years service, much of it beyond the call of duty, he left the Project in autumn 1983 to work for British Waterways as the keeper for nine years, of a swing bridge with a railway line across the Stainforth & Keadby Canal at Vazon, and then, until his retirement, as lock-keeper at Keadby where the same canal meets the river Trent.

It is difficult to imagine what a challenge those early days were for him. First and foremost a barge skipper, he was faced with having to manage staff and young people who had expectations that did not take into account the dangers and restrictions of Yorkshire's canals and tidal rivers. There was pressure to accept as many bookings as possible and the resulting workload was enormous. But unless *Sobriety* was on the move seven days a week, how could the Project justify its grant? Thirty five years later in an interview at his home he said:

> *My six years as skipper were very rewarding but hard work. Would I do it again? Yes. It gave me an insight into how youngsters who had been physically and mentally abused, responded to going away on a converted barge. They could learn new skills such as cooking, learning to steer or just sitting and talking. One lad told me his parents had gone off to Brazil and just left him behind. I was a boatman first and last, taught by my grandfather on the old steam tug* Welshman. *What did I know of social work? My priorities were looking after* Sobriety; *she was an old lady even then. Now she is 102. I'm nearly 80 and also need a new cylinder head. I have lots of happy memories and hope* Sobriety *will continue to prosper.*

But in spite of Brian's skills of navigation, there was always the potential for disaster.

During the summer of 1981 the Project had persuaded Hull College of Higher Education to make a promotional TV film for showing to school staff, local authorities and anyone who might donate funds. The idea was to give insights into the benefits of *Sobriety* expeditions. Peter Adamson, a leading presenter on Radio Humberside, had volunteered to speak the commentary and we had lined up an impressive gallery of 'talking heads'. Maxwell Bird, Chair of Humberside's Education Committee and always amused by the idea of a council barge, exhorted schools to toe the line, while Michael Pinnock and his young people from St.George's Road Intermediate Treatment Centre in Hull, described their adventures in the waterway wilds of South Yorkshire. Meanwhile away from the TV studio, on the Humber, *Sobriety* had left Hull's King George Dock to rendezvous with the college camera crew somewhere near the Humber Bridge which was due to be opened by the Queen four days later. On board was a group from King's Mill school in Driffield. The children, in the care of the head of the school, Peter Montgomery, a veteran user of *Sobriety*, had severe learning difficulties and were on the barge to enjoy the stimulation of adventure and new endeavours. *Sobriety* passed under the bridge as the tide was beginning to ebb and ran quietly aground on a submerged concrete jetty built to be a temporary berth for the construction company's rescue boat. If she had arrived ten minutes earlier she would have passed over the jetty; ten minutes later she would have bumped against it. The barge was so safely grounded that everyone on board got on with their lunch. The problem was elsewhere.

July 17th was the day of the ceremony of opening the Humber Bridge, but Freeman Fox & Partners, the Resident Engineers, could not find in their schedule of Her Majesty's visit, any reference to the presence of a barge called *Sobriety*. Was it a marker for the Red Arrows who were to fly over the bridge while the Bishop of Hull led the congregation in a prayer for those in peril on the sea? Was it the base for a detachment of special forces sent to guarantee the safety of royalty? The Engineers were not amused by these speculations and sent word that they knew of a friendly company of explosives experts who would come and dynamite the unfortunate vessel if it was not removed on the next high tide. The good thing was that we were on the company's private compound, protected from reporters who might have in mind a scoop of juicy editorial in preparation for the Queen's visit. The bad thing was that there was a high spring tide that evening; thereafter the tides would be lower. If *Sobriety* was not going to be high and dry for a fortnight and the Project derided by the nation, she had to be pulled off the jetty when the tide was highest at 9.00pm. After a few 'phone calls, Brian secured the services of Gillyot & Scott's tug, *Gillian Knight*, named after the Gilbert and Sullivan contralto singer who might well have swapped her part as *Buttercup* in *HMS Pinafore* for the greater comedy of *Sobriety*. Freeman Fox lent us their rescue boat, and the two vessels under the direction of *Gillian Knight*'s skipper Tommy White, tugged and pulled together. Like Ko-Ko's prisoner in The Mikado, *Sobriety* 'squirmed and struggled and gurgled and guggled' but finally gave up the contest and splashed angrily into the river.

I was sorry but proud when Brian left us. Arriving at the Project six years earlier, he had shown all the marks of institutional living, walking slowly with long strides, asking approval for every trivial decision and unsure whether to be compliant or defensive. By the time he went to new employment in autumn 1983, he had re-married and had a life of his own. The Project owed him a debt of gratitude for his pioneering efforts.

An age of exploration

Fifty seven feet long, eleven feet wide and the smaller of the two vessels, *Eden* was visiting less accessible centres in the region. She went up the river Ouse to Ripon via the Ure whose tributaries come down from the hills above Wensleydale. She went through the Pennine tunnels from Leeds to Salford much to the alarm of oncoming boats, and she completed the twenty one miles from Wakefield to Sowerby Bridge on the Calder & Hebble Navigation. Meanwhile *Sobriety* continued to navigate the Humber estuary and its related rivers and canals and as a flippant introduction to the new age, I use the indulgent language of luxury cruise advertisements to reveal other destinations:

Do you have the courage to sail with the Romans?

After embarking aboard *Sobriety* and *Eden* from our potato store on Goole Docks, we shall pen down with ships and barges through Ocean lock into the Ouse seaway and take the tide to Blacktoft jetty where legend says the spies Burgess and Maclean joined a ship for Russia. For us, the end of two leisurely hours listening to the boring yarns of skipper-brothers Paull and Norman Church in Blacktoft's Hope & Anchor, will see the flood tide take us up the river Trent to the village of Torksey. After viewing its famous viaduct which once carried the Manchester, Sheffield & Lincolnshire Railway, we shall enjoy an alfresco supper and sing-song with lock mistress and folk guitarist Cillvia Sweetdreams.

The next morning, after *petit déjeuner à l'ecluse*, Cillvia will take us to Torksey's Civil War battered castle and the site where twelve hundred years ago a Viking army camped in preparation for war with King Alfred of Wessex. Under the guidance of our lock mistress, we shall operate Torksey lock to give us fairway into the Foss Dyke, a Roman canal hand-dug for grain ships sailing from The Wash via Lindum Colonia (Lincoln) to York.

In the city, our two boats will berth in Lincoln's 'Left Bank' Brayford Pool where we are advised to keep a lookout for poolmaster 'Old Frosty' who has the power of life and death over new arrivals. After making faces at an imp perched up in the cathedral's gothic choir, and trudging up and down Steep Hill with its almost vertical gradient, we shall return to the boats for a 'centurion's snack' of salted beef and porridge made with goat's milk.

Sobriety and *Eden* will now go their separate ways, *Eden* through the Glory Hole into the river Witham, past Anton's Goyt to Boston, and *Sobriety* back to the Trent and upstream to Nottingham passing the vicious Cromwell weir which can capsize a vessel in seconds.

Or would you rather chug into Yorkshire's industrial past?
A journey to the final frontier of the waterways!

We shall assemble near the cement works on Goole's Dutch River Side with views across the primeval landscape to the world heritage site of Thorne Moors, enhanced by the unique triangular pit-head of Thorne colliery. After meeting our now familiar skipper-brothers, Paull and Norman Church, we shall embark on the Tom Pudding tug *Wheldale* and sing a lament for the coal industry from the repertoire of the late Gezz Overington — 'The Day the Devil Paid a Call'.[10]

Following the picturesque Goole to Knottingley canal westwards, we may find ourselves playing 'chicken' on the approach of a 700 tonne tanker barge from Leeds, hurrying to Goole to catch the tide to Immingham and another load of oil. Today's destination is Beaver Ponds, the 'Cowes' of Humberside, where yachtsmen race to win the coveted Hole-in-the-Dyke trophy. Here we shall leave our tug and be welcomed aboard *Eden*, an open plan vessel specially designed to take us south through the New Junction canal built in 1905 by William Hamond Bartholomew, engineer for the Aire & Calder Company.

As our resident experts press the red, yellow and green buttons to raise and lower the bridges and barriers, we can wave sympathetically to the waiting traffic. After navigating an aqueduct high above the swirling waters of the river Don at Kirk Bramwith, we tie up under Doncaster's by-pass in preparation for an *Early Bird Skate* at the town's ice rink followed by an optional visit to the *Chest Press*, *Leg Extension* and *Vibration Plate* at the nearby Fitness Village. There is a £50 surcharge for this experience.

Day Three sees us at pretty Sprotborough Lock, scene of the notorious 1987 "It was me, gov" incident, when twenty eight policemen arrested themselves for exceeding the twelve passenger limit on the pleasure barge *Cuff*. After a few tedious hours of French Cricket, we take the river Don beneath the A1 motorway's towering viaduct, past miles of derelict factories, until we reach our berth in Rotherham next to its magistrates court and the lock which serves as the entrance to the hazardous Sheffield Canal.

While Paull prepares *Eden* for the challenge of the Tinsley Flight, Norman will lead a discussion which allows him to boast about how he will cope with the difficulties of getting us through the perilous Ickles, Holmes and Jordan locks en route for the canal basin and its amazing straddle warehouse. At a dizzying 150 feet above sea level, the same height as the top of the tower of Holy Trinity Church in Hull, the basin marks the end of the canal and the climax of our week on the 'final frontier' of the waterways.

There is truth in these make-believe descriptions of *Sobriety*'s and *Eden*'s itineraries. The waterways of Yorkshire and the East Midlands occupy an area bounded by Nottingham, Halifax, Ripon and Hull and do not beguile visitors in the manner of the rivers and canals of the south of England. With some exceptions, the north east waterways are the product of the age of heavy industry and lack the quiet charm of the Cotswold canals or the Kennet & Avon Canal from Bristol to the Thames via Bath. The teacher or social worker bringing her children or elderly residents to the Project, had to see that benefits were less likely to come from an appreciation of passing scenery but more likely from activities ashore and, as we have seen, from a menu of activities on board. Benefits could not be taken for granted. Somehow the Project and visiting staff had to 'turn a sow's ear into a silk purse'.

Blacktoft Jetty – a wild and lonely spot on the Lower Ouse where it was rumoured the spies Burgess and Maclean boarded a ship for Russia.

Tim Watson

The references to the tanker barge and 'our skipper-brothers' may be tongue-in-cheek but they show why the Project needed professional skippers to navigate broad canals and tidal rivers used by ships and commercial barges. As John Hughes observed on his grammar school trip to Leeds, the 45 ton *Sobriety* was a demanding servant even in the hands of an experienced captain. On the leisure canals, a few days of tuition can turn a reasonably confident adult into a narrowboat steerer capable of teaching children to manage and steer the boat and work the locks. On the north east waterways, a group's contribution to handling a barge is limited. Staff are dependent on a professional boatman for information about where they can go and what they can do. As a result, this person had the power to make or ruin an expedition. Another problem was that the men or women with the understanding to help group leaders achieve their aims and who were willing to contribute to the benefits of the expedition, were sometimes not very proficient at handling barges. Others had an outstanding record in this respect, but as Brian Calvert observed, had not been trained to work with teachers and social workers. When they did have both the skills and the personality, then we flew!

Kevin Rokahr met all the requirements of the post. Having been a deckie learner on Hull trawlers, he arrived at the Project just after Brian's departure and with all his good humour, was able to understand what *Sobriety* was about and how it fitted the curriculum of the special schools. Here he is sharing a trip in 1985 with Jonathan Fogell, second master of Derringham school for children with moderate learning difficulties. This abridged version of a story told by Jon under the title *A Life of Sobriety*, was originally published in full the same year, in the newsletter of the National Council for Special Education.

I was woken by the noise of the water pump. It was like a Honda 50cc motor bike revving six inches away. At first my muggy head was confused but I quickly realised where I was and why this torture resounded in my eardrums. Kevin, the skipper of Sobriety, *has promised to wake me up with a quick burst of the water pump. I now realised why he smiled whilst making this promise. He was to wake me in the agreed manner when the children had emerged from their bunks and could be neither coaxed nor threatened back to them.*

The air seemed unusually cold that morning, much colder and duller than recent mornings when I had risen at around 7.00am. After dressing hastily I climbed the vertical steps of the cosy wood panelled forecabin and clambered on to the deck of Sobriety. *Goole Docks seemed strangely at peace. The morning calm was broken only by the gentle clatter-clang of distant milk floats and the biting breeze on my unshaven face. As I approached the hatch to the main cabin I could hear the murmurings of children also trying to face the morning.*

I didn't linger on deck; it was far too cold for that. I descended the steps into the lounge-cum-dining classroom of Sobriety. *Kevin stood close to the Aga, as he does habitually in the pre-breakfast muddle. His eyes looked as strained and heavy as mine felt. "There's a cup of tea for you," he muttered to me. I thanked him and after a sip or two, waiting for him to start up a conversation I said, "What time did the kids get off to sleep?" He gazed into*

*his cup as though he was beckoning the leaves to tell his fortune. "About half past three",
he groaned at last. Again I waited for the conversation to start but there was none. After
several more sips of tea I ventured, "What time is it now?" Kevin stared at his watch for
several seconds as if debating whether or not the watch was telling the truth. He decided
it was and sighed with only slight emotion, "Quarter past five". As I looked up in disbelief
I saw that all but one of our pupils was sitting down fully dressed, waiting for breakfast to
commence.*

Jon then goes on to explain his design of activities on and off the barge and outlines the
educational purposes that were so important for skippers to understand:

This story serves to illustrate the impact that Sobriety *has on pupils. Having organised
residential trips to camps and hostels, I was well used to the first day energy that the pupils
find from somewhere. The excitement induced by this barge surpassed all others I had
seen. It can't be put down to the nature of that particular group. I took a different group of
youngsters on* Sobriety *last year with very much the same results. I think on that occasion
they slept until 5.40 on the first morning.*

*My programme of activities was designed around the needs of a group of 11/12 year
olds. I wanted to work on coping skills and so the pupils planned, shopped for and cooked
every meal. There were lots of activities that involved finding their way round unfamiliar
towns.* Sobriety *was excellent for this because it berthed close to the centres of Doncaster
and Rotherham. I also wanted to broaden the leisure experience of the pupils. To this
end I think I was successful because the television stayed off all week without even one
complaint. This was our week's programme. It helps to demonstrate the variety of activities
that are available:*

	Morning	*Afternoon*	*Evening*
Monday	Packing up bus. Last minute equipment checks.	Horse riding at stables near Newbald.	Sail round Goole Docks with friends.
Tuesday	Sail to Doncaster. Spotter sheets competition.	Exploring town centre.	Treasure hunt and ghost stories.
Wednesday	Diaries and postcards home. Sail to Rotherham.	Visit Herringthorpe leisure centre.	Visit Spurley Hey youth club.
Thursday	Abbeydale Industrial Hamlet.	Free time in Conisborough. Sail to Barnby Dun.	Bonfire singsong followed by midnight walk.
Friday	Sail to Goole. Joined by Humberside County Council Leisure Services Committee.	Pack and clean up	

*Setting off back to school on the Friday afternoon I felt my usual sense of anti-climax.
Several of the pupils cried openly because their holiday was over. Paul, an undersized 12
year old with an oversized heart, said it had been the holiday of a lifetime, and nobody
disagreed with him.*

In the late nineteen eighties Jon Fogell left Humberside to become head of East Quinton school for children with emotional and behavioural difficulties (EBD) in Sussex. From there he went to be chief educational psychologist for the East Sussex authority but came back to Yorkshire in 2003 as Head of the East Riding's Behaviour Improvement Unit at County Hall, Beverley.

The unexpected bonus is Jon's accomplishment as a raconteur of moving and instructive stories from his years in special education. Here are some of his best. Not all of them are funny. Some are sad, but they are all instructive:

Fourteen year olds Peter and Raymond were in year 8 at Derringham School, Hull. During a few spare hours on a Sobriety trip, after fishing from the barge, they had gone to play football. When they returned, Peter noticed that his friend's tin of bait was still on the deck and took it downstairs to Raymond's bunk. Not being closely acquainted with the pre-pupa stages of the maggot life cycle, Peter was not to know that the occupants of this particular tin of bait were getting fed up with being earthbound and had ambitions to take to the air. When Mr Fogell went into the dormitory, some were still exploring the inside of sleeping bags while others were buzzing excitedly with their new freedom.

Their teacher was very angry with Peter, and the children shared his anger. Their view was that someone had upset Mr Fogell. They thought Peter had been playing the fool and wanted to punish him. But Peter went on his knees and said that he had only been trying to be helpful. He had not wanted Raymond's bait to get lost and did not know that the tin would get knocked off the bunk. So Mr Fogell, seeing that Peter had acted with the best intentions, admitted he was wrong and apologised to Peter and the rest of the group.

Jon makes the point that keeping discipline is a complicated exercise and that children's intentions are just as important as the effects of their behaviour. He says that the episode taught him not to jump to conclusions but to take the trouble to find out what had really happened. Children's pain at injustice should not be taken lightly. He also says that it was the family atmosphere on *Sobriety* that made the rescue of Peter's reputation so important.

Life is tough for children in special education and they can easily be crushed, as when some Derringham children went into a sweet shop in Goole. One of them, Albert, asked the shopkeeper, "How much is a Twix?", then he asked, "How much is a Mars Bar?" He got the reply, "Can't you read?"

At another time the barge displays miraculous powers:

Alan was a biker's son and came to Derringham school each day dressed like a Hell's Angel. He was a very quiet boy and terrified of school. In his terror he used to be sick three or four times before lessons began and always arrived in the classroom with a bucket. He and his friend Freddie came to school on the 'daft bus' as it was known to the less kind residents of Hull's Bransholme estate where the two boys lived. On one of Jon's Sobriety expeditions, Alan discovered that he could not only make a reasonable cup of tea but that he was a good cook. More crucially he had forgotten about the bucket. The trip had changed his relationship with his teachers and with the other children.

In this story are the shades of Jim Hogan's pot boy we met in Chapter 1 and of the young people changed by City Challenge in Chapter 2. Consciously or unconsciously they battle against the odds and then discover to their surprise that they have hitherto unrecognised strengths. They never look back. That is what, Jon says, *Sobriety* was and is about. On a lighter note we hear of a colleague at Derringham School being quizzed by a boy:

"Have you any brothers and sisters?" "Yes five brothers and a sister." "That's seven. It means a lot of dads have been coming to your house." "No, only one dad." "One dad to seven children? That's disgusting!"

No doubt the boy's family tree would take some unravelling by future historians but the story highlights the isolation of some children from accepted, some might say, 'middle class', values, and leaves them unprotected from ridicule and unfair treatment.

Jonathan sums everything up:

If I were to list the benefits the pupils gained from their week on Sobriety, I would need reams. How they felt about it was reflected in a sense of co-operation and commitment that went beyond anything seen in this group of children. The point about the opening story is that to provide this sort of experience takes a lot of hard work on the part of teacher and pupils, but the educational harvest is sure to be there in the end. John Holt commented on school ethos recently, 'The challenge for the future is not to make the home environment more like the school, but to make the school less like school'. Sobriety is nothing like school and as a learning experience it takes some beating!

Questions

What were the successes and failures of the early *Sobriety* project? Was there any evidence that the project's educational objectives were achieved? If so, where and how?

If you were a youth leader or teacher responsible for the education of children who were in trouble with the police, what would be your priorities?

How might the curriculum for children with additional learning needs differ from a mainstream curriculum? Should children with additional learning needs be taught in mainstream schools?

Sobriety's development was organic in the sense that it arose out of day to day considerations at a very grassroots level. Would you have organised things differently?

Chapter 5 Notes

1 I am aware that the description, 'with learning difficulties', has been replaced by the more positive 'having additional learning needs'. At the time when these events took place the former description was current, so for the sake of consistency I have continued to use it. The same applies elsewhere to the outdated term 'mental handicap'.

2 In 1983 Intermediate Treatment was introduced by the Department of Health to fund alternatives to custody for children. £15 million funded 98 new diversionary projects during the following two years. As a result custody rates fell dramatically.

3 For the same reason as in note 1, I have kept to the title in use at the time.

4 For further discussion and summary see *Action for Children: Young People: 21 years of policy*: John Pitts, Vauxhall Professor of Socio-Legal Studies, University of Bedfordshire. Also publications of *Beyond Youth Custody*: www.beyondyouthcustody.net

5 The (restored) Bull Leaping fresco from Knossos, capital of the Minoan empire, now in the Heraklion Museum, Crete.

6 *A History of the Diocese of Sheffield*: Mary Walton: 1981.

7 David Lunn now lives in Wetwang in the East Riding of Yorkshire and is an authority on the history of local villages and their places of worship. His latest book, *The Wetwang Saga: The Story of Fridaythorpe, Fimber and Wetwang: A History of England in Two and a Half Parishes* is 'not just for those who have heard of Wetwang. The careful study of the villages makes it an invaluable guide to the history of nearly every village in England'. ISBN 978-0-9562495-0-00: Published by High Wolds Heritage Publications and available from the author, 28 Southfield Road, Wetwang.)

8 The Rainbow Boats Trust was an organisation set up in 1975 by HRH Prince Charles to replicate *Heulwen* (Welsh for sunshine), a community boat built by Camell-Laird that provided trips for disabled children on the newly re-opened Montgomery Canal.

9 The full story of the Tom Puddings is in the book, *The Railway on the Water* published by the Sobriety Project in 1992 and available from the Yorkshire Waterways Museum (Tel: 01405 768 730) at £12.00. A revised edition, 2015, is in the press.

10 With thanks to the respective estates of Gezz Overington and Goff Sherburn and to Steve Gardham and the Sherburn family. My thanks also to Bill Sowerby for the notation on page 84.

Chapter 6

VOLUNTEERS YOUNG AND OLD
SKIPPERS GOOD AND BAD

The youth of a nation are the trustees of posterity – Benjamin Disraeli
Stuff a mod with green onions; they smell better – Motto on a punk badge

A Royal Visit

In the early afternoon of March 5ᵗʰ 1986, as arranged by Humberside County Council's civic office, *Sobriety* and *Eden* berthed in Hull's Albert Dock to await the arrival of their Royal Highnesses the Prince and Princess of Wales.

During the morning Diana had visited the Lonsdale community centre, while Charles had been entertained by the Brethren of Trinity House. After lunch the royal couple were to meet on the quayside of Albert Dock. Diana would go aboard *Sobriety* while Charles would inspect *Eden* which was still being fitted out by young people on a back-to-work scheme organised by the National Association for the Care and Re-settlement of Offenders (NACRO).

Down below on *Sobriety* were the children and teachers from Carnforth special school in Grimsby and young people from Compass Youth Training Scheme (YTS) in Hull: on *Sobriety*'s deck were skipper Kevin Rokahr and his wife Linda, and John McGrory, the Project's benefactor, and his wife Marie: waiting in *Eden*'s saloon were Geoff Walton, Ted Pindar who was in charge of fitting out, apprentice Terry Clarke, and several skippers. On the quayside was a large crowd of royalists and well wishers.

The *Hull Daily Mail* gave an account of the visit under the heading *The Princess and the Punk*. It was not the first time that 'punk' had featured in the chronicles of *Sobriety*. During his barge progress through Sheffield diocese, Bishop David Lunn had had a similar encounter recorded on that occasion by the *Guardian*. The *Hull Daily Mail* said:

The Princess and the punk came face to face down at Hull's Albert Dock. The culture clash happened when Prince Charles and Princess Diana visited the Sobriety *Project which is supported by the Prince's Trust.*

On board Sobriety, *a converted Humber keel, the royal couple met 17 year old punk, Maz Cooke, a trainee at Compass Youth Training on Hedon Road. The Princess's bright mauve dress was almost a perfect match with Maz's pink mohican style hair. A collection of badges pinned to Maz's black leather jacket, caught Diana's eye, especially one which bore the cryptic legend 'Stuff a mod with green onions, they smell better'. But the pair got on well together and Maz said afterwards, "I thought the Princess might be a bit posh but she was very down to earth and chatty".*

Three other girls from Compass YTS also met the royal couple — Angie Gray who presented the Princess with a bouquet, Fiona Edmonds and Donna Dunn. As part of their YTS training, they had spent two weeks aboard Sobriety last summer with a group of elderly women from Carr Head residential home, Bridlington.

Apart from a faulty crane on the Dog & Duck slipway in Goole which had resulted in *Sobriety* falling into the water and creating a tidal wave big enough to empty the canal, the weeks of preparation had paid off. The only hitch was the appearance ten minutes before the arrival of the royal party, of a perfectly innocent individual from KiddeThorn who had chosen that afternoon to deliver a fire extinguisher to *Sobriety*'s engine room. Humberside Police divers who had been spending a week patrolling Albert Dock, presumably in a midget submarine, were not impressed and hurried the poor man away for 'further questioning'. He was of course soon released.

Training And Recruitment

Of greater interest to everyone were the two groups of young volunteers from Compass YTS and our skipper apprentice Terry Clarke, who was learning the art of navigation. In 1986 the Project was employing nine skippers and Terry was the youngest of the group. The post of apprentice dated back to Brian Calvert's time when it became obvious that for the person in charge to be 'all hands one', (a barge captain's term for 'on your own!'), was not satisfactory. The first person recruited to assist with navigation was Dean Brigham who came straight from Riverside special school at the age of 16. He stayed for three years during Brian's regime and then found a job as a shop worker. At this point, in 1981, the Project's management committee requested financial support for the salary of an apprentice skipper from Boothferry Borough Council, the second tier local authority created by 1974 local government re-organisation. The proposal was approved and Terry was appointed. However we were determined that the post should be a stepping stone either to greater responsibility within the Project or promotion to work outside it. He had not been appointed simply to be cheap labour for the skipper.

To widen Terry's experience we arranged placements, first with British Waterways who had jurisdiction over many of the Yorkshire waterways and then with John Whitaker & Son, whose tanker barges carried fuel from Immingham to Leeds. He attended college on day release and achieved a credit in the Part 2 Certificate in shipbuilding craft studies as well as a St John Ambulance certificate in first aid. To improve his personal confidence we asked him to attend a City Challenge course and he returned from this with glowing reports from his tutors. Five years later in 1986, after an illness from which he fully recovered, he left us for a better paid engineering post at Drax power station. Boothferry Borough Council however, continued to grant aid the Project at the same level of support until the second round of local authority re-organisation in 1996.

Manpower Services Commission rules said that the skippers we could recruit after advertising in local job centres, must have been unemployed for at least a year and were eligible to stay in a post for two years if they were promoted to supervisor. It was expected that at the end of this time they would have acquired adequate experience and skills to find permanent work. Among the recruits were some personalities who did not always live up to the declarations of character and experience they had made at interview. Others were so competent and helpful that we wanted to keep them. A few were quite simply rogues. They all took some managing and had to understand that 'customer care' was to be taken seriously.

At the time of booking I would arrange a planning meeting, generally on the premises of the visiting group, to discuss the details of the expedition. The skipper in charge of the trip would attend and explain to the group staff that constraints on the tideways might sometimes be the fault of the moon rather than the skipper. The meeting also allowed crew and young volunteers to understand staff aims and objectives and for everyone to agree on times, dates and special arrangements. My guiding principle on such occasions was that all surprises were bad ones.

I would try to be on hand on Monday mornings when the groups were leaving on the boats from the potato shed HQ in Goole Docks, and again on Fridays when the groups returned. This gave me the opportunity to deal immediately with any problems raised by crew or group staff. Before they left for home, staff would be given a questionnaire to complete after doing a *post mortem* on the trip with their clients or young people. Their replies coming about a week later, would be discussed with crew and any problems dealt with. It did not always work. I was quite happy to have hard hitting debates with *Sobriety* staff but when problems were created by visitors themselves, it was less easy. I tended to bite my lip and wait until the group's next visit was being planned. At that point I would have the opportunity to find out more about the problems of the previous expedition.

Jim Bolton — A Forward Looking Educationalist

At this time, from the mid nineteen eighties until the turn of the millennium, *Sobriety* and *Eden* were booked every week and weekend except for the Christmas holiday when the Project closed. But in spite of popularity with schools, youth clubs, and social services groups in the region, income from trips came nowhere near covering costs. The MSC was being abolished and to keep the boats moving, we had to find money from elsewhere. I decided it might be profitable to pay a surprise visit to Jim Bolton, Humberside's assistant director of education for schools. He had helped with the arrangements for City Challenge and had come bearing gifts of chemical toilets for the nascent Project. With little regard for protocol I recruited four of our skippers to join me for a visit to County Hall where, in those days, there was open access to officers and members (The suppliant visitor knocked on the office door, walked in, declared undying love for the department or political party and stated the case for funding). Accordingly the five of us walked into Jim's office and sat down to await his arrival. He was dismayed to find his office occupied by four scruffy boatmen and their stroppy leader but it worked, and within six months the LEA had settled on an annual grant to the Project, equivalent to the support coming from Social Services. The subsidy was in addition to the payment of my own teacher's salary.

The late Jim Bolton was larger than life. He told me himself about a day when he and his colleague Rex Stott had been visiting schools in the Howden area and, thinking it would be instructive to measure local opinion, arrived at the bar of a Howden hotel. He said that he and Rex normally pretended to be Bible salesmen, but on this occasion they were entrepreneurs from London, thinking of expanding their businesses north into Humberside where wages were lower. They explained to their audience that they had come to get to know the area and find a good secondary school for their children. What was customers' opinion, they asked, about the quality of local provision? Jim would not tell me what the customers said but he did tell me some of their names so that I was able to draw my own conclusions. On the assumption that most people's humour was as brutal as his own, he was not averse to playing practical jokes when he thought it might be useful.

On another occasion, unwarily, I made an arrangement to see him on the day that coincided with the Christmas end-of-term party at County Hall. As I made my way towards the education department which at that time was on the first floor, I heard a lot of shouting. I had to step aside, while a man I assumed was a member of staff, ran down the stairs three at a time. Jim explained that he (Jim) was in the process of paying back one of his education colleagues who had made his life a misery during the previous few months. The office assistants had been asked to pretend they were speaking from London. Jim was then able to torment his victim with a message that an official from the Department for Education & Science (DES) was on the phone waiting to put him through to the secretary of state. The call was to be taken downstairs because of problems with the telephone system. As soon as the hapless officer arrived to take the call, the pretend secretary told him that the minister had gone into a meeting but would ring him back. Twenty minutes later the routine was repeated and again the officer was told he was just too late. The DES 'official' said that although the minister did want to speak to him very urgently, he had gone into a meeting with the Prime Minister and it would be two hours before he was able to ring again. Would that be convenient? As Jim pointed out, by that time, everyone in County Hall would have gone home — except 'PR', who presumably is still waiting for the summons of a lifetime. A greater seriousness prevails these days and the social media looks over council shoulders, but it was good while it lasted.

Before the formation of Humberside in 1974, Jim had promised that the best features of the West Riding's extra curriculum policy would be carried forward into the new LEA. He was as good as his word and by the early nineties, Humberside's support for *Sobriety* amounted to £150,000 a year. The real changes came in 1996 with boundary changes that led to the abolition of Humberside and the restoration of an East Riding. Sadly 'Jimbo' as he was affectionately known, died at a comparatively young age and was much missed.

Learning To Manage — The Hard Way

For the most part, the skippers and other staff recruited through the Manpower Services Commission were loyal, eager to promote the Project and popular with the organisations and agencies using the boats.

Alf Acaster and Eric Punter had worked for British Waterways for thirty years on the Yorkshire canals and rivers. They were competent and professional in their relations with visitors and an example to all who worked with them. There was charm in senior skipper Kevin Rokahr's dry humour and with an accident free record over many years, he was the safe pair of hands so vital to *Sobriety*'s future. Linda Thornton ran the office for more than 20 years. Without her delightful personality and attention to detail, the Project could not have moved forward at the speed it did. Ted Pindar was workshop supervisor, a joiner by trade who had the inventiveness of a Greek when it came to solving mechanical problems. Known as 'Ted in the Shed', he kept a small boat for his own use on the river bank in the nearby village of Hook; it was called *Ouzeizit?*

Skippers in the nineteen eighties were used to a rough and tumble relationship with employers and managers. As far as they were concerned I was no different from any other employer. They would present their demands and I would listen, sometimes with scepticism. I always tried to argue on the basis of evidence rather than whim or attitude and to make decisions that seemed fair to both sides. A longstanding bone of contention was the quality of meals. From the point of view of visiting staff, skippers would have to be happy with what was offered; the group programme could occasionally cut across meal times and at those times cooking was not a priority. On the other hand there were occasions when meal preparation had been left completely to chance and everyone ate sandwiches for the week. We thought we had solved the problem by agreeing a framework of overnight allowances to cover meals and other expenses but the arrangement became too expensive and we had to consolidate the payments into salary increases. In the knowledge that *Sobriety*'s rates of pay were lower than those of commercial operators, we did try to increase salaries according to an agreed framework. Staff who lived in Hull found it difficult to cover the cost of their return fares to Goole, so we agreed to subsidise travel expenses for as long as they were working under MSC rules. To the benefit of skippers as well as groups, we maintained the boats to high standards of safety, efficiency and comfort, and by the early 1990s had just about eliminated engine and equipment failure. It was in the Project's interest to manage and train its staff with care, especially since those under the MSC regime, might well be on the way to other work and have only a passing interest in *Sobriety*. We knew that while a boat was away, its skipper who was out of reach of management, had a powerful influence over the people on board, and this did not always accord with the ideas and standards of teachers and social workers. A boatman might be proficient in his own trade but at a loss to understand what lay behind the obligations and protocols of the staff in charge of his passengers. The planning process I have mentioned, but it was necessary to spend more time on philosophy and purpose than was available at those meetings. In this respect people like Jon Fogell, and Roger Coates, Jon's head at Derringham school, were invaluable. They were delighted when arrangements were made for skippers to go and spend a day in their school, observing the methods and disciplines that contributed to good practice and ultimately to more successful expeditions on the barges. Even so, *Sobriety*'s happy band of boatmen contained one or two strange and unpredictable characters.

With a handlebar moustache and cockney accent, Stan Waddilove had been skipper of *Hiddekel*, a barge which carried bank re-inforcement stone up to Rawcliffe on the tidal Aire, a river reckoned to be unnavigable in its lower reaches. He was obsessed with speed and told me proudly that he had been the first person to be prosecuted for exceeding the speed limit on a motor bike on the new Humber Bridge. I had to forbid him to install stainless steel wagon exhausts with fins on each side of *Sobriety*'s wheelhouse. He wanted to give the impression of a barge that could go as fast as a wagon if it was driven hard enough. On a journey back from Leeds he was so concerned with the power under his feet that he did serious damage to a lock and brought back several metres of telephone wire draped round *Sobriety*'s mast which he had forgotten to lower before setting off for Goole. Enough was enough when I found him using a sledge hammer to drive *Eden*'s engine shaft into its stern tube.

Another episode was more reminiscent of the hooliganism visited on Falaraki, the notorious seaside resort on the island of Rhodes. The two boats were travelling together into south Yorkshire, a practice which always made me nervous because two boats together changed the dynamic on board from family to crowd, and the four skippers on duty to becoming their own group rather than part of the 'family'. But I had to acquiesce because the use of *Sobriety* and *Eden* together, allowed a college or school to bring a complement of 24 instead of 12.

Sharing the boats were 20 girls from one of Humberside's colleges, four female staff under the direction of a leader, and four boatmen in separate accommodation. During an evening when everyone was in a Rotherham cinema, the two young *Eden* skippers rifled the girls' luggage for cameras, removed their own trousers and took pictures of one another's backsides. They then returned the cameras to where they had found them. The girls of course, had no knowledge of this until the pictures were developed, printed and handed round their respective families. Not a particularly amusing diversion during Sunday tea! I learned of this mischief from the lecturer in charge of the group. It was a case of gross misconduct and after due process, both men were dismissed. One of them thought he had been dealt with unjustly and reported the events to the *Hull Daily Mail*. The editor telephoned to ask if I had any comment on an article that was to be printed in the evening edition under the headline 'Fun and games on charity barge'. I did my best to explain what had happened and asked him not to print the story. I then spoke to Bob Kernohan, the *Hull Daily Mail* reporter for Goole and he persuaded his colleague that printing the article would have a grave effect on the Project's future.

More serious was an incident that could have resulted in a tragedy of the same proportions as the Lyme Bay disaster in March 1993 which saw four young people die while canoeing with their leaders in bad weather; or the misadventure on the Leeds & Liverpool Canal at Gargrave when three young people with learning difficulties died inside a narrow boat which had filled with water after getting stuck under a lock cill.

Sobriety was coming down the river Ouse from York to Goole with a group of elderly and disabled people from a local authority home in the south of the county. As they approached the village of Cawood where there is a swing bridge, the tide was ebbing, giving the barge a speed of about six miles an hour over the ground. It was a bright and sunny day and the old people were enjoying the last day of their holiday sitting together on a long seat on *Sobriety*'s deck. The Cawood bridgekeeper asked the skipper over the radio if he would like the bridge to be swung.

He had observed that *Sobriety* was coming down river on the first of the ebb and that she would not be able to get under the bridge; the water level would be too high. The skipper however, said he did not think it would be necessary and maintained his speed. It was at this point that Providence intervened. Helping with the old people's holiday was a young man who was coming to the end of his sentence at Hatfield Youth Custody Centre (YCC) near Doncaster. He had been given temporary release by the YCC to take part in the Project's Helper Scheme as part of his preparation for leaving the institution. Because it was getting near lunch time he thought to begin the process of helping the visitors downstairs into the saloon, some by lift and others by the stairs. The last of them was safely below when *Sobriety* did indeed go under the bridge but at such speed and with so little room to spare, that the steel girders of the bridge raked the deck and smashed to pieces everything that stood more than half a metre high, including the wheelhouse and the long seat where the old people had been sitting. It was the worst 'near miss' in the history of *Sobriety*. I knew about it before the barge arrived back in Goole; the York river manager had phoned me. When we asked the skipper why he had not gone along with the bridgemaster's suggestion that the bridge should be swung, he said he did not know. On 11th September 1998 I reported to the Project's safety sub-committee and to the Marine Accident Investigation Bureau (MAIB):

Incident at Cawood Bridge, North Yorkshire :

September 10th 1998

At about 8.00 a.m. on Tuesday 7th September 1998, Sobriety *left Ocean Lock, Goole, for Selby and York, a journey on the Upper Ouse of about six hours. A group of residents and staff from The Willows residential home in Barton-on-Humber had come on board the previous day and were looking forward to their holiday. On Tuesday night, according to plan,* Sobriety *berthed in the Selby Canal. On Wednesday she arrived in York and lay at Marygate Landing. On Thursday she left York, bound for Goole. The tides were big. This indicated a fast ebb and a return to Goole by early evening.*

During the Thursday morning the weather was good and the residents were sitting on deck. All of them were in their eighties or nineties. One of them was blind. As Sobriety *was approaching Cawood Bridge they went below for lunch.*

The duty skipper was in the wheelhouse. He has forty years experience on the Ouse and Trent and has the Maritime & Coastguard Agency's Boatmaster's Licence to navigate vessels down river as far as Grimsby.

As he approached Cawood Bridge, the bridgemaster asked him if he wanted the bridge swung to allow Sobriety *passage. He also said that there was at that time of the tide about 7ft 6in air draft. The skipper said that that would be enough and went ahead. The tide was still in flood and rising. The air draft was not sufficient and* Sobriety's *deck was raked by the bridge.*

The collision immediately deformed the frames of the Velux windows which are made of re-inforced glass. The glass broke and fell into the saloon. The vessel continued under the bridge and the cradle containing the Salter float was then broken. The float itself was also damaged. Sobriety came to rest with the wheelhouse against the bridge. The rest of the vessel was under the bridge and the tide was rising.

The only person on deck at the time was the assistant skipper, Paul Derbyshire, who seeing the certainty of collision went to the saloon hatchway and prevented anyone from coming up the stairs. At the moment of the collision he threw himself down the companion way and avoided injury to himself.

The bridgemaster immediately called North Yorkshire Police who asked the Rescue and Ambulance Services to attend. A group of paramedics came on board and examined the old people. None were injured but two of them were in a state of shock. However all of them later expressed a wish to continue with the holiday. As the tide fell, Sobriety was able to continue on her way to Goole and she arrived at Ocean Lock at about 6.30 p.m. The Willows group remained on board on Thursday night and left the Waterways Museum on Friday morning at about 12 noon.

Staff and Passengers:

There were 12 passengers and 2 crew: Terry Rooke (57), Skipper, Paul Derbyshire (26), Assistant Skipper, Stephen Jelley (20) Volunteer from Hatfield YCC, June Fitzjames + 3 staff, 7 residents (2 in wheelchairs).

Mrs Fitzjames was previously Officer in Charge of Rosecroft residential home in Brigg and has used Sobriety on many occasions in the last fifteen years. Paul Derbyshire possesses the MCA Boatmaster's Licence. Sobriety was carrying a full complement of lifejackets, a Salter float and a self inflating life raft on hire from Cosalt. Her fire extinguishers were inspected January 1998. Her VHF radio was working properly and the vessel had a serviceable anchor.

What went wrong?

The skipper should have known that 7ft 6in was not suffiicient air draft. The highest point of the vessel with the wheelbox lowered is 9ft. The tide was running up and the vessel which was going down river, had good steerage. The skipper has no explanation for why he did not wait for the bridge to be swung.

Recommendations :

Early meeting of Safety Committee to make comments and discuss further action against background of existing Rule Book.
Date to be fixed for emergency exercise…preferably in November
Question of wearing of lifejackets to be reviewed.

Further action:

Letters to Paul Derbyshire and Stephen Jelley thanking them for their quick thinking.
Inform insurers by 'phone.
Ring Mrs Fitzjames and enquire about residents.

The incident remains a mystery. The skipper was an experienced and skilled man who had worked for the Project for five years and had a thorough knowledge of the tideways. One might argue that if the bridgekeeper was so convinced that *Sobriety* would not get under the bridge, he should have swung the bridge anyway, but that is academic. What is not academic is the debt we owed to the young man from Hatfield YCC who unwittingly saved us from catastrophe. He was not accompanying the old people as a 'treat' for good behaviour. He was there because someone believed that the experience would bring out the best in him and set down a marker in his life which he could refer back to and say, *"Yes, I'm proud of having achieved something that never came into my wildest dreams."* It was another echo of City Challenge, another hyacinth in bloom.

They Have Sent Us A Criminal

The person who had faith in Stephen Jelley and many other young offenders like him, was Bob Trafford, principal officer of 'Hatfield Young Offenders' as it was called by prison officers, which had recently changed its name from Youth Custody Centre to Young Offender Institution (YOI). Bob's 'curriculum' ignored the bloodlust of the tabloid newspapers and the philosophy of the 'short sharp shock' which he believed did nothing to keep young people away from crime. Instead he promoted a regime to 'bring out the best from the negative, the unsure and the apprehensive'. His own reward he said, was to hear a seventeen year old say, *"I didn't think I could do that"* or *"People treated me normal"*. After twenty five years of working in prisons he had come to the conclusion that 'we undersell our young people and discount the experiences that can change lives for the good'. Here is Bob describing one of his *Sobriety* volunteers:

Gary, twenty years old, released, now living independently: first court appearance at the age of thirteen: poor home situation: arrived Hatfield serving eighteen months: thirty five previous convictions: his third custodial sentence. After six weeks at Hatfield he absconded and lost thirty eight days remission. During the next few months he was placed on five Governor's reports and lost another fourteen days, fifty two in total. Some months later he was given the chance to work as a social orderly, renovating bicycles and helping at the Sobriety Project. He spent six days on Sobriety barge with two different groups of primary school children.

The teachers' reports vindicate Bob's faith in him:

Gary was a pleasure to have on board with us. He was pleasant and amiable and built up a good relationship with the children. He helped with all the chores without being asked and showed a lot of initiative and responsibility. He was interested in the outdoor activities and discussed these carefully with the children. The second half of the trip Gary continued with his excellent start. He quickly began to relate to the new group who thoroughly enjoyed his company. He used his initiative and acted quickly to avert what could have been a nasty incident with one child. He was keen to offer help where it was needed and was always pleasant and friendly.

Shortly after returning to the YOI, he received notification that his parole had been refused. However some time later he attended a City Challenge course and by this stage there was nothing but purposeful thinking. His efforts earned him restoration of forty two days of remission and he now runs a successful industrial cleaning business in York and employs ex-Hatfield trainees. Three other reports show a remarkable contrast in behaviour. First, his social enquiry report prior to sentence:

> *There can be little doubt from his records that the courts have tried a variety of sentences with no remorse shown for his behaviour.*

Then his pre-discharge report:

Enjoys his work with the disabled. A likeable rogue who I hope does well.

And finally from his supervising probation officer:

> *Gary came out with a very positive attitude and a determination to keep out of trouble. I note in particular, his success on education and his attendance at the* Sobriety *Project. Both gave him back his self respect and his belief in himself. This is the most positive YOI feedback that I have completed for a considerable time.*

There is another effect, this time on staff, as they see beyond the stereotype of the delinquent. Bob Trafford remembers bringing a young man to *Sobriety* in preparation for a trip beginning the same day. Two weeks later he received a 'phone call from a lady apologising for her negative thoughts. She said she had gone to another member of the staff and said, *"They have sent us a criminal."* She ended the 'phone call by asking, *"Can we have another of your boys next year?"*

Bob asks the hard questions. Why do politicians have a tendency to tar all offenders with the same brush and to regard prison as the default answer to every crime from shoplifting to murder? His view is that we categorise far too easily. How can we pre-judge young people simply on the basis of age?

He says give them responsibilities, give them a purpose, give them hope, and when we do, the results are amazing. But society at large thinks differently. It seems to prefer retribution to reform. He invites those who see *Sobriety* and similar projects as a soft option, to try living for a week with ten people who are mentally disordered in the confines of a canal barge. As many of his trainees proved, it is anything but soft.

At a meeting about funding Bob was asked, *"How many successes would you get for £2000?"* He says he could not believe the question. *"How do you price a sense of worth, personal achievement or indeed a simple smile?"* was his reply.

Hatfield is now an open prison for adults as well as young offenders and most of the men coming to *Sobriety* are in their last two years of sentence. Subject to satisfactory risk assessment, they are eligible for extended periods of community work. During their final year in custody they can look for paid work that will be their bridge to release. At this time when they have the opportunity for paid 'outwork' while still serving their sentence, they can be haunted by the indiscriminate stereotyping that destroys pride and hope for the future.

Tabloid Bloodlust

Peter Carter had been a pit deputy in the Yorkshire coalfield with responsibility for the safety of miners. He was serving six years in Hatfield for badly injuring a man he had discovered in bed with his wife. With remission for good behaviour, he had come to *Sobriety* during the last two years of his sentence. His agreeable manner and enthusiasm for hard work soon made him good management material for Doncaster Borough Council's refuse department which he joined after leaving the Project. Rising quickly through the ranks he became a supervisor responsible for work rotas and timekeeping and it was inevitable that he would have to discipline employees who did not comply with the Council's rules. Predictably, one embittered operative discovered that Peter was in prison and reported the fact to the *News of the World* which then named him on its front page and gave advice to its readers that if they lived in Doncaster, they should lock up their children and protect their households from the depredations of this criminal at large. The final outcome was that he was dismissed by the Council, a victim of the gutter press with no means of redress.

What a pity that custody is now the only 'curriculum' that satisfies Tabloid bloodlust. Now that the prison population exceeds 86,000 what a pity England can't follow Scotland by handing down community punishments to offenders who are no danger to society; what a pity that more enlightened politicians and prison staff are continuously having to risk-assess policies in the light of the media interest they may provoke.[1]

Always shy of publicity for obvious reasons, *Sobriety* has tried for the last thirty years, to provide an alternative 'curriculum' for the prisons and young offender institutions in its catchment area.

Under the supervision of Keren Banfield, prison work co-ordinator, a 2006 project called *Bridge to Release* saw eight men a day from HMP Moorland (Open), (now the re-named HMP Hatfield), doing unpaid community work at *Sobriety*'s museum for five or six days a week. During the year there were thirty nine prisoners benefiting from the scheme which allowed them to provide skilled and unskilled services to the community. The list of projects, begun and completed, is impressive:

- Repair and replacement of outfall sewage pipe
- Interior and exterior maintenance of *Opportunity* and *Sobriety*
- Refurbishment of portacabin, and construction of door grille

Hatfield YOI at work.

- Renewal of emergency lighting and other work to bring museum up to new standards
- PAT testing of all electrical equipment
- Design and installation of seating and stanchions to bring the tug *Wheldale* up to passenger carrying standard
- Re-design and refurbishment of workshops for delivery of multi-skill engineering NVQ qualifications
- Building of new gas store in line with regulations
- Maintenance and care of gardens and building
- Management of café
- Minibus driving
- Boat navigation and accreditation to national standards
- General assistance with weekend opening

The work was carried out in line with sentence management and was part of an individual's training and re-settlement plan prior to release. Qualifications gained during the year were recorded as follows:

- Complete Crew Certificate accredited by National Community Boats Association   12
- Certificate in Community Boat Management accredited by National Community Boats Association   4
- VHF (marine) Radio Licence   6
- Basic First Aid   4
- First Aid in the Workplace   3
- Released from prison during the year   2
- Finding paid work after *Bridge to Release*   30

In her end of year report, Keren said that the work requires skill and application and is good preparation for individuals who wish to look for paid work. She felt that opportunities for prisoners coming to the end of sentence and undertaking unpaid community work should be greatly extended. Her report ends with her conclusion that 're-offending can be reduced by allowing prisoners to re-integrate into the community on a resettlement programme designed to give them stability on release'. Nothing new there, but prisons are finding it a harder and harder aspiration to live up to. She asked two of her participants to comment on their time with the Project. The one said:

Being able to leave the prison and attend Sobriety *Project to help and work with a team*

Volunteers from HMP Hatfield replacing a storm drain.

Restoration of Tom Pudding tug *Wheldale*.

gives me a huge lift and a feeling of how good it is to actually achieve something once again. After serving just over two years in closed conditions and then being moved to open conditions was a relief in itself. Being chosen to go out on unpaid community work at the Sobriety *Project has been just the tonic I needed. For me it not only gives me re-integration it also enables me to use my brain again. Without this I am not sure how I could prepare and get ready for work once released. All I can say is prisons need this sort of rehabilitation project.*

The other said:

I am a prisoner serving a sentence of eight years. I was in closed conditions for three years and thought I would never get out. I am now in open conditions and giving back to the community through a charity called 'The Sobriety *Project'. It is only through doing unpaid community work there that I have had a chance to better myself and give back to the community. I am grateful for the opportunities provided and glad to have the chance to re-think my lifestyle prior to release.*

In 2015 the 'hyacinths' in the prison curriculum are wilting. Skills training and education are under threat and some open prisons are imposing more restrictions on opportunities for end-of-sentence rehabilitation schemes. A widespread opinion is that if the NHS or the Education Service were in the same sorry state as the nation's penal institutions,[2] there would be a public outcry. Society at large has always had it in for 'criminals' (in some quarters hanging would still be too good for shoplifters) but recent governments have seemed incapable of carrying through any radical improvements. With appalling lack of political will they pay lip-service to reform but in reality are frightened of causing offence to tabloid editors and the public which buys their papers. In Chapter 11 we shall look at *Sobriety*'s response to the problems of women in prison, but for now we turn to a similarly forgotten group of people who for years have languished in the neglect and humiliation associated with mental illness.

Calm Amid The Storm — The Doctor's Tale

Gus Plaut was a volunteer with a difference.[3] He was in his mid sixties, a Fellow of the Royal College of Surgeons and Fellow of the Society of Medical Writers.

He was also the founding trustee and benefactor of a charitable trust registered in his name and it was through this that the *Sobriety* Project came to his attention. The first time he and I met was in York, one evening when *Sobriety* was visiting the city. He then asked his trustees to give the Project an annual subscription and volunteered himself for work on the boats. He had a soft spot for Hull, having lived there after his parents had fled Nazi Germany, and during the time subsequently, when his father was Professor of Economics at Hull University. Always in favour of giving volunteers a challenge I suggested that he should accompany two groups of people on the barge who would benefit from having a medical practitioner on board. The first would be the men living in the Church Army Hostel on Trippett Street, and the second would be Hull MIND.

After the two trips he wrote an article for *Sobriety's Review of 1986* under the title *Calm amid the storm* and under the pseudonym of 'The Ship's Doctor'.

The People

Peter and Steve, skippers of *Sobriety* who subsequently moved to *Eden*

Susan, a Duke of Edinburgh's Award volunteer

Barry and Don, skippers of *Eden* who subsequently moved to *Sobriety*

Ewan and Liz, leaders of MIND group

Mark, a Duke of Edinburgh's Award volunteer

John, Mike, Shirley, Nick, Deidre, Margaret, Jenny, Ian, Linda and Janet, all MIND members.

April 1986

Thank you for arranging the trip on Sobriety *with our friends from Hull. It was an interesting and enjoyable experience. The last few days were especially pleasant, the weather was ideal, and it was a sheer delight to cruise down the canals and admire the country scenery. The trees were just beginning to bud and the sheep and lambs were frequently seen. Often no house was in sight other than perhaps the lock-keeper's building.*

We did have some problems and both staff and crew have mentioned that they would appreciate a note to you from me. I shall name people by their first names, as we knew each other in this way, like a big happy family.

We left Goole on the Saturday. The original arrangement was for Peter and Steve to be the crew for Sobriety. *Susan and I were the volunteers on this barge.* Eden *was crewed by Barry and Don. Ewan and Liz were leaders and Mark was the volunteer. Rotas were made up for duty by the various people on each boat, so that everyone would take their turn in preparing breakfast, lunch or tea, and also for shopping and for cleaning the boat (although the latter turn was not always strictly adhered to).*

The first meal on Sobriety *consisted of a hamburger, mashed potato and peas. It was not a success. No cooking fat had been supplied and the hamburgers were dry and shrivelled. The mashed potatoes had been prepared from Smash. The green dye of the tinned peas ran all over the plates. Our friends from Hull were hungry enough to eat it all, but Steve was clearly seen to look at the food in absolute disgust, and to empty his plate straight into the waste bin. Sunday lunch was a sausage, mash and a tinned vegetable and not much more interesting. Steve complained to me that he expected better food for a Sunday dinner. Part of the purpose of the trip was of course, to teach our friends to cook and to look after themselves, and so it was almost inevitable that their efforts would be poor at times.*

There were clashes of temperament and Ewan arranged for himself to travel on Sobriety *and for me to move to* Eden. *As you know, Peter found the hassle unbearable and left, but returned the following day. The crews were changed so that Steve, and Don who is a vegetarian, thus adding to the problems for the cooks, were on* Sobriety, *and Peter and Barry were on* Eden. *Peter and Barry were on my last trip to Lincoln with the men from the Church Army Hostel, and worked together happily. The other crew also, as far as I could make out, managed to work together without problems after the re-arrangement.*

Our next problem was John who comes from a small residential home and was very confused. On Saturday night he strayed from the boat and was picked up by the local police. Fortunately he was found by our search party and taken back to the boat. He was on Eden. *Just before midnight on the Sunday we heard the noise of water running in the cabin. It transpired that John had got out of bed to go to the toilet, but had been unable to get out of his sleeping bag and had soaked it. A spare bag was found by Barry and the drenched sleeping bag was put into a black polythene bag and sealed for future cleaning. John was made comfortable, put back into bed and tucked in. I woke in the early hours to the noise of water being sprayed into the cabin. This time John had lost his way to the toilet and passed water onto the cabin floor. It was difficult to see exactly where but we soon mopped it up and put him back to bed. I had the impression that he had stood rather too close to the bunk of Nick but Nick assured me that his bed was dry. The next morning he discovered that his sleeping bag had indeed been wetted by John. On the last day of the trip, Ewan found that his change of clothes which he had left in a drawer on* Eden, *had also been soaked.*

Clearly it was impossible to allow a repeat of incidents of this kind and John remained completely confused. Ewan, after discussion with me, telephoned the residential home in Hedon where John was a resident and arranged for the proprietor of the home to collect him. Ewan tried to explain this to John but he denied the incidents, said that I had been lying and lashed out at me. John then picked up the fire extinguisher and tried either to club Ewan with it or to throw it through the window. Fortunately Mark came to our rescue. Our other friends were cleared out of the cabin and after a short struggle we were able to take the fire extinguisher from John and calm him down. He walked up and down disconsolately for most of the day, at first glaring at me whenever he saw me, but later he seemed to have forgotten all about the incident. He was collected as arranged in the evening.

Mike on Sobriety *had become very depressed on the Monday and Ewan considered that there was a clear risk that he would commit suicide by taking an overdose of the tablets that he had in his case. I went over to* Sobriety *at Ewan's request to assess Mike and I agreed entirely with Ewan that to keep Mike on the boat was unacceptable. Ewan tried to phone a local doctor to arrange for Mike to be admitted to a local mental hospital and was advised to take him to the casualty department at Leeds hospital. He did this and Mike was seen and examined at length. Ewan was advised that urgent admission was certainly necessary, but it was recommended that he should be sent to Broadgate Hospital near Beverley, where Mike had been a patient.*

I therefore took Mike to Beverley by train the following day. I kept a constant eye on him and even accompanied him to the toilet. He was examined by the psychiatric registrar and he arranged his immediate admission to the hospital.

Ewan tried very hard to stimulate the group to take part in activities but it was not easy. In Leeds the group visited the museum and also the local radio station. They went to the cinema one evening. Visits to the local pubs were more popular and some members went every night.

We played a modified version of Trivial Pursuits one afternoon and a card game of Chinese Patience another day. We had a very successful game of cricket in the park at Thorne. I am sorry to say that I was caught out on my very first ball.

On the Wednesday night I was fetched out of bed shortly before midnight because Shirley had tripped on the kerb on the way home from the pub. She complained loudly and bitterly about great pain in her right knee. It was feared that she had broken her leg and that an ambulance should be called to take her to hospital. I examined her and found no evidence of any fracture. I therefore bandaged the knee and gave her some pain killing tablets. She was put to bed and fell asleep shortly afterwards. I am pleased to say that she was walking although with a limp, the next day, and that she took part in the game of cricket the day after that.

On trips of this kind I carry a small supply of emergency medications. There were minor emergencies, including an asthma attack, a sore throat, one or two bruises, some bowel upsets and Nick unfortunately had several epileptic attacks. He always wore a lifejacket on board of course.

Our least pleasant experience was having to clean the small toilet on Eden. Unfortunately one of our friends missed the lavatory pan completely – both ways. I cannot understand how it is anatomically possible to do this in the very confined space of this small room. However for our friends nothing is impossible. I cleaned the room one evening, helped by Barry, but left this unpleasant duty for other helpers on the other two occasions.

You may like my impressions about Mark and Susan as they are both involved in the Duke of Edinburgh's Award. I found them to be likeable youngsters. Mark is in the sixth form at school and about to take A levels. He hopes to go into the RAF and train as a pilot. He seemed a very capable lad and was bright and helpful. It seems a good choice for him, and I wish him success.

Susan is only seventeen. She wants to be a nurse when she leaves school. She seemed to have the right disposition for this. I asked her whether the problems with our friends on the boats had made her change her mind but she assured me that they had not.

Liz the other leader, had previously worked with Ewan at the Centre and she knew many of our friends. She was a great help. She kept the various medications and administered them at the correct times. She helped with washing, tidying hair and of course the many duties involved with looking after everyone.

You may like a few remarks about the other members of our boat.

Deidre unfortunately is markedly mentally handicapped and regularly takes a large number of tablets. She also suffers from asthma.

I found it difficult to understand Margaret, not only because of the way she speaks but also her problems. She has, I believe, three children in care. One of them is in Wakefield and she tried to visit him when we moored in that town. She told me that she went to the house but was not allowed to see him.

Jenny was something of a problem. Her constant inconsequential chatter and need for attention both day and night, was exhausting for us. Fortunately she settled down after the first few days when she was given a sketch book and crayons. She drew simple pictures of a river, her cat, her mother's washing and similar things.

I knew Ian from my previous trip. He enjoyed the holiday. It came as a great surprise to me to see him play cricket with almost professional style. Ian has never been able to work, and has spent twenty five years in hospital. He enjoys the freedom of the hostel where he now lives but it is clearly necessary to keep an eye on his personal hygiene and his finances. We are fortunate that the staff of the Church Army hostel and especially Stewart, the resident care manager, are able to do this.

Linda also seemed to enjoy the trip although she had some respiratory problems. These were not severe.

Janet and her husband Nick were at first affected by the hassle but once this was resolved, enjoyed the trip and were generally helpful, although Nick as mentioned, had several epileptic attacks.

I always enjoy river or canal cruises and the variety of the locks fascinates me. No two seem similar. Mark, Ewan and I helped the crew to work some of the locks. I disgraced myself to one of the lock-keepers when I walked onto a freshly painted white line but the paint came off my shoe long before I returned to the barge. One of the other members sat on a freshly painted part of Eden and for the rest of the trip had thick dark blue horizontal lines on the backs of her thighs.

My most important observation was that patients who are discharged into the community from a mental hospital, sometimes have nowhere to go and have little knowledge about caring for themselves. Some became permanent residents of the Hostel for the Homeless in Hull. The hostel warden was a very caring young man who had previously been unemployed. Ideally he and his team should have been trained in the care of mentally ill people, and the hostel should have been larger and better equipped. But then it would have been a mental hospital! I asked some of our fellow passengers whether they preferred the warmth and comforts of the mental hospital to the cold walls and hard bunks of the hostel. They preferred the hostel. There is an old proverb 'A bird prefers a mere twig to a golden cage'. The answer to the best care of chronically ill mental patients is difficult to find.

I shall send you some photographs of the trip as soon as they are developed, for you to keep. It was a trip I shall never forget, with its difficult and lighter moments. I hope that you will invite me again to join one of your projects.

Dr Plaut died in 2006 at the age of 86. His charity supports the Project with an annual grant.

Coltman Street Centre, Hull

Putting aside the drama of these odysseys, narrated in very Jewish style by an accomplished raconteur, we have to ask the question as to what, apart from an expectation of resilience, were the effects on the people from MIND and from the hostel. I think the answer can come only indirectly from Coltman Street Day Centre, another establishment in Hull, which also catered for men with serious mental health problems.

Phil Teale, its officer in charge in 1987, listed the two aims in his curriculum as firstly, giving a holiday to those of his clients who would never have the opportunity or the money for a holiday of any sort, and secondly, stimulating the same people to develop 'daily living and domestic skills'.

His people were among the poor of the world. There was Peter who was involved in a tragic accident some years previously and ever since had been in a state of depression, sometimes very severe. He lived with his parents in a remote house in the country with no close neighbours and no one of his own age to relate to. Phil said he needed this break away from his parents. As a result of his week on *Sobriety* he was now beginning to get on better with people and was looking for a more independent way of life if he could find accommodation and escape from his isolation.

Cyril who found walking almost impossible, suffered from depression. In spite of his painful feet, he would make the effort and walk considerable distances to remain with the group. He lived in hostel accommodation but maintained contact with his mother who could only get around in a wheelchair. He could be seen any weekend pushing his mother along in her chair despite his sore feet.

Mally had a mental age of somewhere around eight and would always need strong support. He just lived from one trip to the next. Phil said they would no sooner get back than they would hear, *"When are we going on the barge again?"*

Phil went on to say that there were seven other members in the party, all with varying degrees of mental disability including schizophrenia, agoraphobia and depression. The barge holiday was the chance for everyone to socialise and get to know one another better. As a result there would be someone who would now hang back and wait for Cyril, even if it meant missing some football on the telly. Indeed thanks to the efforts of the volunteers, they all enjoyed a disco as they motored up the Ouse to Goole one evening. Phil commented, *"You should have seen Cyril dance when he had some of the stuff other beers cannot reach."*

They were also learning to do the chores. He said, *"We have two watches for the duties that have to be done. One day a team of seven, including staff and volunteer helpers, will be responsible for cooking and cleaning. The washer-up one day will be cooking the next, and on his third day of duty, will be a cleaner, so that everyone will have an equal share of the tasks that have to be performed."* His final verdict:

> *The benefit of this week to the men was immeasurable. Each helped the other as in any normal situation. The week finished as usual with everyone without exception, looking forward to the next expedition in May 1988.*

A Helper Scheme

Three years previously, Harold Heywood, Director of the Royal Jubilee Trusts,[4] came from London to St Thomas's Centre in Old Goole to meet the Project's young volunteers — the likes of Philip, Mark and Susan who featured in Gus Plaut's account of his holiday with Hull MIND.

At this early stage many volunteers were from sixth forms and a few were serving time in young offender institutions (YOIs) or were on probation. Others were in further education or government training schemes. Bob Trafford's Gary from Hatfield YOI would have personal difficulties to overcome while Mark and Susan found the challenge in the group itself. The reason for Mr Heywood's visit was that the Trusts had given £3500 to the Project 'to help young people help others' and he wanted to hear first hand in their own words about the difference the grant had made, not just to the people they had been working with, but to their own lives. More than 200 young volunteers would be involved in this *Helper Scheme* during its first three years from 1984.

The process of volunteer recruitment would begin with an introductory letter from the Project to the head of the youth club or other organisation for young people. After phone calls to discuss possibilities, one of *Sobriety*'s staff would visit the centre and meet the young people asking to take part. The volunteers then had to spend a day prior to the expedition with their host group, getting to know everyone and becoming acquainted with expectations and arrangements. An A4 size booklet enabled them to keep a diary in the form of drawings and photographs which were just as acceptable as a written account. This was to make sure that the confidence of young people who had reading and writing problems was not undermined. The record also contained space for host staff to make a brief report on a volunteer's achievements.

The benefits to young offenders from Everthorpe Young Offender Institution (now HMP Humber), as well as those from Hatfield, were real and consistent, above all a spur to confidence and obligation that would help them 'on the outside'. But as ever, the success of the placements depended on the staff of the institution taking the trouble to select individuals who would make observable progress. These staff members were usually in a position where they needed to avoid publicity and not risk a turn of events that could harm their own establishment or *Sobriety*. (In the last chapter, we saw in the story of Peter Carter how easily that could happen). The result was that in spite of royal interest through the Jubilee Trusts and later through the Prince's Trust, *Sobriety*'s Helper Scheme never achieved the critical mass to challenge the tabloid newspapers and pressurise the politicians into a change of policy. It remained too much of a well guarded secret. Occasionally, however, the cover was blown. In the mid nineteen nineties the Project was operating a sea going sailing barge, *Audrey*, more of which in the following chapters. Michael

Howard was Home Secretary and John Clarke, a no-nonsense Scotsman, was governor of Hatfield YOI. In Hull, a group of hearing impaired (deaf) children and their teachers, led by head of unit John Parker, were preparing to spend two weeks aboard *Audrey*, sailing on the Ijsselmeer in Holland. They would go to Rotterdam by North Sea Ferry from Hull, take the train to Amsterdam and join *Audrey* at the lock where the North Holland Canal joins the Ij (pronounced 'eye') river. It was an opportunity for two well tried and experienced volunteers to be provided by the YOI. The two weeks were a great success and on his return, John Parker wrote a report on the outstanding contribution made by the two young men and sent copies to the Home Office, congratulating the Prison Service on having such far sighted policies to make the venture possible. Within hours of receiving John Parker's letter, the Home Secretary was on the phone to the governor, asking why two felons serving sentences in one of Her Majesty's penal institutions had been allowed to go abroad. John Clarke beat off the attack by pointing out that *Audrey* was a British ship, that the placement had done nothing but good and that the Home Secretary was of course at liberty to make of him a public example if he so wished. He heard nothing more and retired with dignity at the appropriate time with his pension intact. Like the teacher we met earlier who could not understand the boy's poem about his dead father, the politician seemed only able to recite the rules protecting his position. The expedition was a very small cuckoo in the penal curriculum but John Clarke made the best use of it and in the following year sent three more of his 'inmates' to Holland to work again for a week with John Parker's deaf children, and for a second week with a group of old people with dementia from Beverley.

From the mid-nineteen-eighties there were boundless opportunities for volunteers, made possible by the range and number of agencies using the boats for residential expeditions. *Sobriety* and *Eden* were fully booked through the year and most groups were living on board

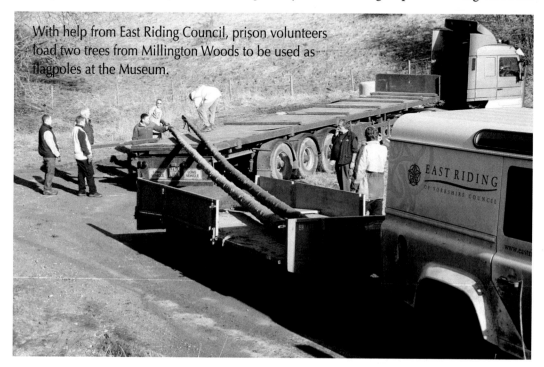

With help from East Riding Council, prison volunteers load two trees from Millington Woods to be used as flagpoles at the Museum.

for five days, sometimes for as long as a fortnight. Christmas was the only break. But this level of booking did not happen by magic; it was the result of persuasive marketing and unwavering attention to the aims and objectives of participating organisations, some of which returned to the Project year after year. Taken from the *Sobriety* Project Review of 1988, the year before *Audrey* came into operation, an analysis of the boat schedule shows 69 groups using the Project for five days or more, a five percent increase on the previous year. Almost all of them came from Humberside which in 1996, was replaced by the current local authority areas of Hull, East Yorkshire, North Lincolnshire, and North East Lincolnshire. Other groups came from Kirklees, Sheffield, Doncaster and on two occasions from Newcastle-on-Tyne. Beneficiaries were invariably on low incomes and showed evidence of dependency. The list from 1988 below, is comprehensive, but the mix is somewhat *ad hoc* and different terminologies may be in use today. The figures denote passenger days – that is the number of people in the group multiplied by the number of days of stay:

- People in rehabilitation from drug or alcohol dependency, ex-offenders and homeless people   1068
- Members of single parent families   60
- Adults with mental health problems attending day centres or living in residential establishments   240
- Children with additional learning needs from schools, units and foster homes 648
- Children from primary and secondary schools   276
- People with additional learning needs from training centres, colleges of further education, hostels and community support units   696
- Young people from youth groups, centres, young offender institutions and playschemes   1392
- Disabled people attending day centres   228
- Old people living at home   528
- Residents of homes for the elderly   588
- Linked groups (five clients and five young people)   228

The number of passenger days in this year was 5952, a high point for residentials and the last of the years when the Project was operating two boats from a potato shed on Goole Docks. In 1989, the centre of operations became the new Waterways Adventure Centre on Dutch River Side in Old Goole. The figure was exceeded in the following years but only because until the mid nineties, the Project was operating three residential boats and a day boat based on the new HQ. Most groups were delighted to host volunteers. They made them welcome and encouraged them to earn their keep. From young people's accounts, it appears that the most challenging groups brought the most resolute response. Here were shades again of Jim Hogan's pot boy and of the City Challenge students working with families on the Buttershaw estate in Bradford.

"You shouldn't judge people by first impressions," concluded 18 year old Velma Kazer. Velma was a volunteer working with children from Fountain House, a pupil referral unit (PRU) in Hull, for young people with behavioural problems who could not be taught in mainstream school. Arriving on *Audrey*, she was startled to find the party had been reduced by two; one of the pupils

had 'done a runner' and the other had been locked up by the police for stealing bikes. Her story continues:

After berthing that evening in King George Dock and an attempt to trade me for a couple of crates of vodka with the crew of a Russian ship, we went to Paull for some fish and chips... On Wednesday we headed for Hull and swapped the four boys for four more boys and three girls.

She says that at this point all her fears re-appeared. The three thirteen year old girls were wearing more make-up than she'd ever worn and were swearing continuously. They called her a 'snob' and kept everyone awake, talking until 4.00 in the morning. At South Ferriby they were fascinated by a body being taken out of the water and tried to persuade the police to give them a closer look. However Velma persevered and had some success in trying to show them she was normal. By the end of the week she felt she had a greater understanding of such children and says she 'would not have believed that three days away from school and home could effect such a change on their attitudes especially towards outsiders. The experience had opened her eyes and perhaps made the children slightly more thoughtful. Velma was at university and already possessed plenty of self confidence. In prisons and young offender institutions however, low self esteem is commonplace, so in 1992 it was decided that, notwithstanding the benefits to young people in full time education, men and women from YOIs should be given priority of access to the volunteer scheme. Staff reports on the young people speak for themselves and are a riposte to popular demands for the re-instatement of flogging and transportation.

From the staff of Derringham School, Hull:

Both members of staff found Jason to be very helpful, polite and friendly on the trip. He worked extremely hard from early in the morning to last thing at night. He used his initiative in dealing with all kinds of situations and accepted us as a group for what we were. He was very patient and tolerant and befriended the children. He continued the second half of the week as he began, and we found him to be absolutely brilliant in all situations. He was very understanding and patient with the second all girl group and showed a maturity beyond his years. Our thanks to him for his help. We would like him as a member of our crew any time.

And from Brighowgate Salvation Army Men's Hostel in Grimsby, the staff wrote:

I would like to say that Mark is the most hard working, well mannered and loyal member of the group we have ever had on any of our trips with the Project. I cannot help feeling that he displays qualities that are well beyond his years, He has been very sensitive to the needs of the men and on many occasions has gone the extra mile to encourage them. He has also taken time to listen as well as talk to them. I know that this has been appreciated by all concerned.

These commendations are just two of many. Why on earth had these young men been sent to prison? When it costs more than £40,000 a year to keep an individual in custody, why cannot successive governments invest in developing schemes that are cheaper and more likely to reduce re-offending?[5] Why does the legislature seem to lack the political courage to devise sentences that are more discriminating? Why does incarceration apparently remain the default disposal? Here is Bob Trafford, Hatfield's principal officer, once again observing that 'the effect the involvement has had on our trainees is greater than the service we offer. In the majority of cases it is the first time lads have become involved in any kind of charity work and they are pleasantly surprised to find they can give without receiving a financial reward'. What a waste of inherent talent when young people are confined, bored silly, to the regime of a penal institution instead of being 'sentenced' to a form of community service that will commend them to employers and help them become good citizens.

Bartholomew House, Goole, was a short stay hostel managed by the Community Psychiatric Service of the Scunthorpe Health Authority. Like the members of Hull MIND, its residents suffered acute symptoms of mental disorder. In early September 1992 a young woman from Askham Grange, a re-settlement prison near York, spent a week with them on *Sobriety*. Bartholomew House staff said about her:

Karen has tried very hard during this week and has made efforts to get to know everyone on the barge. She has built good relationships with a couple of people in particular. The age range of clients on this holiday is from 12 to 92 years and Karen has proved able to adapt to their various needs. She has carried out willingly any activities asked of her, and has used her initiative where required. During the week we have found her trustworthy, reliable and flexible.

The staff of Parkside School, Newcastle-on-Tyne which educates profoundly disabled children, also gave their views about another woman from Askham Grange:

Tonia was a valuable member of our team. She worked hard, doing everything she was asked to do. Once she had worked out the routines and individual needs of the children, she was carrying out many tasks without having to be directed. She was very good at seeing what jobs needed doing and had no difficulty in getting on with staff or children. She was kind and considerate and aware of the need to preserve the children's dignity, coping extremely well with a very difficult group of children and a close-knit group of staff. We have all thoroughly enjoyed working with Tonia and will do our best to keep in touch.

One who escaped prison by the skin of his teeth was a young man whose history contributes to the case studies in the Inland Waterways Advisory Council's (IWAC) 2009 report, *Using the inland waterways to combat the effects of social exclusion:*[6]

This man's formal education was not a success. In his early teens his aggressive behaviour led to exclusion from mainstream school, statementing and attendance at pupil referral unit. He then acquired a police record for stealing, fighting, drinking and drug taking and arrived in 'the last chance saloon' of the Youth Inclusion Programme run by the local authority's Youth Offending Team (YOT). He was referred to Sobriety for 'diversionary activities' and soon showed that although he wasn't a team player he did want to be a leader.

The programme supported by the Youth Justice Board and agreed by the inter-agency panel of Connexions (formerly the Careers Service), Humberside Police, YOT and school staff, was that each week, Callum should do boat related activities for three days, literacy and numeracy for one day and personal skills including cookery for one day.

Suddenly in the course of a four day residential on Sobriety, he organised and cooked an evening meal for twelve people. The skipper who hitherto had regarded him as a yob, was amazed. The event signified the boy had changed.

In 2006 he enrolled full time with Hull College and in 2007 was voted Student of the Year. His reading and writing has improved, he is now earning money at a pickle factory in Selby but realising the journey he has travelled, is keen not to leave it at that. He wants to train to be a firefighter.

One wonders whether the outcome would have been the same if he had been sent to YOI or prison.

The next stage in the development of the Helper Scheme was to take another leaf out of City Challenge and make the placements more demanding. The suggestion was that a group of young people from a mainstream school, YOI or youth training scheme would take responsibility for organising a week's holiday for one of the groups using the boats. Once again Hatfield showed the way. During the period of its connection with *Sobriety*, the YOI had developed links with Thorne House, a local residential home for people with autism. In 1988 and 1989 the YOI organised two weeks of holidays on the boats for four young people from the home — Stephen, John, Jackie and Lisa. Helpers were Chris, Alan and Gilly from Hatfield and overseeing the venture was Neil McCunnell, a prison officer, and Colin and Tracy, staff at Thorne House. *Audrey*'s crew was Mark Peacock and Colin Walden. A charming account of a day sailing the Humber was written by Chris, one of the young men from Hatfield:

We were all up this morning at 7 o'clock and after breakfast we got ready to set off from Albert Dock on the 8.50 tide. When we were clear of the dock the engine was turned off and we put up the sails. At least we tried, but didn't do too well, so Mark the skipper called us into a group and explained how to put them up properly. It was hard enough trying to get it right ourselves but when we tried to show our friends from Thorne House, that was one experience I wouldn't have missed for the world. It took us able bodied lads about twenty minutes to get them up but when we showed the others, they had a go and yep, it only took them ten minutes. That just goes to show that disabled people are as good if not better than all us able bodied people.

After the sails were up John took the helm with a little help from Gilly, but after an hour the wind dropped and we started to drift the wrong way down the Humber. We turned the engine on and motored into King George Dock. Once we were in the dock, Jackie and I went down into the galley and started the dinner. If I remember correctly we had shepherd's pie, carrots, peas and Angel Delight to finish, and even if I do say so myself, it was extremely nice and I think everybody enjoyed it.

Combined Urban Challenge

In an attempt to keep the City Challenge flag flying, the Project hosted two full blown Urban Combined Challenge courses in the autumn 1991 and 1992, based at its new Waterways Adventure Centre (later to be re-named the Yorkshire Waterways Museum).

Twenty four students from all parts of the UK, were recruited by the Outward Bound Trust and the courses, staffed jointly by the Trust and *Sobriety*, were sponsored by Yorkshire Electricity. The programme was a departure from the format of the nineteen seventies and eighties and something of a return to the original Leeds courses of the late nineteen sixties which had included outdoor activities. At that time, the general opinion among students was that climbing, abseiling and the like, which City Challenge had inherited from its parent body, detracted from the real business of working among destitute and needy people in the inner city. As a result the outdoor activities were discontinued. The three components of the 1991 course however, were rock climbing and sleeping in rough shelters for two days on the North York Moors, a canal expedition to Rotherham involving people with chronic disabilities and thirdly, placements with local families and in hospitals including Rawcliffe Hall. When in Goole, students slept on *Sobriety* and *Eden,* and used *Spider,* a barge borrowed from South Yorkshire Police, as a dining room and common room.[7]

For Jackie Needham, a nurse at Goole & District Hospital, the challenge was unusual and a surprise. Unlike other members of the course, she did not have much in the way of outdoor skills but she did know how to care for people with severe mental health issues. Here, she reflects on the physical challenges of the 1991 course:

The next couple of days were occupied with physical challenges such as orienteering, rock climbing and abseiling. Rock climbing was the biggest challenge I came across throughout the course. After setting up the equipment it looked reasonably easy but I found it very difficult. My first couple of attempts were disastrous but I was determined to climb the rock face before the day was through. Eventually and with a lot of support from the rest of the group, I made it. The next challenge was to get down. The thought of abseiling was even worse than climbing up. After my legs had stopped shaking, I managed the journey down. At the end of the day I felt a great sense of achievement. I could see the funny side of my ordeal.

She then goes on to describe preparations for the barge expedition which would include twelve residents of local hospitals and adds, *"I felt that because the rest of the group had supported me the previous week, and had helped me through my challenges, so now it was my turn to offer support to them."* And from what she says, they would need it:

Many of our guests were quite dependent and needed assistance with ordinary activities such as eating and washing, dressing and going to the toilet. This came as a shock to some of the group and they thought they would be unable to help with these tasks. Very quickly everyone seemed to find themselves a job such as washing the dishes in order to get out of helping with our guests. As the weekend went on, the group was encouraged to help

Telethon Louise cruises Railway Dock Goole.

with the tasks they felt so unsure about. Eventually everyone was helping and in many cases without realising they were doing so.

Tracey Martin, a student on the previous year's course felt very anxious and frightened because she had never dealt with any kind of disability before. The four guests delegated to her barge team were Minnie, Tom, Richard and Syd and were suffering from dementia. They came from Goole Mental Health Day Hospital which provided a five day service of respite care for the relatives and friends who were caring for them. Minnie and Tom could walk and were continent, but Richard and Syd were in wheelchairs and being incontinent, needed twenty four hour care. Tracey says that a twenty four hour timetable was set up by the group. This meant getting up at 4.00am to carry out a four hour shift one night, and getting up at 12.30am the next. On top of the day's activities it was exhausting. She recalled that as she came to her last shift on Saturday night, one of the group left a message which kept her going:

Dear Rota Group,

Sobriety *barge 11.30pm 27th October 1990*

Look I know it's been a rough night but what I was thinking was that despite everything we are still a good reliable team who respect each other and get on perfectly. Bear this in mind whatever happens. This team includes Phil, Angie, Tim, Sarah, Tracey, Alan, Anthony, and Terry and Kevin the crew, plus our welcome guests, Minnie, Tom, Syd and Richard.

Her verdict on a course which had tested her personal resources to the limit, was plain and straightforward, *"I just wish everyone could have seen what I saw: the gentle old men and ladies needing constant care and love."*

Earlier in 1990, a thirteen year old girl, Louise Conlon, was coming with her father on occasional visits to *Sobriety*. During one of these visits she wrote a poem about her dad who at the age of forty was suffering from Alzheimer's Disease.

Castaway

The lost mind in its prison
A solitary confinement
Propped between his mind and his body.
He opens his eyes
And lets the thoughts and his world enter
Until despair drives them away.

Eating food from a world of his own,
Drinking water from a cup of his own
Which his head filled with bitterness
In the sky where he looks
Sleeping at night with a dream of his own
But nobody cares.

Like the days when he came early,
Like the nights when he sat down
And 'Castaway' they called 'Hey, Castaway!'
And mocking voices from the other world
He ran when he saw them clearly,
Or out of sound
Past the lake and past the shops,
Laughing when he looked at them strangely
They gazed in mockery.
But in his imaginary world
He dodges the danger of his thoughts
With the dreams in his head.

As we have seen, it was with such people that the students of the courses based at *Sobriety*'s new Waterways Adventure Centre were working. They spent their time trying to communicate with their guests, breaking open the prisons and breaking down the barriers. They came from many different social backgrounds and while some had great ambitions, others had none. What they discovered was that the common purpose of being responsible for their disabled guests, did break down the barriers that would normally have existed between them.

In a final farewell to Outward Bound City Challenge and to the Combined Challenge courses organised by *Sobriety* in the early nineties, some of the students interviewed by a local newspaper can have the last word:

Andy, a 23 year old telecommunications engineer, admits to having been worried about working with disabled people and men from prison. But the course has opened his eyes. His fears, he now realises, were unfounded.

Omar who works in Hull with the unemployed, says the course has made him more aware of himself and he feels a better person for it. The group discussions were especially important. "If any issues cropped up that caused any bad feeling, there was group support. It is a team experience," he explains.

"It's very unlikely I'll offend again because I've realised I've got something. I'm not a down and out", says Tony, soon to leave Everthorpe. "The course has rehabilitated me. I feel I've got a lot to offer".

Chris from Hatfield YOI, also feels a changed man."It's going to help us when we get out. I can prove to myself I can do something with my life. It's self confidence".

The interviewer summed it up:

Not everything the students have learned about themselves has been pleasant. There has also been hard work and on occasions friction, resentment and disagreement. But all that is part of the experience. In a world where pain and unhappiness is too often based on intransigence, the students' new found awareness of themselves and other people becomes all the more worthy.

Questions

Some organisations 'suffer' volunteers because they provide free labour. Others are entirely voluntary and have no paid staff. What is your experience of volunteers? Does volunteering have a place in the broader curriculum of prisons and young offender institutions. Could volunteering be a more widespread alternative to custody?

There is no doubt that the so called red top newpapers occasionally overstep the mark, as in the case of Peter Carter who went to work for Doncaster Council as a serving prisoner on 'outwork'. Did the Council act fairly in dismissing Peter? Could he or the prison have had any redress against the newspaper concerned?

What are Bob Trafford's suggestions for a young offenders' curriculum? Do you agree with him?

Do local authorities and government have a duty more systematically to provide facilities and activities for people suffering from mental illness like the men attending Coltman Street Centre or the people on Gus Plaut's canal expedition?

Chapter 6 Notes

1   A recent report aired on BBC Look North put the re-offending rate of people released from Hull Prison at 70%. See also *Hull Daily Mail*, August 13th 2014:

Figures released by the Ministry of Justice show around 30 per cent of all offenders in the city – including those given suspended sentences and community orders – return to a life of crime within a year. Twelve per cent of criminals are re-offending within just three months.

Today, the Ministry of Justice vowed to tackle the 'unacceptable problem' after describing re-offending rates in Hull as 'staggering'.

Justice Minister Andrew Selous said: 'Currently, offenders sentenced to less than 12 months in prison get no statutory support upon release and have the highest re-offending rates'.

Read more at: http://www.hulldailymail.co.uk/Staggering-number-Hull-criminals-offending-year/story-22711854detail/story.html#hBIHxwLgbJekX91G.99

2   In 2001 the *Guardian* ran *Behind Bars* a week long series of G2 articles on the English penal system. Occasional details may be out of date but it remains an excellent layman's guide to prisons, community and the press: 29th January–2nd February 2001.

More recent is *A conveyor belt to hell* written by a former inmate of HMP Manchester (*Guardian* February 8th 2014) which looks at the reasons for death in custody of young prisoners.

A third item worth attention is Youth Justice Timeline on the website *Beyond Youth Custody* by Dr Tim Bateman and Professor Neal Hazel. They say :

This timeline sets out a brief history of youth justice in England and Wales from the first attempts to separate young offenders from adults in the criminal justice system a little over 220 years ago. Although not intentionally focused on custodial provision, many of the significant events concern attempts to reform, replace or divert children from various types of institution. The recognition of the need for resettlement support after custody is also a recurring theme – from the embryonic youth justice system to the present day.

www.beyondyouthcustody.net

3   From Parr's *Lives of the Fellows of the Royal College of Surgeons: Gustav Siegmund 'Gus' Plaut was a consultant surgeon at Tooting, London. He was born on 2 September 1921 to Ellen Warburg and Theodor Plaut in Hamburg, both from eminent Jewish banking families. His father was dismissed by the Nazis and took the post of Professor of Economics at Hull University where Gus was educated at Hymers College. He went up to Gonville and Caius College, Cambridge in 1940 where he obtained a double first in natural sciences, and went on to win the Price entrance scholarship to the London Hospital. He qualified with the Andrew Clarke prize in clinical medicine, and after junior posts, did his National Service in Freetown, Sierra Leone. Following demobilisation he went on to do junior surgical jobs at Addenbrooke's, London Hospital, Chase Farm and the Gordon Hospital in London, from which he passed the Edinburgh and English fellowships and then did a series of locum posts, including one in the Anglo-Ecuadorian oil fields. He had great difficulty in finding a regular consultant post, eventually being appointed at Tooting in 1960. A most entertaining and agreeable companion, Gus was a keen Territorial and spent much of his energy in charitable work, with Rotary and the Soldiers, Sailors, Airmen and Families' Association. He was a keen sailor and swimmer. Always very modest, he concealed his intellect and his wealth with great urbanity. He married Ivy in 1977, who predeceased him in 1999. He died on 17 January 2006.*

4   In 1985 these were The Prince's Trust, The Queen's Silver Jubilee Trust and the King George V Jubilee Trust.

5   On August 13th 2014 the *Guardian* and other newspapers drew attention to a privately run prison in which 'Prison inmates were held without electricity or running water for two days.' The same day saw the publication of 'a troubling report from the prison and probation ombudsman into self-inflicted deaths among young adult inmates, which found suicide risk assessments and monitoring arrangements were poor in too many cases'.

6   The report was commissioned by the Department for Environment Food and Rural Affairs (Defra) but is generally critical of Government's failure to recognise and invest in the inland waterways as a resource to restore the social and economic equilibrium of disadvantaged individuals and communities. The report is available on the Defra website. Look for the abbreviation, IWAC or use/paste the link: http://www.bcu.org.uk/files/IWAC_Using_Inland_Waterways_to_Combat_the_Effects_of_Social_Exclusion_Apr09.pdf

There is an inference also that British Waterways (now the Canal & Rivers Trust) is too preoccupied with its own survival to be a likely agency for progress in this regard.

7. The decision to include outdoor activities was right. The course was of only two weeks duration and it was necessary to speed up the sense of interdependence that characterised City Challenge. This was best done by a programme that took students into challenging situations from day one, and it appeared to work.

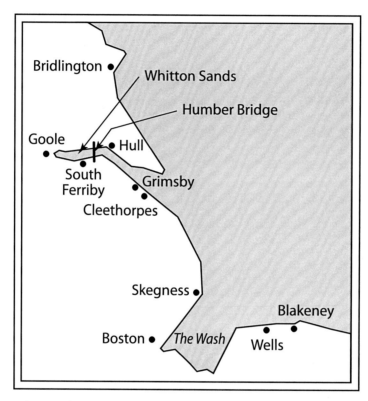

The Humber and east coast was *Audrey*'s usual cruising area.

Chapter 7

THE SAILING BARGE *AUDREY*

We Buy A Lightship

John Hainsworth was head of VI form and head of the German language department of Wolfreton School. Located on the western outskirts of Hull, Wolfreton was a 12 form entry comprehensive school, one of the biggest in the UK, with 400 post 16 students studying for A-level GCE and other qualifications. For several years John made good use of *Sobriety*'s Helper Scheme which he used as a way of removing the social blinkers from his students who came largely from the leafy suburbs. Though many had no first hand knowledge of the poverty which afflicted Hull's council estates, they possessed the energy and imagination to become first class volunteers. They learned quickly, wrote good reports and had noticeably more to contribute to school and classroom when they returned from their placements on the barges.

John was also secretary of the Humber Keel & Sloop Preservation Society (HKSPS), an organisation devoted to sailing the survivors of the keels and sloops that until the nineteen fifties were the principal trading vessels on the Humber and its tributaries.[1] Foremost among the Society's ships were *Comrade*, a square rigged sailing barge which had its home in Beverley Beck, and the sloop *Amy Howson* which was berthed on the other side of the Humber at South Ferriby. Both ships had been rescued from the breaker's yard and brought back to sail by volunteers. The Society was not only preserving the remnants of history, it was introducing its volunteers to the mystique of the river and the skills held dear by mariners working the coasts of Britain and Europe since mesolithic times.

For the *Sobriety* Project, the appeal of a sailing ship was overwhelming, and justified at a practical level by the argument that *Sobriety* and *Eden* were fully booked throughout the year and another boat was needed. But there was also a missing dimension to the Project's work, and John Hainsworth and his

Audrey under sail on the Humber.

139

Audrey in dry dock at Goole.

colleagues would help make it good. From 1910 until 1939 when her engine was installed, *Sobriety* had been a square rigged sailing barge like *Comrade*. Now she would be re-rigged and, with the help of the Society, recall a legacy of the Humber and east coast currently denied to the Project.

The challenge of *Sobriety* and *Eden* was for individuals to live and work together and wherever possible to participate in activities *en route*. But what the two motor barges could not offer, was involvement in navigation. On leisure canals, young people could steer a boat, open and close locks, tie up when and where they wished and generally be responsible for making a success of their expedition. By contrast, responsibility for navigating an iron barge of 45 tons deadweight, had to rest with professionals who understood the unruly nature of the Yorkshire waterways and knew how to manoeuvre craft in confined spaces. And as we have seen, even they could make mistakes.

Sobriety in sail on the Humber would create the opportunities absent from the Project's menu of activities. It would reduce dependence on shore-based recreation and under the direction of the skipper, allow 'crew' to manage the sails, work with the weather and tides and experience the bleakness of the estuary. As a new and different world, it would be a taste of the sea.

But alas, it was not to be. Associated British Ports routinely made available one of its dry docks and *Sobriety* was given a close inspection by Colin Screeton, *Comrade's* sailing master, accompanied by the Project's appointed surveyor, Nigel Ling. Reluctantly they concluded that too many structural changes would have to be made to the hull and accommodation, the cost of conversion would be huge, the work would be impossible without specialist contractors, and perhaps most discouragingly, the barge would be out of action for at least a year. A more sceptical view was that we were afflicted by madness, and that the 15th century remedy of boring a hole in our skulls might relieve the insanity. But the illness was too advanced and the only cure would be to find another way of 'taking to the ships'.

Colin Screeton admitted to having dreamed of a third sailing barge for his Society, the third 'Toby Jug' as he called it. He explained that while the likes of *Comrade* and *Amy Howson* were keels and sloops designed for inshore trading, there was a third kind of Humber barge known as a 'billyboy' that with a ketch rig, high bulwarks, and leeboards, could leave the Humber and sail to east coast ports as far south as London. To Colin's knowledge there were two of these vessels still in existence; one was *Brilliant Star* which had belonged to the Eastwood family of barge owners since 1905 and was berthed on the river Ouse at Selby. The other was *Saira*, built for the Barracloughs, another famous barge owning family in Hull, and lying at Thorne's Lane wharf in Wakefield, not far from what is now the Hepworth Gallery.

With the owner Selwyn Eastwood's permission, I was able to get aboard *Brilliant Star*. She was not in good condition and her lines had been ruined in later life by being lengthened. *Saira* on the other hand, had elegant lines and appeared to be in reasonable repair. Associated British Ports once again did the dry docking and it was now *Saira* that was made ready for inspection. The verdict was the same as for *Sobriety* and worse. She turned out to be what is cruelly known in the trade as a 'rust bucket'. We were lucky she had made the journey to Goole without sinking. The outcome of *Saira's* inspection was a big disappointment. Long and graceful, she was a genuine billyboy built in Hull in 1899 for coastal trade, and would have been proud under sail, a splendid advertisement for the maritime history of Yorkshire and Lincolnshire. Perhaps we missed an opportunity. Within weeks she was purchased by a group of young people and taken under her own power to Cornwall. A year or two later however, we heard she was lying derelict on a west country beach. No doubt she could have been brought back to Goole but only at great cost, and in spite of her attraction it was sensible to let her rest in peace.[2]

As 'snoops for a sloop' we were hanging on to Colin Screeton's coat tails, but it was a process which highlighted the shared interest of the two organisations and would have important practical benefits for *Sobriety* once we had found a third vessel. And indeed another possibility was to hand. Listeners to the BBC's *Round Britain Quiz* scratch their heads looking for connections between people and events that appear to have nothing in common. So it was that in our search for a sailing ship we found an unlikely link between a fish and chip shop proprietor on Hull's Preston Road, a seventy year old derelict lightship at Beverley, and a refugee from Nazi Germany who had led a commando unit in the British Army.

The 'chippie' proprietor was John Dean, who was also a Hull lighterman and managing director of Dean's Tugs & Workboats; the lightship at Beverley was in retirement from marking the sandbanks in the upper Humber; and the wartime commando was Alan Marshall, chair of the *Sobriety* Project committee and managing director of Huttons of Hull, a UK company providing stores and equipment to ships all over the world.

This unlikely association was the outcome of Colin Screeton's solution to the puzzle of where to find a billyboy. *"Lying in the river Hull, just outside the lock into Beverley Beck,"* he said, *"there's an old lightship. She belonged to the Humber Conservancy and has been well looked after. With a few alterations, like removing her light tower, she would make a handsome sailing ship. Her bulwarks would make her ideal for the lower estuary and her flat bottom would sit her nicely once again on the Humber sands. If you can raise the funds, the Society will help with technical advice and, albeit as a replica, we shall have our billyboy."*

A survey by Broderick, Wright and Strong in Hull, assured *Sobriety's* committee that she was built like a battleship and in good condition. John Dean was the lightship's owner and asked for £4000 for her as seen. Alan Marshall paid the bill. In the Project's *Review of 1986* I wrote:

In June this year we heard it might be possible to acquire one of the former Whitton lightships. (At low tide, Whitton Sands form a barrier to ships wishing to navigate the Trent or the Ouse from the east, and the Humber from the west). The archives of Associated British Ports record that Humber Conservancy Light Vessel No.10 *was built by Thomas*

Watson of Gainsborough in 1915 and that her first assignment was the Middle Whitton station. Her lantern was illuminated by burning paraffin and she had a crew of four. After being moved to Upper Whitton she was retired about seven years ago.

On *Sobriety*'s visits to the Humber during the nineteen seventies, this lightship was a familiar sight to passengers who would attract a friendly wave from her crew. After going into more detail about the suitability of the vessel's accommodation for groups of young people, I noted in the *Review* that the Project had received approval from the Manpower Services Commission (MSC) for a Community Programme team to undertake the conversion. Work would begin in late January 1987 and be completed by the November. David Robinson, assistant sailing master of *Amy Howson*, would be the supervisor. In an article in the same journal, David got quite excited:

Properly rigged and with an auxiliary engine, Audrey, *as she has been christened,[3] will make a marvellous ship to take sailing. Crewed by competent and enthusiastic sailors, Audrey could exploit and encourage the potential of many groups. Inherently safe with bulkheads, ample freeboard and generous bulwarks, she has on station as a lightship, endured more than half a century of the worst the Humber could give her. As a free sailing ship she is more than capable of being the vessel to thrill and enthuse her human cargo and race through the waves as they once charged by her.*

Early in 1986, *Audrey* was towed by the river barge Jolly Miner from Hull's Old Harbour up the Humber and Ouse to Goole where she was welcomed by the *Sobriety* committee, staff and the local press. Her berth was to be on the east side of Aldam Dock next to the dredger Goole Bight, just outside 35 Shed. The shed, which was occasionally used to store potatoes, would become the workshop for the project. One of *Sobriety*'s staff, Ted-in-the-Shed Pindar, as he became affectionately known, would supervise the workshop, David Robinson would be in charge of work aboard the vessel and he would be assisted by Norman Garner, a local joiner who was out of work. Helping informally with advice about masts and rigging would be Cyril Harrison, sailing master of *Amy Howson* and David's father-in-law. With generous financial help from the MSC, thirteen people, mainly from Old Goole, who had been unemployed for at least three months, would be recruited to learn some of the skills of shipbuilding and to get the ship ready for her future life of cruising the Ouse and Humber between Goole and Cleethorpes.

Not Cleethorpes Again!

Middle Whitton No.10 may have been happy bouncing around in the Humber for seventy years but there were problems to be solved before she could begin her new life. Born-again *Audrey* would face some tough preliminaries to conversion. Her accommodation and deck was beyond repair. The steelwork was good but the timber was rotten and would require nothing less than complete replacement. The layout of her living area would need to be changed to accommodate boys and girls as well as visiting staff and her crew. As a lightship she had no means of propulsion; two anchors had kept her on station when the tide was in; her flat bottom and bilge keels[4] had made life safe and comfortable for her crew when the tide was out. But dry docking or relocation had required the services of a Humber Conservancy towing vessel. In her new life she would need not only masts, rigging and sails but an engine reliable enough for manoeuvring in the close quarters of docks and marinas where she would encounter shipping and expensive cruisers, not to mention coping with the weather and tides of the Ouse, Trent and Humber and possibly the east coast.

This was only the beginning of problems to be faced. In response to recent tragedies involving sail training ships, notably *Marques*, a British registered barque that had sunk in less than a minute with the loss of 19 crew during the 1984 Tall Ships race, the Maritime & Coastguard Agency had introduced *The Code of Practice for the Construction, Machinery, Equipment, Stability, Operation and Examination of Sailing Vessels of, up to 24 metres in load line length, in commercial use and which do not carry cargo or more than 12 passengers*. This meant *Audrey*! The code did not become mandatory until 1993, but insurers would have taken a dim view of any organisation trying to avoid compliance. Then there was the question of who would sail her? Could we manage with volunteers or would we need one, two or even three full time skippers? Thirdly, how would we pay for materials for the conversion as well as for staff salaries? The Manpower Services Commission would allow 10% of its payments to be be spent of the purchase of timber, steel and equipment but that still required letters to be written to trusts and foundations and much lobbying of Hull City Council and Humberside County Council. Lastly there was a far-fetched hope that one day she might leave the estuary and sail beyond the sunrise to Europe, the Baltic and the Mediterranean, but for the moment *Audrey*'s cruising and insurance limits were fixed by two imaginary lines, one for summer, between Cleethorpes pier on the south bank of the Humber, and Patrington church, west of Spurn Point in south Holderness, and one for winter, between Paull just down river from Hull, and New Holland on the Lincolnshire coast.

The MCA's new code of practice, normally referred to as the Blue Book to distinguish it from the Yellow Book or Code of Practice for Small Commercial Motor Vessels, and the Red Book or Code of Practice for Small Commercial Work Boats, was going to cause us some headaches. Foremost was the question of stability. The code had not been written for the likes of *Audrey* but for yachts and sailing ships designed for sea passages in rough weather. The prescribed 'critical angle of heel' or extent to which a vessel could heel over but still be expected to right itself, was fixed in the regulations at a minimum of 105 degrees. In the case of a racing yacht this would mean that even though its main mast was in the water the vessel would not capsize and would be capable of returning to the vertical. *Audrey*, with her flat bottom, was not capable of such gymnastics. Some practical incline tests using concrete weights and a computerised formula for calculating the point at which she would capsize, suggested that in spite of plenty of stability in good weather, her critical angle of heel was a mere 87 degrees and far outside the permitted limit for going to sea. But *Audrey*'s crew and Nigel Ling, a ship's surveyor with an uncompromising but common sense approach to the prevention of accidents, thought otherwise. One of the factors in the calculations was a ship's area of sail, a determining factor for whether *Audrey* was a sailing ship or simply a motor vessel with auxiliary sails. Quite by chance, *Audrey* did not have enough sail to bring her entirely within the scope of the Blue Book (by chance, because her sails had been made well before there was debate about her cruising area). She was a motorised candidate for the Yellow Book which prescribed a critical angle of heel of only 85 degrees. The final conclusion of the Maritime and Coastguard Agency and insurers was that she should be regulated by both Blue and Yellow Books: the Blue in respect of her sails and the Yellow in respect of her hull and machinery. The MCA was further reassured by the *Sobriety* trustees' decision that *Audrey* should never be at sea in a wind strength of more than Force 7. As far as I know she was the only ship to come under both codes of practice and was regularly inspected by MCA personnel in the ports where she berthed.

So it was 'Goodbye Cleethorpes!' and 'Hello Holland, France, Ireland, Scotland and the east coast of England to London and beyond!'. Here now was a ship to exchange the restrictions of the inland waterways of eastern England for the freedom to visit the East India Company's ports on the Ijsselmeer in Holland, the islands of Mull and Skye in the Inner Hebrides, Derry-Londonderry in Northern Ireland or Boulogne-sur-Mer in the Pas de Calais of northern France. *Audrey*'s cruising ground would now be legally defined as no more than 60 miles from a safe haven within the coastal waters of the UK, and mainland Europe between Brest on the Brittany peninsula and the River Elbe which flows through Hamburg. The definition was intended to discourage over enthusiastic skippers from setting sail across the North Atlantic or through the Bay of Biscay.

Between 1988 and 2003, *Audrey* carried more than 7,000 young people, mainly from low income families living on Hull's council estates, to destinations on the continent of Europe and the British coast. In all aspects of their work her crew were outstanding and maintained the respect of sea and harbour authorities in every port the ship visited. Throughout the 15 years of her operation there was no serious accident, nor was the ship exposed to any serious danger. For young people, *Audrey* represented an experience which they would otherwise never have been able to afford. Through her, the closed world of Hull's council estates was able to give way to the romance of the open sea and the discovery of worlds beyond the concrete jungle. But let us return to when *Audrey* appeared as a virtual wreck in Goole Docks, and pick out the highlights of the year it took to turn her into a sailing barge, technically labelled 'a billyboy, gaff rigged as a ketch'.[5]

The Work Proceeds

There was a prodigious amount of work to be done in a very short time and management of the workforce was going to be as difficult as solving the problems directly connected with the ship. This time there was no Geoff Walton to take charge, and although David Robinson did his best to supervise the truculent band of brothers from Old Goole[6] who were the hard core of the Community Programme workforce, he was no match for their cunning and occasional ill discipline. Admittedly this was reactive and jocular rather than malicious but enough to slow down and frustrate the work. Ted Pindar was someone who would stand no nonsense but as the only professional joiner and plumber on site, he had enough on his plate. Cyril Harrison, with his 40 years of navigating the Humber, commanded immediate respect but was available only to advise and help with aspects of the work relating to sailing. As for me, I was still teaching a part timetable at school and in the days before mobile phones, had no direct communication with Ted or David in 35 Shed. I did visit *Audrey* most days but generally in the aftermath of what might be called 'a management episode,' several of which come to mind.

Audrey's light tower had been removed while she was berthed at Beverley Lock but further engineering work requiring use of a dry dock, was needed to prepare her for the installation of engine, shaft and propellor. Yet again Associated British Ports provided the facility, together with the services of two shipwrights, to manage the procedure. The dock, adjacent to the river Ouse, first had to be emptied during the ebb tide to allow the water to run into the river. The ship then had to be measured and the blocks on which it was to rest, hauled into position at correct intervals on the dock floor. With the opening of the sluices at the time of high water in the river, the dock was re-filled, whereupon the shipwrights, using ropes and the sighting marks at each end of the dock, pulled the ship into its exact position above the blocks. After this they inserted long square props engraved with Roman numerals and known as shorings, between the ship and the dock walls to stop the ship toppling over. After the dock had been emptied and the vessel was correctly settled, the procedure which had taken the best part of a day, was completed when the shipwrights made fast the ropes to bollards located above the dock. The ropes would remain in place until the ship was undocked. The depth of the No.2 dry dock in Goole, which was suitable only for small coasters and barges, was about seven metres and the length of each rope from *Audrey* to the dock side was also about seven metres.

So it happened that on a day in mid February when the ropes were speckled and stiff with ice, I arrived at the dry dock to find one of the welders who had worked with Geoff Walton on the *Eden* conversion, hanging by his crossed legs and hands from the rope joining *Audrey*'s starboard quarter to the bollard on the dock side. He was working his way hand over hand towards the ship. Completely transfixed, I was fearful that if I called to him he would lose concentration and fall onto the stonework below. At this point he would have been killed or so gravely injured that the rest of his life would have been spent in a wheelchair. Miraculously he arrived unscathed at his destination and I was not compelled to discover whether *Sobriety* would have been found partly responsible for his fate.

The second incident was not so much serious as mischievous. Since the time of *Audrey*'s conversion, Aldam Dock has been re-designed as *Boothferry Terminal*, a huge concrete platform for the storage and movement of containers. 35 Shed has gone and with it the Number 3 compartment boat hoist and the little brick building or lobby furnished with a fireplace and chimney that housed some of the equipment for operating the hoist. By the late 1980s, the lobby on Aldam Dock was surplus to the port's requirements and, with ABP's agreement, served as a 'snaproom' where the *Audrey* team could have tea breaks and lunch. During one of my routine meetings with Ted and David to discuss their plans for the week, Ted said, *"Look, there's red smoke coming from the the lobby chimney."* When the colour of the smoke suddenly changed to white I said, *"We've elected a new pope."* Further investigation revealed that having run out of wood to keep the home fires burning and not wishing to go into the cold to forage, our inventive employees had used the next best combustible material to hand, which was paint. Not any old paint but expensive red oxide costing twenty pounds a gallon even in those days. The red oxide created the red smoke; the water used to douse the flames which would otherwise have incinerated everyone and everything in the building, provided the white smoke. Henceforward until its demolition, the lobby was known as the 'Sistine Chapel'.

It was fire that featured in another incident involving ABP staff and in particular the port manager, the late Colin Silvester, who was also a member of *Sobriety's* committee. It should be remembered that port managers are lords of all they survey and are not to be offended or crossed even for the most trivial reasons. They occupy a very large office and sit at a very large desk near a conference table which can seat twelve in rank of importance, the most lowly being invited to sit furthest from the chief. On the walls there is a display of documents tracing the port's history back to the Iron Age with photographs of cranes and forklifts showing that compared with ABP's ports, Shanghai and Rotterdam are but rustic backwaters. Finally there is a single chair facing the large desk which is reserved for those in need of correction. It was into this chair that, following a summons from Sheila Cade, Colin's secretary, I found myself placed. After a few courtesies and mutual enquiries about health and progress, the conversation went like this:

"Tell me Bob, how do you make sure Audrey *and 35 Shed are left safe after work?"*

"All the equipment is put away and the shed locked."

"Do you know what time I was woken up this morning?"

"No, when?"

"2.30, by Humberside Fire Brigade!"

"Oh dear."

"There was smoke coming from the Number 3 boat hoist. It was spotted by a passer-by who happened to be sober and had the presence of mind to go to a phone box and ring 999. Your welder didn't do his job very well, did he!"

"Yes, no. Of course not."

"Never mind apologising, I'm very angry."

"Yes, understandably."

"Yes, he should have done a better job and made sure the bloody hoist burned down!"

We then both moved to the large conference table and sat together for morning coffee. Colin was not being irresponsible. The interview amounted to a practical joke, but behind it was the problem of an obsolete piece of 19th century machinery getting in the way of port development. It just happened that the machinery was listed Grade 2* and in the top ten per cent of England's protected monuments. I understood Colin's frustration but, as a fan of the Number 3 Hoist, I could not share his disappointment with our welder's performance. We will look more closely at the problem of Goole's boat hoists in Chapter 10 but for the moment we will return to *Audrey*. The final tribulation came with an episode that took place just before Christmas when the ship was all but finished and the workforce was coming to the end of its contract with *Sobriety*.

Alf Codd was a young man who had tragically lost an arm in a road accident. He lived in Old Goole and had been out of work for some time before joining *Audrey*. Wishing to celebrate the festival and being proud of the ship to which he had given so much time, he organised an undercover collection of scrap metal from the dockside with the intention of having it weighed in by Chummy Jarrold, an Old Goole scrap metal merchant who would pay him for the metal, and thereby subsidise a treat for Alf and his friends at the Macintosh Arms, a dockland pub close to 35 Shed. The fact that much of the 'scrap' was chain belonging to ABP and needed for the operation of quayside machinery was lost on those commissioned with stockpiling the 'blood' metal in an empty oil drum left by *Goole Bight*, the dredger berthed next to *Audrey*. Alf saw the drum needed its lid removing and pestered David Robinson to make the necessary perforations. Then with a head full of fantasies associated with free beer, he eagerly bent back the lid of the drum only to cut his finger. Perhaps a plaster would have stopped the flow of blood but David thought it best to avoid any danger of tetanus and took the victim to the local A&E department where he was comforted with two stitches and a neat bandage. Alf settled down as planned to an evening in the Macintosh Arms, after which he returned home to enjoy Christmas.

I too, was enjoying Christmas until I received a letter from the Nottingham branch of the distinguished trade union solicitors, Robin Thompson & Partners,[7] alleging common-law negligence by the *Sobriety* Project in allowing one of our employees to use an oil drum as a container for scrap metal, and claiming loss of wages and convalescence fees in respect of the injury to his finger. It was all too daft for words. Alf cut his finger while stealing the scrap: the employment scheme had finished on the day of his injury, so how could solicitors support a claim for loss of wages? As for convalescence, he did have only one arm and would have had some short term inconvenience as a result of the bandaged finger. The solicitors assessed his total claim to be about £4000, roughly the equivalent of £8000 today. I rang Fred Wright, our friendly head of insurance at County Hall who had steered us through the fiasco at York, and his advice was to fight the claim. Burstalls Solicitors in Hull were hired to make our case, which, after some exchange of correspondence with the plaintiff's solicitors, would go before a judge at Doncaster County Court and require the services of a barrister.

The string of witnesses for the plaintiff were cross-questioned by *Sobriety*'s counsel and found to be so contradictory in their stories that by lunchtime, plaintiff's counsel was saying publicly that it was useless to carry on. But we were ambushed in the afternoon when our two supervisors, David Robinson and Norman Garner, bungled their stories. Terrified by the Old Goole infantry seated just below them when they were in the witness box, they went to pieces under questioning. The judge awarded costs of £30,000 against *Sobriety*; Alf himself received £100 on the grounds that he had behaved negligently and contributed to his own injury. That was the end of it. I felt aggrieved and indignant but it was a lesson for the future.

A Weather Man's Amusement

With two hundred year old pitch pine for decking, masts of Norwegian Spruce donated by the Earl of Yarborough from his Brocklesby Park Estate and sails sewn by James Lawrence, Sailmaker in Brightlingsea, Essex, *Audrey* was now ready to put to sea, and although for the moment, 'sea' meant the Humber Estuary, we celebrated her arrival with a dockside Gala Evening on July 15th 1988.

The *Sobriety* Project has always operated on the premise that most surprises are bad ones and makes plans accordingly. This particular evening however, the Furies were determined to get us. The Gala Evening was to be the occasion of *Audrey*'s commissioning and Lord and Lady Yarborough had kindly agreed to perform a ceremony which was intended to bring together the volunteers, employees and funders who had supported *Audrey*'s change of life. A small group had started work on arrangements during the previous September. 36 Shed, near the Number 3 boat hoist, was to be the venue. There were holes in the roof at one end but this would only enhance the atmosphere. Guests would dance on the quayside or free of care, would sip wine and be witty under the warm sun of a July evening. We would be singing *Auld Lang Syne* in the moonlight and *Audrey*'s floodlit masts and rigging would remind us of adventures to come.

By early July everything was organised. Goole Amateur Operatic & Dramatic Society, directed by Doreen Chappell MBE, and underpinned by Clary Shirtliffe's staging, were to present a cabaret based on a decade of musical comedy: the jazz group *Blue Brass* had polished its trombones and re-strung its guitars: it was believed that vocalist Rosie Cross had cancelled an appearance at the Royal Festival Hall to sing for us: California Gardens in Howden, had force-fed 60 conifer trees to 'green' the occasion: Compass Youth Training Scheme in Hull was filling the vol-au-vents: Boothferry Borough Council's works department had come to a standstill following our raids on its stores of cables, chairs, tables, road barriers and platforms: George Farmery, a local builder was going bankrupt because we had borrowed all his scaffolding poles: Associated British Ports had lost a container which was eventually found behind 36 Shed full of dancing girls: the lighting and microphones were set and we all held our breath as they were switched on, wondering whether the overload would cause the meltdown of Drax power station.

At 7.30, as our 300 guests began to arrive, some from as far away as Coventry and Sheffield, a Weather Man could be heard sniggering behind the Number 3 Hoist. In spite of his sniggering turning to guffaws, the civic guests were invited onto the platform to make speeches and to witness the panegyrics. Lord and Lady Yarborough were the Guests of Honour and the Mayor and Mayoress of Boothferry and Alan Marshall, Chair of *Sobriety*, welcomed them. The Mayor of Goole and her Escort were in attendance, as was the Chair of Humberside County Council and his Lady. The Lord Mayor of Kingston upon Hull, as Admiral of the Humber, replied to Alan Marshall's welcome and it was during her speech that we noticed that our other 290 guests, who earlier had surrounded the dais, were now specks on the horizon, retreating into the leaking end of 36 Shed. The raindrops were getting bigger and without warning, the platform party, sometimes known rather disrespectfully as the 'chain gang', also decamped to the Shed, chased by frustrated photographers from the *Hull Daily Mail* and *Goole Times*.

While the more conscientious guests had been standing attentively listening to the speeches, a less polite group of 'gannets' had been making early forays into the supper. The rain put an end to their games, but the damage was done. Even the most well spread table cannot withstand the removal of sausage rolls and jellies by the dozen. Even an acre of well filled vols-au-vent will succumb if they are removed seven high on cardboard plates. 'Disgusted, Tonbridge Wells' was quite loud in his disapproval. He had paid £6.00 for his ticket and all that was left were a few wishbones and a wet sandwich. Even the offer to send out for chip butties would not console him.

And so it went on. The cabaret lifted our spirits, *Blue Brass* played enthusiastically and the evening was rescued by the two young disc jockeys, Rosie Cross did her turn and Lord and Lady Yarborough remained unruffled even though the ship they were bringing into commission was only 100 metres away but might just as well have been in Yokohama. By midnight most people had enjoyed themselves; certainly everyone had given the Project their friendly support. But I am also sure that many went home relieved it was over.

By Monday afternoon, Boothferry Council was back in business, George Farmery had rescued his scaffolding and ABP had found its container. All that remained was the Weather Man doubled up with laughter in the leaking end of 36 Shed.

Audrey Sets Sail

Two months later in September 1988, under the command of Cyril Harrison, Sailing Master of the Humber Sloop *Amy Howson*, *Audrey* made her maiden voyage as a replica billyboy, designed to give a taste of maritime adventure to disadvantaged young people.

The first group to use the ship was from Perronet Thompson High School, a brand new 1300 place comprehensive on Hull's North Bransholme estate which with a population of 40,000 was one of the biggest local authority estates in Europe. Keith Watson was the school's newly appointed special needs co-ordinator and keen to establish the importance of outdoor residential experiences for children from socially disadvantaged families. The idea of the week was to give as many pupils as possible the opportunity to spend time aboard a sailing barge and to be away from home, perhaps for the first time. The staff decided to split the week and take two groups of eight boys for two and a half days each. (Boys were chosen, because at the time of booking,

Waiting for the tide at South Ferriby where the River Ancholme flows into the Humber.
Tim Watson

staff did not know the accommodation layout of the new barge). The sixteen most needy pupils were approached and given a letter asking permission from parents. The response was a hundred percent and deposits of a few pounds were soon paid. *"At the same time,"* Keith said, *"we tried to offer financial assistance where there was hardship and in this case the school paid for two boys."* Planning the trip was as exciting as the trip itself. A visit to Goole Docks and the barge on the day the sailmakers were sewing the sails by hand on deck, fuelled enthusiasm to fever pitch. Every day, Keith said, he would be followed down the school corridors and asked over and over again the same questions about clothing, food and times.

Perronet Thompson was a community school with a library and cafeteria at its centre. That meant that parents were regularly in and out of the building. Keith saw this as an opportunity to involve the pupils in organising an exhibition about barges and the Humber. The results were surprising. The boys cajoled the librarian into finding lots of books on waterways and barges. They collected wildlife posters and photographs, made a model of *Audrey,* and for two or three nights worked until the library closed at 6.30. Two parents came in to see what they were doing and ended up helping. The project showed that without a lot of effort on a teacher's part, a new experience could motivate the most difficult pupils, not to mention their parents. The group travelled to Goole by train, a new experience for several pupils who had never been out of Hull and a lesson in 'rail and sail'. (The line from Hull to Goole runs along the bank of the Humber and the journey takes 30 minutes compared to the three hours that it would take to sail back to Hull on *Audrey*).

With a 'crew' paralysed with excitement, *Audrey* sailed down the Humber to South Ferriby, going through the lock and having the road bridge lifted just as tea-time traffic was at its peak. To the boys' delight, over 60 vehicles were queueing at the bridge and it was clear that skipper Cyril Harrison took some pleasure in obstructing such 'fast modes of transport'. With *Audrey* berthed in the river Ancholme, the evening was spent playing board games and chatting about the day. School staff were surprised by the way the boys readily tackled the washing up and sorted out their cabins without a lot of fuss and moaning. Yet it was quite obvious that most of them seldom washed up or tackled even the simplest cooking tasks at home. Next morning they awoke to find the weather quite misty. No one was more disappointed at the thought of not sailing than Cyril. He was looking forward to getting all the sails up and having a go. So it was a combination of his keenness combined with a slight improvement in visibility and a lot of pestering from the boys that the ship set sail from Ferriby lock at mid-morning.

With half the sails hoisted, a strong ebbing tide and the engine out of gear, *Audrey* made rapid progress down river. Cyril was pleased with the way the ship was performing. He would like to have made full use of the ebbing tide and gone further but the mist was looking thick towards Grimsby so he dropped the sails, turned against the tide with the engine in gear, and slowly punched his way back past Saltend and King George Dock towards the Humber bridge. All the time, the boys were asking questions:

"Why does the tide turn earlier further down the river?" — *"Where is that ship from?"* — *"What is it carrying?"* — *"What are those birds?"* — *"Can we get out on that sandbank?"* — *"How many people want tea?"*

With a turn of the tide imminent, the group listened to Vessel Traffic Services Humber talking on the radio to ships waiting to enter the estuary from the Bull Anchorages. When the tide turns, it does so with a rush and *Audrey's* speed suddenly increased without any change in engine power. The ship was soon back under the Humber bridge and making a bee-line towards South Ferriby Lock. Cyril was in a hurry to catch the tea-time traffic but misjudged the depth of water and the ship came to a halt on a sandbank. While *Audrey* was flat bottomed and would soon float on the rising tide, the yacht behind her came to a more abrupt halt when its keel dug firmly into the sand. According to Keith, the next half hour proved to be one of those situations that could never be planned by the most resourceful educationist. The fast incoming tide scooped away the sand from the downriver side of the barge and piled it up in a huge mound at the other side. He said it was a geography teacher's dream demonstration of the movement of fluid mud.[8] Meanwhile the yachtsman was panicking, so Cyril radioed the coastguard who promptly appeared on the south bank of the river in his car along with a policeman. An empty fuel barge bound for Immingham from the Trent, stopped and offered assistance. All this time the excited observers on *Audrey's* deck were drinking tea and coffee and laughing and joking in a display which must have aggravated the stranded yachtsman. After a short time *Audrey* lifted enough to sail off the sandbank, followed shortly afterwards by the yacht whose skipper, it appeared, was a stranger to the river and not aware of its dangers. Arriving in the lock at South Ferriby, Cyril was disappointed to find he had missed the best of the traffic but threatened to be away early in the morning so as to catch everyone on the way to work.

With further trips in mind, Keith raised the question of the ebb and flow of the tide and a corresponding need for patience. The tides on the Wednesday morning, when the groups were changing over, meant that the new group had to arrive by 9.30 or they would not get into the lock. They arrived with very little time to spare and before they knew, were out into the Humber with all sails raised. Conditions were near perfect and visibility excellent. With a fair wind and tide, *Audrey* was quickly at the Thorngumbald lighthouse. (The village of Thorngumbald is well inland and the lighthouse is a long way from it). The river was much rougher than on previous days and, said Keith, some boys found it unpleasant, much to the amusement of the others. With the boat pitching and rolling it was also more difficult to train the new team in the tea-making traditions. However they excelled themselves and soon matched the output of their predecessors.

Thursday was the best sailing day of the week. Conditions again were near perfect. Cyril and the crew were by now quite familiar with the vessel and the boys enjoyed helping to hoist the sails, drawing out the bowsprit and taking a turn at the helm. They arrived at Goole hungry and tired, but still maintained their barrage of tea and questions. After a sit-down fish and chips in town, Keith was delighted when the boys thanked the proprietor without any prompting. This was the more surprising since they had just commented that the video shop next door had no grille on the window. So why had no one put a brick through it? *"They would have round our end,"* they said. Keith hoped this was just bravado in front of their mates; their attitude during the rest of the trip had been, almost without exception, exemplary. No more so than on the Friday morning when, after they had cleaned the barge, they went to Goole Leisure Centre to clean themselves up before catching the train home, back to the 20th century, their housing estate and their space-age school. His final verdict on the trip:

> *Pupils learn about themselves, their friends and their teachers. We learn about the pupils and our colleagues in a way that no 9-5 situation can ever allow. There are now 16 grateful lads following me around school asking 'When can we go again?'*

However, not all of *Audrey*'s cruises had quite the same satisfactory ending.

A Different Experience

Situated in Longhill, off Holderness Road in east Hull, is the Anglican parish church of St Margaret of Scotland built in 1959 at the same time as its parent estate. Associated with the church was a regeneration venture sponsored by Hull University and called *Link-Up at St Margaret's*. Like many inner city church projects, the scheme catered for people who were on their uppers and had no means of support. Sometimes they were just out of prison, sleeping rough and at the mercy of local hooligans; sometimes it was families which had slipped through the benefit system and were at the end of their tether.

In summer 1998, nearly ten years after the Fountain House cruise, Barrie Allsop and staff of the *Link-Up Trust* asked some of their regulars if they would like a few days on *Audrey*, sailing the east coast. The outcome was a dozen volunteers who joined the ship at Hull Marina with the idea of sailing to Bridlington and back. Among them were Lawrence Guymer and his three children. Lawrence's opinion of the sea and ships was far from romantic and a corrective to the view that mankind was born to sail, or that everyone who steps aboard a sailing ship is endowed with a 'stiff upper lip'. He sets the scene:

> *I visited the boat with Barrie our leader and then took my kids to see the boat. The night before we went I didn't sleep because I was knackered and tried to keep awake. Every half hour I checked the church to make sure the food was safe. We'd had a break-in the week before and they'd stolen all the food…*

Leaving the marina they put out into the estuary:

> *The colour of the water was brown and dead dark while we were on the Humber. When we got to sea it became clear. It was nice, two kinds of different colours. It was separate, running like a zig-zag. They were coloured at one end, kind of blue on one side, the other brown and then frothy at the end.*

With this surfeit of colour he began to feel sick but then had his attention drawn to 'a big war castle in the sea'.

> *It was a very funny shape, concrete and black. I thought it was an oil thing but Barrie said it was for scanning planes and things in the war'.*

Whatever it was. it did not help Lawrence Guymer's state of mind:

> *I was tired, sick, had toothache and when I was on deck was cold too…I told Barrie I wanted to get off at the next stop and go home but the sailor (Audrey's skipper) said, "We're going to leave at 9.30 in the morning." "Are we going across the sea again?" I asked. "Yep",he*

said, "and we're going to spend the night out there." I said, "No, I'm not going."

I did a bad thing because I didn't want to stay on the barge. I pushed up the skylight and one of the lads got my clothes and I walked away with the three of them. It was raining. I told the kids to go back because I couldn't take the responsibility of getting them back home.

But rescue was to hand:

I got a lift when I hitched and he took me to another village. I was standing waiting for a lift. My lighter was so wet I couldn't smoke. I chucked it away and went to a pub for a light and spoke to the manager and told him about Audrey. *I told him I was sick and that I'm never going on a boat again and he laughed and laughed. He got me a box of matches and gave them to me 'cos I had no money. I said I was trying to get a lift and would sleep in a 'phone box if I couldn't. As I was walking away he called, "Jock get yer bag!" I said, "Yes! I've got a lift".*

There were three fellas and one said he'd take me home but I was worried 'cos they'd been drinking. The bar man said not to worry, they were good blokes. They drank coffee and we left at about 2.15. I was home by 3.00 and glad to see the flat.

I've learned noffink, but I did learn to put the sails up, drive the boat, steer it, look through binoculars and wash hundreds of dishes. I don't like the sea. I'll never go in a boat again.

This was a man who espoused adventure, 'but not as we know it'. Another was Tim Harding who before he became head of Burton-upon-Stather Primary School in North Lincolnshire, was naïve enough to think that if he got his children to play at being pirates, they would not *behave* like pirates:

We'd split the week on Audrey *with another school* (three nights each), *and inevitably, the theme for the week was 'Pirates'. As a keen young teacher I decided that many curriculum opportunities could be linked to this, including compass reading, and wouldn't it be a great exercise to leave a treasure map on the boat for the next school to find? They would follow our clues to a beach and be able to discover gold! Well, a box of Terry's All Gold chocolates at least! We just needed a beach.*

After docking at Grimsby, we all dressed as pirates and amidst strange looks from the other passengers, took the Number 9 bus to Cleethorpes. However, for a ship-bound pirate crew, the attractions of splashing in the sea and playing football far outweighed the importance of the educational aims of their curriculum minded captain. So it was with much resentment and grumbling that they were coerced into learning the points of the compass!

"Look," I said, wanting them to do this exercise, "Here's the compass. Let's just get this done. Just bury something in the sand and I'll check your instructions by following the clues. We'll bury the real treasure for the other school to find and then we'll go and have fish and chips."

After a lot of mutinous glances, shuffling around in the sand and mutterings of 'Four steps east, three steps north, two steps west', one of the group finally came over to say they'd finished. "Right", I said, "That's great! Now, what's the treasure I'm looking for?" And of course, they'd buried the compass!

Philosophy And Practice

A radio conversation between *Audrey*'s skipper, Paul Cooper, and Vessel Traffic Services (VTS)[9] Humber in July 1993:

> *VTS: Good morning* Audrey.
>
> *PC: Good morning VTS.*
>
> *VTS: You and your passengers are having a game of cricket on Hull Middle Sand. I'm sure you know the Humber is the second busiest estuary in the world and that there are shipping lanes either side of you?*
>
> *PC: Yes.*
>
> *VTS: Have a good day* Audrey.
>
> *PC: Thank you VTS.*

It was not a part of the daily routine of VTS to discuss the pros and cons of playing cricket or of giving *Audrey*'s hull a quick coat of black varnish in the middle of the Humber. Not many prospective England players have stood at a sandy crease a hundred metres from a moving P&O car ferry nor has the England & Wales Cricket Board yet advised its umpires on what hand signal will indicate 'ball lost at sea'.

Paul thought it would be exciting to beach his flat bottomed ship as the tide went out. VTS obviously thought he was a cuckoo but did not want to be a spoilsport. The exchange illustrates how staff and volunteers routinely believed in the value of adventure and took every opportunity to nudge their young people into it. It takes us back to Tom Price's comment, "*Anyone can make adventure training safe by taking all the adventure out of it. The best safety lies not so much in the avoidance of danger but in learning how to deal with it.*"

Reedness Light on the Lower Ouse – a marker for ships on their way to or from the port of Goole.   Tim Watson

The episode shows the regard the navigation authorities had for *Audrey*. VTS keeps discipline on the river but appeared to be disarmed by the skipper's well placed confidence.

Who were *Audrey's* skippers? Paul Cooper had a degree in fine art and a fascination with English ecclesiastical architecture. He also had experience of the seaways and coasts of western Europe. Mark Peacock was a veteran of the Fastnet Race: Bob Wride who later became deputy head of one of Hull's pupil referral units, combined his remarkable skills as a teacher with a mature knowledge of sailing: Mel Parish was the son of a sailing school proprietor and married to a prison officer. Many of the sailing volunteers were the same: Mike Dixon for example was a river pilot. With qualifications and experience up to the Royal Yachting Association's highest awards of Yachtmaster Ocean and Yachtmaster Instructor, they made a team which would have given any conventional sailor a good run for his or her money. What was extraordinary was that they exchanged the brotherhood of competitive sailing for working with stroppy children on a flat bottomed boat that had a habit of drifting sideways in an unfavourable wind. In a 1990 article *Havens I have known*, Mark Peacock gave his own view of the ship:

At first I cursed the shallow draft of Audrey *when trying to sail into the wind and wondered why we couldn't be sailing a modern weatherly yacht with a reasonable draft. Looking back though, her shoal draft [10] when she was originally conceived was definitely forward thinking. The ability to explore outside the main shipping channels, has enabled crew to plan more interesting and varied cruises to the tidal muddy havens.*

As a child I can remember my grandfather taking me down to his old wooden yacht moored at Winteringham Haven. He would reminisce about when the haven was festooned with the masts of Humber keels and sloops trading into Winteringham. The wild grassy banks, the dilapidated staithe and the peace still exist there today. The place seemed to me to be an ideal stop-off. The groups were able to get away from the bustle of Hull and Grimsby with the ship lying peacefully alongside the staithe during a long summer evening.

Another favourite is the passage inside Read's Island [11] from South Ferriby to Whitton Ness. Wild deer roam the windswept landscape, whilst on the water's edge you will see shags elegantly perched on the flotsam washed up by the tide.

Describing the character of the estuary he says:

There are days when it is warm and sunny with not a ripple on the water, yet twenty four hours later it becomes cold, overcast and depressing, with a rough sea. What does this mean for the groups who use Audrey? *Well, quite simply it sometimes makes them feel more remote and isolated than they would on a canal cruise. They gain an awareness and understanding of tides, wind and weather, which pose certain constraints on where and how far we can sail. Best of all it is physically demanding.*

And looking to *Audrey's* future he concludes:

Paul Cooper will continue his explorations into the muddy backwaters in his quest to fulfil his roaming, adventurous nature. And myself? Well, if possible I would like to poke Audrey's *nose out past Spurn Point to stretch my sea legs on a short coastal passage.*

Of Audrey, The Wash, Onions And The Baby's Head

Mark would not be disappointed. On the glorious 12th August 1991, with a volunteer crew of teachers, youth workers and *Sobriety* committee members, Paul Cooper took *Audrey* on a seven day voyage out of the Humber. The destination was Wells-next-the-Sea on the Norfolk coast and the purpose was to pave the way for schools, youth groups and any organisation with adventure in mind. The long suffering author of this edited ship's log is Paul himself:

Monday August 12th

> *Audrey's skipper was to be found in a queue outside ASDA pondering the coming week's weather and wondering why there are so many people at a supermarket at that early hour on a Monday morning.*

> *The same hot and bothered skipper was now surrounded by enough food to feed an army and wondering if the cheque written in the shop would bounce and if anybody would turn up for the planned cruise.*

> *A jolly smiling face peered down the companion way and introduced itself and the body to which it was attached, as John Pacey. As the day progressed more eager faces arrived, paid their share of the food bill and were despatched to complete the chores that have to be done before sailing. The weather looked good and the now relieved skipper was solvent once again. To celebrate, he cooked two monstrous shepherds' pies, the like of which have only been seen in the Beano comic's Desperate Dan.*

> *With all sails set in a light north westerly,* Audrey *slipped quietly through the dark and over Skitter Ness with one watch on deck and the other two watches drifting slowly off to bed.*

Tuesday August 13th

> *The appearance of the skipper, the dawn and a fair tide was a coincidence which was not missed by the two previous watches. The appearance of bacon sandwiches cooked by the skipper to offset the unfair accusations made about the order of the watches, was welcomed by all except two of the crew.*

> Audrey *anchored off Hunstanton and found herself plagued by hoverflies and jet skiers after a perfect passage completed entirely under sail. After a lunch of pizzas, green salad and hoverflies, some members of the crew rowed ashore to sample the delights of the town and to perform shopping chores.* Audrey *penned into ABP's Kings Lynn dock where by comparison with some ports, the lock men here were helpful and interested.*

Wednesday August 14th

> *Daniel George, the Kings Lynn harbourmaster, arrived in time to foil a plot to serve fried lettuce to the skipper for breakfast and presented an heraldic plaque of Kings Lynn docks to the ship.*

> *Unfortunately the day's plan to explore the Parlour Channel, Dogs Heads, and Wainfleet Haven were abandoned because of* Audrey's *windward performance in a strong sea breeze. Under the direction of the skipper, the alternative plan of practising man overboard manoeuvres under sail was put into effect. It attracted a surprisingly large audience of*

fishing boats, ships and helicopters, much to the embarrassment of the skipper who retired below to shower and shave. On this occasion the recovery record of four minutes and thirty seconds was not broken. Early evening saw Audrey *still under sail passing through the Freeman Channel towards Boston while her crew successfully bartered with some fishermen a bucketful of onions (of which* Audrey *had a reasonable quantity) for two bucketfuls of cockles.*

Thursday August 15th

After lunch and sailing with a fair south-westerly breeze, conversation revolved around the measurement of the boat's speed. This resulted in an equation for calculating Audrey's *speed by dropping an object off her bow and recording the time taken for it to pass her stern. The objects thrown overboard to test the hypothesis were the few onions still remaining in* Audrey's *galley and were selected on the grounds that they were environmentally friendly, scientifically constant and expendable. The experiment was considered a success and new heights of nautical technology achieved when* Audrey's *speed through the water was plotted at 35 knots!*

Wells harbour was extremely busy and Audrey *had to moor alongside a sand dredger. It was a manoeuvre which unfortunately awoke its rather grumpy skipper who said he was moving in the next half hour. This upset plans for a last night together on the town and as some crew had to be left aboard, Wells holidaymakers were able to view the crew running in shifts between* Audrey *and the Golden Fleece. John Pacey rang home and then announced he was to be the father of twins. Celebrations followed while other members of the crew continued to dash back and forth.*

The dredger finally moved off and after Audrey *was safely moored against Wells quay, there was much wetting of the babies' heads using John's own rum which he had bought as a present for his wife.*

Friday August 16th

Audrey *went from Wells over the bar with the sea breaking on Bob Halls Sand in a stiff north-westerly, an impressive sight, but not apparently, as impressive as when the seas are 'puddinee', a local expression for when strong northerly winds cause large seas to break over Wells Bar itself and make exit from the harbour impossible. While still motoring north, most of* Audrey's *crew crashed out, making the decks look like those of a plague ship.*

There was a change of watch inside the DZ buoys off Donna Nook.[12] *Then the wind died to nothing and with Spurn lighthouse and the Humber entrance buoys in sight,* Audrey *motored home in the late afternoon sun.*

Saturday August 17th

Crew drifted slowly away and the skipper, burdened with the remaining onions, meandered home, pondering the coming week's weather, what shopping he needed, and hoping that the experiment of taking Audrey *out of the Humber would result in extended cruising grounds for* Audrey's *usual clients.*

The continuing story of this ship and the people it carried constitutes a book in its own right. *Audrey*'s crew, and particularly Paul, forever had their eyes on new horizons and the promise of greater adventure. As a result, the 'clients' prepared for their cruise in excited anticipation, often for months. Few were disappointed, for as we have seen from the first trip out of the estuary, her crew were never going to be mere chauffeurs; they would become youth workers, cooks, nannies, cleaners, couriers and counsellors, sometimes taking on the responsibilities of all of these on the same voyage.

People get lazy during days at sea in good weather and at worst, amuse themselves with grumbling and gossip. A sea passage is not like a canal cruise with amusements ashore; until it reaches port, the ship is the only world. Staff and volunteers began to realise that when the sails had been raised and the breakfast dishes washed, there was time to fill. Hence the arrival of *Audrey*'s art workers in 1992.

Richard Downes was the first, recruited and employed to make everyone laugh. Performances of Mozart's comb concerto and Beethoven's saucepan symphony quickly turned the North Sea into a concert hall and the art workers into characters from *Fitzcarraldo*, the opera freak in Werner Herzog's film who drags his ship *Molly Aïda* over an Andean peak to Lake Titicaca. On a trip with young people from Hull's Orchard Park estate, Richard recalled his impressions:

> *As we tangle with people hauling sails, avoid surging booms and mingle with children mad with excitement, we create a cacophony of sounds, arrays of masks and numerous kites. Add to this a flotilla of submersible bin liners otherwise known as small boats, fresh windsocks, and even the occasional procession.*

The muddy waters of the Humber are more exciting when your willow and plastic sculptures are skimming the surface behind the ship. The windy sky is much more exciting when the kite you've been making all morning is ducking and diving above the barge. Spurn Point is thrilling and romantic when Audrey *rests her flat belly on the sands. Framing the distant anchored ships with driftwood sculptures, building softened brick henges and simply doing the largest beach drawing ever seen was a real buzz and time brilliantly spent.*

Warren Pirates.

As art worker, Richard felt he had a position of neutrality between boat crew, children and visiting staff. This allowed him to train staff and introduce different ideas and ways of working. Sheila, for example, was on her first solo trip as a youth leader, and produced a huge fish made out of willow and papier maché. Through spending time getting to know one another and doing things together, people found that art is not simply being able to draw. By the end of the week it was more about 'Look at that!' and going through a process of change. But an art worker could be challenged in more ways than one. A freshly painted skull and crossbones hoisted to the mast top, gained the notice of a member of HM Coastguard who promptly threatened a £500 fine. Luckily the skipper was on hand to argue.

Richard held that sensitivity was needed in assessing a group but that the artist should push where necessary. Success meant providing an active focus and enabling people to work together. And quite often, he said, they were doing this for the first time with that particular mix of people or in that particularly strange environment. Providing an enthusiastic and creative focus was the crux of his job. It was a position which allowed individuals to discover new things about themselves while they were part of a group. They found it was acceptable to play a small vital part or a big loud part. Making art in a group can allow this to happen and it frequently does.

Holland — The Ijsselmeer

Meanwhile during the winter of 1992 Paul Cooper and Mark Peacock continued plotting new adventures:

As another sailing season draws to a close, Audrey *and her cold wet crew look happily towards a period of warmth and rest, to a time of reflection, discussion and future planning conducted in soft easy chairs by the fireside. While composing maintenance lists and work schedules, my colleague Mark Peacock has floated an idea which is beginning to excite and dominate the thoughts of the ship's permanent crew. The idea is Holland or more precisely the Ijsselmeer.*

The Humber is a fascinating river full of wildlife, open skies, industry and commerce. It is a wonderful if hard cruising ground for a sailing barge. However because of its ribbon-like nature and strong tides, a week on the Humber entails an amount of motoring understood by the sailing fraternity but difficult to explain to the lay people who use Audrey. *As the years go by, many of the groups who sail with us are second, third and fourth time users, all of whom have enjoyed the river. It was with this in mind that the idea of taking* Audrey *to the Ijsselmeer was conceived. The Ijsselmeer is a large inland lake with access to the Waddinzee and the Frisian Islands made famous in Erskine Childers'* Riddle of the Sands. *Many of the Ijsselmeer's towns were Dutch East India Company ports on the Zuiderzee and date back to the early 17th century. In 1932 the Zuiderzee was enclosed and the new lake became the Ijsselmeer. Sea locks give access to its northern end; the network of Dutch inland waterways begins at its southern end. It is 50 miles long, twenty miles wide and non tidal. In fair weather it should make an ideal cruising ground with many places to visit under sail and without the excessive motoring which is routinely dictated on the Humber.*

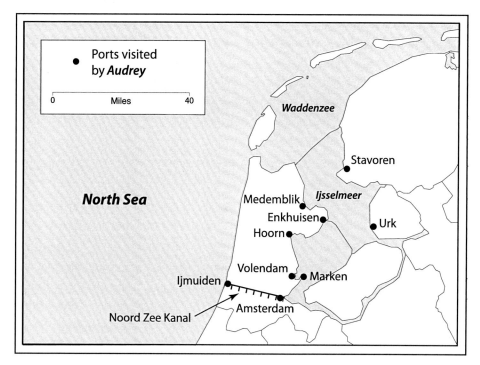

The following year, 1993, under the title *"Well, we went!"*, Paul wrote an account of *Audrey's* first crossing of the North Sea and of the groups which sailed with her.

With the first part of her season completed in home waters, Audrey *sat in Hull Marina on 14th May, fuelled, watered, and supplied, awaiting delivery of her crew. And a crew she received, sailors all, with a wealth of experience — ex Merchant Navy officers, professional engineers, marine radio experts. Indeed such a vast spread of knowledge may have seemed excessive for a passage which hundreds of small yachts from the east coast complete every year. But I for one was glad that the 75 year old Whitton lightship was so crewed for her first North Sea crossing.*

The voyage turned out to be uneventful. Strong winds gave us a short hop down the coast to Wells-next-the-Sea in Norfolk. After a couple of days of waiting, light easterly winds restricted us to a 30 hour motor sail across to the Continent, a rather tedious form of travelling for people who prefer to sail. It was made worse by fog during the night as we crossed the shipping lanes. The fog persisted well into the morning and during our approach to the Dutch coast, the ship's radar, acquired during the winter, did much to relieve the tension that such poor visibility can create on a small boat. And there we were, motoring down the Noordzee Kanal from Ijmuiden to Amsterdam in the warm afternoon sunshine, sceptics confounded, problems overcome and a couple of days in hand to explore a little of Audrey's *new playground…*

Seven days after leaving Hull, Audrey *was moored in the Noord Hollands Kanal, opposite Amsterdam's Central Station. Mark and the volunteer crew had gone home and the remaining crew member had washed his socks, sorted out some minor domestic problems, become accepted as a regular at the local café, Ot'en Sien, and was waiting once again to see if anyone would arrive. And they did arrive, Monday after Monday for nine weeks – happy, tired, excited and full of questions…Shopping, sailing and swimming filled the weeks for most groups, along with visits to clog factories and museums. A walk to buy fresh bread and look round the town where we moored, became the normal morning activity before sailing off for the day.*

Nine organisations, from inner city primary schools to hostels for homeless teenagers, used Audrey *this summer. Every week was different; some had good weather, some got wet; they have tales of disasters and humorous stories, but they all had a great time and I hope benefited from the experience.*

Soon it was all over. The last group boarded the train for Europoort as a new volunteer crew arrived for the passage home. From the crew's point of view the venture had been a success, an opportunity which we hope to offer other organisations next year. All that now remained was to return Audrey *to the Humber.*

All that remained! The weather was appalling and the forecast worse. Strong westerly gales and horrific seas hammering the Dutch coast were not what we were looking for. It would be days and frustrating days before the weather and sea would moderate enough to allow us to go home. The question was whether to sit it out in Amsterdam or to use the time to explore part of Holland's inland waterways. We chose to explore the waterways: down the Noordzee Kanal to Spaardam, along the Zijkannal past thirty opening bridges to Gouda, following the Holland Ijseel to the river Maas, past Rotterdam and finally arriving in Maassluis near Hoek van Holland. Mark Peacock, trapped on his own yacht, replaced Bob Wride who had to return home by ferry for his family holiday. So, with an improving weather forecast and six days later than planned, Audrey *pushed her nose out into the North Sea at Hoek. Twenty four hours later she motor sailed in a light south westerly towards Cromer before turning off the engine and sailing straight up the Humber to Immingham. Here she arrived to a welcome of fierce winds and rain, thirty six hours after leaving Holland.*

In celebration of a Hull school's Dutch expedition, 'an anonymous Kingstonian' composed this doggerel, '*Why It's James's Mum*'. After ruthless editing, it is reproduced here:

Sunday arrived, our trip had begun
Departing from Hull on the ferry Norsun
James' much troubled mum stayed to give us a wave
Then it was off to the disco to join in the rave

Monday found us on Audrey and heading for Hoorn
Under crew supervision of Bob, Mark and Sean
The next day we sailed to the port of Enkhuizen
Where Melvyn and Kelly engaged in some German

We took it in turn to do all the chores
To cook, clean the toilets and sweep all the floors
The food on occasions was tasty and nice
Especially the meal of overcooked rice

We all got along though it has to be said
Little Alan at times nearly did in your head.
On occasions he brought us quite close to the brink
But took it so well when thrown in the drink

It's Sunday again so to Hull in the (Nor) 'sun
And who's first to greet us
Why it's young James's mum

Audrey's *Secret Diary*

Paul Cooper continued to produce reports and articles while running *Audrey* and many of them found their way into the Project's Reviews of the Year which were published each December. Especially entertaining was one of his stories ghosted by *Audrey* herself under the title *My Secret Diary*. In it the ship recounts her own view of events. Paul is variously Grumpy, the old man, the boss and 'him up top':

Dawn broke bright and clear, at least I assume it did, as sunrise in early August is a little earlier than I care to contemplate, let alone experience, especially when I'm snuggled against a very comfortable Scottish pontoon. The crew seem to be stirring so I'd best be up too.

We're off. Still a bit early for me, but the guests have been banging about for the past hour, and after supping his requisite three mugs of tea, the old man has decided to head up the Forth. I've never really understood why we have to leave at such uncivilised times. Tides, whoever or whatever they are, always seem to get blamed. One day I'll find them and have words.

Well this is a breeze, if you'll excuse the pun, as it is warm and calm. Not a breath as I motor gently under the most massively engineered bridge I have ever allowed the old man to pass under. Not the most delicate of structures by contemporary standards, but impressive nonetheless. Yet another flurry of activity in my galley. Is it possible to overdose on tea I wonder.

What a beautiful day. Some of the guests can even keep me tracking in a straight line, but it's too nice a day to make a fuss and after all they didn't keep me awake last night. Considering it was their first night, they weren't bad at all. Not like those 'people' last week. I might not invite them again!

Tried to say hello to an old battleship as we passed, but it turned out to be a fortified island made to look like one. Very strange! The boss seems to be considering stopping at another small island. Nothing on it but a ruined abbey as far as I can see, but then he's a bit odd like that. War and religion! What a perverse species the old man belongs to.

Still heading east. We didn't stop after all. I could do with stretching my sails a bit after having them stowed for the past few days but there's still no wind. It's hot and most of the guests are chilled out on my deck. A rather odd expression, 'chilled out', and one I have only recently come across; wholly inappropriate I would have thought, given the temperature. 'They' used the expression a lot last week during their interminable bickering, but it didn't seem to have any effect.

I do wish these dolphins would bugger off. I've never actually hit one but they do come awfully close to my nose on occasions and the concentration required to avoid them is exhausting. Why can't they just pop their heads out of the water and watch us glide by like the seals did earlier?

Spurlash! And that's that for now. I had words with 'him up top' a while back, about the early start this morning and he agreed, reluctantly, to let me anchor for a rest. A nice spot to relax, off a sandy beach, protected inside a rocky reef and opposite a tiny harbour. I refused to allow him to take me into the harbour as it is patently too small. The harbourmaster's launch, a nice chap, friendly and helpful like all the boats I've met round here, told me that the outer wall makes a safe mooring and that I'm welcome to use it. I'll tell the old man later, to get back in his good books. Calling me mutinous was a bit strong.

Peace! For a while at least. Everyone's ashore, in town or swimming off the beach, leaving just me and the mate watching the world drift by. Nice.

Cleared North Berwick about an hour ago and am now circumnavigating the most amazing rock mass I've ever seen. I'm so close, the guests can almost touch it. It's too close but I daren't say anything to the boss. As I approached I was apprehensive about my decks, but the gannets wheeling overhead are much better behaved than those filthy seagulls you get everywhere.

This is wonderful! A breeze filled in from the southeast while I rounded the Bass Rock and I'm now heading north under full sail. It's a glorious evening with a full red sun setting over the mountains to the west, marred I might add, by Grumpy pacing my deck mumbling about tide times, boat speed and lack of sail area. A stately pace suits my mature nature and the guests I invite, and if he wants to go thrashing around on a modern plastic girl racer, then let him! Let's see how much tea he would be able to drink then.

I wonder where we are going. The Fife coast is rather unprepossessing apart from loads of small fishing ports dotted every mile or so. I have fisher friends in Pitanweem but there are so many boats coming and going all through the night that although it would be nice to moor up with my old mates, I would prefer to sleep somewhere quieter. St Monace maybe. Very quiet. Too quiet for my current guests!

Well, that was a bit frantic. The past couple of hours were so relaxing that I must have dosed off. I awoke just in time to start my engine and stop the boss sailing into the harbour. I know we've been to Anstruther before; but in the dark with inexperienced guests on board, it did not seem prudent. Fortunately my intervention does not seem to have put any further strain on our present rather tense relationship.

Took the ground half an hour ago. Strange how in some places the water comes and goes. The guests who are all ashore now, were slightly intimidated by what I would consider an excellent, admittedly vertical, wall ladder. They'll come across far worse before their voyage is over! However, I'm sure they'll cope. It's amazing how quickly landlubbers adapt to life on board.

After everyone had gone to bed, the old man, while doing his rounds, thanked me for being on the ball as we approached the harbour, so I told him about the harbour wall at North Berwick and we are now back on the best of terms. It didn't seem sensible to mention my short nap. It appears I'll be up to watch the dawn break again tomorrow. Something to do with those tide things I suppose.

This make-believe log reflects a project at peace with itself and enjoying a rhythm of work ordained by tides and seasons. What perhaps made *Audrey* special was her crew's willingness to reconcile educational objectives with the necessities of navigation and encouragement of young people with no knowledge of the sea. The inheritance of twelve years of development was a tradition that balanced the expectation of adventure with the capabilities of individuals. Crew and volunteers were not afflicted by notions of 'the stiff upper lip' exemplified a hundred years ago in the gentlemen heroes of John Buchan's Richard Hannay novels, and which even in the nineteen nineties were still the undeclared aims of some training organisations. The single-mindedness which drove Scott to the South Pole and Mallory to Mount Everest created leaders and heroes but as a principle of education took no account of differing levels of physical and mental development. Like the pot-boy's officers described in Jim Hogan's *Impelled into Experiences*, it never permitted discovery of the strengths of those who were not singled out for advancement.

Audrey was conspicuous for its faith in the likes of the pot-boy and for encouraging teamwork in place of competition, and endeavour above success. The result was respect, not so much for the crew's sailing prowess which should be taken for granted, as for their humanity and good judgement.

The cover of the Project's 1991 *Review of the Year* shows *Audrey* anchored in Tetney Haven at the entrance to the Louth Canal in the lower Humber. In the foreground are boys from Fountain House pupil referral unit wading on a sandbank, but this time, they were aground closer to the shore. Standing on deck is Colin Walden, *Audrey*'s first skipper, who, through grant aid of his salary by the Carnegie United Kingdom Trust, became *Audrey*'s Course Leader in 1989. Having taught biology for a few years in a school in St Albans, he had decided to change tack and capitalise on his sailing experience with the Ocean Youth Club.

He found the practicalities of sailing in unknown waters a little daunting but had a clear idea of how he wanted to see *Audrey* develop:

I honestly forget who it was suggested to me that skippers were bus drivers and groups on board were passengers, but it stuck with me. It underestimated what we as boat crew can contribute to those who sail with us. The bottom line when it comes to outdoor or experiential education of any kind, is to place people young or old, in demanding situations where the degree of support is so managed that they must draw on and develop inner strengths.

He went on to say that *Audrey* was an ideal vehicle for combining a setting of adventure with 'the social environment of group members, leaders and professional instructors' and that the ship was only a 'bus' in the sense that she carried people into these two realms. Working his way towards what this meant in practice, he said that group leaders differed in understanding from those with well developed notions of what they want their group to achieve, to the group leader with little or no understanding of why they are on board, except to say that it will be a good experience. Both present problems: the first may have expectations we cannot hope to meet: the second may be such a poor leader that anything gained will be by chance.

As a consequence, crew had to be able to understand and describe the schemes *Audrey* could offer. They also had to manage expeditions in such a way that opportunities for development could easily be 'manufactured' (like playing cricket on a sandbank!) and lastly they had to be able to perceive and record changes resulting from the experience. Good day-to-day organisation would create the best chance for a successful expedition and would be based on themes relating to the management of the ship: personal safety: sailing: cooking and cleaning: use of spare time: natural forces: natural beauty, and the history and geography of the Humber.

Colin concluded:

Personal development schemes are notoriously difficult to describe, simply because they assume both pre-determined and accidental benefits. On Audrey *we have the added difficulty of working with all kinds of contrasting groups : young and old: varying abilities in different spheres of activity: trained and trainee: in prison and free. We should not underestimate the value of* Audrey *to youth leaders, teachers and trainers. The opportunity for them to live and work with their young people often enables them to make a completely new assessment of individuals and it often enables the young people to make a new assessment of their leader or teacher.* Audrey *is a vehicle for personal development and it is our responsibility to develop our techniques.*

This was a manifesto which would describe precisely how the ship would operate for the next 15 years. It is a tribute to Colin's foresight that such practical questions were answered early in the ship's history.

Questions

Audrey's commissioning was attended by several civic dignatories? How important do you think it is to have the support of a local authority in projects of this kind? Does support always have to be financial?

Were you surprised that the arts featured so centrally in *Audrey*'s curriculum? How important was this dimension?

Do you subscribe to the view of *Audrey* expressed by Colin Walden?

What made the ship and its crew distinctive even at this early stage of development?

Chapter 7 Notes

1   For further information contact: *Amy Howson & Comrade*, Sluice Road, River Ancholme, South Ferriby, North Lincolnshire DN18 6JQ. *Tel*: 01482 703947. *E-mail*: info@keelsandsloops.org.uk. www.keelsandsloops.org.uk

2   In May 2013 *Saira* was lying at Barnstaple and for sale at £6,500. Her original lines had been ruined by the construction of a deckhouse but she was apparently still afloat.

3   *Audrey* was named after Audrey Stritt, a colleague of Alan Marshall and co-director with Alan, of Baltec UK (1987) Ltd. which traded with countries bordering the Black Sea.

4   A bilge keel is used to reduce a ship's tendency to roll. Bilge keels are employed in pairs, one for each side of the ship. In commercial shipping the bilge keel is the form of a strake, or small keel, running along much of the length of the hull. They are typically fitted one on each side, low down on the side of the hull, so as not to increase the draft of the vessel. (Wikipedia.org)

5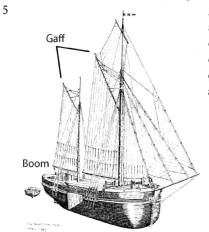

A ketch is a sailing craft with two masts (both rigged fore-and-aft): a mainmast and a shorter mizzen mast. A gaff rig is a configuration of sails in which the sail is four-cornered, fore-and-aft rigged, controlled at its peak by a spar or pole called the gaff. The gaff enables a fore and aft sail to be four sided, rather than triangular and as a result carries 25 percent more sail area.

6   Old Goole is a community separated from the town of Goole by the Dutch River. As Goole South it has for many years been in the top 10% of the most deprived wards in England determined by property, health, educational achievement, employment and crime. However, its reputation as a byword for trouble, is unfair.

7   The trade union lawyer Robin Thompson (1924-2002) devoted his life to the struggle for workers' rights, including health and safety and legal protection at work. Tony Benn called him 'one of the most important figures of his generation'. See firm's website.

8   See the Journal of Coastal Research (Summer 1989): *A Two Dimensional Model of the Movement of Fluid Mud in a High Energy Turbid Estuary* by Nicholas Odd and Alan Cooper.

9   Vessel Traffic Services Humber, part of Associated British Ports and based at Spurn Point, manages and directs shipping in the river – anything from a supertanker discharging oil at the monobuoy off Immingham to a small pleasure boat coming into the Humber from the river Trent. Vessels are required to contact VTS on marine band radio channel 12 to ask permission to enter the river, and to state their intentions.

Associated British Ports (ABP) is the Competent Harbour Authority for the Rivers Humber, Ouse and Trent from the Spurn Light Float, in the approaches to the Humber, to the road bridge known as Stone Bridge at Gainsborough on the River Trent and the railway bridge at Skelton on the River Ouse.' – (Pleasure Craft Navigation website)

10 'Shoal draft' is a measurement of clearance in shallow waters. .

11 Read's Island: Lying in the upper Humber just off South Ferriby, the island was formed from Pudding Pie Sand and offered 300 acres of grazing land for cattle and deer. At one time there was a farmhouse and a university study centre. In the storms of 2008 the island's area was reduced by half and is now in rapid decline. It is home to a significant proportion of Britain's avocet population. It is named after Mr Read, the first farmer to introduce cattle.

12 DZ buoys mark the area of a torpedo range.

Chapter 8

LOG OF *AUDREY* 2000 - A MILLENNIUM VOYAGE

Introduction

The title was intended to catch the public's imagination but the real purpose of a round-Britain cruise was to develop new ideas about group recruitment and cruising areas while still leaving time for the Project's established clients. It was designed to be an advertisement for the benefits of residentials and by extending its 'customer base,' to bring new life to a project that was now in its fourteenth year. In July 1999 a circular letter went out from *Sobriety*:

> *Applications are invited from schools, youth, community and women's groups, arts and multi-media organisations, and older people's friendship groups, based in Yorkshire & Humber, to participate in a* Millennium Round Britain Cruise *aboard the sailing barge* Audrey.

> *Each leg of the cruise will last for a week from Sunday to Saturday. The voyage will take 16 weeks, beginning at Goole on 14th May and returning to Hull on September 2nd, in time for Hull's annual Shanty Festival. The ship will call at most ports in the UK including Castletown on the Isle of Man and Bangor in Northern Ireland. During Week 4 she will visit Dunkirk in France. She will not sail round the north coast of Scotland but will go through the Caledonian Canal and the Great Glen.*

> *Artists from all disciplines including sculptors, textile makers, printers, painters and digital imaging designers will facilitate the compilation of a* Ship's Log. *Museums and galleries along* Audrey's *route will be used to trigger creative interpretation of the journeys made by boats similar to* Audrey, *the cargoes they carried and the stories surrounding them.*

> Audrey *was built in 1915 to be a lightship on Whitton Sands in the Humber. In the late eighties she was rigged and rebuilt to resemble a Goole 'billyboy'. (This was a type of vessel which sailed from the Humber, carrying cargoes to ports on the British coast.) In 1998 her residential accommodation for 12 passengers and two crew was re-fitted at a cost of £90,000. Facilities include flush toilets, shower, fridge/ freezer, 240v. sockets, hot water and central heating. The ship is licensed to go to sea. Her crew have many years' accident free experience of coastal sailing and are employees of the* Sobriety *Project.*

> *Groups interested in participating should contact Bob Watson at the Waterways Museum (01405 768730) as a matter of urgency. They will be sent a detailed itinerary and arrangements will be made for a meeting. The price will be subsidised but groups will need*

to raise £1500 towards the costs of running the ship and to provide their own food and transport.

In the September 1999 a budget of £45,000 was approved by *Sobriety*'s trustees. During February 2000, participant organisations, artists, museum curators and crew, agreed the itinerary and themes for the sixteen weeks.

The Log of *Audrey* 2000 is a composite account of a four month journey round the English, Welsh and Scottish coasts with visits to France, the Isle of Man and Northern Ireland. Excerpts from *Audrey*'s log books describe the places visited and selective references explain the background of the groups. Following the success of Hull artist Richard Downes in turning *Audrey* into a young people's circus, it was obvious that a lively artistic dimension would be required for *Audrey* 2000. So during 1999, photographers, painters, sculptors and textile specialists who had experience of working with young people and who could cope with being at sea for a week, were recruited. In the Log they describe their successes and frustrations. The young people give their opinions. Insights from teaching colleagues, reports of Ofsted inspections and articles from newspapers add to the picture. The loss of some records has created gaps in the narrative but this should not hinder the reader's enjoyment.

The Log is also an account of how *Audrey 2000* attempted to capture the imagination of young people, representing a view often repeated, that adventure, hand in hand with creativity, is indispensable to the curriculum. Whether experienced through sailing, the arts or any other field of activity it invariably leads to new enthusiasms and discovery of new fields of endeavour. As Sir Ken Robinson, international adviser on education in the arts, says, "*The real driver of creativity is an appetite for discovery and a passion for the work itself.*"[1] For all its participants — young people, teachers, youth workers, volunteers and professional crew — *Audrey 2000* was an opportunity to feel new passions. As well as a voyage round Britain it was, for many of them, a very personal 'inward odyssey.'[2]

Through the experiences and events recorded in the Log, the *Sobriety* Project was giving young people an opportunity not only to discover the culture and history of the British coast and its hinterland, but also their own abilities and talents, however obscured by personal circumstances. The voyage with all its surprises was intended to bring out the best in them, and for a few days to reflect a new beginning, never forgotten, through the community of a sailing ship. While crew and volunteers looked after *Audrey*, enforcing her rules and protecting her passengers, the artists connected the young people with their surroundings and offered them the freedom to interpret their feelings and relationships on the voyage, through the medium of painting, photography and sculpture. They were the door to a new world. On the other hand the teachers and youth workers accompanying the groups were part of both worlds; they supported the crew in the enforcement of the ship's rules, and the artists and young people in the quest for inspiration. It was a fine balancing act conducted with the utmost professionalism, perhaps best summed up by a teacher in special education who said, "*I was sick and hated every minute of it but we shall be back next year.*" In this chapter there are excerpts from Ofsted inspections that do not always tally with the dates of group expeditions. The reason for this apparent inconsistency is that I have selected reports which broadly shed light on the background of the voyagers and contribute to an understanding of the narrative. Here is a selection of excerpts from the Log:

Week 1: 14th-20th May, 2000 — Ship's Artist: Elaine Aske

Hull – Boston - Kings Lynn – Blakeney – Wells - Great Yarmouth - Southwold - Orford - Ipswich

Fountain House Pupil Referral Unit, Hull

Ofsted Report of Inspection, 22nd October 2008.

> *The Pupil Referral Unit (PRU) provides for pupils who have experienced significant difficulties in coping in mainstream schools. The roll is unstable because during an*

academic year, as many as 100 pupils may attend the unit for varying lengths of time. A third of pupils are dual registered with their mainstream schools. Other pupils in Year 10 have been permanently excluded from one school and will move to another school in the city. A small number of pupils in Year 11 who have been excluded, remain at the unit as do all other pupils who have been excluded twice from mainstream schools. A third of the pupils are girls and the pupils are almost all of white British origin.

*There were many reasons **why** these children were attending a PRU or a school for children with emotional and behavioural difficulties (EBD). On the surface: misbehaviour in class, no acceptance of school rules, truanting and minor crime. At a deeper level: family circumstances and attitudes, loneliness, disorientation and lack of love and friendship. A tiny proportion of pupils have chemical or electrical malfunctions in their brains resulting in Asperger Syndrome, Tourettes, or Attention Deficit Hyperactive Disorder. On the other hand, some have never been taught how to behave properly, and the rest, the vast majority, have or are experiencing life circumstances that nobody should be expected to put up with.*[3]

Sunday 14th May — Paul Cooper: Skipper

There was a light southerly wind and the sky was hazy but bright as we penned out of Hull Marina with the good wishes of Brian Wilkinson, Lord Mayor of Kingston–upon-Hull and Admiral of the Humber, and the cheers of our friends and supporters. Sixteen weeks and two thousand miles lay ahead of us. If we sailed the same distance westwards we'd be across the Atlantic and off the Newfoundland coast. As we followed the east Hull waterfront, past Paull Haven and the

Audrey leaving Hull on her milennium voyage

Saltend gas terminal, the P&O North Sea Ferries brought our adventure to mind. *They* were on their way to ports in Holland and Belgium; *we* were going to France, the Isle of Man, Ireland and the west of Scotland.

At about 8.00pm we reached the mouth of the Humber and made fast to the buoy next to the estuary lifeboat not far from the lights of the Easington gas terminal. Our first 'crew' were children from Fountain House, a pupil referral unit in Hull. They were veteran fishermen.

Monday 15th May

We awoke to mist which thickened to fog and sailed with a light south east wind down the Lincolnshire coast to the North Well buoy at the mouth of The Wash, famous for its cockle beds, whelks, brown prawns and seals. In the late afternoon we moored on the west wall in the town of Boston which lies on the river Welland about three miles upstream from Boston Sluice'.

Elaine Aske: Artist

I introduce myself. *"I'm Elaine, an artist."* Carl says, *"I don't do art, Miss."* So that appears to be that. Later on, as I'm sketching Craig steering the boat, Carl watches me and asks something about the sketch. *"Ah, but you don't do art,"* I remind him. By the end of the day I have at least two friends. Only Carl remains elusive.

They were up to tricks in the night and Denno (Paul) was the victim. Two lads took the top off the toothpaste and smeared it all over him while he was asleep. It stung! This was cruel and unnecessary 'sport' at the expense of one of their friends and with the help of crew, I organised a mid morning session for them to say what were their motives for this unpleasantness.

Tuesday 16th May — Paul Cooper: Skipper

Next to us was an Everard ship, one of a fleet of small coasters with headquarters at Gravesend. Many were built in Goole until its shipyard closed in the early eighties. The captain offered us hospitality and took the children on a tour of his ship. After a visit to the museum which celebrated the voyage of the Pilgrim Fathers, we left our berth in Boston and with the sun setting behind us over The Wash, sailed for Thornham, a little village on the north Norfolk coast about ten miles from Wells-next-Sea.

Wednesday 17th May

Assisting our diehard crew from Fountain House was Bob Wride a teacher from the same school and a former skipper of *Audrey*. There was also a volunteer, Alan Shaw, a retired planning officer, Tony Papademetrie, a youth worker from Kent, employed for the duration of the cruise, and me. At 4.00am we set all of *Audrey's* sails except her tops'l, and with a south westerly force seven, sailed for Great Yarmouth. We covered the fifty seven miles at an average speed of eight and a half knots and arrived on Town Hall Quay at 12 noon. It was our best sail on *Audrey* in ten years. We were surrounded by river wharves and rig supply boats. In dry dock was the paddle steamer *Waverley*, far away from her home on the Clyde.

Thursday 18th May

Our destination was Walton Backwaters in north Essex. It was a dramatic evening. To get there we had to cross the Harwich and Felixstowe shipping lanes and keep out of the way of some of the biggest container ships afloat. But we saw no ships. Thunder, lightning and heavy rain obliterated everything. Only the radar told us they were there.

Elaine Aske: Artist

The storm clouds hung down like a forest of black mushrooms. You could tell when you were about to hit one and enter the rainy zone. Forks of lightning completed the colour. Terns, Brent geese, shelduck, oyster catchers, cormorants, a flock of dunlin, and gulls entertained us as they made their way to roost. The children's main interest though, was the fishing: crabs galore crowded round their chunks of smelly mackerel. Baggy even caught a starfish.

Paul Cooper: Skipper

Walton Backwaters are surrounded by dunes and fenland and marshy creeks. Saltmarshes and ancient oyster beds surround the hamlet of Frinton where we would spend the night. Samphire sometimes known as sea asparagus, is part of the diet here. The place is in the middle of nowhere but only a few miles away are the cranes and containers of Harwich and the habitations of 'Essex Man'.

Author's comment

Unlike the arrangement of many yachts and sailing barges, *Audrey* had no wheelhouse. Crew held to the belief that young people, staff and volunteers should be free to take the ship's wheel whenever possible . They were never in favour of steering by invitation. Every time they introduced *Audrey* to a group, their preface was 'we are all in this together', meaning that duties would be shared. Crew would take their turn to cook, do the dishes and clean the toilets; children and young people would steer and hoist the sails. It was a style of management in which authority was manifested through service and was an eye opener for children who had a low opinion of themselves. When Denno said to Paul that he could steer the ship as well as anyone else, it was evident we were making progress.

Friday 19th May — Paul Cooper: Skipper

We navigated Harwich Harbour and the ships and sea-cats and the place where the river Orwell and Stour flow together, until we arrived at Pin Mill and *The Button Oyster*. This is a public house which predates drive-in takeaways by about two hundred years. You grab your beer as you sail past the open window. Further up the river Orwell we passed Thames sailing barges and the Royal Navy's training ship HMS *Ganges*, before coming onto Neptune Quay in the middle of Ipswich .

Elaine Aske: Artist

We glide under the Orwell Bridge — a delicate white span of two central columns with rows of double pillars at each end. A few minutes later we enter the first lock in Ipswich docks. The gates gently close behind us as we wait for the water level to balance out, *"Shit, man, its raining again,"* exclaims one of the boys. The rain turns to hail as the lock gate opens to let us into the docks.

Craig: Fountain House Pupil

We went the first night to Spurn Point where we anchored and went fishing. We were tied to a yellow buoy with a chain. It was banging all night. It did my head in.

Next day we were at sea for a long time. It was good steering the barge. Denno was posing, trying to look good. We ended up at Boston in a small dock next to a ship called *Hoocrest*. We went for a look round the ship. The captain took us into the engine room and his cabin which was quite small.

Fred was the volunteer from Holland but really from Liverpool. He was funny. Alan was another volunteer. They helped us do the cooking and steering. They were sound blokes. On Friday we went to Ipswich. We passed loads of ships with containers on them and a ferry that came very close to us. It had a tunnel under it. The trip was great and I can't wait until September when we are going again.

Bob Wride: Fountain House Teacher

Since the cruise I've had time to reflect on the merits of taking a group of young people with challenging behaviour on a residential which would test the resolve and relationships of even the most patient group. Staff had aired concerns about the distance they would be from any school support. The trip had been introduced to pupils at the start of the school year and had been an incentive to good behaviour and effort in all aspects of school life.

Life aboard was very pleasant and the weather was kind. The young people were busy steering, and below deck were cleaning and preparing meals. It was very interesting to see the way they were able to communicate with adults and enjoy their company, something which is missing in their everyday life. The school has used *Audrey* again since sailing to Ipswich and the pupils all asked if Alan would be able to sail with them again, which he did. It is a tribute to the excellent work done by kind and interested adult volunteers who are prepared to sail with some very difficult groups.

The opinion of the lads was that they had thoroughly enjoyed the trip and staff agreed that the group had been amenable. Their good behaviour would result in similar ventures in the future.

Week 2: 21st-27th May — Ship's Artist: Elaine Aske

Ipswich – Maldon – Brightlingsea - Gravesend - St Katharine Dock (below Tower Bridge on the Thames)

Tweendykes Community Special School, Hull

From Ofsted's Report of Inspection 21st-22nd September 2006:

Tweendykes is a school for pupils with severe learning difficulties, profound and multiple learning difficulties and autistic spectrum disorders. Consequently, pupils' attainment on entry to the school is well below average and necessitates a developmental curriculum. There are significantly more boys than girls in the school. A small minority of pupils attend school from a neighbouring local authority, but the majority live in Hull. A large percentage of the pupils are eligible for free school meals and six pupils are in care. Almost all are white British. The school has been awarded the Sportsmark 'Gold and Positive'.

Author's Comment

The school's expectation of the voyage was that pupils would develop confidence. Far from being frightened they would be bursting with excitement and their imaginations would be captured. In contrast, teachers in mainstream schools often report that children appear to be losing their imaginations when reading. No pictures come into their minds, just words. Some are saying that the combination of computer games at home and the rote learning of supplied answers at school

Tweendykes School at the wheel.

are depriving some children of the ability to visualise. A gloss on this was a letter to the *Guardian* (22nd June 2013) from Roger Carpenter, Professor of Neuroscience at Cambridge University:

The tick-box mentality underpinning GCSE and A level, rewards reactive rather than proactive responses. Here at university it now takes two years to get even our best students to approach a problem analytically and imaginatively, rather than expecting us to supply the correct answer to memorise. The problem is partly an attitude encouraged by regimented teaching methods designed for tick-boxes, and partly because in order to think, one needs something to think about.

The Tweendykes children had plenty to think about.

Monday 22nd May — Paul Cooper: Skipper

At 1.00am at the request of Ipswich Port Control, which, like Vessel Traffic Services Humber, is part of Associated British Ports, we moved from Neptune Quay and tied up between bollards 8 and 9 on Cliff Quay. At 6.45pm we began the return journey down the Orwell under the supervision of Port Control whose closed circuit television cameras never sleep. There was a warm south westerly wind as we made our way to Walton-on-the-Naze. Although not much more than a beach, it has the distinction, like Immingham, Glasgow, London Bridge, and Dover, of being a Standard Port. This means that it is used as a regional reference point for tidal information.

The coastline was flat and sandy as we passed Clacton-on-Sea and anchored in Bradwell Creek under the shadow of the nuclear power station. We ate in *The Green Man* whose gloomy interior reminded us of *The Admiral Benbow* in Treasure Island. Bradwell village has the oldest parish church in England dating back to the Battle of Maldon in the ninth century.

Tuesday 23rd May — Elaine Aske: Artist

Wayne paints the sea with a variety of marks and colours. Then Sam follows my instructions to draw half a circle with four handle-lines radiating out from the hub where my finger touches. Martin, the volunteer, is steering. He is wearing a green coat, depicted by Sam with two vertical lines and a circle for his head. I ask each child which part of *Audrey* interests them most and help them to translate that into a two dimensional representation. Carl does a picture of the colour green, then expands into other colours round the outside. He wants a purple crayon but there isn't one, so I show him how to hold two together, dip them in turps and swirl them round. He does the same with a green and red to form a brown: a perfect abstract, worthy of an exhibition. I draw the mouth for him to copy, but instead he adds two eyes, perfectly positioned. I draw fast lines in the air accompanied by noises to symbolise the spikey hair, and he copies me perfectly — sound effects included. We continue this way with an oval for the body and straight lines for legs. Michael works out a clever way to get the oil pastels out of the box by pressing down on one end. He chooses yellow for the hair and repeats his action for getting out the orange. A touch of blue for the shoes and the effect is complete.

Author's Comment

The artist shows the essential skills of task analysis, beginning with an understanding of the children and then leading them to learn for themselves. This is an indispensable process in any teaching but comes into high relief when the children have severe learning difficulties.

Paul Cooper: Skipper

We navigated the Bradwell swatchways[4] in drizzle which soon turned to rain, sailed past Southend and in the late afternoon arrived at Tower Bridge. The berth was in St Katharine's Dock, home of the sugar trade until Rotterdam replaced London as the distribution port for Europe. It was no easy matter getting into the lock. We seemed to be competing with a flotilla of cruisers from Henley-on-Thames, as well as the Thames barge, *Lady Daphne,* and an assortment of small dredgers and trip boats.

Elaine Aske: Artist

When we entered the Thames proper, cars slowly paraded over the pencil line of London's Dartford Crossing. Fans of delicate wire appear to hold it in place. From a distance it's like an architect's drawing. The next bridge is Tower Bridge. It is tall and town hall-like.

Paul Cooper: Skipper

The popularity of this part of London has resulted in big price increases in the cafés and restaurants. I set about finding somewhere for the children to eat in the evenings and discovered the restaurant of the *Thistle Hotel* which dominates St Katharine's Dock but from whose interior is a light and airy view of the Thames . The staff gave us a warm welcome.

Wednesday 24th - Friday 26th May — Elaine Aske: Artist

Audrey's crew fixed transport to The Dome at Greenwich by making an arrangement with the managers of one of the Thames waterbuses! The children found The Dome awe inspiring. Inside

the 'Play-Zone' there are short queues for every computer controlled game. Sam wants to try the mouse-ball that generates printed musical notes on a canvas sheet and plays them on an open grand piano. The queue is quite big and the

Audrey following a Thames Barge into St Katharine Dock, London.

group is moving on, so I daren't encourage him to stop. We try another game with a giant jigsaw made out of our two faces.

Paul Cooper: Skipper

Using *Audrey* as a base, the Tweendykes pupils toured London in open top buses, had a picnic in Green Park, visited Madame Tussaud's and went to an IMAX cinema and watched *Creatures of the Deep*.

Elaine Aske: Artist

Andrew finishes first so he comes up on deck to work with me. I dig out wire, pliers, egg trays, aluminium foil and glue left over from day one. The egg tray cups are shaped like The Dome, so he fashions a replica with just four wire projections twisted to represent the external 'tent' poles. I add a bit of glue for good measure and ask him if he would like to make some like this to tie together and form an independent piece of sculpture. The answer is, *"No — I want to make a robot."* Ah, well — I can only do so much.

Paul Cooper: Skipper

On the ship meanwhile, there were oil filters to be changed and rigging to be tightened.

Week 3: 28th-June 3rd May — Ship's Artist: Arkady Shepard

St Katharine Dock – Gravesend - Whitstable - Margate

Gilshill Primary School, Hull

From Ofsted's Report of Inspection 7th-11th July 2003 (See introductory Note 5):

> *This large, urban, primary school has 420 full-time pupils on roll, almost entirely from white British families. The tiny minority of bilingual pupils speak English fluently. When they start in reception, children's skills and knowledge are average. The children's family backgrounds are broadly average. Although unemployment in the area that the children come from is higher than usual, some families do not take up their children's entitlement to free school meals. The percentage of children who need help with learning or behaviour is average.*

Tuesday 30th May — Arkady Shepard: Artist

Later in the day we all went to Tate Modern. In the entrance was a sculpture of a spider with her eggs. It stood about forty feet tall and made you feel that spiders were in charge of the world.

I did like some of the Bridget Riley pieces as they created a three-dimensional effect on a two-dimensional canvas using paint. The children said that the work was simple and they could do it without thinking. So even though they didn't like much of the exhibition, they were inspired by its colours and shapes and some began to work with pastels using squares of colour.

Wednesday 1st May — Paul Cooper: Skipper

We kept well clear of the wreck of the munitions ship *Montgomery*, a casualty of World War II. It is said that the cordite in the shells has now mixed for so long with salt water that it has produced enough nitro-glycerine to send the whole of the Isle of Sheppey to kingdom come. After Sheerness we passed *Radio Caroline*, the original pirate radio of the nineteen sixties. As we came alongside the tidal landing at Queenborough we met a little girl who said there was a big fish under the landing that no one had been able to catch. She helped us with our ropes. The Isle of Sheppey is a strange and remote place, so close to London but like a foreign country whose inhabitants speak another language.

Tony Papademetrie: Skipper

We had just secured a bow line when one of our volunteers, Tony Atkin, fell in the water while trying to secure the stern line. He maintained his grip and we were quickly able to recover him. He was not injured and the tide helped keep the stern out while we rescued him.

Author's comment

It is perhaps worth mentioning here, that volunteers, artists and groups, on arrival at the ship, were given a full safety briefing and specific directions about what to do in the event of the more common emergencies.

Thursday 2nd June — Arkady Shepard: Artist

Many sat in their cabins on their bunks, others in the galley and on deck writing down ideas, creating clay models and pencil drawings. Sophie was sewing and padding her own little orange fish. There was a fish shop by the harbour where we bought mussels and sea bass for supper.

In the museum the children enjoyed the waxwork of a diver and oddments salvaged from the sea. Manda, the curator, came with new purchases for the museum — a diver's knife and torch. The children were quite dazzled by the pieces and surprised how heavy they were. Later, I found two of them sitting happily drawing the model ships in their glass cases.

Friday 3rd June — Tony Papademetrie: Skipper

A calm and sunny day took us round the North Foreland to Ramsgate where we arrived in the late afternoon.

Week 4: 4th-10th June — Ship's Artist: Arkady Shepard

Ramsgate - Dunkirk - Calais – Boulogne - Rye - Newhaven

Grimsby College, Department for Students with Additional Learning Needs

From Report of Ofsted Inspection 3rd -13th November 1999:

> *Grimsby College is a large general further education (FE) college offering a wide range of provision… There are 2,850 full-time students and over 11,889 part-time students following FE programmes; a total of 35,000 enrolments. Provision for dyslexic students is good and students with learning difficulties and/or disabilities are supported well.*

Author's comment

The group using *Audrey* had moderate learning difficulties (MLD). Some had recently left school and were nostalgic for the family atmosphere that can characterise so much in special education. Others were approaching the time when they might expect to find work whether in the open labour market or in sheltered workshops. The week therefore had one objective — to get the students to the point where confidence became second nature.

Monday 5th June — Paul Cooper: Skipper

This was a long day. It began serenely enough for me, with a nostalgic breakfast in a greasy spoon café at the top of Kent Steps, recalling the brief but happy time I had spent in Ramsgate as a charter skipper.

By mid morning we had reported to Dover Coastguard that we were intending to cross the Channel to Dunkirk. Our destination was Le Musée Portuaire in the old town. It was the day that the 'little ships' were returning to England after their final re-union. We passed them in mid Channel being escorted by British and French warships but never saw them. The weather was getting grim. At 7.00pm we arrived in the harbour and were instructed to make our way to a berth just behind the museum and next to a French warship named after the Dunkirk pirate, *Jean Bart.*[5]

We had just berthed when we had two distinguished visitors. One was Marcel Carpetière, President of the French Historic Ships Association: the other was the President of the Old Gaffers Working Boats Association. They had been attending a reception on *Jean Bart* and immediately dragged us off to a local bar where we were joined by the *Chef des Pompiers* (Fire Brigade Chief) in full regalia, and several officers from the ship. Suddenly an assistant dockmaster appeared and told us we must move *Audrey*. Another warship was scheduled to come onto the berth.

Tuesday 6th June

In the morning we visited the Musée Portuaire, Dunkerque, where we were given a warm welcome by its Director, Mme Isabelle Roussel and her staff. The collection consisted of fleets of model ships from different parts of the world beautifully displayed with space between each case and clear historical notes. The museum education department then became home to the Grimsby students who, under the tuition of our artist, Arkady Shepard, constructed more model ships to rival those on display.

Arkady Shepard: Artist

Within 20 minutes we began our tour of the museum with our English speaking guide. She explained to the whole group about the history of Dunkirk and its harbour, how it built ships and transported goods, and was home to a naval fleet. Not everyone was able to take in everything but there was enough to look at — models of boats, and pictures from the 1st and 2nd World Wars.

Paul Cooper: Skipper

At 3.00pm with bands playing in the rain and a south westerly wind blowing force 3 to 4, we followed *Jean Bart* out of the lock *en route* for Calais, thirty miles down the coast. We berthed on a tidal quay in appalling weather at about 9.30pm but the harbourmaster asked us to move. He said that the trawler fleet was coming out. At 3.00am we penned into the dock and then slept for ever.

Arkady Shepard: Artist

I spent time helping them re-draw their pictures in a larger scale and to come up with ideas for the design of a flag for *Audrey*. I also got a few others to join in, especially Brian. He was a very quiet young man and didn't say anything without being pushed. I got him to play with the idea of using a set shape and repeating it in various sizes and positions on a page. He sat there as carefully and precisely as he could, drawing and colouring his piece of work. Christopher sat creating a multitude of flags on one page. I have never seen anyone so patient at drawing tiny things. Stephen wasn't interested in drawing so I got him to sing a sailors' song that he knew.

Thursday 8th June — Paul Cooper and Tony Papademetrie: Skippers

The Sandetti Bank lies in the English Channel roughly half way between Ramsgate and Ostend. Hidden at best by only five metres of water it is a hazard for shipping and was marked for many years by the Sandetti Lightship. In 1989 the last of the lightships went into the care of the Musée Portuaire in Dunkirk and was replaced by Sandetti Automatic which features in the BBC's shipping forecast.

After leaving Calais at 6.30, in perfect morning sunshine for the crossing from Dunkirk to Rye, *Audrey* was near the Sandetti Bank just opposite Cap Gris Nez when her duty skipper noticed a large white bow wave moving fast towards him from the south. He thought at first it might be a fisheries protection vessel but when he saw the guns on its foredeck, wondered if Somali pirates had finally got the better of the Royal Navy. The gunboat came in close and ordered him to drop sails and maintain course. Four French customs officers with sub machine guns and two immigration officials with side arms then transferred to an inflatable and came aboard. Below deck they found seven young people with a learning disability, two college staff sitting in their dressing gowns waiting to start breakfast, and another member of staff being sick. Agitated but undeterred, the boarding party demanded to see the ship's manifest and ordered all passports to be collected and put on the table with the cornflakes. Two were missing, one belonging to Tony Atkin, *Sobriety*'s committee chair, and the other to a student. Tony put his passport on the pile, then decided to remove it and got a slap on the hand for his pains. For the student, things were more complicated. He didn't have his passport and he didn't know his date of birth or the address of the sheltered accommodation where he lived. One of the immigration officers wanted to arrest him but was dissuaded by his colleagues, and after a rather sullen stand off, the visitors declined any further hospitality and departed, chuntering about British disregard for bureaucracy. By evening *Audrey* was in Rye.

Author's Comment

As well as sharing the pleasures and chores of life aboard ship, the students had heard a foreign language, met gun carrying officials from another country, learned about the importance of passports, found that the law operates on the sea as well as on land, discovered why you need to remember your address and perhaps why trying to stay calm is a good idea.

Friday 9th June — Paul Cooper: Skipper

We passed the site of the old Royal Sovereign Light and arrived in Eastbourne's new marina at about 10.00am.

Arkady Shepard: Artist

We're making a map of the voyage by layering with the use of see-through material on top of the paint. This is a good way for many of the students to join in and make their mark.

Last night Claire got a bit upset that she couldn't take her picture to Newbury where she lives. But telling her she would be in an exhibition made it better. I gave her a few sheets of drawing paper and this cheered her up. It wasn't only that. I think it was telling her that the fun doesn't stop with me. She has now begun something she enjoyed and can pursue it in her spare time. Janet said she wanted to continue drawing and I gave her some tips to get away from drawing from pictures and magazines.

Week 5: 11th-17th June — Ship's Artist : Andrea Bretherton

Brighton – Littlehampton – Portsmouth – Yarmouth - Poole

The Warren Young People's Resource Centre, Hull

We're not about telling young people what to do. Through conversation, we aim to build an environment of mutual respect and trust. The Warren has a way of working with people, a philosophy that is upheld by everyone; it is there to help build a safe and welcoming environment so all young people can thrive and unleash their full potential. (The Warren: How we work)

Monday 12th June — Paul Cooper: Skipper

The plan was to make for Littlehampton or Shoreham but the sea around Beachy Head was so bad that we put into Brighton. On the way we came across HMS *Essex* rescuing a broken down jet skier.

Tuesday 13th June

We left Brighton at 4.00pm and arrived on the old wharf in Littlehampton after five hours of appalling weather brought by a south westerly force five.

At about 4.00am, one of the Warren members was returning to the ship when she fell from the wharf ladder onto the boat. Crew were in bed and unaware of the incident. She was later questioned and asked how she was. Apart from being shaken up and bruised around her left eye, she declared she was fine and did not need treatment.

Wednesday 14th June

We made our way through terrible weather past Selsey Bill and into the lee of the Isle of Wight. Our first landfall was Camber Dock just inside Portsmouth Harbour near HMS *Warrior*. The berth could only be described as a hell hole and we determined to find somewhere more suitable for the Warren young people who had suffered bravely. Haslar Marina was our eventual destination. There were excellent facilities and the staff were most helpful.

Thursday 15th June

We woke to a warm and sunny day and with a light westerly wind, sailed past Cowes to Yarmouth on the Isle of Wight where the ferries come from Lymington. We fished for mackerel and had a barbecue on deck.

Friday 16th June

In fog and using the radar, we passed through the Needles Channel towards Poole where we arrived at 3.00pm. We then had to deal with a complete failure of the electrical system, having been misled by a faulty meter reader and an inadequate battery charger.

Week 6: 18th-24th June — Ship's Sculptor: Kath Shortland

Poole – Weymouth – Torquay – Plymouth

Turn the Tide students, The Waterways Museum and Adventure Centre, Goole

The students were largely resident in Goole or the surrounding villages, over 25 years of age, and suffering severe disadvantage in the labour market because of learning disabilities or mental health problems or chronic health conditions. Some had been caring for aged relatives for many years and some may have been offenders. Others may never have had permanent employment and some had been dock or shipyard workers of the 1970s and 1980s who were made redundant and had not worked since. They often lacked the personal skills required by employers in service industries. They were not on a mainstream pathway and generally had no knowledge of what re-training opportunities were available. They had no transport of their own. Those with mental health problems, especially depression, had become 'invisible'.

Based on an application to the European Social Fund: 1999-2000:The *Sobriety* Project.

Author's Comment

One of *Audrey's* volunteers, Mike Dixon, who had been touring England on his Honda 50 motor cycle arrived in Torquay at the same time as the Goole students. Completing the party was Kath Shortland with the portable forge she had brought from the Waterways Museum in Gloucester.

Week 7: 25th June-1st July — Ship's Sculptor: Kath Shortland

Penzance - Padstow

The Warren Young People's Resource Centre, Hull

Tony Papademetrie: Skipper

We left Penzance at 2.45pm, and at 6 o'clock the following morning rounded Lands End and the Longships Lighthouse in the company of a basking shark. The sea was dead calm and the sun was rising over the moors. The diminutive Padstow harbour is in the form of a tiny square and is surrounded by restaurants, one of which is owned by Rick Stein, the famous chef, and gives the town its nickname, *Padstein*.

Jo Beneton: a Warren worker from east Hull

She said the voyage was, *'truly memorable'. 'It brought the group together and it was brilliant to see some of the country, as all I ever see is The Warren and my house. It is beautiful out there'.* (*Hull Daily Mail* 2.9.2000)

Author's Comment

The Padstow harbourmaster refused permission for the forge to be fired up on his quayside. He decided it would be a danger to shipping.

Susan Redington: a Warren worker

She said, 'The weather was awful and we were all seasick but it was the best experience of our lives.' (*Hull Daily Mail* 2.9.2000)

Week 10: 16th-22nd July — Ship's Artist: Graham Marsden

Newport – Fishguard – Aberystwyth – Barmouth – Caernarvon – Liverpool

The Hinge Day Centre for Homeless Young People Goole

We are a community charity providing support to the residents and young people living in Bridlington and Goole. The Hinge operates an open door policy for anyone, any age, any issue. We pride ourselves on being able to provide direct support which is unavailable or has been refused elsewhere. We provide cooking and laundry facilities, an IT suite, community drop-in, preparation for employment, life skills training, support for independent living

The Warren Young People's Centre Hull in Tenby harbour.

and housing and benefits advice. We are open 5 days a week between 9.30am and 4.30pm. www.thehinge.org.uk

Author's Comment

Graham Marsden, a textile specialist from Manchester, became a member of the team in a very short time. The broad sweep of his diary covers all aspects of the two weeks he spent with The Hinge and with Leeds Groundwork, a group of young people committed to making practical improvements to their local environment.

Sunday 16th July — Graham Marsden: Artist

It's a beautiful sunny day, and when we arrive at the service station on M1, I see the group spread out on the grass by the car park. They'd made the drive much quicker than anticipated and assure me that it's not me that's late. *"What sort of artist are you?"* asks Rob, the driver, *"Watercolours?" "No,"* I say and try to explain what I do as a community artist.

Monday 17th July

Leave Tenby at 6.00am. Cloudless sky, rapidly becoming bluer by the minute. Sun throwing a dazzling, silver finger from the horizon to the boat. After breakfast I explain the plan for the banner and encourage the group to try sketching bits of the boat or the views of the coast. With some success.

Great excitement, *"Dolphins, dolphins,"* shouts Michael, waking me up. It is magic. As always these wonderful creatures have created a buzz of joy and wonder. More people have a go at sketching. The results produce pleasure and frustration. After lunch we make sled kites and they fly from the stern. Another good buzz as the two red and blue sky dancers follow us for an hour or so. It is hot, baking hot! No wind for sailing though. We pass several beautiful lighthouses, gleaming white. One looks very art deco, another like a minaret, almost mediterranean.

Tuesday 18th July

Requests are already in for more kite making, preferably stunt kites. I haven't the materials for these but try a small Chilean fighter kite without success. There are a couple of attempts to turn the steady flying sleds into stunt kites. Rob can make his do a loop. Eventually we lose both. They hit the sea and the drag breaks the bridle line. After the kites there is a short session on deck, working on large sheets of paper and card to plan each of the fourteen 12in x 9in pieces that will make the border of the banner. The next job is to work up the central 24in square and the designs for the borders. Each person is doing a design based on yesterday's sketches or new ideas from this morning.

The approach to Pwllheli is spectacular. The mountains of Snowdonia rise up behind sandy beaches to meet clear blue skies. The tide is not high enough to get straight into the marina, so we head for the beach and run aground in a metre of water.

The Hinge members are enthusiastic about the banner. Some work on it for lengthy sessions, others dip in and out. We then get out some shadow puppet materials and start cutting out simple outlines, to everyone's great amusement. I get out the screen, Jacky holds a torch, and I put up a puppet. Everyone goes on deck to watch through the skylight. We do an impromptu show about The Hinge and a giant dolphin. Lots of laughs.

Thursday 20th July

We leave the anchorage quite early. The effect of tide and wind is to make the boat scurry round in circles as the tide changes. It alters the view of the shore and adds to the wonder of living on a boat. The route is through the Menai Straits and for the first time we are quite close to other craft, all of them yachts or power boats. People wave, including the crew of a French yacht, *Gigo l'Eau*. It's exciting going under the Britannia Bridge. There's just enough headroom for the main mast. We arrive at Conway and dock in the centre of town. *Audrey* sits on the mud.

The centre panel is now on fabric. On the metal foredeck Mike and Rob help me to fix eyelets in the background canvas.

Friday 21st July

The boat leaves at 4.00am to catch the tide. Approaching Liverpool is very different from the other stops. I wonder what sailors felt when they approached after months away or were going away on long voyages.

Saturday 22nd July

We spend a long time taking photos of the group and of the banners. The photo session is a celebration of the group's achievements. There is a lot of pride which is evident in the way the banner is handled. Hurried goodbyes. It's been a fantastic week and a wonderful experience.

Richard Chatten: Hinge Customer

I was a bit a wary about coming on *Audrey* because I've never been on a boat on a river, never mind the Irish Sea. When I found out the boat was held up at Tenby because of bad weather, I was very nervous. When we got to Tenby, I met eight people I had never seen before and an artist we'd picked up in Manchester. I thought, 'Art on a boat?' I didn't think I'd be able to stand upright, never mind draw!

I'd never done any drawing since I left school ten years ago so doing it felt really strange. I thought Graham was going to push drawing down our throats but when I got talking to him, I changed my mind. The idea of a banner was a good one. We could pick what we wanted to draw then paint and I surprised myself by what I did. The bond has got stronger and we are all real good friends even though there is a little age gap.

The banner looks great and really signifies what we had done on the trip, which will carry on after I've left *Audrey*. I've re-learned a talent I thought I had forgotten. I don't know if I'll do any art when I get back to Goole but it made the trip a better experience which I really enjoyed.

I've never been out of Goole much at all and this trip has made me want to do it again. It's been a time I'll never forget.

Tony Hutchins: Hinge Customer

I thought to myself, *"Oh no! This is going to be crap!"* But as we started to get on with it, my thoughts and perspectives changed. Now I've seen the completed banner, my opinion is that we have made a good effort. As for the rest of the trip, it's been a whole new experience getting to know everyone. I would hope we could all do it again sometime as I'm quite gutted we're going home.

Robert Tandy: Hinge Customer

We went to Conway Castle and in Liverpool we went to the maritime museum in Albert Dock. It was a brilliant trip. There were some people I didn't know and as you're on a boat you have to deal with that and make an effort. You find yourself becoming a team very quickly and I would certainly say it's something that will definitely benefit me in the future. (*Goole Courier* 8.9.2000)

Week 11: 23rd–29th July — Ship's Artist: Graham Marsden

Liverpool – Castletown, Isle of Man – Bangor, County Down – Troon

Groundwork Leeds

Groundwork helps young people to take an active role in their schools and communities by providing learning experiences linked to the environment, which can also have positive effects on their confidence. There are projects and services for primary and secondary schools to help young people to understand their influence on the planet, beginning with exploration of their local natural environment. We provide an alternative curriculum for young people at risk and encourage them to get into further education or training. For unemployed young people, we have programmes of training to help them into employment. (*Groundwork website*).

Graham Marsden: Artist

The group is on board. There are four young people and two staff. Soon we are leaving Liverpool with a large crowd on either side of the lock to wave us out. And then the long passage down the Mersey and out to sea to the Isle of Man. We hoist the mainsail and jib and the whole boat is transformed: beauty and power together. The monotonous drone of the engine is replaced by the sounds of sea and wind and creaking timber. We are sailing into the night.

Monday 23rd July

Dawn comes up quickly. The mast lights make streaks across the rigging and I do some sketching as well as steering. We arrive at Castletown early enough to catch the tide and dock at the end of the harbour wall.

My schedule is to do a full day workshop at the Nautical Museum which backs onto the estuary. We have a guided tour of *Peggy* a 200 year old armed schooner which is the museum's star attraction.[6] After lunch some of the Groundwork group visit the museum while James and Matthew do a little painting. Gail negotiates the loan of a sea kayak and happily paddles round the mouth of the estuary. Swans swim up and down the river and a lone heron keeps its watchful eye on us from the opposite bank.

Tuesday 24ᵗʰ July

We sail through a mackerel shoal. Soon we've caught 20 fish, including a record four on one line, and three haddock, before arriving at Ardglass in the afternoon.

We decide on the name of the group — 'Kippax Krew'. (Kippax is the area of Leeds the group is from). One of them works on ideas for lettering for the title. I encourage the boys to work up earlier sketches and they are reasonably pleased with the results. One of the young women has started a fabric collage of a life jacket. By the end of the day's voyage we have lots of ideas.

Ardglass is a busy working port. We berth next to a deep sea trawler which dwarfs *Audrey*. After mooring we are greeted by three seals. The largest swims up to the boat. A boat arrival obviously means food. We oblige with a few mackerel from our catch, mainly to attract the other seals but also to set up photo and video opportunities. Just as with the dolphins of last week there is now a 'star' feature for this leg — Sydney the seal.

Wednesday 25ᵗʰ July

As the morning progresses and the sun comes out we gather on deck to plan the other banner design. Good ideas start to flow and we reach a consensus. I want to try fabric appliqué work and large blocks of painted colour for both speed and interest. Before reaching Bangor in County Down we start cutting out paper templates for the mackerel that are in the design.

Ian Wilson at Bangor Heritage Centre gives us a guided tour of the museum and provides us with another feature for the banner — a 9ᵗʰ century handbell from Bangor Abbey. Ian considers it to be the prize of the Centre's collection, a link to the period when the abbey was an important centre in the Celtic Church.

Thursday 26ᵗʰ July

Ian from the museum and one of his assistants turn up with scones, freshly baked from their restaurant, and to look around *Audrey*.

As soon as we leave the marina Paul starts to raise the sails. *Audrey* is under full sail, racing across the Irish Sea. We cut out fish from shiny, metallic fabrics and paint them with 3D paints. The group think they look good.

The core of the week is again reinforced: it's the boat, and living and working on it. We are under sail all day then it's back to the motor. The grandeur of the scenery almost makes up for the drone of the engine after the magic of the wind. The night is spent at an anchorage by the lock. Some people fish. Three of us paint the lettering on the banner, working on the galley table.

Friday 27ᵗʰ July

A cold, grey, misty start. The loch is very still and mysterious but after an hour or so the sun breaks through. The coastline is full of rich purples, greens and brown. Throughout the trip it has always been a pleasure coming from below deck to discover a new horizon.

We motor up the Scottish coast and I'm confident of pulling all the elements together. Gail completes a couple of rubbings with wax crayons on calico of one of the coils of rope on deck. These will be used in the central part. Nat has finished cutting out the felt letters and the only remaining elements are the Bangor Museum bell and an Isle of Man logo. It can then all be stuck together.

We arrive at Troon marina about 2.00pm. *Audrey* always attracts a lot of interest wherever we go and I like being a part of its eccentric difference. Except for Bangor the marinas are out of town and do not compare with the beauty of harbours like Fishguard and Tenby, or the working hustle of Ardglass. Nor do they have the winding streets with the promise of interesting buildings.

Saturday 28th July

Paul gets us all together for the distribution of certificates and postcards. I photograph the banners which Alan will arrange to be taken to Goole in *Sobriety*'s mini bus on Sunday. Groundwork's minibus arrives and we finally leave *Audrey* and Troon at 1.00pm. Soon the bus is quiet as everyone sleeps for the first hour of the long journey to Leeds.

Week 13: 6th-12th August — Ship's Artist: Barbara Shepard

Oban – Fort William – Caledonian Canal – Fort Augustus – Inverness

St Michael's Youth Project Orchard Park Estate Hull

Author's Comment

Orchard Park estate lies to the north west of the city and for many years has been the focus of regeneration initiatives by Hull City Council. In the middle of the estate is St Michael's anglican church, a centre of activities for young people, which fills the gap left by the council's decision to abolish its youth service, consequent upon HM Treasury cuts to local authorities.

Paul Cooper: Skipper

The journey was along the Caledonian Canal with nine girls from Hull. They were the younger members of the youth club with an age range of 11-12 years. The leaders were Irene Howard and Geoff Gledhill, both long standing volunteer workers, who live in the same area as the members and know their families.

Monday 7th August — Barbara Shepard: Artist

The weather was drizzly and re-location to Oban meant we had limited time to visit the War Museum. However the children were undeterred and museum staff were more than helpful and welcoming. I used the visit to introduce the application of water colour techniques, using colour wash.

We set off for Mull in a chilly, fine mist. The children enjoyed steering the boat then after lunch we did some painting, concentrating on portraiture. I discovered in the morning that the girls had a fairly short concentration span so decided to find out more about their capabilities by experimenting. I wanted them to get the hang of using water colours rather than poster paint or gouache. This would develop their skills for scenery painting. We used crayon and wash and pencil and wash applied with sponge and brush on poorer quality paper.

Tuesday 8th August

I began my day with Tai Chi on deck as usual. The girls were watching me from below and were interested to learn it. The weather was misty and cold and some hands were numb, so I started hand massage. Later below deck, I introduced some shoulder massage which we did in pairs. It put them in a better state of mind for picture making. From my experience as a therapist, children's physical and emotional discomfort is often overlooked.

Wednesday 9th August

We left Corpach at 8.30pm to begin the 54 foot ascent of the locks called Neptune's Staircase. Because it was raining and drizzling, I began a large canvas picture working with four girls — Marie, Gemma, Lucy and Rachel. We decided on the theme and worked out a composition. Initial drawings were made on paper and the various elements were traced out. These were then cut out and arranged on the canvas. The girls each had a say in the process and then arrived at a consensus. The overall composition was mapped out before lunch.

Thursday 10th August

Sailing through Loch Ness, we arrived at the Foyers waterfall by 3.00pm in brilliant sunshine. There was a great place for picture making on the picnic tables facing the loch. We made studies in pastels and water colour. Sarah and Nicola carried on painting for more than three hours.

Friday 11th August

During the morning Gemma, Marie, Lucy and Rachel finished the large canvas. I was pleased they had seen this project through to a conclusion. The others were impressed with the canvas picture and keen to do something similar so we worked for five hours without a break. The girls stuck with it and did a really good job on the Loch Ness monster and the dolphins. I am sure that they were not used to working like this, but as the week progressed it was evident that their concentration span had improved. I was pleased we'd finished all three canvases. I was also delighted that the girls had had the opportunity to work on the larger pictures and had co-operated with each other.

Week 14: 13th-19th August — Ship's Artist: Barbara Shepard

Inverness – Macduff – Stonehaven – Dundee – St Andrews – Arbroath

Universal Connections South Lanarkshire

Universal Connections is part of South Lanarkshire youth service with branches in Hamilton, Rutherglen, East Kilbride, Douglas, Larkhall, Whitehill, Carluke, Lanark and Cambuslang.

Boys — Barbara Shepard: Artist

Before the start of the trip I had been in contact with Alex Curry, team leader at Universal Connections and youth worker Frank Fallows. Alex told me their programme would be divided into two. The first three days would be for boys, with two workers, Frank and Jim, and the last three days would be for girls. Frank would remain, while Jim would be replaced by Sharon. Later I discovered that both groups were composed of youngsters from different youth projects and didn't know each other or the workers.

Alex indicated that he wanted the young people to be engaged in a co-operative project. I protested. I knew it was unrealistic because there would be too little time to produce this kind of work in three days. Between settling in and preparing to leave, we would be left with one day for picture making which would limit the chances of getting to know the youngsters well enough to produce co-operative work. Also there were other activities to be taken into account, like fishing and visits ashore, not to mention the possibility of sea sickness. It was difficult to get this across to Alex but I would take things as they came.

Sunday 13th August

The first group arrived at 1.30pm and brought a good supply of art materials and film with them. The boys were aged 13-16. After boarding with their belongings including cards, dominoes and a guitar, they had an induction talk by the skipper. I was struck by the friendliness of the group and the relaxed manner of the staff. Frank seemed to have a rapport with the young people. The boys had been travelling a few hours and were hungry. Galley arrangements were designed to involve half the group in cooking under the guidance of Jim, an ex-army chef, and the other half in cleaning up.

The views were magnificent. After a little relaxation I decided to retrace my steps with a couple of the youngsters and both cameras. Frank and a few more boys decided to join us for the walk and the photography. The evening sky was stunning but it quickly got dark and we were without a tripod. However we managed to steady ourselves on whatever was available — a wall, a tree, or a boulder.

The excursion was a good start to the trip but an incident later that evening rather spoilt things. I took exception to some of the language in common use with a few of the older boys. Darren and Tom in particular, were habitually using offensive language, most of it quite sexist. I'm sure it was a result of high spirits and not meant to offend, but it was persistent and I felt uncomfortable. This led to a discussion involving the two workers who were keen to point out that such language was inconsiderate and unnecessary. I am not sure how helpful the discussion was because the lads became extremely defensive. Eventually we reached a slightly better stage of understanding but it led to some surly responses during the rest of the trip. I am not sure how this could have been avoided other than by my making no comment in the first place.

Monday 14th August

We left Inverness with a beautiful view of the locks. The lads were really excited and on deck before breakfast so I set up the Nikon and tripod to make good use of the time. We went through the locks into the Moray Firth and were thrilled by the wildlife. The boys were using the ship's binoculars to spot the seals and birds. We were enthralled by dolphins and very excited when they came closer.

Tuesday 15th August

At 5.00am the boat set off from Macduff. After being very active through the night the boys spent the whole morning asleep on deck under a sunny sky on a calm sea. I had art materials and cameras set up, but to no avail as they were completely out of it. The two Davids, Tom and Grant were feeling queasy, and David Moony was throwing up.

Meanwhile Frank had spent much of the day in bed in an unsuccessful attempt to recover from a virus infection. He was concerned not to infect the crew and decided to cut short his stay on the boat.

Eventually we arrived at Stonehaven and went shopping. I purchased compasses, protractors and film. On my return Frank had been collected by relatives and had left the ship. After tea I agreed to take six of the lads swimming, an arrangement that had been promised by Frank. I did not have any details of the pool timetable and we found that it was not available to youngsters at that time of day. We made our way back to the boat by 9.45pm, via the amusement arcade and pizza takeaway.

Wednesday 16th August

I felt especially concerned about one of the older boys who had been diagnosed as ADHD (Attention Deficit and Hyperactive Disorder) and took the drug Ritalin to control it. This tended to make him stumble around in a stupor. He also had emotional problems which Frank said had to do with problems in his home life, and led him to bully and ridicule the younger boys. In the mornings he showed an interest in Tai Chi and I tried to encourage this as a possible way of introducing some calm and balance into his life.

I think that by and large the boys had enjoyed the trip. The experience of being on the sea was thrilling for them. Between bouts of seasickness they were in extremely high spirits. On such a short trip they were never calm enough to produce the kind of work that Alex had planned. However they did have some interest in the photography and I think that a full week, with a healthy Frank Fallows and another female worker in addition to me, would have helped counter balance the testosterone levels on the ship. The boys cleared out their belongings and swapped places with the girls who arrived at about 12.30pm.

Girls

There were two new workers, Sharon and Ann. Ann had stepped in at the last minute to cover for Frank. By this time it was too late for us to catch the tide to Arbroath. Paul decided we would stay put until the next day, so in the afternoon we shopped for food and returned to make tea. This left some time to do some drawing and painting from the Celtic and Pictish design books I had purchased at Fort Augustus. The girls took to it really well, even those without any particular flair.

Thursday 17th August

We set off from Stonehaven early. It was fine weather. I set out the art material with the scenic studies and Celtic designs but in a very short time, most of the group were out of it, feeling seasick or tired. One by one they dropped out and either went to their bunk after being sick, or huddled on deck under duvets. The exceptions were young Teresa, Sharon the youth worker, and the crew. This was a sleepy day but one or two girls perked up and we did manage the odd photo. Towards the end of the afternoon, Debbie, Lee, Teresa and Louise managed to make some watercolour studies. Lisa joined in later. While we were docking at Anstruther there were some good views of buildings and ships. Twelve year old Kirsty who was not keen on painting and drawing, was interested in the mechanics of using the 80-200 mm zoom lens on the mounted Nikon camera.

The evening was spent walking round town and whistling at local lads. These girls were up for fun and they were a really good crowd, just hanging out and enjoying each other's company. Sleep didn't come easy though, and they were awake into the early hours chatting on deck.

Friday 18th August

They finally made it to bed by 3.30am. We set off from Anstruther at 8.00am but we were late rising. Some inquisitive seals and dolphins were spotted near the boat and created some excitement.

Later in the morning we beached *Audrey* in St Andrews Bay. Three of the girls Teresa, Debbie Lee, and Lindsey waded ashore. When they returned, I joined them in the water. Maggie, Kirsty and Lisa tried to climb down the ladders and join their friends in their watery frolics but were beaten back by the cold. This was a really enjoyable interlude and at about 11.45 we set sail for Dundee. The weather had now become more overcast and the girls renewed their interest in picture making. Working in water colours, using a technique in which they were becoming accomplished, they made copies of Celtic designs and postcard pictures of dolphins.

We arrived at Dundee late in the afternoon to find the dock unexpectedly derelict. After tea, the lack of scenic areas to visit, prompted artistic effort in fits and starts on the dining room table. At one point I accompanied a few girls off the boat to visit the local petrol station for some supplies. When we got back, the picture making was still in full swing and continued throughout the evening. Mary Ann who had been seasick all through the trip did not put down her brush until after midnight.

Saturday 19th August

The boat was heading to Arbroath, an altogether pleasanter place. Before returning home, the girls wanted to copy my movements and do Tai Chi with me on the dockside. I thought this was a perfect ending to the trip and felt appreciated for my part in their adventure.

The short project with the girls had been successful. Although they had worked on individual pieces and it had not been possible to create a mural, we had nevertheless achieved a lot in a short time. They needed little encouragement to get involved and give of their best and I was sad that given their level of talent and enthusiasm, we did not have the opportunity to test them further. I thoroughly enjoyed myself and the company of those involved

Week 15: 20th-26th August

Arbroath – Anstruther – Berwick on Tweed – Lindisfarne – Blythe – North Shields

The Harding Family

Author's Comment

Following a very late cancellation for Week 15 of *Audrey 2000* it was suggested that Tim Harding, Head of Burton Stather Primary School in North Lincolnshire, and his family should entertain the north east coast from Arbroath to North Shields with songs they would compose 'before the mast'. An orchestra of Hardings, namely Tim and Amanda, Eleanor (13), Charlotte (11) and Emily soon produced *The Audrey Suite* which in Tim's words:

> ...begins with the Audrey *theme composed by Emily and Tim during the voyage. The theme recurred with different instrumentation to reflect the changing landscapes. Interspersed with the theme were three local folk tunes from the areas visited. The first, The East Neuk of Fife was given a traditional Scottish flavour. Go to Berwick began in a traditional manner and was set against a new song, The Proud Walls of Berwick, but gradually moved into a more up-tempo rendition of the tune. Finally The New Road to Tynemouth was completely re-worked to reflect the new, more cosmopolitan modern developments to be found along the banks of the Tyne. The words of the accompanying song reflected on the passing of the old dockyards and the regeneration of the area.*

Amanda Harding

Charlotte and Eleanor made a sign advertising live music on the boat at 7.00pm and we put it above the boat on the quayside. Seahouses was by far the busiest place we've come into — teeming with holidaymakers — so it looked like a good venue. We then set up all the instruments on deck just as we had done at Anstruther. Quite a crowd gathered as we started to play. A fishing boat came into harbour with the crew dancing and they tooted their whistle to join in. We also had boys in a rowing boat alongside listening to us. Some people arrived who said they had heard us in the town. They had then walked down to see us, so we had to do an encore.

Author's Comment

Not surprisingly Burton Stather school derived its success from an active curriculum inspired by its headteacher. The Ofsted report of January 2001 said:

> *The school provides a very good range of extra-curricular clubs and activities. Older pupils are involved in musical groups, for example, orchestra, choir and jazz band. They put into practice the skills they learn in lessons and through instrumental tuition. They perform with verve and enthusiasm. Sporting activities are strongly represented and these extend pupils' physical skills, help them to develop a sense of fair play and encourage teamwork.*
>
> *Older pupils take part in residential visits. These provide activities to support the geography and history curriculum in Year 5 and adventurous outdoor activities in Year 6. The residential element, one night for pupils in Year 5 and several nights for pupils in Year 6, promotes personal organisation and independence. Challenging activities encourage self-discipline and co-operation.*
>
> *Pupils are encouraged to use their talents for the good of the school and the wider community. The school has developed a justifiable reputation as one 'that does things'. It has contributed to a multi-cultural arts project and a poetry publication. Pupils take part in festivals, competitions and functions and give performances for the pleasure of others. Together with teachers and parents they have developed a wild life area. These opportunities contribute strongly to pupils' social development and enrich their learning.*
>
> *Pupils are proud of their school. By the time they leave, they have developed levels of maturity and confidence that stand them in good stead for the next stage of their school life'.*

Tim Harding: Headteacher of Burton Stather Primary School, North Lincolnshire

We all left *Audrey* with, to a greater or lesser extent, a sense of achievement, survival, enrichment and a fund of memorable experiences. Sailing through the mist and then seeing Dunstanburgh castle as dolphins swam in the bow wave, is something I'll always remember!

Author's Comment

The time on *Audrey*, Tim said, would be remembered seven years later, by his daughter Charlotte,[7] who, *'became a professional musician and composer. She won the very prestigious Queen Elizabeth the Queen Mother trophy awarded to the top student at the Royal College of Music. As soon as she got access to music software, she wrote her first concerto in 2007 and almost inevitably it was called*

'Voyage', inspired of course, by Audrey.[7] The concerto was premiered by world-class saxophonist, Richard Ingham, with the orchestra of St Andrew's university, and subsequently published by Reed Music in 2011. It is now being played by accomplished saxophonists worldwide'.

Paul Cooper: Skipper

Audrey penned into Hull marina at 6.30pm on 2nd September 2000 after a journey of 2000 miles round the British Isles. It had been a chance remark about the coming millennium and an unrelated encounter with an admiralty chart catalogue that had sent her on this *fin-de-siècle* odyssey. Sixteen weeks of highs and lows:

> *Beautiful sunrises — Misplaced children — Gallic customs — Barbecues in the rain — Private traumas — Fair winds and long sails — Lots of motoring — Rain — Friendly receptions — Outstanding professionalism — Dolphins round the boat — More rain — Beautiful sunsets*

Author's Comment

I will let Tim Harding give his headteacher perspective:

> *I feel that experiential teaching and learning, whilst diminishing in schools for apparent reasons to do with Health & Safety, the new alleged 'rigorous' curriculum, league tables, teacher overload and judgement by 'results', is actually becoming more important for the new generations of 'screenagers'. We now live in an age when skimming stones, climbing trees and eating around a table and sharing experiences, views and opinions, are often novelties for children.*

> *On Audrey, I think we all, literally and figuratively, saw things from a different perspective. This was real learning, away from the page, screen or pedagogue, combining curriculum content in a thoroughly comprehensive environment, interlaced with social experience and learning. And at the teacher's discretion where appropriate, this learning could be effectively linked to the activities of the classroom.*

Audrey Afterword: What Did The Project Achieve?

Reflections on *Audrey*'s millennium voyage lasted several months.

On December 2nd 2000, three months after the ship's arrival back in Hull, Councillor Patrick Doyle, Leader of Kingston upon Hull City Council, was the main speaker at an *Audrey* 2000 Open Day in Hull's Guildhall. Praising the Project's work in Hull over 20 years, he said, "Sobriety *helps people to think for themselves, to acquire personal convictions and have the courage to take risks.*" On the same occasion, the Harding family, who had entertained the east coast from Arbroath to North Shields during the penultimate week of the voyage, launched a CD: *Audrey 2000 — A Musical Voyage* with themes of the sea. A display of banners and photographs, and presentations by the voyagers completed the celebration.

Perhaps however, the real legacy was unseen, intangible and private, belonging exclusively to individuals who had dormant talents brought to life by the voyage. They seem to have had much the same experience as established artists in their early years. Among these was contemporary artist Bob and Roberta Smith (also known as Patrick Brill) who went on a school visit to the

Whitechapel Art Gallery where the curator presented him with a huge sheet of paper and said forget about the paintings downstairs, just make something huge. That was the day he thought, *"This is for me."* Similarly Turner Prize winner Elizabeth Price recalls pieces she made during school, all of them redolent of the efforts of *Audrey*'s budding artists: a poster of Jesus (wearing flares) admonishing children to put litter in bins: a powder colour painting of a Coca-Cola bottle, and a gold foil collage of Tutankhamun. She says, *"It was my way of growing up and of joining in."* [8] This may seem a long way from the deck of a sailing barge in rough weather but as several of *Audrey*'s artists said to young people when they joined the ship, *"You have to begin somewhere and who knows where your endeavours will end."*

Taking a theme of 'reaching out', Martin Wainwright, former Northern Editor of the *Guardian*, wrote in *Sobriety*'s Review of 2000:

> *This Millennium year has seen the virtues of* Sobriety *taking to the high seas with* Audrey*'s momentous tour of the national coast. This was important symbolically because of its emphasis on reaching out and not just contemplating our own Yorkshire navels however satisfactory they may be. Reaching out whether to Doncaster's prisons or to distant harbours in Devon and Cornwall is central to the ethos of* Sobriety. *In fact in some fanciful moments I rather wish that some modern-day Christian Fletcher had hi-jacked* Audrey *and sailed her to America to spread the word of the Project there.*

'Reaching out' continued into 2001 with the ship's crew planning a 14 week voyage to Poland for 2004. Their inspiration was the enlargement of the European Union which had contributed so much to the Project's development during the previous decade. They presented *Destination Gdansk* as a natural by-product of the historical links between Britain and northern Europe. After describing the connections between medieval England, Flanders and the Hanseatic League, they suggested that *Audrey* should visit cities on the littorals of Holland, Germany, Scandinavia and Poland, including the ancient port city of Lübeck, so that young people could learn about the trade links represented in the collections of their respective museums. (see Appendix 6)

The idea was romantic on paper but sadly would come to nothing. The *Sobriety* Project could not afford to keep *Audrey*, and within two years she would be sold at a knock down price to become cheap accommodation. The only community project in Yorkshire to use the open sea as an adventure playground for local young people, would come to an end.

The development of *Audrey* culminating but not quite ending, in a circumnavigation of Britain to celebrate the millennium, was the subject of many articles in the *Sobriety* Project's Reviews of the Year. The people who told the stories were proud of the game they were in and eloquent in its interpretation and as editor of the narratives up to 2003, the year when she was sold, I can only try not to distort their message and to safeguard their reputation and record. I said:

> *My sadness is the result of our decision to cease the operation of our sailing barge* Audrey. *With net outgoings of more than £60,000 a year, the project has become impossible to justify in its present form.*

I am grateful for the impact the ship has made on the young people of the region. Since 1987 they have come from pupil referral units, young offender institutions, youth groups on big council estates and schools and colleges, to spend a week working together with a common purpose. As part of the millennium celebrations in 2000, Audrey sailed round the UK in 16 weeks. During the nineteen nineties she took young people from the back streets of Hull, Bradford, Leeds and Sheffield to sail the Scottish west coast and the Ijsselmeer in Holland. It was fun to hear children who had never before left their home city, talking about Enkhuizen or the Isle of Skye as if they were familiar places just down the road. About 7000 young people who would never have thought of going to sea have been deeply affected. They have experienced a new environment, a release from routine and a pleasure of teamwork and discipline they could not have imagined.

Two groups of people have been immediately responsible for this. Firstly they are the ship's staff and volunteers. Among the latter were those who left home in the winter to scrape and black varnish Audrey's hull and those in the summer who were given the task of working with the most difficult groups of young people. My tribute to Audrey's staff is that throughout fifteen years of sea and river passages, equivalent in distance to sailing round the world, there has been a sustained tradition of achieving the highest standards in all aspects of the ship's operation. A thread of honest appraisal and determination has characterised her development both as a passenger vessel and as an educational resource for Yorkshire and Humberside. We have been fortunate to have staff who combined proficiency in ocean going sailing with understanding of young people. Paul Cooper and Mel Parish, her skippers in recent years, became institutions on the Humber and in ports around the UK. Their professionalism and skill inspired respect for Audrey's work of adventure and learning. They led and managed teams of experts, outstanding among whom in the nineties were Mark Peacock and Bob Wride who helped build the tradition, and more recently, Tony Papademetrie and Graham Waite, who maintained it with enthusiasm and affection.

In the background but also crucial to Audrey's success over 15 years, have been charitable trusts and statutory authorities investing money in the work. Many of them contributed to a major re-fit of the ship in 1998 and on June 1st that year, came to the Waterways Museum to applaud her re-commissioning by HRH The Duke of Edinburgh.

Rescue Plans

The immediate reason for the project's demise was easy to grasp; she simply could not pay for herself, and although it may sound like carelessness, it was never intended that she should.

From the beginning, *Sobriety*'s committee was determined the ship would serve the interests of organisations and individuals on restricted incomes. *Audrey* would recruit and welcome people living in the parts of Yorkshire that were socially and economically well below the national average in respect of any broad measures of education, health and employment. For *Audrey*, as for the rest of *Sobriety*, the people who would have priority would be those who were hard-up and unlikely ever to have the opportunity to enjoy the sea and inland waterways. In defence of a policy to benefit people on low incomes which some nowadays would regard (wrongly I think) as misguided, it should be remembered that the groups did make every effort to contribute towards the cost of the ship's operation and managed to pay about £60,000 a year. That they raised this by special efforts and approaches to grant making bodies says something about *Audrey*'s appeal. Against an expenditure of £90,000 however, it was not enough to prevent her being put on the market when the *Sobriety* Project as a whole was in serious deficit.

Was there an alternative? Nigel Ling, without whose forward thinking *Audrey* would never have left the Humber, was adamant that the best and most profitable arrangement would be to lease her on bareboat charter. This is a legal agreement or charterparty which makes the hirer responsible for all expenditure associated with the vessel including insurance, repair and staff costs. His opinion was that the proposal to sell was irresponsible. He agreed that it might be necessary to take the ship out of service and pay off her staff but certainly not to take the irrevocable step of disposal. If a charterer paid £5,000 or £10,000 a year, the asset would create a net income rather than the net loss resulting from sale, especially since it was a fully certificated going concern. He also thought *Audrey* would take a long time to sell and that the Project would be lucky to realise more than £50,000 less broker s fees. An irreplaceable asset would have been lost as well as the income that it could generate from charter. We would in effect have burned our boats.

The committee acknowledged Nigel's opinion and took it seriously. The market for *Audrey* would be restricted. She might have masts and sails but still had the hull of a lightship, and although she had won the Humber Barge Race in 1998, a yacht she certainly was not. Nor after conversion could she be considered an historic ship like a Thames barge, and eligible for membership of an exclusive club. She was what she was; a lightship converted to sail and fitted with accommodation appropriate to her use as a community boat. She was in a niche market. Thinking that we might pursue some kind of 'timeshare' arrangement, I approached the Open Lock Project, a training provider in Greater Manchester, and Basics Plus in Scarborough, which had a long history of using *Sobriety* to help people with additional learning needs get into employment. In June 2003 I outlined my proposals in letters to the principals of the two organisations, Glen Rees and Avis Turner. I said that *Audrey* was to be sold to raise much needed unrestricted funding [9] but that I should like her to remain a 'community boat' which catered for the developmental needs of young people. I suggested that with access to capital from the European Regional Development Fund [10] they might agree to set up a small consortium so that Open Lock, Basics Plus and *Sobriety* had an equal share in responsibilities for running costs. I continued:

Trustees have put Audrey *on the market at £150,000. As you know she is in superb condition and has been maintained to the highest standards. If the Open Lock Project and Scarborough each paid £50,000 using ERDF, then Sobriety would keep a one third share. The main revenue cost is for staffing which could be the subject of a revenue application to the European Social Fund. If the ship worked for 38 weeks in the year and was also used in the winter as a river and canal boat, she could earn £60,000. If this could be achieved there would be £24,000 left to find — split between the three organisations. There are many possibilities and I'm open to suggestions, but the bottom line is that she is to be sold and that her staff, Paul Cooper and Mel Parish, are to be made redundant. I still hope it may be possible to arrange things so that their goodwill and expertise are not lost to the cause.*

As an example of how the ship might be used, I outlined the elements of a training course which if sensitively adapted, might suit their students:

- Introduction to boats and their terminologies
- How to live on a boat – teamwork, hygiene, safety, routines and procedures
- Ropes and their care
- Leaving and returning to moorings
- Communications and look out
- Steering the ship – fixed marks, compass
- Sail and engine – deckwork, mechanics
- How decisions are made – importance of information:
- Tides, charts and collision regulations.

When *Audrey* was in Scarborough however, she would also meet the requirements of the resort's *Renaissance* programme [11] by running trips round the bay, providing a harbour venue for performing arts and exhibitions, advertising neighbourhood links with the sea, participating in civic and corporate functions and being available for weekend and week long residentials. Each organisation would 'own' the vessel for up to 15 weeks and dates would be finalised by the end of November.

A third idea briefly discussed with Ian White, British Waterways regional manager for the north east of England, was that his organisation might agree to purchase the ship and then lease it back under a charterparty to the *Sobriety* Project.

My suggestions were politely considered but rejected; the three organisations were just as worried about revenue expenditure as *Sobriety*, and were unwilling to risk their capital. Avis Turner did try to persuade several of her supporting charitable trusts to come in on the venture but they remained sceptical. In the end *Sobriety*'s trustees who had waited patiently for a good outcome, decided that financial pressures would not allow any further delay and that *Audrey* had to go. In a last ditch attempt to provoke interest, I sent a circular to voluntary organisations in the Yorkshire and Humber region.

The circular came to the attention of youth worker Graham Pearson who purchased *Audrey* for £60,000 in September 2003. The ship was to be his home and with a berth in Hull marina, he had every intention of sailing her on the Humber. It was however not a realistic undertaking for someone outside the yachting fraternity and after a couple of years she was back on the market. She is now home to a family in London and berthed on a private wharf downriver from Tower Bridge on the river Thames. She gives the appearance of being well cared for.

Post Mortem

Audrey was perhaps her own worst enemy. Not only was she unglamourous, neither did she commend herself to organisations in search of flagships and exclusive symbols. She was insistently a community barge with an appeal to people who would have been terrified at the prospect of joining an ocean-going yacht. She was not in any sense exclusive; all were welcome and the planning that took place before and during a cruise was designed not to present passengers with competitive targets and humiliating comparisons but to ascertain how best to extend their opportunities to shine. For people who sometimes had a low opinion of themselves, it was not mandatory to learn the skills and disciplines of sailing; what was expected was that everyone on board would pull together in different ways to make the trip a success. There was no prescription about what constituted success; that was the business of individuals. Crew were there to make and adapt arrangements to meet staff objectives for the young people in their care. This helped to take away fear of the unknown and was a congenial experience for everyone. It transmitted informality and by giving the school or youth club the feeling that *Audrey* belonged to them for the week, removed barriers of hierarchies and allowed problems to be solved quickly without posturing or difficulties of communication. On the rare occasions when staff were inadequate, this relationship enabled crew to step in and become responsible for all aspects of the trip.

There was an example of this intervention when a school in Hull commissioned *Audrey* to help a group of young people to improve their reading, writing and numeracy. The ship was on the west coast of Scotland and the weather was fine. The young people were looking forward to a week navigating the 60 miles of the Great Glen from Corpach at the foot of Ben Nevis to Inverness on the east coast. Their leader in charge however, was unpleasant and for two days sat on deck speaking neither to children nor crew. Without fuss the two skippers rang the school and asked for the man to be instructed to return home. In the words of the crew to the head of department, *"We will make it a good week for the children."* And they did.

On another occasion a fifteen year old girl had a miscarriage while the boat was moored in one of the havens on the south bank of the Humber, a terrifying experience for one so young. The wife of one of *Audrey*'s crew who worked for Hull's teenage pregnancy unit was able to come and help the girl while crew looked after the other children who all came from families needing Social Services support.

An equally distressing episode occurred one summer evening when *Audrey* was at *Sobriety*'s museum in Goole. Under the eyes of visitors, a boy from a children's home 'kicked off' and had to be restrained and calmed by two members of the home's staff, one of whom was quite seriously hurt. With the additional help of a local student volunteer who had been helping with the children, crew were able to take a lead in occupying the other children until professional help arrived.

This closeness to client groups was *Audrey*'s hallmark. It reflected the philosophy and practice of the other parts of its parent organisation and indeed of community boat organisations on the inland waterways, but in its use of the sea, it was different.

Unlike *Audrey*, many sail training organisations were exclusive, recruiting middle class young people and educating them to the highest possible standards in the sailing discipline. Young people with a learning disability, mental health problems or a history of offending would find it difficult to get a place on a cruise, and even if they did, might find themselves in hopeless competition with people more familiar with the terminologies and routines of a training ship. Jim Hogan's pot boy was a rarity!

One might be justified in asking why then, with all its credentials for community development, *Audrey* was not underpinned by enough support from statutory bodies like Hull City Council and Yorkshire Forward to guarantee her survival. This could have been made available for a few years at least, that is until local authorities were overtaken by the economic downturns in the closing years of the decade. Whilst it would be curmudgeonly not to acknowledge the huge contribution that both of these public authorities made to the work of the *Sobriety* Project over 20 years, it became apparent that both had their own fish to fry.

In 1995 Sir Robin Knox Johnston had founded the Clipper Round the World Race. Many of the participant yachts were sponsored by and named after famous cities and when it was decided that the race should begin in Hull, Yorkshire Forward saw an opportunity to promote the Humber sub-region by building the yacht *Hull and Humber*. It cost £300,000 and crew for the race were recruited from the Hull business fraternity and the employees of Yorkshire Forward. They each paid £10,000 to take part in one of the 13 legs of the cruise, a wonderful experience for those who could afford it. *Sobriety* was approached by Blue Banana consultants who had been hired to promote the venture to schools and youth groups. We asked if our young people could get a ride on the boat. The answer was that they could follow the race on a map.

Hull and Humber did well in the races and with more public and private sponsorship to hand, from Hull Primary Care Trust which paid for the boat, and from City Vison and Yorkshire Forward which covered the outgoings, the City Council set up its own sail training charity, *CatZero*, with its yacht *One Hull*. Unlike *Audrey* it had no problem leaving the Humber; one of its first cruises was to Iceland and Greenland. The website introduction reads:

> CatZero (*formerly known as* One Hull) *is the 72 foot Challenge Round the World Racing Yacht which is at the heart of the scheme. The yacht is insurance Category Zero, from where it gets its name, and can sail anywhere in the world, in all conditions. We take this intrepid, adventurous attitude into our work with young people. Purchased using capital funds from NHS Hull, the yacht is primarily used with groups of young people as a tool to build self-confidence, teamwork and co-operation. However, the* CatZero *yacht has now successfully been able to develop a number of exciting racing and other challenging adventures throughout the year, available to private and corporate clients. From discovering fabulous Norwegian Fjords to skipping over the waves in the world famous Fastnet race,* CatZero *continues to set challenges, explore new horizons and push boundaries the world over.*

Interesting that the yacht, rather than the people that might use it is described as 'the heart' of the scheme. There is also a rather downbeat notice:

CatZero is not currently running any courses on the North Bank for young people aged 16-18 not in education, employment or training but we are looking for funding to run such programmes in the area, in 2013 and beyond.

This is followed by an invitation to apply for a place in the Rolex 2013 Fastnet Race. It says that interested young people should contact *CatZero* as soon as possible. Presumably, the applications would come from those who could pay for their place and who have some serious experience as yachtsmen. Some upbeat recruitment editorial [12] appeared in local newspapers in autumn 2014 but the fact remains that in contrast to members of *Audrey*'s groups the partcipating young people would be fit and bright. No one sailing to the Orkneys aboard *CatZero* would be one of the regular attenders at Coltman Street Day Centre, the mental health facility in Hull described in Chapter 6, whose members had spent a week on *Sobriety*.

With three of her four skippers qualified to the level of Yachtmaster Ocean and one who had sailed twice in the Fastnet Race, qualified to Yachtmaster Instructor, *Audrey*'s crew was not lacking in expertise and as we have seen, the ship more than met Maritime and Coastguard Agency standards of safety for a sea going vessel. Added to this the Project had no difficulty in recruiting young people from some of the sub-region's most deprived areas and had shown historically that it was capable of achieving numerical and outcome targets set by both city and government. In other words, as Patrick Doyle had said in 2000, it was very good at working with people who had problems that were widespread in Hull: high unemployment, bad health, truancy from school, low educational attainment and small business failure. Why did not the city council and Yorkshire Forward commission *Audrey* to help with the solution to these problems? It would be unfair to accuse them of pandering to the romantic inclinations of the corporate sector but the £15,000 that CatZero is said to charge annually for a company to display its logo on the hull of the yacht would certainly have helped *Sobriety* balance its books.

What Made Audrey *Special?*

Early in 1998 *Audrey* had been given a full re-fit in dry dock at Beverley and then on June 1st of that year had been re-commissioned by HRH Prince Phillip at the Waterways Museum in Goole. In the Project's 1998 Review, under the title of *Winds of Change*, Paul Cooper took an opportunity to analyse current trends. Some of his conclusions took us back to Colin Walden's ideas about *Audrey* eight years before and are of the utmost importance:

For me Audrey *offers an unusual social experience in what for most people is a strange and exciting environment. Many organisations use the ship with the idea that the venture alone will enable them to achieve their aims. Others use the opportunity to work towards specific objectives which may assist with the achievement of longer term aims.*

However I want to sound a word of caution in becoming too involved in the development of 'off the peg' programmes. I think that individuals take away from our cruises many different memories. Some of these are clear challenges to prejudice and preconception, some cannot be pinned down and are downright uncomfortable, and others are therapeutic and amusing. However, they are all part of personal development and I don't want an unquantifiable and personal experience to be ruined by an obsession with 'measurable outcomes'. We live at a time when the simple memory of a sunset over the Western Isles is not enough. It has to be recorded to provide evidence of authenticity. It would be a shame if the Project's concern with objectives led to a devaluation of the overall experience. If we market 'objectives' rather than the total experience, we will then go on to say that certain 'objectives' are suitable for certain people. And then we are starting to become exclusive because funding will follow the targets and re-inforce the selection of the objectives.

Audrey *has always accepted all comers. Although this policy has sometimes created difficulties for crew, the commitment to being 'open to all' has allowed groups and individuals to take from the experience what they need. Within the limits of safety, propriety and common sense, I want this experience to remain as open and accessible as it is.*

Tim Harding, head of Burton-upon-Stather Primary School put a high value on this openness:

For me, the inclusivity of the Project was a huge feature. Here was something that everyone could enjoy, learn and benefit from, whatever their background or ability level (my interpretation of inclusivity is something that includes everyone, as opposed to the narrower concept of including less able people in mainstream activities). At whatever level, intellectual or social, the Audrey *experience had a great deal to give.*

Whilst, understandably, the Project had an emphasis on groups from disadvantaged backgrounds, the children that I took on these boats were village children from a spectrum of social backgrounds. And the more privileged children gained just as much from the experience as the less advantaged; these were unique experiences. Even the more privileged children would very rarely have the opportunity to do what we did — sail on the Humber, viewing their village from the water, with a group of peers.

He also said that for his school, his four trips on *Audrey* and two on *Sobriety* were some of the most effective, valuable and memorable experiences of his teaching career:

From a curriculum point of view, Audrey *provided endless planned opportunities to cover much of the required curriculum content across a wide variety of subjects: from English (factual ship's logs and descriptions of environments), to poetry and stories (as well as lots of drama!), to maths (compass reading and speed calculation), to science (dipping for water samples at various points up and down the estuary) to art and music. The list could go on and on.*

Then there were the many spontaneous learning opportunities, which ranged from "What's that bird called?" (Answer: "Don't know. Go and ask the skipper!") to the fascinating talk given by one of the crew members of an Arctic Research vessel we moored next to in Grimsby docks. We all learned about the importance of research on krill and its effect on the whole eco system. This led to a fabulous impromptu lesson on food chains on the deck of Audrey *as we sailed back to Hull, using paper plates from the galley laid out in a pyramid pattern, with the children drawing and writing the names of the different creatures in the Arctic marine food chain and understanding how the demise of one layer would affect all the other layers.*

The boat environment also provided a setting where the need for rules and discipline were easier to understand, the consequences of ignoring them being immediately visible over the side! This helped to foster that all-important sense of occasion that all children (and adults) need, which is that there are times when we can all be silly, and times when for a reason, we need to be sensible or behave in a certain way.

But thoughtful and popular as the professional crew were, and perfect as *Audrey* was in providing the *Sobriety* Project's own brand of social education, some cracks had appeared. Critically, there was a downward trend in bookings in the spring and autumn of 1999. In another *Review* article *Of Mice and Marlin Spikes* Paul attributed this to several factors: *Audrey*'s absence from the Humber which may have devalued the experience she could offer in local waters, staffing reductions in the organisations which used the ship, and thirdly, changes in working practice created by Ofsted's increasingly tight grip on the school curriculum through classroom testing. There also appeared to be a change of heart about residential experiences. Following some well publicised tragedies on the inland waterways and coast, teachers and youth leaders began to feel exposed to the risk of litigation. The teachers who had as pupils benefited from outdoor residentials now began to feel vulnerable. A tradition held dear by generations of staff in state schools since the nineteen twenties, was beginning to die.

I do not know whether the Project failed to market itself forcefully enough or whether being based in Goole was a disadvantage or whether a flat bottomed ex-lightship was not the right symbol of status for public and corporate authorities. I do know however, that the sight of a replica 'billyboy' in full sail on the Humber, consistently brought a sense of pride to everyone associated with her during the fifteen years of her operation from 1988 to 2003. But not everything is lost. Just as the name 'City Challenge', was hi-jacked to introduce less imaginative initiatives, so 'Billyboy' lives on in the name of Germany's best selling high quality condom highlighted recently in a 'Buy one, Get one free' promotion.

Questions

The artist accompanying Glasgow's *Universal Connections* appeared to be less than happy. Would you have done anything about this?

Would you have sold *Audrey*?

What was lost?

Chapter 8 Notes

1   Article by Ken Robinson (*Guardian* 18th May 2013) entitled *Gove extols creativity-but he has no idea what it is.* (Michael Gove was Secretary of State for Education in the coalition government 2010 – 2015).

2   *Outward Bound the Inward Odyssey* is the title of a book by Zelinski and Shaefer, published in 1991 by Beyond Words Publishing Inc.

3   For a full description of Fountain House Pupil Referral Unit as it was in 2000 see Ofsted Inspection Report 20th-23rd March 2000. Page 16 paragraph 30 lists a range of extra curricular activities:

   The unit provides residential experiences for some pupils, for example, on a sailing barge. Several pupils offer valued support to a local school for severely disabled pupils, helping others less fortunate than themselves in swimming lessons.

   It is worth noting however that the unit was not subject to the requirements of the National Curriculum.

   However, few after school clubs and residential visits are provided. As a result, opportunities are missed to provide pupils with experiences for them to practise their independent living skills in real situations. (P.4 Curriculum and Other Activities Ofsted Report 2006). The school seems to have gone backwards from 2000 in this respect, but to have remedied the problem by the time of later inspections.

4   Dialect in eastern England for a channel of water lying between sandbanks or between sandbanks and the shore: OED.

5   Jean Bart (1650–1702) was a French sailor who served the French crown as naval commander and privateer. Many anecdotes tell of the courage and bluntness of the uncultivated sailor who became a popular hero of the French Navy. He captured a total of 386 ships and also sank or burned a great many more. The town of Dunkirk has honoured his memory by erecting a statue and by naming a public square after him. (Wikipedia)

6   *Peggy* is an 18th century manx yacht built for George Quayle of Castletown between 1789 and 1793. For over one hundred years following Quayle's death, *Peggy* was interred within the boathouse he had built for her, effectively forgotten. Interest in her grew during the 20th century, and after World War II she was given to the people of the Isle Man to be held in trust by Manx National Heritage. She remains preserved in the boathouse, now part of The Nautical Museum in Castletown. She is clinker-built and was schooner rigged with a bowsprit. A set of her spars is preserved with her, along with her armaments of six cannon and two stern chasers, and the winding gear employed to draw her into the boathouse. She is the oldest surviving schooner in the world.

7   Charlotte Harding: see also page 2 of the Goole Courier 3.5.2007

8   See *Guardian (Review section)*, 15.12.2012

9   Unrestricted funding: Charity Commission rules require organisations that have been given funds for a specific purpose to spend it on that purpose. These funds are 'restricted'. Other funds are 'unrestricted'. Audit reports are required to discriminate between the two kinds of funds.

10 ERDF: European Regional Development Fund normally available only to areas of deprivation and designed to support infrastructure development.

   ESF: European Social Fund available on a competitive basis to eligible organisations for support of training and labour market entry. (See also Chapter 13; Europe)

11 *Renaissance*: a government initiative assisting local authorities with the economic development of market towns (as opposed to cities and rural areas)

12 *South Holderness Gazette*, 2.10.2014.

Chapter 9

DUTCH RIVER SIDE

Location Location

At the times of the spring and autumn equinox, Goole is two and a half metres below the average height of high water in the Yorkshire Ouse, a threat which would seem to give the town a good chance of being an early victim of rising sea levels preceded by some unusually high prices of house insurance. However, reinforced river banks and expertly managed systems of drains and sluices have removed the threat and the town is safe. Playing a critically important part in the drainage is the river Don, a tributary of the lower Ouse, known locally as the Dutch River, which rises on the Derbyshire moors above Sheffield, and flows through south Yorkshire until it reaches Goole. Just before joining the Ouse seaway, the river divides the town in two, the original 1362 settlement of Old Goole being to its south, and to its north, the Aire & Calder Company's town and docks which were built in the eighteen twenties and thirties. The lower reaches of the Don are in fact a man-made diversion dug in the 1630s by Dutch engineers hired by King Charles I to drain the royal hunting grounds around the village of Hatfield near Doncaster. A walk

Dutch River Goole. Tim Watson

along the north bank of the river, past the Goole to Doncaster railway bridge, leads to an ancient sandstone milepost set in the bank, which says that the distance to Sheffield is 38 miles. But this is a treacherous waterway, a drain as much as a river and while it might be only a dribble at low water, the power of its six knot incoming tide can smash to pieces any vessel getting caught against the bridges at Goole and Rawcliffe.

On the other side of the isthmus, north of the Dutch River, is the more benign Goole to Knottingley section of the Aire & Calder Navigation, a broad canal opened in 1826 to fanfares and celebrations following the survey of its line by John Rennie, the engineer for London Bridge. On land between the canal and the river, known as Dutch River Side (not Dutch Riverside for it is the river not its bank which is Dutch) and a few hundred yards west of Bridge Street, is the Yorkshire Waterways Museum, *Sobriety*'s headquarters since 1989 and conveniently isolated from the town but linked to the docks and waterways by the boats and barges berthed on its waterfront.

Someone walking a dog along the rough road up Dutch River Side in earlier years would have seen on her right, the pump house supplying hydraulic pressure to the boat hoists, capstans and lock gates and uniquely, by an extension of the pipework, to the organ of Goole parish church. Next would have come a dry dock and behind it the Number 5 Boat Hoist, one of five 'brothers' which were the destination of the coal-carrying Tom Pudding compartment boats. A few yards further on were the offices and workshops of the British Waterways Board (BWB) which, since taking responsibility for the waterways under the terms of the 1948 Transport Act, had built and repaired the compartment boats. The same Act however had put the care of the hoists into the hands of the British Transport Docks Board, a slightly perverse arrangement which 40 years later would cause problems. Then came the timber ponds excavated for the purpose of seasoning pit props, but now a marina full of little boats for use at weekends, and bigger boats in use all the time, known by their inhabitants as 'live-aboards'. At this point our dog walker would have reached an area derelict with rusty fences, concrete blocks, caterpillar infested rosebay willowherb and lines of orphaned compartment boats awaiting a last waterless journey to the Scunthorpe steel furnaces. Beyond here she would have encountered a cement works with chutes and piles of sand, and wagons keeping the concrete wet in their revolving drums, ready for delivery. Finally she would have arrived on rough ground narrowing into the westward towpaths of the two waterways.

On the other side of the Goole to Knottingley canal opposite the proposed site for *Sobriety*'s HQ was the inland waterways equivalent of the North Atlantic Garbage Patch, a place where barges came to die. Foremost were the hated BACATS (barge aboard a catamaran) which, in defiance of Hull's dockers led by Walter 'Catseyes' Cunningham, had by-passed the Humber ports and carried cargo direct from Rotterdam to Rotherham.

This was a forgotten part of Goole with nothing to interest tourists or local people except perhaps a few bored drunks or clandestine lovers in search of a safe haven.

The marina just about managed to keep going and the boat hoists had the attention of students of industry, but there was little else to attract visitors. In fact, given its proximity to the noisy and pugnacious clientele of the pubs close by — The Dock Tavern, The Mariners' Arms, The Cape of Good Hope and The Vermuyden — it was an area to be avoided, and our ambling dog walker would have been wise to choose a rotweiler as her companion. But even though there was as yet no museum café to offer her tea and scones, this mixture of commerce, history and recreation was perhaps already a museum. It just needed to be discovered.

A Sobriety *Centre*

In August 1986 I was summoned to a meeting which had been organised by Enid Thompson, administration assistant in Boothferry Borough Council's economic development department. Those present included planning officers from Humberside and two architects, Peter White and Chris Bolton from BWB, who had come from their offices at Hillmorton Locks in Warwickshire. The meeting wanted my views on the possibility of developing this small part of their waterway empire as a recreational amenity and centre for the study and display of Goole's history as a canal port. Their drawings showed a star shaped *Sobriety* centre consisting of six shipping containers coming to a common point under a geodesic dome which, with a campsite and berths for the Project's boats, was to turn this neglected strip of land into an adventure area for the public, and a landbase for *Sobriety*. When the idea was put later to the Project's trustees, they did not take long to approve the plans. In the Project's *Review of 1987* they said:

> In other circumstances we might have thought that this would be an unnecessary and expensive development. We already have secure berths in Aldam dock and the use of a former potato shed as a workshop and storage area. Associated British Ports however, have plans to re-develop the Aldam dock quays as container handling areas. 35 Shed and our berths will no longer be available.
>
> Another matter for serious consideration is that the Project has nowhere for visitors, no meeting rooms, no library and no office accommodation. Now that we are employing 25 people, many of them on government work creation schemes, running two vessels and soon a third, and dealing with many different groups, a landbase has become indispensable.

The proposal was given further support by the publication on the 19th December 1987, of an economic development study of Boothferry by the Leeds based consultants *Pieda* Ltd, which noted that in 1983 the borough had the lowest level of tourism spend of any district in the region. It went on to recommend support for a *Sobriety* Project based on Dutch River Side:

> At present the number of visitors to the Project is limited. However, plans for a heritage centre interpreting the history of Goole and the waterways offers scope for a significant increase in activity. If properly presented and marketed, we believe that it would be possible to attract 30,000 to 50,000 visitors a year. This would require a number of actions, namely development of displays incorporating items from the exhibition currently housed in Goole library. Priority should also be given to fitting out a vessel suitable for short tours of the port.

Things soon began to happen. A Community Programme team sponsored by the National Society for the Care & Re-settlement of Offenders (NACRO) arrived on site with sickles and

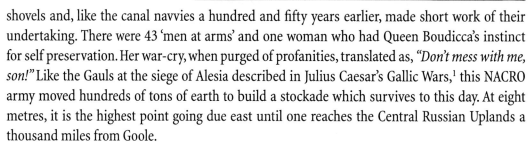

The *Sobriety* Centre, Goole.

shovels and, like the canal navvies a hundred and fifty years earlier, made short work of their undertaking. There were 43 'men at arms' and one woman who had Queen Boudicca's instinct for self preservation. Her war-cry, when purged of profanities, translated as, *"Don't mess with me, son!"* Like the Gauls at the siege of Alesia described in Julius Caesar's Gallic Wars,[1] this NACRO army moved hundreds of tons of earth to build a stockade which survives to this day. At eight metres, it is the highest point going due east until one reaches the Central Russian Uplands a thousand miles from Goole.

Enid Thompson was also a member of *Sobriety*'s management committee and encouraged trustees to smile sweetly on the council's plan for Dutch River Side. In the article *Reclamation: how it happened*, written for a local newpaper, she gave an eloquent account of how the project had been nursed through BWB and government:

> *Some four years ago in 1985 when John Barber the chief executive of Boothferry Borough Council met the chairman of British Waterways at a luncheon engagement, their conversation naturally turned to Goole's links with the waterways and the Board's plans for developing its derelict land as an amenity for Goole and as a tourist attraction.*
>
> *Across from the town's dockland, there leads from Bridge Street a roadway which is sandwiched between the Aire & Calder Navigation and the muddy banks of the river Don. It goes past a dry dock and through drab workaday surroundings. If you lift your eyes over the river bank there is a reminder of a Dutch landscape stretching away across the flat treeless waste of Goole moors. A pattern of dykes divides the land. In the other direction commercial barge traffic chugging along the canal comes into view at the timber pond. The parish church spire rises above the skyline flanked by the jibs of cranes. Wagons on the by-pass can be seen but not heard. It is this mixture of flight and fancy that gives life to Dutch River Side.*

The first improvements to this derelict 'corridor' started in September 1986. On the land betweenthe Tilcon (concrete) works and Smiths boatyard it was planned to provide better access for vistors and facilities for recreation by creating footpaths, a picnic site and car park together with shrubs and trees for screening. British Waterways gained approval from the trade unions for the work to be done by the Goole NACRO team under the government's Community Programme. This gave employment and skills training to townspeople who had been without paid jobs, as well as an opportunity to create wider social and economic benefits for the older part of Goole. Materials and equipment were obtained from local suppliers. The wages of the workforce were paid by central government and the cost of materials was met by Boothferry Borough Council which contributed £5,000, and British Waterways which found the balance of £10,000.

The second phase of the project involved the drainage of land between the Tilcon site and the railway bridge. This area seemed to qualify for grant assistance under another government scheme for reclaiming disused industrial land. Only recently has emphasis been placed on clearing sites purely for environmental use but the council applied early in 1987 for a 100% derelict land grant from the Department of the Environment so that this area could be rescued. Enquiries of British Waterways revealed evidence of its former industrial purpose. Excavation materials and dredgings had been tipped there over 50 years ago when Ocean Lock had been constructed. Part of the land had been occupied by Orchard Cottage built for a canal employee. Other land had also been used from time to time for dumping materials and for breaking up old Tom Puddings. A number of Goole horse marines had owned stables there. Happily the Department of the Environment accepted that the site could be fully funded and the total costs of £9,600 for clearance, drainage and re-seeding were met from the government purse. Although the application was submitted in September 1987, moneys could not be allocated until the next financial year but work eventually received the go-ahead in April 1988. It was intended to be completed in time for the civic opening of the Sobriety Centre in May 1989.

As the groundwork was completed and plans for a Sobriety HQ took shape, other issues arose associated with the history of Goole and its distinctive sense of place. The commercial demands of the port required the demolition of the Aldam Dock compartment boat hoist which was Grade 2*. As a condition of the removal of this historic edifice Associated British Ports undertook to keep the sole remaining compartment boat hoist at South Dock in good repair for visitors to inspect.

The next chapter in this revival story will concern the part the area has to play as a tourist attraction. The proposed Waterways Adventure Centre will occupy a focal point which will strengthen the Sobriety Project's links with enterprise, education and the local community.

The Architect

This was all very well but if the Borough's plans for this 'focal point' were to be realised, we had to find an architect and a builder. Always imaginative, Peter White suggested we talk to Chris

Jones, head of Hull University's school of architecture. Peter and I were soon invited to provide a brief for final year students who, based on their understanding of *Sobriety*'s requirements, would construct models in wood and cardboard to be submitted as coursework for their degrees. The resulting designs, inspired by the students' own cultures from around the world, went on display in Goole library. One of the most remarkable, conceived by a student from Indonesia, consisted of a design for a series of elevated walkways and platforms, presumably intended to protect visitors from the jungle below, or perhaps to protect the jungle from the depredations of visitors. But exciting though the models were, this was Goole not a Disney location on the other side of the world, and when the problem came to the notice of a Hull businessman who had spent his life in maritime commerce, we had our marching orders.

In 1985 Alan Marshall was the newly elected chair of *Sobriety*. After resigning from being managing director of Hutton's, the international ship chandlers, he moved into premises near Minerva pier on Hull's waterfront. From here, with his friend and co-director Audrey Stritt, he founded a company called Baltec (1987) Ltd, whose chief trading partner was the Bulgarian navy based in the Black Sea port of Vanya. I had met him a few years earlier while he was still at Hutton's. We were wanting to improve *Sobriety*'s life saving equipment so that crew could confidently tackle any emergencies arising when the barge was on the lower Humber, in the vicinity of Grimsby and Cleethorpes for example. During an idle dinner hour at school I had written to him without any introduction, asking if he could give or lend us a liferaft up to SOLAS (Safety Of Lives At Sea) standard. Without fuss he presented the Project with a 25 person self inflating raft complete with rations, and medical supplies that would have kept the Black Death at bay. (He did however arrange for the morphine to be removed.) When I went with our treasurer, Sydney Wilks, to thank him, he took us on a tour of the warehouse which provisioned a number of cruise liners, among them the *QE2*. Quantities for each ship were enormous: two tons of cheese, 1,000 bottles of whisky, 100 hams, 100 miles of toilet roll, and so on. However, for most of his time at *Sobriety* he was running Baltec and it was my habit to go to his office each week and give an account of what we were up to. It was not unusual as I reached the bottom of the stairs, to hear him shouting down the telephone in German at some hapless contractor. In the middle of our discussion he would typically be buying wetsuits from a factory in California to sell to the Russian navy in Vladivostock or, after purchasing of a floating power station in Norway, be arranging for tugs to tow it to the coast of Sierra Leone. He was larger than life and his generosity matched his personality.

Part of Alan's charm, which certainly took some getting used to, was his forthright approach to problems. At the time of the fall of the Soviet Union, he said to me, *"You know what the problem is in Moscow? It's full of bloody Germans!"* When I looked puzzled he explained that it was German traders who were 'invading' the Russian capital, not British companies as it should have been. In an equally direct manner, he expressed his opinion of the 'moonbase' design for *Sobriety*'s new centre: *"What the hell do you think you're doing?"* he asked, after I had brought him up to date with the most recent ideas from the school of architecture. *"My son in law, Brian Ferguson, is an architect and will design it for you"*, he announced. There was no arguing.

Brian Ferguson was at that time senior partner in Ferguson, Cale & Sayell, a firm of architects in Knaresborough, North Yorkshire, which had designed the Harrogate Conference Centre. He was nearly as much under Alan's thumb as I was, and quickly produced a design which he introduced (using the appropriate jargon), in *Sobriety*'s Review of 1988:

> *The building aims to provide a combination of playful geometry with recollected images of yesteryear's sailing vessels. Internally the plan generates comfortable work areas while allowing flexible interaction between these and the activities in the central hall.*

> *The site originally resulted from the formation of the Dutch River and is a barrier to it. The load bearing quality of the ground therefore is poor and special techniques are required to create a suitable foundation for the building. The method being employed is vibro-compaction whereby the ground substrate is stabilised and improved by the introduction of 'stone columns' which in turn provide support points for the structural elements including a re-inforced concrete raft which extends to the full area of the ground floor.*

Brian Ferguson's building, which in 2001 he brilliantly doubled in size following a generous grant from the Heritage Lottery Fund (HLF), is architecturally among the most interesting in the region. There is no brickwork; its walls are timber-clad breeze blocks and its roof, supported by a pattern of beams, is clad with aluminium which reflects sunlight, ideal for the deployment of solar panels. Since 2001 the Fund has also sponsored several Young Roots projects brought forward by the museum.

The Builder

The architect also had some ideas about builders. He suggested we get in touch with John Laing plc, which had a reputation for broad based philanthropy and was still being run from its offices in Mill Hill, north London, by members of the Laing family. The company, which had just built Goole's new hospital and Perronet Thompson School in north Hull, was closely associated with the family's grant-making trusts. One of them, the Beatrice Laing Trust, promoted charitable work with ex-offenders as well as giving support to other unpopular causes. A further consideration was that the main interests of the company chairman, Sir Maurice Laing, were the Church of England and sailing, making it evident that an approach to the company had to come from our patron, Bishop David Lunn. His letter to Sir Maurice prompted a reply by return, a cheque for £10,000 towards *Sobriety*'s general funds and the promise of practical help with construction. At the subsequent meeting between the bishop and Laing's managing director, Brian Gregory, the Project was given the choice of recruiting a workforce which his company would manage, or of contracting with John Laing which would forgo its usual profit and do the work at cost, estimated to be about £60,000. In one of today's vulgarisms it was a 'no brainer', and very soon a Laing site office inhabited by foreman Ellis Ward arrived on Dutch River Side and the work began.

Compared to many projects of its kind, the works were generally trouble free. Ray Owen, the manager of Laing Yorkshire, took a personal interest in problems and there were no delays. Even so there were the usual tensions between architect and builder especially in connection with the more difficult aspects of construction such as the roof beams. Laings made it clear that they would have preferred to have designed the building themselves! Costs rose in the end to £204,000, more than three times the original estimate, partly because there was a mini boom in the building industry and sub contractors were able to charge higher rates than previously, and partly because on the *Sobriety* side, our failure to tell the architect precisely what we wanted had resulted in several expensive extras, such as the 110 volt circuits for workshop machinery. The contract required stage payments and anyone who has built a house even with a bank-supported mortgage, knows that these can be a nightmare. With £90,000 left to raise at the time of the opening ceremony we nevertheless managed to meet our obligations as far as the last £11,000. In the end the company decided that enough was enough and generously released the Project from this debt. It was during my final visit to Laing's offices in Leeds to hear the news of this decision from Ray Owen that I noticed a leaflet saying that the Yorkshire Schools Exploring Society was looking for a chief leader for its 1993 summer expedition to Qinghai on the Tibetan Plateau in China. I applied and was appointed.

Nearer to home on Friday 19th May 1989 at 3.00pm, 'and afterwards for afternoon tea', the *Sobriety* Waterways Adventure Centre was opened by Councillor George Barker, Mayor of Boothferry. In his speech to about 100 guests the Mayor praised the work of the architect and builder and thanked, among many benefactors, Humberside County Council which had contributed £25,000 and Hull City Council which had given help through its Inner Area Programme. He went on to say:

With this design the architect and builder have taken the Sobriety *Project into the 21st century. Their pride and enthusiasm for the job remind* Sobriety *that it must go on being a bulwark in the service of people who are conspicuously disadvantaged.*

But in his foreword to the *Project's Review of 1990*, on the broader subject of the 'new' Dutch River Side, David Lunn had this to say:

People used to smile gently at the Chinese for drawing their maps with their country, the Middle Kingdom (between earth and heaven), at the centre of the world. But now scientists help us to understand that each of us is at the centre of a universe that is infinitely expanding in all directions. I tell you this to help you understand that Goole is the centre of the world and at the real centre of Goole — twixt river and canal — is the headquarters of the Sobriety *Project. Stand there with* Sobriety, Eden *and* Audrey *coming and going and you soon know that you are where it is all happening.*

And so we are reminded of the way in which so many of the major concerns of mankind — the environment, disability, the use of resources, the role of experience in education (the list could be a lot longer) — find some sort of focus within the Sobriety *Project. I look forward to the future with confidence, trusting that the charity will never lack an army of dedicated helpers.*

This 'army' would appear in due time but it was a strange experience moving into the new world of a new building. The Project had occupied a windowless cubby hole at Goole Grammar School and a slightly brighter one at St Thomas's, each of them accommodating only one person at a time, standing up. Now we had empty space galore and our obligation was to fill it with people, sitting down as well as standing up.

Men in Prison: The heavy lift of a Tom Pudding at the Museum — Supported by the Heritage Lottery Fund

Goole: Traffic on the Dutch River and the Hull to Doncaster railway.

Arts And The Environment

I took seriously Boothferry Borough's prescription that the Centre should tell the story of the town and port and recruited two sixth formers from Goole Grammar School who seemed to be at a loose end — Jason Redman and Tyrone Forrest, and Nick Jagger, a young teacher from Reade School, Drax. With Samantha Williams and Martin Turner, two budding artists from the Marshland villages, we set about collecting, reading and reproducing items to put on display. The young people understood the brief and worked very hard to fulfil it. Sam Williams was good at pen and ink drawings and reproduced in her own hand, as the cover for a small brochure, the Japanese artist Hokusai's *Great Wave off Kanagawa*. Nick and the two boys worked on reproducing photographs we had borrowed. It was a process which in the days before digital cameras, required a good deal of patience and the photographer 'to get it right first time'. The subjects of our study, and eventually of an exhibition, were the Tom Puddings, hoists and the life of Goole docks before the days of containers. Then we had three important breaks.

The first was an introduction to the Wakefield historian and collector, John Goodchild, and the second was acquaintance with Mrs Lily Crabtree, wife of the late Harold Crabtree who had been the Aire & Calder Company's archivist. In 1990, John, who is now vice-president of the Wakefield Historical Society and a leading authority on the history of the West Riding, was holding court on an upper floor of Wakefield library. He sat surrounded by his collection of documents and photographs which he had acquired from the families of West Riding industrialists, and accompanied by his dog which lived under the table and thrived on doughnuts. John was an hospitable historian and only too pleased to help us study the documents that told the story of

211

the West Riding waterways during the 19ᵗʰ and 20ᵗʰ centuries. He made us work hard but in such a way that we enjoyed and remembered what we had learned. It was his informal tuition that gave us an understanding of Goole's emergence as a canal port and of its subsequent metamorphosis into an inland distribution centre.

Our acquaintance with Lily Crabtree was the result of a letter to the *Goole Times* in which we asked readers to let us know if they had any maps, pictures or brochures which might be displayed in the hall of the centre. Mrs Crabtree telephoned and invited us to come and inspect her late husband's personal collection. There were three Marks & Spencer carrier bags full of documents among which was the manuscript for a book about the Tom Puddings. In 1993, with the help of Mike Clarke, a researcher and historian living in Lancashire, the book was published by *Sobriety* and introduced by Sir Keith Stuart, Chairman of Associated British Ports. Mrs Crabtree paid the costs of publication and the book, entitled *The Railway on the Water*, has been recently revised and is available from the museum. The other contents of the carrier bags were primary sources for the port's history, far too important to be left to interpretation by amateurs, and after some heartsearching we offered them to Goole library. When the staff said they had no room for them, we realised we had some new responsibilities!

The third surprise was a renewed link with the Lankelly Foundation and with the Carnegie United Kingdom Trust which had been supporting the development of *Audrey* by grant aiding the salary of sailing leader Colin Walden.

Just after moving into the Centre I had received an invitation to an open day for museum contractors at York University. Knowing no one and in doubt about my reason for attending, I was reassured to come across the familiar figure of Geoffrey Lord, the Carnegie UK Trust's treasurer and secretary. I told him the Project's interest in Goole's history and he said, *"If you write to me about this, we will see if we can fund an arts and environment Project."* A few weeks later, with hours to spare in Stockport, waiting for specialist engineers to finish repairing *Eden's* gearbox, I made a haven of the town's public library and letting rip with my pen, beefed up the history of the Tom Puddings to the point where it might have displaced *Alice in Wonderland* as the nation's favourite fairy story. The Carnegie trustees liked it and in November 1989 made a grant of £7,000 to:

> *…initiate a project which would involve local people in a celebration of the history of the Aire & Calder Navigation's compartment boats and the way of life of those who, for more than 120 years, brought these 'trains' down to Goole. The project which now has the name, The Railway on the Water, has so far involved about 30 volunteers, some of them disabled. The project will not have a final end product. Rather it is a process now beginning which it is hoped will continue for many years. Its 'customers' among others will be the children of the region's primary schools.*

On July 6ᵗʰ 1990 we launched a 38 page booklet, unsophisticated in appearance but a cuckoo's nest of entertainment, stories, songs and tit bits of history, doubling as a resource for primary school teachers. It was called *The Railway on the Water — A Guide to the Tom Puddings and the Sobriety Waterways Adventure Centre* and contained an introduction to Goole docks, which could

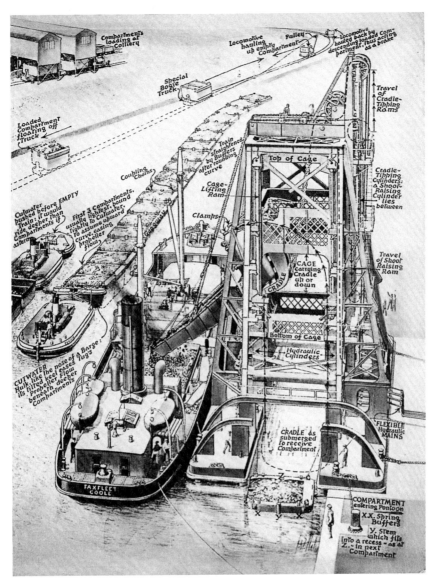

The Tom Pudding system explained.

be visited by boat. The booklet also contained explanations of dockland installations and tape recordings of songs written, sung and recorded by the late Gezz Overington who at that time was working as a teacher with the Royal National Institute for Blind People. He was blind himself and had close family links with Tom Pudding families. One of his more amusing compositions was *The Day the Devil Paid a Call*. (The words of the song and notation are on page 84). Written at the time of the 1984 miners' strike, it tells of the Devil arriving aboard the Tom Pudding tug *Kellingley* in 1962 and contains a reproach to Alfred (Lord) Robens, Chairman of the National Coal Board in Clement Attlee's post war government. But the real target was Prime Minister Margaret Thatcher's policy towards the coal industry.

Another feature of the booklet was excerpts from interviews with retired Aire & Calder skippers, and residents of the company town, recorded by *Sobriety* volunteers. They had some interesting reflections on sex equality, privatisation, health, housing and working conditions. Harold Addy had worked for BWB:

> *After transport was nationalised in 1948 our (British Waterways) area manager tried to negotiate a contract with the Yorkshire Electricity Board. He guaranteed a regular coal tonnage and even offered to build the necessary hoists if they awarded us the contract, but the YEB gave the business to a private company. That stuck in our throats.*

> *I knew of a woman who worked the canal alongside her husband. He thought he was the skipper when in fact she was the boss. She once competed against the men in a sculling race and won. Her name was Mona Riley. She is still alive and in her nineties.*

Douglas Hawksworth was one of an earlier generation who had been employed by the Aire & Calder Company:

> *I took up employment with the Aire & Calder in 1929 when I was 20 years old. I joined a Teamfly at Whitley Bridge. We loaded 96 tons of bran and maize which was brought from Croysdale's flour mill by horse and dray. The sacks were handed down to us and we had to back it in and tow it in such a way to keep the craft even. We used to run to Huddersfield, Dewsbury, Saville Town, Horbury Bridge and Feeney Cut and believe me, my back and neck were always hurting.*

Goff Sherburn was not going to romanticise:

> *Pay was poor so if there was overtime we took it even if it meant working Sundays and seven days a week. I had five children and Sunday pay bought a pair of children's shoes and a fish and chip for the whole family. I could start work at 4.00 a.m., come home at 10.00 p.m. to collect my pack-up and be away again. Me and my crew would take it in turns to sleep until we got to where the work was. I hardly saw my first two children growing up.*

> *In 1956/57 when we had a big freeze, we worked day and night to keep the canals open. We did nothing other than break the ice for a fortnight on the Keadby canal until we got orders to pull out. If we stopped for a couple of hours we had to break the tug out with a*

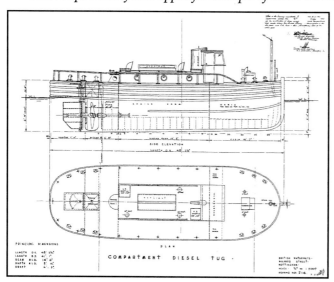

> *sledgehammer. The ice was thick enough to take the weight of a horse and cart. The job could not be done wearing gloves because we were working with chains. You can imagine what chains are like covered in frost. They stuck to our fingers. I've seen lads cry because their hands were so*

Engineeering drawing showing the design of a compartment diesel tug.

Winter of the Aire & Calder: Tom Pudding tug towing barges.

cold. I've seen skin come off fingers stuck to chains and men be unable to stop shivering, teeth chattering and unable to grip anything. We used to have a pot permanently on the stove. A mate would bring his shotgun and shoot anything in sight – rabbits and game birds mostly. I know we shouldn't have, but we took turnips and carrots from the farmers' fields on the canal sides. Everything went in the pot.

Until his death in January 2015, Goff Sherburn was a regular volunteer at the museum with his son Chris Sherburn, a folk musician who plays the concertina, and partners with Bella Hardy.

Alf Shires joined the Aire & Calder when he was 15 but had to wait until he was married to be made up to skipper. This was at a time when a man had to have a wife who could work as mate. He recalled:

We could beat the railway where time was concerned. A load of woollen rags could be loaded during the day at Humber Dock in Hull, brought up to Goole and hung onto the tug that left at 6.00pm. We would tow that tug to Castleford where a horse would be waiting which would pull us up to Dewsbury and the rags would be on Dewsbury market by 10.00am. Same with Tetley's Grit (crushed maize) for the brewing of bitter beer. Load it at Hull one morning and have it at Leeds and going into Tetley's at 8.00am the next day.

The houses built by the Aire & Calder were unusual. The visitor entered the house at street level, walked along a corridor, went down the stairs and emerged into a yard which was generally damp and unpleasant. Wilhemina Porter's family lived in one of them:

The back lane went right down below the level of the house and the street. We had one bedroom which was divided into two. A living room was on the level with the street and there were some steps and a cellar. We used to live in the cellar and kept the middle room as a bedroom. We had a really long yard and the toilet, a box lavatory, was at the end. The nightsoil men used to come and empty the toilets at midnight.

Ken Sargeantson, a local builder who later became curate of Goole, was able to explain in great detail the routine for collecting nightsoil. In 1997 he had been demolishing the only cottage in the nearby village of Swinefleet which did not have a flush toilet. In the course of the work he found the *privy* seat, a 'one holer' as he called it, and decided that the best destination for this piece of sanitary heritage would be the Waterways Museum. The story continues in his own words:

> All this set me thinking about my younger days when, for the majority of households in Crowle where I was born and brought up, the privy or closet was part of everyday life and only a few well off households had the benefit of waterborne sanitation. Where we lived on Commonside was just a hundred yards from Fred Mason, a farmer and dealer. Fred, and his father before him, held the contract for many years from the urban district council to remove nightsoil as it was politely called, from 'all dwelling houses in the town of Crowle'.
>
> Fred's eldest son Geoff was the same age as me and for a good many years we were best mates. After leaving school at 14 Geoff worked with his dad on the smallholding for part of the week and then went out with the horse drawn dilly cart for five nights a week. Fred and Geoff between them emptied the contents of every privy in the town at least once a week throughout the year. As we got older we started going to the pub but Geoff always had to be on his way by 10.30. Their work was done in darkness in order to give as little offence as possible to the public.
>
> The system worked like this. All that went in at one end came out at the other, via the privy and the ash pit which was usually a brick enclosure built onto the back of the privy. The ash pit also served as a dustbin. All household waste was thrown into the pit and this included the dust and ashes each day from coal fires. In former times householders had made their own arrangements with people like Geoff's dad to dig out the rotted down contents of ash pits and dispose of them. They paid the going rate for an average load that would fill two carts.
>
> There were thousands of gallons of effluent from these nightly expeditions and so when the fields were empty of crops during the winter, the loads of nightsoil would be spread as manure. Many farmers welcomed this free service. Spreading was effected by setting the poor old horse to go as fast as he could. The attendant driver would run alongside the dilly cart turning a crank handle which was linked to the collecting cylinder, until the contents of the thing were all out. And remember all this was done under cover of darkness with only the light from a paraffin stable lamp for illumination. With the modernisation of the collecting process, the vehicles could not tip the stuff on the fields like the old horses did, so the council decided that the refuse tip on Field Lane would be suitable for disposal of nightsoil. The result was that the old tip became a lake of sewage which attracted hundreds of rats. In the autumn of 1947 I used to visit the tip with my mates to shoot at rats with our little 410s. The road foreman, Bill Barraclough, who was responsible for the tip as well, brought us a box of 500 cartridges when he discovered what we were up to.
>
> All this came from a little old privy that was seeking a final resting place. I hope it survives for many more years, not in giving sterling service as it has in the past but as a visual reminder of how things used to be.

Concluding the *Railway on the Water* booklet was the infamous report on *The Sanitary State of the Town of Goole* written in August 1871 by Dr AD Holmes, Medical Officer of Health. The report was prompted by the latest of several outbreaks of cholera since 1832:

> *In the canal are many ships, amongst them cattle steamers; the sailors leave when the ships are in the basin but some caretakers are always on board. I am told that cattle steamers have occasionally cleaned out their holds in the basin, and when one of the servants of the Aire & Calder was explaining to me the rules framed to prevent fouling of the canal water, I pointed out to him within a few feet of the pipe which led the water from the basin for the supply of the houses, a large tract of filthy oily scum. Nor is this all; as the dock gates are usually opened every tide, some brackish water must enter, and with it sewage from the outfall which is close to the dock gates.*

> *The Sanitary Authority for Goole is the Vestry of Snaith, the parish in which it is situated — which is the Sewer Authority — and the Guardians of the Union of Goole, the Nuisance Authority; but practically, the only action in sanitary matters ever taken in Goole by an official body has been taken by the Board of Guardians. So far as I could learn in conversation with residents, the Vestry of Snaith Parish is ignorant that by statute there devolves on it most extensive powers in relation to the conservancy of health of the inhabitants of Goole.*

> *The Aire & Calder Company as owning much property and employing large amount of labour, has naturally great influence outside its legal powers and morally, has a corresponding responsibility.*

We now had an archive of documents and a collection of recorded histories, photographs, prints, paintings and newspaper extracts. Close by there were also three large 'objects': two early compartment boats and a hoist.

The compartment boats had been rescued by Tony Conder, Director of the National Waterways Museum at Gloucester, and the hoist, belonging to Associated British Ports was sited on derelict ground that in the future, *Sobriety* would lease from the company and sub-let to Goole Model Boat Club. The boats and hoist were not in our collection but we quickly became eager to protect and promote them as representatives of the Aire & Calder's 120 year old transportation system. To do this we needed volunteers, and it was not difficult to recruit several people who were stuck in unemployment. There was Jackie

Tug, jebus and pans in Goole Docks *en route* for museum.

Trainee Skippers.

who worked at the Centre for five mornings a week, painting, varnishing and general maintenance. She said:

If I didn't come here in a morning I'd probably stay in bed. The days are long if you've nowhere to go. The people are nice here; I get on with them and look forward to coming. I'm hoping to get on a City and Guilds course in decorating. So the experience is really useful.

Another volunteer, Andy, was recovering from a long spell in hospital and wanted to get back into circulation. Gill Pirt, who spent two days a week, 'drawing together the volunteers who are already involved with the Project and developing ways in which others can become involved', later wrote that, 'The atmosphere was always welcoming with the emphasis firmly on the needs of the people who use the Centre'.

It was becoming apparent that *Sobriety* would never have clients, only volunteers, responsible to the Project for the work they did and to themselves for what they would get from the experience.

In the meantime Alan Marshall had discovered hidden among brambles at the back of his company's premises, a lifeboat which had been built at Lymington in 1964 for service with the liner *Sea Princess*. Made of fibreglass, it had carried seating and rations for 150 people attanged in tiers. Knowing that it would provide a service to the public who would pay for short tours up the canal and round the docks, he put it on a low loader and brought it to Goole. Exclaiming *en route* that it looked like a 'pregnant turkey' he followed it on its slow journey along the M62 from Hull and was on the quayside when it was craned into the water. With the support of John McGrory who had made the original donation of the barge *Sobriety* to Goole Grammar School, the Project received £40,000 from Yorkshire Television's 'Telethon' towards the conversion of this little boat. It was commissioned to carry 12 passengers and named *Telethon Louise* by Louise Conlon from Sheffield who wrote the poem about her father's sufferings with Alzheimer's Disease.

A Museum

The next stage was to move this activity onto a more substantial footing by appointing staff to be responsible for the development of the *Railway on the Water* arts programme. The Lankelly Foundation again rose to the occasion and voted funds for the post of Arts & Environment Officer, a position filled after advertising and interviews by Isobel (Izzy) Kitt who was a sculptor with an MA in Fine Art and had worked at Brandesburton Hospital and Hull Prison. With her appointment things began to move quickly. So did she!

I would not have believed anyone who told me that I would be in the midst of 68 children and 12 helpers, going through six sessions of arts activities in a single day. And this while the visiting head pleaded with me to stop the children making things. His 50 seater coach could only hold a limited number of boats, coal hoists and posters.

We now have lots of groups using the Centre including the 'Happy Snappers' and 'Circle Dancers' from the community psychiatric service. We might perhaps, in the not too distant future, have a Dirty Art Room. Then I can really let go and branch into plaster work, pottery and scrap sculptures and might, perhaps might, clean up my office.

After 'Splash' weeks, fire breathing Chinese dragons, street performances, and queues of visiting schools including one from Manchester, Izzy got her wish in 1994 when the Project acquired for £2,000 a dumb barge (which by definition had no engine) 83 feet long and 18 feet wide, from Bunny Lewis, the engineer to the Ffestiniog Railway in Wales, who lived two villages up the canal from Goole.

To use Sir Alec Clegg's word again, this barge was the most enormous 'hyacinth' of creativity. For one small child it was 'a big room in a little boat', just like Dr Who's *Tardis*. Ted-in-the-Shed Pindar who looked after the workshops had first noticed it lying with derelict craft on the other side of the canal. Built as a lighter in 1923 for carrying grain to Rank's mill on the river Hull and listed as RHM (Ranks Hovis McDougal) *No.58*, it was pleased to have its name changed in 1994 to *ROOM 58* and to become an exhibition gallery and arts centre, complementing the new building. Reviewing 1994, Izzy described the highlights of *ROOM 58*'s year:

This year the barge has housed two exhibitions, a drama week and dance workshops. Schools have come on day visits to learn about the port and its history. Andy Dakin's sculptural installations of step ladders prompted children to ask if they were part of the barge, and if so, how did they climb a 180 degree bent stepladder. Harry Malkin's exhibition of mining memories from his former working life went down a treat and his talk about life down the pit was interesting and moving. During September, ROOM 58 was shunted down the Ouse and Humber so that she could take part in Hull's Sea Shanty Festival. At her berth in the marina, she was home to shanty singers and choirs from Holland, France and Britain.

Izzy's background in conceptual art gave her a head start in working with schools. Her skill in explaining ideas through the use of objects meant that she was able to appeal to children's imagination in such a way that they could *become* engineers and make things. The

Artist's Preview aboard
ROOM 58 floating gallery.

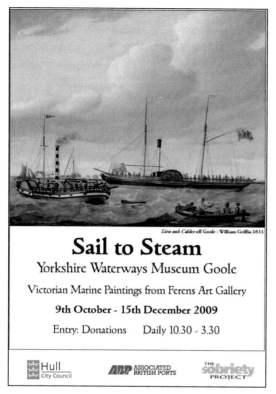

Lise and Calder off Goole : William Griffin 1835

Sail to Steam

Yorkshire Waterways Museum Goole

Victorian Marine Paintings from Ferens Art Gallery

9th October - 15th December 2009

Entry: Donations   Daily 10.30 - 3.30

Hull City Council   *ABP* ASSOCIATED BRITISH PORTS   THE sobriety PROJECT

Sail to steam exhibition.

process gave them insight into some of the industrial features of the port that they had seen on their tour of the docks and gave them the confidence to ask questions about function and design as well as materials and methods of construction. It was an approach which gave them a good deal of enjoyment and led to a greater understanding of the purpose and workings of locks, barges, hoists, bridges, cranes and other dockland installations. Another project involved the use of pinhole cameras as an introduction to photographs of 'how we used to live'. It enabled the children to make images without having to own expensive equipment. When they compared old and new they began to see how much had changed; they looked twice at their grandparents' pictures and saw a way of life different from their own. It was a style of education which let loose children's imagination, curiosity and sense of wonder. It was in contrast to government directed classroom practice which foists on children the facts and information they need in order to be successful in tests and meet the politicised expectations of league tables and PISA (Programme for International Student Assessment [2]).

An annual average of 3,000 children came with their schools between 1995 and 2000. Izzy also went *to* the schools. Some, on the Hull estates, had few visitors and did not have the funds to make the journey to Goole. Her philosophy was that a museum should have a heart, not be obsessed with output targets and sales.

The predictable outcome of having a collection of boats, objects and photographs in an historically interesting part of the town, a building to put them in, eager volunteers including some from prison, popular arts and educational activities and a member of staff to make it all happen, was that *Sobriety*'s Waterways Adventure Centre would inevitably become a museum. Barbara Woronçow, Director of the Yorkshire & Humberside Museums Council and her staff took us through the required protocols and assessments and in 1995 we received museum registration. A cartoon at the time showed Mick Stanley, our new curatorial adviser and Principal Keeper for Hull Museums, handing back a scruffy piece of clothing to Izzy Kitt with the caption, *"I don't think that needs cataloguing; it's Bob Watson's best jacket."* This change of status however, was not universally popular. One of *Sobriety*'s trustees arrived for a meeting and enquired, *"What's all this museum nonsense?"* There was the same reaction the following year 1996, when the East Riding of Yorkshire Council which succeeded Humberside as the administrative authority, made it clear that it regarded the new museum as a threat to its own collection in Goole library, inherited from the former Boothferry Council. This was in spite of having previously turned down the collection of Aire & Calder documents. The new authority need not have worried; *Sobriety*'s museum was established as a way of showing gratitude to the local community for having supported the Project through its infant years. But in spite of the Waterways Museum changing its collecting policy to accommodate the authority's wishes, the resentment festered, and only as late as 2006 would the hatchet be finally buried. The council was probably unaware that the previous administration had proposed moving some of the contents of Goole Museum, known more widely as the Garside Collection, lock stock and barrel to *Sobriety*'s museum on Dutch River Side. With insufficient room for proper storage or display, this was an offer the Project had to decline.

Just before its demise, Boothferry Borough Council received a small windfall from the European Regional Development Fund and decided to spend £15,000 on showcases and displays for the hall of the Centre. The design was in the hands of Izzy Kitt, Mike Clarke and Mike Cox, a museum professional who had worked for Vivien Duffield. (Mrs Duffield was the philanthropist founder of EUREKA, the children's activity centre in Halifax and heir to the Clore shoe empire). The 'set' was constructed and dressed by Museum Council staff and remains today much the same as when it opened in 1995. One of its most interesting features is the mock-up of the forecabin of a Humber keel which contains the original furniture from *Sobriety* and meets John McGrory's wishes that it should be displayed in a museum. Another exhibit to catch the public's attention is a life size mannequin of a barge skipper made by Karre Furrer, a sculptor colleague of Antony Gormley, designer of *The Angel of the North*. In a shed at the back of the Railway Tavern in Albert Street which was awaiting demolition, she spent a month making such an accurate likeness of local historian Brian Masterman that when he brought his young grandchildren to see it, they burst into tears. For several years we would move the faux Brian around the building and site, always with an open newspaper in his hands and a fag end in his mouth. At conferences and public events we would place him at the back of the proceedings, causing one visitor who had arrived late and was standing next to him, to declare loudly that, *"this guy's bloody dead!"* Karre made him for £350. It would have been completely beyond our means to have commissioned and paid the going rate for such quality of work.

Under Izzy's direction and with guidance from Mick Stanley, *Sobriety* Centre had achieved the standards required for registration by the Museums & Galleries Commission and was renamed the Waterways Museum, later being changed once more to the Yorkshire Waterways Museum

Wheldale Crew with Dr Fiona Spiers, Regional Director of The Heritage Lottey Fund (Yorkshire and Humber).

Wheldale's engine room. Ernie Sherburn and brother Goff carry out an inspection.

as it is known today. Fame and recognition came first in 1996 when staff efforts were rewarded with National Heritage's Unilever Prize for Best Museum of Industrial & Social History. The judges said:

This museum sets out to educate people, particularly children, able bodied and disabled, in the history of the port of Goole and the canals. The museum building is complemented by a barge whose former grain compartment has been converted into an exhibition space and education area. As an enterprising and accessible experience admirably fulfilling its aims the judges decided to award it the Unilever Prize.

They added that:

This is an amazing museum and it is easy to run out of superlatives in attempting to describe it. There is an obvious sense of commitment and caring from all concerned and a sense of fun and humour pervades the whole enterprise.

On November 4th 1996, accompanied by Goole and Howden MP, David Davis, who at that time was Minister for Europe, we received the award from Heritage Minister Peter Brooke at the Museum of London. With the arrival on stage of a phalanx of local authority worthies eager to take credit for achievements rightly belonging to their museum curators, David cried in apparent despair, *"Not more bloody councillors!"*

It was however not exclusively with children's education that the Waterways Museum made its mark. It was using the objects in its collection, large and small, indoors and outdoors, to give pleasure among others, to people with impaired intellect who were in danger of becoming isolated and forgotten. Former long stay hospital patients and others with mental health problems could find a new 'medicines':

Yorkshire Coble *Gemini* awaiting restoration.

circle dancing, aromatherapy, lace making, photography and video activities, poetry and story telling, dressing up, and looking at household equipment used on the barges fifty years ago. [3] In the same spirit Yorkshire Arts Circus organised a writing weekend on *Sobriety* which went to Castleford in West Yorkshire. In three days the group produced *Wash in the Calder and Rinse in the Aire*, a prose and poetry account of their trip illustrated by photographs that they themselves had taken. Within a few weeks the book was published in paperback and came at a friendly price in local bookshops. The new museum showcases also played their part. With the purpose of getting the local community involved with the museum, *My Story* invited people who lived in the Boothferry area and bargee families connected with the port to loan objects and documents for research and display.

In her article for the 1995 *Review*, Izzy took a light hearted look at progress under the title 'We are fully registered':

> *Those of you who can remember our museum's humble beginnings and my earlier reports of grappling with acquisitions, identification, understanding industrial archaeology and documenting artefacts, will be conversant with 'The Novice's Guide to Museum Registration' otherwise known as 'Put away the polish mum and put on the little white gloves'. Unfortunately it did not include the dancing shoes, only the sweet words – Mylar, acid-free envelopes, hygrometers, calibration kits, buffered tissue, and little snippets of conversation for use at a cocktail party like, "Did you know that you can get a micro chamber impregnated with charcoal which absorbs fumes released by unstable photographs and photocopies?" It is sad I know, but I believe I have become, as they say in the trade, a 'character'. I am also reminded of our yearly visual arts and workshop programme. It has been all go, with exhibitions by local historical societies, art clubs and national artists. Outreach work in schools and residential homes has become an annual occurrence, with over three hundred and fifty people in day centres, hospitals and nursing homes benefiting from our reminiscence sessions.*

> *ROOM 58 was in Hull once again for the International Sea Shanty Festival. At the end of the week the barge stayed in the marina so that the nearby Adelaide and St Charles' primary schools could take part in Around the World in Eighty Days drama workshops. The sessions were funded by Sobriety, Yorkshire & Humberside Arts, Boothferry Borough Council and Humberside County Council's community budget.*

> *The Community Council of Humberside also had an open evening on ROOM 58 for the councillors and officers of the new East Riding unitary authority. The weather was dreadful with heavy rain and winds battering the barge. We did not sink. If we had, we might have been changing history rather than documenting it.*

For the Yorkshire & Humberside Museums Council, the Waterways Museum was the 'new kid on the block' and an example of how collections could be brought to life for the benefit of communities. Curators from as far afield as the new maritime museum in Liverpool were coming to learn our secrets, but in all honesty we had to explain that we had done things the 'wrong' way round. With an existing record of work with community groups and schools, *Sobriety* staff were easily able

Yorkshire Waterways Museum foyer.

to balance the technical aspects of museum development with the marketing of a social service. There was no history of precious curators defending their collections against all comers. The museum had emerged from the community and still connected to it, had the responsibility to interpret and make sense of what the collection represented; a wooden rudder was an early nineteenth century barge with horse and captain: a toolbox was the skills of its owner: a flag was the company which employed men on the docks and ships: the compartment boats were King Coal, and so on. The message to visitors was that the objects might have some aesthetic value in themselves but that they had a much greater value as pathways into history.

For several years the Project had no museum specialist and this perhaps was an advantage. Izzy Kitt's qualifications were in fine art. Prior to coming to *Sobriety* she had used her skills as a sculptor to make life more bearable for the men in Hull prison and the 'patients' as they were then known, in hospitals for people with a mental illness or handicap. She was well equipped to take the collection to the community without getting bogged down in purely curatorial disciplines. Her direct and uncomplicated approach was still something of a rarity among museum professionals and she was considered by some, like our mentor and adviser Mick Stanley, to be ahead of her time. The result was that this little museum stuck in the middle of nowhere, in a town whose name was something of a national joke, went on to win awards in the face of competition from much more prestigious institutions. (see Appendix 7)

A result of our publicised success was an arrangement between the Museums Council and Buckingham Palace that The Duke of Edinburgh would come to see us during a visit to Yorkshire in June 1998. It was a lively affair. He landed by helicopter on Vermuyden School's rugby pitch and came straight to the museum where he toured the displays, met men from Hatfield Young Offender Institution and chatted with primary school children and the slightly older winners of his Award. After attending a reception for the 'great and good' on *ROOM 58*, he re-commissioned *Audrey* and steered her into Goole docks where his car was waiting. The *Hull Daily Mail* was as usual in attendance and recorded the occasion with pictures and editorial, commenting that:

Regular skippers Mel Parish and Paul Cooper were quite happy to hand over Audrey *to a VIP sailor more at home in the Solent than in the land locked waters of the Aire and Calder Canal. "I only wish I could stay on board for the first cruise," the Prince told his audience. And then, "I would like to congratulate the* Sobriety *Project for all it is doing in many fields, and I hope it will make a real difference to the lives of many young people in this part of the British Isles."*

The *Goole Times* on the other hand put on its front page a picture of the Duke leaning over the wasted timbers of a fishing coble that Izzy had rescued from the field of a landowner near Lelley in South Holderness. After noting that the vessel was 'a long way from being seaworthy' the paper caught the Duke's parting comment to a rather knowledgeable boat builder, *"I'll make an appointment to come back in ten years and we'll have a look at how you're getting on."* His prescience was remarkable. It would be just ten years before the coble's restoration would be complete.

Another of Izzy's museum acquisitions in the mid nineties was the tug *Wheldale* which, with sister tugs similarly named after West Riding collieries, had pulled the Tom Puddings up and down the Aire & Calder Navigation between Leeds and Goole. The tug was purchased for £15,000 from Hargreaves, a company based in Castleford which had a fleet of its own more modern vessels transporting coal from Kellingley pit to Ferrybridge power station. Purchased with the help of PRISM, the fund for the preservation of industrial and scientific material, *Wheldale* became a magnet for volunteers with the same affection for tug restoration as railway enthusiasts show towards derelict locomotives and rolling stock. The family of Goff Sherburn led the way and it was heart warming when local skippers who in their working days had been moving coal for a living, happily entered the new world of tourism and turned *Wheldale* and the compartment boats into one of the museum's main attractions. In 2012 *Wheldale* went under her own steam down the coast to London and took part in the Thames river pageant organised in celebration of the diamond jubilee of Queen Elizabeth II. BBC's *Today* presenter, Mishal Husain, was the tug's guest for the day, a cheering presence during ten hours of foul weather.

With the development of the museum there appeared a small problem of identity. The image of a waterways museum was uncomplicated and tangible. Everyone knew what it ought to be like and it was easy to advertise. Brochures, award ceremonies and the paraphernalia of marketing brought it to the public's attention as an attraction they ought to visit. Less easy to communicate were the aims and practices of the Museum's parent body, the *Sobriety* Project, whose very name was misleading. There was a temptation to take the easy way out and to refer in conversation to the Waterways Museum rather than to

Wheldale in East India Dock London with Canary Wharf in the background. The occasion was Queen's Diamond Jubilee Pageant on the River Thames. Above a title 'Austerity', the picture made the front cover of the Project's *Review of 2012*.

Sobriety. People then asked what was the relationship between *Sobriety* and the museum. The answer was simple, *"The Yorkshire Waterways Museum is part of the* Sobriety *Project. The Project, not the museum, is the charity."* However a selection of references from the visitor lists in the annual reviews shows how from 1995, it was the new museum that succeeded in attracting the rich and famous.

David Brooke, founder of Brooke Bond Tea, came to vet us as possible recipients of his charity; the cricketer Freddie Truman raised £1400 for the Project; we had the second visit of Philip Jelley, administrator of the L. J. and Mary C. Skaggs Foundation in San Francisco and the museum was suddenly $10,000 better off; Petroc Trelawny, renowned Radio 3 presenter, spent an afternoon at the museum and interviewed everyone in sight, then came sixty members of the Leeds Chinese community who were rather puzzled: The Director of the Science Museum, Sir Neil Cossons, opened the rebuilt Dutch River Side road: Martin Wainwright, Northern Editor of the *Guardian* and past chair of the National Lottery Charities Board gave a talk on *ROOM 58* entitled *Pigs, Prostitutes and the Press*: Chris (Lord) Haskins, Policy Adviser to Tony Blair came on a whistle-stop tour to find out how we thought the government could support the voluntary sector: under the auspices of Yehudi Menuhin, Yorkshire Electricity brought a small orchestra of young disabled people to give an atonal concert on *ROOM 58*: the Director and staff of the Pushkin Museum in St Petersburg arrived as guests of the Museums Council.

A museum which combined history with social work and attracted 'volunteers' rather than 'clients' also received significant donations of artefacts, sometimes complete collections. Peter Smith's collection from Wakefield, for example, contained a cast iron milepost with the letters MSLR on one side and S&SYN on the other. It referred to the brief period in the eighteen fifties when the Manchester, Sheffield & Lincolnshire Railway owned the Sheffield & South Yorkshire Navigation. More recently David Woodward, proprietor of A&E Woodward, marine engineers in Lime Street Hull, presented the museum with a single cylinder *Elwe* barge engine, while the National Waterways Museum at Gloucester repatriated a model of a hoist and ship which had last been seen leaving Goole in a British Waterways Board van in 1965.

The growth of the collection led to an increase in visitors and a correspondingly greater reliance on volunteers to assist with exhibitions, school visits, boat trips, conferences, the café, reception and the gift shop. One of these, Steve Drewson, was finishing a sentence at Everthorpe prison. For a year he travelled each day to the museum and eventually took charge of the *ROOM 58* exhibitions programme. At job interviews after release he talked about his work with *Sobriety* and went on to do a degree course in furniture design.

In an article for *Sobriety*'s Review of 2000 Barbara Woronçow, on the verge of retirement, gave her verdict on the museum:

Although most museums are currently working hard to make their collections more widely accessible to a broader range of new audiences, few can match the tremendous commitment of the Waterways Museum in putting people's needs first. The thread of social inclusion, often with people who have little or no experience of what museums have to offer, runs right through the work and activities of the museum. Whether it is pathways to employment or developing the skills of young offenders, the Sobriety *Project has set new standards for community involvement in museums which directly help to fulfil the government's objectives for the cultural sector as a whole.*

In educational terms the museum has responded strongly to the shift away from merely schools-based education to lifelong learning for all at every level of ability. The opportunities offered by the museum are not confined to the building and its collections, but also encompass visitor and hospitality services, horticulture and the restoration of historic craft. This breadth of practical activity, with something for everyone, places the Waterways Museum in a strong position for the future. Its historic collections are unique in the region and provide an uncommon opportunity for water based as well as land based heritage interpretation. In the past too many museums have attempted to be all things to all people at all times. The clear focus of the Sobriety *Project on the key priorities now set at both regional and national level should help to provide a solid basis for the never ending quest for core resources and additional project funding. The museum can be proud of its achievements to date from very modest beginnings, as well as being confident that it is doing its utmost to contribute to national and regional strategic objectives.*

In contrast, Bill Rigby who had been senior education officer for schools in the Humberside administration and in 1989 had overseen the re-organisation of 59 of Hull's schools, hailed *Sobriety* as a trail blazer of independence from local authorities and governments. He said:

The Project sits in pride of place within our locality's contribution to civil society, promoting not only enjoyment and education for all through the rich portfolio which is now established, but also a set of values which commend an approach to life set apart from materialism and self seeking opportunism. I have spent half a professional life within the formal sector, thinking that the community can be served effectively in that way. It is now clear to me that a local authority could not recognise or embrace a value if it pushed it into the 'cut'. Community development through voluntary agencies presents a very untidy picture which offends the neatness of a local authority development plan. The Waterways Museum and Adventure Centre is unique with no comparable activity – anywhere. Its contribution is forged by a response to its unique location and the unique set of people who contribute to its work.

The ten years from 1996 to 2006 would see *Sobriety* cold shouldered by East Riding Council. This, with a consideration of other threats and how they were overcome, is the subject of the next chapter.

HM The Queen's Diamond Jubilee Pageant. Tom Pudding Tug *Wheldale* passing the Royal Barge.

Questions

'What's all this museum nonsense?' said one of *Sobriety*'s trustees.

Would you have developed a museum?

Why?

Why were other museums fascinated by the Waterways Museum?

How could the Yorkshire Waterways Museum contribute to the achievement of *Sobriety*'s original purpose?

In what ways can a museum benefit from links with its local community?

Chapter 9 Notes

1   The siege of Alesia took place in September 52 BC. Alesia was a major centre and hill fort of a Celtic tribe, the Mandubii. The siege was laid by an army of the Roman Republic commanded by Julius Caesar.

Alesia was a hill-top fort surrounded by river valleys, with strong defensive features. As a frontal assault would have been hopeless, Caesar decided upon a siege, hoping to force surrender by starvation. Considering that about 80,000 men were garrisoned in Alesia, together with the local civilian population, this would not have taken long. To guarantee a perfect blockade, Caesar ordered the construction of an encircling set of fortifications around Alesia. About 18 kilometres of 4 metre high fortifications were constructed in about three weeks. This line was followed inwards by two four and a half metre wide ditches which were four and a half metres deep. The one nearest to the fortification was filled with water from the surrounding rivers. These fortifications were supplemented with mantraps and deep holes in front of the ditches, and regularly spaced watch towers equipped with Roman artillery.(Wikipedia)

2   See *Times Educational Supplement* 26th July 2013. The article, *Is PISA fundamentally flawed*, is by William Stewart. He says:

But what if there are 'serious problems' with the Pisa data? What if the statistical techniques used to compile it are 'utterly wrong' and based on a 'profound conceptual error'? Suppose the whole idea of being able to accurately rank such diverse education systems is 'meaningless', 'madness'? What if you learned that Pisa's comparisons are not based on a common test, but on different students answering different questions? And what if switching these questions around leads to huge variations in the all-important Pisa rankings, with the UK finishing anywhere between 14th and 30th and Denmark between fifth and 37th? What if these rankings — that so many reputations and billions of pounds depend on, that have so much impact on students and teachers around the world — are in fact 'useless'?

3   These activities also had a following of participants sponsored by the Heritage Lottery Fund through its ever popular Young Roots training scheme. In the hands of energetic young people the collection could be used to great social advantage - no longer mere 'heritage', but a living connection with 'The way we used to be'.

A Cuckoo
in the Curriculum

Part 3

Changing Agendas

Perseverance Persuasion And Providence

Chapter 10

THREATS

My friends, as I have discovered myself, there are no disasters, only opportunities. And, indeed opportunities for fresh disasters — Boris Johnson, Mayor of London

In the life of many voluntary organisations there are episodes which threaten both their future and their jealously guarded independence. For small charities like *Sobriety* which lack the resources and power not to appear a 'pushover' to large public concerns, these episodes occupy an enormous amount of time and the longer they last the greater is their capability to divide and weaken the resolve of supporters and trustees. It is then the lot of a chief officer or director to imitate the proverbial swan and paddle frantically below the surface while appearing calm and serene above it. To illustrate the point here are six accounts of events which threatened the Project in different ways: a combined heat and power incinerator: the abolition of two supporting local authorities: a threat to transfer the project director (me) to work at county hall: the collapse of a river bank, the fight for the future of Goole's remaining compartment boat hoist and plans to site windmills on the Project's towpath nature trail. Just as hair raising were other threats but they were solved in a matter of days: £13,000 embezzled by a finance officer to pay off gambling debts: an assertion by HMRC that the Project owed £75,000 in unpaid VAT and a proposal to lower the height of a dock swing bridge which if unchallenged, would have put an end to the museum's boat tours of Goole docks. In addition to these and always dominant, was the struggle to raise the funds to keep the *Sobriety* Project in business — between 1973 and 2010, a total of £11.5 million, which represented an average fund raising requirement, often from a standing start, of £292,000 per year

An Incinerator?

"We often have difficulty with local people"
ProjectManager of Energy Power Resources commenting at a public meeting
on Goole's hostility to the construction of a waste incinerator in the town.
E pulvere lux et vis (light and heat from dust)
Inscription on a Victorian incinerator in Shoreditch, London

I was always suspicious of men in suits who arrived on the museum car park in black BMWs and began to make notes on clipboards while remaining in their cars, or worse, began to look round the site without introducing themselves. They were distinguishable from the men from the Revenue who like Wyatt Earp, wore hats and long black coats, (possibly hiding long black rifles). They came to secure payment of outstanding debts. We always made them welcome if only to divert their attention, if that were possible, from announcing that our 'goods were to be taken into distraint' until they had been paid what we owed.

On this occasion in August 1997 however, two 'suits' did introduce themselves. They were employees of a waste to energy company, Energy Power Resources (EPR). Pointing to the canal bank opposite, one said, *"We've come to build a combined heat and power incinerator. Construction will begin next year and the plant will be operational by 2001."* His colleague added with a grin, *"And your building will make a good interpretation centre for the plant."* Their visit turned out to be the beginning of two and a half years of public meetings, demonstrations, petitions and MP briefings arranged by local people determined to resist a development which was being supported by the local authority. Together with Associated British Ports and British Waterways, the East Riding Council had an eye for the financial benefits the project would bring: £176,000 annually in business rates and for ABP and BW an increase in traffic through the port. Effluent tankers on the canal may have inspired one of Goole's aldermen to say, twenty years previously, that the town was reduced to being the anus of the West Riding, but the threat of an incinerator receiving waste not only from the four Humberside authorities but possibly from the near continent, and in some people's imaginings from as far away as South America, made Goole 'the waste capital of Yorkshire' if not of western Europe and beyond. At the end of it all the medals for bravery went to Enid Thompson, introduced earlier, who had *Sobriety*'s interests at heart, and Simon Jarrold, a local newsagent who was fearless in his hatred of conspiracy and well known for his affection for the town. His shop was always full. Customers arrived to buy newspapers but after two minutes of his oratory, became eager messengers for the *No Campaign*. It was hardly 'nimbyism'. The proposed site was not in Goole's back yard; it was in its front garden.

But what justified such opposition? Surely no one could object to a project which promised to turn waste otherwise destined for landfill, into electricity, and provide hundreds of new jobs in the region. Goole's location on the M62 and Aire & Calder Navigation made it an ideal 'hub' for the transfer of waste from lorries, ships and barges and EPR had plenty of experience of building and operating similar plants in other parts of England.

However, such an imminent threat to the future of the museum meant that as Director I had to report to *Sobriety*'s trustees the contents of an environmental impact assessment produced on EPR's behalf by Barton Willmore Surveyors in Cambridge. My comments on this statement formed the broad basis of *Sobriety*'s early objections and its subsequent part in the *No Campaign*.

The surveyors began with an appraisal of similar plants in Corby and Fife where chicken droppings were the 'waste to energy'. They said there was also a combined heat and power plant owned by the French *Compagnie Generale des Eaux* running successfully in Deptford in the London Borough of Lewisham. Its proposed 'brother' in Goole would burn 400,000 tonnes of waste each year, comprising daily deliveries of about 1100 tonnes of rubbish by more than 200 heavy goods vehicles between 7.30am and 10.00pm.

In their 150 page document Barton Willmore failed to make any substantial reference to the Waterways Museum which lay less than 600 feet across the canal from the proposed site, part of a former nature reserve known as Glews Hollow which had been filled in by Boothferry Borough Council to provide space for business units. The appendix to the environmental assessment contained an aerial photograph of Dutch River Side which clearly showed the location of the museum. Bearing in mind that EPR representatives had personally visited the site and possibly that Barton Willmore staff had parked there, this was an astonishing omission. The 125 feet high main building with its chimney of 235 feet would deprive the museum of any hope of maintaining its visitor numbers which at that time were about 15,000 a year. With their decline would go the jobs of the twenty or so people who worked either as volunteers or paid staff and the dark prediction that the building would be used to promote the incinerator would come true. At the administrative level the scheme certainly did not take into account a government directive that developments were acceptable as long as there was no adverse effect 'on places where people congregate'. Sections 4 and 5 of the report which dealt with 'visually conspicuous buildings' suggested that the skyline could not be made worse, a perverse observation in view of the fact that it included three Grade 2* listed buildings. The 'salt and pepper pot' water towers, one of them built in the art deco style, and the lines of dock cranes silhouetted against the sky, were for many visitors lasting and agreeable memories of the town and port. Again the company's claim appeared to be in ignorance of government policy that 'developments must include adequate measures to ensure that there are no unacceptable visual impacts.'[1]

In the same spirit, a pond on the Project's towpath nature trail which was home to great crested newts and like the museum, about 600 feet from the incinerator site, was dismissed by the surveyors as being an unsuitable environment for the species to breed. They could not have known that a few years later the reconstruction of the adjacent railway bridge would be delayed for six months in order to protect the newts' habitat.

Project staff were also concerned about noise, especially during the projected two and a half years of construction. To our surprise, Barton Willmore stated that South Airmyn Grange at half a mile distant from the site was the nearest place of residence. They had not understood that when *Sobriety*'s boats were on their berths it was usual for at least a dozen people to be sleeping aboard. Finally there was nothing in the report which even resembled a plan for dealing with the effect that an explosion or other serious accident would have on people visiting or working on the other side of the canal.

If these were the immediate worries of the *Sobriety* Project, the town had wider concerns, especially with air pollution which it was thought would increase the already high number of people suffering from asthma and other bronchial conditions. Job losses were also a possibility. A recent arrival on the industrial estate was the manufacturer of ingredients for major confectionery companies. In a letter to members of the East Riding western area planning committee in August 1997 I recalled a meeting with this company's managing director who had told me that if the incinerator were built, his factory would have to close. Claims that the plant would create jobs were also regarded as specious. They would be limited to part time posts for cleaners and attendants while the recruitment of skilled employees would take place far from Goole. Connected with arguments about employment was the question of the town's image. Within easy travelling distance of regional centres like Hull and Leeds, Goole looked well set to welcome new residents who preferred their home life to be in the environs of a small town rather than a city. Goole could be a commuter 'hub' just as much as a centre for waste disposal but it could not be both.

On December 22nd 1997, I represented the town and Project in a lone protest outside the main entrance to County Hall Beverley. Feeling self conscious but determined, I handed to the Director of Planning, 5,000 notes of objection written by Goole residents and requested that these be brought to the attention of his committee when it met in January.

Protest accelerated during 1998. *The Hull Daily Mail*, apparently wanting to make sure that if Goole escaped EPR's designs, Hull should not be its next target, reported on June 2nd under a heading 'Protest along the royal route' that:

> *Protesters fighting plans for an £80 million waste to energy burner in Goole, failed to mar the royal visit. A dozen banner carrying 'No' campaigners formed a peaceful picket before the Duke of Edinburgh's motorcade swept by on its route to the waterways museum and adventure centre. The anti-incinerator activists stood at the roadside as the official cars made their way yesterday morning to the Dutch Riverside venue. "We weren't there to lobby the Duke, of course", said 'No' secretary Simon Jarrold. "But we were there to make our point to the many councillors and council officials who were attending the ceremony at the waterways centre. And there's no doubt that they would have seen our protest and understood the message that Goole people don't want this incinerator."*

In August the same year a letter went from the Project to the East Riding authority's strategic development services manager rehearsing the familiar arguments but making a particular point about tourism:

> *For many years the Project has taken pride in finding employment for local people by putting Goole firmly on the tourist map. The canals, rivers and industrial heritage of the area are an irresistible magnet and as a result of investment by Boothferry Borough Council, Associated British Ports, the Yorkshire Tourist Board and the EU, more than twenty jobs have been created and sustained over the last ten years.*

Some organisations were more cagey than *Sobriety*. The Hull & Humber Chamber of Commerce Industry & Shipping claimed that because many of its members were 'undecided', it 'could not take an official stance on the subject'. Unsurprisingly there was tension between the need to follow public opinion and the Chamber's business interests. However when its voting figures were analysed using methods for determining electoral opinion it was discovered that there was a 2:1 majority against EPR's proposals. Less equivocal was the MP for Brigg and Goole, Ian Cawsey, who got on a train and went to Deptford to inspect the much vaunted South East London Combined Heat & Power (SELCHP) plant and to ascertain the views of local people. He and they were not enthusiastic. Six years later in 2003, while protests against SELCHP continued undiminished, a local source said:

The combined heat and power system was designed for a district heating scheme that has never been implemented and the plant generates only electricity. The plant can generate up to 35 MW of power using a steam turbine. It can take up to 420,000 tonnes per year of municipal solid waste. In 2002 SELCHP was subject to direct action by Greenpeace UK. It was concerned about the potential negative health effects of the dioxins produced during the incineration of waste at the site. The plant was shut down for three and a half days when protesters entered the main tipping hall and climbed the chimney. The standoff was resolved when bailiffs entered the building and removed the protestors. As a result of the action both Liberal Democrats on Lewisham Council and the Shadow Environment Secretary Peter Ainsworth pledged their support to the campaign.(Wikipedia report)

If events in Goole had taken their course it is possible that the protests would have been ignored and on the recommendation of the Joint Waste Management Advisory Committee representing the authorities of Hull, the East Riding, North Lincolnshire and North East Lincolnshire, the planning authority would by the end of 1999 have approved construction. The conclusion of the campaign and of EPR's plans for Goole, came out of the blue. Discovered in the previous administration's contracts with two food manufacturing companies based in Glews Hollow, but unknown to the East Riding's senior management team, was a clause forbidding any odorous or contaminating industry. In the wake of the closure of Goole shipyard, the contracts also restricted occupation of the estate to manufacturing businesses employing fewer than 12 people. Even though EPR's plans had been supported by the Treasury's Private Finance Initiative (PFI) for companies prepared to work jointly with government on capital projects, this clause represented a stipulation that could not be challenged. Waste to energy burners were not 'clean' in the sense intended by Boothferry Council and nor was Energy Power Resources a manufacturing enterprise or small employer.

It was a cause for reflection that if the incinerator had been built using PFI funds, EPR would have been locked into a contract to burn waste at least until 2023. It was an unforeseen disclosure that ended nearly three years of uncertainty and allowed the *Sobriety* Project to breathe again. For the moment it was safe, at least from this particular threat, but there were others, present and imminent.

'England's Newest County'
Humberside County Council promotional slogan

The County of Humberside never stood a chance. As a child of the Redcliffe-Maud Report on the reorganisation of local government implemented by the Heath government in 1974, the infant authority was from its beginning regarded as an attack on the identity of Yorkshire and Lincolnshire. The fact that it made good economic sense to combine the north and south banks of the Humber under a county administration with second tier districts was neither here nor there. The Humber Bridge, dubbed the 'bridge to nowhere', was denigrated as a white elephant and even Prime Minister John Major, in his 1992 speech to the Conservative party, abandoned his usual courtesies for a cheap jibe, to ask, *"Can you imagine Len Hutton walking out to bat for Humberside?"* Restoration of the Yorkshire and Lincolnshire birthright was demanded long and loud from that first day when the old East Riding council chamber at Beverley was invaded by 'yellow bellies' and 'codheads' from the other side of the Humber. Why there was no similar fuss about the West Riding's replacement by a string of metropolitan districts from Rotherham to Bradford is a good question. Perhaps it was the rural and much less cosmopolitan nature of the new county that made it a sitting duck for abolition in 1995. It was just twenty one years of age.[2]

During the same twenty one years *Sobriety* passed from infancy to an adulthood that made it one of the bricks of the authority, albeit on occasions, a loose brick! Under Humberside it achieved financial stability as a result of contracts to give practical support to social services and education policies as they changed and developed over a wide geographical area. St Thomas's Centre in Old Goole was one example: another was the boats providing residential expeditions for schools, old people's homes and voluntary organisations based in all parts of the county. The Project's management group included local authority officers and members who presented the *Sobriety* case to colleagues with conviction and imagination. The only other voluntary organisation to enjoy the same high level of patronage was The Warren in Hull which took under its wing young people who had fallen on hard times through the effects of unemployment or leaving care or being kicked out of their homes by parents or landlords.

Recognition by Humberside was hard won. It was a continuous and sometimes frightening exercise in public relations but it paid off to the extent that *Sobriety* became one of the authority's models of how to work well with voluntary organisations. By the late nineteen eighties, *Sobriety*, like The Warren under the leadership of Keith Russell, was receiving up to £150,000 per year in grant aid and contract work. The boats flew the flag in all the districts of Humberside and from two of these, the City of Hull and Boothferry Borough, the charity received an additional £30,000. It was useful and enjoyable to have access to members and to be near the top of the list when officers were looking for a home for budget underspends. *"Could you use £45,000 to help us with mental health services in Goole?"* asked the area social services team manager. Then there were invitations to events such as the civic service held annually in one of Humberside's principal parish churches and to a reception given by the Queen and Prince Philip on the Royal Yacht *Britannia*. The Humberside civic office had also suggested to Buckingham Palace that *Sobriety* would fit nicely with Prince Charles' and Princess Diana's visit to Hull. On another occasion two trustees were guests of honour at the passing out parade of air cadets at RAF Leeming. The base was looking for a worthy recipient of its charitable funds and from a telephone conversation with staff at county hall had learned about the *Sobriety* Project.

In acknowledgement of these privileges we made a point of inviting councillors to spend time on the boats as well as to visit the museum. Successive Lord Mayors of Hull, as Admirals of the Humber, braved the weather of the estuary for a view of their city from the river. With the necessary Department of Transport permissions, 40 county and city councillors boarded *Sobriety* for a journey up the River Hull while the city engineer, acting as their tour guide, drew attention to the state of repair of the ten bridges between the river mouth and the northern suburbs: the chairs of Humberside's education committee visited York and Lincoln by boat: the Mayor of Grimsby travelled up the estuary with the residents of two homes for old people in the borough: a picture of *Audrey* hung in the Lord Mayor's Parlour in Hull's Guildhall and a photograph of *Sobriety* barge reminded members in County Hall, Beverley, of the magic of the waterways. Until a few months ago, amazingly, the photograph was still there.

But the anti-Humberside rumblings persisted and in 1982 the Local Government Boundary Commission for England advised the Secretary of State for the Environment that, 'a review of the Humberside county boundary was warranted'. The Commission carried out the review but found that 'Humberside County Council could not be shown to have failed'. However a report eight years later in 1990 indicated that sixty three percent of respondents thought that the creation of Humberside was 'bad' and only fourteen per cent that it was 'good'. Also in 1990 a general local government review for England was announced. The Commission recommended that as a priority Humberside and its districts should be abolished and, with the objective of saving money, be replaced with four unitary authorities: Kingston upon Hull, East Riding of Yorkshire, North Lincolnshire and North East Lincolnshire. The MP for Brigg and Cleethorpes, was particularly vociferous in support of abolition, saying, *"I want to see the word Humberside expunged from the English language."* Whilst few voices were heard in its defence, the word 'Humberside' was not however, expunged from the language. There still remained Humberside Police, Humberside Airport, Humberside Fire & Rescue and BBC Radio Humberside. The area covered by the despised county also became the foundation for the Hull and Humber Ports City Region, supported by the Humber Economic Partnership which was comprised of representatives of the four districts of the former administration. The Royal Mail for its part continued to divide the area into North and South Humberside but as late as August 2013, seventeen years after the abolition of the former county, the MP for Beverley could still say, *"We are proud to live in the East Riding of Yorkshire, not Humberside."* He stepped up his campaign for a change of address after the head of the newly privatised Royal Mail refused to meet him to discuss the matter. The argument continues. In 2015 the Coalition Government suggested that the four authorities on each bank of the estuary should be combined into a region serviced by an elected mayor. The suggested name was 'Humber'.

Without the support of the Humberside local authority, *Sobriety* could never have developed as it did. The relentless reviews and shrill opinions demanding Humberside's abolition were unnerving, and whenever possible the Project put itself in line of county's defence, writing to schools and other groups to say what we saw as the advantage of working within a big local authority. I found it difficult to find any sensible reason for re-organisation. It appeared to be the result of sustained nasty temper fuelled by ethnic fantasies about Yorkshire and Lincolnshire and to have little to do with social and economic benefit, or even with administrative efficiency. Moreover when the actual break up came on April 1st 1996 it was unpleasant; the new authorities could barely make ends meet and *Sobriety* had to join a scramble for funds to replace the Humberside and Boothferry grants and contracts. All sorts of promises were made and solutions aired but the truth was that the new authorities wanted services to be provided locally. At that time, before the days of 'outsourcing' this was an impossible restriction on *Sobriety's* activities and became a nightmare that would last another four years.

Compounding the problems was the fact that Goole had no home in the new landscape. Located just south of the river Ouse which had been the boundary between the West and East Ridings before 1974, the town had been administered partly by the West Riding based in Wakefield, and partly by Goole Urban District Council. But with the implementation of Redcliffe-Maud these administrations had disappeared. The consequence was that unlike other areas of Humberside, Goole was an orphan.[3] Before 1974 the Grimsby and Scunthorpe areas had been solidly part of Lincolnshire just as Beverley had been the county town of the East Riding. In 1996 they were able to return (almost) to their previous homes.

The Boundary Commission's response to the Goole problem was to suggest four solutions. These were to join with Selby District and become a unitary authority, or be absorbed into the existing Doncaster Metropolitan District (which the Commission favoured), or to be joined to the two tier County of North Yorkshire administered from Northallerton, or to become part of one of the new unitary councils, either North Lincolnshire, based in Scunthorpe, or the East Riding, based in Beverley. The Commission tested local opinion and there was a majority in favour of the last of these options, with a preference for North Lincolnshire coming a close second. The reincarnated East Riding was none too keen to receive Goole into its midst; it did not conform to the image that Beverley and Driffield had of themselves. But when it became apparent that the level of deprivation in the town would open the door to a bigger share of central government funding, the opposition died down. *Sobriety's* staff and trustees had promoted the case for the new authority and welcomed the balance of public opinion in its favour. They also expected that the Project would have the same relationship with this council as it had with Humberside County Council. Why it did not is uncertain, but it *is* certain that its wings were to be clipped and the easy going association it had enjoyed with former members and officers was to come to an end. The reasons were probably political, administrative, financial and personal: political because *Sobriety* had been supported primarily (but not exclusively) by Humberside's Labour group: administrative because Humberside had largely been run by its members and the senior officers of the new authority decided that officers would be in charge: financial because there was now no economy of scale and cuts had to be made: and personal in ways that need some explanation.[3]

The Director's Tale

My first mistake was appearing to question the level of salary of the new authority's chief executive. The BBC television presenter, the late Richard Whiteley, came to the museum to interview staff and young people who had taken part in waterway residentials sponsored by *Children in Need*. At the end of the interviews he asked how *Sobriety* was coping with the changes in local government and in particular what did I think about the proposal to pay a salary of £110,000 to the East Riding s incoming chief officer. I replied naïvely that £110,000 would enable a good number of children in need to enjoy a week away on the boats. I later heard from colleagues that my remarks had not gone down well at county hall.

A few months later a community education officer who had oversight of the East Riding's two museums, Goole and Skidby Mill, made a written report to his committee that the Waterways Museum was a threat to the Garside Collection displayed in Goole Library. Although the report was nonsense, it created a climate of competition rather than collaboration and led to councillors and officers taking positions. More secretive and notorious was the action of another officer who wrote to the Heritage Lottery Fund in an attempt to undermine an application for a grant towards the cost of *Sobriety*'s museum extension. It was fortunate that his efforts were ignored but neither incident endeared *Sobriety* or me to the myrmidons in Beverley. Nor did opposition to the incinerator. *Sobriety*'s opposition was regarded as an irritating waste of time.

Perhaps not surprisingly my position as director was soon brought into question when I received instructions from John Ginnever, the LEA's new chief education officer, to leave the Project and report for work at county hall. The origins of the problem went back to 1973 and are of interest in showing how *Sobriety* did not escape the changes and fashions in the education policy of central government nor the complications of a relationship with local government. The report of a seven day employment tribunal held in Leeds in January 1999 provides a framework for describing some aspects of a dispute which began in 1996 and lasted for three years. The bottom line for the authority was that it had to save money. It also felt that it had a duty to tidy up the arrangement with the *Sobriety* Project inherited from Humberside; there was no place in the new regime for voluntary sector mavericks or staff it could not control.

The first formal contact with the East Riding of Yorkshire Council (ERYC) came with an invitation to Norman Young and me to attend a special committee in Beverley at which we were to discuss *Sobriety*'s future with members and officers. As well as being vicar of Barnby Dun near Doncaster, Norman was *Sobriety*'s chair and also had responsibility for industrial mission in Sheffield diocese. While preparing for the meeting we found a courageous ally in Professor Arthur Pollard who held the chair of English at Hull University and was chair of ERYC's education committee. He made the case in our favour but predictably got nowhere and the total grant to the Project was cut from the £100,000 it had been in the last days of Humberside and Boothferry, to £30,000. The amount constituted a grant towards *Sobriety*'s work in the fields of social services and education and was not intended to cover the costs of my salary which because I was a seconded teacher, was protected by TUPE.[4] (This is shorthand for the legislation which protects employees when a business is transferred from one owner to another; in my case the transfer was from Humberside to ERYC.) However the Director of Education came to the conclusion that protection was a sleight of hand to secure more money than *Sobriety* was entitled to. He said it was his intention to terminate my secondment whereupon I should report for duty at county hall. If I did not comply with what he regarded as a 'reasonable instruction' it would be assumed that I was absent from work without leave and my salary would be stopped pending the outcome of disciplinary procedures. This sounds altogether very high handed (and it was) but one has to remember that here was a 'foreign' director. Coming from a post in Newcastle, he had no knowledge of *Sobriety*'s work and was determined that it was not going to run rings round his policy for the new LEA. In his defence it should be noted that these latest changes in local government were resented by many employees of the former county and its districts, even to the point of them wiping the hard drives of computers so that the information contained in them could not be used by the incoming councils. It was not a good time for *Sobriety* to be asking for favours from one of four new local authorities picking over the bones of Humberside. However in order to come to a balanced view of the dispute we need to look at the history of the Project's relationship with Humberside County Council.

The barge *Sobriety* was given to Goole Grammar School in 1973 for young people actively to enjoy and learn about local waterways and the characters associated with them. The barge and its development became part of a faculty of social and community studies of which I was head. At this time there was no formal link with the authority and I was responsible solely to the head of the school. Although there was interest from the education department, it was the contract made in 1979 with Humberside Social Services that created a direct connection to the council. In 1984 the LEA followed suit and wishing to support the expansion of *Sobriety* beyond the school, agreed to pay half the cost of my salary from central funds. In return I would be teaching a half timetable and running the faculty; the rest of my time would be spent promoting and organising the use of the barge by schools, social services groups and youth organisations throughout Humberside. In respect of both aspects of the post, the head of the school would continue to be my manager. Although this was not a satisfactory solution to the problem of *Sobriety*'s development, or fair to the staff of the faculty, it did show the local authority endeavouring to find a structure to accommodate the sort of untidy arrangement not uncommon in the voluntary sector at the time.

Then in 1985 Peter Teed retired. The new head was sympathetic but he was not going to tolerate a part time teacher as head of faculty. The authority acknowledged this and a year later agreed to my working full time for *Sobriety*. At this stage I was a teacher, seconded from the school to run the Project, based at the St Thomas's centre in Old Goole, with a salary and travelling expenses paid by my employer which was now Humberside education department. Through the good services of its senior education officer Bill Rigby, the authority again did its best to define relationships. In a letter to *Sobriety*'s management committee in July 1986 he said that I would be responsible to the trustees 'so far as the Project and its terms of development were concerned, but in regard to those aspects of (my) Project directorship which affected the education authority (my) links were to be with the director of education and his representative'. This letter brought to an end the Project's links with the school except that in the circumstances of it (the Project) being wound up, I would return to a teaching post in Vermuyden School still on a protected salary.

1988 was a year that tested to the limits the ingenuity of Humberside LEA in protecting the Project's interests as well as its own. This was the year of LMS, (Local Management of Schools), which transferred responsibility for school management and budgets to boards of governors. Local authorities meanwhile continued to pay teachers' salaries. The trouble was that LMS did not fit with the cost of a teaching post being kept in cold storage at Vermuyden School on the off chance that it might be needed. When the problem was raised subsequently by its head,

Edwin Hoey, the LEA tried to undo the tangle by saying that the *Sobriety* trustees should think of themselves as a school with a devolved budget and take from the LEA the duty of employing me. In the words of the 1999 employment tribunal's report:

> A meeting of the Sobriety management committee took place on 6th March 1991 whereby it was agreed to accept responsibility for the employment of its director 'subject to appropriate grant aid being made available'. At a further meeting on the 24th June, Mr Bill Rigby in his capacity as a senior education officer, spoke of the project having a similar relationship to a school under local management of schools. At a meeting of the Humberside education evaluation and operations sub committee, (minute number 9254), it was proposed that in future the committee's support for the project be funded through grants and that the project's director be employed by the council of management.
>
> A (further) letter dated 31st May 1991 from Mr Rigby, went to Mr Watson making it clear that the grant that year came from two sources in the previous year's budget, namely the director's salary with on-costs on the one hand, and grant aid on the other. In future years however this distinction would not be made.

For the East Riding in 1996 this was an arrangement too far. Three years later it would argue in tribunal that there were no statutory powers available to a local authority to devolve its management responsibilities to any organisation other than a school while retaining its liabilities as an employer. For John Ginnever the alternatives were clear. Trustees could take over the management of the post but if they did so they would be responsible for its costs. And these costs would have to be found by trustees; the LEA might contribute in grant aid but there was no obligation to do so. If on the other hand the organisation's trustees did not feel able to find the funding, the post would remain protected but the LEA would retain all employment rights and would be justified in redeploying me to county hall if it chose to do so. In these days when the new council was grappling with reorganisation it was not going to turn a blind eye to an arrangement which denied it control over an employee who, it was stated clearly in a letter from Humberside's director of education in November 1994, was on the council's own books. Either I was employed by the Project in which case the Project should pay for me and take its chance on being able to afford the salary or I was employed by the council, in which case it was at liberty to change my place of work and job description. If I was being paid by the LEA I ought be working directly under the supervision of LEA staff. During the year of shadow councils in 1995 Bill Rigby fought a rearguard action with a letter to the transition team to say that I 'was regarded as being in the employment of the Project itself while (my) contract remained with the county council'. This was yet another attempt to undo a tangled knot but again the new director was having none of it.

The break-up of Humberside also generated a less domestic but equally insoluble problem. *Sobriety*'s work had taken it to all parts of a county which was under a single administration but the changes brought to power four new administrations with much more limited budgets. In the light of this it was reasonable for the East Riding to ask how much the other three were going to contribute. In the end North Lincolnshire managed £7,000 for one year, Hull City Council did its best for several years but North East Lincolnshire could hardly afford to meet its statutory obligations, let alone offer support to an organisation fifty miles away in Goole. *Sobriety* was indeed based in the East Riding but it did not mean that its council had to foot the bill for work in other areas.

My own position was that I was nervous about *Sobriety* taking over responsibility for my remuneration. I had spent thirty years teaching and running the Project, all of it in the service of Goole, Humberside and the LEA, and with a family to consider, the prospect of losing the security of a monthly salary was worrying. On the other hand I had a dread of losing the excitement and freedom of developing the Project and coming up with ideas to help solve its often quite big problems. When I refused to move to Beverley, the LEA stopped my salary; it was only reinstated two months later through the good services of two trustees who were on friendly terms with the East Riding's chief executive. In return for a subsequent agreement between the council and the management committee that it would take over all aspects of my employment, I was paid off with early access to the local government pension scheme. These discussions coincided with the visit of the Duke of Edinburgh to the museum in 1998 and it was a strange experience to have as guests the local authority officers who were appearing to undermine the Project's work.

My application to an employment tribunal which was heard in Leeds early in 1999, was an attempt to put right the perceived injustices of the previous three years. The council hired John Bowers QC to put its case. We drew many complimentary remarks from the members of the tribunal but, perhaps inevitably, we lost. However, the fact that the proceedings lasted a full seven days suggested that our side had put up a good show.

The East Riding's hidden response was to forbid its staff to have any contact with the Project for the next seven years. There were no links or contracts with the local authority until the return of Jonathan Fogell from Sussex in 2007. For a number of years after leaving Derringham School in Hull he had been East Sussex LEA's expert in the management and education of children with emotional and behavioural difficulties. Now he was coming to the East Riding to head up its behaviour improvement team. The doors he opened for the Project are described in the next chapter

The Road On Dutch River Side

When *Sobriety* moved into its new home in 1989 we discovered our neighbours were not just the cement mixers next door; there were also lorries arriving to load coal arriving by ship from Australia and to transport it all over Yorkshire. When they turned from the quay and swung into Dutch River Side, they spilt coal on the road. As cars, bicycles or feet became drenched with coal slush, visitors on their way to the museum wondered, *"Is this the beginning of the advertised 'reality experience' of the Industrial Revolution?"* Even British Waterways, landlords of this Caldaire Terminal, who were very attached to plans for the revival of freight on the waterways, agreed that being steeped in 'black gold' might not be the best introduction to their tourism investment further up the road. After the north east regional manager, Ian White, was sprayed with melting snow and coal, the operation was moved elsewhere. Either that or Australia had run out of coal. In any event it was a relief, and museum visitors no longer arrived looking like miners emerging from the coal face.

British Waterways at this time was a good friend, paying for the road to be re-surfaced at a cost of £75,000 and paying for the track running along the canal side on the museum site to be laid with granite setts at a cost of £11,000. Meanwhile however, waiting to cause a disturbance like the weather man at the launch of *Audrey*, was a river goblin lurking in the north bank of the Dutch River. Staff driving and walking to work noticed cracks appearing in the re-surfaced road, some of them quite wide. Those with a detailed knowledge of Chapter 16 of the Book of Numbers in the Old Testament assumed that like the unfortunate Dathan and Abiram they would soon be swallowed up and become lost in the realms of darkness. Others made a no less dramatic observation, that the river bank was sliding into the river. And it was. Ian White said later that in thirty years working for BW, this was the only engineering challenge that had kept him awake at night. If the bank had collapsed, Old Goole would have been immediately flooded to a depth of several feet. Work began urgently. It cost £7 million and involved driving 40 foot steel piles down to the bedrock for the one third of a mile length of the road. For a year there was no way of getting to the museum except by the boat which we organised to leave from the boat hoist every hour. "*It is great to visit a museum cut off from the rest of the world,*" said our visitors, "*Can we stay?*" At the end of the works BW gave us £11,000 compensation for lost business.

The No. 5 Compartment Boat Hoist, South Dock, Goole

Confrontation between grassroots organisations and public authorities or big business is the stuff of local politics and makes good headlines in local and regional newspapers. Letters and reports of public meetings sustained the incinerator story in the *Goole Times* for months on end. The weekly episodes created a battlefield mentality in which each side was probing the enemy's weakness and turning any information to its own advantage, making the outcome more dependent on rhetoric than evidence. Those in contention resembled opposing fans at a football match or members of parliament on the front benches at prime minister's questions. Argument is much more difficult to manage however when the opponent is a longstanding and generous friend. The cause of the argument was the deterioration of the Grade 2* listed compartment boat hoist which had been designed by the Aire & Calder Company in the 1860s and built by William Armstrong of Newcastle; the disagreement was with Associated British Ports (ABP) which, like its predecessor the British Transport Docks Board (BTDB), had assisted every stage of *Sobriety*'s development since 1973. These two organisations, the one public until 1984 and its successor, a stock exchange listed company from the same year, had looked after the Project as if it were their own. There was a 'special relationship' which found expression in concessions and solutions that were always free of charge. Examples were numerous: plumbers and electricians made available to install services into *Sobriety* barge: part of 35 Shed in Aldam dock handed over as a workshop and base for the boats: permission given for *Telethon Louise* to take the public on tours of Goole docks: successive port managers becoming active members of the Project's management committee: a site found on the dock estate for the six month re-construction of

Eden: financial support for publication of the Project's Review of the Year and for special events such as the tug *Wheldale's* participation in the celebrations on the Thames to mark the diamond jubilee of HM The Queen: access granted to berths in King George and Albert docks in Hull: the area occupied by the Number 5 Boat Hoist let *pro bono* to the Project. The list goes on but perhaps the biggest gift was the business expertise of retired port managers Sydney Wilks and George Robinson, Sydney being *Sobriety* treasurer during the nineteen eighties and George chair between 2002 and 2010.

Why was the hoist so important, locally and nationally? Simply because it was a symbol of the labour of past generations that made the port a prosperous investment. It broadcast the message that Goole had been the centre of a system unchanged in 120 years, that transported coal to London. For the Yorkshire Waterways Museum it was an attraction that fitted the curriculum of schools and brought income from the general public. Insofar as *Sobriety* owed its existence to the Goole community, it felt duty bound to do everything possible to protect a monument which was fascinating to young children, academics and everyone in-between. The Tom Puddings and hoist together, still cry out for a series of children's books to rival *Thomas the Tank Engine*.

The problem of the hoist's future never threatened the relationship with ABP, but it did make *Sobriety's* Director realise that going on the rampage against 'the enemy' could be counter productive! So here is the story of what was a virtual tight rope walk, based on my letter to Zafar Khan, ABP's Group Corporate Finance Manager, in July 2003.

I began with a statement about the purpose of the letter:

Further to our telephone conversation two months ago I am writing to ask that the Chief Executive and Board of Associated British Ports take urgent action to discharge their

Number 5 compartment boat hoist with accumulator tower and the guiding light which originally marked Trent End (the confluence of the rivers Trent and Ouse) — South Dock Goole.

statutory responsibilities and corporate obligations by repairing the Number 5 Boat Hoist in South Dock, Goole, which is a Grade 2* listed industrial monument belonging to ABP and among the most important fifteen per cent of the nation's historic buildings, and publishing, financing and implementing a rolling programme of measures to safeguard the hoist's future.

Then followed some facts about the monument:

The port of Goole was designed and built between 1820 and 1826 by the Aire & Calder Navigation Company. In 1865 its engineer, William Hamond Bartholomew, designed a system of coal transportation to enable the company to compete with the railways. It consisted of a train of linked compartment boats pulled by a tug, which carried the coal from most of the West Yorkshire mines to Goole Docks. At Goole the compartments boats or Tom Puddings were shunted one by one into position under a hoist driven entirely by hydraulic power. At a given signal each boat in turn was lifted in a cage to a height of about fifty feet. On a further signal the boat was tipped so that its contents slid down a chute into the hold of a waiting ship. The cage containing the boat was then returned to the water. The routine would continue until the ship had a full cargo for its voyage to the Metropolitan Gas Works in London.

The importance of the system in providing light and heat to the capital is outlined in the Railway on the Water, *a book published by the* Sobriety *Project in 1993 with a foreword by ABP's then Chairman, Sir Keith Stuart.*

From the point of view of the canal historian, the nationalisation of docks and waterways unwisely divided responsibility for maintaining the system. The compartment boats and tugs went to the British Waterways Board and the hoists to the British Transport Docks Board. But whereas much of BWB's inheritance dated from the period of canal mania in the early nineteenth century, BTDB's interest — and later ABP's — was in developing port facilities to meet the requirements of international trade. ABP was not geared up to cope with dockland heritage. The result was that in 1986 when waterborne coal movement came to an end, the two year old ABP found itself having to face the financial burden not only of the repair of the Number 3 and Number 5 Boat Hoists, but of 19 other listed buildings and items of machinery on the Goole dock estate, most of them 150 years old. These were Ouse and Victoria locks, Shed 19 known as 'The Cathedral', a crane known as 'Old Fifty', three dry docks, three swing bridges, four workmen's cabins, a railway turntable, a train of railway wagons with their accompanying wagon hoist, a pump house for the dock's hydraulic system with two wood clad accumulator towers for maintaining the pressures and finally a 'Pug' locomotive for use on the dock's narrow gauge railway. This was more of a museum than a port and it was little wonder that the port authority threw up its hands in despair when it needed to extend its quays to accommodate containers and install modern cargo handling equipment. The Heritage Lottery Fund instinctively demurred from helping, saying it could not make grants for the conservation of buildings that were not in public ownership. Tony Conder, who until 2000 was director of the National Waterways Museum in Gloucester, came to discuss the problem with George Robinson while he was still Port Manager.

Tony and I thought it judicious to stick to the future of the Number 5 Hoist rather than open the question of what might happen to the rest of the 'collection'. But we made no headway. George said these monuments belonged to the nation, not exclusively to ABP and therefore the nation should contribute towards their preservation. Who could argue? George and his port manager colleague in Hull, Mike Fell, were no philistine executives; George was and is one of the UK's leading authorities on ship registration and is volunteer treasurer for a society in Liverpool which has restored the art deco tug *Daniel Adamson*, while Mike Fell is the author of several books and monographs on canals and railways. George became *Sobriety*'s chair in 2002 and in the Review of that year looked back on his career:

In 2002 I retired from a career in ports which began and ended at Goole, a journey which did not cover great distances, Hull and King's Lynn being the geographical limits of my career but which embraced sweeping changes in the way ports are organised, the way cargoes are shipped (and the ships needed to carry them), and above all the people who keep the whole job going.

I first set foot in Goole in the middle of November 1967 only a few months out of university. I arrived in a stately manner in my 1960 Morris Minor, registration number 6262 PT. It was just young enough to have the one piece windscreen but still sported signal arms known as trafficators. To indicate a right turn required a hearty thump on the door pillar in order to raise the mechanism above a drooping 35 degrees.

My weekly pay was £18.18s.10d., enough to live in fine style at the Clifton Hotel where the goodly Mrs Connor presided over a mixed bag of trainees and a few elderly residents. Stay over on a Sunday and enjoy as a bonus all the wedding leftovers from the day before. What were my first impressions? A town which, like Spike Milligan's Puckoon, *had 'its body on earth, its feet in water,' a hive of activity where ships floated high above Aire Street: a watery maze of docks and inlets with a small armada of continental traders revealed round every corner: tracks full of coal wagons feeding the hoists on Railway Dock, and of course the fleets of Tom Puddings heading for the three boat hoists.*

I was sent up the sidings to collect tickets off the wagons and punch the weights into a Mark 1 adding machine, and was persuaded to climb the 'shake rattle and roll' heights of No. 5 Hoist. Tom Hunter presided over the port which was at that time in national ownership, the position of port manager being probably the most prestigious office in a settlement which was created as a port first and as a town only second. 'The Port and Town of Goole' the road sign still proclaims as you arrive. The natives were friendly...a fine bunch of foremen, clerks, porters, shunters and all manner of 'workmen' helping to keep the job going smoothly with an impressive in-born ability to re-jig plans at short notice to cater for a late or cancelled arrival or an urgent sailing.

I have always kept notes of shipping and if I look back to those first few weeks in Goole I see reminders of the main trades — Byland Abbey on the bacon-and-butter run from Copenhagen: Suffolk *bottled Carlsberg onto trailers which rattled up the road to the local depot:* York *on the Antwerp run:* Habicht *in from Hamburg and Bremen:* Oriole *on the old Bennet Steamship Company's route to Boulogne:* Beijerland *for Harlingen:* Chichester Cross *being fitted out at Goole shipyard:* Assidity *in dry dock:* Havelet *and* Caernarvonsbrook *among many colliers loading black diamonds for the power stations of the Thames and South Coast. And no end of bog standard Dutch and German coasters carrying timber, minerals and all manner of general cargo.*

The seas were rough this autumn and news came from Hull of four trawlers lost with only one survivor from their crews. It was a sad and sobering reminder of the constant perils of the sea which have touched Goole on too many occasions. And it was to Hull that my career took me for the next 30 years with just a short interlude in the pleasant lowlands of King's Lynn. Coal shipments from Hull had ended although some of the hoists had yet to be demolished. Trade was split between European and Baltic; it was Goole but on a larger scale. The deep-sea traffic was in oilseeds, grain, hardwoods, fruit and all kinds of manufactured goods on the export lines. I think there were over 5,000 dockers and the port handled about 5 million tonnes of cargo each year. Life was never dull due to the constant battle to get the job done and ships back to sea. This was an atmosphere that provided a good training not only in cargo operations but also in human nature and man management. Mind you, it was a topsy-turvy world in which 'the managed' seemed to make all the rules. To this day I remain astonished by the gulf which then existed between employers, customers and the workforce. There was no concept of common interest and destiny. But the Thatcher years brought much delayed changes in the form of privatisation which has brought new financial pressures and disciplines to the ports, and of course the reform of dock labour. And underpinning all this was the change to larger ships with ro-ro trailers and containers taking the lion's share of sea traffic, whether within Europe or deep-sea. This is an evolution which favours ports with deeper water, 24 hour access and many acres of land to absorb the cargoes which would have once been craned directly from hold or quayside onto transport by road, rail and canal even as a ship was discharging.

So when I had the opportunity to return to Goole at the beginning of a new millennium, what did I find after such a long absence? Well, a few familiar faces from 1967 and a dock system which had been knocked about a bit (like the faces) but which was still essentially the same. The main physical changes were the demolition of all the old multi-storey warehouses and traditional wooden sheds in order to clear space for containers, timber and heavy machinery. No longer any coal of course, but there were reminders in the two preserved hoists. This was still a port which had extended its boundaries even into the canal which begat it, but which was constrained by two rivers on the south side and by the town and railway line on the north and west sides. I found a great bunch of customers and workforce working in harmony with cutomers' requirements. Now there's a change for the better! And, perhaps surprisingly, nearly three million tonnes of cargo being handled each year, nearly double that of the busy port of the late 1960s but all done with the impression of not being busy and one of the effects of the changes in packaging, handling and manpower in the last quarter century.

In 1991, as part of the modernisation overseen by George, ABP wished to develop Aldam Dock as an area for container storage, a plan which required the removal of the Number 3 Hoist from its 1903 site. English Heritage and the local authority planners gave permission for it to be dismantled on condition that it was re-erected near the waterways museum. This of course would have been a very expensive undertaking even if at all feasible, and so with the support of the museum, the conditions of the agreement were changed to allow ABP to demolish and dispose of the hoist. In return the company was to 'refurbish and conserve in perpetuity the Number 5 Hoist in South Dock' (originally sited in 1912 at the far end of West Dock but moved to South Dock in 1922). Secondly it was to support the establishment of a charitable trust — The South Dock Compartment Boat Hoist Company Limited — whose trustees appointed to oversee the long term future of the hoist, would be museum professionals, planners and local people with an interest in Goole's history. Thirdly ABP was to build a small facility for visitors on the Number 5 site and lease the whole to the charity at £50 annually for 28 years. The Number 5 Hoist itself remained ABP's responsibility and was not included in the lease. Its Aldam dock brother Number 3, like the Tom Puddings before it, went to the Scunthorpe steel furnaces. After delaying until 1996 ABP finally got round to doing repairs to what was now the sole surviving hoist, and to its next door accumulator tower. The work cost £128,110 but it was carried out in the winter and the paint used was sub standard for the purpose. Meanwhile the museum took the lead in setting up the new trust and ABP leased the site to it, but apart from this, nothing was done. The trust requested a schedule for the continuing maintenance of the hoist but this was not forthcoming and the visitor centre which was to contain static displays and accommodation for small groups of schoolchildren was declared to be too expensive.

The following year, 1997, again as part of its modernisation plans, ABP demolished another listed building, this time a lock office standing on the island between Victoria and Ouse Locks and integral to their style and design. Demolition had taken place without the permission of the planning authority and ABP was asked to make matters good. It said it would meet the complaint by asking the museum to move the bricks to the hoist site where they could be used for the construction of the visitor centre. However the visitor centre remained unbuilt and the bricks, left in piles on the hoist site, were eventually sold.

Next came a swing bridge. It had been built in 1892 as part of the town's principal industrial thoroughfare and carried a main road south to Scunthorpe. After many years of mechanical failure, especially during hot weather when the fire brigade had to be called to cool the bolts connecting the bridge with the road, it was decided that it should be replaced. Again English Heritage and the planning authority instructed ABP, 'to preserve, interpret and create public access' to the re-constructed bridge which was to be placed on a site near the hoist. Once more the trust and the museum supported a submission to English Heritage that no useful purpose would be served by preserving it. English Heritage agreed and the planning authority gave ABP permission to sell it for scrap. The listed 19 Shed was the next to go, but this time the company took the trouble to obtain the proper permissions. However ABP was taking all and giving nothing. In spite of twelve years of concessions which had assisted the commercial development of the docks and saved the company the cost (estimated by some to be about two million pounds) of re-erectiing and maintaining the Number 3 Hoist together with the bridge and the lock office, it resolutely refused to publish and implement a programme of measures for conserving the Number 5. It was at this point that sympathy for ABP's position began to evaporate. The company could have created an annual budget to meet the costs of maintenance which in the medium and longer term would have saved it money and trouble. In September 2002, following a survey of the structure, it did tell the South Dock Compartment Boat Hoist Trust that £10,000 a year had been made available but never disclosed how the money was being spent. However, in autumn 2003 the Trust was told that the survey and the removal of pigeon droppings from the control cabin had used up £5000 of the allocation. The Trust was also told that the survey was commercially sensitive and had to remain confidential to ABP. The inference from this was that the report of survey also contained plans for other listed structures, in particular the wagon hoist in Railway Dock, and that the publicised neglect of these structures would generate unwelcome interest.

Towards the end of my letter to Zafar Khan I elaborated on the hoist's prestige in the local community and said that as a result of occasional donations from the L. J. and Mary C. Skaggs Foundation in San Francisco, the Compartment Boat Trust and the museum had been able to recruit and manage a group of volunteers, many of them former employees of ABP, who had designed signage, built fencing and produced leaflets dealing with the history of the Goole coal trade. Foremost among them were members of Goole Model Boat Club who were helping to maintain and manage the hoist site through their own activities. They had dug a boating pond and raised funds from the Heritage Lottery Fund to display a Tom Pudding on land. They had also refurbished a mooring post, a hydraulic capstan and constructed a shelter and toilet for public use. The museum had acquired and restored the tug *Wheldale* which carried visitors round the docks on Saturdays and Sundays throughout the summer and for the previous fifteen years had looked after the last four remaining compartment boats. I ended the letter perhaps rather pompously by drawing attention to the statement of social responsibility on ABP's website. It said :

Railway wagon hoist, Goole.

ABP willingly carries a considerable burden of preserving many historic buildings and features of interest. It is only one of the ways in which ABP can contribute to the life of communities that have grown up around its ports. ABP is the custodian of a unique commercial heritage.

In 2006 the company replaced the wood cladding and roof felt of the hoist. The cost was not made public but it was considerable, and everyone connected with the preservation campaign was pleased to see ABP's change of heart. Its current report on corporate responsibility shows how the company is supporting initiatives in training, employment, charitable endeavour and community work but meanwhile in 2014, after eight years of exposure to wind and rain, the Number 5 Compartment Boat Hoist and its accumulator tower in South Dock Goole are again falling into disrepair. Would it not be nice to think that arguments about the resources needed to guarantee the hoist's future could become a thing of the past? This will only happen however if Associated British Ports comes clean about its policy and intentions.

The Towpath Nature Trail

The trail follows the towpath for two miles along the bank of the Goole to Knottingley section of the Aire & Calder Navigation. It starts at the museum and goes past the cement works, under a railway bridge and westwards first to the village of Rawcliffe Bridge and then as far as the flyover carrying the M18 from its junction with the M62, in the direction of Doncaster and south Yorkshire. Thanks to the ambition of two volunteers, Elaine Pittaway and her husband John, an empty and monotonous canal bank became a pathway of discovery for schoolchildren and their families. Following an award of £800 from the Civic Trust in 1996, they planted rowan, oak, silver birch and alder in an otherwise barren landscape. Then came Tom James, a retired local authority manager with brains and energy, and Sean Hutchinson a Railtrack signalman from Bridlington, who led groups of young people from Rotherham and Leeds Groundwork to build an iron age boardwalk through reed beds full of bullrushes. They constructed a viewing platform around the pond belonging to the great crested newts and after sowing a meadow with wild flowers, planted a willow coppice for use in the fabrication of baskets and coracles. A willow barge was built by children with additional learning needs and owl boxes made a home for kestrels as well as barn owls. Finally, illustrations of birds and insects were wrought in iron fencing alongside the canal where an amphitheatre of standing stones became an open air classroom.

But the trail was also interrupted by history, a piece of it borrowed from the opening stages of the First World War. For an episode in the Discovery Channel's *Heroes* series, the company produced a re-enactment of Private Sydney Godley's rearguard defence of British soldiers retreating from Mons on 23rd August 1914, an action for which he was awarded the Victoria Cross. They identified a location just south of the North Eastern Railway bridge next to the Knottingley & Goole Canal, which bore a close resemblance to the land between the Nimy railway bridge and the Mons-Condé Canal in Belgium where Private Godley placed his machine gun.

Further up the trail was the village of Rawcliffe Bridge and the Black Horse public house, these days much improved, which was home to as much intrigue as the Admiral Benbow in *Treasure*

Island. One of its 'lock-in' customers was 'Yabber' Walker who as a result of being knocked down by a train on the single track level crossing, argued in court that the train had arrived early; it was the train driver not he who was to blame. Across the canal from this pub, whose landlord claimed all the mild beer to quench his own thirst, was a chemical works specialising in the production of vitamins for use in cosmetics. It was said that workers at the plant became so contaminated with Vitamin B that they were as hirsute as Great Apes.

Less direct than some threats, but nevertheless unwelcome, was British Waterways' decision to allow a renewable energy company to erect a trial mast for a windfarm on the trail. It was a proposal which affected no one but visitors to the museum who wished to enjoy a seasonal canalside walk. Not having any control over land owned by BW, the Project was left to argue alone that it was perverse to allow windmills to be sited on a trail that had taken ten years of voluntary endeavour to develop. There were so many alternative sites in the vicinity, far from habitations and footpaths, that would be more suitable. However, the end came when the British Airports Authority objected to the proposal on the grounds that the mast would be in the flight path of aircraft approaching Doncaster's Robin Hood Airport. It was a lucky outcome to an unpublicised battle.

There was another battle, however, which we lost: the fight against vandals. Adrian O'Neill who worked full time on the trail, provided a vivid example of the problem in the 2002 Review of the Year:

Sadly I must report that two baby barn owls were mercilessly slaughtered in the night. Both suffered air gun wounds to the head and eye. They died alone in fear and in pain. Their bodies were found by visitors to the museum and have been sent for post mortem examination. The perpetrators of this despicable crime go undiscovered and unpunished.

Barn owls are what we call a schedule one species. This means they are among the most endangered species in the country. What it also means is that they have the full protection of the law. Offenders are liable to a fine of £5,000 per bird and a custodial jail sentence.

To add further to the most profound sadness felt by all involved, both birds were within a week of fledging. It was perhaps learning to fly that killed them. If they had not been able to fly they would not have left the nest box and would not have been a target. On the other hand if they had permanently left the nest, they would have escaped this horrible death.

The truth was that before the nature trail was even conceived, this section of the canal bank had been the haunt not just of drunks, addicts, thieves and vandals but of people who would shoot anything for a free meal.

There were plans for the trail to become designated as a local nature reserve and to protect it with closed circuit TV cameras but British Waterways was unwilling to grant a lease. It might have needed the land to secure the rental from a windfarm developer.

Questions

The effect of local government re-organisation in 1995-1996 was to create a good deal of anxiety for *Sobriety*. Should the Project's approach have been different?

When George Robinson was port manager for Goole he said that the Number 5 Boat Hoist was part of the nation's heritage and that the nation, rather than Associated British Ports, should maintain it. Was he right?

Chapter 10 Notes

1   I am grateful for information about the Glews Hollow contracts to Steve Robinson, Chief Economic Development Officer, Boothferry Borough Council and to Enid Thompson, his assistant.

2   The Leader of Kingston upon Hull City Council, Patrick Doyle, once said to me that the 'Ridings' agitators would have been seen off if Humberside's HQ had been in the Guildhall in Hull rather than in the former East Riding offices in Beverley.

3   The suggestion that Goole might be administered by a local authority based in Northallerton sixty miles away, prompted the placing of a large sign on Ocean Lock, 'Welcome to Goole, Gateway to the Yorkshire Dales'.

4   Transfer of Undertakings (Protection of Employment)

Chapter 11

WOMEN AND CHILDREN IN TROUBLE

Brian Tinsley And Liam Ventris

In losing access to school, they have lost one of the most precious things in their lives. If these young people are helped to recover some faith in education, then the Sobriety team will have done an immeasurable service for the whole community. It's a job worth doing. — Jonathan Fogell, Headteacher and Education Psychologist

These young people often do not want to go to school and school sometimes does not want them. So what's to be done? In short they have to change but so does the community.

Brian Tinsley was a handful, a very large handful. He was 6ft 2in by the time he was 14 and a steamroller in attitude as well as appearance. Like Jon Fogell who hailed originally from Blackpool, he came to East Yorkshire from Sussex. But his and Jon's paths did not cross until after the boy's expulsion from the school in the seaside town in East Yorkshire where his parents had a B&B. Apart from teenage growing pains, his problems arose from his conspicuous size, red hair and accent. He was often teased by other children and sometimes retaliated with his fists and got into trouble, a situation which offended his sense of justice and made him resent the teachers who regarded *him* as the bully. A pupil referral unit (PRU) was his remedial destination but his underlying state of mind was misunderstood and he was bounced from the PRU into a private establishment in Hull which did little to help. He was now effectively banned from receiving an education and could have roamed the streets for months. The seafront amusement arcades might have been an irresistible attraction, introducing him to others on the edge but in fact he took a job delivering wheelie bins and it was ironic that the local authority that should have ensured he remained in education, was unwittingly paying him to occupy his time. However through the efforts of his parents and his own 'savvy', rather than through any help offered directly by the education service, he managed to stay out of trouble and was eventually directed towards the LEA's Behaviour & Inclusion Team. Headed by Jon Fogell and staffed by teachers with experience in special education, the unit served about thirty children who like Brian, had been abandoned because they were regarded as unmanageable. But as was evident later, difficult to manage should not have meant uneducable. In fact he was very intelligent and eager to pursue a career in marine engineering. Perhaps more sinned against than sinning, he needed an environment which created an expectation of good behaviour not through the commands of exasperated classroom teachers ending with, 'because I say so!', but through being part of a small educational community which was not afraid to put practicalities above principles or the interests of the child above those of the institution.

And so, in 2006, Brian came to *Sobriety*. He was with the Project for a year and travelled each day by train from Bridlington to Goole, a long journey which gave him time to have debates with any of his fellow passengers who would rise to the occasion. When he 'kicked off' at the museum he required the undivided attention of at least three staff, not to restrain him but to cope with his quarrelsome nature. Jon said that he was in many ways a typical Sussex lad. He could argue the hind leg off a donkey and would have run rings round any opponent in a debate. He also showed a stubbornness that is celebrated in the old Sussex chant, 'We will not be druv'. It is a phrase which indicates determination, but in the head of a stroppy teenager, it is a trait which can drive teachers to distraction. By the end of his time he was working as a sous-chef in the museum café and getting ready to go into further education. While acknowledging all the effort the Project put into him, I think that one of the most effective agents for his improvement was the group of men from Hatfield prison who came to the museum for pre-release training. They stood no nonsense and quickly convinced him that boasting would get him nowhere; in their own way they gave him firm advice for the future, *"Stay out of trouble or you'll end up where we are."* Not surprisingly he never returned to full time formal education and left the museum when he was 16 to go to college. His mother and father were delighted and so were *Sobriety* staff.

His own verdict was down to earth:

Hi, my name is Brian Tinsley. I started at the museum sometime in the summer on a training programme due to me being suspended from school. Since starting here my horizons have opened a lot more. I started learning my Complete Crew Certificate with Paul Cooper. I successfully passed that and am currently doing my Certificate in Community Boat Management. One of the things I have to do while I am here is to research a training course so I'm going to do one with the Sail Training Association on board one of their ships called Stavros *which I am currently raising sponsorship for. Well I have learnt lots and no doubt with Bob Watson about, will learn lots more, including his riveting stories.*

But the story does not end there. A few years of study led him to gain a degree in marine engineering and a post with Ximax Environmental Solutions. He is also a volunteer member of crew of the Bridlington lifeboat and the proud father of a very bright little girl called Izzy.

Just prior to Brian Tinsley's appearance there had been a change of heart at Beverley. The director of education, John Ginnever, had returned to Newcastle to be a volunteer with the Duke of Edinburgh's Award. At the same time, George Robinson, now chair of *Sobriety*'s trustees since 2002, wrote to the East Riding's chief executive to ask for help for the Project. (Sanctions are not always restricted to international relations). It was a bold move but made more acceptable by George's credentials as a former port manager. The Authority replied with two suggestions: firstly there should be a meeting between Project trustees and staff and senior officers of the council: secondly a firm of consultants should work with *Sobriety* staff to appraise the strengths and weaknesses of the charity's recently completed 2005-2008 business plan. These conditions of assistance were readily agreed and were followed by a meeting on *ROOM 58* with the head of East Riding Children's Services and a representative of the council's economic development department. The meeting brought to mind Prime Minister Harold Wilson's encounter with Rhodesia's Ian Smith on HMS *Tiger*, but it was friendly and business-like and resulted in a request by the Authority for the Project to help with the education of young people who had been excluded from school. Jonathan Fogell was named as contact for the project. He later said:

> *I believe there has not been a better time in recent years for schools to use Key Stage 4 flexibility to take advantage of the facilities of the* Sobriety *Project to contribute to alternative learning programmes, outward bound style adventure and other curriculum enrichment possibilities.*

> *I have been delighted to renew my relationship with* Sobriety *barge, the splendid waterways museum in Goole, and east Yorkshire generally. I am just left with one nagging thought. I have been told that many an educationalist works twice in the East Riding, once on the way up and once on the way down. It's good to be back!*

Meanwhile in London in the same year 2006, Ian Cawsey, Goole's MP in succession to David Davis who had moved to Haltemprice and Howden after some constituency boundary changes, was discussing *Sobriety*'s plight with Martin Havenhand, CEO of Yorkshire Forward. The upshot was an allocation of £17,000 to the East Riding Council to pay the fee of Meadowhead Projects, a company based in Blackburn and appointed to carry out the business plan review.

In three months of meetings and consultations with staff, trustees and outside agencies, Simon Ryder and John Murray, the directors of Meadowhead,[1] used their experience and imagination to re-invigorate the Project and make the process of change undeniably enjoyable. It was a signal to me to be less autocratic and a turning point for staff who discovered a new energy and confidence. The consultancy also changed *Sobriety*'s relations with the local authority which now declared itself open for business.

The immediate development arising from Meadowhead's final report was a contract for contracts by which Yorkshire Forward would recognise *Sobriety*'s efforts to set up agreements with local authorities or other public bodies. The Agency would make a grant of £20,000 a year for three years as an incentive for *Sobriety* to get into the market place and spread the word about what it could do with young people who were isolated and adrift.

One of these was Liam Ventris, a fourteen year old pupil at Bridgeview, a Hull school for children with behaviour, emotional and social difficulties.[2] During 2007 Liam was putting in limited attendance at school and leading the staff a dance. But conveniently he lived in Old Goole, having fled for unknown reasons from Orchard Park estate in Hull. His teachers thought that a few months at *Sobriety* would help him re-balance his life. Part way through his placement he wrote, disarmingly :

> *I started at the Yorkshire Waterways Museum in the summer on a training programme from school when I first came to look around the place. Since then, I have learned more*

about boats. Since starting here my eyes were on the boats. Then after twenty one weeks of coming here I had got my Complete Crew Certificate (CCC). After this I went on to do cooking with Ricky who was a volunteer from prison working in the café. He taught me lots of food to cook outside the place. Then Colin, a new member of staff, came to work in the woodwork shop so I asked to work with him and will be here for over 50 weeks and still learning more.

So if you would like to come then please come by all means. Lots of nice people are here so don't be shy. The food is nice and lots of things in the kitchen are nice. Please come and we'll be pleased to meet you. From coming here I got my CCC and my first aid course and have learned lots of food to cook. I meet a lot of new people who can help you with what you need help with, so thanks for reading this and I hope sometime to meet you.

Liam was enjoying himself. He fitted well into the life of the museum and had high hopes for the future. With the help of Bridgeview staff who visited him each week we were confident he would soon take the opportunity to go back to the classroom. But it was not to be. Rather than seeing his placement as a step on a journey back to mainstream education, the school decided that *Sobriety* was a privilege he had to earn. He was told that he could continue his association with the Project only if he spent part of the week in lessons at Bridgeview. If he did not attend school he would be truanting and as a consequence would be banned from attending the museum. It was a decision bound to lead to confrontation. The boy refused to comply with the school's demands and continued to arrive at the museum each morning.

At this point I had a meeting with two senior staff from Bridgeview who threatened me with the police if I did not enforce their ban. They said that if Liam did not go to school, he should be left to his own devices. If he got into trouble with the police and was arrested that would be one solution to his problems; *Sobriety* was not to be his bolt-hole.

The predictable outcome was that he hung around outside the museum for several weeks and spent the time with his friends drinking lager on the canal bank. In the end he disappeared and presumably returned to his roots in Hull. The school's stance may have been the result of internal disagreements among staff but it was unforgivable that an establishment set up for no reason other than to cater for the likes of this boy, could abandon one of its most wayward pupils just when he was beginning to make progress. Recent Ofsted reports suggest that the school has changed out of all recognition since 2007. I hope it has.

Youth Service In Decline

With the collapse of Fannie Mae and Freddie Mac[3] in the US mortgage market and economic crises besetting Europe, 2008 was the beginning of a period when local authorities would reduce or abolish their provision of leisure time activity for young people. A parliamentary select committee found that the average per capita funding for children at school was more than £4,000 a year while for youth services it had been cut to below £80.[4] The effects were probably felt most acutely in northern cities like Hull whose council under duress, voted for complete abolition. Speaking for the government however, civil society minister Nick Hurd claimed that it was, *"Okay to lose some of the (youth) services that had been slashed due to cuts, because they were crap in the first place."* [5]

Whatever the truth about quality, it is noteworthy that in Goole, with the exception of a youth centre which was part of the grammar school, no voluntary youth clubs survived beyond the nineteen eighties. Up until then, at least one had been open each evening of the week. Two were in Old Goole: one was in St Thomas's church hall run by sisters of the convent and favoured by young people who were the descendents of the Irish immigrants who had built the town and waterway: the other in Cottingham Street primary school was open for two nights a week and organised by a town councillor who was the caretaker of another local primary school. In Goole itself young people could 'hang out' at the YMCA on North street or at the 'Parish' in St John's church hall: there was also a Sunday night session on the same premises. Goole & District Youth Club found a home in the two ground floor rooms of the science block (now demolished) at the grammar school. Volunteer staff had daytime jobs in teaching, managing businesses or public service. One of them was Harry Bagnall, a former butcher turned priest who was curate of Goole. Later, at the time of the Falklands war, Harry was appointed to be vicar of Port Stanley. The young people were a healthy mixture of boozy rebels, children of dock workers and those with ambitions to higher education. Some fitted all three descriptions. But whoever they were and however they behaved, they found a home in one or other of these organisations. There were children in the two secondary schools who had never left their immediate neighbourhood and it was the duty of the voluntary youth service to open their eyes to new horizons and provide a nightly alternative to wandering the streets.

Despite complaints that there was, 'nothing to do in Goole', the clubs were places where activities could be requested and organised, sometimes by members and sometimes by staff bringing opportunities to their attention. In the background was the West Riding Three Rivers Area Youth Service managed by George Dodd and his assistant, David Mantell, who later became chief youth officer for Barnsley. They made funds available for special events and equipment - the Super 8 film projector used for publicising Rawcliffe Hall for example, and part bursaries for young people to attend Outward Bound or City Challenge courses. Meanwhile Ken Sedgwick, head of City of Leeds youth service and a semi-professional drummer, led a group of young people from all parts of the county to tour northern France as 'strolling players'. Nearer home, after a good deal of hand wringing by its management committee, Goole & District Youth Club got permission and funds to organise an all night session featuring the now famous folk guitarist Mike Chapman whose distinctive style was to play an American steel guitar laid across his knees.

During the period there was overlap but also clear difference between the formal school curriculum and the remit of the youth service and it was this difference that made youth work distinctive. In a Youth Advisory Council report on the purpose and content of the latter, published by the Ministry of Education as long ago as 1945, there was an emphasis on conversation and informality and a concern for non-vocational education. [6]

Informal education of this kind is probably more not less difficult than formal class-teaching and its technique needs to be deliberately learnt. It needs to be said also that discussion must be honest and fearless. The argument must be followed whithersoever it may lead, for the developing mind must not be arbitrarily stopped short by any prejudice or preconception on the part of the leader. His function is to encourage the development of a questioning and questing attitude to life rather than a receptive and submissive one. At the same time he must remember that he is dealing with minds which are immature and often unformed and one of his most constant duties must be to give them the respect and protection which are their due. Inside this framework there is very little which can or should be excluded, from social security or sex, to town-planning or religion. The responsibility of the leader is an obvious and heavy one.

It is strange that these principles and methods, which were once acknowledged to be indispensable for effective youth work, now only survive in a curriculum for children who are excluded, suspended or expelled from school.

With the loss of the Youth Service in many areas, informal provision is in decline and what funding is available tends to be sport related or linked to specialised activity groups that will not tolerate rebellious behaviour. On the other hand many schools are test orientated and concentrate their most gifted teachers on children who will achieve grade C or above at GCSE. Children who are troublesome and not candidates for a GCSE grade may be corralled into quarantined units separate from the rest of the school and ultimately from society. The kind of youth work envisaged by the Youth Advisory Council and many others during the last six decades, has finally become a curriculum reserved for children in trouble. But even that is under threat. There is no widespread public understanding of unco-operative children and there are fewer and fewer charities or institutions prepared to work with them. The reason may be that the so-called contract culture leads organisations to shy away from work that has no guaranteed outcomes and may result in the withholding of performance related payment. As an exponent of an alternative curriculum designed to meet the educational needs of children who have been excluded from school, it may well be that *Sobriety* is, like the cuckoo, one of a vanishing species. We must surely do everything in our power to make sure that it and voluntary organisations doing the same work, are not allowed to fail. If Society were to inherit a generation of young adults seeking revenge for having been ignored, it would be facing more than summer riots [7] in London and Birmingham.

Although it may not always appear to be the case, these young people's problems are often temporary, and with care and patience can be set aside. We may also find that an alternative curriculum can bring alternative achievements to match the best of their less troubled peers. But let us return to an account of *Sobriety*'s progress in these fields of social education.

Refugees From The Classroom

Brian Tinsley and Liam Ventris turned out to be the latest of an advance guard of children with similar problems who would attend the museum, generally to relieve their school of students requiring disproportionate attention, or occasionally to hide a pupil whose behaviour might compromise an Ofsted inspection. From its beginnings in the early seventies the Project had been working with young people but this new contract signified a new relationship with the LEA.

The standard arrangement for students who were not permanently excluded from school was that the week would be split between school and *Sobriety*. The placement was recognised as a complement to classwork, thus avoiding the misapprehension that attendance at the Project was merely a reward for progress at school and preventing children from falling into the same trap as Liam. Along with term-time provision were two other programmes — one for children who were at a loose end during the twelve weeks of holidays, the other for young people at serious risk of offending.

Leading the team of volunteers and staff as *Sobriety*'s youth work co-ordinator was Karen Beaumont who was and is a most gifted youth leader. In her dealings with young people, she was in the wording of the 1945 report, 'honest and fearless', encouraging them to have a 'questioning and questing attitude to life rather than a receptive and submissive one' and giving them the 'respect and protection which were their due'. Not surprisingly she was repaid with their trust and friendship.

Reviewing the achievements of 40 children during 2012, she maintained that accreditation, if used carefully, could demonstrate skills and attitudes needed by employers, give public recognition of success and prove to the world that hands-on learning can achieve amazing results. Certification derived from an understanding of individuals who might have difficulties in school but who nevertheless have the pride and ambition to become good people. It was the unconventional *timing* of their development that was the problem. As Eric Morecambe famously retorted to the pianist André Previn, *"I'm playing all the right notes—but not necessarily in the right order."* These children had first to get to the piano but by the time they had left the care of Karen and her team, they were playing some combinations of notes in quite sweet harmony. Never complacent, she said, *"While the Project has always been successful in engaging and encouraging young people, we have now stepped up a level to ensure they all gain formal recognition for their achievements."*[8]

There were also public events to mark the group's achievements. Two students, Jack and Callum, went to Aston Villa football ground for the presentation of the Keep Britain Tidy Award. They had a tour of the club and attended a gala dinner to accept the award on behalf of the Project. Charley and Tom went to London to help with a film for the National Lottery where they met McFly. The film was then shown on TV during the presentation of the Community Spaces Award. These two students became members of a youth advisory board representing 70 projects in the UK. They visited Halton, Altrincham and Birmingham to carry out appraisals on behalf of *Catch 22* which is a programme to help young people steer clear of crime or substance misuse. With six other board members at a conference in London, they facilitated workshops for 100 adults on how to run environmental projects.

Awards were also earned for work in the community: planting flowers on the approach to the train station in aid of *Goole in Bloom* and planting trees at the museum and on the nature trail with Goole Lions. At the *Drop In*, the children created a sensory yard, and at the allotment they organised the Big Lunch. A project for the summer months, Community Spaces Lasting Legacy, provided volunteering and training opportunities for young people aged 16 to gain qualifications in preparation for the job market.

With an eye on the future Karen noted that:

With funding for Community Spaces Challenge due to come to an end, we had to look at ways of maintaining our work in the community. We did some trials of mini enterprises and held a plant sale that required several thousand bedding plants to be grown. Ninety hanging baskets were sold and we made a profit to put towards the Big Lunch. The young people also set up a business in concrete garden furniture and paving. It got off the ground and orders came in. We also grew cut flowers which were very popular and we shall increase production next year. Lastly we took the produce from the community allotment to make chutneys and jams and this completely sold out. The year also saw members of the group take on another allotment. They had to design the garden, erect fences, and make and lay paving, all of which gave them new skills. Of course it was not all work and no play! With help from the Lankelly Chase Foundation, there were barge residentials to Leeds, York, Castleford and Doncaster, one of which was paid for and filmed by the BBC for Children in Need.

Her review continued with thanks to the people and organisations that had made the work possible:

We worked with Goole High School, Goole Community Group, the Youth Support Service, Barclays Bank, Goole Lions, Positive Futures, East Riding Voluntary Action Services and Catch 22. Without the expertise and skill of the staff team at Sobriety the environmental projects would not have been a success. But the biggest thank-you goes to the young people of whom I am extremely proud. It is no wonder some of them have begun to believe in themselves, to know what they can achieve and to want to aim higher.

Making no apologies for using accreditation, she said to those who would sneer or argue:

These achievements bring a look of pride on young people's faces when they are presented with the certificates at presentation evenings. We see the same pride in their parents and families. It is a priceless moment and one to be cherished.

Like Bob Trafford, the prison officer at Hatfield Young Offender Institution, she said that for some children it was the first time they had been recognised for any achievement. Commenting on their preparations for the Big Lunch on the Project's allotment which was attended by, 'a staggering 452 people', she said the police and community support officers were amazed at the age range and variety of backgrounds of the young people attending the event and by how well they got on together, adding that two local councillors had praised them for their hard work. More importantly, she said, the community's perception of them had changed. They were no longer seen as anti-social louts. People were no longer afraid to say 'Hi' to them on the way to the shop.

Like the staff of St Thomas's Centre in earlier years she was definite about the value of rewards:

Young people receive points for getting involved and making a commitment to change their attitude and behaviour. This is not always easy. Peer pressure and other factors sometimes mean they have to wait for rewards, while others who have engaged positively from the outset go off on trips. I have heard people argue that negative behaviour should not be rewarded. But it's not the negative we reward, it's the positive, and I will wholly defend their right to rewards. These children are invariably making life changing decisions.

Finally she gave her verdict on the last few years:

The education placements have been successful. They have helped prevent young people from being excluded from school and supported those who have been permanently excluded. They have said that the projects have helped them stay in school, keep out of trouble with the police, changed their views of life and given them the desire to achieve.

Damian East

Damian East was what in education circles used to be known as a late developer. Violence at home was routine and Damian brought it with him to school. He was statemented at eleven and soon judged to be an impossible challenge for mainstream schools. Then like Brian Tinsley he was sent to a pupil referral unit and expelled from it. Also considered uneducable by the Authority, he arrived at *Sobriety* and caused such mayhem in the workshops that Paul Cooper and I found ourselves summoned to a meeting with Social Services at a local police station to discuss Damian's placement with us. In his account below he dismisses the episode with, *"I still did misbehave a bit."* However Karen and her tutors persevered. So did Susan Walker in the kitchen, David Maw on the allotment, Colin Derbyshire in the workshops and Rachel Walker in the Museum all take their share of responsibility. If *Sobriety* was to be Damian's curriculum they would 'draw him out' only by 'kindness and encouragement'. Fascinated by the boats, he soon obtained qualifications to take passengers on tours of Goole Docks on *Telethon Louise*. He also joined the Sea Cadets and did a course at Rosyth where he gained a level 2 certificate in the Royal Yachting Association's power boat exams. At the same time he was involved with a group in Bradford which was sponsoring a man with a severe stomach disorder to canoe from Yorkshire to Bristol. Damian was asked to be the skipper of the boat which would travel with him. He is now studying at Bishop Burton College of Agriculture and has become a father. During the last five years the time and patience given to him by Project staff have accompanied him everywhere. Here he is in 2013:

I have been coming to the Waterways Museum since I was thirteen. I was sent here by my school because I was misbehaving and the school thought it would be good for me. I liked being at the museum although I did still misbehave a bit. I did woodwork, went out on the boats and worked in the kitchen. I enjoyed it because it was more hands-on and not sitting in a classroom all day. At school the teachers gave me a bit of grief. At the museum I fitted in better with the people there and passed qualifications in first aid, food hygiene, customer service and a crewing certificate for the boats. I also did a certificate of personal effectiveness. I felt I had achieved something I would not have done at school. Later on I also used to come to the museum to help out on weekends.

I was surprised and excited to be asked to go on Wheldale *at the Queen's Jubilee Pageant in London. John Springer, a Quaker friend of* Sobriety, *had offered to sponsor me. Before going to London I helped to get the tug ready. When it left for London I was happy that it was going but also a bit concerned for those on it. On the day before the pageant I went to London on the train. This was the first time I've been to London on my own. At Kings Cross I was unsure of what to do next and got on the wrong tube but eventually found my way. Feeling really excited I got on a water taxi which took me to* Wheldale *and was immediately handed a paintbrush to help smarten the boat. In the morning, after I'd slept under the cabin stairs and got dripped on by rain, we waited for the passengers. About two o'clock we set off. By then some of my clothes were hung up in the engine room to dry.*

It was weird. All the way down there were thousands of people, on the banks, on buildings and on roofs. I was proud to be there. After two hours I was wet and tired but still feeling good. I was gobsmacked that I was only a few feet away from the Queen, I had not expected see her that close. The Queen is someone you see on telly. After Tower Bridge I sat talking to Mishal Husain from the BBC who had been on the tug with us all day. She was as good looking in real life as she is on the telly. Back in the dock I went with some of the others to a party for all of the boat crews. On the Monday I caught the train back to Goole. On the train home, I was happy that I had been on the pageant but sad it was over.

Charlotte Rejected

But what of *girls* in trouble? In its section on the value of residential courses, the 1963 Newsom Report, *Half Our Future*, says that girls 'in particular are often desperately anxious for guidance in matters of speech and behaviour, in dealing with everyday social situations and personal relations' and that courses away from school can often be the setting for this. Guidance for the girls referred to *Sobriety* came invariably from Karen and other women staff. Often unable to cope with the level of work, these young women had kept their heads down in primary school and by the time they arrived in secondary education were a long way behind other students. Add to this a home life where everyone was at loggerheads, affection at a premium, and for a minority, the problems associated with leaving care. The residue was a yearning for understanding, frustrated by a realisation that they were not going to be candidates for the crucial GCSE Grade C that some believed would bring them the prosperity and happiness they craved. And institutions were sometimes less than sympathetic.

Charlotte was 13 when Bristol Social Services made her subject to a full care order and placed her in a home in Selby. The order stated that she was not to have any contact with her natural parents who had mistreated her from an early age. Understandably her first reaction to being taken into care was shock and fear and she misbehaved. She assaulted a member of staff and threw a television through a window, neither of them serious offences but she was bound over and saddled with a criminal record. At the museum however, she became an outstanding member of the group. Like two of the boys she was elected to membership of *Catch 22*'s youth advisory board and had a responsibility for appraising youth projects all over the UK. At 16 she left school and applied to a further education college to study for a qualification in community care. She had completed a full term's study and was looking forward to the second term when she would be doing work experience in a nursery belonging to the East Riding of Yorkshire Council. But in spite of not having committed any offences after the age of 13 (she had now turned 17), the Council turned her down and she had to give up her college place. It was an appalling decision, just as it was appalling that at such a young age she had been given a criminal record which, under current legislation, would follow her for the rest of her life. From that time, things went wrong. Her father arrived on the scene and the support that she was receiving from Social Services was withdrawn, leaving *Sobriety* staff as the only people she could trust and depend on. In the end with so much stacked against her she gave up coming to the museum and went to live with her father in Leeds. That was the last that was heard of her. It was a double whammy. If she had been able to continue with her course, Social Services would have been duty bound to support her until she was 21.

Who knows what Charlotte and children like her will do with their lives? Karen's work and the work of those like her is crucial for the economy, safety and culture of the nation. Government would do well to support such endeavours with more enthusiasm and critically, to desist from the divisive policy of putting schools in a position where they have to discount the future of children who are playing the notes in a different order.

Women In Prison: A Curriculum For The Damned?

After years of abuse and drug taking, Daciana Cojocaru was arrested for conspiracy to murder. She jumped bail and was on the run for 10 years. Eventually she was extradited to the UK from Germany and was sentenced to eight years in prison. After six years in closed conditions she became eligible for re-settlement and arrived at Askham Grange near York. Her sentence plan allowed her to do community work in preparation for release on parole and she was referred, by the prison's Head of Learning & Skills, to *Sobriety*. The aim of the placement, supported by

charitable trusts, was to restore her confidence and give her the skills to get a job and lead a law abiding life. She took to the training with enthusiasm and gained the qualifications necessary to manage a small passenger boat. She also took driving lessons and attended further education college for one day a week. She was released in September 2008 and is now secure in full time work and earning a salary large enough to run a car, visit her daughter and grandson, and pay her share of rent for a house that she shares with a work colleague. Daciana's experience demonstrates why UK Government Ministers should give public support to waterway projects that are delivering exactly the benefits identified by the Cabinet Office as policy priorities.[9]

Tony Hands and Daciana Cojocaru

In *A Prison Journey* [10] written for the Project, Daciana described her experience of the four prisons in which she had served her sentence. Her article highlighted the particular problems women face during their time in prison and is reproduced here in full:

HMP Styal, Wilmslow, Cheshire

In September 2004 I started an eight year prison sentence at HMP Styal. On arrival I was ushered into a grubby reception area and locked in a room with a number of other new detainees. It was like a cattle market.

I was then led to another dirty room where two officers held an old blanket in front of me and ordered me to strip off all my clothes. I was ordered to do a full turn so that the officers could see the back of my body. When they were satisfied that I was not concealing any contraband I was ordered to get dressed.

After this I suffered further humiliation; another two officers emptied my personal belongings onto a table and went through them as if they were rummaging through a jumble sale, making comments like "Too short, too dressy. Where do you think you're going with this lot?" Meantime they made two separate piles out of the only possessions I had left! One pile was clothing and toiletries I was allowed to take with me. The other was to be given to family or friends to take away.

Then it was my turn for the duty doctor on reception! He asked me if I was on any drugs? I replied "No". He asked if I was on any medication. I answered "Yes" and told him about the prescribed medication that I had been receiving through my GP. He told me this would all be stopped until I was seen by the prison doctor. I was then sent away with a plastic cup and told to give a urine sample. That was that! No physical examination or other questions. I had been dismissed.

A number of us were then marched off to Y Wing. We had been given prison plastic bags in which to carry our belongings. Y Wing was the next step after reception and horrendous. The inmates called it 'Beirut'! It was like a war zone, if not worse. Alarms were constantly going off all day and night. Drugs were readily available and bullying was a part of everyday life. Threats of aggression were constant. 'De-crutching' had occurred on more than one occasion. This is when a woman suspected of carrying drugs inside her vagina, has them forcibly removed by other women. I have never personally witnessed this but the practice was common knowledge. Some women even set fire to their cells. I had a sense of foreboding, a feeling of being thrown to the wolves. It was a mad house.

On the wing we were locked in our cells sometimes for twenty four hours a day. If an argument occurred the whole wing was locked up rather than just the women causing the trouble. I had to share my cell with another woman. There was absolutely no privacy. We had to do everything in front of each other. This meant we had to use the toilet, change our monthly sanitary towels and wash ourselves in full view as there was no curtain or divider — just a toilet and sink in the corner of the cell. It was humiliating and degrading and against any declared notions of human rights.

Officers were unfriendly and unapproachable. Basic requests such as wanting to speak to a probation officer or personal officer or to see a doctor, had to be made on an application form. This application system was, and is still is, a total shambles. Applications get lost in the system because there are too many forms to be processed! I asked to see the doctor and it took me eight weeks to get an appointment. And that was only because I moved from Y Wing to a house and was able to go to the health centre and make the appointment myself. Otherwise it would have taken longer.

There was absolutely no support from officers. They did not know what was going on from one day to the next. Rules changed daily and either there was no communication down the line or they didn't bother to read notices. So if you asked two officers the same question you would get two different answers. When talking to officers I got an impression that some were despondent about their job while others were quite happy and even said things like, 'Where else can you get paid for drinking tea?' This sort of officer had no understanding of the women.

When I arrived on Y Wing nothing was explained to me. No one told me where or how to get my food or mail, or phone calls or how I went about getting work, or what choice of work or education was on offer. Nor was I told that I had to apply for these things. This kind of information had to come from other prisoners.

Later I was moved to a self-catering house. This was excellently set up. The mood of the women prisoners, their attitude and the environment were very positive — a huge contrast to living on the wing. The house units consisted of 20 to 25 women. The system was one of the best I have known since being in prison. I had my own room, I could cook my own food, do my own washing, plan my own sentence and organise my own education. And make my own appointments! Here I finally got the feeling that there was a lifeline.

Being placed in a prison near to my family allowed me to have one visit a week. The visits at Styal were not the best but they did help me mentally and emotionally during those first days of incarceration. I don't know what the visits are like now but I'm sure more could be done for women with children. It's also remarkable that there is nothing in place anywhere in the system for grandmas! As a grandmother I know how much my daughter and grandchildren depended on me and I know how much of a wrench it was for my grandchildren not to have me involved in their daily lives.

The education department ran a wide range of useful and interesting courses. Day, evening and weekend classes were accessible to some of the lucky women whose risk assessment allowed 'free-flow' — meaning that if they are trusted, prisoners can walk around the prison alone, but only to and from designated places of work or education classes. The courses included numeracy at all levels, computer literacy, business administration, hair, beauty and other related activities, gymnastics and distance learning through the Open University. The IT centre, which was run separately from the education department, published its own prison newspaper. If you worked on this you had the opportunity to work towards an entry level qualification in journalism. I started a number of courses: NVQ Level 3 business administration (available to all classroom orderlies), several computer courses and a distance learning course.

I had settled into Styal and was progressing positively. However Styal is a local jail, so seven months into my sentence, having finished the normal offending behaviour programmes — enhanced thinking skills, anger management and so on — I was informed one five o'clock tea-time that I was to be moved to HMP Buckley Hall in Rochdale. I couldn't understand why. I felt I was being punished for something else. Apparently it was to do with numbers. I have to add that while in Styal, a lot of women live in daily dread of the news that they are the next to go! This was an anxious time. I was frightened of being moved. My first thought was of how Jews and gypsies must have felt when waiting and wondering when and if they were going to be sent to a Nazi camp! It was a frightening experience not knowing how long I'd got left before they came to ship me out from familiar surroundings and everything I'd been working on. How far would they send me from my family?

HMP Buckley Hall, Rochdale

As I had had a positive attitude to my sentence from the outset, being put on a wing in Buckley Hall was upsetting and unsettling and set me back in my personal sentence plan.

I have witnessed women self harm when they have been told they are being shipped out. One woman smashed her arms through the house window and was then dragged off to the segregation unit only to be immediately transported out with both arms bandaged. I arrived at Buckley Hall three months later and she was still in the prison segregation unit. I let her know that I had arrived and was on the induction unit. When she came to visit escorted by a female officer, she told me she was too afraid. In the five months I was in Buckley Hall I watched as this woman changed. At Styal she was very motivated and positive. At Buckley Hall on the wing she was self harming on a regular basis and very weepy and withdrawn.

The wing situation is not good. Sometimes there would be up to half a dozen 24 hour watches on one wing! This is when a prisoner is at such a risk to herself that an officer has to be present and write down in File 2052 everything she does — her mood, who she's spoken to, when she took a shower, even when she goes to the toilet. Every night the alarm was going off because a woman had attempted to kill herself. That was still happening with the officers present on their watch. Living on the wing at Buckley Hall was very difficult in a number of ways. If one needed to use the toilet during the night, it was not acceptable to flush it afterwards. This was because the walls were so thin everything could be heard throughout the wing. If someone snored they would have problems with their neighbours. I could hear everything my neighbour did including all her bodily functions and daily ablutions. Drugs were easily available here too. Bullying and intimidation by both prisoners and some of the staff seem to be an acceptable form of behaviour. Sometimes there would be only one wing officer! We would be locked in our cells for 24 hours on these occasions. Luckily there were curtains in front of the toilets here. More single rooms too. The education staff were very helpful but unfortunately their education programme was very limited and the classes very small. I was employed as classroom assistant in the English language class. My only achievement at Buckley Hall was one module on a basic computer course. I could not carry on with my more advanced courses because they didn't do them there, nor did they do the NVQ Level 3 in business and administration. This was frustrating. I couldn't understand why I had to be moved from a prison where I was doing good, positive, rehabilitating coursework that would help me get decent legitimate work on release, to another prison that didn't do any of the same courses. But I was one of the lucky ones. Women had to pester to get into education at Buckley Hall due to the size of the building that was used. Though the premises were unsuitable, I must add that the education staff were very good. This has been the case throughout my journey within the prison system but there has been little or no consistency of provision.

After five months at Buckley Hall we were all informed that the prison was going to become a men's establishment. We were given forms to make requests for the prison we would like to be transferred to. We were also warned that a decision would depend on how full that particular prison was. In the event lots of women were moved to prisons that were far from their homes and families and this caused more distress to many inmates, me included.

HMP Drake Hall, Stafford

I arrived at Drake Hall semi-open prison. This was a good prison. The governor grade staff were approachable and I saw one of them every day of the ten months I spent there. They made the effort to mix with the women; everywhere and everyone was accessible. If I needed to see health care, resettlement, probation or education officers, I just had to put in an application or simply ask an officer to phone and make me an appointment. As usual that would still depend on which officer I asked. In all prisons there are officers that will not do anything but lock us up and then complain about us having too many privileges. Again the education programme didn't offer much of a choice and the classes were never full. Sometimes there were only a couple of students in a class even though there was a waiting list for that particular course. Sometimes a class would be closed because there were no students! The department itself was well laid out and there were plenty of computers. Only ten women were allowed out to attend college. The choice of work within the prison was library assistant, packing for a catering company, counting nails and screws, laundry, waste management or gardens. There were limited choices of community work and the prison's location made it difficult for women to find paid employment. However there was a lot more freedom of movement here. There was also a rehabilitation unit. The self harm rate was less than at Styal and Buckley Hall, due perhaps to the layout of the prison and there being fewer restrictions.

Drake Hall is a collection of houses, a lot like a Butlins holiday camp! I know this because I went to Butlin's once as a child and that's what Drake Hall reminded me of, especially its tannoy system which started at 7.30am and was used to tell women where they had to go. The last call at 8.00pm was to tell women to go to their houses for final roll call. We could do our own washing; there was a machine and dryer in each house, a TV room and a toaster in the kitchen. Single rooms and double rooms were an option. The more I think about it the more I believe that it is down to the governor on how good the performance of officers and prisoners is. The layout of the prison is also important but the officers and board of visitors have to take initiatives and mix with the prisoners. The governor has to know his or her staff and be on terms with everyone. There was a good feeling at Drake Hall but it was a shame about its location. This caused a lot of difficulty for visitors as there was no public transport to the prison and information to prisoners and families was severely lacking.

I was given permission to revamp the prisoners' information room. I repainted, re-stocked and refurbished it, turning it into a Prisoners' Advice Bureau. I did this happily and instead of it being open just a couple of evenings a week, I opened from 8.30am till 8.30pm seven days a week. I encountered a lot of obstacles at first from some officers but others were impressed. The women could get information and help in a responsive, friendly way. If I didn't know the answer I would go and find it out. I have been in prison long enough and am mature enough not to allow myself to be intimidated. If I had any problems I would speak to a senior officer or a governor about it. It was a good service that would be invaluable in other prisons.

Some women didn't like to go to the officers for anything, especially when they first arrived at a new prison. Women would tell me they didn't feel they were getting the right answers from them or that they would be told to go away and come back later, only to find when they did, that there was no one in the office. That's not unusual. At Styal, Buckley Hall, Drake Hall and even Askham Grange, it's the same. Everything depends on which particular staff are working or not working. Some staff are downright bullies. I have even seen and heard threats from staff to prisoners. I have personally been threatened. They let you know they can make your life miserable. They can cause silly things to happen. Visit applications, canteen sheets, RDR (resettlement day release) applications, licences for community or paid work or college, can all go missing. They just don't get processed and this causes no end of delays and upset for both prisoners and families.

HMP Askham Grange, York

Reception here is one of the best. I wasn't strip searched and was treated with dignity and respect when I arrived and that made a lot of difference. However as usual the whole risk assessment process starts again! I was given appointments with probation, housing, education and family workers. It took three months to get my risk assessment but within that three months I got my computer studies finally completed. Other than Styal this was the only prison that offered the classes I wanted. All other normal prison courses are also on offer. The head of learning and skills is a dedicated woman and very hands-on. She a great believer in education and family ties being the back bone of rehabilitation.

Unfortunately some of the new Prison Service Orders (PSOs) hinder or prohibit a lot of what Askham Grange used to be about. This is especially true for the prisoners sentenced under the old parole regulations. Women at Askham Grange are generally very focused about their sentence and have reached a point of trust where they can go out to do community work. Some are in full time paid employment at local businesses earning a full wage. Is it not a waste of resources for these women to have to remain behind in prison when they have proved not only that they can be trusted but that they can take on responsibilities? Why are we not allowed out on a tagging system at this stage? Would this not be more beneficial for our community and families? Parolees under the old regulations have a lot more to lose than the short term prisoners that get tagged.

To be honest, for many women, prison doesn't work. It has only worked for me because I have used every possible channel and opportunity to get what I can from the system. Many a time I felt I was fighting a losing battle as no prison I went to offered a continuation of the course

I had already started at the previous establishment. There is nothing to be gained from being locked up with raging drug addicts that don't want to be rehabilitated or with prison officers that intimidate and bully. Small units like Askham Grange with more specialised civilian staff running the gaol can work and encourage women to rebuild their lives. The prisoners can even do a lot of the jobs that the officers and OSG's (Officers Support Grade) are paid to do. Gone should be the days of quasi militarised regimes. It's help and support that women need. I am successful because I am stronger than most of the poor shattered women in these places. Yes I do believe that some people should be locked up and yes there are some extremely good officers. But there is also widespread unfairness within the sytem and some of it is due to the new Prison Service Orders which treat women like men. I believe the government is breaking its own code of practice when it comes to fair treatment. We must be allowed access to our families and partners, have support from housing agencies and employers if we are to be successful upon release. Isn't this what we all want?

Reports Of Visits By HM Inspector Of Prisons

Daciana wrote this account just before her release in autumn 2008. She hoped it would strengthen the view held by many involved in the administration of justice, that if there is to be a reduction in women's re-offending, some aspects of the prison system will need reform. High security institutions may be effective in protecting the public from dangerous criminals but many women's prisons in their present form do little to assist the process of re-settlement. It is not the purpose of this chapter either to praise or criticise the Prison Service but it may be useful to compare some of Daciana's observations with reports by the Chief Inspector of Prisons during the period of her sentence, 2004 to 2008. Daciana had seven areas of concern, some common to many women's prisons and some a problem for particular institutions. She was distressed by reception procedures at Styal: unhappy with accommodation on the wings at Styal and Buckley Hall: dissatisfied with the limited education provision at Styal, Buckley Hall and Drake Hall: upset and angry about shipping out: contemptuous of the attitudes of some prison officers: frustrated by lack of information: and finally, bewildered by new prison service rules limiting women's re-settlement opportunities. Excerpts from inspections of the four prisons give credence to her story:

Reception

From Report of Full Unannounced Inspection of HMP/YOI Styal 19th – 23rd January 2004

Other elements of support for women in the early days of custody were missing. The reception area, as at the last inspection, was too small and cramped, with insufficient privacy. There were no effective first night and induction procedures, and women described how they learnt routines and rules from each other, if at all. Some basic elements of care could be overlooked. There was over-reliance on prisoners to provide support that should have been embedded in prison routines and procedures.

Accommodation

From Report on an Unannounced Full Follow-up Inspection of HMP & YOI Styal: 26th October – 4th November 2005

The conditions and support on Waite wing, half of which was occupied by detoxifying prisoners, remained wholly unsatisfactory. The recently-opened CALM (care, assessment, learning and motivation) centre provided an excellent environment for the 30 women who were able to access it. But the wing was once again overcrowded, and for most women, the regime was inadequate: we found 100 of the 165 residents of Waite locked in their cells during the core day. Interactions between staff and prisoners remained limited. On the houses, there was a much more open and active regime, but there were nevertheless unaddressed problems of bullying.[11]

Education

From Report of Announced Inspection of HMP Buckley Hall: 16th – 24th February 2004

The quality assurance of education and training was very weak. There was little ongoing accreditation of national vocational qualification units and inadequate verification arrangements in hairdressing had led to incorrect accreditation of prisoners' work. The arrangements for sharing good practice were inadequate and the college's policies and procedures were not effectively adhered to. We found significant weaknesses in the quality assurance arrangements covering training and work.

From Report of Announced Inspection HMP Drake Hall: 3rd – 7th September 2007

Vocational training leading to qualifications was linked to most work activities, but uptake was low. The range of provision was broad, although the learning and skills strategy failed to take sufficient account of sentence plans or employment potential. The English-for-speakers-of-other-languages provision was underdeveloped. There were enough work activities but allocation to work was not systematic and the quality of jobs varied. Achievements were generally good, but attendance in many lessons was poor. Vocational training leading to qualifications was linked to most work activities, but uptake was low.

Relations with prison officers

From Report of Announced Inspection of HMP Buckley Hall 16th – 24th February 2004

While staff–prisoner relationships overall were positive, there was a residue of serious disrespect towards women prisoners by a minority of staff, both residential and educational. This manifested itself in inappropriate comments and behaviour, both of which needed to be challenged and eliminated.

Shipping out

From Report on Unannounced Full Follow-up Inspection of HMP & YOI Styal: 26th October – 4th November 2005

Prisoners' responses to questions about transfers and escorts were significantly more negative. Twelve per cent of prisoners said that they had spent more than four hours in a van, compared to 7% in 2004. Only 6% of women said that they had received sufficient comfort breaks, and 89% found the vans uncomfortable. Only 10% of women said that they had received written information about what would happen to them before they arrived.

Daciana commended Askham Grange, the last prison on her five year journey, for the education and work opportunities it made available to women in the final two years of their sentence. But she also said that recent PSOs, designed to control outwork in men's prisons, had the effect of limiting women's freedom to do voluntary and paid work in the community and were a barrier to women's re-settlement. Five years later in July 2013 the Justice Parliamentary Select Committee agreed, saying that the government's reforms had been 'designed with male offenders in mind' and treated women as 'an afterthought'.

Presenting Askham Grange as a national exemplar, the Chief Inspector said at the beginning of her 2008 Report of Inspection that:

Askham Grange, near York, is one of two women's open prisons holding around 100 women who are close to release, in some cases after having served long sentences. It has always had positive inspection reports, but on this occasion its performance can best be described as outstanding. It is the only adult prison which we have assessed as performing well across each of our four tests of safety, respect, purposeful activity and resettlement.

And in the final paragraph of her introduction she says:

Open prisons, despite their relatively compliant population, are not always positive and supportive environments. Too often they are merely waiting rooms on the way to release. Askham Grange was far from that; it provided a holistic and individualised approach to managing the transition from custody back to the community. This is a credit to its staff and HMP Askham Grange managers. It is also a message to the prison system about the kind of establishment and the kind of approach that most benefit prisoners, particularly women prisoners.

The Link With Askham Grange

In autumn 2013 the Ministry of Justice announced through the *Women's Custodial Estate Review*[12] that Askham Grange would close. One hopes that the decision was not influenced by the potential sale value of the buildings and grounds. With a location in the upmarket village of Askham Richard, three miles from York, the prison could easily be converted into an exclusive hotel and conference centre. However, that is speculation. Less conjectural was *Sobriety's* close association with the prison from 1991 until 2008, the year of Daciana's release. It was a connection sustained throughout the years by the determination of Sue Blackburn, head of Askham's physical education department, to provide work experience and volunteer placements for the women in her charge, who, like the young people described above, needed a long time to get on their feet. Successive governors had full confidence in her judgement and there were rarely any hiccups.

Back in 1992 as the link was being established, a young woman called Alison Nicholls attended a City Challenge course at *Sobriety*. The course director, Mike Berners-Lee,[13] signed off her report:

Several of the participants in the City Challenge course held at Sobriety *Centre came from prisons. One of them came from Askham Grange open prison where she had a reputation for bullying. She returned from the course to discover she was due to be sent to a closed prison. On the strength of her progress on City Challenge the decision was reversed. She now works three days a week with adults with learning difficulties and takes people with special needs horse riding in her spare time. Staff say that her behaviour at the prison has been transformed.*

It is difficult to believe that Daciana suffering her tribulations at Styal in 2004, and Xenia, an Askham volunteer working at *Sobriety* in 1999, were held within the same jurisdiction. Xenia explained:

I am currently serving a custodial sentence at HMP Askham Grange. In July I was offered a placement at the Waterways Museum which would allow me to work out of the prison for three days a week. When I first started I felt very nervous and not sure how people would treat me. As time went by I felt less alone but was quite intimidated by the apparent size of the outside world. In just a few months away, it seemed to have grown.

During my time in prison I have completed NVQ levels 1 and 2 in business administration with a view to getting employment when I am released. Although I have worked previously, I had never worked in an office until I arrived in Goole. While working at the Museum I have gained work experience that has gone a long way to help prepare me for a return to the real world. I work as a receptionist, greeting customers as they arrive, serve in the gift shop and assist with spreadsheets for monitoring visitor numbers. Now I know that there are people who will give me a chance and treat me as a human being instead of as a number on a list. They also trust me and help me to get on with my life, proving that there may be such a thing as rehabilitation.

Another Askham resident, Jeanette Elm did work experience on *Eden* with an organisation working with homeless people in Hull. She earned this report:

Jeanette has looked after the only female resident on board. As a result of her patience and drive, our resident started to make her own choices, was more assertive and went shopping to buy the food for a meal for nine people. With Jeanette's help she costed and bought the food and prepared the meal.

Some Solutions

By 1999 *Sobriety* was feeling sufficiently confident of the difference it was making to women's re-settlement, to apply to the European Social Fund (ESF) for assistance to increase the scope of its courses. (For details of the Project's broader relationship with Europe, please go to Chapter 13). The confidence was based not only on its good relationship with the prison but also on the successful completion of a series of measures sponsored by Europe to benefit people who had been out of work for a long time, sometimes for years. Known as *Waterways Work for Women* the proposed measures were designed to do everything possible to help women near the end of sentence overcome the barriers preventing them getting into work. The Project's experience was that the three most important requirements were motivation, accommodation and a job. Motivation could only come through an enjoyable programme of preparation for release; in their search for accommodation and work, women had to have enough belief in themselves to overcome prejudice and be judged for who they were, not for what they had done in the past. Added to this was a need for accredited training that met skills shortages in the labour market, free child care and transport, and help with interview techniques and CV writing.

Unashamedly *Sobriety* set out its stall. Once again the waterways would be the attraction and focus for recruitment, training and employment. During the heady days of the Manpower Services Commission, the Project had employed nine boat*men*; there had been no female skippers working for the Project at that time and in 1999 there were still none. Further afield, the waterways had not changed in this respect since the time of the Vikings. There were no women in positions of practical responsibility on boats anywhere in Yorkshire, an oddity of the private [14] as well as the voluntary sector. I was accused of preaching patronising feminist dogma by some of our skippers but the regional labour market predictions were there for everyone to consider; there would be 100,000 new jobs in tourism between 1999 and 2003. The Yorkshire waterways were recognised to be a 'honeypot' for heritage and recreation and the job vacancies would have to be filled, so why not by women? Nor was it fantasy that there was substantial prejudice against women from prison. In 1998 North Yorkshire Training & Enterprise Council had done an attitude survey in which 41% of employers said they had no *suitable* vacancies.

Sobriety would combat these problems with a fullblown programme of activity approved by Askham but offering, in addition, child-care at Goole College for women who had babies or young children with them in prison. The scheme would also cover the running costs of a minibus, based at Askham and driven by one of the women, to bring beneficiaries and children each day from York. Meals, refreshments and protective clothing would be available to students free of charge.

Below are extracts from answers to questions on the ESF application form. They are illustrative of the 'eurostyle' required to complete the section on support measures and activities. Many gallons of midnight oil were burned in researching and answering the questions in this and similar forms.

In line with the ESF Objective 3 prospectus and the Regional Development Plan (RDP 7.57) this Priority 5 Measure 1 project will target 30 inmates of Askham Grange

Women in prison – Learning the ropes.

prison near York who, through being offenders, come from a socially excluded group. They will be coming to the end of a custodial sentence and will either be returners to the labour market who lack skills or whose skills are outdated or they may be lone mothers whose caring responsibilities are a barrier to them being active in the labour market. 25% will be from community ethnic minorities. This meets the recommendations of the RDP p.46.6.6 that there needs to be a greater focus on specific groups of women facing the greatest difficulties: lone parents and women with no qualifications.

The purpose of Waterways Work for Women *will be to raise women's horizons. By getting them away from the prison into the new world of the waterways and into meeting people from different social and intellectual backgrounds, the project will be the first rung on the ladder to enable women offenders to enter a labour market in which 'most new jobs require a higher level of skill than those which they replace' (Yorkshire Forward Skills Action Plan (SAP) 1.15). Each beneficiary will follow a 300 hour programme at the Waterways Museum at Goole; individual timetables will vary according to women's needs and commitments.*

The programme will tackle skills gaps (SAP p.26) of practical skills, ICT, communication and customer handling. Accreditation will follow, not confront, beneficiaries. To allow flexibility and freedom to choose, a 'pick and mix' menu will be available as follows:

Taster day trips and residentials, boat handling and management leading to the Certificate of Community Boat Management, a qualification approved by the Maritime and Coastguard Agency, to build confidence and develop management skills:

'Front of House' and customer care leading to the Welcome Host certificate of the Yorkshire Tourist Board:

Digital Arts using AppleMac computers – a rewarding and enjoyable way of learning ICT skills:

First Aid at Work and Food Hygiene certificated courses:

Engine maintenance certificated by the Royal Yachting Association:

Other courses leading to Open College Network (OCN) Levels 1 & 2 will be waterway crafts, willow weaving, museum conservation, numeracy and literacy. The emphasis is on informal and experiential learning in order to increase confidence to the point where a woman can say about a new employment challenge 'Yes, I could do that'.

The outcomes of a previous pathway to employment, *Turn the Tide,* justified the decision to make an application to Europe. Between 1996 and 2000 there had been 113 beneficiaries of which 97 were long term unemployed for three years or more, and 37 were offenders. Of these, 17 found employment, 57 went into further training and 41 gained basic qualifications in preparation for work. The ESF Verification & Audit section of Government Office for Yorkshire & the Humber concluded its inspection of the project with '*We have informed the Head of the European Secretariat of the positive impacts the project has had on the local community and the exemplar systems you have in place*'. On the strength of this, the application for EU assistance for *Waterways Work for Women,* was successful.

One of its beneficiaries was Chrissie Buckley who was coming to the end of a life sentence. She had served 17 years and was now resident at Askham. Having spent many years earning qualifications that would benefit her on release, she had finally studied for a PhD in research methodology. Together with prison staff and colleagues from the Learning & Skills Council (North Yorkshire), she suggested that *Sobriety* might undertake a project to ascertain to what extent some women due for release and others after release, had found the *Sobriety* approach useful in their re-settlement. The result was *Spring to Release*, a 32 page report of a year long enquiry into the effectiveness of *Sobriety* in '*helping women serving a custodial sentence to overcome the barriers to subsequent employment. These barriers are often caring responsibilities, isolation, accommodation, finance and inflexible training programmes.*'[15] The intended purpose of the report was to influence the future planning of both organisations. Some of the findings however, highlighted a problem to which there was no immediate solution:

What the women appeared particularly to appreciate was the qualifications gained from their education and training at Sobriety *and the receipt of a certificate as proof of their achievement. The benefit of this was twofold. Firstly it boosted their opinion of themselves by providing evidence of their capabilities. Secondly it was an addition to their CV and evidence to prospective employers of what they had accomplished.*

However the practice of having to declare a conviction when applying for employment was such that many ex-prisoners chose not to do so if they could avoid it, despite knowing the risks of losing their job if their non-disclosure was subsequently discovered. Consequently they would not be able to explain why they had attended a boat management course in a location which could be many miles from their home town — and therefore had to omit this potentially valuable piece of information from their job application.

The first of two case-studies in *Spring to Release* showed how prison rules could be a serious hindrance to women wanting to find accommodation for themselves and their children. In one instance the rules, arbitrarily interpreted, were also a serious hindrance to *Sobriety* and begged a question of trust:

Ellen was due for release from Askham in July 2003. She had her little boy Sam with her. Her other two children — two daughters, had gone into local authority care when Ellen was put in prison.

Prior to becoming eligible for release on licence she had been working conscientiously for several months in the museum café. To prepare for her release, find accommodation and arrange to see her children, Ellen requested a home leave. At the instigation of the prison governor the home leave board which considered such requests, informed her that she was not eligible for tagging because the address she had given was not acceptable.

To assist a woman who was known and trusted by the Project, staff contacted local estate agents and found accommodation for her in Goole but although she was going on a daily basis to Sobriety, *the prison refused permission for her to view the premises. The letting agents could not hold the property.* Sobriety *again found suitable accommodation. In the end she was released four months late, with £47.00 for her and her son. There was no*

275

furniture in the house. The Project paid the £800 bond for the property until such time as Social Services could provide the money. Staff then assisted with the furnishing. Social Services visited and approved the property and Ellen was able to have her daughters with her as well as her small son.

There was less implied criticism of Askham Grange in the second of the report's case-studies it but showed the importance for all women of pre-release work placements outside the prison whether as volunteers or paid employees:

Jane and her little boy Jason were residents in Askham's mother and baby unit. Jane went to the Sobriety *Project early in her sentence. Jason travelled with her and was able to spend the day in the local nursery thanks to a place paid for by the Project. She was released in 2004 and, having built an excellent reputation and rapport with staff at the museum, was offered full time employment to give her enough time to get on her feet, find accommodation and work nearer her home. It was a success story made possible by a combination of Jane's determination and Sobriety's assistance. Had she not been a beneficiary of* Waterways Work for Women *and chosen to remain working in the prison, the outcome would have been very different for her family.*

In 2002 Ann Hodgson followed Norman Young as chair of *Sobriety's* trustees. At the time, just prior to her retirement from the Prison Service, she was governor of HMP Moorland. In the foreword to *Spring to Release* she said:

We are very grateful to the Learning & Skills Council (North Yorkshire) for generously funding this research. Having started my career in the prison service working in the maximum security wing for women in Durham prison, it is ironic that the author of this published research should have been one of my charges at the beginning of her sentence. Little thought was given then in 1988 to prisoner re-settlement, especially of women, and it is to her credit that she has used her opportunities in custody and developed skills to produce this in-depth report.

In 2003 with the prison population exceeding all predictions, there are approximately 11,000 women entering prison each year, the majority serving sentences of less than 12 months.

One of the protective factors against recidivism is having employment. However women who have served a custodial sentence find this especially difficult to achieve. One of the key performance indicators of the prison service is now the number of discharged prisoners going into employment or further education. So it is pertinent that a piece of research should be commissioned which looks into the barriers facing women offenders getting into employment using the Sobriety *Project's* Waterways Work for Women *as an indicator and evaluation tool.*

In the same foreword the Chief Executive of British Waterways, Robin Evans, acknowledged the part the waterways could play in women's re-settlement:

In recent years there has been a phenomenal revival in the interest and use of Britain's inland waterways. More people than ever before want to live, work and socialise near water. Our waterways are publicly owned and managed to maximise public benefit. They have a very broad appeal and are a resource that can be adapted for an extraordinarily wide range of activity. It is therefore perhaps not surprising, but wonderful nevertheless, to learn of the Sobriety *Project's* Waterways Work for Women *and how in this report it has been used to influence future policy in helping discharged prisoners back into employment.*

This is an important piece of research that deserves wide circulation, not just among the professionals within and around the prison service. As a result I hope that we shall see even more use of our waterways for activities like this that clearly deliver real social benefit.

Daciana was the last of the line. Having looked after the link for nineteen years, Sue Blackburn left Askham, albeit only temporarily, and by 2009 the prison seemed to have lost interest. At the same time *Sobriety* had renewed its acquaintance with the re-named HMP Moorland, (now HMP Hatfield). There was never a formal divorce but the drift apart had begun with publication of *Spring to Release,* which while suggesting a number of improvements to *Sobriety,* was not uncritical of the prison's education department. Transport also became a problem; it was easier for staff to monitor the progress of women doing community work in York than to be spending half a day travelling to and from Goole. There was a feeling that the Project was too far away and too independent for the prison to be able to keep a proper eye on the projects in which women were involved. And finally there were 'the men from Moorland' who appeared an unhealthy threat to a woman's reputation.

The Chief Inspector's reports give the impression that Askham Grange was a first class institution that gave its residents the best possible chance of re-settlement but it was only as a result of the good judgement and care shown by Sue Blackburn in her selection of volunteers that *Sobriety* was able to assist so wholeheartedly in this process. After she resigned there was no one to carry the banner and maintain the tradition.

After Daciana's release I made two final visits to the prison, neither of them particularly pleasant. The first, at the invitation of staff, involved a meeting with prison managers from Libya who on the instruction of Muammar al Gaddafi were enquiring into ways in which the country's prisons could be improved. I was asked to acquaint them with *Sobriety*'s part in Askham's re-settlement framework. However, the group did not show enthusiasm for ideas so detached from the reality of its own appalling record that any re-settlement concessions must have seemed stupidly indulgent.

My second visit was in the company of the Yorkshire Grantmakers' Forum which before the untimely death of its founder, Peter Marshall, met every few months to bring members up to date with voluntary sector developments that their respective charitable trusts might wish to support. On this occasion the Forum, which like its national counterpart, the Association of Charitable Foundations, had a lively interest in penal affairs, was learning about life in a women's prison. One of the afternoon sessions choreographed by two of Askham's male staff, was introduced by shouting and whistle blowing. Then appeared three women being chased into the hall and ordered to sit in a line together. The men stood some distance away on each side of the line and barked out questions in a manner that would have been more appropriate to a circus ring or parade ground. In the course of the barrage the women confessed to the reasons for their imprisonment: one was a drug addict, one was a prostitute and the third had embezzled money. When asked if they were sorry for their crimes they meekly rehearsed the benefits of being locked away from evil influences . When asked to say what it was like to go into prison for the first time, their descriptions matched word for word Daciana's account of her arrival in the reception block of Styal, but in addition, acquainted us with the evils of prison transport — how they were manacled to plastic seats and with no toilet provision, had to urinate where they sat. The cast then left the hall. For me it was an awful performance which had humiliated three women in front of a large audience and I stood up and said so. It was sexist to the point of being creepy and was a denial of the women's right to have any independent opinion. Psychologically they were at the mercy of the two officers. I had a conversation with them during the tea break and asked if they were aware of any implications or sub-plots of their drama. They said they were not. Most members of the audience accepted that what they had seen represented a proper and just punishment for wayward women. I was glad to get in my car and go home.

To conclude, in her introduction to *The Story of a House — Askham Grange Women's Open Prison,*[16] Helena Kennedy QC says :

> *Over the years many of my female clients have served time at Askham Grange and it has always been a source of relief when they were allocated a place there rather than in one of the larger institutions. The women acknowledged that while this smaller prison was not a not a holiday camp, the ethos upon which it was founded encouraged rehabilitation, the acquiring of new skills and the sustaining of relationships with family and friends beyond the prison gates. They knew they would be more than just a number there and it mattered to them.*

> *We are living in a climate which is increasingly punitive towards those who have fallen from grace and committed crime. The call is for more imprisonment and tougher conditions. Prisoners are demonised and in the collective imagination seen as unlike the rest of us. The whole direction of penal policy is based upon retributive justice and all the knowledge we have gained about effective and successful ways of diverting offenders from crime is being abandoned.*

> *Fortunately, enlightened pockets of good practice still exist. They succeed against the odds to maintain education programmes and therapeutic work for prisoners with little encouragement and inadequate resources. Askham Grange is one of those places. The story told in this book (The Story of a House) is more than the story of a house: it is the story of punishment's failure and the success of rehabilitation. It is all about human redemption and the ability to change. This is a story to be told and told again.*

It is to be hoped that the closure of Askham Grange represents the emergence of a new direction of penal policy and not merely an opportunity to save money at women's expense. If the proposed community support which is to replace the prison, mirrors its best features then we shall be rid of an outdated institution. If not, there may be many women carried to and fro by the tide of media opinion who will wish they were back 'inside'.

Let us finally leave prisons with the brief report of a lecture given in November 2013 to the Yorkshire Philosophical Society by Andrew Ashworth, Professor of English Law, Fellow of All Souls College, Oxford and until 2010 Chair of the Sentencing Advisory Panel.

The prison population in England and Wales has doubled in the last twenty years. The average length of sentences is up over the same period and life sentences have risen from 8% of the total to 17%. Currently we have more 'lifers' than the rest of Western Europe put together. Crime has reduced but there is no evidence to support the idea of 'more prison less crime'. Germany, Sweden and Finland have the lowest prison rates and low crime. Mandatory minimum sentences force courts into imposing too heavy terms of imprisonment. Youth sentences are down, with courts using the full range of alternative measures; no crime wave has resulted.

These were just some of the arguments in favour of radical reform of sentencing guidelines in this country. This wide ranging talk analysed the meaning of imprisonment and the situation in various crime categories, female crime in particular. Some arguments were compelling but there was a notable absence of detailed answers. Press attitudes were seen as one bar to any move away from present practices; papers could be expected to characterise reduced use of prison as a 'criminal's charter'. Professor Ashworth suggested that 'it will take a courageous politician to take on the Daily Mail and make the right decisions.'[17]

Questions

Do you have any sympathy for Bridgeview's way of tackling the Liam Ventris problem?

If you had been headteacher of this school for children with emotional and behavioural difficulties, would you have taken the same actions?

If you were head of the prison service what three reforms would you introduce?

The Museum from the compartment boat 'jebus', with *Sobriety* on the left and *ROOM 58* centre.

Chapter 11 Notes

1 The company is now known as Akronym Partnership Limited and has played an important part in setting the ground rules for a partnership of waterways-related organisations in the East Riding and North Yorkshire.

2 Bridgeview was not a school under East Riding control.

3 Leading American mortgage brokers.

4 *Guardian,* 16.12.2013

5 *Telegraph,* 4.12.2013.

6 1945 report: In anticipation of the Sex Discrimination Act which came 30 years later, the Council would no doubt have welcomed the suggestion that in the excerpt below 'she' would be as good as 'he'.

7 Polly Courtney's excellent novel *Feral Youth* was written in the aftermath of the 2011 riots in London which were sparked by the police shooting of Mark Duggan.

8 Karen Beaumont's records showed that sixty three young people each received Assessment and Qualifications Alliance (AQA) unit awards: five gained Award Scheme Development and Accreditation Network (ASDAN) Level 2 Certificate of Personal Effectiveness (equivalent to grade B GCSE): ten gained Health & Safety in the Workplace: twelve gained Food Hygiene Level 2: twenty gained ASDAN short course awards: nine gained Barclays Bank money skills certificates and thirty seven gained Volunteering for Young People within East Riding (VYPER) awards at bronze, silver and gold level. In addition the group as a whole was joint national winner of Community Space Challenge, the sole national winner of the Keep Britain Tidy Awards and winner of the East Riding of Yorkshire Council Chairman's Award for the Environment.

9 See *Using Inland Waterways to Combat the Effects of Social Exclusion,* Inland Waterways Advisory Council, April 2009.

10 *Sobriety* Project Review of 2009.

11 For her first months at Styal, Daciana was accommodated in the Y spur of Waite wing.

12 National Offender Management Service, October 2013.

13 Son of Sir Tim Berners-Lee, pioneer founder of the World Wide Web.

14 Denise Howard, daughter of Len Howard, proprietor of White Rose Cruises (predecessor of YorkBoat) did employ Askham women on the company's boats but to my knowledge they never became skippers.

15 Page 4 of Introduction to *Spring to Release*: December 2003

16 Edited by Brian Lewis and Harry Crew: Yorkshire Arts Circus 1997. Harry Crew was the very popular governor of Askham at that time. Like John Clarke at Hatfield YOI he took a broad view of problems and had a calming effect on the institution.

17 Annual report for the year 2013 of the Yorkshire Philosophical Society (p.39).

Supplementary note

I finish this chapter by appending some startling press excerpts about relations between HM Inspectors of Prisons and Government which may illustrate Professor Ashworth's final point:

Since taking over from Dame Anne he (Mr Hardwick) has shone an unforgiving spotlight on the deepening crisis in jails, where smaller numbers of staff are holding a record inmate population.

It is no surprise, as Mr Hardwick recently told *The Independent,* that suicide levels are rising or, as he warned in his annual report, that a 'political and policy failure' had led to a 'rapid deterioration in safety' behind bars.

David Ramsbotham (A previous chief inspector) was visiting a jail in Cambridgeshire when an urgent fax from the Home Secretary arrived for him. It was a copy of a statement Jack Straw was about to deliver to MPs. The final paragraph contained the news that he would shortly be 'retiring' as Chief Inspector of Prisons. His feud with Mr Straw — they were barely on speaking terms by then — was the most spectacular falling-out between a chief inspector and a minister. But his experience was far from unique. Lord Ramsbotham's predecessor, Sir Stephen Tumim, did not have his contract renewed by Michael Howard. His successor, Anne Owers, served for nine years but her increasingly pointed reports made uncomfortable reading for her political masters.

Chapter 12

EMPIRE

Swinton Lock Adventure Centre

'When constabulary duty's to be done, a policeman's lot is not a happy one (a nappy one)…'
W. S. Gilbert: *Pirates of Penzance*

When South Yorkshire police were not arresting themselves for overloading their barge *Spider T* with 25 policemen on the river Don near Doncaster, they were running a waterways project in Rotherham, designed like the *Sobriety* Project, to deter young 'hooligans' from getting on the wrong side of the law. Sergeant Keith Bown was the volunteer organiser of a group of colleagues who rescued *Spider T* from her grave in the canal at Castleford in 1989 and set up Rotherham Community Barge Association. *Spider T* or *Spider* for short, was the same shape as *Sobriety*, a floating bathtub which would certainly not have aroused the envy of a Thames barge skipper. The vessel had been built in 1927 on the Lincolnshire side of the Humber for the Tomlinson family of Hull. To differentiate their *Spider* from other *Spiders*, they had put a T for Tomlinson in the name of this early product of Humberside.

By 1995 there were other 'constabulary duties to be done' and the police were finding it difficult to manage a project which, like *Sobriety* twenty years before, possessed a generous supply of growth hormone. The project was creating a lot of work. It was employing a skipper who had worked on commercial barges and belonged to a genus that was not the most easily managed in the natural world even if individual members of his species had a reasonable pedigree. Learning the ropes as well as bad habits from *Spider T*'s captain was a Mexborough lock-keeper's son who was apprentice to the trade and doing well. The principal youth officer for Rotherham, Geoff Eagle, had eased the situation by seconding one of his workers, John Turberville, to help with staff discipline and project development, but Keith Bown and his colleagues wanted to hand over responsibility to a more broadly based committee than either the local authority or the police could muster. The new committee found itself struggling; those with the time did not have the expertise and those with the expertise did not have the time — and both were needed not only to manage the staff but to look after safety, make arrangements with the groups wanting to use the barge and to have sufficient understanding of *SpiderT*'s purpose to raise funds for which there was widespread competition. The people holding the purse strings were senior officers of Rotherham Metropolitan Borough Council and they were not going to see money squandered on projects that could not fulfil their contractual obligations. The committee was not blind to the competition and asked for *Sobriety*'s help.

In winter 1996 I attended a meeting of the trustees of the Rotherham Community Barge Association and was asked directly if *Sobriety* would be willing to take over responsibility for *SpiderT*'s work in Rotherham. We agreed that without the direct support of the police, the organisation would be in danger of not being able to survive in the longer term. It had nevertheless become too much of a top-down initiative concerned with the technicalities of boating rather than with exploring new ideas that would put it in tune with the needs of the wider Rotherham community. In short, the committee had become more pre-occupied with the barge and its staff and less able to have an eye to the expectations of its users. In spite of a huge commitment on the part of the part of the police volunteers, it had not developed a capability to make forward plans or to capitalise on collaborative partnerships and networks. So when asked this question, I hesitated and said that even though in principle it might be possible, there would have to be agreement between both groups of trustees and their staff. Still in doubt I discussed the proposal with Izzy Kitt who had recently been appointed deputy director of *Sobriety*. She could only see advantage in having an interest in South Yorkshire. It would extend *Sobriety*'s capacity to influence youth service, education and social services policy in a deprived urban area. Moreover there were borough officers eager to help, who would support funding bids to continue the work begun by the police. *Sobriety*'s trustees took the view that expansion would benefit everyone as long as there were funds to support it. John Turberville and I did some research into what was available from Europe and found that the European Social Fund (ESF) under its Priority 4 Measure 3 was investing in 'capacity building'.[1] In plain language this meant that we could apply for funds to give *SpiderT* a new lease of life. The project would be called *Spider*'s Web (What else?) and standing on its own feet would take measures to improve the prospects of long term unemployed people. The bid, in *Sobriety*'s name was appraised by an independent panel and an award of £35,157 was made to cover the period January to December 1998. The brief was to build the capacity of Rotherham Community Barge Project so that it could itself develop pathways to benefit target groups in Rotherham and district. The longer term obligation was obvious: to direct our energies to considering what the project would have achieved by the end of the year. What did we want to achieve? What would make the *Spider's Web* training project distinctive? What would be its future at the end of ESF funding? Little by little, with the blessing of both groups of trustees and the local authority, *Sobriety* was acquiring responsibility for *Spider* and it would be *Sobriety* that had to answer these questions.

My own connection with Rotherham went back twenty years to City Challenge. During that month long course with its surprises and minor disasters described in Chapter 2, I got to know the Borough quite well. The excitement of working in the turmoil of an urban area with its characters and conflicts had left me with a good deal of affection for the place. The preparatory work with agencies and institutions that would find placements for the City Challenge students had been done by Ron Day and his colleagues in Rotherham Youth & Community Service based at Blenheim House, and at the municipal offices in Howard Street. The generation of officers in the late nineties were as welcoming as their City Challenge predecessors. They were Geoff Eagle already mentioned, Tammy Whitaker, in charge of *Young People Sharing Rotherham's Future*, and Simon Shaw who was local manager of round three of the government's Single Regeneration Budget (SRB). It is true that an Irish worker in a hostel for homeless men persisted in addressing me as 'Mr Goole' but otherwise *Sobriety* staff never felt like foreigners. I think there were two reasons: firstly, we followed the lead of local people and secondly the project was driven by the adventure of replicating *Sobriety* in a 'foreign land'.

Six months were spent spreading the word, helping crew to see how they fitted into the bigger picture and using *Sobriety* to embark from Rotherham on residentials and day trips. (Her usual berth was on the canal outside Rotherham courthouse). We also had to make a decision about the future of the barge, *Spider T*. Without improvements which at the time we could not afford, she would not pass our 'caravan' test. Her galley, lounge, showers and sleeping accommodation were well below the standard that visiting groups had come to expect and within a few months she had been sold for £500 to Mal Nicholson, a classic car enthusiast from Scunthorpe.[2]

On June 11th 1998, when the sun should have been shining brightly on Rotherham, it was raining hard. A desultory group of children from Dalton Junior School stood under the railway bridge that crosses the canal near the town centre and sang cheerful songs for the Mayor and Mayoress who were guests of honour at the launch of the *Spider's Web* project. *Sobriety* barge was in attendance, carrying young people from Goole as well as a few waterlogged sandwiches, all too reminiscent of *Audrey*'s commissioning nine years previously.

After the launch we began to search for suitable premises. Lynn Horsman, an itinerant probation officer and development worker who did the spadework in the early days of the project, reported in *Sobriety*'s Review of 1998 that:

> *This has proved to be a formidable task which so far, has taken more than a year. Ideally, we would like premises alongside the canal and we are still hopeful that this can be achieved. Over the months the search has involved members of the team spending hours walking, cycling along the towpaths and scouring the town centre. Perseverance has paid off to some extent. The proprietor of Philip Howard Books Ltd has allowed us to use some office space in the basement of his shop. This has helped us to keep our ears to the ground and to keep in touch with local gossip and events.*

But it would be nearly another year before we found the right building. The bookshop basement was a good start as office accommodation but useless for meetings and activities. The next stop was the upstairs room of SuperCigs in the town centre where the nearest waterway was a fountain in the middle of a roundabout. This was followed by a British Waterways shed agreeably situated on the side of the Sheffield canal but disagreeably close to the viaduct that carried the M1 over the waterway. Finally and much to our delight, British Waterways decided it no longer needed such an imposing presence on the canal at Swinton[3] and within a few months we had leased its premises near the junction of the Barnsley and South Yorkshire canals. The building was ideal; there was a workshop, kitchen, store, toilets, offices, project rooms, parking space and frontage onto the Navigation where boats could be berthed. To the south, next to Swinton lock, were the headquarters of E. V. Waddington, barge owners and carriers of cargo between Rotherham and Goole.[4] To the north was a large empty space bordering the canal, also belonging to BW, which in time would become a public park. On our own site to the west, were workshops, retained by BW for the moment, but which would eventually house small businesses specialising in the arts. An invasion by Goole staff and volunteers armed with paint brushes and hoes soon turned the building and its canalside garden into *Sobriety's* South Yorkshire protectorate. A plan was evolving; Swinton Lock Adventure Centre would become an independent charity incorporating the original aims and objectives of Rotherham Community Barge Association. By the end of 2004 it would have separated from its parent body and become an autonomous charity.

Sobriety might now have a landbase in the Borough but what would be its purpose? Who would use it? What were the problems for the local community that a waterways project could help solve? If we were to raise sufficient funds to guarantee the future, answers to these questions had to be forthcoming. So in preparation for an application to the National Lottery Charities Board (NLCB) we did our research and asked local people what they thought. Meanwhile when the area became eligible for Objective 1, a European structural fund reserved for less affluent parts of the EU, the Borough also had to look for answers to questions about the future of Swinton. Led by Angela Warburton, its area regeneration officer, residents and councillors attended meetings in the upstairs offices of our new HQ.

The evidence provided by the meetings gave us a fair idea of Rotherham's broader problems. With the demise of coal mining and the decline of the steel industry the area had lost the foundation of its prosperity. Small companies which supplied the two industries had folded and the resulting unemployment which in the 1980s was as high as 85% in some parts of the Borough, had led to the failure of small retail and service businesses. The statistics told part of the story. In 1999 the unemployment rate was twice the national average and the sixth highest in the UK: twenty nine percent of unemployed young people aged 16-24 did not have any qualifications and according to Rotherham Economic Bulletin published in February 1999, the number of young people aged 16-25 who were not going into employment or further education was increasing. The Racial Equality Council and the Black and Asian Community Forum said:

> *Structural unemployment will remain a major issue in Rotherham. There continues to be a lack of awareness of the abilities and potential of those from the Black and Asian community and those with disabilities.*

The Rotherham Multi Cultural Centre was quoted as saying that Pakistani women did not participate in the labour market because of lack of access to employment opportunities. From a more detached standpoint the Regional Development Plan (RDP) for Yorkshire & the Humber 1998-1999 argued that:

> *Difficulties in employability are compounded by other problems including low levels of attainment, and disaffection; individuals have difficulty in competing and many do not have the necessary skills, knowledge, experience and attitude.*

The solution proposed in the RDP was:

…growth in service sector employment which will require well motivated individuals
with transferable skills, good literacy and numeracy and competence in interpersonal
skills. Solutions will need to be based on outreach work, engaging individuals on their own
terms; activities will need to be timetabled to suit participants.

All this was food and drink to an organisation versed in the requirements of European contracts but it was not enough simply to be regurgitating reports which read like a politician's speech. We needed first hand evidence and accordingly turned to voluntary and statutory bodies working with distinct groups in the Borough. The list was comprehensive: Eastwood and Oakhill community support group working with black and Asian people: Rush House, a unit for single homeless people: Swinton Community Association: Barnardo's, providing for pupils excluded from mainstream schools: Mencap which helped people with learning disabilities to get into training and employment: the Asian Youthwork Project dealing with the problems faced by young Asian women: community support teams for people with mental health problems including dementia: the Asian childcare project for women and children: Rotherham Conservation Volunteers and the Archway Foundation befriending isolated older people who had mobility problems. A final cry from the heart came from an employment centre manager in the suburban village of Kilnhurst:

There is a need to relieve the distress of unemployment among older people, many of whom
possess traditional skills which are no longer required by employers.

Most influential was a report, *Swinton Shaping the Future*, commissioned jointly by the *Sobriety* Project and Swinton Youth Action. Funded by the Dearne Valley Community Forum and published in 2000 by Hayton Associates, the 81 page document was a survey of the attitudes and interests of young people aged 11-17 attending Swinton Comprehensive School. It came to the melancholy conclusion that:

Many of Rotherham's young people feel cut off from the labour and education markets
and locked into a society where crime is on the increase and optimism among the young
is decreasing. They feel they have little or no ownership in the design, implementation and
management of leisure and cultural activities.

On the strength of this research and other evidence it was agreed that the people to benefit from the project would be young people, single parents and children, 'men on the scrap heap' aged over 50 and permanently redundant, socially isolated old people with long term illness, and Asian women and their children. They would all be on low incomes and living in deprived wards in the Borough.

Once the funding was secured we had to find someone energetic and persuasive to run the new Swinton Lock Adventure Centre. *Sobriety*'s management committee appointed Helen Rhodes who was already part of the education team at the waterways museum. After VSO in a Ugandan village, she had taught students with additional learning needs at Bishop Burton College of Agriculture near Beverley. She had then come to *Sobriety* to be responsible for its towpath nature trail and at an administrative level to make sure that the Project's accreditation systems matched students' abilities and were reliable indicators for employers. A mark of her resilience was that, coming from a farm at the foot of the Yorkshire Wolds, she would get up at 3.00am to help with lambing. It was a successful appointment. She was quick witted, friendly and led from the front. The report she wrote in 2001 for the *Sobriety* trustees shows how in the words of the RDP, she was promoting 'growth in service sector employment by engaging people on their own terms' and giving them a start on the first few rungs of the employment ladder:

Two hundred and sixty five students have been involved in activities which have included first aid and basic food hygiene. A three month course in community boat management which if successfully completed, qualifies a student to operate a narrowboat on UK canals, has been very popular. There have been Open College Network accredited courses in aromatherapy, holistic therapy, and vocational courses in catering, pottery, leatherwork, clog making, waterside craft, digital imaging, black and white photography and watercolour painting. The centre has also developed in other ways during the year; the café is now up and running and has a good reputation for homemade lunches and buffets. We hope before Christmas to have installed a tiled mosaic designed by Nova Mills,[5] our arts worker, and made by students on the pottery course. Work on wheelchair accessible moorings has begun and will also be finished before Christmas. There have been three residentials. The first saw a group of young people cruising the inland waterways between Rotherham and Leeds. The second was more adventurous; a group of young people referred to the centre by Swinton Comprehensive School joined Audrey in Arbroath then sailed along the Firth of Forth to Leith. Many of them had not been out of Rotherham but I know they all gained a lot from the experience and are keen to repeat it. Then later in the year, nineteen regular attenders at the centre, from Brinsworth Comprehensive joined Audrey for a week on the Humber. The weather was perfect!

The summer holidays saw fun packed activity weeks with 154 young children enjoying dance, puppet making, photograms, digital imaging, drama, and desert island castaways.

At the end of her report she paid tribute to two people who were leaving:

Nova Mills leaves the centre at Christmas to take up her new life as an artist in Germany. We wish her all the luck in the world. She will be greatly missed by everyone at Swinton, staff and students alike.

Izzy Kitt also leaves the Project at Christmas to take up her new post as manager of the National Community Boats Association and I would like to thank her for her friendship and support over the last four years and on behalf of the team at Swinton Lock, for her enthusiasm and drive that has developed this centre from a partly used office block into a thriving waterways resource.

A year later Simon Shaw, local authority manager of SRB Round 3, a funding programme entirely devoted to *Young People Sharing Rotherham's Future*, was able to say:

Sobriety staff have provided excellent direction for this land based ship and are constantly attracting funding into the project. I work closely with officers of Yorkshire Forward, the regional development agency, the European Social Fund and Government Office for

Yorkshire and the Humber, all of whom have seen Swinton Lock at first hand to witness the impact it is having on regeneration targets. It is one of those projects that funders enjoy visiting because it gives good value for money and real activity — outputs which are sometimes in short supply elsewhere.

Complementing Simon's remarks and mentioned previously in Chapter 12 was the Verification & Audit Report by Government Office ESF audit manager, Cathy Cundall and her colleague Gillian Bray. In the introduction to the report the two auditors said without qualification that:

The Sobriety *Project had exemplar systems in place to administer the ESF projects. It was clear that the overall project management of the* Spider's Web *project and* Turn the Tide *was very good and that comprehensive records had been maintained throughout all stages. Above all, the two projects had made a very positive impact on the local communities they served.* Turn the Tide *and* Spider's Web *had achieved a considerable amount in terms of the training, guidance, support and bringing communities together in a relatively short period of time. This is a credit to the dedication of management, staff and volunteers that work for the* Sobriety *Project.*

Commenting on the financial records relating to the two projects, Cathy Cundall said:

Evidence was seen of the working papers and it was clear that very comprehensive financial systems had been introduced by project management to financially monitor the projects. The visiting team was able to follow the cost breakdown through to the financial records maintained for both the Spider's Web *and the* Turn the Tide *projects.*

And finally and most importantly, her assessment of beneficiary outcomes:

Above all, the Sobriety *Project has achieved commendable success with the individuals that are assisted by the support, training and counselling offered by the organisation. A number of people that come to them with dependency on drugs or drink, or who may have mental health problems, have secured employment or may have just gained more confidence to take an extra step forward.*

In 2004, *Sobriety*'s responsibilities in Rotherham were coming to an end. On Thursday 1st July the management committee of Swinton Lock Adventure Centre, by transfer of undertaking (TUPE), became the employer of four staff and accountable for the proper administration of the newly registered charity's funds. Following Helen Rhodes' departure there was a new person in charge, Ruth Midgley, who had been involved with Voluntary Action Rotherham. In contrast to the previous seven years however, the months before independence were fraught with disputes about income and possessions more characteristic of a divorce court. Celebration was replaced by argument. *Sobriety* retired as gracefully as possible but even now eleven years later, some of its staff remain *persona non grata*. Sad as this may be, the re-named Swinton Lock Activity Centre has survived the youth service cuts afflicting many local authorities since 2008. It is still in business, winning awards and holding to the principles and practice that led to its foundation.[6] I think *Sobriety* and Rotherham can be justly proud of what began with a derelict barge and ended with a youth and community centre in the forefront of using the waterways to fight social exclusion. At a personal level I can only offer a retrospective variation on Geoff Walton's verdict on *Eden* in Chapter 5:

> *If the people who sail in this 'land based ship' get half as much pleasure out of her as the pain we had getting her built, then she will be as happy a ship as she is beautiful.*

Waterstart: Thorne-Moorends

A *Sobriety* visitor climbing the few steps to the top of the Yorkshire Waterways Museum's stockade might have looked south to the low lying peatlands of Thorne Waste and remarked that in the middle distance, until they were blown up by demolition contractors in 2004, had stood the mothballed remains of Thorne-Moorends Colliery, interesting for an unusual design of pithead but equally noteworthy for being a symptom of the decline of the British coal industry. The town of Thorne had a history dating back to Roman times, whereas its daughter village of Moorends was built in the early twentieth century to house the legions of mineworkers arriving in the coal rich area of Doncaster. After producing coal for fifty years the mine became flooded and in 1956 was temporarily closed, leaving the village isolated and many of its inhabitants out of work. Plans to renovate the mine shafts came and went, but the re-construction of pit head gear in the 1980s gave hope that the colliery might soon be back in production. However, later proposals were overruled and the mine was finally abandoned in 2002, leaving the estates of Moorends to their destiny.

On the political front, Thorne, Moorends, and their next door village, Stainforth,[7] became such hard-core Labour enclaves within the Goole parliamentary constituency that in 1983 their committees de-selected Edmund Marshall MP on the grounds that his socialism was too moderate. Boundary changes after 1997 saw Thorne and Moorends leave the Goole constituency and move respectively into Don Valley & Doncaster North. There were two groups involved in community regeneration in the two constituencies, one local, the other national. The local initiative was headed by the Thorne-Moorends Regeneration Partnership, founded in 2003 and in all but name a council for voluntary service, which had access to European funding. The national body was the Coalfields Regeneration Trust (CRT),[8] brainchild of John (Viscount Lord) Prescott, which was attempting to put life back into an area where South Yorkshire police said 90% of young people had links with drug dealers. CRT Regeneration Manager, Andy Lock, suggested that *Sobriety* might repeat its Swinton success by developing a similar waterways project in Thorne and Moorends. In a Review article in 2003 he noted that the work of *Sobriety* was well known to the Trust and that:

> *The innovative and creative way in which it (Sobriety) worked with young people, vulnerable groups and the wider community had many selling points....there were several occasions when the Trust would contact Swinton Lock and ask to showcase the project to the great and the good in order to help raise the Trust's profile...*

Meanwhile the Thorne-Moorends regeneration team obtained the funds from Europe to match the CRT's subvention, and *Sobriety* could get to work once again to find premises and appoint staff.

As soon as the Trust announced in 2004 that it was making the Project a grant of £100,000 to build a new broad beam boat for use in tackling some of the area's educational and social problems, we went to local boatbuilders Louis and Joshua, at that time owned by the late Mike Lewis, and together designed *Waterstart*. It was to be 55 feet long and 10 feet wide, allowing it to navigate most of the northern waterways.

Courses and events associated with the project would only come to life if they were enjoyable and adventurous. *Waterstart*'s new manager, Marc Salter, indicated how the boat's design had to fit its purpose:

Below decks there will be a computer lab to encourage people of all ages to learn new skills in digital photography, video editing and web publishing. It will provide a futuristic learning environment for traditional boat handling courses. Looking ahead, it will allow us to generate a higher level of participation amongst community groups and students, as well as catering for further expansion. We have already experienced huge interest in the new boat and remain convinced that 'If we build it, they will come'.

There were no bunks in *Waterstart*; residential expeditions could take place on *Sobriety*. The vessel would accommodate people who had to use a wheelchair. It would be a training vessel for volunteer skippers and would have an emphasis on getting women into the labour market. The boat was commissioned in April 2005 by Councillor Richard Walker, Mayor of Thorne, and Peter McNestry, Vice Chair of the Coalfields Regeneration Trust. Peter brought along his friend, Ed Miliband, prospective parliamentary candidate for Doncaster North, a safe seat in a General Election but harder to manage in the cut and thrust of constituency meetings.

As at Swinton there was a problem finding suitable premises. The Thorne-Moorends regeneration team led by Dr Rama Isaiah, was housed in Thorne's old police station and very politely we had to turn down the opportunity to conduct our business from a redundant police cell. Much more cheerful were two retail units in Finkle Court in Thorne which became available to rent. They served as a base for staff and volunteers for the next six years.

Development took much the same path as at Swinton. Here is Marc Salter again, writing in the 2005 Review:

During the summer, eighty children from pupil referral units spent time on Waterstart *boat with laptops and digital cameras. In October we were invited by Thorne Town Council to be the boat of honour at the official opening of the new footbridge across the Thorne canal by HRH The Princess Royal. With the additional support of the Learning & Skills Council South Yorkshire, we are meeting the needs of skilled individuals displaced from coal mining, waterway transportation and other occupations, to find new vocational and recreational interests.*

Typical of *Waterstart*'s older volunteers and beneficiaries was Tony Hands, a self employed salesman in Doncaster with his own TV accessories business. Profits were in excess of £100k per annum but a catastrophic loss of memory resulted in bankruptcy and the loss of his wife and two teenage sons. Caught in a vicious circle of stress and loneliness he was referred by his doctors to a therapy group run by the Doncaster Primary Care Trust. It was through this group that he came into contact with *Waterstart* and trained to take charge of a small passenger carrying boat. He did not get his memory back but his cognitive skills returned, he found a council flat and was looking forward at some stage to getting a part time job with *Waterstart*. His observation was that the project 'brought him back from the abyss'. His doctors agreed.

For seven years from 2003 *Waterstart* provided training and adventure for many hundreds of people coming from deprived communities in the Doncaster area. Outstanding among these was Tina Morris who was voted Adult Learner of the Year 2004 by the National Institute of Adult Continuing Education.[9] With no qualifications or hope of employment she had been attracted by *Waterstart's* advertised opportunities for training. Like Tony Hands she worked her way through a series of courses leading to the Certificate in Community Boat Management[10] and finally became a fully qualified skipper who could take responsibility for passengers on the inland waterways. One of Tina's students was Carol Watkins who said:

For me these projects put back the human into humanity and give individuals a life transforming experience. Everyone is treated with dignity, compassion and empathy and has the opportunity to gain enough confidence to outgrow the labels which limit and thwart personal growth.

In spite of such accolades there was a problem — money. By August 31st 2010 *Waterstart's* current funding would terminate and there was nothing to take its place. Economic downturn was in its second year, cutbacks were widespread and only well established and well known projects could hope to survive. There was an irony in this. The problems that *Waterstart* had been intended to solve, arose from the isolation of the Thorne-Moorends community. Now *Waterstart* itself was isolated. The Swinton centre had been close to the hearts of the officers and members of Rotherham Council, but although *Waterstart* staff had worked hard to make friends with local politicians and service managers, there was no similar relationship with Doncaster council; the project had focused on the expectations of the Coalfields Regeneration Trust rather than on policies of the local authority. When viewed from a distance, *Waterstart* was not particularly distinctive; it was not manning the barricades or as members of the ruling party might have said, 'doing our work'. Moreover Doncaster Youth Service had operated the narrowboat *Adam's Ark* in the Yorkshire dales for many years and the fact that this was run entirely by volunteers may have increased its appeal to the council. An added difficulty was that Marc Salter had recently left the project to work for a community organisation in Goole. However, Swinton had survived Helen Rhodes' departure so there was no reason why the remaining staff at *Waterstart* could not keep things going, at least in the short term.

On 5th March 2010, in an attempt to create a future for the organisation, I presented a report to *Sobriety's* trustees and asked them to consider the possibility of making *Waterstart* independent so that it could be developed by local people in line with local priorities. (This had been the intention from the beginning but we had not quite got there). Staff were in favour of the proposal and eager to get to work. Neville Nichol, the boat manager, and Shirley Roberts[11] who ran the office had both been volunteers when the project began and had a big investment in its future.

Run by local volunteers, the project would be in a better position to raise funds, particularly at a time when grant making trusts had reservations about supporting 'umbrella' or 'infrastructure' bodies like councils for voluntary service, which is what *Sobriety* might have appeared to be.

I then set out a timetable for recruiting a management group which would write and publicise a business plan and prepare to register *Waterstart* as a charity. The new organisation would be launched in August 2010.

Writing in 2009, Shirley Roberts was definite about the level to which the project had found a place in the local community :

One of our young volunteers, Stewart Beaumont, had a presentation at the Waterstart *office. He was given a motor scooter from Kick-Start, a gift voucher from* Waterstart, *and best of all, a job offer in a car body workshop. He had been long term unemployed but through his Complete Crew Certificate training, his confidence was restored to the point of proposing marriage at the presentation to Samantha, a young lady he met on the boat while both were doing their training. Luckily she accepted. There wasn't a dry eye!*

The last three months have seen regular team meetings in the training room involving all staff and volunteers to discuss the future of the project and fundraising. We have made a strong relationship with our Primary Care Trust, our outputs for CRT and Neighbourhood Learning for Deprived Communities are progressing and new contacts have been made to achieve relevant targets. Volunteers have come from all walks of life and have acknowledged the new sense of purpose they have found. During the two years, six volunteers have found full time work. One said to me, "I've got my life back." Another said, "I have a passion about the project; it's not about money, it's about people and changing lives."

A note also came from the Intervention Manager of Hatfield Visual Arts College:

We both feel excited by the prospect of our students attending Waterstart *and we can send you plenty of them to work with. I look forward to working with you in the very near future.*

Waterstart was not a lame duck project. There was growing opinion that it *must* continue after August 31st 2010 and individuals were giving the impression that it would. My view was that the *Sobriety* Project had a duty to support them and, at an appropriate time, hand over a large measure of responsibility to a local group.

To this end, I had a meeting in April 2010 with the Director of Doncaster Council for Voluntary Service to discuss governance, and to get information about local charitable trusts and other sources of non statutory funding. I also told my own management committee that we needed to contact the voluntary and private agencies which had used *Waterstart* during the previous two years and arrange meetings. There was a possibility that the Primary Care Trust might consider a contract to begin by the end of May.

I had thought that on the strength of all this, we were in with a chance, but in the end it ran out of steam; Neville Nichol resigned and, after looking after the project for the remainder of

2010, Shirley also resigned. Neither of them were in the first flush of youth and we can only be grateful that they put so much time and effort into their work. The third member of staff, Alison Baker, having rescued herself from unemployment, moved to the waterways museum and for three years worked full time with people with additional learning needs. Her time as a Butlins redcoat stood her in good stead!

Surewaters Selby

I first met Neil Skinner in the Golden Lion in Leeds when he was working for the Industrial Common Ownership Movement (ICOM)[12] in the early nineties. The organisation was not Marxist but certainly more Fabian than Conservative. It believed that 'by combining personal, community, and business development, it could bring to many disadvantaged people the opportunity to go into business on the basis of economic democracy, equal opportunities, and social inclusion'. At that time, ICOM also had regional responsibility for introducing voluntary organisations to the aims and objectives of the European Social Fund (ESF) and for the selection of projects that the Fund might support.

The ICOM regime was rigorously fair. Organisations competed for funding. There were no deals behind the scenes. Independent panels representing the public, private and voluntary sectors, marked the answers to the questions on the application forms. Projects were then listed in rank order and depending on the *ecus*[13] available, a cut-off point was fixed and projects told either that they had been successful or that they were on the reserve list for underspends. It was all a bit like promotion and relegation in the football league. One of Neil's duties was to run seminars and provide individual tuition, but because ICOM had only limited space, the meetings were sometimes held in a room in the Golden Lion, not far from Leeds station. However when government policy changed and ESF project selection was in the hands of the Treasury and sub-contractors like Jobcentre Plus and A4E (Action for Employment), there was no longer a need for ICOM to act as an adviser.

A few years later in 2002 Neil re-appeared as assistant head of economic development in Selby District Council[14] with responsibility for the administration of LEADER+.[15] This was another European funding regime intended to benefit rural communities through local projects selected either by an independent board or by a council's economic development department. Project activity, which was generally monitored and audited by the local authority, might be related to any of a number of themes: tourism, heritage, healthy living, small business development or even regional co-operation, sometimes across national boundaries. Like Andy Lock from the Coalfields Regeneration Trust, Neil had been a witness to *Sobriety*'s work with long term unemployed people. At a meeting on *ROOM 58* at the museum he expressed the hope that the Project might use LEADER+ to extend opportunities to people living in disadvantaged parts of Selby district. Europe would provide one half of the budget and the other half, the match funding),[16] would come from Surestart, a government programme launched in 1999 which was aimed at tackling child poverty at a local level in a way that met local needs. Although Selby district consisted largely of 'leafy suburbs', there were central areas of the town and the outlying community of Brotherton that had high deprivation levels. It was in these two areas that Melanie Davis who headed up Surestart, and Neil who headed up LEADER+, thought *Sobriety* could help.

With additional backing from Jill Carswell, co-ordinator of Selby's Association for Voluntary Services, who promised help with publicity, the *Surewaters* project began quietly in 2003. Preparations were much the same as for Swinton Lock and *Waterstart* but unlike those two projects, *Surewaters* would limit its activity to the pleasures of boating, thus obviating the need to appoint staff to manage a land based centre. On September 1ˢᵗ 2002, I wrote to Neil Skinner about a possible lease of a boat:

> *I visited Selby Boat Centre on Saturday and met Simon Banks who is now running the business following the death of his father earlier in the year. He is a very personable young man who is obviously working hard to make a success of boat hire and other services in an area of England that is not exactly Kennet & Avon territory. I am very happy that we're going to be supporting him.*
>
> *The 50 foot narrowboat he has offered, is called* Pegasus *and is clean, tidy and well appointed. It can be moored at the boatyard where it will be safe, and there is plenty of room on his premises for minibus and car access. We haven't entered into any agreement, pending your consideration of our application.*

Melanie Davis and Neil approved the respective applications and two staff were appointed: Marcia Haigh as manager and Jess Fussey as skipper. Marcia had a background in social work in Barnsley and Jess was a plasterer by trade who had a boat of his own moored in Castleford and was familiar with local waterways.

The pattern of activities based initially on *Pegasus*, was comprehensive. Marcia said that the most rewarding aspect of the project was the variety of people she and Jess were working with: lone parents and their families: Surestart families who wanted to get the best for their young children: people with additional learning needs or mental health issues, often both: anyone unemployed or under-employed: people whose lives were limited by caring, and isolated low income families in villages.

What I really enjoyed hearing so soon after Marcia's appointment was an account of *Surewaters'* three day residential training course for 14 to 16 year olds on the Aire & Calder. It rained as usual on the Yorkshire canals but this had not deterred the young people or their social workers. She described them as a credit to everyone and said, *"They all achieved their Complete Crew Certificate and without exception have all been back to see us in the school holidays."*

Marcia did not stay long with the project. She was a gifted manager who had her eye on posts of greater responsibility. She was popular in Selby and, together with Jess Fussey, had put *Surewaters* on the map. By coincidence she was followed by another Haigh — David Haigh, not related to her. The other change was the boat. Hull City Council had recently presented the *Sobriety* Project with two vessels that were redundant to requirements. One was a 7-foot-wide narrowboat called *Opportunity*. The other was broader in the beam and had been named *City of Hull*. Both had been built at what is now the City Council's construction centre on Studley Street in Hull. The first time I saw *Opportunity* it was about 150 feet in length, having been a project for welding apprentices whose tutors had clearly been less concerned about design than the exercise of welding. The vessel had an engine but no interior accommodation until *Sobriety* fitted it out for use by *Waterways Work for Women*. *City of Hull* on the other hand, had a comfortable and spacious interior ideal for families and disabled people, and it was this vessel that went to Selby.

In 2005 David Haigh recorded 102 day trips on the Selby Canal which is famous for its wildlife and regarded by many as one of the prettiest canals in the north of England. Built by William Jessop and opened in 1778 the canal is 6 miles long and has two locks, one at the southern end into the river Aire at Haddlesey and the other giving access to the river Ouse in Selby. As Goldilocks said, it was 'just right' for young families. Parents with babies and toddlers were collected by boat from a quay near the town centre and for most of the trip, sat in the bows looking out for ducks. For some families it was their first visit to a canal and a chance of a few hours of peace and quiet. As well as parents and children invited by Surestart there were people coming from hostel accommodation who enjoyed steering or looking at wildlife, or just talking or reading. One man said that the gentle movement of the boat helped him to overcome his habitual insomnia and get some sleep. There were also about 25 volunteers who learned to maintain *City of Hull* and prepare it for a trip. They learned the theory and practice of ropework, mooring and 'letting go', the rules of the road, how to steer and manoeuvre a narrowboat, what to do in emergencies, and above all, how to manage their passengers. To take charge of a trip, volunteers had to have the Certificate of Community Boat Management and possess some knowledge of marine diesel engines. *Surewaters* skipper, Jess Fussey, was very popular and had a kindly sense of humour which went down well with his passengers, *"We loved the feeling of warmth on the trip"*, said Vicky, *"Fun is important in everyone's life but especially for someone with a mental health problem."* Commendation also came from Selby's Labour MP, John Grogan[17] who said, *"This is a very innovative project and of particular relevance to Selby whose existence and heritage are due to its place on the river."* In February 2008, happy to keep a political balance, staff entertained Shadow Cabinet Minister, Francis Maude, to lunch. He was visiting with Nigel Adams, Conservative candidate for Selby. As Jess said of the occasion, *"Surewaters was in the spotlight but not on the radio. The interviewer turned up three hours late."*

Surewaters was never a campaigning enterprise; it was more a modest community project which stuck to helping Surestart and LEADER+ meet their community objectives. It was happily limited to two staff, a boat and basic office accommodation in a centre for small businesses not far from the canal. There had never been an intention for it to become independent of *Sobriety* and it would last as long as its funding. This was a painful consideration for staff who were keen to keep the project going. Support from LEADER+ as part of a pan Europe programme for rural development was always going to be limited to three or four years but the funding from Surestart looked at one stage as if it might continue. However when Government policy changed from supporting activity programmes to running children's centres, *Surewater's* future looked less secure.[18] Melanie Davis, by now consultant children's centre manager for Selby, explained it all in an article[19] entitled 'Family Fun and Learning with *Surewaters*':

For the past three and a half years, Surestart Selby District has supported and worked with the Sobriety *Project. With LEADER+, it has provided funding for the* Surewaters *canal boat. Having this resource as part of our programme has enabled staff and families to learn about our local canal and canal boats, as well as giving our parents and carers the opportunity to raise their own self-confidence and spend quality time together.*

As our local programme funding is reduced over the next few years and is focused more towards Children's Centre work, then our opportunities to provide funding may cease. But I wish and hope that in some way we can mainstream this wonderful service and spread its good work to more and more people in Selby. I intend to stay on the Sobriety *Trustee Board and work to this end.*

In January 2007, QA Research published a 50 page report: *Surestart Selby District–Evaluation of Surewaters–Final Report*. There were some brave words at the end of its executive summary:

Parents have benefited from being able to access training and there are clear examples of Surewaters *equipping individuals with the renewed self confidence to seek employment.* Surewaters *has also given opportunities for parents to socialise and meet new people, thereby reducing the isolation by many parents in rural areas. The relationship between delivery partners has been positive...*

The termination of the Surestart and LEADER+ contracts did not deter Jess from trying to make ends meet. He advertised the project to groups who would not previously have been eligible, as well as to existing customers, and for a time not without success. But it was not enough to cover running costs and in 2010, after seven years, *Surewaters* had to close. *City of Hull* was sold in January 2011 and Jess himself was made redundant in 2013. Melanie Davis is now a member of Selby District Council and Neil Skinner is its Policy and Performance Manager. LEADER nationally is very much alive and a new programme having close ties with the European Regional Development Fund [20] and overseen by Local Enterprise Partnerships, began in 2015.

Like *Waterstart*, *Surewaters* was a victim of the 2008 downturn and subsequent cuts, but that is not the whole story. Since 1979 when *Sobriety* signed an agreement with Humberside Social Services to provide residential expeditions for children in trouble, it has been a contract-making charity and from this policy have come many benefits, not least a predictable income. (Whether the income was enough to cover expenditure is for the moment beside the point). However, tempering the excitement created by signing a contract, is the knowledge that when the arrangement ends there may not be funds available from other source to continue the work. Some community boat projects are not willing to take this risk and rely entirely on volunteers rather than paid staff. They are able to pay their way without recourse to any funding other than what they raise from local goodwill and occasional open ended grants from councils and trusts. This has not been *Sobriety's* way. Trustees have taken the view that contracts utilising the Project's resources, keep it in the eye of regional and national developments. Survival depends on two factors. The first is mutual attraction between contractor and project and the second is the comprehensive and successful achievement of outputs and outcomes. I will comment further on this in the next chapter. It may be, however, that had *Surewaters* been bought and operated by Surestart and Selby District Council from the beginning, it would have had a better chance of survival. The contrary view is that the unfamiliar curriculum of community boating is perceived by governments and local authorities as a luxury that can be discarded in hard times.

Trade Routes Hull

A pathway to employment project for hard-to-reach adults sponsored by the European Social Fund (ESF) and the European Regional Development Fund (ERDF): January 2002– December 2005

"Unless you want to work in a shop, there's nowt. I've just left school and I can't find anything. My GCSE's weren't bad either" — the answer to a question about job prospects, from Laura who lived in the Hull suburb of Bilton. More cynical was Mark from Preston Road who when asked about obstacles to finding work, said, *"People just can't be arsed. I can get more money living on social with housing and stuff. There's no incentive".* Denise, a resident of Hessle Road, was positive, *"The school that I work at have actually paid for me to go and learn more because I got off my bum. I know there is places 'cos me friend went on one at an adult education place and it didn't cost owt to learn computers".*

These comments were recorded during a street survey carried out by *Sobriety* in August 2001 as part of an evidence gathering exercise for applications to the ESF and ERDF. The people interviewed were from Hull's PACT areas,[21] neighbourhoods mainly in the suburbs where the problem of unemployment was so acute it could be tackled only with help from Europe. Each area had its own PACT board, elected by residents, that approved or rejected applications for the funds allocated to it by Hull City Council. There were eight boards in total and each had to be visited and persuaded that *Sobriety*'s activities would improve the social and economic prospects of its residents. In spite of having a good reputation in the city, the Project was still an outsider. Not without justification, some boards were suspicious that their funds would be spent maintaining the organisation's normal running costs rather than directly on measures to regenerate their area. Putting *Sobriety*'s case to residents was not easy, but we had a secret weapon in a woman called Sally Brotherton who, as the Project's student development worker, had been running a project for 16 to 19 year olds. It was called *AdventureSail4All* and was based in a disused sandwich shop close to Hull marina and *Audrey*. Sally was familiar with the challenges facing the PACT areas and with a little encouragement from *Sobriety*'s education officer, Sue Kiel, managed to persuade six out of the eight committees to go along with our plans. Things were not always how they seemed. A member of the East Hull group who appeared to have been bored by the presentation, began to speak. We were ready for the worst when he said none too enthusiastically *"I've known about this Sobriety for some time"*, and then with a smile, *"My daughter's been on it and…"*; we held our breath — *"it's bloody brilliant!"*

The application process did not end with public relations. Completing the 94 pages of an application form and business plan constituted hard labour for three months. But it was worth it. The secretary to the ESF/ERDF decision panel rang me to say that we had scored 98% on the 'question papers' and that our answers were the best he had ever marked. We were to be given £577,032 to pay for a 300 hour pathway to employment programme for each of 150 unemployed people living on the PACT estates.[22] It would be called *Trade Routes*.

The first thing we did was appoint staff and move out of the sandwich shop where a small mezzanine gallery had served as an office. The new HQ was to be two floors in Riverside House, a building next to the former ticket office for the Humber ferries, recently vacated by United Towing and, during the nineteen eighties and nineties, Alan Marshall's centre of operations. When Sally decided that her future lay in London, we invited Lynn Horsman to take responsibility for *Trade Routes*. Four years previously Lynn had done the preparatory work in Rotherham which led to the establishment of Swinton Lock and had worked in Thorne-Moorends to prepare the way for *Waterstart*. We also appointed a driver for the minibus and an administrative assistant for the office.

The client group was diverse. Individuals came from the city's big council estates, mainly through referrals from homeless and rootless projects, probation, prison, bail hostels, MIND and other mental health agencies. They often had drug or alcohol problems and in a few cases were ex-offenders. The majority needed a great deal of encouragement and support to take part in activities. They were often disenchanted with society and had a lifestyle different from 'normal'. They would roam the streets during the day and sleep in the same hostel only if they went back in time to obtain a bed. Otherwise they would be sleeping rough. Others would get thrown out of their hostel for breaking the rules. Several had quite serious medical conditions such as epilepsy, depression or other health problems which occasionally led to admission to hospital. Some of the East Hull beneficiaries were in Hull prison and one of these completed the 300 hour course in full. Thirty other offenders living in PACT areas were referred through MIND and probation.

The minibus was a great help. It enabled a significant minority to finish the course and obtain useful qualifications; others did not manage to keep up attendance and in spite of good intentions, were overwhelmed by personal circumstances. Lynn and her small team did try and keep track of students after the programme but many were itinerant and moved on without leaving any information about where they were going. All of them needed friends and a lot of staff time was spent in listening and offering practical help. The progress of four people who took part in all the activities and found jobs, makes the point.

Chris was on probation for a minor sexual offence. He was living at the Homeless & Rootless Project on the east side of the River Hull not far from the tidal barrage. On the boats he shone, gaining his Certificate of Community Boat Management (CCBM) and VHF radio certificate. He became a volunteer and helped to organise open days. Towards the end of *Trade Routes* he found himself a flat and began training to drive heavy goods vehicles. Another beneficiary was Mel who was long term unemployed. After a few months he gained a Certificate of Community Boat Management, became a volunteer and began to train as an adult education tutor. Lindsey, referred by MIND, was a single parent with a child of school age. She began with a course in Yoga, progressed to gaining a Complete Crew Certificate and then joined *Women with Wings*, a course exclusively for women, run by Hull Women's Centre on the Bransholme estate.

Steve also had been without work for several months. He completed the 10 week course, obtained all his boat qualifications and then emigrated to New Zealand to study.

The activity programme was designed to strengthen confidence but also to lead to qualifications that would interest employers even if they were not directly relevant to the job for which a student was applying. Taster sessions provided information. Arranged for the same purpose were open days, one of which was attended by more than 200 people and included a 'superstition' workshop run by local author, Alec Gill. Other workshops at the same event taught ropework, roses and castles painting and music making. BBC Radio Humberside and the *Hull Daily Mail* helped to spread the word and occasional family fun days were based on a pirate theme. These special events publicised the project and attracted agencies and potential beneficiaries.

Students could do courses in tai chi, yoga, photography, wildlife conservation, Indian head massage, VHF radio, navigation and roses and castles painting, but the most popular course was learning how to handle *City of Hull* which was now based on the River Hull at Tickton near Beverley. Students who got the hang of things, went on to help other students by assisting the tutor and sharing experiences. Courses not externally accredited were supported by in-house certificates which introduced what for many was an unfamiliar sense of achievement. Beneficiaries very much enjoyed the day sails on *Audrey* and *Sobriety*. From these, students progressed to extended residentials on *Audrey*, sailing down the east coast and working as a team to take responsibility for running the boat. They planned the menus, bought the food, took part in planning meetings, did the catering and took their turn on the night watch.

Inevitably there were problems which affected the outcomes of the project. The first was the instability of some of the voluntary agencies referring hard-to-reach clients. They suffered from lack of funding and as a result, from continuous staff changes. They could close at a moment's notice. There were also problems with some of the hostels which would book a time and place for a meeting and then not turn up. Internal to *Sobriety* was the disappointment that *Trade Routes* and *Audrey* did not reach the point where they could share the same premises and collaborate. However, in spite of difficulties, a minority of students developed skills and interests directly as a result of the project and were propelled out of 'skid row' into worthwhile occupation. The statistics[23] did not tell the whole story but they were an honest indication of the project's efforts to solve some of the most intractable problems of inner Hull.

With positive outcomes for 56 students I do not know whether *Trade Routes* was good value or not. Government would probably say it was not. Some would say that more sophisticated techniques of measurement might perhaps have painted a different picture; but they might also have been misleading. Some charities would not have risked undertaking what they would regard as a lost cause, and when they read between the lines of the application, would have considered *Sobriety's* enterprise to be foolhardy. Whether or not the project was sufficiently successful to become a curriculum for similar schemes depends on the old question about the nature and purpose of measurement. If landing a job is the sole measure of success in a payment by results contract, it also raises the question of who *will* work with the sort of people recruited into *Trade*

Routes. There were so many personal building blocks to be put in place before *Trade Routes* beneficiaries became ready for employment.

For me the matter is summed up by Chris Collins, a beneficiary of the scheme, who said, *"When I came on the course I had no home, no job, no friends, no hope. The course has given me self respect. I'd tell anyone to do it because of what it's done for me."* It would be interesting to know how many of the 94 'untraceables' would have agreed with him.

Isara: York

The Celtic name for the River Ure which after joining with the River Swale at Little Ouseburn becomes the River Ouse flowing through the City of York.

When Paul Cooper came back from two years self imposed exile in Lancashire[24] following the sale of *Audrey* in 2004, he was asked by two women living in York, Susie Gridley and Kathryn Smith, if *Sobriety* would help them set up a community boat project in the city. Kathryn had learned boat handling with Jess Fussey in Selby: Susie came from a family that was fascinated by the inland waterways. Paul and I had always found it remarkable that York had not been at the forefront of community boat development in the north of England. It was true that the York Association for the Care and Re-settlement of Offenders had set up a project in the 1980s based on a redundant crane barge *Reklaw*, (the name of its owner spelt backwards) but after a year of squabbles between trustees and their fundraiser, the project had fizzled out. Some later attempts to make the river Ouse attractive to community groups were limited to ideas and never acquired any practical substance. It was a pity because there was no shortage of good will on the river, especially among pleasure boat operators like Denise Howard, the proprietor of *YorkBoat*, who provided work placements for the women in prison at Askham. The city council's tourism

York: The *Isara* Team

department welcomed *Sobriety* and *ROOM 58* to its River Festival, and the conservation authority, British Waterways, already had an investment in community boats through its contract with the National Community Boats Association. Paul and I shared the view of the two women that a boat project for York was long overdue and we agreed to help. Unlike *Sobriety's* other outposts of empire, York's project soon to be named *Isara*, would stand on its own feet from the beginning. *Sobriety* would help with advice, attend meetings and lend its boats when requested but would not take responsibility for operations or finance. The founding members would have their own independent project. There were five, all women under 30, a feature which made *Isara* unique in the UK and distinguishable from the normal run of boating groups, community or otherwise, whose largely male all white membership has an average age of somewhere between fifty five and ninety. In addition to Susan Gridley and Kathryn Smith, there was Vanessa Langford who worked for the city council in its community arts department, Rosie Whitworth from the mental health sector who specialised in community re-integration, and Stephanie Prentis who had experience of working with long term unemployed people and had written funding applications. It was, one might say, a 'dream team' which gave considerable cheer to *Sobriety's* director whose battle to establish *Waterways Work for Women* had made debate about gay marriage look pale by comparison.

A series of open days in summer 2009 based on *Sobriety's* boats introduced *Isara* to York. Concluding her press release Kathryn Smith said:

> Isara, *which draws members from the local council and children's services, hopes that the interest sparked by this summer's visits will show the need and desire for such a project in the city.* Isara *believes that the waterways are a resource for everyone to enjoy, not just the tourists and the wealthy. In the 1950s, walkers on Queen's Staithe in York looked across at the premises of T. F. Woods & Co. and saw painted on the front in bold white letters the exhortation to the people of York to 'Use the Ouse'. Nearly 60 years later* Isara *is going to make that happen.*

The committee was now matching its development plans with York City Council's *Without Walls — Inclusive City* which highlighted the need for voluntary organisations to work with excluded and vulnerable groups. The report drew attention to the Joseph Rowntree Foundation's *A Study of Town Life* (1999) which showed that 20% of the York's population was in poverty and 17%, according to the 2001 census, was disabled.

The summer activities in 2009 went down well and the responses to questionnaires gave a guide to the verdict on *Isara*. It was certainly an attraction for young people at risk of exclusion from school; they crewed a boat and were happy to obey instructions, something they had lost the habit of doing in the classroom.

Isara also provided a venue for the Youth Offending Team to run workshops for families in crisis. Spending two days on a boat compelled family members to work together and face their problems. A dad's group had discussed parenting problems. Alzheimer's patients found the boat was a calming influence which brought them close to nature. Their carers made a video and used it to encourage conversation about the trip and patients' past associations with the river. A member of a group with severe mental health problems said, *"While on the boat I felt safe all the time."* Vanessa Langford had used some of her community arts budget for a local artist to work with children's groups and a parent in a speech and language session reported, *"My daughter had such a good time she told Grandma about it and talked about it for three days afterwards."*

The committee was doing everything right. It registered *Isara* as a charity which would 'use the inland waterways to combat the effects of social exclusion through the provision of organised cruises, courses and other activities relating to canals and rivers for the benefit of persons of all ages resident in the City of York and North Yorkshire who are disadvantaged by reason of income or other social or economic disadvantage such as illness disability or longer term unemployment'. In 2009 it produced a business plan for 2010-2011. The eight page document gave details of the strategy for acquiring a boat, appointing a co-ordinator, fund raising and longer term development.

Then the women's personal circumstances changed and one by one they slipped away, leaving only Kathryn Smith who was *Isara*'s chair, to continue the work, an impossible task for one person. Paul and I became pre-occupied with *Sobriety*'s own problems and it was not long before meetings were being postponed or cancelled.

Where did it go wrong? For three years there was excitement in the York air and many alliances and promises were made, but the working group was too small and too restricted. So, too, was each year's activity. Limited to the summer months the project had no momentum during the remainder of the year. It went into hibernation and in the end there was no one to wake it from sleep. However *Isara* is still alive as a legally constituted charity with bank account, business plan and, above all, friends for whom time on the boats was memorable. The project awaits another group of enthusiasts to bring it back to life.

Questions

Here were five community boat projects. Did they take into account local conditions and culture when they were being set up?

Did each project succeed in its own terms?

Could anything else have been done to extend their lives?

What distinguishes these projects from *Sobriety*, in terms of long term sustainability?

Chapter 12 Notes

1   Through the nineteen nineties and the first years of the millennium, South Yorkshire was the recipient of European financial support reserved for regions with more than average economic problems. After passing through the Treasury and the regional development agencies to authorised distributors, these funds could be allocated to local projects that had made a good case for assistance. The money in the gift of the Coalfields Regeneration Trust for example, was dedicated to the repair of communities in the aftermath of the miners' strike against pit closures, which had brought violence and hatred to so many towns and villages.

2   During the last fifteen years Mr Nicholson has restored *Spider T*'s sailing rig and transformed her interior. Each summer she leaves the Humber to sail the English and Scottish coasts between Spurn Point and the Moray Firth and makes the occasional trip to the Netherlands.

3   Swinton is a Rotherham suburb on the border with Doncaster, not to be confused with the more famous suburb of the same name in Manchester.

4   In the nineteen seventies the redoubtable Victor Waddington had pressed BW to make improvements to the canal that would allow crew to operate locks and bigger boats to pass through them. His sons, Tony and Steve, have been generous supporters of the *Sobriety* Project for many years.

5   Nova Mills was one of 230,000 people who lost their life in the tsunami which overwhelmed Bali in December 26th 2004.

6   See: www.swintonlock.org.uk

7   It used to be said that a teacher who could survive the classrooms of Stainforth, could teach in any school in the UK.

8   Coalfields Regeneration Trust (CRT); not to be confused with the new Canal and River Trust originally abbreviated to C&RT but now plain CRT. However, to avoid confusion, the abbreviation C&RT is used in this book.

9   Adult Learners' Week is the UK's largest festival of learning. Its overall purpose is to raise demand for learning and skills. It highlights the benefits of learning, for work, for enjoyment, and for personal development. The initiative continues to be the largest drive for learning of its kind - celebrated in over 55 countries across the world. It was founded and co-ordinated by the National Institute for Adult Continuing Education.

10 The Certificate of Community Boat Management (CCBM) was developed by the National Community Boats Association and approved by the Maritime and Coastguard Agency. It is a recommended training course in the MCA's Code of Practice for Small Passenger Boats.

11 Neville and Shirley, both of them generous and enthusiastic employees of the *Sobriety* Project, died in 2014. The Project remembers them with affection.

12 Industrial Common Ownership Movement : see Wikipedia for general comments.

13 *ecu* : the European Currency Unit, predecessor to the euro but never in circulation - rather like the Bitcoin - except that it was used only by governments and their appointed agents.

14 In 2015 Neil is Head of Corporate Policy and Performance at Selby District Council

15 LEADER: 'Liasons Entre Actions de Développement de l'Économie Rurale' in Europe.

16 Match funding: Although not always quite working out in practice, financial support from Europe is on the basis of intervention; that is to say that a project will have already obtained a percentage of the total required from other sources and Europe makes up the difference. The intervention rate, as it is known, is set nationally at 50% for LEADER, but may vary locally as a result of horse trading between projects.

17 In the light of constituency changes in 2010, John Grogan said he would not be contesting the seat in the 2015 general election. He is now the Labour candidate for Keighley and Ilkley.

18 The report *Every Child Matters*, proposed a switch from Surestart local programmes to Surestart Children's Centres, which would be controlled by local authorities and would be provided not just in the most disadvantaged areas. More recently, cuts in the Government's funding to local authorities in England have led to fears that up to 250 Surestart centres would close. When he was Secretary of State for Children, Schools and

Families, Michael Gove admitted that funding for Surestart has not been protected. A number of local councils announced cuts to their Surestart budgets, and ministers said they wanted to refocus the scheme to help the most disadvantaged families. There is now a proposal to extend Ofsted inspection to two year olds. This will no doubt solve all the problems! When we reflect on all this, we ought perhaps to think back to Ken Baker's removal of Home Management and Childcare from the school curriculum.

19 *Sobriety*'s Review of 2007.

20 The European Regional Development Fund (ERDF), often known as Objective 2 (ESF is Objective 3), funds capital infrastructure for training and business development.

21 The eight Hull PACT areas were Riverside, Bransholme, East Hull, Preston Road, Sutton and Bilton, West Hull, Wyke, and North West Hull. The word 'PACT' was not an acronym but represented an agreement between residents of specific geographical areas and the City Council.

22 About £12 per beneficiary hour to cover staffing, rent of premises, small capital items and running costs.

23 *Trade Routes* numerical outcomes:

Total beneficiaries:	**150**		
Male:	116	Into work:	15
Female:	34	Into education:	12
In-house qualifications:	9	Seeking work:	8
Open College Network:	20	Remaining unemployed:	18
VHF radio certificate:	7	Volunteering:	3
CCBM:	5	Subsequently untraceable:	94

24 Paul's exile led to him managing the waterway and marine activities of Care Afloat, a private business based in Skelmersdale in Lancashire which was responsible for the education and personal development of twenty or thirty severely damaged and disturbed children. The organisation provided residential care for children from all parts of the UK and had as its adventure resources two narrowboats and a sea going yacht. The ratio of staff to children was very high, sometimes as many as seven staff to one child. Paul's job was to link the organisation's land based curriculum with the opportunities for training and development available on the boats. The *per capita* fees chargeable to local authorities could reach £200,000 per year (2003 figures).

The other Brian Masterman

Sykehouse Lock on the New Junction Canal, 1996

The last steam-powered compartment tug *Waterloo* abandonned on the Medway, 2014

Chapter 13

WHAT DID SOBRIETY EVER DO FOR EUROPE?

Some Explanations

Any impression that *Sobriety*'s curriculum was good value must be qualified by the observation that only staff with a rather specialised personality disorder can find pleasure year after year in a way of life that embraces insolvency as a daily possibility.

Lying awake in the early hours, the fund raiser confronts the ghosts of creditors often appearing as tax inspectors and bank managers accompanied by fretful accountants and bailiffs. And then on a day when the nightmare will turn into reality, the phone rings and this martyr to cashflow learns that her organisation has been successful with a Lottery application. Respite though is short lived. In a few months the ghosts will return.

Most voluntary organisations and charities do not depend on staff adrenalin for survival. They have income from sales and donations and their trustees purr with satisfaction at board meetings. That *Sobriety* was an exception to this tradition was brought home to me at a fund raising conference organised by York Council for Voluntary Service. The speaker asked people in the two hundred strong audience if they had a mortgage or other personal debts. Most hands went up; mine stayed down. We were then asked if our respective organisations had a substantial debt or overdraft. All hands stayed down; mine went up!

The purpose of this chapter however is not to complain about penury but to consider one particular source of income that has enabled *Sobriety*'s staff and trustees to achieve their purpose and even be inspired by the challenge of having to make ends meet. They have held to the belief that if the Project's activities were up to date and relevant to the needs of the community, then the money would follow. So far they have been right. By 2014, forty one years after its foundation, *Sobriety* had raised £11.5 million to sustain its work. Donations from small charitable trusts and what is loosely termed 'turnstile' income [1] were important sources of revenue, but as a charity serving the Yorkshire and Humber region, [2] the Project was also well placed to make contracts with local authorities and Europe as well as bidding to the Lottery and large charitable trusts that were prepared to support less popular causes.

The value of these contracts is evident from the projects described in previous chapters but rather than repeating material to be found in any manual of fund raising, I will comment on some of the more intriguing pitfalls and complications associated with them. Europe is always a good whipping boy in our island debates, but not until 2007, the year of the notorious downturn in global finance was it accused of links to witchcraft. *No broomsticks — it's the 21ˢᵗ century* was a *Guardian* news item during that year:

> *Romania's witches have branched out since the country joined the European Union in January, offering spells which increase one's chances of obtaining EU grant money. Florica, the witch from Pitesti, says, "It's a new type of spell that we had to work out, of course". Her preferred method is to splash a success-causing potion directly on to application papers, at a cost of about £40. Witchcraft, she insists, must move with the times. "You cannot pretend you are a real witch if you cannot help a businessman get the European Union funding he wants."*[3]

Oh that it were so easy! Not even the EU recognises witchcraft or wizardry as an occupation eligible for support from its Regional Development Fund.

The years 1996 to 2005 saw *Sobriety* receive £1.5 million in contract income from Europe, a total that does not include the contributions to European sponsored projects from other sources. If this 'match' funding at 40%[4] is included, the total is obviously greater. Between July 2000 and July 2002 for example, *Waterways Work for Women* attracted £165,000 directly from the European Social Fund (ESF) but *Sobriety* had to raise £66,000 to complement this, making the total cost of the scheme about £230,000. Organisations providing match funding were often public bodies or charitable trusts, or in years of plenty, *Sobriety* itself. On the few occasions when the Project did produce its own match funding, it had to furnish the accountable body[5] with an audited certificate stating that the allocated funds were in place and not earmarked for other purposes. In other words one could not spend the same money twice. The match funds also had to be 'clean', untainted by association with any other European fund however remote, otherwise Europe would be match funding itself.

And here we come to a problem. When allocated to a project like *Waterways Work for Women* the match funding became subject to ESF rules even though it originated elsewhere. Difficulty arose when the 'partner' had to claim additional outputs and outcomes in return for its money. Failure by an organisation to recognise that there were two sets of requirements could result at best in it having to repay the funds and at worst being guilty of fraud.

Was Europe worth all the trouble? Yes. The range of *Sobriety* initiatives sponsored by Europe has been impressive. Most applications have been for resources to remove barriers to employment, or for community capacity building, or to give unemployed people the personal skills to become active in the labour market and apply successfully for jobs. All projects used the waterways as a resource to achieve the prescribed outcomes. The Social Fund recognised that for many individuals this could be a long process and might require the organisation providing the training, itself to be trained and guided. The community barge charity in Rotherham was one such organisation and we may recall that *Spider's Web* had the remit to build the capacity of Rotherham Community Barge Project so that it could develop pathways to benefit sub target groups in Rotherham and District.[6] The work with *Spider T* was a stage removed from the people who would ultimately benefit, but it was they who had to be borne in mind as the project progressed. ESF was not there to prop up ailing waterway projects; it was there to get people into work and if unemployed people were attracted by an opportunity to do their training on a canal barge, then this was an unusual resource that could be used for their benefit. And generally, *Sobriety*'s relationship with Europe was distinctive if not unusual.

"What do you know about Objective 4?" Neil Skinner asked me in 1997. *"Nothing,"* I said. To someone not used to eurobabble, the question would have been meaningless but now that like many others in the public and voluntary sectors I was becoming a euro-addict, it was a question that filled me with anticipation. I hung on to Neil's next pronouncement. *"It's the Objective that Maggie Thatcher refused to allow into the UK but now there's been a change of mind and the doors are open. The ESF Unit is going to explain everything at a day conference in Birmingham. Why don't you go and see if there are any possibilities?"* I said I would.

In 2007 the UK government changed its administration of EU funding in favour of a more centralised regime and re-organised the framework so that EU funding was sometimes indistinguishable, at least in name, from any other source of money. Ten years earlier in 1997 however, there were five Objectives which, far from being controlled by Balkan witches, had down to earth aims, priorities and measures across the continent to improve people's skills and help them become more economically active. Numbered 1 to 5, the Objectives, had their own separate programmes of financial assistance and were known (and still are) as the Structural Funds. They were set up to implement the policy of the EU to reduce regional disparities in income, wealth and opportunities. The poorer regions received most of the support but all regions were eligible for funding under the policy's various programmes.[7] The communities in which *Sobriety* based its work gained a great deal from the contracts designed to help communities achieve these Objectives for themselves.

Objective 1 targeted parts of the Union where the average domestic income was less than 75% of the European average. In the UK the beneficiary regions were Cornwall, Merseyside, South Yorkshire, the North East and the Highlands and Islands of Scotland. It was under Objective 1 that *Sobriety* was able to secure some of the money to open the Swinton Lock Adventure Centre.

Objective 2, with the sub-title of European Regional Development Fund (ERDF), supported capital projects and was available to areas which taken as a whole had not reached a common standard in business innovation, entrepreneurship, protection of the environment, and tourism. In the early nineties Boothferry Borough Council was able to allocate funds from this Objective to help set up the Waterways Museum, and in 2002 Hull City Council did the same for *Sobriety*'s training programme for unemployed people on Hull's council estates.

Between 1996 and 2007 *Sobriety* was also a successful applicant for Objective 3, usually known as the European Social Fund, to help specific groups of unemployed people return to the labour market: for instance men and women leaving prison, people with additional learning needs and women facing barriers to getting into work.

The shortlived Objective 4 was designed to provide training in areas that would make small and medium size businesses more competitive.

Objective 5 was the only structural fund closed to the Project and was intended among its other priorities to support hill farming. Even with the most energetic of volunteers in the flat lands of East Yorkshire and one member of staff's long experience of lambing, an application under this Objective would have been a flock too far. Neil Skinner's Objective 4 which helped with the development of small businesses, was more to the point.

Small Business Development

The best times for a fund raiser come not from sitting in front of an application form chewing a pencil but on realising that one's organisation might have the answer to a problem that funders agree needs to be solved. It is a question of researching different aspects of the problem and thinking clearly about plans for its solution. All a bit like Advanced Level GCE plus an element of imagination and the will to give substance to an application.

I went to the Objective 4 conference which, as was the custom in those days, was held not in a posh hotel but in a community centre not far from the city's infamous Bullring. As I listened to the presentations I began to relate them to what was happening in Goole and during the lunch break aired some ideas with colleagues from the ESF Unit. They said we should apply. On the train home I knew, as Neil had said, that the door was opening to a major project. It might be more orientated to Goole's business needs than *Sobriety*'s charitable objects but it would increase respect for the Project and lay the foundations for future activities. I was always careful not to underestimate the importance of local support whether it came from the community or the business sector. *Sobriety* may have been a charity but it had to be run like a business and through an Objective 4 sponsored training programme it could become a better business.

In 1994 the British Government had introduced the Single Regeneration Budget (SRB) which brought together programmes and initiatives from several Government departments. The aim was to simplify the funding process and provide resources to support regeneration projects carried out by local partnerships. Through a series of funding rounds, its purpose was to enhance the quality of life of local people in areas of need. In acknowledgement of the necessity for small businesses to secure loans in circumstances where banks might hesitate, Round 2 of SRB in Goole brought together local business people, council personnel and workers in the voluntary sector, to form Goole Development Trust. But there was a catch; the Trust had to raise the money that it was going to lend.

John Branford's *Humber Renown* entering Castleford Flood Lock

Tim Watson

Meanwhile on Dutch River Side, *Sobriety*, never introspective, was turning its attentions to see how it could collaborate with other residents of the strip of land on which it had its museum and nature trail. There were ten in all: British Waterways, conservator for the Goole to Knottingley canal: Tilcon concrete mixing company: *Sobriety's* museum: Goole Boatyard (a marina): Associated British Ports (ABP): the engineering firm owned by Shane Murphy: the Acaster family's water transport business: Branford Barge Owners: the South Dock Boat Hoist Company, and at the Dog and Duck, Viking Marine. We held a few meetings on *ROOM 58* which were well attended and shared our views on common problems. For the freight carriers it was a shortage of trainee skippers and loss of wharfage, jetties and cranes where the waterway authority had sold or leased its land for housing or tourism development; for ABP it was the need to expand the dock estate and for the smaller concerns it was marketing and cashflow. The meetings broke the ice and gave us insights into one another's work and the confidence to develop a loose alliance of firms with a common interest in the waterway. When it was announced that the new South Dock bridge would have an air draught[8] that would make it impossible for the museum's tour boat to enter Goole docks, the group persuaded ABP to make modifications to the bridge design.

To sum up, here was a development trust that badly needed resources to make loans to infant businesses that had been repeatedly turned away by the banks. Here also was a group of local waterways companies which could work together on projects of common interest. Put the two together and in principle we had a good basis for an application to Objective 4;[9] it would be *Goole SME Collaboration Project*.[10] Six months of meetings, arm twisting and endless draft applications led to a project which allowed 15 SMEs to train owner managers and employees in basic skills, information technology, communication and leadership. £163,000 came from the Social Fund to help achieve the Objective 4 outcome of successful adaptation to change and increased business competitiveness. But the total cost of the project was about £300,000 which paid for 300 individuals each to receive 36 hours of training. It was unique to Goole and set the scene for Goole Development Trust under its directors and new manager Roger Millar, subseqently to raise millions of pounds to help businesses across the Humber region. For efficiency and value for money the Trust was, and is, reckoned to be, one of the best in the UK.

Co-Financing

Since the late nineties the application process for European funds has been much simplified by being brought under the direct control of local authorities and private companies. Gone are the days of sitting in front of a blank sheet of paper knowing that the next three months would consist of little else but researching answers to questions on the application form: answers which might in the end run to more than 100 pages. The hand holding and advice networks have gone but many local authorities are now eager to work with local people to design and run European projects in a way that would not have found favour in the past. This is not an entirely mercenary change of heart illustrated by the cynical adage that 'partnership is the suppression of mutual hatred based on the need to secure funding,' but in their pursuit of partnership, local authorities and the new Canal & River Trust[11] need to remember that many voluntary and community organisations have a sense of independence that can appear unintelligible to the statutory sector and they would do well to take this seriously. Meanwhile the growth of partnerships has generated creativity and excitement and is nothing but welcome.

With the Government's changes to the administration of the EU Structural Funds in the UK, applicants were relieved of the obligation to find match funding. Through a package of 'co-finance', public bodies like the Learning & Skills Council[12] became responsible for letting and monitoring contracts with organisations that previously would have applied directly to the sector managers like ICOM described in the previous chapter. The money came from two sources — Europe and the UK Government, and was handed over to selected public and private agencies for distribution according to agreed rules. *Spring to Release*, the report on the problems faced by women leaving prison, was co-financed by the Learning & Skills Council, North Yorkshire. The LSC published its prospectus and *Sobriety* responded with detailed proposals which were accepted by the LSC. A contract was signed and throughout the eighteen months of the project, from conception to publication, the LSC gave the advice and guidance that would make the report a good example of co-operation between the voluntary and statutory sectors.

From 1995 to the present, *Sobriety* has been responsible for eighteen projects delivered according to EU and UK rules. The average expenditure on each of 955 beneficiaries has been £1571: 422 beneficiaries have gained qualifications that either helped them into further training or to find work: 133 have gone into employment directly as a result of the EU supported courses: others have taken up voluntary work or gone into further education: a small number did not complete the courses. As we have seen, beneficiaries faced barriers to work additional to simple unemployment. Their progress created a record of which *Sobriety* can be very proud. Occasionally however, we had a fight on our hands.

One of the drawbacks of re-organisation was the increasing reluctance of co-financing agencies like the LSC to make contracts with small organisations. The argument was that the selection of so many projects and the monitoring of so many outcomes were not cost effective and put too much strain on staffing. A common solution was for the LSC to sub-contract these responsibilities to private companies. They were often set up for no other purpose than to make a profit, but their contracts required them to recruit huge numbers of beneficiaries and get them into work or further training. Having such tight *per capita* profit margins, they were not themselves in a position to work directly with the likes of *Sobriety*'s clientele, and did their best to persuade local voluntary bodies to achieve the prescribed LSC targets on their behalf. Some paid peanuts, paid late, their monitoring was inadequate and they had no real interest in the people who needed help. The less they could pay their sub-contracted charities the more they could keep for themselves. Such an impersonal and unscrupulous purchase of outputs and outcomes was a long way from *Sobriety*'s philosophy of assistance and not at all in the spirit of the European Social Fund. *Sobriety* was the victim of two of these scams. Hull Local Labour Initiative went bankrupt before it could settle its debts and the *Sobriety* Project lost £2000. It then gave itself a new name and was given a new contract! More seriously the Care Sector Trust made false claims in *Sobriety*'s name among others, and became the subject of an enquiry by Humberside Police. I was angry that *Sobriety* had been led up the garden path but sad that one of the culprits, a former

Home Management pupil at Goole Grammar School, had got herself into such a mess. Another quite different episode showed the need for careful research when dealing with public institutions answerable to European bureaucracy. Encouraged by the success of several projects designed to help women return to the labour market, *Sobriety* made an application for co-finance to the Learning & Skills Council South Yorkshire.

Under the terms of Objective 1, money was being made available to help women with some exceptional barriers to employment. They would be residents of bail hostels, or women recovering from drug and alcohol addiction or individuals who had never had a job. *Sobriety* made the application in the early part of 2002 when the LSC was desperate to

Waterways Work for Women

find projects to address issues of gender imbalance in the labour market. Advertisements had appeared in *South Yorkshire Funding News* and the LSC had organised a conference at MAGNA[13] on, 'Tackling Women's and Men's Segregation in the Labour Market'. *Sobriety's* subsequent proposal to design and run a course for 60 women across the sub-region was praised by the LSC as 'cutting edge,' and some early results were included in its publicity material. But *Sobriety* and the LSC soon knew they had bitten off more than they could chew. By September 2004 which marked the end of the course, we were still short of 15 beneficiaries. In the light of this failure, the LSC was demanding the return of £19,234. It was an uncomfortable situation. To persuade the commissioning body that it was an unfair demand would take some hard thinking and some good communication.

In the note accompanying its invoice, the LSC argued that it had to account for the use of EU funds and that if a project did not meet its targets, then money would have to be repaid. However the LSC's statement left some leeway to the extent that because co-financing included funding from sources other than Europe, the LSC might have some local discretion. In my letter to its external funding manager I drew attention to this possibility and also to the Sixth Report of Session 2002-03 (Vol.II) of the House of Commons Work & Pensions Committee which showed that *Sobriety's* predicament was not unusual. The committee had requested submissions from statutory and voluntary bodies on the impact of co-financing. Its final report had stated that '*The actual practice of CFOs*[14] *is not suitable for dealing with inclusion work. It is modelled on unproblematic training provision, it is output and contract driven, inflexible and not designed to empower control of activity by outside agencies, which is key to inclusion.* The fact that such opinions were being aired at the time of the introduction of co-financing, suggested the LSC should have known there was risk in what it certainly regarded as an experimental course. My contention was that it should have built in sufficient contingency to deal with the risk.

Following the Work & Pensions Committee's verdict, it also seemed reasonable to ask that if it was the LSC that was making the rules, and not the European Commission, would not the funds the LSC had been given make more impact if they had taken into account the personal circumstances of the potential beneficiaries? Rounding things off with a rather indelicate question, I asked if the LSC believed that those who are most disadvantaged benefit more if they are in European funded courses than if they are in courses that are purely nationally funded.

Strangely the letter seemed to have the effect of letting the LSC off the hook as well as *Sobriety*. I was relieved that after a meeting in the lovely straddle warehouse overlooking the terminus of the Sheffield Canal, at which the LSC withdrew its demand, we parted friends and pledged our eternal allegiance to the European project. The issue never descended into a row and we remained on good terms with the LSC until its abolition in 2010.[15]

Let it not be assumed however that we had neglected our duties; many women from complicated social circumstances enrolled into the project and made notable progress. As we have seen, one won the NIACE (National Institute of Adult & Continuing Education) Adult Learner of the Year Award and found work as a skipper with *Waterstart*, *Sobriety*'s community boat project in Thorne. Several were having problems of re-settlement from prison and I reflected that it would be surprising if the European Commission were to censure LSC South Yorkshire for including these beneficiaries in its balance sheet for EU audit, when the cost of keeping an individual in prison for a year was more than £37,000. The EU subsidies notoriously handed out for the planting and uprooting of olive trees seemed a far cry from the mean streets of the UK's northern cities.

Leader: The Beneficiaries

On roadsides all over Europe from Dublin to Sophia, from Hamburg to Sicily, are signboards recording the EU's assistance with national and trans-national projects.

Some of these signboards carry the distinctive symbol of LEADER, the acronym for *Liaison Entre Actions de Développement de l'Économie Rurale*. But all that is meant by this elaborate advertisement is that the EU is helping a particular area to find solutions to problems in its rural economy. LEADER has existed for many years and we have seen how when match funded by Surestart in Selby district, it enabled *Sobriety*'s *Surewaters* project to provide a service for families in isolated rural communities.

But response to changes in national and local needs has always been one of the characteristics of Europe's funding programmes and in 2008 the time was ripe for the East Riding of Yorkshire Council to ally with Ryedale District Council and parts of Scarborough in North Yorkshire and apply to the Department for Environment, Food and Rural Affairs (Defra) for LEADER funding to support an expansion of rural tourism in the three areas. The hope was that visitors from other parts of England and from Europe, including those disembarking from the ferries in Hull, could be induced not to make a beeline for York and the stately homes of the West Riding, but to enjoy the beaches and open skies of Yorkshire's east coast, perhaps walk and cycle between the villages of the Yorkshire Wolds and discover the wetlands of the Humber and Yorkshire Derwent. The bid also created an invitation to visit one of the 17 waterways which lace the area and have their origins in Britain's industrial revolution. There was plenty of history; it just needed improvement of local facilities and amenities to make it attractive. The outcome was the launch and development of *Coast, Wolds, Wetlands & Waterways* (CWWW) through which nature tourism (not naturism) would be encouraged, the area's heritage promoted further afield and availability of overnight accommodation extended. The intended result was that B&Bs, craft shops, cafés , pubs, local art galleries, churches, woodlands, footpaths, bridleways, seabird sanctuaries and all the rest of the rural economy would benefit. And it has happened. During the five years of the scheme, hundreds of organisations and communities have received assistance. Sceptical taxpayers should be reassured that the investment and distribution of the £2.8 million[16] allocated by Defra has not been haphazard. In a selection process just competitive enough to make it interesting, projects have had to make presentations to a decision making board representing the private, statutory and voluntary and community sectors, and to submit to some very humane monitoring in the interests of making sure they have done what they said they would do. *Coast, Wolds, Wetlands & Waterways* has been a remarkable success with not a whiff of the failures or bureaucratic burdens routinely reported by eurosceptic politicians and media. The project has succeeded in doing what it set out to do and has paved the way for similar investment. But what did *Sobriety* do to help?

The disputes between the Project and the local authority during the late nineties had been stuffed into the recycle bin and thanks to the efforts of Jon Fogell and others, the Project was now acting as an educational refuge for children excluded from mainstream schools. In addition to winning the East Riding Chairman's Award[17] in 2003 and again in 2012, the Project was actively contributing to the Authority's youth work provision and assisting with an inter-agency project sponsored by the Youth Justice Board and the East Riding Youth Offending Team. Against a background of increasing collaboration I found it a welcome surprise to be asked my views on how the local waterways could complement the proposals for CWWW. At a meeting of the authority's Transport Overview & Scrutiny Committee early in 2009 to which I had been invited by Claire Watts, the manager in charge of external funding and policy, I offered some ideas.

I referred to the 17 waterways in the area[18] listed below, which even if some were no longer navigable, could still play a part in the economy of nearby communities:

River Humber from Blacktoft to Broomfleet; Yorkshire Ouse from Blacktoft to Barmby-on-the-Marsh; Market Weighton Canal and the River Foulness (pronounced 'Fulna') from Broomfleet to Spaldington; River Aire from Snaith to Cowick; River Derwent from Barmby-on-the-Marsh to Halsham and beyond; River Don known as the Dutch River where it flows through Goole on its way from Snaith and Cowick; Knottingley & Goole Canal between Goole and Pollington; Driffield Navigation and canalised River Hull from Ticton to Driffield; Hedon Haven; Pocklington Canal from East Cottingwith to Pocklington; Gypsey Race from Duggleby to Bridlington; Hornsea Mere; Leven Canal; Frodingham Beck; River Hertford adjoining the mesolithic site of Starr Carr.[19]

Like the coast and wolds, most of these rivers and canals lent themselves to some aspects of enlightened exploitation for tourism, health, small business opportunities, boating and wildlife conservation. They often attracted volunteers and, as we have seen elsewhere, could be a useful resource for helping people on low incomes get into work or training. Moreover in some areas there were well established groups like *Sobriety* or the Beverley Barge Preservation Society that were already channels for waterway based community development. In Driffield and Pocklington there were longstanding plans for improvement and promotion of their respective waterways and on the high wolds, the Gypsey Race chalk stream was a focus point for churches, farmers, parish councils and residents to collaborate in solving local problems, not least the lack of rural transport and access to broadband. There were also interesting riparian developments which used the waterway as a resource for land based activity. The Number 5 Boat Hoist at Goole with its associated tug and compartment boats was not just an attraction but stood on a site occupied and maintained by a model boat club which recruited local people of all ages and backgrounds. What did not exist, I argued, was a common aim of all these organisations to help one another. They tended to work in isolation and rarely to communicate with groups not in their locality or outside their field of interest. The *Coast Wolds Wetlands & Waterways Project* could help to change this.

Another question I raised in a letter to Annie Hadfield who in 2008 was director of the rural programmes team, concerned arrangements for the selection of projects:

Prior to the LSC and local authorities taking over the administration of applications to the EU, project selection was an open process. Bids had to fit with published guidance and were scored by an independent panel with representatives from the public and voluntary sectors. The scoring regime was communicated well in advance, each application was marked twice and a rank order of successful and failed bids was published. This included a reserve list of projects which would be funded if money became available. The process was fair, transparent and widely appreciated. Bidding had to be integrated into an organisation's business planning. Questions were designed so that applicants could not write answers unless they had done the homework on need and delivery.

I suggested that some elements of this process might find favour with local communities if complemented by help from LEADER staff. The letter was well received and contributed to the recognition that aside from financial probity and audit, LEADER would not get the best out of voluntary and community groups if the Authority appeared to be telling them what to do and if it made money available only to those groups which did as they were told.

I need not have worried. I had five enjoyable years of working with local authority officers led by Dee Mitchell, an accountant with previous experience of a South Yorkshire charity. From the beginning, they devolved their powers to a decision making board elected by a local action group. The arrangement worked well because groups applying for funds could see that the process was fair and thorough; decisions were not made in smoke filled rooms nor was money allocated on a whim. All organisations, public, private and voluntary, were given a hand to develop their ideas and, if successful, to manage the paperwork which inevitably arises from any EU project. The word soon got round that here was a user friendly application process. Not surprisingly the success of so many projects led to projected overspends which at Defra's instigation were recouped from underspends in other parts of the UK.

Two examples of projects appeared in CWWW'S March 2010 bulletin. The first was the Riverside Pop-in Café in St Andrew's Church, Paull, which lies on the north bank of the Humber and is home to a fort built to deter Napoleon from mounting an estuarine invasion. The circular noted that Paull had been classed as an area with 40% deprivation and had lost its post office, local shop and a pub. It also stood to lose its church unless the money was found to carry out urgent repairs. The money was found and the repairs were completed. At this point LEADER was able to step in and help with a grant of £41,000 towards the capital cost of turning part of the church into a café for visitors and local people. The second example was *Making best use of the CWWW area's inland waterways,* and was described as a 'key legacy project outstanding for the establishment of an inland waterways partnership of public and private bodies to secure the economic and social future of the area's waterway heritage'. As if to confirm this in 2011, the project went on to win first place in the partnership category of the Waterways Renaissance Awards, a national competition sponsored by The Waterways Trust and British Waterways.

During 2009/2010, the first year of CWWW, 24 projects were supported with a total income from all sources of £2,700,000. My comment as chair of the new waterways partnership was that 'through a combination of help from the full time LEADER team and the imagination and determination of applicants, funding has been allocated to projects in North and East Yorkshire which fit precisely with the *Coast, Wolds, Wetlands and Waterways* criteria. None of these schemes would have gone ahead without the LEADER contribution to the funding jigsaw'.

Simon Ryder, the consultant who had helped to dig *Sobriety* out of its impasse with the East Riding, was now invited by the LEADER team to prepare the ground rules for the partnership. He and his colleague Lyn O'Sullivan spent six months meeting organisations connected with the 17 waterways. They recommended that there should be an executive committee elected by two forums, one of which would deal with technical matters such as drainage and navigation and the other would give its views on possibilities for social and community development. They also prepared information templates to give an overview of each waterway and helped the committee ensure that LEADER funds were voted for the salary of a full time co-ordinator. James Cokeham, who had qualifications and experience in planning, design and marketing, was appointed on a three year contract in 2010 and fulfilled admirably the expectations of the members of the partnership, the local authority and the LEADER team. He took very seriously the advice offered by the Inland Waterways Advisory Council in its *Working Together — Effective Waterways Partnerships.*[20] By the middle of 2014 when he accepted a permanent post in the Authority's department for economic development, he was able to hand over to Annabel Hanson, his successor, an association that was making waves locally, and at a national level was attracting increasing attention for the diversity of its waterway interests. James left two legacies: a new spirit of collaboration among partners and a *Waterways Strategy 2012-2020*[21] which was seminal in its comprehensive appraisal of the LEADER investment. In 127 pages it detailed exactly what had been achieved since 2010 and provided an

LEADER Waterways Partnership. Award winner in
Waterways Renaissance Awards: Birmingham City Library.

agreed road map for supporting the future development of the waterways in the East and North Yorkshire LEADER area. The Strategy was launched in the presence of 150 invited guests at Bishop Burton College of Agriculture on 29th November 2012. This was my welcoming speech:

Any launch is an important occasion and I feel I ought to be wearing a big hat, like Chris Patten, last governor of Hong Kong, who described the governor's hat he was supposed to wear on ceremonial occasions but didn't, as 'a topi with a dead pigeon on top'. The Chinese government found his modesty very difficult to cope with because he didn't fit their idea of how an imperial governor should behave. Nor does this partnership fit with the usual idea of partnership, a word I have been brought up to believe and have said elsewhere, symbolised suppression of mutual hatred in the interests of acquiring funds.

Your most welcome attendance here today (and this includes colleagues from South Pennines and other faraway places), says that you appreciate the philosophy and practice of the partnership, and with no such repressed hang-ups, are keen for it to continue. This is what the Strategy is about. It is a longish written statement of aims and objectives for the coming years, put together and agreed over the last six months by 68 members of the partnership. Some are closely associated with the East Riding and North Yorkshire Authorities and others represent national organisations, statutory and voluntary interests big and small, all with their own ideas and ways of working, who think that the partnership will help them do their work better. Members attend the community forum which brings forward projects for consideration by the executive committee to see how it can help; others are enthusiastic about the technical forum which gives advice to the executive on the feasibility of projects.

The next stage is for your organisations, however different in size or objectives, to get to know one another so well that you don't have to rely on James Cokeham and his assistant,

Heather Clunie, to make things happen. The implication is that you want the partnership to continue after the end of LEADER funding in September 2013 and that you have done something about it by contributing carefully and imaginatively to the Strategy.

It was not always so. When we began four years ago, there was no partnership. Even if they knew of each other's existence, organisations did not generally work together. And sometimes ignorance was bliss because it became apparent that some organisations that did know one another, also hated one another. There was nothing magical about the process of setting up the partnership, just lots of hard work and friendly persuasion, as John Edmonds our main speaker knows. He can run masterclasses in getting individuals and groups to work together, having been president of the TUC in 1998 and later, chair of the Inland Waterways Advisory Council which in a moment of 'we can do it better ourselves', the Coalition Government decided this year to abolish.

Now let me entertain you with a down to earth picture of what the partnership has been doing. I'll take a cue from the names of the barges that early in the last century traded on the waterways that you represent here, except perhaps on the Gipsey Race, Europe's most northerly chalk stream which is only big enough for model boats.

Humber barges were named after sound, non-conformist virtues such as GRATITUDE *and* PERSEVERANCE *and I think it would be a good idea if projects were asked to adopt these names as an indication of their* INTEGRITY. *Perhaps consideration of the process of allocating names to projects could go on the next agenda of the executive committee. Taking excerpts from my foreword to the Strategy, let us give the projects mentioned there some suggestions for the names they may adopt.*

In spite of years of setbacks to their plans, 48 Driffield residents attended a recent meeting of the town's newly formed canal partnership to show their enthusiasm for re-opening the whole length of the Driffield Navigation for public use. The 'Blessed Forty Eight' will be represented by DAUNTLESS, ENERGY, EFFORT *and definitely* NIL DESPERANDUM *and* DEFIANCE, *and if things go awry, even* MAYDAY!

The Pocklington Canal Amenity Society and a small steering group associated with the Market Weighton canal are pressing forward with plans to stimulate economic and social benefits in their respective communities. In their case, PRODESSE, *the Latin for 'To make a profit', seems appropriate, as well as* RISING HOPE *and* ECONOMY.

People in Snaith, a small town near Selby, are well ahead with a scheme to make the banks of the river Aire more attractive to visitors. I think FRUITS OF INDUSTRY *would fit them well.*

In Goole there is an established project using waterway related activities to help young people prepare themselves for work. EXPECT *and* BE THANKFUL *are good descriptions of the Goole project as well perhaps as* Review *when its budgets are under scrutiny.*

Further north, the Chalk Rivers Trust and Derwent Action Group, and local residents and professionals connected with the river Hertford, a man-made stream adjacent to the mesolithic site of Starr Carr, are wanting to make the best of opportunities for tourism without losing sight of their obligations to the natural world. ENTERPRISE *and* EVER READY *are obvious;* UNIQUE *and* RESOLUTE *look likely.*

With commendable foresight and imagination, members and officers in the East Riding of Yorkshire Council and North Yorkshire County Council adopted a plan to secure LEADER funding from Europe. This is obviously a reference to Dee Mitchell, our LEADER leader of Coast Wolds Wetlands and Waterways, and so DIVINE or even VENUS would not be going too far.

Under the leadership of its full time co-ordinator and the guidance of an elected executive committee representing different waterways interests, the partnership has a record second to none. DUX, *the Latin for leader, describes James Cokeham, our co-ordinator, and is a continuous reminder of our origins.*

BARROSA, *not to be confused with Jose Manuel Barroso, President of the European Commission, is an antidote to too much Euro-enthusiasm, being the name of a Peninsular War battle in 1811 in which a single British division defeated two French divisions.*

The executive committee will be represented by I KNOW *and the launch of the strategy by* DEI GRATIA *(Thanks be to God),* OLIVE BRANCH, SUCCESS *and* UNITED. *Any attempts to scupper it will require the combined forces of a* HUMBER WITCH *and* NERO *himself!*

Please enjoy the conference and get your questions ready for the panel at the end — a panel which will be very LIBERAL *but not an* EVANGELIST *for* AUSTERITY, *nor even for* SOBRIETY.

With grateful thanks to LEADER and the two Authorities of East Riding of Yorkshire and North Yorkshire, I now declare the Waterways Strategy well and truly launched for your contemplation and celebration. Please tell your friends that a graphic novel version of the strategy will be appear in January 2013.

Just as whimsical in its title but less so in content was *Becks, Banks, Brains and Drains* which is described in the Strategy as:

…a project to help local communities explore the River Hull's drainage history — the rows of raised banks, the complex network of dykes, pumping stations and outlets that raise or lower the water levels. It will uncover the local stories of the 'brains' behind the development of the drainage system — the people whose ingenuity turned inaccessible marsh into farms and communities. It will give local people the opportunity to research and interpret the history of the drains in their area, leading to better understanding of how they worked in the past and developing local solutions to drainage and flooding in the future.

The project was the brainchild of The Hull Valley Drainage Heritage Group [22] which in 2013 published a superbly illustrated book also called *Becks, Banks, Brains and Drains.* LEADER provided encouragement for the project and subsidised the book.

Not mentioned in the Strategy was the twinning of *Coast Wolds Wetlands & Waterways (CWWW)* with Le Musée du Canal de Berry situated in the hamlet of Magnette near Montluçon in central France. The link formed part of a LEADER transnational co-operation project with

Val du Cher[23] in the Auvergne region. The Yorkshire Waterways Museum's involvement with Europe made it central to the success of several aspects of CWWW, one of which was to work with a similar museum in France against the broader background of community economic development. So during April 2011, two LEADER colleagues and I spent three days in Val du Cher discussing with French colleagues how we could work together on schemes that would benefit both organisations. Whereas in

LEADER Project: Musée du Canal de Berry

east and north Yorkshire community use of waterways could be restricted by vested interests whether riparian or bureaucratic, in Val du Cher it was rural indifference and emigration of skilled workers that hindered development. The hope was that co-operation between the two institutions at a practical level would lead to collaboration at a problem solving level.

The Musée du Canal de Berry was similar in size to the Yorkshire Waterways Museum. Its attractions were the canal barge *Frène* and a complex of buildings designed for the transportation and burning of lime. *Frène* was pulled along the canal by a donkey which was stabled on board. On arrival at Magnette the limestone would be offloaded into small railway wagons and carried the short distance to a kiln.

The link flourished for a couple of years and featured an exchange of artefacts, a film about the two museums and a travelling exhibition. But knowing what an impact *Audrey* had made with her adventures, I was disappointed that *Sobriety*'s museum did not develop a more permanent link with Val du Cher and allow the narratives of the two museums to lead to a deeper economic and cultural relationship. Our French colleagues were charming. Their enthusiasm for the link was matched only by their hospitality and a grasp of English that put my knowledge of French to shame. The Val du Cher authority also subsidised several projects which strictly speaking were CWWW's responsibility. There was unfinished business here. In more affluent times *Sobriety* might have devised a permanent youth exchange programme to give some of the young people attending the Project an opportunity to spend time in France and perhaps to have arranged curatorial exchanges between the two museums.

As for LEADER's benefits to *Sobriety*, there were contributions totalling £70,000 towards two capital projects: the conversion into a floating classroom of the motor barge *Service*, given on permanent loan to *Sobriety* by the Waddington family in Swinton, and the restoration of a Yorkshire fishing coble which had been rescued in the late nineties by Izzy Kitt from a field in the village of Lelley, not far from the seaside town of Withernsea.[24]

Over seventeen years, Europe gave the Project the obligation to look far beyond its own concerns to the future of individuals who came its way.[25] In so doing the Project enhanced its reputation and guaranteed its own future. But there were other networks and affiliations which contributed to the same end — the National Community Boats Association and the Inland Waterways Advisory Council.

Questions

What made European funding distinctive? If funding had been requested exclusively from government, would *Sobriety* have been able to initiate *Waterways Work for Women* or to obtain the money to get the *Spider* project and subsequently Swinton Lock Adventure Centre off the ground?

If Britain were to leave the European Union what would the consequences be for organisations like *Sobriety* and indeed for local authority run schemes like LEADER? Would government come up with the cash?

Chapter 13 Notes

1 'Turnstile' income is revenue from what the Project sells — boat trips, café meals, conference facilities, paintings, items from the gift shop, occasional services and so on. The income is 'unrestricted', meaning that it does not have to be spent on a particular purpose or activity. Grants from charitable trusts on the other hand, are often linked to agreed objectives or to the purchase of items of equipment and are quite often 'restricted'.

2 The term Yorkshire and Humber enables us to include the two authorities to the south of the Humber, North Lincolnshire and North East Lincolnshire.

3 Reproduced in *Sobriety*'s Review of 2008 – page 18.

4 The intervention rate varies according to the rules of a particular fund. In some ways the term 'match funding' is a misnomer. Europe assumes that you have for example, 60% of the money needed to run a project. It then will 'intervene' by making available the outstanding 40% to enable the work to go ahead. In practice most projects depend on Europe for the initial slice of funding and fill the gap from other sources. However in most application forms one has to bring evidence to show that without ESF or ERDF a particular project could not go ahead.

5 The accountable body — an intermediary such as a local authority or sector manager like ICOM (see Chapter 13). This body would select projects and monitor target delivery and finance.

6 Sub target groups. The 'target' group would be people who were unemployed. The term 'sub target' group would describe beneficiaries who were not only unemployed but also had some additional handicap preventing them from getting a job. This could be lack of literacy or customer service skills. It might even be their sex. Some unemployed men might be discouraged from filling vacant posts for nursing auxiliaries because they did not have any understanding of hospital routines or women might not feel confident to apply to become HGV or bus drivers.

7 European funding framework. I am indebted to Wikipedia for some details here.

8 Air draught: the space between the top of a vessel and the bridge above it. Other instances of co-operative action were road improvement, dealing with noxious cargoes, certification of skippers and use of slipways and dry docks.

9 Objective 4 had a short life (1998-2000) but *Sobriety* made the most of it. The application was submitted in spring 1999.

10 SME: small or medium size enterprise. The definition below is supplied by the European Commission:

Company category	Employees	Turnover	or	Balance sheet total
Medium-sized	< 250	≤ €50 m		≤ €43 m
Small	< 50	≤ €10 m		≤ €10 m
Micro	< 10	≤ €2 m		≤ €2 m

Goole SME Collaboration Project involved all three categories.

11 The Canal & River Trust is a charitable body that was set up to look after the waterways of England and Wales. The transfer of ownership from the previous government-owned British Waterways, took place on 2 July 2012. It is expected that the inland navigations managed by the Environment Agency will transfer to the Trust in 2015.

12 In 2001 the 72 Training and Enterprise Councils (TEC) in the UK were replaced by the Learning & Skills Council (LSC) which like the TECs, had sub-regional HQs. The LSC South Yorkshire was based in the straddle warehouse overlooking Sheffield Canal Basin and the LSC Humberside in The Maltings, Hull. The LSC and all its sub-regional branches were abolished in 2010.

13 A steelworks heritage centre in Rotherham, South Yorkshire.

14 CFOs – Co-Financing Organisations

15 From a letter containing these arguments from me to Nigel Brough, External Funding Manager, LSC South Yorkshire, 6th November 2004.

16 The figure of £2.8m did not include the match funding element required of most projects. If this had been included the total would have been about £4m.

17 The Chairman's Awards are presented annually by East Riding of Yorkshire Council to companies within the East Riding of Yorkshire in recognition of their achievements in enhancing the economy of the area. Nominations can be put forward by the public or by the individual companies concerned, as well as officers and members of the council, using the following criteria:

>   Creation of new jobs within the area;
>   Investment in training and their workforce;
>   Investment within the area;
>   Recent expansion of existing business;
>   Success as a small business;
>   Promoting equal opportunities.

(East Riding of Yorkshire Council nomination form)

18 For purposes of LEADER, Old Goole (Goole South ward) where *Sobriety* had its museum, was regarded as a separate rural community. Market towns such as Goole, Beverley and coastal resorts of any size were not eligible for LEADER funding. They had to find other programmes of assistance.

19 A good general reference book outlining the history of some of the waterways in the list is *The Canals of Yorkshire and North East England* by Charles Hadfield published by David and Charles in 1972. The two volumes are still widely available on the second hand market for about £30.

20 Working Together — Effective Waterways Partnerships (IWAC March 2010) contained summary guidance: Seek clarity and consensus in defining your purpose; Agree an appropriate structure at the outset; Plan appropriately what you propose to do; Agree a strategic plan as part of 'signing up' to your partnership; Take all possible steps, even small ones, to reduce the risk of future financial uncertainty; Communicate effectively at all levels and with all stakeholders — make it a priority; Recognise the need for both champions and conciliators within the leadership of the partnership; Involve the local community; Be clear about the partners' roles and be open and honest about problems; Be committed to deliver the benefits which you envisaged at the outset; Adopt a 'can-do' attitude and stick with it

21 *East Riding & North Yorkshire Waterways Partnership: Waterways Strategy 2012–2020* is available from East Riding of Yorkshire Council, County Hall, Beverley HU17 9BA.

For the names of the barges I am grateful to Michael Ullyat who listed them in his book, *Flying Sail.*

22 The group is led by Ian Reid PhD (Hull), Professor of Physical Geography at the University of Loughborough and Chair of the Parish Council at Beswick which lies in the River Hull's flood plain, and Colin Walker, Rural Policy and Strategy Officer, East Riding of Yorkshire Council.

The book is available from East Riding Council's Rural Programmes team. EU rules stipulate that the book must be free of charge but I have no doubt that donations of about £10 might be welcome.

23 The title of Duke of Berry in the French nobility was frequently created for junior members of the French royal family. The Berry region now consists of the départements of Cher, Indre and parts of Vienne. The capital of Berry is Bourges.

Situated along the Canal du Berry in the heart of Val du Cher, the museum was established in 1978 on the site of the old lime kilns by the Association of Lay Reugny. René Chambareau and a group of volunteers have brought together hundreds of artefacts over a period of 25 years from more than 400 donors. Documents, tools, paintings, lock gates and two barges illustrate the way of life on France's narrowest canal. The museum will be a delight for students of nineteenth and early twentieth century industry and transportation.

Val du Cher website: http://comcom-valdecher.planet-allier.com/musee_du_canal.html

24 The Yorkshire fishing coble *GEMINI* is an example of a type of inshore fishing boat working on the east coast of England between the Tyne and the Humber. Flat bottoms allow the cobles to be launched from a beach and their high bows give protection from choppy seas. *GEMINI* was built for the Pockley family of Flamborough in the early 1980's by Joe Gelsthorpe at his Barmston workshop. She was registered on the Hull fishing register as H 485 and after being sold away from Flamborough, lay rotting in a field at Lelley in the East Riding for a good many years. On one of her forward timbers is engraved the name 'Pebble Boats', the trading title of the boatbuilder who produced a number of wooden cobles for customers all along the east coast.

With generous help from LEADER and a grant from the Association of Independent Museums, *Sobriety* was able to hire the services of Jimmy Cliff a wooden boat builder of Alan G Pease Boat Repairers and Builders in Goole. Jimmy worked through the winter of 2009 to restore *GEMINI* and in places where the frame could not be salvaged he reproduced a new section by hand so that the original lines were restored. The new planks were then steamed into shape and fitted one by one. To aid its long term conservation and show off its lines to best advantage the coble is displayed at the museum, out of the water under an architect-designed canopy also paid for by LEADER.

25 *The Guardian* Saturday 12th January 2013 printed under the title *What's the EU done for us? This lot…..* a letter from Simon Sweeney, Lecturer in international political economy at the University of York:

At last we may get a debate on Britain's relationship with Europe (Leader 11th January). What did the EEC/EU ever do for us? Not much apart from: providing 57% of our trade; structural funding to areas hit by industrial decline; clean beaches and rivers; cleaner air; lead free petrol; restrictions on landfill dumping; a recycling culture; cheaper mobile charges; cheaper air travel; improved consumer protection and food labelling; a ban on growth hormones and other harmful food additives; better product safety; single market competition bringing quality improvements and better industrial performance; breakup of monopolies; Europe-wide patent and copyright protection; no paperwork or customs for exports throughout the single market; price transparency and removal of commission on currency exchanges across the eurozone; freedom to travel, live and work across Europe; funded opportunities for young people to undertake study or work placements abroad; access to European health services; labour protection and enhanced social welfare; smoke-free workplaces; equal pay legislation; holiday entitlement; the right not to work more than a 48-hour week without overtime; strongest wildlife protection in the world; improved animal welfare in food production; EU funded research and industrial collaboration; EU representation in international forums; bloc EEA negotiation at the WTO; EU diplomatic efforts to uphold the nuclear no-proliferation treaty; European arrest warrant; cross border policing to combat human trafficking, arms and drug smuggling; counter terrorism intelligence; European civil and military co-operation in post-conflict zones in Europe and Africa; support for democracy and human rights across Europe and beyond; investment across Europe contributing to better living standards and educational, social and cultural capital.

All of this is nothing compared with its greatest achievements: the EU has for 60 years been the foundation of peace between European neighbours after centuries of bloodshed. It furthermore assisted the extraordinary political, social and economic transformation of 13 former dictatorships, now EU members, since 1980. Now the union faces major challenges brought on by neo-liberal globalisation, and worsened by its systemic weaknesses. It is taking measures to overcome these. We in the UK should reflect on whether our net contribution of £7bn out of total government expenditure of £695bn is good value. We must play a full part in enabling the union to be a force for good in a multipolar global future.

A Cuckoo
in the Curriculum

Part 4

The Future

Chapter 14

THE WATERWAYS:
PARTNERSHIPS POLICIES AND POLITICS

Waterways For All?

This final chapter has a perspective on the inland waterways as a national resource for combating social exclusion and disadvantage. While the waterways were built in the nineteenth century to be a reliable artery for trade at a time before tarmac and motor transport, the first half of the twentieth century saw the abandonment of sails and horses and the widespread introduction of the diesel engine as the motive power for barges and narrowboats. Since the Second World War, freight transportation has been in decline and a new purpose for the waterways, brought to public attention in a 1996 report, *Britain's Inland Waterways—An Undervalued Asset*, has been found in leisure and tourism, This has been accompanied by a realisation that if the canals and rivers of the UK could be a playground for boating enthusiasts, they could also provide a medium for education and training. A 2009 report for Government by the Inland Waterways Advisory Council said:

> *Crewing a boat is a new and exciting experience for most people and immediately engages interest. The variety of required skills means that most people however lacking in confidence, can find a suitable niche, while the efficient operation of a boat requires co-operation and team work. Canal and river boats move slowly, safety concerns are easily handled and crew members can be given early responsibility without feeling under unreasonable pressure.*

> *Inland waterways also have the additional advantage of being local to many communities…(meaning) that people can be helped within their own community and this brings considerable social benefits.*

As well as showing how these uses of the waterways have been developed nationally over the last thirty years largely through the efforts of the National Community Boats Association (NCBA), the chapter also sheds light on attitudes and policies that threaten the success celebrated by the poet and lyricist Benjamin Zephaniah in his foreword to *Glide*,[1] a collection of poems and stories about the canals written and collected by primary school children living in the Handsworth district of Birmingham:

> *When I was a young boy at school in Birmingham I used to go down to the canal and gaze in wonder. I just knew that the canal was not made to be so empty, and so I would wonder*

what it was used for. Why was it there and what did it do? Then a teacher told me about the history of the canal and the people who would have used it. This only helped to fuel my imagination and interest in this mysterious place… With our new-found confidence we must continue to appreciate our environment fully and take to the waters. I see the inland waterways as another way of enjoying the city and a new way of appreciating the space we live in; we must go for it — it's ours. I'm with Glide *because* Glide *sets out to support the Black community in embarking on this new journey. It's all about an increased understanding of our needs and a willingness to break down barriers.*

Glide was published in 2004 by the NCBA at the same time as the Inland Waterways Amenity Advisory Council (IWAAC) had been expressing a worry that government was not doing enough to promote the inland waterways among minority ethnic communities. IWAAC's 2001 report, *The Inland Waterways: towards greater social inclusion* had taken the view that government departments should work together to do everything possible to 'increase the social value of waterways and remove barriers to increased use by those who are economically, socially, physically, sensorily and in any other way disadvantaged'.[2] A further IWAAC[3] report had shown that exclusion was not confined to the communities represented by Ben Zephaniah;

The evidence reveals that those from the Asian communities are less likely than other ethnic groups to visit waterways. In Blackburn, for example, a 1999 study by Groundwork found members of the Asian Muslim community 'adamant in their dislike of the canal' and not surprisingly, few made visits. The BW (British Waterways) Birmingham survey also provided evidence that Asians are both less likely to visit waterways and have a more negative perception than those from the white or black communities.

This meant that whole sections of society had come to the conclusion that the canals were not for them. After all, the commonest sight on the waterways was of a white middle aged man at the wheel of an expensive cruiser. Was not this a sign that the inland waterways were the playground for the well off? When was the last time a black or disabled person or even a woman had appeared on the front cover of a waterways magazine steering a boat, or for that matter doing anything.

IWAC found itself re-stating the problem as recently as 2009. In *Using the inland waterways to combat the effects of social exclusion*[4] it maintained that:

To date the story of social exclusion and the inland waterways has mostly been very gloomy. In the face of uncomfortable changes in society including the fragmentation of families, the increase in the prison population and the alienation of young people in some ethnic groups, the Government has given increased priority to policies to regenerate communities and enhance community cohesion. Unfortunately the contribution that could be made by the waterways was not recognised in Waterways for Tomorrow[5] *and has not been recognised since.*

The following year, in 2010, the incoming Coalition Government, intent on showing its political muscle, consigned IWAC to a widely advertised 'bonfire of the quangos'.[6] Other public bodies sent to burn at the stake by Defra included the Potato Council and numerous agricultural wages boards considered to be past their sell-by date. It was a sad ending to an organisation whose corporate intellect and determination had kept the future of Britain's waterways well and truly anchored in broad social policy and always with the best interests of users and navigation authorities at heart. Apart from its chair who received a modest honorarium, IWAC members were unpaid volunteers. In 2010, the last year of its life, the organisation cost the taxpayer a mere £137,570 probably less than the annual cost to navigation authorities of removing shopping trolleys from their waterways. For the first time for forty two years it meant there was no independent body advising on the future of the inland waterways in England and Wales.

In 2011 the Coalition Government produced *A New Era for the Waterways* — a report which was intended to introduce a new look British Waterways prior to its re-organisation into the Canal & River Trust. However, the document skated round questions of social exclusion by making watered down references to volunteering and economic development. Nowhere did it grasp the nettle and publicly endorse IWAC's recommendation that the NCBA's work in communities should be supported. (see Appendix 2 for a full statement of NCBA's position)

In spite of the of the Government's declared commitment to localism, it was getting more difficult for organisations to influence national policy, a trend illustrated by the disgraceful decision to publish *New Era for the Waterways* before the formal public consultation period had ended.

But who had been raising the dust? NCBA never afraid to fight exclusion but living permanently on the margins of influence and IWAC tasked by parliament with bringing evidence of need for change and improvement but regarded as unnecessary by the Coalition Government as politicians loosened their ties with the waterways. I had the pleasure and privilege to be involved with both of these 'dissident' organisations; firstly as chair of NCBA for several years and then as an enthusiastic member of IWAC [7] led until its abolition, by John Edmonds.[8]

But it is now time to consider community boats in general and the National Community Boats Association in particular.

Community Boats

In 2007 I made a presentation to the Inland Waterways World Canal Conference in Liverpool under the title *'Access for All' is not enough*. I wanted to show how local waterways can be used not only as a recreational resource but further exploited to help communities achieve regeneration and inclusion objectives in a popular and effective way. I went on to explain:

Social inclusion is not only about providing wheelchair ramps and towpaths with good surfaces; it is also about actively inviting, including and involving excluded people in the pleasure and excitement that draws us to the canals and rivers of Britain. More than that, it is then about using the waterways to help improve health and employment prospects, increase training opportunities, reduce crime and bring many people living on big estates in cities their first experience of the countryside. It's the seeking out and the follow-up that make the difference. Put another way, 'Boating for All' is a utopian aspiration unless we reach out to the communities and individuals who can benefit most from the magic of the waterways and positively encourage them to get involved. An easy first step is often through community boating.

As a result of cuts and changing fashions numbers are beginning to decline, but in 2015 there are about one hundred community and voluntary organisations in England, Scotland, Wales and Northern Ireland, not all of them NCBA members, now using the waterways as a resource to meet the social and economic needs of their locality or region. Examples from the four nations of the UK show the scope of the work. The first is Belfast Barge.

> *On a barge in Belfast's river Lagan is* Lagan Legacy, *a charity that was established to save artefacts from Harland & Woolf, the world famous shipyard which built over 2000 ships including* Titanic. *Rather than pass the records to a national archive, the charity decided that it would itself display the documents and tell the Lagan story. The* Belfast Barge *at Lanyon Quay is now home to the charity's permanent exhibition using artefacts and oral histories to tell the* Greatest Story Never Told *about the river and the city's industrial heritage. A schools programme has been developed by teachers working with charity staff to meet national curriculum requirements. There are guided visits to the barge and spoken histories have been put together by shipyard workers who wanted to get involved. An outreach programme takes stories and artefacts from Belfast's common heritage into the classrooms of schools in unionist and republican areas which are unable to afford the cost of transport to the barge.* Lagan Legacy's *place in the community is confirmed by the number of seafarers who come to thank the organisation for its conservation of their untold story, a narrative that is part of a brighter future for Belfast and Northern Ireland.*
> (Lagan Legacy brochure)

When I visited *Lagan Legacy* in the course of assessing projects entered for the Waterways Renaissance Awards,[9] I was much moved by meeting a man from England who had come to the province as a soldier in the British Army during the worst times of the Troubles. He loved Ireland so much that he decided to stay in Belfast and after leaving the army, worked his way up the academic ladder. After O-Levels, A-Levels, a first degree and then a PhD in Irish history, he was appointed to a post at Belfast University and in his spare time now works as a volunteer for *Lagan Legacy*.

A similar project involving the mid-Wales town of Brecon in celebration of the 200 year old Monmouth & Brecon Canal was *Brecon Gateway* entered for the same Awards in 2010. The canal had contributed to the Industrial Revolution in south Wales; the network of horse-drawn tramways and railroads linking the canal with the Heads of the Valleys iron workings, provided the theme for a project to attract local people to the waterway through the creation of art works. There were four parts: at a welcome point for visitors was a seat in the shape of a working boat with maps and information linking the town to the canal and Brecon Beacons National Park: a mosaic at Brecon Basin showed imaginary scenes from the history of the canal, based on drawings by children from Ysgol y Bannau who had listened to the childhood reminiscences of a local narrowboat captain: Brecon Brownies had worked with a professional sculptor to design and build a life-size wooden sculpture of a man and his horse-drawn tram: and finally there was *Matthew's Passion*, a specially commissioned drama about a boy who lived beside the canal. A cast of sixty adults and children from Theatr Ffynnon,[10] all with additional learning needs, performed the play in Brecon's canalside theatre in front of an audience of 750 people.

In Scotland the Seagull Trust holds sway with centres at Ratho, Falkirk, Kirkintilloch and Inverness all providing day cruises for disabled people of all ages. In July 2003 a new residential holiday canal boat, *Marion Seagull,* was launched. The new boat allowed families to cruise the lowland waterways for a few days at their leisure. As a result of successful promotion and fund raising, all trips were offered free of charge.

On the Wirral peninsula in north west England the Wirral Community Narrowboat Trust, winner of the community and volunteering category in the Living Waterways Awards in 2014, has been operating for 30 years. The charity's two boats can be hired for day or residential expeditions and are crewed by volunteers who work to a nationally recognised code of conduct for community boats. The group's website states, 'Our trips have proved very popular and many of our clients, mostly senior citizens, youth groups and disabled people, return year after year to enjoy the tranquility of the canals and countryside'.[11]

An Association

It took until 1985 for *Sobriety* to emerge from its Goole Grammar School cocoon and spread its wings in search of life elsewhere. A circular in the same year from Barrie Slowen, a teacher working for Coventry Waterways Scheme, announced that in Milton Keynes was a narrowboat charity eager to discover other 'multi-user groups'. This was a term invented by the British Waterways Board to classify boat operators who did not fit its standard categories of licence fee payers, such as 'private' or 'commercial,' and served as a general description for charities or other voluntary groups. (The term 'community boat' was not yet current on this side of the Atlantic even though it had been in use since the 1930s in the United States). So a multi-user group we were and it did not take long to be saddled with the obvious acronym of MUGS. However at a meeting in the small museum of Canal House Coventry in December 1985, the MUGS from London, the Midlands and Yorkshire decided that the label would do nothing to commend their high minded ambitions to those in authority, and after a vote of twelve to three in favour of change we became the Community Boats Association (CBA).[12] It was later alleged by one member present, that the three against were diehards for tradition whose pleasure in their youth had been to spend a week cruising what were at that time the the open sewers of the Birmingham canal system and then to sit smelling each other in the unventilated intimacy of a narrowboat cabin.

The early meetings of the Association allowed members to share experiences and compare problems. Not the least of concerns was the development of standards and qualifications that would make the waterways a safer place for the many organisations attracted to members' boats. We were aware that the Royal Yachting Association and the Department of Transport had their own courses and examinations but we needed certification that would guarantee proficiency in the additional discipline of boat and group management. The eventual outcome was the Certificate in Community Boat Management[13] which British Waterways and the Maritime & Coastguard Agency later recommended as a qualification to complement their own regulations. Within the Maritime & Coastguard Agency (MCA) we had a good friend in Julie Carlton who, in addition to providing the secretariat for the public inquiry into the *Marchioness* disaster,[14] was the convenor of the working group which developed the MCA's Small Passenger Boat Code. Immediately after its publication in 2002, Julie and her colleague took the Code on a tour of the UK and made presentations to the community boat organisations likely to be affected by it.

Until January 2002 when the Association was the beneficiary of a grant from the National Lottery and able to employ four full time staff, the organisation was held together by two volunteers: Paul Treble who ran the Disabled Afloat Riverboats Trust in Gloucester, and Barrie Slowen already mentioned, who was a pioneer of community boat development. Another who held office in early days was Miranda Jaggers whose Thames-based *Richmond Venturer* had been converted to community use with a wave of the wand by Anneka Rice in her TV series *Challenge Anneka*. Tim Snowden and Jenny Thorne of Hillingdon Narrowboat Association in London were also involved, as were Ron Bailey and Roger Hobson, senior colleagues in Doncaster Youth Service who headed up CBA training and qualifications. In the nineteen eighties it seemed that all aspects of community boating were experimental. There were no approved measures of competence; we had to devise accreditation that was flexible enough to test performance on different kinds of inland waterways from the tidal Humber to the sleepy canals of the Welsh borders, and then provide the training to meet the standards which we ourselves had approved. VAT, insurance and the EU's Working Time Directive had to be demystified and British Waterways and the Association of Pleasure Craft Operators had to be persuaded that our free or discounted expeditions were not threatening their livelihood. It helped that meetings were attended by an increasing number of members and were held at venues all over the UK. Barrie Slowen caught the spirit of the times:

> For the rest of the eighties when the culture of individualism was in full swing, more and more people came to the CBA's quarterly meetings at different waterways venues around the country. Project workers wanted to talk about common problems and issues relating to their work with the widest possible range of community groups and the use of an equally diverse range of craft. They wanted to share their ideas about safe practice when their user groups were on the water; they were keen to make it easier for people with disabilities to get on board; they wanted to know how they could develop resources for the National Curriculum and how better training could improve group safety and welfare. The list seemed endless but they discovered that there was a spider's web of social and educational spin-offs for users and operators if they kept talking to each other.

Barrie had far sighted ambitions, one of which was to persuade Coventry LEA to pay for a residential boat on the Canal du Nivernais.[15] One of the prettiest waterways in France, it would encourage the city's schoolchildren to learn French and enjoy French culture. For the Community Boats Association he set three aims:

> To make sure that as many people as possible knew about the work that was taking place on community boats. To government ministers, managers, TV companies and newspaper editors, the CBA would show its best side by highlighting model projects:

> To spread the idea that by spending intensive periods as part of a group, a residential experience on one of the CBA's boats could be a catalyst for change in a person's life.

Experience has suggested that community boating was an effective medium for volunteers and individuals in groups to raise their self esteem and re-assess their attitudes and aspirations:

These thoughts were probably less commonplace than they are today but there was prescience in his conclusion:

I cannot avoid suggesting that a political sea-change is needed before any government will begin to experiment with initiatives as an alternative to more and more prisons, to more schools being razed to the ground by their own pupils, to some inner cities becoming no-go areas and to many elderly people becoming isolated in their own communities.

While Barrie Slowen had the ideas, Paul Treble looked after the stamps and photocopier, producing leaflets, agendas, minutes and occasional papers for debate. With a membership of 120 organisations, this was no mean undertaking and required an approach that left members in no doubt about who was the boss. Paul was a kindly person, intensely proud of the Association and nothing if not decisive. (He still runs a successful enterprise based in Gloucester that uses other projects' boats to provide residential holidays for the Association's traditional clients.) Not all members however, including some in senior positions in local authorities, were used to taking orders, and found it difficult to submit to Paul's administrative demands. Things finally came to a head at a meeting in a Salvation Army Hall in Mirfield on the Calder & Hebble Navigation, where, under a large wooden shield proclaiming the Army's 'Blood and Fire' war-cry against sin, battle commenced between trustees. My own view was that Paul had too much to do and was receiving little help from his critics. Through first rate administration and a professional knowledge of IT he was holding the organisation together and deserved better acknowledgement of his efforts.

There was however a brighter side to the conflict; the Association had hitherto relied entirely on a volunteer to maintain its secretariat, an arrangement that was rapidly becoming impractical. On the other hand and in spite of wearisome argument, the CBA remained forward-looking and continued to plan for the future. It was a combination of problems and opportunities that appealed to Marks & Spencer plc and was an important factor in persuading the company that the donation of a salary of a part time worker would be a cause that met all the requirements of its community involvement policy. For the six years from 1994 to 2000, M&S supported the work of the Association with a grant of £8000 per year and it made all the difference; Barrie was released from his post with Coventry LEA and became the Association's training officer while Paul was able to hand over some of the admin and get back to his daytime job of being an IT consultant.

Hartshill – Salad Days

In 2001 when M&S support came to an end, the Association applied to what was then the Community Fund of the National Lottery and was awarded a three year grant which, when match funded by British Waterways, enabled the Association to employ a manager, two members of staff to look after training and marketing, and a full time clerical assistant. Taking a lead from David Fletcher, its chief executive, and Ian White, north-east regional manager, British Waterways did everything it could at this time to support community boating. It saw the Association's work as a natural extension of its own purpose to get as many people as possible onto the waterways, but also felt an obligation towards individuals who were denied a normal life, often suffering the added handicap of a low income. It also had regard to an organisation which, through its own efforts during the previous fifteen years, was becoming a national voice for community boats. However BW's support did not end with match funding the Lottery grant; it made available an office and meeting rooms in its Grade 2 listed premises at Hartshill on the Coventry canal near Atherstone, having first spent forty thousand pounds on repairs and decoration. In autumn 2002 after advertising in national media, the trustees appointed Izzy Kitt to manage the new staff and develop the Association. She was well qualified for the post.

Ten years previously Izzy had come from teaching on Hull prison's remand wing to be *Sobriety*'s Arts Development Worker. At the time she was completing her MA in sculpture and put her experience to good use to establish a waterways museum in *Sobriety*'s new HQ. One feature of the museum was a derelict grain barge, acquired for £2,000 from a wandering engineer, which she turned into a conference and exhibition space doubling as a project workshop for schools. 1998 saw her taking the initiative to replicate *Sobriety* in Rotherham through months of meetings with local residents, regeneration professionals and sympathetic British Waterways managers. Through the late nineties she was also managing the process of building a £650,000 extension to the Waterways Museum which required endless negotiations with the regional development agency, architects, museum professionals and the Heritage Lottery Fund. After the extension was opened in autumn 2001 she successfully applied for a Millennium Fellowship to research and publish *A Beginner's Guide to Social Inclusion* for The Waterways Trust.

When she took up her appointment with the Community Boats Association in January 2002, the many challenges included three years of internal power struggles which had weakened the organisation's capacity to develop training and public relations. Her policy was to ignore the factions as far as possible and to support the new team at Hartshill to improve services to members. The Association added 'National' to its name and the marketing and training officers went off on grand tours round the country to give personal advice and occasionally some money to community boat groups needing their services. Since by the end of 18 months the team had met most of the outputs required by the Lottery, Izzy sensibly decided to consolidate progress by applying to the West Midlands Social & Economic Partnership (WEMSEP) for a research grant of £75,000 to get 15 groups in the Birmingham area to identify the essentials of a successful community boat project. There were three important outcomes: *The Lifejacket*[16] was a handbook for members; a national conference in Sheffield paved the way for a more democratic future, and *Glide* gave NCBA a groundbreaking link with the black community in Birmingham. Staff and members turned out in force to represent the Association at national rallies and exhibitions where they handed out teeshirts and children's goodies and gave information to curious visitors including on one occasion, Timothy West and Prunella Scales. When the Maritime & Coastguard Agency turned its attention to small passenger boats, Izzy represented NCBA on the working party in Southampton and backed policies that would safeguard members' interests as well as encourage them to aim for high standards of operation. By the end of 2003 however, she knew that the good times could not last; the end of the three year Lottery grant was looming and it was important to plan for the future. The Association needed to turn its attention to social enterprise and be ready to make contracts with bodies like WEMSEP which were less about waterways *per se* and more about using the waterways to assist outside organisations achieve their own aims. On the other hand the reports *Reducing Re-offending* and *Every Child Matters*, pointed the way to possible work with prisoners' families and new developments in training. The result was *Family Learning on Water* (FLOW) and a *Y-Afloat* youth programme being tested and launched.

Having sorted out issues of governance and registered NCBA as a centre for Criminal Records Bureau checks, the Hartshill team successfully managed the setbacks caused by a follow-up Lottery application being turned down. Soon after the departure of David Fletcher and Ian White from British Waterways, the Association received notice of BW's intention to charge £11,000 a year for the lease of the Hartshill office. It was an absurd demand and forced NCBA to move its office to the Yorkshire Waterways Museum in Goole, far away from what had been a convenient central location in Warwickshire. The premises subsequently had no tenant and BW had no income. Other money saving measures protected the training programme by allowing the Training Officer to become self-employed, and the cost of member services was reduced by making more use of e-mail and telephone. The budget was managed so that to the outsider it had the miraculous substance of the loaves and fishes in the story of the Feeding of the Five Thousand. Another great hope was that the Association would support the idea of regional committees. When it became impossible on a tiny budget employing part time staff, to continue the work of developing community boat projects through visits and special events, Izzy saw regionalisation as a way of spreading the message of good practice and of giving young people the opportunity to feel part of a young people's waterway movement. In this connection she was proud to be invited to Doncaster Mansion House for the annual presentation of NCBA certificates to young people by the elected mayor. It confirmed her belief that the Association

National Community Boats Association – Trustee meeting at Ratho on the Forth & Clyde Canal

needed imaginative and energetic leadership to reflect social diversity and capture the interest of young people. The same conviction sustained her through the hard times and enabled her to raise enough money to maintain development during her time in office. So what went wrong? Why was an application to the Lottery for further funding so surprisingly rejected?

It was clear at the time and is still clear that Hartshill policy uncompromisingly followed NCBA's founding principle to promote equal opportunities on the waterways. *The Lifejacket* training manual went far beyond mere advice to steerers; its introduction stated unequivocally that NCBA:

> …*is particularly concerned with improving access to boating for disadvantaged people*
> *from disadvantaged communities. It promotes the inland waterways…as an opportunity*
> *for meeting individuals' social, educational and recreational needs.*

A quarterly magazine, *the cut*, edited by Hartshill's marketing officer Dave Bailey between 2002 and 2005, was a fine example of eye-catching journalism which used short articles, pictures and up-to-date news stories not only to link NCBA groups with one another and the 'outside' world, but to encourage new groups onto the waterways. Similarly *FLOW, Y-Afloat,* the publication,*Glide*, a women's forum led by Jenny Thorne, and the participation of trustees and members in national exhibitions and events, were all evidence of the team's determination to challenge the curiously widespread, *"We've always done it like this."* Writing as chair in the February 2003 edition of *the cut*, I tried to set the agenda for the coming year:

> *For my part I intend that the coming year will be exciting but not comfortable. Changes in*
> *governance are needed : we should be preparing new structures to support the timeshare*
> *groups: the Training Standards panel needs re-direction: membership criteria need reform*
> *so that groups which boat only one a year can join us: officers for election at the AGM*
> *should have to produce a manifesto based on NCBA's vision: the staff team needs to expand*
> *and perhaps find new premises in Birmingham: the claim to be national should be justified*
> *by the appointment of regional support workers: more money needs to be raised and a*
> *working group set up to help with this.*
>
> *In short we need internal structures that better meet the expectations of partners in a*
> *changing outside world, and committee members and staff who are fluent in the language*
> *of the new market place and can move freely among its traders. That way NCBA members*
> *will get the best bargains and be able to sell their product to a queue of customers.*

Grandiloquent if you like but vital for the 'equal opps' branding' that Dave Bailey was trying to give the Association through his design of logos, displays and indeed his very likeable manner which was far from stuffy. (As if to advertise his free and easy approach he spent several hours during an NCBA open day at Hartshill handing out brochures while wearing the suffocating costume of a interplanetary ape.) Behind the scenes however, were members of the Training Standards panel who regarded all this as trivia, irrelevant to what they saw as the main purpose of NCBA. Accreditation of training procedures had been the exclusive business during the eighties and nineties and should remain so. When, in a meeting about governance, the chair of the panel appeared to be saying that he and his colleagues would take over the management of the Association and raised his fists, it was clear that this was an attempt at a *coup d'état*. It was a re-run of the spectacle in the Mirfield Salvation Army Hall, frequent enough around the world, but less frequent in a suburb of Nuneaton. I was relieved when James Bryan, a heavily built training officer with the Metropolitan Police who had recently been elected vice-chair, came to the rescue. The outcome was that the reformers won the day, but victory was at a cost. The old guard crept away to nurse its wounds and probably conspired eighteen months later, to scupper any hope of a second successful lottery application.[17] In the meantime at the 2004 AGM I made a nervously confident report to members:

> First of all, your trustees have set big store by instituting a structure of governance guaranteeing that NCBA can take its place alongside other similar national networks. Without a recognisable and respected mechanism for making democratic decisions no organisation can survive for very long.
>
> We now have a body of 12 trustees recruited from the regions who attend meetings and make responsible decisions. There are also three sub-committees reporting to the trustees. The training committee now chaired by Eddie Warburton and advised by Paul Bryan, the new national training officer, is carrying forward the work of improving our accreditation schemes through the Open College Network: it is also bringing forward proposals for new kinds of endorsements, for people with a disability and groups operating on tideways.
>
> Jenny Thorne has headed the Women on the Waterways committee which is tackling barriers, sometimes never even acknowledged, to women's participation in community boat management. A smaller personnel committee has been dealing with staff appointments, terms and conditions, and remuneration.
>
> The smooth operation of the democratic process is characterised by flow of ideas and debate about priorities. A well attended conference in Sheffield in October 2003, entitled *Planning for the Future*, set us two priorities — region based development and national sustainability. The process of achieving these has begun. Early in February 2004 forty member organisations participated in a week of regional events in Glasgow, Doncaster, Runcorn, Leicester and London. A follow-on programme is being repeated next week in the same centres... We all look forward to even greater involvement that will lead eventually to regional committees and possibly to the appointment of regional staff.

A post mortem on Hartshill might say there was nothing unusual about splits between traditionalists and reformers. Examples from history and contemporary politics are too numerous to mention, but I think it was a pity that NCBA was deprived of the momentum to put many of its (to most people uncontroversial) proposals into effect. There was so much unfinished business, a fact that was brought home to me by a request from IWAC to look into possible practical links between prisons and community boats along the lines of *Sobriety*'s arrangement with HMPs Hatfield and Askham Grange. First I discussed the possibilities with a senior official in the Department of Justice then after doing research into the prisons that might be interested, I contacted respective Education or Task Force officers with some outline suggestions. Without exception the prisons were up for it. It was the boating organisations that showed themselves to be reactionary and prejudiced. I did not blame them entirely; they were faced with having to make a decision out of the blue. During the Hartshill period there would have been better preparation and early personal contact between prison staff and groups.

After Hartshill

Be this as it may, it would be wrong to give the impression that NCBA died with the departure of Izzy Kitt and her team. After a short interval the torch passed to volunteer vice-chair, James Bryan, who was a trustee of South West Herts Narrowboat Project. This was a Hemel Hempstead charity based on *Pickles Folly*, a vessel whose name I am assured has no connection with a well known Conservative politician. James became NCBA chair in 2005 and was assisted by vice-chair Trevor Roberts, a longstanding NCBA member who at that time managed the boating side of Bradford Motor Education Project. Trevor was a good manager and had many years' experience working directly with young people. He describes how his journey through community boating began after a conversation with his great friend Eric Gibbs,[18] founder of the Motor Education Project:

> *I was a trustee of the charity that Eric was developing as a diversion-from-crime scheme using motor vehicles to engage young people. I had passed the former offices of Leeds & Liverpool Canal Company on Manor Road Bradford many times but was not aware of any canal. Despite my lack of knowledge I began the task of developing a marine division of the Project based on Eric's argument that boats had engines. My first adventure was to take a group of young people and volunteers on a voyage to London where we were welcomed by a member of the National Community Boats Association, Camden's Pirate Castle. A weekend cruise into the capital introduced us to a new world and gave us ideas of how to develop our project. We met eight boat projects including the people from the Truman Trust in Walsall who were mid way through a two week challenge involving four groups of young people taking two boats on a return trip from Birmingham to London.*

This was the kind of networking that, after taking over from me as chair in 2006, James Bryan highlighted in his AGM address. With National Voice, Training, and Organisational Standards, Networking would be one of the Four Pillars of the Association. To be fair to history, these subjects had always been NCBA's preoccupation; the clever bit was to publicise 'Four Pillars' as a mnemonic to remind people what the Association was about. Looking back he said:

> *NCBA has had an accelerated development over the last few years, mainly thanks to our ability to employ a full-time staff team to work on projects. One of the challenges during that time has been to keep individual members involved and progressing at the same speed as others in the Association.*

Put more directly it was true that failure to secure a second period of Lottery funding had robbed the Association of the means to catch up with itself. The Hartshill team's work had been ground breaking but in spite of its best efforts through *the cut*, visits, presentations and courses, the team had not had long enough to 'spread the word' among organisations that often needed persuasion as much as information. The failure of the proposed link with prisons through the Department of Justice illustrated the point. The team had done its best but with a membership of over one hundred organisations it was a job that was impossible to tackle simultaneously with the kinds of development promised in the original Lottery application.

Communications would remain a problem that would not go away. The successful cultivation of a National Voice often required trustees to approach questions in depth over a longish period with evidence presented well enough to convince other national bodies, not least the government or British Waterways. But the effect was criticism of the board by members for being too 'national' and of the membership by the board for shutting its eyes to matters that were not of immediate domestic importance. In this connection I remember going to a meeting near Huddersfield organised for Robin Evans, British Waterways CEO, as part of his round Britain tour, to tell boaters about BW's plans for the future. The audience seemed to have little time for 'affairs of state' and spent its time chewing the rag about bollards and lock closures. This was in spite of the fact that local area managers held monthly sessions to listen to boaters' frustrations and investigate solutions.

The debate continues. Should the NCBA act as the voice of community boating nationally or should it exist simply to provide training and office services for its members?

However, with the resignation or redundancy of the Hartshill team, both James and Trevor were determined not to allow twenty years of NCBA development disappear without trace. Their first action was to recruit Diane Taylor from the last days of the re-located Hartshill team to be their finance manager. Diane stayed with NCBA for the next eight years, coping with the Association's administration as well as looking after its funds. She was competent with accounts and fearless in her dealings with members, especially the ones who might have thought they could do the job better than her. Another recruit was Derek Stansfield who had been an inspector for the Adventure Activities Licensing Authority in Cardiff, set up in 1996 in the wake of the Lime Bay kayaking disaster.[19] Derek is now chair of the Association and has worked with colleagues to devise, revamp, monitor and accredit training procedures and objectives that 'allow young people to experience exciting and stimulating activities outdoors without being exposed to avoidable risks of death or disabling injury'.

In spite of occasional local difficulties, NCBA remains a popular umbrella for many community boat organisations.

A questionnaire sent out to 68 groups in 2010 requested information about location, training, access, significant users, racial mix, finances and sources of income. Here are some of the more interesting findings from the document:

There were 68 organisations in the Association which operated 116 boats on the rivers and canals of the UK with a total daily passenger capacity of 1,405. Days in the year available to users were 15,314.

Thirty three organisations were accredited training centres with staff qualified to teach and assess qualifications accredited by the Maritime & Coastguard Agency in its Small Passenger Boat Code. The certificated qualifications were Complete Crew, Boat Handling, Community Boat Management, and Trainer's Endorsement.

Of the 68 member organisations 23 worked with offenders, 19 with refugees, 20 with homeless people, 47 with people with mental health problems and, unsurprisingly, 50 with schools.

There were three organisations where white users were less than 40% of total users but only two organisations where Asian users made up more than 35% of the total.

The total number of users of NCBA boats and facilities in 2010 was 76,550. Each individual spent an average of five days (not necessarily consecutive days) with an organisation, giving a total of 749,765 passenger days for significant users. (This total excludes members of the general public who, for example, might pay for historical interest tours of Goole docks). Organisations were supported by 1,709 volunteers and about 200 paid staff.

The primary source of income for 47 organisations was donations, followed by grants (43), trading (31) and service agreements (17).

The Canal & River Trust

Some of these figures are startling and more than justify NCBA's expectation to be taken seriously at regional and national levels, especially in the light of the major event of the last five years — the emergence of the Canal & River Trust as a replacement for British Waterways. On July 2nd 2012 a quango gave birth to a charity.[20] Two years earlier in *Sobriety's* Review of 2010 under the pen name of 'Weedcutter' and the title of *A Cuckoo in the Voluntary Sector Nest?* I had looked forward to the event but also aired some questions:

It's common knowledge in the shadiest and most stagnant backwaters that on 1ˢᵗ April 2012 British Waterways will become a national waterways charity, severing its links with government and joining the great communion of saints and sinners in the voluntary and charitable sector. Already transitional trustees are being appointed and BW staff are preparing to re-design their identity badges. It goes without saying that like many community boat organisations Sobriety *looks forward to working with the new charity to promote and cherish the waterways. But how will the elderly incomer regard its new brothers and sisters? Will it join them in common endeavours or will it try and exploit them? Will it look for help to face and solve common problems or will it go it alone in competition for funds and public support? Never having been through infancy, will it be able to understand the predicament of less influential members of the family to which it belongs? The questions are worth asking because the answers are crucial to the future of community boating and possibly to the future of the new organisation.*

Historically Sobriety's *own relationship with British Waterways has been close. For the ten years from 1994–2004, BW saw the Project as a means of achieving its own aspiration to engage with communities which had few if any links to the waterways. Understandably BW's own priorities never included using the inland waterways to combat social exclusion directly but regional managers were eager to support organisations which knew how to use the waterways in this way. For example, in 2001 BW renovated its Hartshill building and leased it to the NCBA at a peppercorn rent. Then followed a promise of £10,000 a year match funding for a Lottery project to provide NCBA with full time staff to promote and encourage use of the waterways by people on low incomes who might have additional social handicaps or disabilities — young offenders or people with mental health problems such as dementia. Prior to this in 1998 BW joined* Sobriety, *Yorkshire Forward and Rotherham MBC to develop business units and a small park on the side of the South Yorkshire Canal at Swinton as well as making available its former workshops on a 99 year lease, again at a peppercorn rent. In Goole, the Dutch River Side road leading to the Yorkshire Waterways Museum was rebuilt at a cost of £7 million. If these were far sighted investments for improving access to the waterways in the broadest sense, they also showed that BW was happy to support voluntary organisations taking the lead in spheres of development outside its own immediate remit. Good evidence of such an enlightened view of partnership was BW Chief Executive Robin Evans's foreword to* Spring to Release, *a report published in 2003 by the* Sobriety *Project on how women in a re-settlement prison could use work experience on the inland waterways to help them return to normal life.*

Our more recent experience however is of a BW which is harder nosed, more distant, and less inclined to regard itself as partner in the voluntary sector nest. Indeed in respect of its 2010 boat licensing proposals, it is a cuckoo! The reforms which propose the abolition of the 60% licence discount for charities, have brought allegations from community organisations that BW is being high handed and stubborn. In one among many cases, Sobriety's *own licence payment to BW will increase from £4,000 per year to £12,000. Waterways charities will suffer similar unprecedented penalties instigated by an organisation which itself will soon be reliant on public good will. BW is talking of a concessionary phasing-in period but entreaties that the current proposals be scrapped and re-appraised by the New Waterways Charity are falling on deaf ears. BW assures its critics that there is no financial motive for the reform; it is being done to make the administration of the licence fee more manageable. However at its re-birth in 2012, the newly constituted charity will need to raise at least £20 million to complement its income from other sources. BW is promoting the National Trust as a model for its relationship with the public, in the hope that the inland waterways will prove as much an attraction as historic buildings and landscapes; it has created the post of Community Engagement Co-ordinator in its senior team and is revising its approach to volunteering; there is radical talk of prisons and probation being involved selectively with waterway regeneration schemes; interest in local communities has a new lease of life. This is to be welcomed. With it, one hopes, will come the view that more can be achieved by working together than by covert rivalry and exploitation (which is as rampant in the voluntary sector as anywhere else). It would be a pity if, in the interests of short term survival, the new charity promoted itself to contractors as the only reasonable channel for their funding.*

British Waterways did postpone a decision about licensing but its successor, the Canal & River Trust (C&RT), is still trying to get its act together. A full transcript of my January 2011 response to BW's proposals — *How British Waterways' proposals for licence reform will affect community boat charities: the case against the abolition of the charity discount* is at Appendix 3.

One of BW's more absurd proposals in January 2010 was to impose a supplementary fee if a community boat was based, 'within 500 metres of a public car park, public toilets, a pub, a restaurant, a café, tea room or coffee shop, or a visitor attraction such as a garden, museum or shopping mall'. It was suggested that a score-chart entry would determine the extent of liability for extra fees, presumably after a BW official had used his or her tape measure to calculate the distance between the two destinations. Discussions on this subject alone could well have occupied several hours of a BW senior manager's time during the consultation period. A more recent communication from the Canal & River Trust dated 8th December 2013 and entitled *Licensing of Community Boats: New proposals for discussion with representatives from the National Community Boats Association*, in a section entitled *Recognising the value of charitable work*, said:

> Now that we ourselves are a charity we need to agree to all fundraising activity that takes place on our land to ensure that there is no conflict of interest and that waterway visitors are not being overly targeted for contributions.

Vindictive enough, but a more sinister threat followed under the heading *Moorings and Property*:

> It should be noted that where discounted or free moorings are provided or the charity is occupying property owned by the Trust, it is intended to phase in market rate charging for these.

Many community boat organisations have 99 year leases on BW property which in some cases are discounted by 75%. Such an increase would call into question whether they had any future.

The real bone of contention however, was about whether or not a charity was a business. If it charged fees then it was a business, said BW, and should pay a commercial rate. BW and later the C&RT could not grasp that charities are not allowed to operate for private gain and cannot *be* businesses. On the other hand charity trustees, auditors and ultimately the Charity Commission expect them to operate in a *businesslike* manner. A charity is not a business but it may be *like* a business. I would have thought that the concept of a charitable business *not* being a private commercial business would have registered with the new C&RT trustees and managers.

In order to bring to an end four years of deadlock, NCBA suggested to C&RT that the two organisations might do a deal. In return for free licensing of all community boats and a service agreement to pay office costs, NCBA would undertake to act as BW's agent in the regulation of quality standards, boat safety, safeguarding of users and the appropriate training and monitoring of all community boat organisations. The arrangement would have relieved C&RT of the burden of trying to understand community boats and would have provided NCBA with additional income. Trevor Roberts was party to the discussions and makes clear his disappointment:

> The proposals were dismissed by the C&RT Trustees; it certainly appeared that the application of the new licence fees reflected a lack of understanding of the value of [NCBA] projects to the inland waterways. There is no doubt in my mind that the breadth and variety of community boating provides a bridge for C&RT to engage with some of our most challenging communities and hard-to-reach groups. As C&RT develops, if nothing else, it should recognise that NCBA members bring more than 76,000 people to the waterways each year and, with this figure in mind, be less defensive about its licensing policies. The

proposals we submitted, if accepted, would have ensured the protection of some of the most vulnerable people in our society.

I now sit on C&RT's north east partnership board. This gives me an insight into the complexities of running a large organisation, but I am irritated by being asked repeatedly to prove the value of our work, and this in spite of all the reports, presentations and case studies going back nearly 30 years.[21]

One of these reports was *Using Inland Waterways to Combat the Effects of Social Exclusion*. It was commissioned by Defra and launched in 2009 at the Yorkshire Waterways Museum by Dr Christine Johnstone, IWAC member and *Sobriety* trustee. It preceded the abolition of IWAC by one year and the re-birth of BW in the form of the C&RT by three years. It concluded that:

The inland waterways can be used effectively to combat social exclusion. In spite of strong recommendations from IWAC and AINA (Association of Inland Navigation Authorities), little progress has been made. There is a need for a change of perception and understanding by the whole of UK Government and by the navigation authorities: a step change is necessary.

The same report made six recommendations:

IWAC and Defra should continue research into the benefits of using inland waterways to combat social exclusion

The updated policy statement that will replace Waterways for Tomorrow *should contain a section showing the advantages of using inland waterways to combat social exclusion*

The UK Government should recognise and promote the value of inland waterway projects that combat social exclusion

Local authorities, Regional Development Agencies and other public bodies should be encouraged by the UK Government to recognise the potential benefit of using inland waterways to combat social exclusion

The National Community Boats Association should be recognised as the infrastructure organisation for accreditation, capacity building and promotion, and should receive a measure of public funding to carry out these duties

Working with AINA, IWAC should develop models of good practice and these should be widely disseminated to show the practical stages by which partners can begin to use their inland waterways to meet the needs of individuals facing significant social problems

Defra's response to the report is at Appendix 4. The Head of Environment Agency & Waterways, replying on behalf of the Minister, was sympathetic with IWAC's expectation that the waterways should contribute to the battle against social exclusion but otherwise she was quite clear that there would be no government initiative or cash to support IWAC's recommendations. She went on to say:

It will be important for IWAC to continue to work with us so that we can ensure we can highlight and promote this activity to local and regional bodies. But I suspect this will need further hard work over the period covered by the strategy to make further progress.

The report and Defra's response to it were subsequently overtaken by events. A new government was elected and a new national body for the waterways came into existence. Since the publication of *Using Inland Waterways to Combat the Effects of Social Exclusion* nothing favourable to community boating, save occasional grunts of approval, has happened at a national level and there is no reason to be sanguine or optimistic about the future. With the advent of C&RT we were promised a personality change; C&RT would be different from British Waterways. But so far in its dealings with community boating, the organisation has done little either to change its appearance or to rebalance its hormones. What a pity that C&RT's managers do not launch out into the deep of wholehearted support of community boating rather than going fishing for licence fees in a nasty little pond. They should understand that their policies are an obstacle to social inclusion however much they aspire to be its advocate.

The Future Of Community Boats

The economic downturn which took hold of the UK in 2008, led to serious restrictions on local authority spending, and concern by councils that they would have difficulty in maintaining even front-line services. Cuts were made not only to second line services such as museums and galleries but more deeply into youth provision so that some authorities have completely abandoned any attempt at traditional youth work. Also, throughout much of the period covered by this book, many council services have been privatised. The trend has been to create independently governed or owned organisations and then to provide grant aid which could be withdrawn if the organisation was not up to scratch or if the authority became short of money. *Sobriety* has been a case in point; it was never part of a local authority but it did receive funding in its early days in return for an agreement to provide planned activities for children at risk. However in 1993 it was threatened with closure when Humberside County Council decided it needed to save £40,000 of the grant aid currently being allocated to the Project. The threat was only lifted after lobbying of members led, allegedly, to an offer by the chair of the highways department to postpone the construction of a roundabout and use the savings to defray *Sobriety's* threatened deficit.

These days, local authority departments fare no better than voluntary organisations. In 2014 Northampton Borough Council sold an ancient Egyptian statue for £15.8 million from its museum collection as part of a plan to balance its books. The penalties were an Arts Council decision to remove accreditation of the Borough's museums and the withdrawl of a £200,000 grant by the Heritage Lottery Fund.[22] The bottom line for community boats is that councils will not entertain any increase in expenditure unless it is forced on them by central government or assists with a priority service. 'Friends at court' whether members or officers, have less influence than in the past; they have to toe the line in political decisions which offer no room for manoeuvre. The days of experimentation and innovation, so welcome in the nineteen seventies and eighties, have well and truly gone. The *only* route to funding by local authorities seems to be through commissioning and contracts, and, as we have seen in earlier chapters an organisation has to be very fleet of foot and confident of success if it is going to tie its future into arrangements of this kind. Even in circumstances where contracts are feasible, charities say that cashflow is obstructed by long delays, not so much in payments for services, but by the time it takes the contractor to plug loopholes, real or imagined, that relate to legal and personnel matters in the wording of a service agreement. Certainly *Sobriety* has routinely had to wait many months for a document to do the rounds in county hall, before being approved by a committee and signed by the commissioning officer.

Word on the street is that the Canal & River Trust has worked out that there may be material as well as more high-minded rewards for tackling social exclusion.[23] However, its conclusions are made questionable by the suggestion that if a charity's activities take place on C&RT land, then the Trust is entitled to share in the outputs achieved by the charity. This is even if the outputs already form part of an existing service agreement with another organisation. In other words, 'Your outputs are our outputs'. Some would say that at worst, the practice could result in double counting[24] but also that if C&RT took a decision to make the demand to every NCBA member which had a lease on C&RT land, then it (C&RT) would be better off to the tune of 76,000 beneficiary outputs.[25] This would provide a not inconsiderable advantage in applications to Lottery, European or charitable funds, and into the bargain, the outputs would be free. It is to be hoped that such a 'smash and grab' approach will not be entertained. Whatever the pros and cons however, it is disappointing that C&RT, like the Learning & Skills Council before it, appears reluctant to make service agreements with small organisations, arguing that a profusion of contracts is too expensive of staff and office time.

But the problems the NCBA faces are not restricted to relations with local authorities, government, and the Canal & River Trust. There are internal questions common to many 'mature'[26] organisations that need debate and resolution. The first of these is the decline in members, perhaps due to high subscription and certification fees and the difficulty for the trustee directors of communicating with such a widespread and varied membership. The cost of training centre registration is an annual £400 and the fee payable for Complete Crew certification far exceeds the cost of a similar qualification obtainable from the Royal Yachting Association. As *Sobriety*'s Paul Cooper says, *"You don't need to become a deep sea master to take a narrowboat on the Shropshire Union Canal."* NCBA training is in good hands and gone are the days of strife and discord, but as we have seen with Ofsted, there is a common tendency for accreditation bodies to extend their remit to cover activities that are not their business. As far as communications are concerned, the trustees do their best and have the assistance of e-mail and internet that their predecessors in the mid eighties did not have. But NCBA is an organisation with a very diverse membership and cries out for full time staffing just as it did twenty five years ago. What a pity it did not have the chance of a second bite at the Lottery and another three years at Hartshill. It might have made all the difference.

Whatever the reasons, the damage to community boating has already become apparent. *Reach Out Plus*, based in St Albans in Hertfordshire and offering week long holidays to disabled and disadvantaged teenagers on four specially adapted narrowboats, has closed: the Walsall based Truman Enterprise Trust, specialising in training young people to be narrowboat skippers to the standard required by the Certificate of Community Boat Management, has been forced to sell two of its four boats, whilst several projects in the Pennines and the Thames Valley are rumoured to be under threat. Beneficiaries of NCBA's member charities are on breadline incomes or below and they deserve better. It is now up to NCBA to re-capture the enthusiasm of earlier years and C&RT to come off the fence and give the Association its wholehearted support and respect. It would be repaid tenfold if it did so.

Questions

What are the differences at a practical level between 'social inclusion' and 'combating social exclusion'?

What do you think is meant by the phrase 'waterways for all'? Is there a question here for government and for the Canal & River Trust?

How would you deal with the problem facing the National Community Boats Association — how to respond to the needs of member organisations while at the same time developing new ideas that will be of interest to funders and policy makers?

Chapter 14 Notes

1   This 23 page book beautifully illustrated by Samantha Saville is out of print but still available at £2.50 +postage from The Yorkshire Waterways Museum, Goole DN14 5TB info@waterwaysmuseum.org.uk or 01405.768.730.

2   The Inland Waterways:towards greater social inclusion (final report page 7): Inland Waterways Amenity Advisory Council: April 2001.

3   As above, page 9. The Inland Waterways Amenity Advisory Council (IWAAC) was set up by the Transport Act 1968 as a statutory body to advise the Government and British Waterways (BW) on matters affecting the use of the 2,000 mile BW system of canal and river navigations for recreation and amenity. Following a consultative review of the Council in 2003, Government decided in 2004 to retain the Council and make the following changes:
    Widen its remit functionally to cover all strategic aspects of waterway use and development
    Widen its remit geographically to include all inland waterways in England and Wales as well as those owned or managed by, or which receive technical advice or assistance from, British Waterways throughout Britain
    Reconstitute it as an advisory body reporting to Ministers in Whitehall
    Legislation to give effect to these changes received Royal Assent in 2006 and the reconstituted Council, renamed the Inland Waterways Advisory Council (IWAC), became operational on 1 April 2007.

4   Using the inland waterways to combat the effects of social exclusion : IWAC April 2009. Available on the Defra website.

5   Waterways for Tomorrow : Department for Environment Food and Rural Affairs : June 2000. Available on Defra website

6   'quango' originally defined as a 'quasi autonomous non-governmental organisation' — now known as a 'non departmental public body' — NDPB.

7   From the Defra archive: Environment Food and Rural Affairs Committee: Session 2012–2013: Minutes of Evidence.

8   See back cover. John Edmonds was TUC president in 1998.

9   The Waterways Renaissance Awards were organised by the Waterways Trust and sponsored by leading regeneration and construction companies. They now go under the title of Living Waterways Awards and are organised each year by the Canal & River Trust. More information from: Justine.Lee@canalrivertrust.org.uk

10 Theatr Ffynnon is the only theatre company in Wales working solely with adults with additional learning needs. It involves its members both as creators and performers.

11 Information about the four projects is based on their respective websites and my own observations and conversations.

12 In 2001 the Community Boats Association changed its name to the *National* Community Boats Association and began to have a national voice on behalf of its members. Appendices 1,2,3 and 5 contain documents which were expressions of this responsibility.

Appendix 1: Comments on IWAC abolition

Appendix 2: Comments on *New Era for The Waterways*.

Appendices 3 and 5 : Comments on licence reform

13 Barrie Slowen writing in *Sobriety*'s 1999 Review:

The Community *Boats* Association has now been able to establish a national standard for youth workers, care workers, teachers, scout and guide leaders and project volunteers, in fact, anyone who accompanies groups on community boats on non-tidal waterways. The *Certificate in Community Boat Management* (CCBM) was introduced two years ago after extensive field-testing and with the full support of British Waterways. Sixteen training centres have been rigorously inspected prior to becoming eligible to offer the course to local people. Each centre has at least one trainer with the qualifications and the experience to deliver intensive two-day courses throughout the year. Their work is overseen by a centre co-ordinator who is also responsible for promoting and administering the CCBM. 283 people have now successfully completed training and assessment for the Certificate. 5% of candidates were referred for further training. The training centre co-ordinator will plan a number of courses well in advance and offer five places on each course. Students are advised that they are unlikely to pass all 13 units of competence if they have little or no experience of the training boat, or the local waterways, or travelling with groups. Centres encourage students to visit, and can offer hands-on experience in preparation for the CCBM. This pre-training is particularly important where community boats meet commercial traffic or where the local rivers have significant flows at certain times or where the training boat is wide-beamed rather than the more usual narrowboat.

Courses take place over a weekend. Students sometimes have the chance to meet on Friday evening, get to know each other and talk about what is involved over the following two days. Trainers' expectations will be high. They will want students to be familiar with the boat systems such as water, gas, engine and electrics and to know what to do in an emergency. They will expect students to demonstrate boat handling skills in different situations and to know how to deal with a range of problems presented by particular groups. As well as simulated fire, man-overboard, sinking and grounding exercises they will need detailed knowledge of the canals and rivers on which they intend to travel. For example, students will learn where access points for the emergency services are found along the route, and where to find essential services for up to 12 people. The Community Boat Management course is unique. No other qualification covers the safety and welfare of special needs groups on the inland waterways.

To make sure that the national standard is maintained across the UK, the Association's Training Standards Panel, comprising some of the most experienced members, employs a national training officer to visit centres on a regular basis. He reports on best practice, recommends new centres and trainers to the Panel, receives feedback from the candidates and works with the navigation authorities on safety issues.

It has taken a long time to develop a national standard for community boat operators. The Community Boats Association is working hard to have the Certificate endorsed as an industry standard by British Waterways. Next year all 32 trainers will take part in a series of courses aimed at improving their teaching skills.

Perhaps in five years time the *Certificate in Community Boat Management will* become mandatory, but in the meantime, those involved in developing the standard will work towards reducing even further the risks to groups using the inland waterways.

14 The *Marchioness* disaster occurred on the River Thames in London in the early hours of 20 August 1989. The pleasure boat *Marchioness* sank after being run down by the dredger *Bowbelle*, near Cannon Street Railway Bridge. There were 131 people on *Marchioness*, including members of the crew, catering staff and guests at a private birthday party. 51 of them drowned. *Marchioness* was built in 1923 and in 1940 was one of the little ships of Dunkirk. (Wikipedia)

15 The Canal du Nivernais links the Loire basin with the Seine basin following approximately the course of

the river Yonne in a south to north direction. Beginning in the village of Saint-Léger-des-Vignes, the canal traverses the Départment du Nièvre reaching its half-way point at the town of Clamecy and finishes in the town of Auxerre, situated on the River Yonne.

Barrie failed to persuade his LEA that a community boat in France should be one of the city council's priorities but he did acquire a *péniche* himself and made it available to deserving groups.

16 Unfortunately the NCBA website does not contain a comprehensive archive of the Hartshill period but the dedicated browser may find some helpful links. Go to www.national-cba.co.uk

17 In its rejection of the request for continuation funding in 2003, the Lottery did not appear to take into account the Hartshill staff's efforts to involve the membership in its activities. Feedback on the application said there was not enough grassroots support to justify a further three years funding. The evidence presented in this chapter suggests otherwise; in any event a second round of funding was needed for the further development of what *had* been achieved in the three years

18 Eric Gibbs MBE was a Bradford probation officer who wanted to divert young people away from vehicle-related crime in the city. 'Former circuit judge Terry Walsh said: Eric had an unerring skill in identifying that spark in someone whom others had written off as a serial offender.. hence the number of lives which the projects have changed. (Bradford Telegraph and Argus).

19 The Lyme Bay kayaking tragedy was the deaths of four teenagers on a sea kayaking accident in the Lyme Bay area which led to legislation to regulate adventure activities centres working with young people in the UK.

On 22 March 1993, a group of eight schoolchildren and their teacher from Southway Community College, Plymouth were accompanied by two instructors from an outdoor centre on a kayak trip across Lyme Bay, on the south coast of England. As a result of a series of errors and circumstances, four of the teenagers died from hypothermia. The group was swept out to sea, where all their kayaks were quickly swamped.

The subsequent trial resulted in the prosecution of the parent company and the centre manager. The owner of the activity centre and the centre itself were convicted of corporate manslaughter over the deaths. This was the first conviction for this offence in the UK. The owner was jailed for three years, but his sentence was cut to two years on appeal. This tragedy accelerated governmental discussions to end self-regulation of outdoor education centres. The Activity Centres (Young Persons' Safety) Act 1995 was passed through Parliament in January 1995 and an independent licensing authority, the Adventure Activities Licensing Authority (AALA), was formed, funded by the Department for Education & Employment (DFE) and under the guidance of the Health & Safety Executive.

20 *A New Era for the Waterways* was the title of a consultation document launched by Defra in March 2011 which invited comment on the proposed change of BW's status. Appendix 3 contains James Bryan's response to the document on behalf of the NCBA board. In July 2011 the All Party Parliamentary Group on Waterways chaired by Alun Michael MP, published its response to *New Era* as a 12 page memorandum.

21 Trevor has had the courage of his convictions and recently set up *Canal Connections* through which he aims to demonstrate beyond any doubt the potential of the waterways in social regeneration.

22 The Arts Council accreditation scheme is designed to apply standard procedures and codes of conduct to museums and galleries. It covers conservation, acquisitions and disposals, customer care, disaster planning and so on. Only in exceptional circumstances would an accredited museum be given leave to sell items from its collection. The Arts Council obviously did not regard Northampton's predicament as exceptional. For further information contact the Museums Association.

23 Refer to my article *A cuckoo in the voluntary sector nest* in this chapter above, where I ask [whether] *C&RT will go it alone in competition for funds and public support?'*

24 If an organisation 'sells' the same outputs to two contractors it will be sailing very close to the wind. If C&RT were to force charities to hand over the outputs agreed with another organisation (or third party) this would put the charity in an impossible position.

25 At the last count in 2010, the number of people using NCBA boats in the previous year.

26 Mature, I think, in the sense that they are in danger of becoming over-ripe, too dependent on past glory, prone to the view that 'We've always done it like this..' and not giving enough priority to recruitment of young people.

Chapter 15

CONCLUSIONS

Resilient Sobriety

But what of *Sobriety*? Where does its future lie? How can it develop in new ways that are responsive to the spirit of the times without surrendering to the disease of hyperaccountability.[1] Following Peter Fryer's immortal description of social and economic change, I will try and show what are the *rapidly deforming fitness landscapes*[2] on which *Sobriety* has to jump, bounce and sometimes crawl. The intention is to show how *Sobriety* has to cope with change.

We begin with *Sobriety*'s historic aim *to use the heritage, arts and environment of the inland waterways as a resource for education and learning*. Helping to realise this aim at a practical level are two features of the charity which cannot be compromised: a mix of generations working together, and a consistent refusal by the Project to label as 'clients' the people who use its services. It is a question of dignity; they are all volunteers and the philosophy is as important as any contract. Nevertheless the challenge is to agree aims and objectives that are of interest to contractors but which also maximise income, protect cashflow and do not increase core overheads.[3] An example would be service agreements designed to help people with additional learning needs get on a ladder to employment. Individuals work in the museum café, sometimes staff the reception desk, and at other times form part of a group that makes and sells hand crafted items such as calendars and table mats. The purpose of the activities and responsibilities is social, but also, at a certain stage, to encourage individuals to look for employment. The allotment and nature trail, for instance, are attractive settings for the development of some of the skills required by employers.

The Project's longstanding contract for employment training of people with additional learning needs has been with the East Riding of Yorkshire Council's *Worklink*. Both sides worked together over many years to the benefit of everyone involved, but the problem which has begun to affect the arrangement is delay in contracting procedures. In 2013 it took six frustrating months for a 12 page contract not materially different from other similar contracts, to be approved. Operationally everything was agreed and ready to go by the July, in preparation for the start of the academic year, but it was January 2014 before the service agreement was finally approved. To cope with such changes the Project needs resilience as well as good working relationships with local authority officers.

Much of this book has been concerned with the education of young people, especially those who become cast-offs in the year before GCSE. The Project organises about 50 pupil days[4] each week for children who are excluded or at serious risk of exclusion from school and this is a provision that is likely to grow. Activities include working on the boats, personal projects in the workshops, cooking and budgeting, serving in the café, digging and planting on the allotment, conservation work on the towpath nature trail, residential expeditions on the boats and other pursuits and diversions mentioned in Chapter 11. Results are good; most children benefit from understanding the expectations of the Project and experience a kind of authority that is different from classroom based instruction. For this reason *Sobriety* is held in high regard by commissioners such as schools, education welfare services and indeed generally by the East Riding of Yorkshire Council. Referrals have traditionally been made by representatives of commissioning bodies: the deputy head of a school or a member of the authority's Behaviour Intervention Team (BIT). In 2014 however, it was decided that the six organisations wanting to become 'approved providers' would have to bid for children, through a computer portal. The portal sorts the children who will benefit from 'alternative provision' from those who will not, in a process known as a 'call off'. If all goes to plan, the designated children eventually appear on *Sobriety*'s doorstep, in much the same way as characters in *Dr Who* travel between civilisations and then appear in the *Tardis*. But the system has had teething problems and it is not unusual for details of individual children to arrive up to a month after a student has started with *Sobriety*. Some organisations which cannot work in such an unpredictable system, have pulled out, including one in sparsely populated and isolated South Holderness where access to any service is more difficult than in an urban area. *Sobriety*, on the other hand, seems to be coping satisfactorily with the new arrangements.

Another challenge is the raising of the school leaving age to 18. This is not the same as the ROSLA of 1972 when the leaving age was raised to 16 and applied exclusively to schools. This time the law says that young people must continue at school or be in training[5] or in work up to the age of 18; they may be removed from the school roll only if they have another educational destination. The new arrangements in formal education give an opportunity for *Sobriety* to add the teaching of literacy and numeracy to its curriculum for excluded children, many of whom are short of these two basic skills. Theoretically a child could arrive at the Project at the age of 14 and spend the next four years as a student at *Sobriety*'s 'college of the waterways'.

Opportunities also lie in the new format of *Community Payback* which is organised and overseen by the National Probation Service,[6] a body soon to be replaced by 21 private companies and large voluntary organisations. Young people aged between 16 and 18 may now be given an Unpaid Work Order which sentences them to 40 hours of community work. They must attend for 10 sessions of four hours and there must be a training element in the prescribed activities, which in *Sobriety*'s case, if combined with some teaching of numeracy and literacy, will fit well with the day to day requirements of its towpath nature trail, allotments and boats.

There is less justification to be sanguine about prisons. Successive chief inspectors of prisons have been thrown out, resigned or have not re-applied for the post because they see nothing being done to remedy the levels of violence, suicide and boredom that characterise many prisons, boredom being due to lack of resources to maintain a decent prison education service. The Chief Inspector said in August 2014 that, *"self-inflicted prison deaths are not acceptable in a civilised country."* [7] The message for *Sobriety* is to carry on as normal, but this will be in spite of arbitrary restrictions on the work placements and home leave for which prisoners become eligible towards the end of their sentence. The Project's work with serving prisoners goes back without a break to the early nineteen eighties and has been supported generously and consistently by several charitable trusts which see the value in its work. Otherwise it is a side of the organisation which remains in low profile, applauded by prison staff but not advertised or brought to public attention. Perhaps this book will help *Sobriety* to 'come out' and promote the benefits of its prison links. Moves to set up a 'secure college' on the pattern found in the American states of Louisiana and New Mexico would consolidate progress in this respect. If such a college were ever built in the UK it would tackle the lack of literacy and numeracy that handicaps many young prisoners' search for employment. However, to achieve a change to a more enlightened prison education service will require a shift in government policy. While Ministers kow-tow to tabloid 'bloodlust', there will be little progress.

Then we come to the boats. With the demise of the Youth Service and schools having other preoccupations, the importance attached to residential expeditions during the twentieth century, has dwindled. Financial cutbacks, bureaucracy and fear of litigation have added to the decline of a tradition going back to the narrowboat camping holidays of the nineteen thirties. If the wheel turns however and the policies and solutions proposed in this book are adopted, we may see a resurgence of enthusiasm.

And money? Years ago, Sydney Wilks, *Sobriety*'s treasurer who, after a life in the merchant navy 'came ashore' to be a manager for the British Transport Docks Board, used to say to me at our weekly meetings, *"You must keep the money coming in, Bob."* The same message was always on the lips of George Robinson, chair of *Sobriety* for eight years, and of Bernard Fletcher, the Project's treasurer. Bernard is a retired NatWest bank manager from Swinton with the diplomatic skills of a Henry Kissinger. These trustees looked after the Project through thick and thin. They never lost their bottle, they came to see us sometimes twice in a week, and were virtually unpaid members of staff. Following my retirement, their involvement steadily came to an end; George was succeeded by Mick Stanley, a museum consultant from Ripon, equally optimistic and single minded in his encouragement of staff and volunteers, while the burden of fundraising has passed seamlessly to Clare Hunt. Clare, like me in past times, is now programmed to wake up in the night, screaming about electronic application forms and committee delays, but has, nevertheless, raised more than two million pounds in the last four years.

At the time of writing *Sobriety* is going through one of its leaner years in which the difficulty of covering the fixed costs makes an impact on cashflow. At such a time I am reminded of the comment of Philip Jelley, Secretary of the L. J. and Mary Skaggs Foundation in San Francisco, who said to me on one of his visits to the Project that if *Sobriety* was based in the US there would be organisations corporate and public, competing with one another to support its work. The only short cuts to fund raising are in dreams; the only path to success in the process, is knowledge and honesty about the successes and failures of the organisation, passionate belief in what it is about, a good standard of written English, a smattering of creativity, the confidence to express oneself convincingly, a sense of humour, determination to abide by the maxim *Promise less but deliver more*, and above all, patience.

Has *Sobriety* been able to influence policy making at a national level? The answer is no, not in any direct sense. But over the years there has been a stream of individuals and organisations coming to the Project to find out 'how it is done' and the charity has held consistently to the view that the broader curriculum should be vigorously promoted and protected. It has also signalled to museums that they should turn their attention to a greater concern for audience development and access, it has played a big part in the development and survival of the National Community Boats Association and its links with Hatfield and Askham Grange prisons have been a model for prison voluntary sector co-operation. Its interest in the Inland Waterways Advisory Council and authorship, for Defra, of *Using the inland waterways to combat social exclusion* commended a new approach by government and British Waterways to people who were struggling on low incomes and handicapped by social as well as physical disability. It has been a reliable development partner in setting up projects in deprived communities and perhaps above all, has been true to the wishes all those 42 years ago of its founding benefactor, John McGrory.

Has *Sobriety* had its day? By no means — unless we say that children in pupil referral units and young offender institutions, people with a learning disability or mental health problems, men and women in prison and others living in poverty have also 'had their day'.

Unless we say those who don't fit with the expectations of the majority should be abandoned, *Sobriety* will have a part to play in giving hope to people young and old who are forgotten and often despised But it cannot be content to wait for handouts and philanthropy; in a time of change it has first to show the way.

The Russian poet Evgeny Baratynsky, a friend of the poet Pushkin, said, *"Providence has given human wisdom the choice between two fates: hope and agitation, or hopelessness and calm."* My conclusion is that Hope and Agitation are *Sobriety*'s most enduring features.

And Secondly...

I hope that this book has been entertaining, in parts even amusing, and where appropriate, salutary. It has not been my intention to write a polemic. Where policy and practice have been questioned, it has been because I believe they are obstacles to one of the purposes of education made clear in Chapter 1 by Sir Alec Clegg's 'hyacinths,' and in Chapter 2, by young people's experience of City Challenge.

Rawcliffe Hall, upper Nidderdale and the Asian community in Batley and Dewsbury were among the magical experiences in Goole Grammar School, while *Sobriety*, often in the face of threats that, like a computer virus, had the power to destroy everything it stood for, showed how the excitement of cruising the inland waterways and coasts of the UK and Europe could for many create a new reference point in their lives and be a relief from guilt and mental pain.

Nor has the book been intended to belittle the adventure that can be generated within classrooms and institutions. Twenty one years of teaching in a secondary school, especially a year in northern Nigeria, and employment years ago, as a part time tutor in a local borstal, taught me that what brings teacher and pupil together, often in spiritual and intellectual harmony, is the curiosity which is often followed by lightening strikes of discovery.

In a good classroom there is a momentum for teacher and pupils; the teacher leads the way (for a time) but the pupils are hot on his or her heels. It is a place where pretence and intimidation can be replaced by teacher trust and pupil freedom and it is replicable the world over — with any children and in any setting.

At this point, the difference between learning in the classroom and learning beyond the classroom becomes indistinguishable. Some colleagues quoted or described in this book realised this and made common cause against institutions that denied them the 'hyacinths' that education could bring. Remember John Clarke, Governor of Hatfield YOI when he had to answer to Home Secretary, Michael Howard, for permitting the young men in his charge to go to Holland with a group of deaf children, or Daciana, holed up in her rather less than inspiring prison routines, until she said, *"To hell with it"*, and set up a prisoner information bureau at HMP Drake Hall: or the excluded children at *Sobriety* waiting for contract breadcrumbs to fall their way from the tables of government, local authority and school. In a similar manner, the teachers building the outdoor centre at How Stean were convinced of the benefits that study outside the classroom could bring to work in the classroom.

Many of the schools receiving Ofsted accolades and many schools in the independent sector still offer pupils outstanding programmes of extra curricular activities. The forty young people that went under the auspices of the Yorkshire Schools Exploring Society to the Tibetan Plateau in 1993 were all from Yorkshire schools. But when, 21 years later, Sir Michael Wilshaw, head of Ofsted said, *"Secondary schools in England are failing in increasing numbers, with more falling into special measures and tens of thousands more pupils attending schools condemned as inadequate"*, one is bound to look beyond Osted's simple verdict of bad management for reasons why this should be. Could it be that many of the 170,000 children Wilshaw says are attending these so-called failing schools, are finding it difficult to be inspired by a curriculum dominated by examinations and assessments. (Wilshaw's opinion is not made more palatable by Michael Gove's reference in 2013, to the teaching profession as 'The Blob'.)

Children and adults thrive on excitement and while one acknowledges that certain features of the learning process may inevitably be boring, it is the duty of a teacher in any institution, from nursery to prison and university to evening class, to lead and fire the imagination of pupils young and old. To what extent this can happen while education and allied services are under the direct control of faraway politicians is a good question.

However, an example of where classroom learning *is* inspired by out-of-school activity is in the approach of Abingdon & Witney Further Education College in Oxfordshire, to young people who have failed GCSE maths. One of its pupils, Toby Swift, said, *"I left school with a U in maths and did lots of practical work like tree surgery."* In Toby's case there were problems that needed solving in conservation and tree felling — through mathematics. More important for Toby's fellow students was the comment by the college's assistant principal who said, *"We basically tell them that they **can** do it."* Here are shades of Bob Trafford's approach to his young offenders at Hatfield YOI and emphatically one of the themes of this book. Interestingly the college is in Prime Minister David Cameron's constituency.

For my part I am grateful that I was able to work in a school which allowed me to develop, and later serve an organisation that could adopt a curriculum, unfettered by politicians, that children in trouble, adults, prisoners, volunteers and people with additional learning needs could find enjoyable and helpful. My hope is that the message of Sir Alec Clegg's 'hyacinths' will go out near and far as an encouragement to those who want to have a go themselves. I hope they will also feel an urge to challenge a centralised system that is stifling development of the broader curriculum and in Sir Alec's words, *"cultivating failure by praising the adept and ignoring the inept."*

The nearest *Sobriety* will get to immortality. Hieroglyphs are authentic.
The author stands on the afterdeck. Original painting by Viv Morgan.

Questions

Do you agree that the informal or broader curriculum is suffering as a result of too much political control over what is taught in schools?

If you were secretary of state for education what changes would you make to the curriculum and to Ofsted? How would you introduce or reintroduce a broader curriculum? What would it cover that it does not cover at present?

What are the lessons to be learned from the English education system from 1970 onwards?

To what extent is the curriculum of prisons and other institutions also restricted. How and why?

Can charities like the *Sobriety* Project ever be effective campaigners for change?

Would you consider waterways and boats to be a useful resource for personal development?

Chapter 15 Notes

1   A term used widely in Warwick Mansell's book *Education by Numbers – The Tyranny of Testing*.

2   For an explanation see opening paragraph of *Summary History of Sobriety* (Appendix 8).

3   *Core* overheads consist of running costs of museum and boats, and salaries of senior staff (in *Sobriety*'s case, two). As a rule of thumb, core costs have to be met from unrestricted income from charitable trusts, donations or 'turnstile' profit from boats, café and gift shop.

   Project costs are expenditure incurred within a particular area of activity prescribed and circumscribed by contract. *Sobriety* is paid by contractors for contracted results.

   Although in theory payments cover segments of the core, (for example the amount of recorded staff time needed to deliver the outputs of a particular project), in practice project costs often turn out to exceed the costs agreed in the service contract.

4   Children are in the 14-16 age bracket. Very few are full time *at Sobriety*; most attend for between one and four days. The remainder of the week is spent in school or on other placements.

5   Day release at a further education college for example.

6   Under the £450m-a-year probation sell-off, the supervision of more than 200,000 low and medium-risk offenders will be taken over by the private and voluntary sectors in 21 community rehabilitation companies. It is the most radical justice privatisation undertaken by the Coalition Government: *Guardian* 2.12.2014

7   Our jails are bursting at the seams. Violence, self-harm and suicide rates are soaring and rehabilitation has not just taken a back seat, it is out of the vehicle. Many prisoners are spending the working day in their cells. Staff and managers are demoralised: *Guardian* 8.10.2014

Appendix 1

NCBA RESPONSE TO THE DEFRA CONSULTATION ON THE ABOLITION OF THE INLAND WATERWAYS ADVISORY COUNCIL

The National Community Boats Association (NCBA) is the umbrella organisation that supports and represents community boating organisations across the inland waterways network. Community boating organisations (CBOs) provide access and services to the UK's waterways for the benefit of their local community. They work with youth and other community based groups and with individuals and provide specific services for disabled, disadvantaged or excluded people on low incomes. The aim of these organisations is much more than just access to a leisure facility. It could be working in areas of social inclusion, education, rehabilitation (health or offending) and issues of wider community cohesion. They are usually charitable in nature and are often registered charities. They are predominantly voluntary organisations themselves relying on donations, fund-raising and sponsorship from within their operating area. The NCBA's vision is a network of well resourced, well managed community boating organisations that promote access to UK waterways as well as promoting the safe use of community boat services as a resource that promotes social cohesion, protects the environment and supports economic regeneration.

The announcement to abolish the Inland Waterways Advisory Council (IWAC) as part of the government's drive to reduce the number of arms-length governmental bodies without proper discussion or consultation was ill-advised no matter how well intended. No-one doubts that there are many such bodies whose remit and role needs scrutiny and change but there are 'smarter' ways of approaching the issue. The NCBA recognises that DEFRA itself may have had little influence on the formation of the list for abolition or the announcement. **NCBA believes the case to abolish IWAC has simply not been made** and nothing in the consultation document changes that view.

NCBA considers itself lucky that a number of members of IWAC have knowledge and experience of community boating activities. They understand how the waterways can be used as a tool to deliver far-reaching services that go beyond the leisure and (limited) trade uses most people will see possible. There is no doubt that the experiences of these individuals has helped steer some of IWACs discussion and work in ways it otherwise might not have gone. No other waterways body has demonstrated this and there are few signs of that situation changing.

The consultation document states that government recognises the contribution made by IWAC. It describes possible ways in which the work of IWAC could be undertaken; largely through the New Waterways Charity (NWC) itself or organisations such as the Association of Inland Navigation Authorities (AINA). The NWC may have aspirations and even plans to recognise and engage with stakeholders and issues across the waterways spectrum but has not done so yet, is still some considerable way off doing so and has no track record of demonstrating that they will. AINA, whilst no doubt providing a valuable function, equally has no history of engaging with many issues that IWAC has reported on.

With a number of substantial pieces of work very directly relating to the activities of CBOs, the NCBA has high regard for IWAC and its output. It is important to understand that this work is not IWAC supporting the NCBA or its aims but reporting on how extremely valuable the waterways are in the context of the activities NCBA members conduct. Such issues will be critical to the NWC if it is to demonstrate maximum public benefit but, despite this, the NCBA still has to work hard to get that view heard.

With the advent of the NWC, **NCBA considers that the need for an independent body to advise government (and others) has actually increased** rather than diminished. At the very least, government should be seeking a suitably knowledgeable and experienced scrutiny body to ensure the transition to the NWC is successful and the ongoing government grant is being used wisely. The Council of the NWC or even the trustees can hardly be expected to report objectively on this. Coupled with this, there are still a considerable number of navigation authorities (other than BW/NWC) who will clearly not benefit from any work the NWC subsumes. AINA has not shown it has the resources or the desire to engage with this work and an influx of money and personnel to do so rather defeats the objective. Such oversight work could reassure government, stakeholders, users and the public at large that the whole of the waterways are being managed properly and in their best interests. To assert that stakeholders will be able to influence issues through the NWC structure before it is even in place is concerning; particularly when feedback on how those structures will be established is not all positive.

As an independent body, IWAC does seem exceptionally well placed to conduct the review of the proposed Environment Agency waterways transition in 2014 and also subsequent reviews into the success or otherwise of the NWC. In fact, NCBA believes the NWC trustees would be well-advised to seek such a body themselves to provide advice and scrutiny. NCBA does not believe that IWACs activities will be successfully subsumed into the NWC and, even if they are to some extent, that they will be delivered as a considerably less effective 'internal' process.

NCBA does recognise that IWACs functions may need adjustment in light of the creation of the NWC and transfer of the waterways to the civil society. The boating standards appeal panel could be revised in line with the proposals but remain part of an independent body. The wider role of IWAC could be reviewed to include a scrutiny role for all waterways; particularly as some (BW Scotland) will remain in public ownership. Whilst cost is always a factor, the saving by abolishing IWAC is a tiny fraction of what the government will be contributing to the waterways over the next decade, let alone what the public and waterways users will be expected to contribute. As taxpayers, as users and supporters of the waterways and as organisations who believe the waterways have much more to offer than most people understand, **NCBA strongly recommends the government reconsider its position on IWAC.**

James Bryan
Chair, Board of Directors
National Community Boats Association
8 November 2011

Appendix 2

NCBA RESPONSE TO "A NEW ERA FOR THE WATERWAYS", THE DEFRA CONSULTATION ON THE NEW WATERWAYS CHARITY

The National Community Boats Association (NCBA) is the umbrella organisation that supports and represents community boating organisations across the inland waterways network. Community boating organisations (CBOs) provide access to and services on the UK's waterways for the benefit of their local community. They often work with youth and other community based groups as well as individuals and may provide specific services for disabled, disadvantaged or excluded people in our society such as those on low incomes or from minority groups. The aim of these organisations is much more than just access to a leisure facility. It could be working in areas of social inclusion, education, rehabilitation (health or offending) and issues of wider community cohesion. They are usually charitable in nature and are often registered charities. They are predominantly voluntary organisations themselves relying on donations, fund-raising and sponsorship from within their operating area. The NCBA's vision is a network of well resourced, well managed community boating organisations that promote access to UK waterways as well as promoting the safe use of community boat services as a resource that promotes social cohesion, protects the environment and supports economic regeneration.

NCBA is aware of some very well researched and well presented responses; most notably that from IWAC. Given the submission of these, we do not propose to repeat or reiterate that work but comment only on matters which fall within our area of interest and/or expertise.

Charitable Purposes

Almost everything about the NWC will depend largely on the wording of the charitable aims given at the beginning of its governing instrument. These lay down not only the purpose of the charity but influences how it will function as well. Our considerable experience of charitable organisations demonstrates that getting this right is critical. The various purposes and objects need to be in the right order and worded correctly to ensure the right mix and desired impact on the operation of the charity.

The NCBA is concerned about two elements in particular: the importance of 'navigation' in the purposes and the description range of 'public benefit'. Firstly, whilst all other activities on the inland waterways are acknowledged and welcomed, it is the provision of a navigation that provides something distinct from other inland waters and, for example, the ability to navigate boats allows CBOs to deliver their services. **The wording of the charitable aims should be structured to give the provision of navigation primacy over other waterways interests.**

NCBA also recommends that a desire to use the waterways for socially inclusive activities and community cohesion should be more readily articulated in the charitable aims. NCBA members consistently demonstrate that using the waterways can positively impact on education, health, rehabilitation of offenders and social cohesion as well as the more basic requirements of being a properly inclusive leisure pastime. It is noticeable that with the current (BW) structure and processes, inclusion of hard-to-reach groups is almost entirely the purview of NCBA member organisations. Waterways businesses, particularly commercial boat operators, almost universally fail to support full and unfettered access to this national asset by disadvantaged groups. What is worse is that BW, as the navigation and management authority, has done equally as badly in this area. Taking a different approach would not only be the right thing to do but also the sensible thing when seeking public support for a charity and trying to demonstrate a 'public benefit'.

Finance

Other organisations responding to this consultation have undertaken far more detailed analyses of the financial picture than NCBA is able to do and it is not intended to spend time repeating or recalculating those figures. Based on the presumption that all those respondents who have calculated detailed forecasts predict that there will be a significant shortfall in funding, clearly this is an issue no matter what the figures. Lack of proper funding must be a concern to government as well as to any waterways user as the potential for failure of either the waterways network or the NWC governing it would have significant impact on both the waterways community and the taxpayer (who would undoubtedly have to fund any recovery).

The NWC is not starting as most charities do – from small and slow beginnings. On day one it will already be a massive operation requiring many millions of pounds and have many hundreds of people employed to support it. For that reason, stable finance is also critical to success. **It is NCBA's view that the interim trustees should not recommend the launch of the NWC until they are assured that secure funding arrangements are in place that will generate an amount at least equal to that previously attained by BW.**

Governance

NCBA is concerned that the governance arrangements seem to be a best fit to the current BW structure rather than designed to suit the purpose intended; particularly in relation to the Local Partnership Boards. Using the current BW regions fails completely to recognise the organisations using non-waterway boundaries (such as those of local authorities) with whom the LPBs will be expected to engage for support, partnership and finance. Similarly, a BW region could consist of a narrow but long area (the Grand Union being a good example). Anything covering over 100 miles in length cannot be expected to be "local" in engaging with the communities that surround it. **NCBA's view is that some other, non-waterways based, boundaries are considered and that these are drawn up with the specific intention of achieving the "local" and "partnership" aims sought in the proposal.**

NCBA's view is that these boards also need to be the place that truly engages with the local and diverse population surrounding the waterways. Boating can easily be seen as a white, middle-class, middle-income, middle-aged hobby and if the NWC is to gain real public support and demonstrate effectively its obligation as a charity to be for 'public benefit' then breaking this perception will be an important objective. Following the decline of our waterways network as an industrial transport system, many parts of the country that surround those waterways also fell into decline. Indeed, many of the most deprived areas in our cities and towns are within easy reach of a canal. A real effort needs to be made to engage with those communities. To do so both widens demonstrably the public benefit the charity serves and offers increased opportunities for funding in support of working with those groups. However, this issue must be addressed carefully. NCBA members would not wish to be usurped by a new national charity absorbing all the funding without the slightest hope of delivering the activity that directly engages with those local communities. For this reason, a two-pronged approach is suggested. **(1) The NWC must activity seek representation on its LPBs from those communities that are often excluded from waterways activities because of their social position, ethnic background, low income or disability AND those who might seek to use the waterways as a tool to promote health, education or rehabilitation in the wider sense. (2) The NWC and LPBs must support current and encourage new organisations that provide access to the waterways for those groups and deliver services for them using the waterways.** NCBA is eager to work with the NWC to establish an infrastructure to facilitate this.

LPBs appear to have no proper voice at either a local or national level. Inclusion of the Chairs on the council, whose role appears to be extremely limited, does not give a national input from the LPBs and acting only in a consultative/advisory capacity at the regional level seems just to perpetuate the (current

BW) status quo. In order for the LPBs to both attract participants and succeed, the members will need to feel they have a proper voice and responsibilities in the running of the charity. These groups are also who the waterways users will look to for holding local NWC management to account. **NCBA would like to see LPBs properly engaged and involved in the management structures of the NWC (rather than acting purely in an advisory or consultative capacity) and also with a formal relationship to the National Council.**

Similarly, the National Council appears to have extremely limited powers given it is designed to be the representative body of all waterways interests. **NCBA recommends that the relationship between the National Council, the trustees and the NWC management is changed to ensure that the representative body is significantly involved in the formulation of NWC strategy and policy.**

NCBA, as an organisation that aims to support the sharing of good practice, notes that there appears to be no mechanism to do so in the current proposals; either between the National Council and the Local Partnership Boards or amongst the LPBs themselves. **NCBA recommends that some formal process be established for collaboration between the National Council and the LPBs and between the LPBs.**

NCBA considers that using learning from within the third sector is vital to the long-term viability of the NWC. Simply sharing knowledge and experience or more formally partnering with other third sector organisations is undoubtedly a catalyst for success; particularly when wishing to engage with volunteers and the community. NCBA is alarmed that the BW Advisory Forum proposal to BW regarding 'Expert Advisory Groups' specifically excludes the need for a group covering community engagement, youth and volunteering issues other than briefly during the transition stage. **NCBA strongly recommends that these issues are fundamental to the ongoing success of the NWC and should therefore form a central feature of the governance arrangements.** LPBs alone will not attract or represent properly the diversity of waterways users sought. Without a strategic plan for engaging with both waterways users and other communities, the NWC will fail to achieve the inclusive approach it seeks.

Membership

Broadly speaking, **NCBA supports the idea of the NWC being a membership organisation** of some description for reasons of participation and fund-raising. As NCBA clients and user groups are unlikely to become members, we do not propose to comment further.

Volunteering

Provision should be made for the NWC to provide direct and indirect support for organisations bringing volunteers and communities to the waterways whether to volunteer on/for the waterways themselves or to volunteer in other pursuits that use the waterways to deliver some other charitable objective. BW's record at supporting organisations like CBOs is patchy at best. Despite some well intentioned local and personal support from BW staff, corporately BW has failed to recognise the benefits generated by such organisations. Most CBOs are charitable in nature and many are registered charities and, as such, cannot be seen in the same way as businesses that operate for private gain. Organisations with exclusively altruistic aims should be recognised and heavily supported by the NWC. Again, NCBA stands ready to help the NWC establish the processes to do this.

Organisational Culture

One of the greatest challenges facing the NWC will be changing the BW structures, systems and staff behaviours to deliver the culture expected of a large national charity. BW's attitude towards volunteers and charities has historically ranged from good support (usually as the result of a personal connection between individuals) to downright destructiveness. The NWC and its staff at all levels will be expected to listen to and work with the people it is there to benefit whether they become members or not. Apart from anything else, much of any success with fund-raising in this area rests with the relationship between the staff and the user. **The NWC needs to establish a clear set of values and behaviours expected from**

the outset by all staff and volunteers and mechanisms to ensure they are delivered. In the longer term, it may be advisable to seek external support to establish a wider-ranging set of competencies and systems that train and support staff in delivering them.

Staff terms and conditions also need to be reviewed as a matter of urgency to ensure they are benchmarked against a range of suitable organisations. This is particularly important for salaries and benefits paid to senior staff. Whilst the requirement to TUPE staff across to the NWC is acknowledged, progress needs to be made quickly on aligning the NWC terms and conditions with that expected of a similar organisation. TUPE'd staff will, of course, be protected from these changes in the immediate future but the early provision of such a framework will allow for an easier transition later on.

Powers and Duties

NCBA recommends that a panel, drawn from somewhere like the current BW Advisory Forum, are allowed to consider individually and then recommend to DEFRA and the trustees which of BW's current powers and responsibilities should be transferred to the NWC. Duties such as those under the Freedom of Information Act and in relation to landfill taxes must be considered carefully before a blanket transfer is decided. To unnecessarily burden the NWC with the considerable restraints required of a public body would merely encourage its failure. Whilst it might be admirable and even desirable for the NWC to act in accordance with the same high standards that public corporations are held accountable to, if it is not a statutory requirement on a charity then the need to impose such duties should be considered on an individual basis and justification given.

James Bryan
Chair, Board of Directors
National Community Boats Association
29 June 2011

Appendix 3

How British Waterways' proposals for licence reform will affect community boat charities
The case against the abolition of the charity discount

January 18th 2011

Note : The word 'charity' is used to describe a charity registered with the Charity Commission for England and Wales. In this paper it does not cover organisations that regard themselves as charitable but are not registered.

Summary

British Waterways should be aware of the political implications of penalising charitable organisations through its proposed licence fee regime.

BW will appear publicly to be discriminating against charities on the eve of its own transformation into a charity. Is this the way it wishes to be seen to deal with its obligations within the charitable sector?

In view of these political implications NCBA suggests that such a fundamental change should be considered by the new charity and not taken by the existing organisation.

Background
Community Boat Organisations

There are 72 organisations in the Association operating 120 boats on the rivers and canals of the UK with a total daily passenger capacity of 1,476. There are very few community boats having an MCA certificate to carry more than 12 passengers.

Users and target groups are universally on low incomes and include ex-offenders, people with a learning disability,refugees, minority ethnic groups, carers, homeless people, children and young people, families, elderly people, schools and children's services. Organisations are supported by 2,495 volunteers and 240 paid staff.

The size of organisations varies. Some are very small with an income of less than £5,000 p.a. The majority (41) have an income of somewhere between ten and fifty thousand pounds a year. Not all community boat organisations derive all their income from boating activities. In some cases revenue from this source may be small in proportion to the size of the overall organisation.

Some charities have service agreements with local authorities but the majority (46) rely on charitable donations augmented by a modest income from boat trips and refreshments.

Recruitment of groups and individuals is often by self referral or word of mouth recommendation. Websites help with the process.

Association of Pleasure Craft Operators (APCO)

There are 107 members of APCO. Of these, 14 run day trips on passenger boats and 20 are bases for hire of self-drive dayboats.

APCO members also operate restaurant boats and hotel boats but their main business is hiring out narrowboats to the general public for private hire for 'short breaks' for a week or longer.

New customers are recruited as a result of advertising in waterway journals and on websites and by word of mouth recommendation.

British Waterways' proposals

Briefly, the (BW) proposal is that all boats will require the standard pleasure boat licence (the cost of which will be increased by 5.1% and additional 2.5% VAT). There will then be a generic operator agreement and an additional fee for any boat not used solely for private pleasure use.(NCBA statement to members)

In paragraph 3.11 of its consultation paper dated January 2010, BW said 'Fair trading principles have some bearing on our position with respect to concessions for charitable ventures….'

In July 2010 it went further and said in 2.5a '….if it is providing services to the public in order to generate income to support its charitable purpose, then by offering a lower tariff we would be favouring this operation over commercial competitors. This would not be fair.

In 2.5b of the same document it went on to say 'Recent trends within the charity (or 'third') sector throughout our society demonstrate increasing professionalism and improvements in standards. We do not think it right or appropriate that BW should discriminate in favour of certain operations simply because they belong to a category of enterprises which are not solely profit-focused.'

However in a footnote to page 5 a charity may be offered an Operator Agreement at the minimum fee of £150+the standard pleasure boat licence fee if it meets the following conditions:

The boat is used for educational purposes by an organisation

not operating for profit, or by registered charities for charitable purposes for the disadvantaged or people with disabilities.

The boat is used only by or for the class of persons that the boat is intended to benefit.

Any charge for the use of the boat is limited to the costs of the trip.

The boat is not offered to the general public for hire or reward or for carrying passengers for payment on a regular basis.

The last condition was subsequently amended by BW to:

the boat is not offered to the general public for hire or reward for more than 30 days in a year.

BW also said 'The concession will not apply if it would create an unfair advantage over commercial passenger boat operations in the vicinity'.

A gloss on this appeared in an e-mail (12.10.2010) from the Boating Trade Manager (North) who said that if the above conditions were met by one particular organisation, there would be a 60% reduction on the fee which would be payable in addition to the standard pleasure boat licence and Operator Agreement fee of £150. The inference is that on this basis the charity would pay the standard pleasure boat licence fee plus £150 plus 40% of the additional new commercial rate as long as the charity met the conditions above.

In an e-mail (23.7.2010) from BW's Head of Boating, the catch-all condition about 'unfair advantage' seemed to be extended by an answer to the question of what would be BW's approach 'if a commercial operator set up in the same area (as an existing community boat project)? The answer was another question: 'Should we withdraw the concession?'

Within the proposed Operator Agreement structure there is provision for a location element (Proposals January 2010 : 6.4.4) which will affect community boat charities if they are based within 500 metres of a public car park, public toilets, a pub, a restaurant, a café, tea room or coffee shop, or a visitor attraction such as a garden, museum or shopping mall. A score-chart entry will determine the extent of liability for extra fees.

In the pre consultation draft for discussion with trade representatives (21.7.2010) section 5 deals with proposals for skippered passenger boats. It states inter alia that 'We believe that a minimum sum of £150 per year is reasonable for the smallest operators' and goes on in Table 1 to suggest an 'Earnings potential matrix for passenger boats'. Under this regime the smallest operators would pay the standard licence fee + £150. In the example given, a large operator deriving substantial income from passenger boat trips, might pay as much as £4,050. BW decided to abandon this proposal.

Charity or Business?

A charity is an organisation set up for public benefit according to statute and strict regulations. Trustees may not be paid and all income must be acquired and spent in line with the organisation's charitable purposes which are set out in its trust deed.

A business may well benefit the public but it is essentially for private gain. Its directors may spend the company's profits as they wish.

The Charity Commission expects a charity to be run like a business. That is to say it is expected wherever possible to stand on its own feet. Where it cannot, it goes out to statutory and other charitable sources in order to make up the shortfall. However this does not mean that it is a business; it cannot be a business because it is not for private gain. The fact that it may have salaried workers is neither here nor there. A charity is allowed to have employees only to the extent that they are helping to achieve the organisation's charitable objects.

The term 'not for profit' which came from America about 30 years ago is misleading. It is the mark of an efficiently run charity if it does make a profit and within certain limits it may trade in order to do so. A charity which consistently failed to 'make a profit' could find that its auditors did not regard it as a going concern.

The Charity Commission takes an interest in proportionality. If an employee were to be paid an outrageously high salary or a trustee excessive reimbursement of expenses the Commission, which has powers of prosecution, would intervene. This would not happen in the private business sector where salaries and fees are unregulated.

Charities are subject to many laws and restrictions which do not apply to commercial enterprises

The extent to which the BW proposals will affect community boat charities

Taking into account the various conditions, smaller charities which rely entirely on charitable donations will be paying the price of a standard 12 month licence plus 5.1% increase plus £150 fee for an Operator's Agreement. Larger charities will pay the price of a standard 12 month licence plus 5.1% increase plus £150 fee for an Operator's Agreement plus all or part of a full business licence.

In the case of some charities this could mean an increase of £5,000 p.a. or more payable to British Waterways and its successor body.

Recommendations (in italics below)

Competition with commercial organisations

The authors of the reports perhaps should be more aware of the distinctive nature of charities and the implications of the differences between a charity and a business. A sensible business person would trade in an area where she was likely to make a profit. A community boat organisation would normally be established in an area of social and economic deprivation where even making a profit in line with charitable objectives was secondary to meeting urgent local needs.

The question of competition is made to justify removing the charity discount. As far as APCO members are concerned it is unlikely that there are more than five locations where there is competition. The question of competition has raised its head several times in the last 30 years but any misunderstandings between APCO and NCBA have been quietly dealt with behind the scenes. It is a pity that BW has decided use any issues for its own financial benefit.

The effects on some charities for whom passenger boats are only one part of their activities may lead them to abandon dayboat provision altogether. In some areas this would mean that neither the public nor traditional NCBA groups had access to the waterway.

BW should provide accurate details of where competition exists. The NCBA should be given the opportunity to verify the details and come to a working agreement independently of BW, with the APCO members concerned.

A regulatory nightmare?

The conditions are detailed and burdensome for BW as well as organisations. There will be endless argument about definitions. In the Pre-Consultation Draft (21.7.2010) Para 2.5b says 'The concept for a reduced tariff for certain types of activity such as educational trips for school parties or preserving a particular historic boat leads immediately to the need for value judgements as to how much these activities are 'worth'. We believe that this is beyond BW's reasonable competence to judge....'

However BW may well have to have 'the competence to judge' how far away are the nearest public toilets! From what part of an operator's site will the measurement be made? What constitutes a visitor attraction? Who will police the 30 day condition which in any event seems to be an arbitrary figure?

How will the condition 'that any charge for the use of the boat is limited to the costs of the trip' be monitored? What does this condition mean? Are an organisations 'core costs' not retrievable? What have been BW's expectations in this regard? Does BW administer its own finances on this basis?

With any rough appraisal of the cost of office time the business case for abolishing the charity discount begins to look thin.

BW should not tie the assessment of licence fees to such variable and arbitrary criteria.

Historic privileges: the distinctive nature of charities

Charities have historic privileges which enable them more easily to work for public benefit. As a result they:

> receive 100% relief on business rates
>
> are exempt from VAT on advertising
>
> receive donations gift aided by a 28% relief on tax
>
> do not pay income tax

BW should become more informed about the status of charities before proceeding any further with the proposals

The national picture

Local authorities are already terminating service agreements with outside bodies even where the organisation is the sole provider of the service and is making a success of its delivery. Community boat organisations are not usually regarded as 'front line' and are likely to suffer big reductions in income if they have arrangements with their local authority. Revenue coming from direct passenger payments described by BW as 'for hire or reward' is insignificant. Users are people with a very low disposable income.

Cutbacks may well affect APCO members indirectly but their customer base is generally different.

Over the last few years Government has consistently reduced BW's grant in aid.

As an organisation on the brink of becoming a charity itself, British Waterways might consider 'doing as it would be done by'.

A legal standpoint

There may be a basis for complaint to the Waterways Ombudsman if it can be shown that BW is unjustifiably discriminating against charities and possibly acting ultra vires.

British Waterways should check whether Section 43(3) and 43(8) of the Transport Act 1962 (as amended) extends to making what may be an unfair charge on charities. (footnote on page 7 of the BW consultation document January 2010)

Wording used in these reports

Many people find reference to 'the disadvantaged' or 'the less fortunate' slightly offensive. The implication of this kind of wording is that the people described are a sub-class of 'normal' society.

BW should check this aspect of its documents before publishing them.

Conclusions

The reasons for the removal of the charity discount are not based on evidence. The case on behalf of charities has not been heard. There is a reasonable argument that community boat charities should have to pay the standard fee plus a £150 fee for the Operator Agreement but there is no evidence to justify the imposition of commercial rates.

British Waterways and its successor charity should give every possible financial encouragement to community boat charities to find 'new audiences' by using the inland waterways as a resource to combat social exclusion.

Proposals to impose commercial rates on charities should be withdrawn.

Bob Watson MBE MA(Oxon)
Former Director of The Sobriety Project
Former Chair, Waterways Partnership Interim Executive Committee, East and North Yorkshire
Trustee and former Chair, National Community Boats Association
Former Member, Inland Waterways Advisory Council
Panel member, Living Waterways Awards
Author of IWAC Report: Using the inland waterways as a resource to combat social exclusion.

Two case studies

Case study 1

Camden Canals & Narrowboat Association

From John Sheridan, Chair:

We paid for our current licence (expires 02/11) £735.65.

The next one will have gone up (increase in VAT, plus annual rise). BW just give us a figure to pay, including a 'prompt payment' discount.

For 2011 the starting rate (including prompt payment) for a business licence for boat up to 70' 6" is £1,819.04 and 70' 7"+ is £1,878.25. From this we should get a 10% discount for a historic boat and a 60% discount for a boat operated for charitable purposes.

You will see that £2,861, the figure I calculated as applicable to our boat and the way we operate, based on the proposed new formulae and rules about eligibility, is nearly four times what we currently pay, and approx twice what we might otherwise have paid from next month.

I don't know exactly how the current percentage reductions are applied but (£1,878.25 less 10% is) £187.82, plus (£1,878.25 less 60% which is) £1,126.92 = £1,314.74 – less than half what we would have to pay under the new regime.

The difference is less startling, however, if we were to concede that we are not strictly-speaking eligible for the 60% discount, even under the rules that currently apply – with only a 10% discount we'd be liable to pay £1690.43, so the proposed changes would cost us another £1,170.57 – a 69.5% increase. To say that this would be unwelcome, and seems wholly unreasonable, would be something of an understatement.

Case Study 2

Canal Boat Project Harlow

Stort Challenger (57ft self-steer holiday hire)

Current licence £1,722 less 60% charity reduction = £688

Proposed	£748 + £150 + VAT	= £928 (+ 35%)
Or	£748 + £630(if no charity reduction) = £1,378(+100%)	

Red Watch (65ft self-steer holiday hire)

Current licence £1,914 less 60% charity reduction = £764

Proposed	£831 +£150 + VAT	= £1,011(+32%)
Or	£831 + £630 (if no charity reduction)= £1,461(+91%)	

Stort Daybreak (57ft day-boat river only)

Current licence	£1,033 less 60% charity reduction	= £413
Proposed	£449 + £150 + VAT	= £629(+52%)

Dawn Treader (27ft day-boat river only licence)

Current licence	£687 less 60% charity reduction	= £ 275

REFERENCES

NCBA Summary Statistics 2008 (for IWAC): 27.11.2009

BW: Reforming Business Boat Licensing: Public consultation – January 2010

BW: Reforming Business Boat Licensing: Public consultation – Summer 2010 (This was a pre-consultation draft for discussion with trade representatives 21 July 2010)

E-mail correspondence with Sally Ash, Head of Boating between 23rd and 27th July 2010

E-mail correspondence with Richard Delves, Boating Trade Manager (North) on 13th September and 12th October 2010

BW Press Release: Boat Licence Changes for 2011: 25th November 2010

BW: Boat Licence Changes 2011 dated 7/12/2010

NCBA Internal Statement to Member Re BW Licensing Consultation – undated

Summary of Sobriety's licence payments 2008-2010

Waterways World: January 2011: Article – BW Boat Licences Increased by 5.1%

Waterways World: February 2011: Article – The new waterway charity

Charity Commission website

APCO website

Appendix 4

DEFRA response to IWAC Combatting Social Exclusion

Area 2D
Ergon House
Horseferry Road
London, SW1P 2AL
Telephone: 0207 238 4800
Web: www.defra.gov.uk

Mr J Edmonds
Chair, Inland Waterways Advisory Council
City Road Lock
38 Graham Street
London, N1 8JX

8th September 2009

Dear John (by email)

IWAC REPORT ON USING INLAND WATERWAYS TO COMBAT SOCIAL EXCLUSION

You wrote to Huw Irranca-Davies on 23 April 2009 enclosing a copy of IWAC's report 'Using Inland Waterways to combat the effects of Social Exclusion'. I have discussed our response to this with the Minister and he has asked me to reply accordingly.

As you know we are supportive of work which can make use of inland waterways to both increase access but also which can proactively address social exclusion. The case studies contained in the report provide useful and informative examples of how inland waterways have helped a range of people regain their confidence and so help them re-integrate back into the community. Information on various initiatives gives a useful indication of the many organisations which are active in this area.

While we acknowledge the important role inland waterways can play, your report rightly acknowledges that they are not unique in the benefits that they provide and that excellent work is taking place in other sectors away from the waterways.

I think the revised Waterways for Tomorrow will provide the ideal mechanism to enable Government to demonstrate how inland waterways can help to combat social exclusion. At the moment as we continue to work on the structure of the new document I think we will be able to address social exclusion both within the proposed theme on health, well-being and sport and the theme on fairer, stronger more active communities.

The report contains a number of recommendations directed towards Government and I thought it would be helpful if I set out our view on those.

Recommendation 1 – IWAC and Defra should continue research into the benefits of using inland waterways to combat social exclusion

The first stage of the research programme on the social and economic benefits of inland waterways has been completed and one of the outputs is the Benefits Transfer Framework. This will need testing during the second stage of the programme using known case studies and in time it is hoped that it will prove to be a useful tool for local and regional authorities and others in helping them to make investment decisions and to highlight benefits that they had not previously considered including the contribution

367

inland waterways could make to help address the needs of disadvantaged members of the community.

Recommendation 2 – The updated policy statement that will replace Waterways for Tomorrow should contain a section showing the advantages of using inland waterways to combat social exclusion

I have already mentioned that the revised strategy will provide the opportunity to both confirm the role inland waterways can already play and to say what more needs to be done. It will be important for IWAC to continue to work with us so that we can ensure we can highlight and promote this activity to local and regional bodies. But I suspect this will need further hard work over the period covered by the strategy to make further progress.

Recommendation 3 – The UK Government should recognise and promote the value of inland waterway projects that combat social exclusion

As before the revised strategy should be the vehicle for this rather than a separate initiative. I think we should ensure we have a good case study in the strategy which can demonstrate the benefits inland waterways can offer.

Recommendation 4 – Local authorities, Regional Development Agencies and other public bodies should be encouraged by the UK Government to recognise the potential benefit of using inland waterways to combat social exclusion.

Again the revised Waterways for Tomorrow should do this. A key purpose of the strategy will be to promote the benefits of inland waterways to local and regional authorities which may not have fully grasped what they can deliver. The more engagement we can achieve with a wider range of bodies the better chance we have of ensuring we have a sustainable inland waterways.

Recommendation 5 – The National Community Boats Association should be recognised as the infrastructure organisation for accreditation, capacity building and should receive a measure of public funding to carry out these duties.

I do not believe that it would be appropriate for Government to commit to funding any particular organisation. It is also rather unclear from the report how an accreditation system (which in any case would not fall to Defra) would work or what the benefits would be. I acknowledge that securing funding is never easy but hopefully one output from the revised Waterways for Tomorrow will be greater recognition by local, regional and other bodies of the value of inland waterways to help deliver objectives and this might help to re-direct existing funding sources more towards inland waterways initiatives. It is also worth remembering that boats which operate for charitable purposes (and are not in competition with commercial operators) are eligible for a substantial discount on their licence fee, which effectively represents a public subsidy of their operations.

In conclusion I would like to thank IWAC for your report, the conclusions of which we will be able to consider in the context of the revision of Waterways for Tomorrow. I look forward to continuing to work closely with you over the next few months as we take that work forward.

Yours sincerely

Sarah Nason

Head of Environment Agency and Waterways

Appendix 5

 | NCBA RESPONSE TO BW LICENSING CONSULTATION JULY 2013

The National Community Boats Association (NCBA) is pleased to support British Waterways (BW) in reviewing the current system of waterways licences which, for community boating organisations, has always been a slightly disorganised and inconsistent process but it also recognises that these changes may have a negative impact on some community boat operations.

Community boats will always use the waterways infrastructure more than privately owned pleasure boats and often more than commercial hire boat operations as well but they also bring significantly larger numbers of people into contact with the waterways. In addition, Community Boating Organisations (CBOs) make a wide-ranging contribution to an agenda that includes many of the nations (and the Canal & River Trust's (CRT)) social and community cohesion priorities.

Part of the ongoing challenge faced with licensing these craft is that it is not always easy to define what a "community boat" is. Whilst almost exclusively owned or managed by defined organisations rather than individuals, these boats may be operated by registered charities, local authorities or corporate bodies. They may have charitable aims in their constitution or no constitution at all. They might be an educational project, deliver training or work with excluded, disabled or disadvantaged individuals and groups. They may deliver rehabilitation contract services for the health or justice sectors. They may simply offer large residential capacity afloat for community group.

Whilst simplicity in licencing CBOs is essential – particularly for the number of boats involved (being less than 1% of the total number licenced by CRT) – NCBA is disappointed at CRT's lack of willingness to engage with the social, charitable and 'public benefit' benefits of these types of organisation. To do so could only strengthen CRT's own ability to engage with the hard-to-reach groups it craves and demonstrate its own value and contribution to society as a charity. Sadly, the historical approach of British Waterways was frequently more positive in this regard than that of the CRT.

Clearly a complex system of discounts is not easy to administer or police but the alternative proposed by CRT does not appear to resolve this. NCBA is pleased that its proposal of using the Charities Act charitable heads as the qualifying criteria (whilst not necessarily being a registered charity) has been adopted by CRT. These are relatively clear and, where interpretation is in doubt, relevant case law may provide an external 'arbiter'. In the absence of something a little more sophisticated and positive, NCBA supports the central proposal of charging these types of boat the standard leisure boat licence fee. After thee years of discussion, to at least get roughly back to the position we all started in is disappointing but should at least be no more costly.

The 'stings in the tail' of these proposals are (1) the outright ban on revenue generating activity and (2) the failure of CRT to include moorings and service provisions in any agreements.

Generating revenue to support the aims of the organisation by using charitable assets is an entirely legitimate activity. Many (if not most) charities and similar organisations do just this to in order to demonstrate their business-like approach to finance and sustainability. CBOs may well generate revenue to subsidise their target groups; particularly those who are charities themselves or unable to afford the considerable cost of accessing the UK inland waterways by other means.

NCBA strongly objects to CRT's position taken on this matter which appears to be entirely based on a perceived problem of completion with commercial operators using the same waterways. CRT has failed throughout the discussion to provide any evidence of such conflict ever existing. Whilst there have always been individual disputes between organisations using the waterways, NCBA's own research on the matter demonstrates not only that there is no evidence of conflict between CBOs and commercial operators but that these relationships are usually extremely positive and even symbiotic. Notwithstanding this, it is unclear what powers CRT has to stop such legitimate activity and NCBA questions whether such actions could stand up to either legal or public scrutiny well.

The NCBA sees no conflict in navigation authorities providing additional support to organisations seeking to use generated income for the benefit of a charitable objective where the target audience is limited and indeed other authorities do just that. NCBA believes it is entirely proper for licensing bodies to support those organisations delivering on social outcomes as it contributes to their own corporate social responsibility provision and, in the case of CRT, helps demonstrate its own public benefit as a charity because of the client groups CBOs engage with. It is incongruous for CRT to attempt to remove itself from ensuring these operations thrive.

Some organisations utilise CRT land and facilities in providing their operation. There seems to be a variety of arrangements in place from 100 year leases to 'turning a blind eye'. These arrangements will almost certainly have been negotiated locally and may have been in place for many years. Whilst there are relatively few organisations affected by this compared to the total number of CBOs on CRT managed waters, the impact of not honouring such arrangements could be huge. Acknowledging the value of what CBOs deliver is NCBA's prime objective in any discussion rather than adopting a 'poor charity' type stance. Notwithstanding this, the financial impact on those organisations that have historically paid little or nothing for moorings cannot be underestimated. CBOs rarely generate a surplus and, if they do, it can only be ploughed straight back into the work of the organisation. New charges for potentially thousands of pounds could quite simply mean the closure of some of these organisations and CRT should acknowledge that.

It is unclear how CRT intends to police any of the proposed system. Meeting the qualifying criteria, details of the target users, absence of revenue generating activity and robustness of operation will be almost completely impossible to scrutinise in the proposed system. Given the number of people involved and the risks associated with some of the client groups, this is disappointing. Although CBOs are some of the safest on the waterways, this was an opportunity to improve the oversight of such activity.

Finally, NCBA is extremely disappointed at a number of issues relating to the consultation process itself. Although the final proposal papers were delivered to NCBA in June, only a matter of weeks was been offered to respond. CRT decided to deliver the proposals direct to those involved rather than publishing on their website. Several NCBA member organisations have complained they have received the consultation papers late or not at all. Given that part of the issue was the inconsistent and disorganised state of the current licence listings, approaching the communication process in this way was always going to be less than satisfactory,

Derek Stansfield
Chair, Board of Directors
National Community Boats Association

Appendix 6

DESTINATION GDANSK

Although planned in broad detail the voyage never took place, but for those with an eye to the future, here are the details:

North, up the Ijsselmeer to Enkhuizen then via the tidal Waddenzee to Harlingen, the West Friesian Islands and Delfzijl on the river Eems

To Cuxhaven on the River Elbe and across the Elbe estuary to Brunsbuttel, the western terminus of the Noord Ostsee (Kiel) Kanal

Two days to transit the canal with an overnight stop at Rendsburg (Holtenau, a suburb of Kiel, is the eastern terminus of the canal)

On to the east coast of Schleswig-Holstein visiting some of the Danish Baltic islands

A brief stop at Lubeck then round the southern tip of Sweden to Ronne on the Danish island of Bornholm

From Bornholm, a passage of 100 miles to the Polish fishing port of Darlowo followed by coastal hopping via Leba and Wladyslawowo to Gdansk.

Then heads south from the Danish island of Sjaelland to the German island of Rugen and the Mecklenburg - Vorpommern coast. The trip back to Kiel will include visits to the old Hanseatic ports of Stralsund and Rostock.

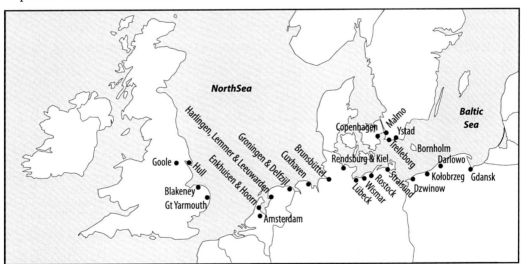

Historical Notes

The proposed itinerary was augmented by notes on the ports to be visited:

Although now heavily silted up, Blakeney was an important port for the wool trade which laid the foundations of England's wealth.

Great Yarmouth's trade rivalled the north European herring fleets.

Hoorn, North Holland on the Zuider Zee was a Dutch East India Company port. The main museum is the Westfries.

Amsterdam: a centre of culture and the principal port of the Dutch East India Company whose history is represented in the Nederland Scheepvaartsmuseum.

Enkhuisen: home to the Zuider Zee Museum.

Harlingen, Friesland: once the Netherlands' most important naval, fishing and trading port, with links to the Dutch East India Company and the Hanseatic League. The Hannemahuis Museum concentrates on the towns shipping and industrial heritage.

Lemmer, Friesland: a small Zuider Zee port and canal entrance to the Friesian lakes.

Leeuwarden, Friesland: an important market town and home to the Fries Museum which has a collection of artefacts from prehistoric Friesia.

Groningen, Friesland: an ancient trading centre with numerous museums including the new Groningen Museum.

Delfzijl, Friesland: a commercial port on the River Eems with strong trading links with the Humber.

Cuxhaven, Germany: port on the River Elbe, a yachting centre and home to a comprehensive maritime museum.

Brunsbuttel, Noord Ostsee Kanal: the western entrance to the canal was built in 1895.

Rendsburg, Noord Ostsee Kanal: historic garrison town halfway along the canal.

Kiel: capital of Schleswig-Holstein, a naval and yachting centre and once Germany's U Boat base.

Lubeck, Germany: historically one of the most important Hanseatic ports. Before German unification Lubeck was a border town in the east.

Kobenhavn, Sjaelland Island, Denmark: a fortress and trading port going back to the early medieval period. Copenhagen has trading links throughout the Baltic and North Sea. It is the political and cultural capital of Denmark.

Malmo, Sweden.

Ystad, Sweden.

Ronne, Bornholm: main port on the isolated but strategically important island of Bornholm

Darlowo, Poland: an historic port, once home to the princes of Pomerania whose castle is now the regional museum.

Gdansk, Poland: as a port and industrial centre, Gdansk has a complicated political and cultural history which is reflected in its monuments and museums, the main maritime collection being in the Morskie.

Kolobrzeg, Poland: a small fishing port and seaside town.

Dziwnow, Poland: a fishing harbour on the River Dziwna.

Trelleborg, Sweden.

Stralsund, Mecklenburg – Vorpommern: a fishing port and Hansa trading town celebrated in its museums and aquarium in the Katharinenkloster.

Rostock, Mecklenburg – Vorpommern: once one of Europe' leading Hansa trading centres this university town is Germany's largest Baltic port and boasts two maritime museums, the Schiffahrtsmuseum and the Schiffbau.

Wismar, Mecklenburg – Vorpommern: an important Hansa port and 17th century Swedish fortress town.

Appendix 7

AWARDS 2003 – 2013

2003

The Waterways Renaissance Award: Certificate

The Waterways Trust

Youth Projects & Education Winner: For demonstrating best practice in the utilisation of inland waterways to raise awareness, involvement and understanding.

Chairman's Award: Certificate

East Riding of Yorkshire Council

Certificate of Distinction: For enhancing the environment of the East Riding of Yorkshire

2007

White Rose Awards For Tourism: Plaque

Yorkshire Tourist Board

Winner - Visitor attraction of the Year (under 50,000 visitors)

Social Enterprise Yorkshire & Humber Awards, Certificate

Social Enterprise Yorkshire & Humber, Supported by: Yorkshire Forward, SEYH, Business Link, European regional development fund, Yorkshire

2008

White Rose Awards: Certificate

Yorkshire Tourist Board: Sponsored by: Yorkshire Forward & Yorkshire

Access for all Tourism Award

2009

Community Space Challenge Award: Trophy & Certificate

Regional Winner: Awarded to: Goole Community Space Challenge: To acknowledge achievements in improving local environmental quality and reducing antisocial behaviour.

White Rose Awards for Tourism: Trophy

Welcome To Yorkshire

Access for All Tourism Award

The Waterways Renaissance Awards: Certificate

The Waterways Trust/BURA, 2009

Education & Learning – Commended: For the project Rooting Around

White Rose Awards: Certificate

Welcome to Yorkshire: Sponsored by Yorkshire Forward & Yorkshire

Winner Access for all Tourism Award

2010

Philip Lawrence Award: Certificate

PLANET (Philip Lawrence Awards Network)

Yorkshire and Humber Regional Finalist: Presented to Goole Community Space Challenge

The Waterways Renaissance Awards: Certificate

The Waterways Trust

Historic Environment Winner: For the project: Railway on the Water – Re launched!

White Rose Award: Certificate
Welcome to Yorkshire
Finalist Access for all Tourism Award

2011
Volunteering Hours Celebration Award: Spade trophy
Catch 22: Community Space Challenge/Big Lottery Funded
In celebration of CSC 100,000 volunteering hours
Yorkshire In Bloom Awards: Certificate
Yorkshire In Bloom
Gold Yorkshire Rose Award: Visitor attraction category
Marsh Volunteer Award: Certificate
National Historic Ships – The official voice for historic vessels in the UK
Presented to: *Wheldale* Crew: For Historic Vessel Conservation

2012
Community Space Challenge Award: Glass Trophy & Certificate
Keep Britain Tidy Network
National Winner: Awarded to: The Sobriety Project
Community Space Challenge: Glass Trophy & Certificate
Community Space Challenge Award: Keep Britain Tidy Network
Regional Winner
Chairman's Award: Glass Trophy & Certificate
East Riding Of Yorkshire Council
Environment category overall winner: Presented to Goole Community Space Project
Goole & Howdenshire Business Excellence Awards: Certificate
Sponsored by Goole High School
Finalist in the category of contribution to the community – Third Sector
Yorkshire In Bloom Awards: Certificate
Yorkshire In Bloom
Gold Award: Visitor attraction category
Yorkshire In Bloom Awards: Certificate
Yorkshire In Bloom
Yorkshire Rose Award: Small Community Category
Diamond Jubilee Flotilla: Certificate
Humber Diamond Jubilee Committee
Presented to The *Sobriety* Project: In acknowledgement of *Sobriety* participation in the Flotilla on the River Humber
Thames Diamond Jubilee Pageant Participant: Plaque
Thames Diamond Jubilee Committee
Presented to The Sobriety Project: For *Wheldale*'s participation in the Thames Jubilee Pageant

2013
Yorkshire In Bloom Awards: Certificate
Yorkshire In Bloom
Silver Gilt Yorkshire Rose Award: Visitor attraction category

Appendix 8

Summary History of the *Sobriety* Project

Sobriety has survived by recognising and taking advantage of changes in the social, political and economic environment of the UK and wider world which in an inspired moment, was described by Peter Fryer, Director of Humberside Training & Enterprise Council, as 'a rapidly deforming fitness landscape'. Like Yorkshire's Aire & Calder Navigation (A&CN), which for two hundred and fifty years expanded its canal and river empire against the threat of railways and rival companies, *Sobriety* has danced to many tunes. Like Harold Wilson, UK prime minister in the nineteen sixties who said he was at his best 'in a messy, middle-of-the-road muddle', it has generally found that it could solve many of its problems by the same muddling along.[1]

The Project has been convinced of its purpose, taken risks, flown by the seat of its pants and not infrequently stood up publicly for what it believed. Like many pioneer organisations it has been on the periphery of statutory policy-making and has never had a secure income. As a consequence, reticence is not one of its strong points.

The story began with Margaret Thatcher when she was Secretary of State for Education. In 1974, during her time in the Heath government, Goole Grammar School changed from being a four form entry selective establishment, drawing children from Hull, Scunthorpe, Pontefract and Selby, under the control of the West Riding Local Education Authority (LEA), to an eight form entry non-selective school with a local catchment area of Goole and nearby villages. Internal re-organisation designed to meet the needs of so called non-academic pupils, grouped together several vocational subjects into a faculty of business, social, and community studies. One of the new faculty's responsibilities was to make practical links between the curriculum and local employers. Goole's docks and waterways which had been disaggregated under the Transport Acts of 1948 and 1968, were major employers in the town and well represented at school careers evenings.

During the 'muddle' of re-organisation which coincided with the raising of the school leaving age to 16, as well as with changes in local government and the emergence of Humberside LEA, there appeared a local business man with the offer of a 1910 Humber barge which he said should be used to keep young people out of trouble and preserve the dwindling heritage of the Yorkshire waterways. It was clear that the vessel had no future for carrying coal but appeared to have plenty of life left to become a travelling adventure centre. Like the psalmist, many school staff 'saw that and fled',[2] but the school was blessed with a far sighted head who saw through the muddle to the opportunities for personal development and employment that this *Sobriety* barge might offer. So by the end of the nineteen seventies, the *Sobriety* Project was in business; the barge was being used for residential expeditions by the school and by local youth groups, and was also marketing itself beyond Goole to help with the education of children with special needs. With special significance for the future was its connection with Humberside Social Services provision for young offenders and children in care.

After ten years of barge residentials on Yorkshire's rivers and canals, the trustees decided it was time to expand; in the early 1980s, *Eden*, a former Leeds & Liverpool shortboat, was purchased for £300 from British Waterways and converted to residential use. Then in 1985 Humberside County Council, British Waterways and Boothferry Borough Council, which was a second tier authority for the Goole area, suggested *Sobriety* might build a canalside HQ on derelict land lying between two local waterways. Again, trustees readily agreed; a building would provide an opportunity to work with young people and other groups when the boats were away, which was most of the time. To speed up the process, David Lunn, Bishop of Sheffield and *Sobriety*'s Patron, wrote to Sir Maurice Laing, chairman of the construction company John Laing. The bishop had his faith rewarded by a Sobriety HQ built by Laings at the cost of nothing but materials and sub contracted labour.

A CUCKOO IN THE CURRICULUM

In 1987, the charity went to sea. A meeting with members of the Humber Keel & Sloop Preservation Society, who were sailing traditional barges on the Humber, had convinced the trustees that we were not making the best of what lay beyond the Humber: especially since much of Hull and Goole's history was concerned with overseas trade. Through the good services of the Manpower Services Commission and Hull City Council, the outcome was *Audrey*, a redundant lightship converted to be a sea-going sailing barge. During the following sixteen years until 2003, the ship would take 7,000 young people from depressed housing estates in Yorkshire on voyages to Holland, France, Ireland and the highlands and islands of Scotland.

In 1994 *Sobriety* set up a waterways museum in its canalside building. Its purpose was to collect and display objects and documents which illustrated life as it had been on the north east waterways and was a way of saying thank you to the town that had nurtured the Project in its early days. The new building immediately opened its doors to anyone wanting to benefit from its activities. People who in other organisations would have been labelled 'clients' were dignified as 'volunteers'. Invariably on benefits and often contributors to the town's high levels of unemployment and illness, they helped with the running of the boats and museum and acquired the confidence to cope better with their problems. The museum soon became a tourist attraction in its own right, albeit with a difference, for it was not a pre-occupation with the waterways that commended it to funders so much as its attempt to find imaginative solutions to the social and economic problems of people on low incomes.

The nineties was a further decade of expansion and spreading the word, which was done through the good services of the European Union after it had recovered from Mrs Thatcher's 1988 'Up yours Delors' speech in Brussels. From 1994, the EU was making money available for projects designed to get long term unemployed people back into the labour market. Famous among these was the Project's Waterways Work for Women which took the view that the Yorkshire waterways had been dominated by men since the time of the Vikings and that by ignoring 50 per cent of the population the regional economy was being seriously disadvantaged. Another EU project set up a *Sobriety* satellite in Rotherham. This was Swinton Lock Adventure Centre which became independent in 2004 and is still in business. It was the product of a *Sobriety* led partnership between the EU, Rotherham Metropolitan Borough Council, British Waterways and the Lottery, and paved the way for *Sobriety* to instigate further collaborative projects in Hull, Thorne and Selby.

At this stage, trustees had to be aware of the danger that, after 25 years, the Project would become 'mature'; that is, set in its ways, convinced it had reached perfection, and expectant of indefinite support from trusts and local authorities. So whilst the decade from 2000 was characterised by severe shortage of funds it was also a period when the Project adopted an approach to business based on the changing requirements of customers and contractors. As a reflection of this policy, about thirty children a week now attend the Project. They are all excluded from school, and for a minority, the charity is a last resort. The East Riding Authority and several schools pay *Sobriety* to help these children return to the classroom and accept a normal school routine. The Project also works with offenders. Up to eight men from Hatfield re-settlement prison near Doncaster work at the museum each day. They are beginning a new life during the last months of their sentence and in order to prepare for life on the 'outside', have to abandon dependence on the prison. The daily routine of the Project also gives an opportunity to other people who have been out of work, sometimes for years, to try their hand at regular employment.

The museum meets national standards for accreditation in conservation, audience development, access, acquisitions and disposals and so on. Museums are not in themselves a frontline service and it has to work hard to pay for itself. The Project promotes enjoyment of the arts not just through exhibitions but through concerts and special events to attract people from Yorkshire and beyond.

Summary History: Notes

1 Harold Wilson said this in a cabinet meeting on 21st January 1975.

2 Psalm 114. 'When Israel came out of Egypt &c' – a reference to the parting of the Red Sea in the Exodus from Egypt.

Appendix 9

CHRONOLOGY

Note: To avoid confusion between BW (Bob Watson) and BW (British Waterways) I have used the initials RW (Robert Watson), in this chronology. The name *Sobriety* is widely used to refer to the organisation as well as to the barge.

1966	RW takes up appointment to post of teacher of Religious Education (RE) at Goole Grammar School (GGS)
1966 - -1971	Responsibility for non examination RE and some Ordinary and Advanced Level GCE Scripture:
	Development of GGS out-of-school curriculum at Rawcliffe Hall and in the Asian community in Batley and Dewsbury:
	Summer holidays spent working on Israeli kibbutz on Lebanon border above Haifa and at the Salvation Army's all night Rink Club in Oxford Street, London.
	Assisted with groups of children on residential expeditions to GGS How Stean Centre in Upper Nidderdale:
	Evening work in Goole youth clubs and at Hatfield Borstal near Doncaster, teaching International and Civic Affairs:
1972	RW seconded to teach English at Government College, Kano, Northern Nigeria:
1973	The Humber barge *Sobriety* presented to GGS by John McGrory, a local businessman:
1974	GGS becomes a comprehensive school. RW appointed to be head of faculty of Social & Community Studies: *Sobriety* continues to be used for excursions down the Humber and on the Yorkshire canals: accommodation installed by British Transport Docks Board and school staff:
1975 – 1976	Barge crewed by volunteers; teachers and retired skippers living in Goole:
1976 - 1979	Brian Calvert becomes full time skipper: his salary funded first by Manpower Services Commission (MSC) and then through contract with Humberside Social Services Department:
1980 – 1983	*Sobriety* workforce has to cope with increasing demand for residentials by education and social services groups: Boothferry Borough Council decides to fund the salary of an apprentice skipper: the organisation takes responsibility for the development of St Thomas' centre for the intermediate treatment of young offenders in Old Goole:
1984	The Leeds & Liverpool shortboat *Eden* acquired from BW in Wigan and rebuilt in Goole by members of the GMB union:
1985 – 1987	*Sobriety* expansion leads to RW being seconded as its first director to work full time for the organisation with small office in St Thomas's centre: Brian Calvert leaves to work for BW: Helper Scheme begins, offering opportunities to young men from Hatfield Young Offender Institution and young women from HMP Askham Grange to assist with groups using the barges. Visit of Prince and Princess of Wales, Albert Dock, Hull:
1988	*Audrey* makes her first appearance as a former light vessel marking Whitton Sands in the upper Humber: purchased for the organisation by Alan Marshall, *Sobriety* chair: converted to sail: accommodation installed by local unemployed people, funded by MSC and Hull City Council:

1989   *Sobriety* Centre opens on Dutch River Side: BW agrees a 99 year lease. *Audrey* based in Hull Marina: other vessels berth at Centre. Colin Walden appointed to skipper *Audrey*.

1991   With the appointment of Izzy Kitt to be Arts Development Worker, the long road to museum registration begins: Paul Cooper appointed to *Audrey*:

1995   *Sobriety* Centre becomes the Waterways Museum registered with the Museums & Galleries Commission: *ROOM 58*, a former Hull lighter, acquired and re-furbished to become a floating art gallery and small conference centre.

1996   Discussions begin with Rotherham Community Barge Association, owner of *Spider T* barge:

            Audrey leaves the Humber each summer to explore the Dutch Isselmeer:

1998   Swinton Lock Adventure Centre opens in Rotherham, a development of *Spider T*, funded by the Lottery and Europe: Helen Rhodes appointed manager: Tom Pudding tug *Wheldale* acquired and restored:

2000   *Audrey*'s Millennium Voyage – 16 weeks circumnavigating the UK 'crewed' by local schools, day centres and youth clubs: volunteers assist the permanent crew:

2001   Izzy Kitt leaves to manage the National Community Boats Association:

2003   Reductions in bookings make *Audrey* too expensive to maintain and she is sold: Waterways Museum renamed Yorkshire Waterways Museum: *Opportunity* and *City of Hull* presented to *Sobriety* by Hull City Council: Publication of research project Spring to Release launched by Robin Evans, CEO of British Waterways:

2004 - 2006   Swinton Lock Adventure Centre achieves independence: *Waterstart* in Thorne–Moorends and *Surewaters* in Selby, open for business: AdventureSail4All and Trade Routes open in Hull: These projects are developed by *Sobriety* to tackle social exclusion in deprived communities: RW appointed to be a member of the Inland Waterways Advisory Council:

2010   RW retires from being *Sobriety* Project director: Paul Cooper appointed to the post:

2011 - 2015   Project continues to provide placements at Museum for men from HMP Hatfield, young people excluded from school and for people with additional learning needs

Index